INTRODUCTION TO ECONOMIC REASONING

INTRODUCTION TO ECONOMIC REASONING

Second Edition

WILLIAM D. ROHLF, JR.

DRURY COLLEGE

ADDISON-WESLEY PUBLISHING COMPANY

Reading, Massachusetts • Menlo Park, California • New York
Don Mills, Ontario • Wokingham, England • Amsterdam • Bonn
Sydney • Singapore • Tokyo • Madrid • San Juan • Milan • Paris

Sponsoring Editor: Marjorie Williams
Assistant Editor: Kari Heen
Production Supervisor: Peggy McMahon
Text Designer: Sally Bindari, Designworks
Cover Designer: Peter Blaiwas
Illustrator: Tech-Graphics
Copy Editor: Carol Beckwith
Photo Research: Christine O'Brien, Mary Dyer
Manufacturing Supervisor: Roy Logan
Senior Marketing Manager: David Theisen

Library of Congress Cataloging-in-Publication Data

Rohlf, William D.
   Introduction to economic reasoning / William D. Rohlf, Jr.—2nd ed.
     p. cm.
   Includes index.
   ISBN 0-201-57261-3
   1. Economics. 2. United States—Economic conditions. I. Title.
HB171.5.R73   1992
330—dc20   92-14605

ISBN 0-201-57261-3

3 4 5 6 7 8 9 10-DO-959493

To my parents, who helped me learn the value of persistence

Preface

Almost one hundred years ago, Alfred Marshall defined economics as "the study of mankind in the ordinary business of life." Today, the ordinary business of life has become incredibly complex. The purpose of this textbook is to help prepare students for that life.

Introduction to Economic Reasoning is intended for students taking the one-term course in introductory economics. Many of these students, perhaps a majority, will take only one course in economics. They have a variety of interests and educational objectives. Some are enrolled in preprofessional programs; others will pursue majors in areas such as business, psychology, or the liberal arts. At a number of institutions, the one-term course also enrolls first-year students in MBA programs and other graduate business programs. Many of these students pursued nonbusiness majors as undergraduates and did not elect to take an economics course. Others desire to review economics before entering the graduate program. Although the students enrolling in the one-term course have diverse objectives and interests, they can all benefit from a course that prepares them to understand economic issues better and helps them to become better decision makers.

The Focus of the Book

How do we prepare students to understand economic issues and help them become better decision makers? I am convinced that we cannot accomplish these objectives by focusing solely on economic issues and short-cutting a discussion of economic concepts. This approach might provide students with ready answers to existing problems, but it would do little to prepare students for coping with new social problems and little to refine their decision-making skills. To accomplish those objectives, we must teach students something about economic reasoning.

Economists are fond of saying that economics is a way of thinking, or a way of reasoning about problems. The essence of economic reasoning is the ability to use theories or models to make sense out of the real world and devise policy solutions to economic problems. If we want students to use economic reasoning, we have to help them to learn and understand the basic economic theories. Without an understanding of economic theory, a course in economics can leave the student with little more than memorized solutions to current economic problems.

The Need to Make Choices

Obviously, we can't do everything in a one-term course in introductory economics. And unless we can keep the student's interest and show the relevance of economics, we can't accomplish anything. So the instructor in a one-term course (and the author of a one-term text) must make choices. He or she must decide what to include and what to exclude, how to balance theory with application, and how to motivate the student without sounding too much like a cheerleader. This textbook attempts to bridge these extremes.

Because economists use theories or models in problem solving, the core of this text is economic theory. No essential micro or macro concept is omitted. Many refinements are omitted, however, so that more time can be devoted to the careful development of the most important concepts. This is one of the distinctive features of the text: a very careful development of the core ideas in economic theory.

Making Economics Relevant

Today's student wants to know why he or she should be studying economics. What problems or issues will it help to clarify? What decisions will it help to improve? In *Introduction to Economic Reasoning*, the relevance of economics is illustrated by the use of examples in the text and through special features entitled "Use Your Economic Reasoning." These features, which are listed in a separate table of contents on pages xxii–xxiii, contain news articles that have been carefully selected to illustrate the relevance of the economic principles being discussed and to provide the student with an opportunity to test his or her knowledge of those principles. Each article is accompanied by a set of questions to ensure that the student gains the maximum benefit from the article, and the features themselves have been designed to make them easy to locate.

Writing Style

In writing this text, my overriding objective has been to make economics accessible to the average student. I have been careful to avoid unnecessarily sophisticated vocabulary and needlessly long sentences. Most important, I have worked to ensure that my explanations of economic concepts are carefully and clearly developed. While professors may adopt a text for a wide variety of reasons, I am convinced that the most common reason for discontinuing its use is because students can't understand it. Your students *will* be able to read this text and understand it.

Aids in Learning

In addition to a clear writing style, the text contains a number of additional learning aids:

1. New terms are presented in boldface italic type and are always defined when they are introduced.
2. "Use Your Economic Reasoning" selections not only generate student interest but also give the student an opportunity to apply the concepts that have been presented and thereby reinforce learning.
3. Careful summaries highlight the contents of the chapter.
4. A glossary of new terms (with page references) appears at the end of each chapter so that a student can easily review definitions and locate the appropriate place to review concepts.
5. A study guide including fill-in-the-blank and multiple choice questions (with answers) and problems and questions for discussion appears at the end of each chapter. This increases the likelihood that the study guide will be used, and encourages the student to review the chapter to correct deficiencies.

Additional Features

1. The demand and supply model (the core of micro theory) is more fully developed than in other one-semester texts, and the student is given numerous opportunities to test his or her understanding of the model.

2. The organization of the macroeconomics chapters provides for maximum flexibility in use. Instructors wishing to employ only the aggregate demand–aggregate supply framework can do so, while those desiring to integrate the Keynesian total expenditures model have that option.

3. Modern developments in macroeconomic theory, such as the theory of rational expectations, are presented in a manner that is accessible to the beginning student.

4. The text contains a section on pricing in practice, which generates student interest and allows the student to see how real-world pricing decisions make use of economic theory.

Second Edition Changes

In the time since the first edition was published, the Soviet Union has been dissolved, the health-care crisis has worsened, the cable television industry has been subjected to reregulation, the United States has experienced another recession, and calls for deficit reduction have turned into demands for tax cuts to stimulate the economy. These and other changes are reflected in the second edition through an updated discussion of the former Soviet Union, new textbook examples, and many new "Use Your Economic Reasoning" selections.

In addition to this general updating, the second edition contains a major revision of the macroeconomics chapters. The aggregate demand–aggregate supply framework is now presented earlier in the text and is developed more extensively than in the first edition. Chapter 10 introduces the aggregate demand–aggregate supply (AD–AS) framework, and uses it to examine the debate between Keynes and the classical economists. Chapter 14 completes the development of the AD–AS framework and uses it to develop a model of the self-correcting economy. Chapter 15 closes the discussion of macroeconomics by using the AD–AS framework to examine the modern activist-nonactivist debate.

The intervening macro chapters (Chapters 11–13) provide additional detail for those who desire it. Chapter 11 presents the Keynesian total expenditures model, and Chapter 12 uses the total expenditures framework to examine Keynesian fiscal policy. Chapter 13 examines money, banking, and monetary policy. This chapter is not tied to the total expenditures model, so it can be used by instructors omitting Chapters 11 and 12.

The intent in revising the macroeconomic chapters is to provide instructors with greater flexibility in choosing how to teach the macroeconomics section of the course. Although the Keynesian aggregate expenditures model is fully developed, the chapters are organized so that this discussion can be omitted by instructors who prefer a more abbreviated coverage of macroeconomics. These options are discussed more fully below.

Strategies for Using the Text

Introduction to Economic Reasoning provides balanced coverage of microeconomics and macroeconomics. The book is divided into four parts. A two-chapter introduction (Part 1) examines the basic economic problem and economic systems. This is followed by six chapters on microeconomics (Part 2), seven chapters on macroeconomics (Part 3), and two chapters on international economics (Part 4).

The chapters in the text are arranged in micro-macro sequence, but an instructor could easily reverse this order by covering Chapters 1, 2, and 3 and then moving directly to Part 3. The remaining micro chapters and Part 4 could then be covered in sequence.

If an instructor desired to shorten the micro portion of the course, Chapter 4 ("The Elasticity of Demand and Supply") and Chapter 8 ("Market Failure") could be omitted with no loss in continuity. Chapter 7 ("Industry Structure and Public Policy") extends the analysis presented in Chapter 6 and could also be skipped if necessary.

The macro coverage of the text can also be reduced. Instructors who want to omit the detailed coverage of fiscal and monetary policy (or who want to concentrate on the aggregate demand–aggregate supply framework) can skip Chapters 11 through 13 and still have a cohesive discussion of macroeconomics. Chapter 13, "Money, Banking, and Monetary Policy," does not require material contained in Chapters 11 or 12, so it could easily be added by those who desire to include greater detail in this area. Likewise, instructors who want to concentrate on the basic Keynesian model can select only Chapters 11–13, omitting Chapters 10, 14, and 15.

International economics is the last part of the book. This material has traditionally been the first to be omitted whenever an instructor found it necessary to shorten his or her course. Today, the growing importance of this subject matter may call for a different strategy. As a compromise course of action, an instructor might cover Chapter 16 ("International Trade") and omit Chapter 17 ("International Finance").

The Instructor's Manual

The instructor's manual that accompanies this book is intended to make the instructor's job easier. New instructors may benefit from the teaching tips provided for each chapter. The manual also contains a chapter-by-chapter listing of additional news articles that may be suitable for writing assignments or class discussion, answers to the "Use Your Economic Reasoning" questions, answers to the "Problems and Questions for Discussion" at the end of each chapter, and a test bank of multiple-choice questions.

Acknowledgments

One author is listed on the cover of this textbook, but there are many people who have helped in its preparation and to whom I owe my thanks.

First I would like to thank the reviewers of the second edition: G.E. Berger, University of South Carolina; Robert P. Edwards, County College of Morris; Peter B. Lund, California State University-Sacramento; Roger F. Riefler, University of Nebraska-Lincoln; James M. Ritgerink, Polk Community College; Eli Shnaider, Florida Institute of Technology; Phil Sorenson, Florida State University; and Donald R. Stabile, St. Mary's College of Maryland. Their comments and suggestions have been immensely helpful to me and are reflected in the content of this revision.

I owe a particular debt of thanks to Steve Mullins, my colleague at Drury College. He was often called on to help me interpret reviewer comments and decide between alternative approaches. His good judgment and ready assistance have made a major difference in the quality of this book.

I would also like to thank those with whom I have worked at Addison-Wesley: Barbara Rifkind, Marjorie Williams, Christine O'Brien, Kari Heen, Peggy McMahon, Mary Dyer, Dick Morton, and Carol Beckwith. Their attention to detail and their personal encouragement have been very much appreciated.

Finally, I would like to thank my wife, Fonda, and my grandchildren, Troy and Alexis, for enduring the boring evenings and missed fishing trips that are part of writing a textbook. Without their patience and support, this edition would never have been completed.

Brief Contents

Detailed Contents

Use Your Economic Reasoning Features

PART 1

INTRODUCTION: SCARCITY AND THE ECONOMIC SYSTEM

This textbook is divided into four parts. Part 1 is an introduction to economics; it is designed to set the stage for the remainder of the text. Here you will discover, among other things, what economics is about and what is meant by an economic system.

Chapter 1 will explain what the study of economics is about and how the knowledge you gain from this course may affect your thinking in many ways. Here you will be introduced to the concept of "opportunity cost"—one of the most important concepts in economics and in everyday living. You will learn about the role of economic theory in helping us make sense out of the things we observe in the world around us. In Chapter 2, you will discover what an economic system is and how economic systems differ from country to country.

With that introductory material behind you, you can begin exploring economics in more detail. Part 2 of the text will examine microeconomics: the study of individual markets and individual business firms. Part 3 will explore macroeconomics: the study of the economy as a whole and the factors that influence the economy's overall performance. Finally, Part 4 will consider international economics: the study of economic exchanges between nations.

THE STUDY OF ECONOMICS

Beginning a subject you haven't explored before is something like starting out on a blind date: You always hope for the best but anticipate the worst. This time, be reassured. No course you take in college is likely to be more relevant to your future—whatever your interests—than this one. An understanding of economic principles is valuable because so many of the questions and decisions that touch our lives have an economic aspect. This is true whether you are evaluating something as personal as your decision to attend college or attempting to grapple with one of today's fundamental social issues: the debate about the proper role of government in the United States, for example, or the future of nuclear power, or the advisability of protecting American businesses and workers from foreign competition. Each of these issues has important implications for your welfare and mine, yet they are just a few of the many complex questions that confront us as consumers, workers, and citizens. To understand and evaluate what economists, politicians, and others are saying about these issues, we need a knowledge of economics. Then we can do a better job of separating the "sense" from the "nonsense" and forming intelligent opinions.

Obviously, you won't learn all there is to know about economics from one short textbook. But here is your opportunity to build a solid understanding of basic economic principles and discover how economists interpret data and analyze economic problems. That is especially important because economics is as much a way of reasoning as it is a body of knowledge. Once you have learned what it means to "consider the opportunity costs," to "compare the costs and benefits," and to "think marginally," nothing will ever look quite the same again. You'll find yourself making better decisions about everything from how to use your time more effectively to whom to support in the next presidential election. Watching the TV news and reading newspapers and magazines will become more meaningful and enjoyable. You will begin to notice the economic dimension of virtually every problem confronting society—pollution, crime, health care, higher education, and so on. Your knowledge of economics will help you understand and deal better with all these problems!

The Economic Problem

The fundamental economic problem facing individuals and societies alike is the fact that our wants exceed our capacity for satisfying those wants. Consider, for example, one of your personal economic problems: how to use your limited income—your limited financial resources. With the possible exception of the very rich, none of us can afford to buy everything we'd like to have. Each of us can think of a virtually limitless number of products we want or "need." Food, shelter, clothing, membership at a health club, new tires for the car, a personal computer . . . we really won't tax our brains if we continue. In fact, economist and social critic John Kenneth Galbraith has suggested that the satisfaction of a want through the purchase of a product not only fails to reduce our wants, but actually creates new ones. Purchase an audio system, for instance, and soon you will want compact discs, headphones, storage cabinets, and the like.

Societies face essentially the same dilemma: the wants of their members exceed the societies' capacities for satisfying those wants. In order to satisfy human wants, societies or nations require the use of *economic resources,* the scarce inputs that are used in the process of creating a good or providing a service. Traditionally, economists divide these resources into four categories: land, labor, capital, and entrepreneurship. *Land* signifies more than earth or acreage; it includes all raw materials—timber, water, minerals, and other production inputs—that are created by nature. *Labor* denotes both the physical and the mental work that goes into the production process. *Capital* is the term for human-made aids to production, including factories, machinery, and tools. *Entrepreneurship* is the managerial function that combines all these economic resources in an effective way and uncovers new opportunities to earn a profit—for example, through new products or processes. Entrepreneurship is characterized by a willingness to take the risks associated with a business venture.

Every society's stock of economic resources is limited, or *scarce*, in relation to the infinite wants of its members. At any given time even the world's richest economies have available only so much raw material, labor, equipment, and managerial talent to use in producing goods and services. Consequently an economy's ability to produce goods and services is limited, just as an individual's ability to satisfy his or her personal wants is limited.

The inability to satisfy all our wants forces us to make choices about how we can best use our limited resources. That is what economics is all about: making wise choices about how to use scarce resources. Therefore we define *economics* as the study of how to use our limited resources to satisfy our unlimited wants as fully as possible. When individuals, businesses, or nations try to make the most of what they have, they are "economizing."

Choice and Opportunity Cost

In order to make wise choices, we must compare the costs and benefits associated with each alternative or option we consider. A particular decision or choice will improve our well-being only if the benefits associated with that decision exceed the costs, if what we gain is worth more to us than what we lose.

One of the fundamental lessons of economics is that all our choices entail costs: there is no "free lunch." Whenever you make a decision to do or have one thing, you sacrifice the opportunity to do or have some other thing. The best, or *most valued*, alternative you must sacrifice in order to take a particular action is the *opportunity cost* of that action. What opportunity are you sacrificing by reading this chapter? Perhaps you could be studying for another class or watching your favorite TV show. The opportunity cost of reading this chapter is whatever you wanted to do most. When your city council or town meeting allocates tax dollars to install sidewalks, it may sacrifice books for the public library, street lights for a residential area, or tennis courts for a local park. Whatever that body would have chosen to do if it hadn't installed sidewalks is the opportunity cost of the sidewalks.

When Congress debates the size of the defense budget, the outcome of that debate affects each of us. If a nation's resources are fully employed, an increase in the output of military goods and services requires a reduction in the output of something else. An increase in military spending may mean a cut in welfare, road construction, or aid to education; it may mean an increase in taxes, which in turn will lead to a reduction in private consumer spending and the output of consumer goods.

Either way, more military output means less civilian output because at any given time there is a limit to the amount of total output the economy can produce. This doesn't necessarily mean we shouldn't spend more on military goods if there are sound reasons for doing so. It does mean we should be aware of what that spending costs us in terms of private goods and services or other government programs. The economist's point here is that we can't make the best decisions about how to use our scarce resources unless we know the true costs and benefits of our decisions. (See "The Fruits of Teen Labor," page 6, for a discussion of some of the hidden costs of a part-time job.)

The Production Possibilities Curve

We can illustrate the concept of opportunity cost with a simple graph called a production possibilities curve. (The appendix on graphing at the end of this chapter explains how graphs are constructed and interpreted.) A *production possibilities curve* shows the combinations of goods that the economy is capable of producing with its present stock of economic resources and its existing techniques of production. Because it outlines the boundaries, or limits, of the economy's ability to produce output, it is sometimes called a *production possibilities frontier*. Any point along or inside the frontier represents a combination of goods that the economy can produce; any point above the curve is beyond the economy's present production capacity.

Exhibit 1.1 shows the production capabilities of a hypothetical economy. The economy's output of civilian goods is measured on the vertical

The Fruits of Teen Labor: Bad Grades, Profligacy and a Jaded View of Working?

Quinn Duffin makes no bones about his priorities. The 18-year-old Evanston (Ill.) High School senior works as many as 38 hours a week as a grocery clerk, for $5.35 an hour. He has bought a stereo, a bicycle, a camera and, with his mother, a 1980 BMW automobile. Meanwhile, he is failing physics and math.

"I'd rather have money than pass a class," he declares.

That attitude, common to many teenagers, worries some psychologists and educators. After a decade and a half of encouraging young people to work, these authorities are concluding that jobs may do more to foster bad grades than to advance the work ethic. They say flipping hamburgers or bagging groceries not only detracts from studies but also provides money for goods that teen-agers don't need—including drugs and alcohol—and gives them a jaded view of work.

"The more kids work, the worse off they are," says Laurence Steinberg, a University of Wisconsin professor of child and family studies.

More Teen Workers

How many teen-age students may be hurting themselves by working isn't clear, but the number of working students is higher than ever—a reflection of rising prices and rising consumer wants. Prof. Steinberg, who is writing a book on teen-age employment, estimates that two in three high-school students hold part-time jobs. Sixteen years ago, he says, only half of high-school students worked.

Nobody denies that working is a necessity for many teen-agers. Melinda Fox, a Connecticut high-school senior, for one, is busy saving money ($6,000 so far) for college; she works in the office of a small manufacturer. Moreover, working long hours at a menial job is edifying for some people. One Evanston senior, Noreen Crittenden, says that working 28 hours a week at a market-research firm has forced her to learn to organize her time. As a result, she says, she made the school honor roll three times in a row. . . .

Yet time and again, teachers tell of employed students' lagging in school. Anne Moniz, a New Bedford (Mass.) High School student who worked as late as 11 p.m. each night as a secretary for an accounting firm, dozed off in classes. Her grades dropped, so she now works fewer hours. In Florida, a survey by the Pinnellas County schools found that 37% of its high-school students who worked were often too tired to go to school or fell asleep in class. . . .

Scheduling Problems

Once employed, many of the students have little choice but to play down school. The biggest employers of teen-agers—fast-food restaurants and grocery stores—often call in workers at the last minute, making it difficult to complete studying. "The employers don't consider the kids' other responsibilities," says Joyce Fischer, an Evanston High counselor.

With teens staying up all hours to earn a few extra dollars, some teachers have lowered their expectations, concludes a study by Linda McNeil, an assistant professor of education at Rice University in Houston. For example, William Hibert, a social-studies teacher at Brookline (Mass.) High School, uses class time for reading that used to be homework and gives one-third fewer assignments than he did 10 years ago.

Even with less homework, students who work more than

20 hours a week are more likely to drop out of school than people who work less or not at all, concluded a 1984 Ohio State University study.

While taking time out for work hurts students academically, the money they earn often hurts them in other ways. A study by the University of Michigan's Institute for Social Research found that the more hours students work, the more likely the students are to use drugs and alcohol, in part because regular paychecks make it easier to buy such things. . . .

On top of bad grades and bad buying habits, the teens are acquiring a bad image of the working world, some authorities fear. In the early 1970s, a number of studies concluded that working was good for U.S. teen-agers. But educators now say they didn't realize that most teens with jobs in the 1980s would be slopping lettuce, tomatoes and mayonnaise onto hamburgers or stuffing groceries into bags.

"These are jobs that are dead-end and dull," says Urie Bronfenbrenner, a professor of psychology at Cornell University in Ithaca, N.Y. "You're not learning anything in these experiences."

Feeling Cheated

That was a problem for one senior at Wilbur Cross High School in New Haven, Conn. The student, who declined to be interviewed for this story, worked his way up to night manager at a nearby McDonald's restaurant, but "he's not satisfied with the kind of money he's making, and he realizes he has gone as far as he can in that situation," says Maureen Howard, his English teacher. "He feels that somehow or other he has been cheated."

The mounting concern is resulting in calls for teens to work less, for parents and schools to monitor the spending of teens' wages and for students to stick to jobs more in line with career aspirations. . . .

But many employers of teenagers profess not to know what all the hubbub is about. Some educators "aren't giving sufficient credit to young people's sense of responsibility and their ability to make intelligent decisions about how they schedule their time and spend their money," insists a spokesman for Wendy's International Inc., an Ohio-based fast-food chain.

In any case, educators may have a tough time getting kids to cut back on work. Says Edward Horwitz, an Evanston High senior who works up to 46 hours a week as a grocery clerk: "The job gives me a kind of excuse. If I don't do well in school, I can always work here." —*Alex Kotlowitz*

SOURCE: *The Wall Street Journal*, May 27, 1986, p. 29. Reprinted by permission of *The Wall Street Journal*, © 1986 Dow Jones & Company, Inc. All Rights Reserved Worldwide.

USE YOUR ECONOMIC REASONING

1. **Identify the economic problem described in this article.** (*Hint:* **What scarce personal resource are these teenagers trying to use to satisfy their wants?**)

2. **What is the opportunity cost of part-time work? Could the opportunity cost involve several lost opportunities?**

3. **Does the fact that there is an opportunity cost for working mean that no student should work? What method should students use to evaluate the desirability of a part-time job?**

EXHIBIT 1.1

The Production Possibilities Curve

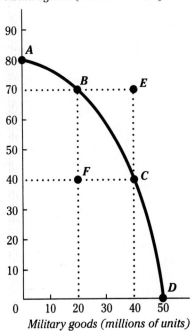

The production possibilities curve, ABCD, shows the combinations of civilian goods and military goods that the economy is capable of producing with its present stock of economic resources and the existing techniques of production. Any point on or below the curve is possible. Any point above the curve is ruled out (impossible).

---

axis and its output of military goods on the horizontal axis. According to this exhibit, if all the economy's resources were used to produce civilian goods, 80 million units of civilian goods could be produced each year (point *A*). On the other hand, if the economy were to use all its economic resources to produce military goods, 50 million units of military goods could be produced each year (point *D*). Between these extremes lie other production possibilities—combined outputs of military and civilian goods that the economy is capable of producing. For example, the economy might choose to produce 70 million units of civilian goods and 20 million units of military goods (point *B*). Or it might choose to produce 40 million units of civilian goods and 40 million units of military goods (point *C*). We can see, then, that the curve *ABCD* outlines the boundaries of our hypothetical economy's production abilities.

Unfortunately, economies do not always live up to their production capabilities. Whenever an economy is operating at a point inside its production possibilities curve, we know that economic resources are not being fully employed. For example, at point *F* in Exh. 1.1, our hypothetical economy is producing 40 million units of civilian goods and 20 million units of military goods each year. But according to the production possibilities curve, the economy could do much better. For example, it could increase its output of civilian goods to 70 million units a year without sacrificing any military goods (point *B*). Or it could increase its output of military goods to 40 million units a year without sacrificing any civilian goods (point *C*). In short, when an economy has unemployed resources, it is not satisfying as many of the society's unlimited wants as it could if it used its full potential.

Even when an economy fully employs its resources, it cannot satisfy all of a society's wants. Any point *above* the production possibilities curve (point *E*, for example, which combines 70 million units of civilian goods and 40 million units of military goods) is beyond the economy's present production capabilities. Society clearly would prefer that combination of products to the combination represented by, say, point *C,* but it can't obtain it. Of course, the economy's production capacity is not permanently fixed. If the quantity of economic resources were to increase, or if better production methods were discovered, then the economy could produce more goods and services. Such an increase in production capacity is usually described as *economic growth* and is illustrated by shifting the production possibilities curve to the right. The outside curve in Exh. 1.2 represents economic growth sufficient to take point *E* within the economy's production possibilities frontier.

Opportunity Costs Along the Curve

We have seen that the production possibilities curve graphically represents the concept of opportunity cost. When an economy's resources are fully employed—that is, when it is operating on the production possibilities curve rather than inside it—larger amounts of one product can be obtained only by producing smaller amounts of the other product. The production possibilities curve slopes downward to the right to illustrate opportunity cost: more of one thing means less of the other thing. We can see opportunity costs changing as we move from one point on the production possibilities curve to another. For example, suppose that the society is operating at point *A* on the production possibilities curve in Exh. 1.1 (or the inside curve in Exh. 1.2), producing 80 million units of civilian goods and no military goods. If the society decides that it would prefer to operate at point *B*, the opportunity cost of acquiring the first 20 million units of military goods would be the loss of 10 million units of civilian goods. The economy can move from point *A* to

EXHIBIT 1.2

Illustrating Economic Growth

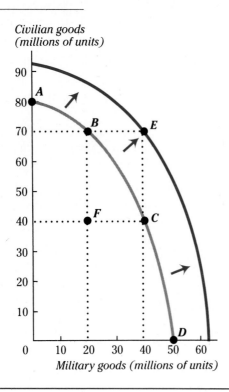

If the quantity of economic resources were to increase or better production methods were discovered, the economy's ability to produce goods and services would expand. Such economic growth can be illustrated by shifting the production possibilities curve to the right.

point *B* only by transferring resources from the production of civilian goods to the production of military goods.

Suppose that the society would like to have even more military goods. For example, suppose it would prefer to have 40 million units of military goods produced each year. According to the production possibilities curve, the opportunity cost of acquiring the next 20 million units of military goods (and moving from point *B* to point *C*) would be a loss of 30 million units of civilian goods—three times what it cost the society to acquire the first 20 million units of military goods. Moving from point *C* to point *D* would be even more expensive. In order to acquire the last 10 million units of military goods, the society would have to sacrifice 40 million units of civilian goods.

The Law of Increasing Costs

Our hypothetical production possibilities curve illustrates an important principle known as the *law of increasing costs:* As more of a particular product is produced, its opportunity cost per unit will increase. How do we explain the law of increasing costs? Why does our hypothetical society have to sacrifice larger and larger amounts of civilian output in order to obtain each additional increment of military output?

The explanation is fairly simple. Not all resources are alike; some economic resources—skilled labor and specialized machinery, for instance—are better suited to the production of one product than another. In our example some resources are better suited to the production of civilian goods and services, others to the production of military products. As a consequence, when the society attempts to expand its output of military goods and services, it must eventually use resources that are not well suited to producing those military products.

To illustrate that problem, let's examine the process of transferring resources from the production of civilian products to the production of military products. Suppose that initially our hypothetical economy is not producing any military output. At first it will not be difficult for the economy to increase its military output. Some of the existing capital resources, including factories, can be converted to the production of military products with relative ease, and many members of the labor force will have skills that are readily transferable to the production of military products. For example, it would be relatively easy to convert a clothing factory to the production of uniforms or to convert an awning factory to the production of tents. Since these conversions are relatively easy, the society will gain just about as much in military output as it will lose in civilian output.

But to continue expanding the output of military products, it will be necessary to use resources that are increasingly less suitable. For instance, consider the difficulty that might be encountered in converting an amusement park to a missile-manufacturing facility or a toy factory to an explosives plant. Much of the equipment that was useful in producing civilian output will be of no use in producing military output. Therefore, while the conversion of these facilities will require society to give up a large quantity of civilian output (many rides at the amusement park and thousands of toys), it will not result in very many additional units of military output.

The point is that because some resources are better suited to the production of civilian goods than to the production of military products, increasing amounts of civilian goods and services will have to be sacrificed to obtain each additional increment of military output.

As you can see, the production possibilities curve tells a great deal about opportunity cost. It shows you that an economy with fully employed resources cannot produce more of one thing without sacrificing something else. It is a forceful reminder that economics is, in effect, "the science of choice." The next section explores the nature of those choices in more detail.

The Three Fundamental Questions

The choice between military goods and civilian goods is only one of the broad decisions that the United States and other nations face. The dilemma of unlimited wants and limited economic resources forces each society to make three basic choices, to answer the "three fundamental questions" of economics: (1) What goods and services will we produce and in what quantities? (2) How will these goods and services be produced? (3) For whom will these products be produced—that is, how will the output be distributed?

What to Produce?

Because no society can produce everything its members desire, each society must sort through and assess its various wants and then decide which goods and services to produce in what quantities. Deciding the relative value of military products against civilian goods is only one part of the picture, because each society must determine precisely which civilian and military products it will produce. For example, it must decide whether to produce clothing or to conserve its scarce resources for some other use. Next, it must decide what types of clothing to produce—how many shirts, dresses, pairs of slacks, overcoats, and so on. Finally, it must decide in what sizes to produce these items of clothing and determine the quantities of each size. Only after considering all such alternatives can a society decide which goods and services to produce.

How to Produce?

After deciding which products to produce, each society must also decide what materials and methods to use in their production. In most cases a given good or service can be produced in more than one way. For instance, a shirt can be made of cotton, wool, or acrylic fibers. It can be sewn entirely by hand, partly by hand, or entirely by machine. It can be packaged in paper, cardboard, plastic, or some combination of materials. It can be shipped by truck, train, boat, or plane. In short, the producer must choose among many options with regard to materials, production methods, and means of shipment.

For Whom to Produce?

Finally, each society must decide how to distribute or divide up its limited output among those who desire to receive it. Should everyone receive equal shares of society's output? Should those who produce more receive more? What about those who don't produce at all, either because they can't work or because they don't want to work? How much of society's output should *they* receive? In deciding how to distribute output—how output will be shared—different societies are influenced by their traditions and cultural values.

Whether a society is rich or poor, simple or complex, democratic or authoritarian, it must have some *economic system* through which it addresses the three fundamental questions. Chapter 2 will examine a variety of economic systems and discuss how they respond to these questions.

Five Economic Goals

A given economic system's answers to the three fundamental questions are not always satisfactory to either the nation's citizens or its leaders. For example, if an economy is operating inside its production possibilities curve, it is not using all its production capabilities and is therefore not satisfying as many human wants as possible. A society with unemployed resources may want to take steps to improve the economy's performance so that it does a better job of fulfilling citizen expectations or, in some cases, the expectations of those in power.

What should a society expect from its economic system? Before a society can attempt to improve its economic performance, it must have a set of goals, objectives, or standards by which to judge that performance. Although there is room for debate about precisely what constitutes "good performance" from an economic system, many societies recognize five essential goals:

1. *Full employment of economic resources.* If a society is to obtain maximum benefit from its scarce resources, it must utilize them fully. Whenever resources are

When labor or other economic resources are unemployed, society must do without the goods and services those resources could have produced.

unemployed—when factories stand idle, laborers lack work, or farmland lies untilled—the society is sacrificing the goods and services that those resources could have produced. Therefore it is doing a less than optimal job of satisfying the unlimited wants of its members.

2. *Efficiency.* Economic efficiency means getting the most benefit out of limited resources. This goal has two separate elements: (a) production of the goods and services that consumers desire the most, and (b) realization of this production at the lowest cost in terms of scarce resources. Economic efficiency is the very essence of economics. If an economic system fully employs its resources but uses them to produce relatively unwanted products, the society cannot hope to achieve maximum satisfaction from its resources. By the same token, if an economy does not minimize the amount of resources used in producing *each* product, it will not be able to produce as many products; consequently, fewer wants will be satisfied.

3. *Economic growth.* Because most people want and expect their standard of living to improve continually, economic growth—expansion in the economy's output of goods and services—is an important objective. If population is increasing, some economic growth is necessary just to maintain the existing standard of material welfare. When a nation's population is stable or is increasing less rapidly than output, economic growth results in more goods and services per person, contributing to a higher standard of living.

4. *A fair distribution of income.* Distribution of income means the way income is divided among the members of a society. In modern economies the income distribution is the primary factor determining how output will be shared. (In primitive economies, such as Ethiopia or Burundi, custom or tradition plays a major role in deciding how output is divided.) Those with larger incomes receive larger shares of their economy's output. Is this a fair distribution of output? Some contend that it is. Others call for redistribution of income to eliminate poverty in the society. Still others argue that nothing less than an equal distribution is truly fair.

5. *A stable price level.* A major goal of most economies is a stable price level. Societies fear inflation—that is, a rise in the general level of prices. Inflation redistributes income arbitrarily: Some people's incomes rise more rapidly than inflation, whereas others find that their incomes can't keep pace. The former group emerges with a larger share of the economy's output, while the latter group must make do with less than before. The demoralizing effect of this redistribution can lead to social unrest.

In pursuing the five economic goals, societies strive to maintain compatibility with their noneconomic, or sociopolitical, objectives. Americans, for example, want to achieve these economic goals without harming the environment or sacrificing the rights of people to select their occupations, own property, and spend their incomes as they choose. Societies like Japan that place high value on tradition may strive to pursue these economic goals without violating the customs of the past. Insofar as the cultural, political, religious, and other noneconomic values of societies differ, the relative importance of each of the five economic goals and the methods of meeting those goals will also differ.

Conflicts and Trade-offs

Defining economic goals is only the first step in attempting to improve our economy's performance. The next step is to decide how to achieve these goals. Often the pursuit of one goal forces us to sacrifice at least part of some other economic or noneconomic goal. That is what economists call a *trade-off*—society gets more of one thing only by giving up, or trading off, something else. This is another way of stating the problem of opportunity cost. The opportunity cost of achieving a particular goal is whatever other goal has to be sacrificed or compromised. Let's consider three problems societies face in pursuing economic goals.

Full Employment versus Stable Prices

The goal of achieving full employment may conflict with the goal of maintaining a stable price level. Experience has taught us that attempting to reduce unemployment generally results in a higher rate of inflation. By the same token, attempts to reduce the rate of inflation often lead to higher unemployment. Frequently, it becomes necessary to sacrifice part of one goal in favor of the other. For instance, society may accept some unemployment to maintain a lower inflation rate. The tradeoff each society makes depends partly on economic analysis, but is also influenced by societal values.[1]

Economic Growth versus Environmental Protection

Conflict frequently occurs between the goals of economic growth and a clean environment. Although most Americans support these two goals, it has become apparent that expansion of the economy's output takes a toll on the environment. For instance, our attempts to expand agricultural output by using pesticides and chemical fertilizers have been partially responsible for the pollution of our rivers and streams. We make trade-offs between economic growth and environmental preservation, trade-offs that reflect prevailing national values.

Equality versus Efficiency

Consider now the potential conflict between income equality and economic efficiency. Suppose a society decided that fair income distribution demanded greater equality of income than presently exists. Many economists would point out that efforts to achieve greater equality tend to have a negative impact on economic efficiency. Remember, efficiency means producing the most wanted products in the least costly way. To accomplish this, the economy must be able to direct labor to the areas where it is most needed, often by making wages and salaries in these areas more attractive than those in other areas. For example, if a society needs to increase its number of computer programmers more rapidly than its number of teachers or nurses, it can encourage people to become computer programmers by making that occupation more rewarding financially than teaching or nursing.[2] If pay differentials are

---

[1] Most economists agree that there is a short-run trade-off between unemployment and inflation that may not exist in the long run. This issue will be discussed in Chapter 14.
[2] In some economic systems these adjustments in wages and salaries would occur automatically; in others deliberate action would be required. Chapter 2 will have more to say about how specific economic systems direct or allocate labor.

reduced in order to meet the goal of equality, a society will sacrifice economic efficiency because it will be more difficult to direct the flow of labor.

Choosing Between Objectives

When our society's goals conflict and demand that we choose between them, it is not the function of economists to determine the best trade-off. The choice between equality and efficiency, for example, is a *normative issue*, involving judgments about what "should be" rather than what is. Setting goals is the job of the society or its representatives. The function of the economist is to make sure that those in charge of setting goals (or devising policies to achieve goals) are aware of the alternatives available to them and the sacrifices each alternative requires. When economists stop talking about how things are and start talking about how they should be, they have entered the realm of values, an arena in which they have no more expertise than anyone else. (See "Oregon Prioritizes Medical Operations In Care Program," page 18, for a discussion of economics and ethics.)

Economic Theory and Policy

Before economists can recommend policies for dealing with economic problems or achieving goals, they must understand thoroughly how the economic system operates. This is where economic theory comes into play.

Economic theories are generalizations about causal relationships between economic variables; through theories, economists attempt to explain what causes what in economics. Theories are also referred to as laws, principles, and models. When in later chapters you encounter the *law* of demand, the *principle* of comparative advantage, and the *model* of command socialism, bear in mind that each of these tools is a theory. One reason why economic theories help economists understand the real world is that they simplify reality. In fact, theories or models are sometimes described as simplified pictures of the real world. By leaving out extraneous details and complexities, they help us see the essential relationships more clearly—much as a map clarifies the shape and layout of a city by excluding unnecessary detail.

When you read the evening newspaper or tune in the news on television, you are exposed to a deluge of facts and figures about everything from housing construction to foreign trade. Without theories to help you interpret them, however, these data are of little value. As an example, suppose we observe that per-capita gasoline consumption in the United States is

Oregon Prioritizes Medical Operations In Care Program

WASHINGTON—Oregon has drawn up a list of health care priorities as part of a closely watched statewide experiment to provide health insurance to more people by rationing care.

The list ranks more than 800 medical procedures and services from those deemed most essential to those considered least vital or cost-effective. The Oregon state legislature in the next few months will review cost estimates of the services and determine a cut-off point at which Medicaid, the public health insurance program for the poor, will no longer provide coverage.

By refusing to pay for some high-cost, high-risk procedures, Medicaid plans to provide basic health benefits to 120,000 poor Oregonians who aren't currently covered by the program. And Oregon businesses have agreed to guarantee the same package of benefits covered under Medicaid starting in 1994.

"We have publicly, honestly and explicitly defined what is most important to us as Oregonians for the health care and quality of our lives," said Bill Gregory, chairman of the state's Health Services Commission, which compiled the list of priorities.

The trade-off is controversial, and before the Oregon plan can go into effect, the U.S. Congress must exempt the state from certain Medicaid rules. It would mark the most radical health care reform efforts in the U.S., where the cost of providing health services climbed above $650 billion last year and more than 30 million people lack health insurance.

Age isn't a factor on the list, which gives priority to life-saving treatments likely to lead to full recovery, such as appendectomies and treatment of bronchopneumonia. It also assigns high priorities to preventive care, such as childhood immunizations; to maternity care and birth control; and to treatment of chronic conditions that improves the quality of life.

It makes hard choices on coverage of terminal illness. Treatment of the early stages of the AIDS virus ranks higher than for later stages. Treatment of patients with acquired immune deficiency syndrome determined to have less than a 10% survival rate at five years, for example, ranks 801 out of the 802 services. Local and regional cancers have higher priority than those that have spread. While heart and liver transplants rank relatively high, certain types of bone marrow transplants are far down the list.

The priority list has left some members of Congress deeply split. Rep. Henry Waxman (D., Calif.), chairman of a House health subcommittee, worries that creating a package of core benefits for everyone could keep Medicare's most needy recipients—poor women and children—from receiving vital health care services.

But Rep. Ron Wyden (D., Ore.) said, "The current health care system for the poor is absolutely indefensible. . . . So many people are being missed that you can't defend the status quo."

The experiment, he argued, would "allow us to serve more people in a more human, rational, cost-effective way."

Currently in Oregon, Medicaid serves only 42% of residents living below the poverty line. A family of four, with an annual income of $6,493 is considered too well-off to qualify. About 18% of the state's population doesn't have health insurance.

The state estimates that, despite the rationing, providing basic health coverage for more people will cost at least an extra $100 million annually, with the state providing more than $40 million. The Oregon state legislators have talked about a payroll tax or a hospital tax to help raise the money. Under a Medicaid formula, the federal government would provide the rest of the funds.
—*Hilary Stout*

SOURCE: *The Wall Street Journal*, February 22, 1991, p. A5. Reprinted by permission of *The Wall Street Journal*, © 1991 Dow Jones & Company, Inc. All Rights Reserved Worldwide.

USE YOUR ECONOMIC REASONING

1. **What statements in this article illustrate that the provision of health care involves an economic problem?**

2. **Oregon plans to provide basic health benefits to 120,000 additional Oregonians by refusing to pay for some high-cost procedures and by raising taxes. What are the opportunity costs of providing benefits to these previously ineligible residents?**

3. **Oregon's health care program clearly involves normative issues. Explain.**

declining. In order to explain this fact, we need a theory. Suppose that after studying the relevant data—number of cars on the road, availability of gasoline and its price—we discover what seems to be a relationship between two facts: As gasoline prices have risen, gasoline consumption has declined. We might "theorize" from this that rising gasoline prices have caused gasoline consumption to decrease.

Testing Economic Theories

We could test our theory by gathering data for a number of different time periods to see if, in fact, gasoline consumption has increased and decreased consistently in accordance with changes in its price. But this test would not include other significant elements. Even if the price of gasoline is a major factor influencing the amount consumed, it is clearly not the *only* factor. It seems likely that over a given period personal income also affects gasoline consumption. If the incomes of car owners remain constant while gasoline prices rise, gasoline consumption may well decline. But if incomes increase during the same period, offsetting the rise in gasoline prices, gasoline consumption will probably remain the same; it may even increase.

To determine whether the consumption of gasoline is in fact related to the price of gasoline, economists have to be able to hold constant personal income and any other nonprice factors that might influence the amount of gasoline consumed. Unfortunately, economists cannot control these other factors as precisely as chemists or physicists can control variables in their experiments. So economists do the next best thing. They *assume* that everything else remains the same; that is, they assume other factors, such as personal incomes, remain constant. This is the assumption of *ceteris paribus,* which literally means "other things being equal." In a sense, what economists are doing is stating the conditions under which they expect a theory to be valid. To illustrate, our theory about the consumption of gasoline might be restated this way: "Consumers will buy less gasoline at higher prices than at lower prices, ceteris paribus—other things being equal." Economists then compare what actually happens to what, on the basis of the theory, they expected to happen. If the facts are not consistent with the theory, then we must determine whether it is because the theory is invalid or because the assumption of ceteris paribus has been violated (that is, because something other than the price of gasoline changed).

Policies and Predictions

Once a theory has been tested and accepted, it can be used as a basis for making predictions and as a guide to formulating economic policy. On the basis of our gas-price theory, for example, we would predict that if gasoline prices go up, consumption will decline and that if prices fall, consumption will increase. We could also use this theory as the basis for devising policies for influencing the level of gasoline consumption. In order to reduce domestic gasoline consumption, for instance, we might recommend an increase in the federal tax on gasoline.

The formulation of policies for dealing with economic problems is the most important use of economic theory and the most important function of economists. In considering this function it is important to remember that usually there is more than one way to achieve a given objective. A society wants to select the policy option that will permit it to achieve its objective at the lowest "cost" in terms of its other goals.

Economists and Conclusions

If you listen to the TV news or read the newspaper, you know that economists do not always agree on matters of economic policy. "You can lay all economists end to end and never reach a conclusion" is a popular saying about the inability of economists to agree on the best economic policy for specific social problems. Laypersons therefore may be skeptical about the contribution that economics can make toward solving society's problems. Because you are going to spend the next few months studying economics, it seems appropriate to take a few minutes now to consider the reasons why economists disagree. Economists may disagree either because they have different views about what *should be* or because they have different views of what *is*.

We've already explained that economists possess no special expertise in choosing goals, in deciding *how things ought to be*. Yet, like all thinking people, economists hold individual values and opinions about which of society's economic goals are the most important. Obviously, economists with different philosophies about what the society should be attempting to achieve will have different recommendations with respect to economic policy. Economists attempt to avoid this source of disagreement by asking political leaders and other decision makers to specify their economic goals; then the economist can suggest policies to achieve those goals.

Economists may also disagree about the proper policy for achieving a chosen goal or combating an economic problem because they disagree about how things *are*—about how the economy works or how a particular policy would work. Suppose, for example, that the challenge is to eliminate inflation. Some economists believe that the major cause of virtually every outbreak of inflation is a too-rapid growth of the money supply. Not surprisingly, the remedy they suggest is a reduction in the growth rate of the money supply. Other economists believe that inflation springs from a variety of causes: too much government spending; "shocks" such as steep OPEC oil-price increases and bad crop harvests; the wage-price spiral, wherein higher wage costs push up prices, and higher prices lead to demands for higher wages. These economists call for a variety of policies to deal with what they see as a multidimensional problem. In the absence of controlled testing, each economic theory retains its supporters, and the debate continues about the merits of one explanation and the limitations of the other.

The fact that economists, like all social scientists, are intensely interested in exploring and debating issues on which they disagree does not mean that they can never reach a conclusion. There are many issues and answers on which economists are in general agreement, so don't let the disagreements about particular policy questions mislead you. The study of economics has a great deal to contribute to your understanding of the world and its many social problems. Approach it with an open mind, and it will help you to make sense out of facts and events you never before understood.

The Organization of the Text

Now that you have some sense of what the study of economics is about, let's take a brief look at the organization of this book. It is composed of four major parts. Part 1 forms the introduction and lays the conceptual groundwork for the rest of the text. Part 2 takes up *microeconomics,* the study of the individual units of the economy. These chapters examine how the prices of particular goods and services are determined and how individual consumers and businesses function. True to its name, microeconomics looks at the small units that make up the whole economy. Part 3 examines *macroeconomics,* the study of the economy's overall performance and the factors influencing that performance. These chapters address such problems as unemployment and inflation and describe what may be done to eliminate these economic ills or at least reduce their severity. Through macroeconomics you will begin to view the economy in terms of the big picture. Part 4 turns to *international economics,* the study of international trade and finance. These chapters explore the reasons for trade and how transactions between nations are financed.

As you can see, economics embraces several specialized areas. Because these areas are interrelated, what you learn in Part 1 will help you understand problems taken up in Part 4. In fact, to a large extent, the chapters in this text build on one another. So please take the time to understand each one thoroughly for an easier and more rewarding trip through economic theory and practice.

Summary

The fundamental economic problem facing both individuals and societies is the fact that our wants exceed our capacity for satisfying those wants. No society has enough *economic resources* (*land, labor, capital,* and *entrepreneurship*) to satisfy its members fully. As a consequence, individuals and societies must make choices about how best to use their limited resources. *Economics* is the study of how to use our limited resources to satisfy our unlimited wants as fully as possible.

One of the principal lessons of economics is that all choices entail costs, that there is no "free lunch." Whenever you make a decision to do or have one thing, you are sacrificing the opportunity to do or have some other thing. The most valued alternative you must sacrifice in order to take a given action is the *opportunity cost* of that action.

A *production possibilities curve* illustrates the concept of opportunity cost by showing the combinations of goods that an economy is capable of producing with its present stock of economic resources and existing techniques of production. It shows that unless there are unemployed resources, producing more of one thing means producing less of something else.

The dilemma of unlimited wants and limited resources forces each society to make three basic choices, to answer the three fundamental questions of economics: (1) What goods and services will the society produce and in what quantities? (2) How will these goods and services be produced? (3) For whom will these products be produced?

In order to determine how well it is answering the three fundamental questions, a society must establish goals or objectives against which it compares its performance. Full employment, economic efficiency, economic growth, a fair distribution of income, and a stable price level are widely accepted goals. When these goals are in conflict, as they often are, the pursuit of one goal commonly requires a trade-off, some sacrifice in terms of fulfilling another goal.

Before economists can recommend policies for dealing with economic problems or achieving specific objectives, they must develop economic theories, generalizations about causal relationships between economic variables. Testing economic theories can be tricky because the assumption of *ceteris paribus* (other things being equal) is often violated. This makes it difficult to determine when a theory is flawed, since the results of an experiment could be biased by changes in uncontrolled factors.

Once a theory has been tested and accepted, it can be used as a basis for making predictions and as a guide to formulating economic policy. When it comes to making policy recommendations, economists do not always agree. They may disagree for one or both of two distinct reasons: because they have different views about what *should be* or because they have different views about what *is*.

Glossary

Page 4 **Capital.** Human-made aids to the production process; for example, factories, machinery, and tools.

Page 20 **Ceteris paribus.** "Other things being equal"; the assumption that other variables remain constant.

Page 4 **Economics.** The study of how to use our limited resources to satisfy our unlimited wants as fully as possible.

Page 3 **Economic resources.** The scarce inputs used in the process of creating a good or providing a service; specifically, land, labor, capital, and entrepreneurship.

Page 17 **Economic theories.** Generalizations about causal relationships between economic variables.

Page 4 **Entrepreneurship.** The managerial function that combines land, labor, and capital in a cost-effective way and uncovers new opportunities to earn profit; includes willingness to take the risks associated with a business venture.

Page 22 **International economics.** The study of international trade and finance: why nations trade and how their transactions are financed.

Page 4 **Labor.** The mental and physical work of those employed in the production process.

Page 4 **Land.** All the natural resources or raw materials used in production; for example, acreage, timber, water, iron ore.

Page 11 **Law of increasing costs.** As more of a particular product is produced, the opportunity cost per unit will increase.

Page 22 **Macroeconomics.** The study of the economy's overall performance and the factors influencing that performance.

Page 22 **Microeconomics.** The study of the behavior of individual economic units.

Page 17 **Normative issue.** A question that calls for a value judgment about how things ought to be.

Page 4   ***Opportunity cost.*** The best, or most valued, alternative that is sacrificed when a particular action is taken.

Page 5   ***Production possibilities curve.*** A curve that shows the combinations of goods that an economy is capable of producing with its present stock of economic resources and existing techniques of production.

Study Questions

Fill in the Blanks

1. Land, labor, and capital are examples of _____.

2. The dilemma of _____ wants and _____ _____ resources is referred to as the economic problem.

3. _____ are combiners, innovators, and risk takers.

4. The term _____ is used by economists to describe the economic resources created by nature.

5. When we sacrifice one alternative for another, the alternative forgone is called the _____ of that action.

6. A _____ shows the combinations of goods that an economy is capable of producing.

7. Economists use economic _____ to make sense out of the facts they observe.

8. When the pursuit of one objective forces society to sacrifice or compromise some other objective, economists say that a _____ exists.

9. Issues involving what "should be" rather than what "is" are referred to as _____ issues.

10. Because economists cannot conduct controlled experiments, they often make the assumption of _____ to state the conditions under which they expect their theory to hold.

Multiple Choice

1. Economics is the study of how to
   a) completely satisfy our unlimited wants.
   b) do the best we can with what we have.
   c) reduce our unlimited wants.
   d) expand our stock of economic resources.

2. The opportunity cost of attending summer school is
   a) the cost of tuition and books.
   b) negative, because you will finish college more rapidly by attending summer school.
   c) the income you could have earned over the summer.
   d) the cost of tuition and books, plus any forgone income and/or recreational opportunities.

3. If something has an opportunity cost, we should
   a) avoid that action.
   b) take that action.
   c) be sure that the benefit of the action exceeds the cost.
   d) be sure that the cost of the action exceeds the benefit.

4. Producing the most wanted products in the least costly way is
   a) full employment.
   b) economic growth.
   c) a fair income distribution.
   d) economic efficiency.

5. Economists have trouble testing their theories because
   a) people are unpredictable.
   b) the real world is too complicated to be explained.
   c) they can't hold constant the "other factors" that might influence the outcome of the experiment.
   d) the necessary economic data are almost never available.

6. Which of the following should not be a function of the economist?
   a) Devising policies to achieve goals
   b) Setting goals
   c) Explaining how the economy works
   d) Explaining how particular goals conflict

7. Economists sometimes reach different conclusions on a given issue because
   a) they disagree about goals.
   b) they disagree about the way the economy works.
   c) a and b
   d) neither a nor b

8. Macroeconomics deals with
   a) the study of international trade.
   b) the study of individual economic units.
   c) the study of production possibilities.
   d) the study of the economy's overall performance.

9. Of the three fundamental questions, the "distribution" question has to do with
   a) who will receive the output.
   b) how the output will be shipped from the place of production to the consumer.
   c) how economic resources are distributed to producers.
   d) what products will be produced.

10. Suppose that you have just found $5.00 on the street and you are thinking of using it to buy a ticket to the movies. The opportunity cost of going to the show would be
    a) nothing—since you found the money, you are sacrificing nothing to spend it.
    b) whatever you would have bought with the money if you hadn't used it to go to the show.
    c) the other activities you would have to sacrifice to attend the show.
    d) b and c

Use the following production possibilities curve in answering questions 11 and 12.

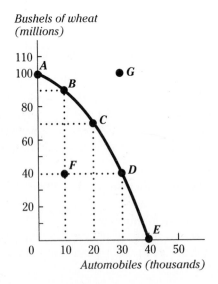

Bushels of wheat (millions)

Automobiles (thousands)

11. If the economy is operating at point *C*, the opportunity cost of producing an additional 10,000 automobiles will be
    a) 10 million bushels of wheat.
    b) 20 million bushels of wheat.
    c) 30 million bushels of wheat.
    d) 40 million bushels of wheat.

12. Point *G* on the diagram represents
    a) an optimal use of the society's resources.
    b) a combination of outputs beyond the economy's productive capacity.
    c) a situation in which some of the economy's resources are unemployed.
    d) the same output combination as point *B*.

Problems and Questions for Discussion

1. List the four categories of economic resources and explain each.

2. Define economics. Why is economics sometimes called the "study of choice"?

3. List and explain the three fundamental choices that each society is forced to make.

4. What is meant when we say that a secretary is efficient? What about a sales clerk? Why is economic efficiency an important performance objective for an economy?

5. Airline personnel are often allowed to make a certain number of free flights each year. How would you compute the opportunity cost to the airlines of these free trips? Might this cost vary from route to route? Might the cost be different at different times of the year? Explain.

6. List and briefly explain the economic objectives recognized as worthwhile by many societies.

7. What are trade-offs? Give some examples.

8. We've just developed a theory. (Actually this theory has been around for quite some time.) It says, "Better-educated people earn higher incomes than less-educated people, ceteris paribus." If we know a high school dropout who earns $200,000 a year, does this mean we should discard our theory? Explain.

9. Suppose we accept the theory given in problem 8 and decide to use it to formulate policies for reducing poverty. Apply this theory by suggesting three policies to reduce poverty.

10. Why is it important to separate the process of setting economic goals from the process of devising policies for achieving these goals? In which process is the economist more expert? Explain.

STUDY QUESTIONS

Answer Key

Fill in the Blanks

1. economic resources
2. unlimited, limited
3. Entrepreneurs
4. land
5. opportunity cost
6. production possibilities curve
7. theories (or models)
8. trade-off
9. normative
10. ceteris paribus

Multiple Choice

1. b
2. d
3. c
4. d
5. c
6. b
7. c
8. d
9. a
10. d
11. c
12. b

Appendix: Working with Graphs

Economists frequently use graphs to illustrate economic concepts. This appendix provides a brief review of graphing and offers some practice problems to help you become more comfortable working with graphs.

The Purpose of Graphs

The basic purpose of a graph is to represent the relationship between two variables. A *variable* is any quantity that can take on different numeric values. Suppose, for example, that a university has conducted a survey to determine the relationship between two variables: the number of hours its students study and their grade-point averages. The results of that hypothetical survey could be shown in table or schedule form, as in panel (a) of Exh. A.1, or they could be represented graphically, as in panel (b) of Exh. A.1. Notice the difference: The graph reveals the relationship between the variables at a glance; you don't have to compare data as you do when reading the table.

Constructing a Graph

The first step in constructing a graph is to draw two perpendicular lines. These lines are called *axes*. In our example the vertical axis is used to measure the first variable, the grade-point average; the horizontal axis is used to measure the second variable, hours of study. The place where the two axes meet is called the *origin* because it is the starting point for measuring each of the

EXHIBIT A.1

The Hypothetical Relationship between Grades and Study Time

HOURS OF STUDY (per week)	GRADE-POINT AVERAGE
32	4.0
28	3.5
24	3.0
20	2.5
16	2.0
12	1.5
8	1.0
4	0.4
0	0.0

(a) Relationship with table

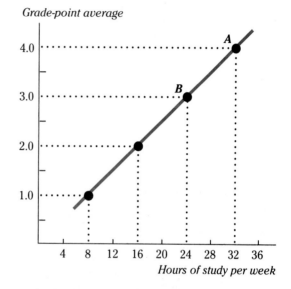

(b) Relationship with graph

Both (a) and (b) illustrate the relationship between hours of study and grades. Panel (a) uses a table to show this relationship; panel (b), a graph. In both illustrations, we can see that the relationship between the two variables is direct; more hours of study tend to be associated with a higher grade-point average.

variables; in our example the origin is zero. Once the axes are in place, we are ready to draw, or *plot*, the points that represent the relationship between the variables. Let's begin with the students who study 32 hours a week. According to the table in panel (a), these students typically earn a grade-point average of 4.0. To show this relationship graphically, we find the point on the horizontal axis that represents 32 hours of study per week. Next we move directly upward from that point until we reach a height of 4.0 grade points. This point, which we will label *A*, represents a combination of two values; it tells us at a glance that the typical student who studies 32 hours a week will earn a 4.0 grade-point average.

We plot the rest of the information found in panel (a) in the same way. To represent the typical or average grade of the student who studies 24 hours a week, all we need to do is locate the number 24 on the horizontal axis and then move up vertically from that point to a distance of 3.0 grade points (point *B*). We plot all the remaining points on the graph in the same way.

Once we have plotted all the points, we can connect them to form a curve. Economists use the term "curve" to describe any graphic relationship between two variables, so don't be surprised when you discover a straight line referred to as a curve. You can see that the resulting curve slopes upward and to the right. This indicates that there is a positive, or *direct*, relationship between the two variables—as one variable (study time) increases, the other (grade-point average) does also. If the resulting curve had sloped downward and to the right, it would have indicated a negative, or *inverse*, relationship between the two variables—as one variable increased, the other would decrease. We would be surprised to find an inverse relationship between these particular variables; that would suggest the unlikely possibility that increased study time lowers the grade-point average!

Practice in Graphing

Basically, all graphs are the same, so if you understand the one we just considered, you should be able to master all the graphs in this textbook and in library sources. If you want some practice, take a few minutes to graph the three sets of data at the end of this appendix.

The first step is to draw and label the vertical and horizontal axes and mark them off in units that are convenient to work with. As you probably know, mathematicians always measure the *independent* variable (the variable that causes the other to change) along the horizontal axis, and the *dependent* variable (the variable that responds to changes) along the vertical axis. Economists are less strict in deciding which variable to place on which axis, so don't be alarmed if occasionally you see the dependent variable on the horizontal axis.

Once you have decided which variable to place on which axis, the next step is to plot the information from the table as points and connect them. Finally, see if you can interpret your graph. What does it tell you about the relationship between the two variables? Are they directly or inversely related? (It's possible they are not related at all. For example, there is probably no relationship between a student's weight and his or her grade-point average.) Does the relationship change somewhere along the graph? The way to become comfortable with graphs is to work with them. Try drawing these graphs to see how easy it is.

1. Graph the relationship between the hourly wage rate paid by the school and the number of students desiring to work in the school cafeteria. Is the relationship direct or inverse?

POINT	WAGE RATE (per hour)	NUMBER OF STUDENT WORKERS
A	$2.50	5
B	3.00	10
C	3.50	15
D	4.00	20
E	4.50	25
F	5.00	30

2. Graph the relationship between the average daily temperature and the average number of students playing tennis on the school tennis courts. How does this relationship change?

POINT	TEMPERATURE (in degrees Fahrenheit)	NUMBER OF TENNIS PLAYERS
A	60	20
B	70	30
C	80	40
D	90	30
E	100	20

3. Graph the relationship between the price of gasoline and the quantity of gasoline purchased by consumers. Is the relationship direct or inverse?

POINT	PRICE (per gallon)	QUANTITY PURCHASED (in gallons)
A	$ .50	15 million
B	1.00	12 million
C	1.50	9 million
D	2.00	6 million
E	2.50	3 million

ECONOMIC SYSTEMS

From the richest to the poorest, every nation faces the same economic dilemma: how to satisfy people's unlimited wants with its limited economic resources. Each society must decide which products and services to produce, how to produce them, and for whom to produce them; in other words, it must establish an economic system. Basically, an *economic system* is a set of procedures for answering the three fundamental questions of economics—what, how, and for whom to produce. We will identify different economic systems according to the following criteria:

Who owns the means of production?

Who makes the economic choices that determine what, how, and for whom to produce?

What mechanism is used to ensure that these decisions are carried out?[1]

The variety of real-world economic systems is probably as great as the number of world nations, but all economic systems lie somewhere be-

---

[1] This is the classification system adopted by Gary M. and Joyce E. Pickersgill in *Contemporary Economic Systems* (Englewood Cliffs, N.J.: Prentice-Hall, 1974), p. 10.

tween two divergent models. At one extreme, the means of production are privately owned; economic choices are made by individuals; implementation occurs through markets. At the other extreme, the means of production are owned publicly, by the state; economic choices are made collectively; implementation occurs through commands from a central authority.

The purpose of this chapter is to give you an overview of how economic systems function. First we examine the two divergent models—pure capitalism and pure command socialism. Recall from Chapter 1 that models simplify reality, making it possible for us to see more clearly how the parts of a system function and interact. Once we have become familiar with these theoretical models, we can compare the economies of the United States and the former Soviet Union against them to discover how they conform and how they deviate from the models.

The Model of Pure Capitalism

Our model of pure capitalism describes a hypothetical economy. As you work through the following sections, remember that you are learning about a theoretical model, not an existing system. As you will see later in the chapter, the United States and other real-world economies don't conform perfectly to either of the two divergent models. Here we will examine the elements of pure capitalism, diagram the operation (or functioning) of the system, see how it answers the three fundamental questions, and conclude by assessing its strengths and weaknesses.

Elements of Capitalism

By definition, *capitalism* is an economic system in which the means of production are privately owned and fundamental economic choices are made by individuals and implemented through the market mechanism—the interaction of buyers and sellers. The model of pure capitalism is entirely consistent with our definition and contains five basic elements, which we will describe briefly.

Private Property and Freedom of Choice. One of the principal features of capitalism is private property. In a capitalist economy private individuals and groups are the owners of the *means of production*: the raw materials, factories, farms, and other economic resources used to produce goods and services. These resource owners may sell or use their resources, including their own labor, as they see fit. Businesses are free to decide what products they will produce and free to purchase the necessary economic resources from whomever they choose. Consumers, in turn, are free to spend their incomes any way they like. They can purchase whatever products they choose, and they can decide what fraction of their income to save and what fraction to spend.

Self-Interest. Self-interest is the driving force of capitalism. In 1776 Adam Smith, the founder of modern economics, described a capitalist economy as one in which the primary concern of each player—of each producer, worker, and consumer—was to promote his or her own welfare.[2]

Smith introduced the *invisible hand* doctrine, which held that as individuals pursued their own interest, they would be led as if by an invisible hand to promote the good of the society as a whole. In order to earn the highest profits, predicted Smith, producers would generate the products consumers wanted the most. Workers would offer their services where they were most needed because wages would be highest in those sectors. Consumers would favor producers who offered superior products and/or lower prices because they would seek the best value for their money. The result would be an economy that produced the goods and services desired by the society without the need for any central direction by government.

Markets and Prices. Capitalism is often described as a market system. This is because a capitalist economy contains numerous interdependent markets through which the functioning of the economy is coordinated and directed. A *market* consists of all actual or potential buyers and sellers of a particular item. It can be local, regional, national, or international. For example, there are numerous local and regional markets for used automobiles, each consisting of all buyers and sellers of such vehicles in that particular area. Similar markets exist for all other goods and services and for all economic resources as well.

Market prices are determined by the interaction of buyers and sellers and serve three important functions: First, prices signal information to prospective buyers and sellers; they tell buyers the relative costs of the various products on the market, and they tell producers how much they can expect to receive by producing a particular product. Second, prices motivate businesses to produce more of some products and less of others. In general, businesses want to supply products that yield the highest profits, the ones with the highest prices in relation to their costs of production. Third, prices

---

[2] Adam Smith's description of the functioning of a capitalist economy appeared in *An Inquiry into the Nature and Causes of the Wealth of Nations,* published in 1776.

help to divide up, or ration, the society's limited output of goods and services. Only those consumers who are willing and able to pay the market price receive the product.

Competition. Adam Smith recognized that for the invisible hand to work—for individuals seeking their own interest to promote the good of all—the pursuit of self-interest had to be guided and restrained by competition. Competition ensures that producers remain responsive to consumers and that prices remain reasonable.

Pure capitalism requires *pure competition,* a situation in which a large number of relatively small buyers and sellers interact to determine prices.[3] Under conditions of pure competition, no individual buyer or seller can set—or even significantly influence—the prevailing price of a product or resource. Prices are thus determined by market forces, not by powerful buyers or sellers, and they change only when market conditions change.

Limited Government Intervention. Pure capitalism is above all a *laissez-faire economy.* (Laissez-faire is a popular French phrase that in this context means "let the people do as they choose.") The model describes no role for government in making economic decisions. Through pricing, the market determines all production and distribution decisions—what, how, and for whom to produce—and competition ensures that consumers will be charged reasonable prices. The only role of government is to provide the kind of environment in which a market economy can function well. For example, government must define and enforce the private-property rights that enable individuals to own and use property.

The Circular-Flow Model

We can represent the operation of a capitalist economy in a diagram called the circular-flow model. Exhibit 2.1 models an economy composed of only two sectors: households and businesses. You can see that these two sectors are connected through transactions, or flows, that occur continuously between them. We'll examine how each sector processes the flow it receives and returns it to the other sector.

The Household and Business Sectors. The household sector is shown at the right in Exh. 2.1. A *household* is a living unit that also functions as an economic unit. Whether it consists of a single person or numerous people, each household will have a source of income and will spend that income. The

---

[3] Further assumptions relating to pure competition will be described in Chapter 6.

EXHIBIT 2.1

The Circular Flow of Pure Capitalism

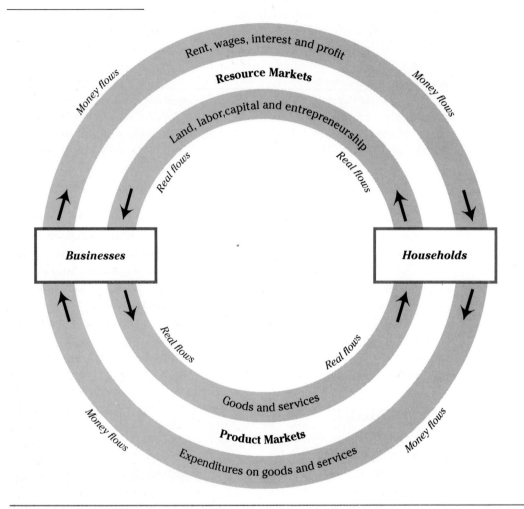

household sector is composed of all the individual households in the economy. Because households own the land, labor, capital, and entrepreneurship that businesses need to produce goods and services, this sector is the source of all economic resources in the model of pure capitalism. It is also the source of consumer spending for the goods and services produced.

The business sector, on the left, is composed of all the businesses in the economy. The business sector purchases economic resources from households, converts them into products, and sells the products to the households.

Real Flows and Money Flows. You can see that two types of flows circle in opposite directions in the diagram. In the outside circle, *money flows*—in the form of rent, wages, interest, and profit—go from businesses to households to pay for economic resources. These flows return to businesses as households pay for products. *Real flows* involve the physical movement of the resources and products. The inner flow in the diagram shows economic resources in the form of land, labor, capital, and entrepreneurship flowing from the household sector to the business sector, where they are used to produce goods and services. The unbroken arrows in the diagram show that these circular flows proceed endlessly.

The Resource and Product Markets. Markets are the key to the operation of a capitalist system because they hold together its decentralized economy of millions of individual buyers and sellers. The interaction of these buyers and sellers ensures that the right products (the ones desired by consumers) are produced and that economic resources flow to the right producers (the ones producing the most wanted products at the lowest prices).

In the resource markets, depicted in the upper portion of Exh. 2.1, the interaction of buyers and sellers determines the prices of the various economic resources. For example, in the labor market for accountants, an accountant's salary is determined by the interaction of employers seeking to hire accountants (the buyers) and accountants seeking employment (the sellers). Changes in resource prices guide and motivate resource suppliers to provide the type and quantity of resources producers need the most. Using our example of labor, suppose that the number of businesses desiring accountants is expanding more rapidly than new accountants are being trained. What will happen to the salaries of accountants? They will tend to increase. As a result, we can expect more people in the household sector to invest the time and money necessary to become accountants. You can see how the price mechanism ensures (1) that the types of labor, equipment, and other resources most needed by businesses will be supplied and (2) that these resources will be supplied in the proper quantities.

In the product markets, depicted in the lower portion of Exh. 2.1, the prices of all products—from eggs and overcoats to haircuts and airline tickets—again are determined by the interaction of buyers and sellers. Prices serve the same function here as they do in the resource market: they make it possible to divide up, or ration, the limited amount of output among all those who wish to receive it. Only those consumers who are willing and able to pay the market price can obtain the product. When prices change, this informs producers about desired changes in the amount they are producing and motivates them to supply the new quantity. For example, when consumers want more of a product than is available, they tend to bid up its price. Producers get a clear signal that consumers like that item; thus they have an incentive to supply more of it.

How Capitalism Answers the Three Fundamental Questions

Now that we have discussed the elements of pure capitalism and have a general idea of the role of markets in such an economy, we can determine more easily how this system answers the three fundamental questions.

What to Produce? One feature of pure capitalism is *consumer sovereignty,* an economic condition in which consumers dictate which goods and services businesses will produce. Because producers are motivated by profits, and because the most profitable products tend to be the ones consumers desire most, producers must be responsive to consumer preferences. To illustrate consumer sovereignty in action, let's consider how automobile manufacturers in a pure capitalist economy would respond if consumer preferences suddenly took a dramatic turn away from standard-sized cars in favor of small ones. If people begin to buy more compacts or subcompacts and fewer full-sized cars, the price of small cars will rise and they will become more profitable, whereas full-sized cars will decline in price and become less profitable. Therefore automobile manufacturers will produce more compacts and fewer full-sized cars: just what consumers want.

Because consumers are free to spend their incomes as they choose, producers who wish to earn profits must be responsive to consumers' desires. As a result, pure capitalism might be described as a system where the consumer is the ruler and the producer an obedient servant.

How to Produce? Automobile producers have a number of options available for manufacturing compact cars and other vehicles that consumers desire. They can produce these automobiles through highly mechanized techniques, or they can rely primarily on skilled labor and simpler tools. They can manufacture car bodies from steel, aluminum, fiberglass, or some combination of the three. In selecting which production technique and combination of resources to use, the capitalist manufacturers will minimize the cost of production—i.e., they will adopt the *least cost* approach—because lower costs contribute to higher profits.

Highly mechanized production methods—
such as those utilizing robots—may be selected if labor is expensive.

The search for the least-cost approach is guided by the market prices of the various economic resources. Because the scarcest resources cost the most, producers use them only when they cannot substitute less expensive resources. For example, if steel is very expensive, automobile makers will tend to use it only where other materials would be inadequate, perhaps in the frame or in other parts of the car that require great strength. Thus the prices of resources help to ensure that resources are used to their best advantage in a capitalist economy. Abundant, cheaper resources are used when they will suffice; scarcer, more costly resources are conserved.

For Whom to Produce? Finally, we consider the task of distributing our hypothetical economy's output of automobiles. We know that only those who can afford to buy automobiles will receive them. The ability to pay, however, is only half the picture; the other half is willingness to purchase, which takes into account consumer preferences. Some of those who can afford a new car will prefer to spend their money elsewhere: remodeling their homes, perhaps, or sending their children to college. Some who seemingly cannot afford a new car may be able to purchase one by doing without other things—new clothes or a larger apartment, for example. Of course, consumers with low incomes will face less attractive choices than those earning high incomes. A low-income consumer may sacrifice basic necessities in order to afford an automobile, whereas a wealthy consumer need only choose between the new car and some luxury item, such as a sailboat or a winter vacation. In the final analysis, those with higher incomes will always have more choices than those with lower incomes and will receive a larger share of the economy's total output.

Capitalism: Strengths and Weaknesses

Before moving on from our discussion of pure capitalism, we will describe briefly some of the strengths and weaknesses inherent in such a system. One of the major strengths of pure capitalism is *economic efficiency*. In a market economy, businesses are encouraged to produce the products that consumers want most and to produce them at the lowest cost in terms of scarce resources. A system that accomplishes those objectives goes a long way toward ensuring that a society achieves the maximum benefit possible from its limited resources.

A second positive feature of capitalism is *economic freedom*. Under pure capitalism, consumers, workers, and producers are free to make decisions based on self-interest. To many, this economic freedom is the overwhelming virtue of the capitalist model.

Economist Milton Friedman, a vocal advocate of competitive capitalism, notes a third strength of the system: It promotes *political freedom* by separating economic and political power. The existence of private ownership of the means of production ensures that government officials are not in a position to deny jobs or goods and services to individuals whose political views conflict with their own.[4]

Pure capitalism also has some shortcomings. First, people are not uniformly equal in ability, and some will succeed to a greater extent than others. In a capitalist system the result is the unequal distribution of income and output. This inequality tends to be perpetuated because the children of the rich usually have access to better educational opportunities and often inherit the income-producing assets of their parents. Such inequality weakens capitalism's claim that it produces the goods and services that the *society* wants the most. It is more the case that capitalism produces the products that the consumers *who have the money* want most.

A second, closely related criticism was voiced by the late Arthur Okun, chairman of the Council of Economic Advisors during the Johnson

---

[4] Milton Friedman, *Capitalism and Freedom* (Chicago: The University of Chicago Press, 1962), p. 9.

administration. In a capitalist economy, observed Okun, money can buy a great many things that are not supposed to be for sale:

> Money buys legal services that can obtain preferred treatment before the law; it buys platforms that give extra weight to the owner's freedom of speech; it buys influence with elected officials and thus compromises the principle of one person, one vote. . . . Even though money generally cannot buy extra helpings of rights directly, it can buy services that, in effect, produce more or better rights.[5]

Third, pure capitalism may be criticized for encouraging the destruction of the environment. Because air, rivers, lakes, and streams are ***common-property resources*** belonging to the society as a whole, they tend to be seen as free—available to be used or abused without charge or concern. The pursuit of self-interest would cause producers to dump their wastes into nearby rivers to avoid the cost of disposing of those wastes in an environmentally acceptable manner. Farmers would select pesticides according to their favorable impact on output and without regard to their undesirable effects on wildlife and water supplies. In this case, Adam Smith's invisible hand fails. The pursuit of self-interest by individuals may not promote the good of all but may instead lead to environmental destruction.

The Model of Pure Command Socialism

The opposite of the model of pure capitalism is the model of pure command socialism. The socialist command economy described in this section represents no existing economic system. Although the economies of the former Soviet Union, China, and Cuba approximate the model of pure command socialism more closely than they do the model of pure capitalism, the match is far from perfect. Like the model of pure capitalism, the model of pure command socialism is simply a tool to help us understand how command economies operate. Again we will examine the basic elements of the model, diagram how the hypothetical economy operates, and see how the system decides what, how, and for whom to produce. Then we will examine the strengths and weaknesses of pure command socialism.

---

[5] Arthur M. Okun, *Equality and Efficiency: The Big Tradeoff* (Washington: The Brookings Institution, 1975), p. 22.

Elements of Command Socialism

We define *command socialism* as an economic system in which the means of production are publicly owned, the fundamental economic choices are made by a central authority, and commands are used to ensure that these decisions are implemented. Four basic elements of pure command socialism support this definition.

Public Ownership. A socialist economy is characterized by state, or public, ownership of the means of production. In the model of pure command socialism, state ownership is complete. The factories, farms, mines, hospitals, and other forms of capital are publicly owned. Even labor is publicly owned in the sense that workers and managers do not select their own employment but are assigned their jobs by the state.

Centralized Decision Making. One of the most distinctive features of command socialism is that economic choices are made by a central authority. This central authority may be either responsive to the feelings of the people (democratic socialism) or unresponsive to their wishes (authoritarian socialism or communism). In either case this authority makes the fundamental production and distribution decisions and then takes the necessary actions to see that these decisions are carried out.

Economic Planning. In the model of command socialism, economic planning replaces the market as the method for coordinating economic decisions. The central authority, or central planning board, gathers information about existing production capacities, supplies of raw materials, and labor force capabilities. It then draws up a master plan specifying production objectives for each sector or industry in the economy. Industrywide objectives are translated into specific production targets for each factory, farm, mine, or other kind of producing unit. Central planning ensures that specific production objectives agree so that automobile manufacturers will not produce one million cars, for example, while tire manufacturers produce only two million tires.

Allocation by Command. In command socialism, resources and products are allocated by directive, or command, and the central authority uses its power to enforce these decisions. Once it determines production and distribution objectives, the central planning board dictates to each producing unit the quantity and assortment of goods the unit is to produce and the combination of resources it is to use. Commands are also issued to producers of raw materials and other production inputs to supply these inputs to the producing units that need them. Further commands direct individuals to places of employment—wherever the central planning board determines that their services are needed—and dictate distribution of the economy's output of goods and services. All the allocative functions that a capitalist economy leaves to the market and the pursuit of self-interest are accomplished through planning and allocation by directive in pure command socialism.

The Pyramid Model

We can represent a socialist command economy as a pyramid with the central planning board at the top and the various producing and consuming units below it. This diagram emphasizes the primary feature of a command economy: centralization of economic decision making.

The outer arrow at the right of Exh. 2.2 shows how information concerning production capacities, raw materials supplies, and labor capabilities flows up from the producing units in the middle of the pyramid to the

EXHIBIT 2.2

The Command Pyramid

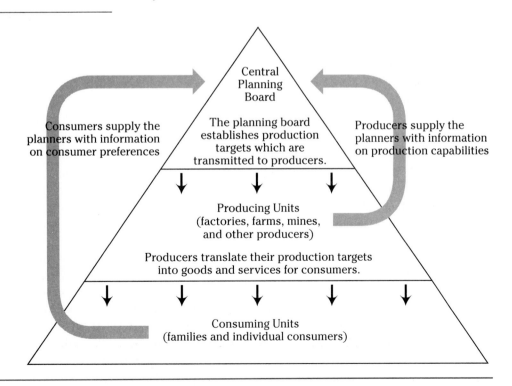

Central Planning Board

Consumers supply the planners with information on consumer preferences

The planning board establishes production targets which are transmitted to producers.

Producers supply the planners with information on production capabilities

Producing Units (factories, farms, mines, and other producers)

Producers translate their production targets into goods and services for consumers.

Consuming Units (families and individual consumers)

central planning board at the top. If it is requested, information about which goods and services consumers desire also flows up from the consuming units at the base of the pyramid (outer left arrow). Production objectives, or targets, are transmitted back to the individual producing units, which then supply the targeted quantity and assortment of products and produce them as specified. Finally, the output is distributed to consumers in accordance with the plan.

How Command Socialism Answers the Three Fundamental Questions

In many respects, the operation of a socialist command economy is easier to understand than the functioning of a capitalist economy. The answers to the three fundamental questions are decided by the central planning board, which then uses its authority to ensure that all directives are carried out.

The central planners can select any output targets, any mix of products within the limits set by the economy's production capacity. Of course, they will have to gather an abundance of information before they have a good picture of the economy's capabilities. They must determine the size of the labor force and the skills it possesses, for example, as well as how many factories exist and what they are capable of producing. Until the central planners have this kind of information, they cannot establish realistic output targets. And even then they will face some tough decisions because, as you already know, more of one thing means less of something else. So if they decide to produce more automobiles, they won't be able to manufacture as many refrigerators and military weapons and other products.

In deciding how to produce each product, central planners must try to stretch the economy's limited resources as far as possible. This requires that each resource be used efficiently—where it makes the greatest contribution to the economy's output. If some resource is particularly scarce, planners must be careful to use it only where no other input will suffice. If they don't do this, they won't be able to maximize the economy's output.

Even with the best of planning, an economy's resources will stretch only so far. The central planning board can allocate the economy's limited output in accordance with any objective it has set. If the planning board's primary objective is equality, it can develop a method of rationing, dividing up the society's output in equal shares to each member. If it wants to promote loyalty to the government, the central authority can give supporters extra shares while penalizing dissenters. Whatever its objectives, the central planning board can use distribution as a method to further them.

Command Socialism: Strengths and Weaknesses

Like pure capitalism, the economy of pure command socialism has certain strengths and certain weaknesses. Some argue that a major strength of command socialism is its ability to promote a high degree of equality in the distribution of income and output. Because the central planners control the distribution of goods and services, they can elect to distribute output in ways that achieve whatever degree of equality in living standard they consider appropriate. Thus it is theoretically possible for command socialism to avoid the extremely unequal income and output distribution that characterizes the pure capitalist model.

Another major strength of command socialism is its potential for achieving economic objectives in a relatively short period of time. As an example, consider the power of the planners to foster more rapid economic growth. If a society wants to increase its capacity for producing goods and services, it must devote more of its resources to producing capital goods (factories and equipment) and fewer resources to producing consumer goods. In other words, society must consume less *now* in order to be able to produce and consume more *later*. Because the central authority has the power to dictate the fraction of the society's resources that will be devoted to capital goods production, in effect it can force the society to make the sacrifices necessary to increase the rate of economic growth.

You probably recognize that the power to bring about rapid economic changes is not necessarily a good thing. The major shortcoming of command socialism, in fact, is the possibility that the central planning board may pursue goals that do not reflect the needs or desires of the majority. If the socialist government is not democratically elected, its goals may bear no relationship to the needs of the general population.

A second weakness in the model of command socialism is its inefficient information network. The system we have described needs more information than it can reasonably expect to acquire and process to ensure efficient use of the economy's resources. The system not only must have a substantial organizational network to acquire information about consumer preferences and production capabilities, but also must use this same network to transmit the decisions of central planners to millions of economic units. On top of this, the central planners have to be able to process all the acquired information and return it in the form of a consistent plan—a staggering task, considering that the output of one industry is often the production input required by some other industry. Finally, they must see that each product is produced efficiently. This complex and cumbersome process is bound to result in breakdowns in communication and decision making. When these occur, the wrong products may be produced or the right ones produced using the wrong combinations of resources. In either case, inefficiency means that the society does not achieve maximum benefit from its limited resources.

Mixed Economies: The Real-World Solution

No existing economic system adheres strictly to either pure capitalism or pure command socialism. All real-world economies are *mixed economies;* they represent a blending of the two models. To illustrate the diversity among economic systems, we will consider two existing economies that are distinctly different from one another: the United States and the former Soviet Union. Our discussion will begin with the United States economy, the system that will occupy most of our attention throughout this text.

The United States Economic System

Because the United States economic system is marked by such a high degree of private ownership and individual decision making, American children learn early from their teachers as well as the news media and others that they live in a capitalist economy. And certainly there is ample evidence to support that viewpoint. Most U.S. businesses, from industrial giants like General Motors and IBM to small firms like your neighborhood hardware store, are private operations, not government-owned enterprises. The United States economy is coordinated and directed largely by the market mechanism, the interaction of buyers and sellers in thousands of interdependent markets. Each of those buyers and sellers is guided by self-interest, which among producers takes the form of profit seeking. Fortunately for consumers, the drive for profits is usually kept in check by another feature of pure capitalism: competition. In most American industries competition, though not pure, is adequate to keep prices reasonable and ensure that consumers receive fair treatment.

Given these elements of pure capitalism, why do we call the United States a "mixed economy"? Actually there are several reasons. First, let us consider the degree of public ownership in our economic system. Although most American businesses are privately owned, some very important and visible producers are publicly owned enterprises. For example, the electricity on which we rely to heat and cool our homes and run our appliances is supplied in part by municipal, state, or county power companies. With few exceptions, we attend public elementary and secondary schools. When we apply for admission to college, we mail those applications via the U.S. Postal Service, often to state universities. If we ride the bus in the morning, that bus is probably the property of a public transit system. In short, although public ownership is by no means the dominant feature of the American economy, it cannot be ignored.

Nor is public ownership the lone feature our predominantly capitalist economy "borrows" from command socialism. Many of our basic economic choices are made or influenced by powerful economic units—government, labor, and business—rather than by individuals, and often these decisions are implemented by commands rather than through markets.

Regulations and restrictions are two means through which the government exerts influence on businesses and consumers. Think of the regulations imposed on automobile manufacturers, for example. They must produce cars that (1) meet specified mileage requirements; (2) conform to certain exhaust-emission standards; (3) can sustain a front- or rear-end crash of a specified force without serious injury to passengers; and (4) include seat-belts plus other safety features. In addition to complying with these directives or commands, automobile producers must conform to the plant health and safety regulations set by the Occupational Safety and Health Administration, and their factories must operate within the various pollution-control standards set by the Environmental Protection Agency. To a greater or lesser extent, most American industries are subject to government regulations.

Government spending and taxing decisions constitute another significant influence on the mixture of goods and services that the economy produces and the distribution of those goods and services among the members of the society. Through its tax policies, for example, the federal government encourages investment in certain industries and discourages investment in others. Our tax system requires that those who earn higher incomes pay a greater fraction of their incomes in taxes, thus altering the distribution of output. Government expenditures for such things as education, national defense, and aid to the poor also have a significant impact on what our economy produces and who will receive that output.

Government is not the only powerful economic unit in our economy. Labor organizations and large businesses have a substantial impact on the way our economy operates. In many industries, labor unions influence market forces and use their bargaining power to force wage increases and negotiate work rules that maximize employment and reduce the likelihood of layoffs. Unions use their political clout and considerable financial resources to lobby for government policies—minimum wage laws and import bans, for example—that enhance their own economic position. Indeed, it is the business of the labor union to attempt to influence to its advantage any market force that has an impact on wages and working conditions.

Powerful businesses exert their own influence on market forces. Under pure capitalism all businesses would respond to prices dictated by the market, but businesses in our economy often use their size to influence the prices of the resources they buy as well as the products they sell. They use advertising in an attempt to influence consumer spending patterns and convince prospective buyers that their product is worth more than the ones offered by competitors. They also use their financial resources and their status as major employers to influence government policies. Like labor unions, powerful businesses use every tool at their disposal to try to alter the economic environment to their advantage.

In summary, the United States economy diverges from the model of pure capitalism in a variety of ways. Publicly owned enterprises make an important contribution to the economy; laws and government regulations significantly influence economic decisions; and powerful labor unions and businesses are able to influence the economic environment rather than simply respond to it. Whether these modifications of pure capitalism are good or bad is a matter for debate. What is clear is that the United States economic system is really a mixed economy. Rather than adhering strictly to the capitalist model, it combines elements of capitalism and command socialism.

The Soviet Economic System

The Soviet Union was recently dissolved and replaced by a loose federation of former Soviet republics known as the Commonwealth of Independent States. Although the Soviet Union has passed into history, much can be learned from examining the Soviet economic system. For decades, the Soviet economy was the economic system that most closely approximated the model of pure command socialism. By studying the Soviet system, we will see just how different an economic system can be from our own and still share the designation "mixed economy." We will also gain insights into the economies of China and Cuba, since these systems duplicate in many ways the old Soviet system. Finally, an understanding of the Soviet system is essential if we are to appreciate the problems confronting the new Commonwealth states as they attempt to construct their own economic systems from the ruins of the Soviet economy. While the Soviet Union has been declared dead, the ghost of the Soviet economic system will haunt the Commonwealth states for a long time to come.

The Soviet economic system had much in common with the model of pure command socialism. Most factories, farms, and other enterprises were owned and operated by the state rather than by private citizens. The fundamental choices about what, how, and for whom to produce were made by the State Planning Committee (GOSPLAN), and GOSPLAN's decisions were implemented mainly by command.

The Soviet Union has been declared dead, but the ghost of the Soviet economic system will haunt the newly independent states for many years to come.

However, even prior to recent reforms (which will be discussed later) the Soviet economy deviated significantly from the model of command socialism; distinct strands of capitalism were woven into the economy's socialist fabric. Consider Soviet agriculture, for example, which operated at three levels: state farms, collective farms, and private plots. Soviet state farms were run basically the same as other state enterprises; they received commands from the planning authority and were expected to meet their production objectives. But collective farms, at least in theory, operated by and for the benefit of their members. (In practice, however, a significant portion of a collective farm's output had to be sold to the state at prices dictated by the state.) The private sector was made up of small plots that peasants farmed in addition to the work they did on collective farms. Although these small plots occupied less than 2 percent of the nation's farmland, they were cultivated intensively and produced roughly one-third of the nation's agricultural output. Part of this output was consumed by the owners, but the major portion was sold in open markets at prices dictated by market forces.

Further elements of capitalism were evident in the labor sector of the Soviet economy, where planners attempted to duplicate some of the wage adjustments that would occur naturally in a free market. Although Soviet planners dictated production goals, they did not adhere to the model of command socialism by issuing directives about who would work at which occupations. Instead, they manipulated wages to bring about the changes they desired. For example, if too few people wanted to become electricians, wages for electricians were increased in order to attract more individuals to this occupation. If there were too many electricians, wages were either reduced or simply not increased when other wage increases were ordered.

Consumer prices were managed in a similar fashion. Rather than command which consumer goods each household would receive, central planners set the prices for each consumer good and allowed households to make their own choices based on their reactions to those prices. Although planners kept some prices artificially low as a matter of policy—the prices of basic food items, for example—they manipulated most prices in an attempt to equalize the amounts available and the amounts consumers desired. Whereas free competitive markets automatically produce this result, Soviet pricing was never flexible enough to precisely duplicate the market process. That is, Soviet prices never changed quickly enough or often enough to ensure that the amounts desired by consumers would exactly duplicate the amounts available.

In addition to manipulating wages and prices, Soviet planners used market-related incentives to achieve their goals. Successful managers, for example, were rewarded with bonuses that might amount to a substantial fraction of their annual income. Payments in kind—a chance for a better apartment or a nice vacation, for instance—also provided incentive for good performance.

As you can see, even before the recent upheaval the economy of the Soviet Union combined elements of capitalism and command socialism. When Mikhail Gorbachev became supreme leader of the Soviet Union in 1985, he was critical of the Soviet economic system, calling it rigid and inefficient. Under his leadership, steps were taken to introduce some additional elements of capitalism. Individuals were allowed to sell services (house painting and home and auto repair, for example), and some small private enterprises such as restaurants were permitted. State-owned enterprises were given more freedom in pricing their products and were given permission to buy inputs and sell their products abroad, without going through the planning board. Political reforms were also undertaken after it became apparent to Gorbachev that economic reform could be accomplished only if accompanied by democratization of the political system.

While Gorbachev's moves to reform the economy were accorded much attention in the press, they were actually modest and piecemeal changes. Proposals for a more thorough reform of the economy were opposed. For instance, in September 1990, a "500-Day Plan" was proposed with the objective of moving the economy to a free market by April 1992. In addition to calling for market-determined product prices, the plan entailed the selling of state-owned property and major cuts in military spending. Gorbachev was unwilling to support the plan, and it was not adopted.

The failure of the 500-Day Plan reflected in part the opposition of those whose power would be reduced—economic planners, top Communist party officials, and members of the military. But it also resulted from Gorbachev's own ambivalence about introducing additional elements of capitalism. While Gorbachev clearly recognized the failures of the Soviet Union, he was unwilling to accept some basic tenets of capitalism—the concept of private property, for example. This ambivalence led to conflicting policy moves. Measures to promote free markets were passed one day, only to be revoked or somehow neutralized on the next. This resulted in chaos for producers, and a substantial disruption in the supplies of goods and services. In short, Gorbachev succeeded in discrediting and disrupting the Soviet economic system without really moving the economy closer to capitalism.

Gorbachev's moves toward democratization were seen by Communist party officials and those in the military as a greater threat than his economic reforms. Several Soviet republics had declared their intention to seek independence, and Soviet citizens were openly criticizing policies of the central government. In August 1991, a handful of Soviet hardliners staged a coup against Gorbachev. But the coup was poorly planned and it met unexpected resistance. As a consequence, the coup failed and Gorbachev was returned to power after only a few days' absence.

The failure of the coup contributed to further disintegration of the central government. The Communist party collapsed, and most of the Soviet republics declared their independence. Gorbachev's power waned, and Russian President Boris Yeltsin—who had achieved prominence by resisting the coup—moved to center stage. In December 1991, the Soviet Union was officially dissolved and replaced with a loose federation of former Soviet republics, the Commonwealth of Independent States. Boris Yeltsin was instrumental in forming the new Commonwealth, and as President of Russia he will play a major role in determining its success or failure.

A major reason for Yeltsin's emergence as a leader was his advocacy of more rapid economic change. As Gorbachev vacillated, Yeltsin criticized and called for quickening the pace of market reforms. But Yeltsin may have underestimated the obstacles to reforming Russia and the other

Antitrust for USSR
Industrial monopolies impede growth in the republics

Monopoly, said Lenin, is the last stage of capitalism. Today, the communist system he founded has bequeathed to its reformers the most monopolistic industrial economy in the world.

This means that the people who are now trying to build nations in place of the old union are trapped by their past. Their republics industrialized in the service of the USSR, not for themselves. Because Soviet central planners favored extremely large enterprises, every republic depends on crucial goods produced by monopolies in other republics.

This combination of monopoly and interdependence worked while the Soviet Union was whole and its authority was unquestioned. Now, the mechanisms of interrepublic trade have collapsed. Central planning and the ruble are both discredited, leaving factories to barter when they trade at all.

The economic system of a superpower has been reduced to using prehistoric methods of exchange.

The rise of ethnic nationalism from the ashes of the communist system has complicated trade still further. Azerbaijan has blocked trade out of Armenia. Armenia, Kazakhstan, Uzbekistan, the Ukraine, and other republics have banned exports. Workers in Azerbaijan oil equipment monopolies and Ukrainian coal mining equipment plants know the importance of their position, and have threatened to strike.

The consequences can be minor, as when Muscovites rioted last year because cigarettes (the filter tips of which are produced only in war-plagued Armenia) were unavailable. That example is less amusing than it seems, though. The Armenia-Azerbaijan dispute has also prevented oil equipment monopolies in Azerbaijan from sending needed machinery to Siberian oil fields.

If a monopoly producer is removed from trade between the republics, the consequences will ripple throughout the economy. The possibilities for such disruptions are staggering, because the number of monopoly producers is so high. A full third of the Soviet production was based on monopolists; thousands of products are made at only one site. Some telling examples:

A plant in Armenia is the only source of a part that is needed in every power station in all the republics. The world's largest polyester factory, in Byelorussia, produces 90 percent of Soviet output. A plant in Moldavia makes 99 percent of die-casting machines. Single plants in Russia produce most of the automobiles (58 percent), trolleys (97 percent) polypropylene (71 percent), sewing machines (100 percent), printing ink (90 percent), combine harvesters (71 percent), oil drilling rigs (two plants produce 100 percent), and all of most grades of boilers and turbines needed by power plants. Factories in the Ukraine build the vast majority of coal hoists (82 percent), coking equipment (78 percent), corn harvesters (100 percent), forklifts (86 percent), and diesel locomotives (96 percent). A plant in Uzbekistan produces 75 percent of cellulose acetate, an important artificial fiber used in rayon, film, and automobiles.

The Soviet Union has left conflicting legacies. Its economic infrastructure, spread across the republics, demands union; its repression of nationalisms and individual rights fuels the drive for independence. The solution must be a mix of political independence and economic union.

Free trade and markets within an economic union of as many sovereign republics as possible is the best alternative, but the reality of monopolies threatens even this solution. Monopolies can charge unreasonably high prices, keeping critical goods away from other enterprises or consumers that need them. As monopolies are privatized, some will fold, some will start to produce other goods, and some will sell their products abroad.

Some Soviet economists argue that these risks make the free market impossible in their country. That is a cop-out, but some precautions are necessary. In addition to the free trade agreement, the republics should sign a compact to locate and monitor supply lines based on monopolies, and . . . provide credits for key goods that may disappear abruptly from the interrepublic market.

In the long run, the free market will bring in new firms to compete with former state enterprises. Still, a developed market economy in the former Soviet Union is decades away. Until it exists, the republics will have to swallow the difficult lesson that sovereignty and prosperity can contradict. For a long while yet, they will owe their standing as industrial nations to monopolies and to each other.

—*Tim Snyder*

(Tim Snyder is writing on Soviet monopoly for the Soviet Disintegration project of the Institute for International Economics in Washington.)

SOURCE: *Christian Science Monitor,* October 2, 1991, p. 19. Reprinted with permission of the author.

USE YOUR ECONOMIC REASONING

1. **How might the existence of monopolies impede the growth of the newly independent republics? Explain why the removal of a monopoly producer would have consequences that "ripple" throughout the Commonwealth.**

2. **Many ethnic rivalries that were suppressed by the Soviet Union threaten to reappear now that it has been dissolved. How might such rivalries interfere with the economic development of the individual republics?**

3. **Mr. Snyder argues that whatever emerges to replace the Soviet Union must provide a mix of political independence and economic union. Why are these two features important? (Note that the Commonwealth of Independent States—which was formed after this article was written—is an attempt to provide precisely this mix.)**

Commonwealth economies. There is no legal basis for private property in most of the states and little popular support for the profit motive. The process of freeing up prices so that they reflect market forces will be painful and unpopular. (At this writing, most prices are still controlled.) Much of the former Soviet Union's productive capacity has been devoted to military hardware; converting it to the production of capital and consumer goods will be difficult. The fact that a third of the former Soviet Union's output consists of products manufactured by a single state enterprise further complicates efforts at reform. Because these enterprises are spread throughout the 15 republics and often supply materials or parts needed by other enterprises, the disintegration of the Union threatens to disrupt or destroy supply links and cause production to plummet (see "Antitrust for USSR" on page 54).

Can the Commonwealth states overcome these problems and move closer to the capitalist model, or will the citizens of these states become frustrated and demand a return to something like the old command system? Will the new independent states be able to cooperate, or will economic or ethnic rivalries cause the Commonwealth to fail? No one can answer these questions. Reformers throughout the Commonwealth believe that market reforms can raise living standards, but the transition to a more market-oriented economy will be slow and painful and success is by no means certain.

The Diversity of Real-World Economies

Compared to the United States and the former Soviet Union, most of the world's economies are characterized by a more thorough blending of capitalism and command socialism. Few, if any, approximate the model of pure capitalism better than the United States, and none matches the model of command socialism better than the former Soviet Union. Exhibit 2.3 summarizes the characteristics of nine national economies. Although this summary is by no means a refined analysis of the cited economies, it captures the diversity of organization of these real-world systems. You can see in the table that a high degree of public ownership usually corresponds with a high degree of central direction and command implementation. But there is no hard and fast rule. The nations appear to mix and match these three features as if they were experimenting to find the best combination for their particular situation.

In recent years many countries that we have come to think of as socialist have shown an increased interest in the market mechanism. We have already mentioned the changes in the Soviet Union, but there are other examples. Hungary, Czechoslovakia, and Poland are among the nations experimenting with a greater role for markets. How far these reforms will progress and whether they will be permanent is impossible to predict.

EXHIBIT 2.3

Characteristics of Some Selected Economies

NAME OF COUNTRY	DEGREE OF PUBLIC OWNERSHIP	DEGREE OF CENTRAL DIRECTION	DEGREE OF COMMAND IMPLEMENTATION
Brazil	moderate	moderate	minimal
China	extensive	extensive	extensive
France	moderate	moderate	minimal
Germany*	moderate	minimal	minimal
Great Britain	moderate	minimal	minimal
Japan	minimal	moderate	minimal
Soviet Union	extensive	extensive	extensive
Sweden	moderate	moderate	moderate
United States	minimal	minimal	minimal

*Describes the former West Germany.

Even if the market mechanism continues to win converts, we should not expect to see a world populated by precise copies of the model of pure capitalism. Each national economic system will remain unique, its own blend of public and private ownership, individual and collective decision making, and command and market implementation. The principles we have explored in this chapter provide a framework for understanding the more than 150 unique economies in the world.

In the remaining chapters of this text we will examine the operation of the United States economy in more detail. To better understand our economy, however, we need to know more about how markets work and how government influences economic choices in our system. We begin to broaden our understanding of markets in Chapter 3.

Summary

An *economic system* is a set of established procedures by which a society answers the three fundamental questions of what, how, and for whom to produce. Although economic systems differ significantly, all can be described according to three criteria: Who owns the *means of production*? Who makes the economic choices about what, how, and for whom to produce? What method is used to ensure that these economic choices are carried out.

Economists commonly use theoretical models to explain the operation of economic systems. At one extreme, the model of *pure capitalism* describes an economic system in which the means of production are privately owned and fundamental economic choices are made by individuals and implemented through markets. The principal features of pure capitalism include private property and freedom of choice, with self-interest as the driving force (held in check by *pure competition*); price determination through markets; and a *laissez-faire* condition of minimum government intervention.

In a capitalist economy, *consumer sovereignty* dictates which goods and services will be produced. If consumers want more of a particular product, its price will tend to rise, encouraging profit-seeking businesses to produce more of it. To produce these products, businesses buy economic resources (e.g., labor) from households, thereby providing households with the money needed to purchase the output of businesses. The circular-flow model of capitalism diagrams this process by showing how the flows of money (money flows) and of resources and products (real flows) circulate between the household and business sectors and operate through product and resource markets.

At the other extreme, the model of *command socialism* describes an economic system in which the means of production are owned by the public or the state, decisions on the three fundamental questions are made by a central authority, and implementation of these decisions occurs through command. The principal features of command socialism include public ownership, centralized decision-making, economic planning, and allocation by command.

In command socialism, the central planning authority gathers information on production capabilities and consumer preference (if the latter is a concern) and establishes production targets for the producing units, such as factories and farms. These units are required to produce the products dictated by the central authority in the manner specified. Output is then distributed according to the central authority's goals. Command socialism is depicted as a pyramid with the central planning board at the top and the producing and consuming units below. The producing and consuming units supply information to the central planners, who use this information to develop production targets and decide how the limited output will be distributed among the potential consumers.

No existing economic system fits neatly into either model. All real-world economies are *mixed* because they represent some blending of the two models. For example, the U.S. economy, commonly described as a capitalist system, contains some elements of a socialist command economy. Public ownership is not uncommon in the United States, and powerful economic units—government, business, and labor—influence many of the fundamental economic choices. And the former Soviet economy, the system thought to exemplify command socialism, contained some elements of capitalism. Free markets existed for certain products, and market-related incentives were sometimes used instead of commands. Most of the world's economies represent more complete blendings of capitalism and command socialism.

Glossary

Page 35   ***Capitalism.*** An economic system in which the means of production are privately owned and fundamental economic choices are made by individuals and implemented through the market mechanism—the interaction of buyers and sellers.

Page 44   ***Command socialism.*** An economic system in which the means of production are publicly owned, the fundamental economic choices are made by a central authority, and commands are used to ensure that these decisions are implemented.

Page 43   ***Common-property resources.*** Resources that belong to society as a whole rather than to particular individuals.

Page 40   ***Consumer sovereignty.*** An economic condition in which consumers dictate which goods and services will be produced by businesses.

Page 34   ***Economic system.*** The set of established procedures by which a society provides answers to the three fundamental questions.

Page 37   ***Household.*** A living unit that also functions as an economic unit. Whether it consists of a single person or a large family, each household has a source of income and responsibility for spending that income.

Page 36   ***Invisible hand.*** A doctrine introduced by Adam Smith in 1776 holding that individuals pursuing their self-interest will be guided (as if by an invisible hand) to achieve objectives that are also in the best interest of society as a whole.

Page 37   ***Laissez-faire economy.*** An economy in which the degree of government intervention is minimal.

Page 36   ***Market.*** All actual or potential buyers and sellers of a particular item. Markets can be international, national, regional, or local.

Page 35   ***Means of production.*** The raw materials, factories, farms, and other economic resources used to produce goods and services.

Page 48   ***Mixed economies.*** Economies that represent a blending of capitalism and command socialism. All real-world economies are mixed economies.

Page 37   ***Pure competition.*** A situation in which a large number of relatively small buyers and sellers interact.

Study Questions

Fill in the Blanks

1. The driving force or engine of capitalism is _____.

2. The functioning of a capitalist economy is coordinated and directed through _____ in which _____ are determined by the interaction of buyers and sellers.

3. In the model of pure capitalism, the pursuit of self-interest by producers is kept in check by _____. The model of pure capitalism requires _____, a situation in which there are a large number of buyers and sellers of each product.

4. Because businesspeople in a capitalist economy are motivated by self-interest, they want to produce the goods and services that will allow them to earn the highest _____. Those products tend to be the ones that are most desired by _____.

5. According to Milton Friedman, competitive capitalism promotes _____ by separating economic and political power.

6. In pure command socialism, the fundamental economic decisions are made by the _____ and implemented through _____.

7. In pure command socialism, _____ replaces the market as the method of coordinating the various economic decisions.

8. It is possible to represent a socialist command economy as a _____ with the _____ at the top and producing and consuming units at the bottom.

9. One weakness of command socialism is its inefficient _____ network.

10. The United States and the former Soviet Union are both examples of _____ _____ economies.

Multiple Choice

1. Which of the following is *not* a characteristic of pure capitalism?
   a) Public ownership of the means of production
   b) The pursuit of self-interest
   c) Markets and prices
   d) Pure competition
   e) Limited government

2. In a market economy the scarcest resources will be used very conservatively because
   a) central planners will allocate such resources only where they are most needed.
   b) the scarcest resources will tend to have the highest prices.
   c) government officials will not permit their use.
   d) the scarcest resources will tend to have the lowest prices.

3. In a capitalist economy
   a) businesses are free to produce whatever products they choose.
   b) consumers are free to utilize their incomes as they see fit.
   c) resource owners have the freedom to sell their resources to whomever they choose.
   d) All of the above
   e) None of the above

4. Consumer sovereignty means that
   a) consumers dictate which goods and services will be produced by the way they spend their money.
   b) central planners allocate a major share of society's resources to the production of consumer goods.
   c) the role of government in the economy is very limited.
   d) all economic resources are used efficiently.

5. Which of the following best describes command socialism?
   a) An economic system characterized by private ownership of the means of production, centralized decision making, and command implementation
   b) An economic system characterized by public ownership of the means of production, centralized decision making, and market implementation

    c) An economic system characterized by public ownership of the means of production, individual decision making, and command implementation

    d) An economic system characterized by public ownership of the means of production, centralized decision making, and command implementation.

6. Which of the following is correct?

    a) In command socialism, the basic economic choices are made by individuals.

    b) In pure capitalism, powerful economic units have a substantial impact on the way economic choices are made.

    c) In command socialism, producers are required to produce whatever products central planners dictate.

    d) In pure capitalism, economic planning ensures that the various production decisions will be consistent with one another.

7. In deciding what products to produce, the central planners in a socialist command economy need not consider

    a) the size of the economy's labor force.

    b) the production capabilities of the economy's factories.

    c) consumer preferences.

    d) the economy's stock of raw materials.

8. Which of the following is a true statement about the economic system of the former Soviet Union?

    a) All prices were set by market forces.

    b) Workers were free to make their own choices about jobs, based on their reactions to wages set by central planners.

    c) Bonuses of all forms were illegal.

    d) All agricultural output was produced on state farms.

9. One reason the United States is not an example of pure capitalism is that

    a) most producing units are publicly owned.

    b) commands are used to implement some economic decisions.

    c) the pursuit of self-interest is a powerful force.

    d) markets are used to coordinate most economic decisions.

10. The 500-Day Plan to reform the Soviet economy

    a) was proposed and fully supported by Mikhail Gorbachev.

    b) called for moving to free markets by the year 2000.

    c) included the selling of state-owned property.

    d) called for expanded military spending.

Problems and Questions for Discussion

1. What is an economic system? Why is it valid to say that no two real-world economic systems are exactly alike?

2. List the characteristics or elements of pure capitalism and explain each. Are any of these elements absent from the United States economy? Explain.

3. How would a socialist command economy answer the three fundamental questions? What elements of command socialism exist in the U.S. economy?

4. Explain the role of economic planning in command socialism. Who is in charge of economic planning in a capitalist economy?

5. Try to draw the circular-flow diagram without looking back in the text. Now label all the parts of the diagram and indicate which flows are money flows and which are real flows. Use the diagram to explain how a capitalist economy works.

6. Draw the command pyramid and label the parts. What does the command pyramid tell us about the way that a socialist command economy functions?

7. If all real-world economies are mixed economies, why is the United States economy commonly described as a market economy, while the former Soviet economy was normally described as a command system?

8. Why might a centrally planned economy such as the former Soviet economy (or the economy of China or Cuba) use economic incentives rather than commands to accomplish some objectives? If they are willing to rely on incentives and markets to some extent, why do they restrict their use?

9. Soviet factory managers were known to deliberately understate their factories' production capabilities when reporting to central planners? How was such understatement to their advantage?

10. The development of high-speed computers might be a more important breakthrough for a socialist command economy than for a capitalist economy. Why?

STUDY QUESTIONS

Answer Key

Fill in the Blanks

1. self-interest
2. markets, prices
3. competition, pure competition
4. profits, consumers
5. political freedom
6. central authority, commands
7. economic planning
8. pyramid, planning board
9. information
10. mixed

Multiple Choice

1. a	3. d	5. d	7. c	9. b
2. b	4. a	6. c	8. b	10. c

STUDY QUESTIONS

MICROECONOMICS: MARKETS, PRICES, AND THE ROLE OF COMPETITION

Microeconomics is the branch of economics that focuses on the behavior of individual consumers, business firms, and industries, rather than the behavior of the economy as a whole. For instance, you will discover how the prices of particular products are determined and how individual firms maximize profits.

In Chapter 3, we begin our study of microeconomics by investigating how prices are determined in competitive markets. You will learn the precise meaning of "supply" and "demand" and how the interaction of these forces determines prices. You will examine how prices can change and learn the functions that price changes perform in a market economy. Then, in Chapter 4, you will investigate the degree of consumer and producer responsiveness to price changes.

Chapter 5 examines the behavior of the purely competitive firm and explores how firms determine the amount of output to produce in order to maximize profit. You will discover the characteristics of a competitive industry and see why competition is beneficial for consumers. Chapter 6 examines how firms acquire pricing discretion, or market power, and how the behavior of firms that possess market power differs from that of purely competitive firms. This chapter also examines the actual pricing techniques employed by businesses and compares them to the theoretical techniques suggested by economists. Chapter 7 considers the "degrees" of competition that exist in different industry structures and explores the impact of those different industry structures on the well-being of consumers. Chapter 8 looks at some of the inherent limitations of a market economy by examining external costs and the origin of problems such as pollution.

CHAPTER 3

DEMAND AND SUPPLY: PRICE DETERMINATION IN COMPETITIVE MARKETS

How do markets work? A market economy is governed by the forces of demand and supply—the interaction of buyers and sellers in thousands of different product and resource markets. These forces determine *prices.* The prevailing prices of goods and services tell producers which products consumers want most. Resource prices tell them which resources to use to produce those products profitably. Because resource prices affect consumers' incomes, they also influence the distribution of goods and services. For example, workers whose skills are particularly scarce can command higher salaries and thereby claim a larger share of the society's limited output.

A competitive market is composed of many independent buyers and sellers, each small enough in relation to the size of the total market so that no single buyer or seller can significantly affect the market demand or supply. In this chapter, you will see how the forces of demand and supply interact to determine prices in competitive markets. Later in the text we will explore the meaning of competition in greater detail and examine the behavior of the purely competitive firm (Chapter 5). But for now just remember that in competitive markets prices are determined by the impersonal forces of demand and supply—not by the manipulations of powerful buyers and sellers.

After you study this chapter you will have a greater appreciation of the role that prices play in a market economy. You'll understand why the price of gold fluctuates and why salaries are higher in some occupations than in others. You'll understand why the prices of fruits and vegetables tend to rise after a poor growing season and why antique cars often command higher prices than this year's models. You will also understand how prices direct the actions of producers and how they determine the distribution of society's limited output of goods and services. The material in this chapter will give you a clearer comprehension of the role of markets and prices in our economy.

Demand

In a market economy consumers are sovereign; that is, consumers dictate which goods and services will be produced. But it is consumer *demand* rather than consumer desire that makes the actual determination. We have already noted that human wants are unlimited. However, wanting an item and being willing and able to pay for it are two distinctly different things. If the item we want carries a price tag, we may have to do without it: We may lack the money to pay, or we may prefer to spend that money on something else.

People who are both *willing and able* to make purchases are the consumers who determine which products a market economy will produce. When they lack either the willingness or the ability to spend their dollars, producers do not respond. Thus the concept of demand includes the willingness and ability of potential buyers to purchase a product. We define *demand* as a schedule (or table) showing the quantities of a good or service that consumers are willing and able to purchase at various prices during a given time period, when all factors other than the product's price remain unchanged.

Exhibit 3.1 illustrates the concept of demand through a simple example. The schedule shows the yearly demand for jogging shoes of a given quality in the hypothetical community of Hometown, U.S.A. You can see that the number of pairs of jogging shoes that Hometown consumers are willing and able to purchase each year depends on the selling price. If jogging shoes sell for $50 a pair, Hometowners will purchase 2,000 pairs a year, assuming that other factors remain the same—their incomes, for example, and their present jogging routines.

Demand Curves

Economists usually represent schedules in the form of graphs. To graph the demand for jogging shoes, we first plot the information in Exh. 3.1 and then connect the points to form a demand curve as shown in Exh. 3.2. A *demand curve* is simply a graphic representation of demand. By convention, we

EXHIBIT 3.1

Hometown Demand for Jogging Shoes

PRICE (per pair)	QUANTITY (pairs per year)
$50	2,000
40	4,000
30	6,000
20	8,000
10	10,000

measure price on the vertical axis and quantity on the horizontal axis. Each point on the curve represents a price and the quantity that consumers would demand per year at that price. For example, we can see in Exh. 3.2 that at a price of $40, Hometown joggers would demand 4,000 pairs; at a price of $30, the quantity demanded would increase to 6,000 pairs.

EXHIBIT 3.2

The Demand Curve for Jogging Shoes in Hometown, U.S.A.

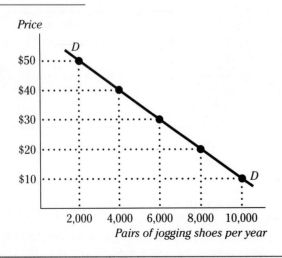

A demand curve is a graphic representation of demand. It demonstrates the inverse relationship between price and quantity demanded.

The Law of Demand

Our hypothetical demand schedule and demand curve for jogging shoes demonstrate clearly what economists call the *law of demand,* which holds that the quantity demanded of a product is *negatively or inversely related* to its price. This simply means that consumers will purchase more of a product at lower prices than at higher prices. That's why demand curves always slope downward and to the right.

Economists believe two factors explain the inverse relationship between price and quantity demanded:

1. When prices are lower, consumers can afford to purchase a larger quantity of the product out of any given income. Economists refer to this *ability* to purchase more as the *income effect* of a price reduction.

2. At lower prices the product becomes more attractive relative to other items serving the same function. This is called the *substitution effect* because it explains the *willingness* of consumers to substitute for other products the product that has declined in price.

To illustrate the income and substitution effects, let's return to our Hometown consumers. Why will they purchase more jogging shoes at $10 than at $50? Because of the income effect, their incomes will now buy more: if the price of jogging shoes declines and other prices don't change, they'll be able to buy more goods and services with their fixed incomes. It's almost as though each consumer had received a raise. And because of the substitution effect, they'll buy jogging shoes instead of tennis shoes, sandals, or moccasins because jogging shoes have become a better footwear buy. Like these hypothetical consumers, we all tend to purchase more of a product at a lower price than at a higher price because of both the income effect and the substitution effect.

Determinants of Demand

The demand curve and the law of demand emphasize the relationship between the price of a product and the quantity demanded, but price is not the only factor that determines how much of a product consumers will buy. A variety of other factors underlie the demand schedule and determine the precise position of the demand curve. These ***determinants of demand*** include income, tastes and preferences, expectations regarding future prices, the price of related goods, and the number of buyers in the market. Any demand curve is based on the assumption that these factors are held constant. Changes in one or more of these determinants will cause the entire demand curve to shift to a new position.

Income

The most obvious determinant of demand is income. Consumers' incomes influence their *ability* to purchase goods and services. For what economists call ***normal goods,*** an increase in income will cause consumers to purchase more of a product than before at each possible price. For example, an increase in per capita income (income per person) will probably cause consumers to buy more steak than before at whatever price exists. We would show this by shifting the demand curve to the right, as illustrated in Exh. 3.3.

Not all products are normal goods, however. An increase in income will cause consumers to purchase less of an ***inferior good,*** thus shifting

EXHIBIT 3.3

Income as a Determinant of Demand

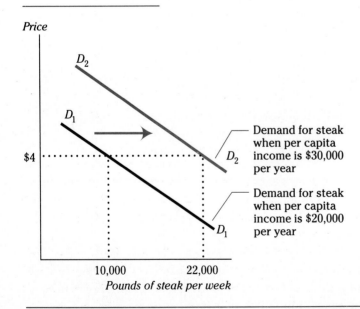

An increase in per capita income will shift the demand curve for a normal good to the right. Consumers will purchase more of the product at each price.

the demand curve to the left. Powdered milk, generic macaroni and cheese, and cheap wine are examples of products that might be inferior goods. When their incomes increase, consumers may choose to buy less of these products in favor of more appetizing grocery items.

Tastes and Preferences

Consumers' tastes and preferences—how well they like the product relative to other products—are also important determinants of demand. A change in tastes and preferences will affect the demand for products. For example, the desire to limit cholesterol intake has altered consumer tastes and preferences for various food products. Today consumers demand less red meat and fewer eggs than in times past, while their demand for fish and chicken has increased. In other words, this change in tastes and preferences has caused the demand curves for red meat and eggs to shift to the left and the demand curves for fish and chicken to shift to the right.

Expectations about Prices

Expectations may also influence consumer behavior. For example, the expectation that the price of an item will rise in the future usually encourages consumers to buy it now. We would represent this by shifting the entire demand curve to the right to show that more would be demanded now at whatever price prevailed. Similarly, the expectation that a product will decline in price is a good incentive to postpone buying it; the present demand curve for the product would shift to the left.

Price of Related Goods

A somewhat less obvious determinant of demand is the price of related goods. Although all goods compete for a consumer's income, the price of substitutes and complements may be particularly important in explaining consumer behavior. *Substitutes* are simply products that can be used in place of other products because to a greater or lesser extent they satisfy the same consumer wants. Hot dogs are a typical substitute for hamburgers, and tennis shoes may substitute for jogging shoes unless one is a serious jogger. *Complements* are products normally purchased along with or in conjunction with another product. For example, pickle relish and hot dogs are complements, as are lettuce and salad dressing.

If the price of hamburgers increased and the price of hot dogs remained unchanged, consumers might be expected to buy fewer hamburgers and more hot dogs. The demand curve for hot dogs would shift to the right. By the same token, an increase in the price of lettuce is likely to have an adverse effect on the sale of salad dressing. Because people buy salad dressing as a complement to salad vegetables, anything that causes consumers to eat fewer salads causes them to demand less salad dressing. The demand curve for salad dressing would shift to the left.

The Number of Consumers in the Market

The final determinant of demand is the number of consumers in the market. The more consumers who demand a particular product, the greater the total demand for the product. When the number of consumers increases, the demand curve for the product will shift to the right to show that a greater quantity is now demanded at each price. If the number of consumers declines, the demand curve will shift to the left.

As we focus on a single demand curve and how consumers respond to price changes, we are assuming that these five determinants of demand do not change. Later in the chapter we will consider changes in these factors.

Change in Quantity Demanded Versus Change in Demand

In analyzing the factors that cause consumers to increase or decrease their purchases of a particular product, it is helpful to distinguish between (1) the impact of a change in the price of the product and (2) the impact of a change in one or more of the determinants of demand.

A change in the price of the product results in a *change in quantity demanded* and is represented graphically by movement along a stationary demand curve. For example, if the price of steak declines from $6 a pound to $4 a pound, consumers will move from point *A* to point *B* on demand curve D_1 in Exh. 3.4. Note that the consumers will now choose to purchase a greater quantity of the product because its price is lower. This is an increase in the quantity demanded. If, on the other hand, the price rises from $2 a pound to $4 a pound, the consumers will move from point *C* to point *B* on the demand curve. Here a price increase will cause a reduction in the quantity demanded.

When any of the determinants of demand changes, the result is a *change in demand*—an entirely new demand schedule represented graphically by a shift of the demand curve to a new position. If consumers develop a stronger preference for steak, for instance, or if the prices of substitutes for steak rise, the entire demand curve for steak will shift to the right—an in-

EXHIBIT 3.4

Distinguishing Change in Demand from Change in Quantity Demanded

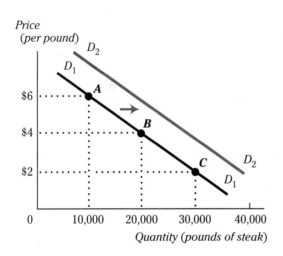

Price (per pound)

D_2

D_1

$6

A

B

$4

C D_2

$2

D_1

0   10,000   20,000   30,000   40,000

Quantity (pounds of steak)

A change in the price of steak will cause a change in the quantity demanded. When the price of steak declines from $6 to $2 a pound, the quantity demanded increases from 10,000 to 30,000 pounds; consumers move from A to C along demand curve D_1.

A change in a determinant of demand will cause a change in demand: The entire curve will shift. The movement from D_1 to D_2 is an increase in demand.

crease in demand. This shift is depicted in Exh. 3.4. An entire demand curve shift to the left would denote a decrease in demand.

Supply

A knowledge of demand is essential to an understanding of how prices are determined, but it is only half the picture. Now we turn to the supply side of the market.

When we use the term "supply" in our everyday language, usually we are referring to a fixed quantity. That's what the owner of the local sporting-goods store means where she advertises a *limited supply* of Fleet Feet tennis shoes or SuperFit swimsuits. But that's not what economists mean

EXHIBIT 3.5

Hometown Supply of Jogging Shoes

PRICE (per pair)	QUANTITY (pairs per year)
$50	10,000
40	8,000
30	6,000
20	4,000
10	2,000

when they talk about supply. To economists, supply is a schedule—just like demand is. Specifically, *supply* is a schedule (or table) showing the quantities of a good or service that producers are willing and able to offer for sale at various prices during a given time period, when all factors other than the product's price remain unchanged.

Exhibit 3.5 represents the annual supply of jogging shoes in the Hometown market area. As the schedule shows, the number of pairs of jogging shoes that suppliers will make available for sale depends on the price of jogging shoes. At a price of $50 a pair, they are willing to produce 10,000 pairs of jogging shoes a year, whereas at a price of $30, they would offer 6,000 pairs. Because supply is a schedule, we can't determine the quantity supplied unless we know the selling price.

The Supply Curve

To transform our supply schedule into a supply curve, we follow the same procedure we used in constructing a demand curve. Here we graph the information in Exh. 3.5, measuring price on the vertical axis and quantity on the horizontal axis. When we've finished graphing the points from the schedule, we connect them to get a *supply curve:* a graphic representation of supply (Exh. 3.6).

Interpreting a supply curve is basically the same as interpreting a demand curve. Each point on the curve represents a price and the quantity of jogging shoes that producers will supply at that price. You can see, for example, that producers will supply 4,000 pairs of shoes at a price of $20 per pair or 8,000 pairs at a price of $40 per pair.

EXHIBIT 3.6

The Supply Curve of Jogging Shoes in Hometown, U.S.A.

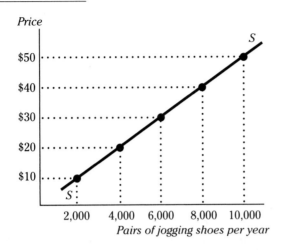

A supply curve is a graphic representation of supply. It demonstrates the direct relationship between price and quantity supplied.

The Law of Supply

You've probably noticed that the supply curve slopes upward and to the right. The supply curve slopes upward because the *law of supply* holds that price and quantity supplied are *positively or directly related*. Producers will supply a larger quantity at higher prices than at lower prices.

Why would producers supply more jogging shoes at a higher price than at a lower price? The major reason is because the higher price allows them to cover the higher per-unit costs associated with producing the additional output. It probably costs more to produce the thousandth pair of jogging shoes than it did to produce the five hundredth pair. It's also likely that it would cost even more to produce the two thousandth pair, and so on. Producers are willing to supply a greater quantity at a higher price because the higher price enables businesses to cover the higher cost of producing the additional units—units that would not have been profitable at lower prices.

Per-unit costs tend to increase with output because some of a business's resources such as its production plant and equipment cannot be expanded in a short period of time. Therefore as the business increases output by hiring more labor and employing more raw materials, it eventually begins to overutilize its factory and equipment. This leads to congestion, workers waiting to use equipment, more frequent breakdowns of equipment, and production bottlenecks—situations where one stage of the production process is slowing down the entire operation. Because of these problems, the cost of producing additional units rises. Producers will supply the additional units only if they can obtain a high enough price to justify paying the higher costs. Thus, the supply curve is upward sloping because a higher price is *necessary* to call forth additional output from suppliers.

Determinants of Supply

The supply curve shows the relationship between the price of a product and the quantity supplied when other factors remain unchanged. However, price is not the only factor that influences the amount producers will offer for sale. Three major *determinants of supply* underlie the supply schedule and determine the position of the supply curve: technology, prices of the resources used in producing the product, and the number of producers in the market. Each supply curve is based on the assumption that these factors are held constant. Changes in any of the determinants will shift the entire supply curve to a new position.

Technology

Each supply curve is based on the existing technology. *Technology* is our state of knowledge about how to produce products. It influences the types of machines we use and the combinations of other resources we select to produce goods and services. A *technological advance* is the discovery of a better way to produce a product—a method that uses fewer resources to produce each unit of output or that produces more output from a given amount of resources. Because a technological advance allows producers to supply a higher quantity at any given price, it is represented by shifting the supply curve to the right, as depicted in Exh. 3.7. As you can see, the development of a better method for producing personal computers will allow computer producers to supply a higher quantity at each price.

EXHIBIT 3.7

The Impact of a Technological Advance on the Supply of Personal Computers

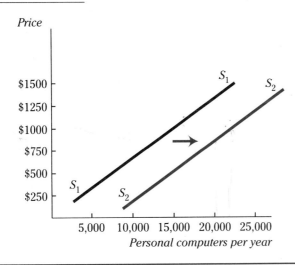

A technological advance will allow producers to supply a higher quantity at any given price.

Resource Prices

Businesses must purchase economic resources in order to produce their products. Each supply curve assumes that the prices of resources remain unchanged. An increase in the price of labor, materials, or some other production input will increase producers' costs and cause them to supply less at any given price. The supply curve will shift to the left. A reduction in resource prices will have the opposite effect; the supply curve will shift to the right because producers will be able to supply a higher quantity at each price.

The Number of Producers in the Market

A third determinant of supply is the number of producers in the particular market: the more producers, the greater the supply. Each supply curve assumes that the number of producers is unchanged. If additional producers enter the market, the supply curve will shift to the right; if some producers leave, the supply curve will shift left.

Many other changes have essentially the same impact on supply as an increase or decrease in the number of producers. A severe frost destroys half the orange crop, decreasing supply; a good growing season enlarges the wheat harvest, increasing supply; trade barriers are lowered and additional beef enters the United States, increasing supply. With each of these changes, the supply curve shifts as it would if the number of suppliers had increased or decreased.

Change in Supply versus Change in Quantity Supplied

Earlier in this chapter you learned the difference between a change in demand and a change in *quantity* demanded. Economists make the same distinction for supply. A *change in the quantity supplied* results from a change in the

EXHIBIT 3.8

Distinguishing Change in Supply from Change in Quantity Supplied

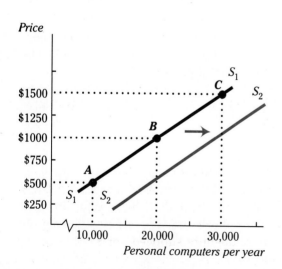

A change in the price of computers will cause a change in the quantity supplied. When price increases from $500 to $1,500, the quantity supplied increases from 10,000 to 30,000 computers per year; we move from A to C along supply curve S₁.

A change in a determinant of supply will cause a change in supply: the entire curve will shift. The movement from S₁ to S₂ is an increase in supply.

price of the product, with factors other than price held constant. It is represented graphically by movement along a stationary supply curve. According to Exh. 3.8, if the price of personal computers declines from $1,000 to $500, the quantity supplied will decrease from 20,000 units to only 10,000 units a year, as suppliers move from point B to point A along supply curve S_1. On the other hand, if the price of computers increases from $1,000 to $1,500, producers will move from point B to point C, and the quantity supplied will expand from 20,000 to 30,000 computers a year.

A *change in supply* is an increase or decrease in the amount of a product supplied at each and every price. A change in supply is caused by a change in one of the determinants of supply and is represented graphically by a shift of the entire supply curve as depicted in Exh. 3.8. If the supply curve shifts to the right (from S_1 to S_2), it denotes an increase in supply; a shift to the left indicates a decrease in supply. (You can test your ability to distinguish between a change in supply and a change in quantity supplied by reading the article entitled "Coal Mine Robots Lift an Industry," on page 82 and answering the questions.)

The Process of Price Determination

Now that you understand the basics of demand and supply, let's put those two pieces of the puzzle together and examine how prices are determined. To do that, we'll consider again the market for jogging shoes. Exhibit 3.9 on page 84 displays hypothetical demand and supply schedules for that product. As you already know, the demand schedule shows the quantities of jogging shoes that will be demanded at various prices, and the supply schedule reveals the quantities that will be supplied at those prices. But which of these possible prices will actually prevail in the market? And what quantity of jogging shoes will actually be exchanged between buyers and sellers? To answer those questions, let's compare the reactions of buyers and sellers to each possible price.

What would happen in the market if jogging shoes were selling for $10 a pair? Because the $10 price would be attractive to consumers but not to producers, 10,000 pairs of jogging shoes would be demanded but only 2,000 pairs would be supplied. At the $10 price there would be a *shortage*—an excess of quantity demanded over quantity supplied—of 8,000 pairs of jogging shoes. Given this situation, some potential buyers would offer to pay a higher price in order to obtain the product. Competition among these

Coal Mine Robots Lift an Industry

WANA, W.Va.—The four-inch carbide-steel claws of a screaming yellow robot tore relentlessly at the coal seam 1,000 feet below the surface, digging enough in 30 seconds to meet the electric needs of a typical suburban house for a year.

The robot's human master, old enough to remember when miners used picks and shovels and loaded coal into carts drawn by dogs, strolled beside, periodically pushing buttons on support equipment.

Coal mining, an unglamorous business known mostly for accidents and bitter strikes, is going high tech, and the resulting productivity gains are important for a nation that is using up its other fossil fuels.

A New Mining Method
The country's deposits of coal are expected to last more than a century, while oil reserves will last only 10 years at current rates of production, assuming no more oil is found. Gas reserves are also more limited than coal supplies. As oil and gas are used up, finding and extracting them become more expensive; by contrast, because of technical advances like the robot, the cost of digging coal is falling. Thus, over the long term, the price gap between coal and oil and gas will probably grow, and coal could become an even more important energy resource.

The robot here, in the Consolidation Coal Company's Blacksville No. 2 mine, 700 to 1,400 feet under the Mason-Dixon line, is perhaps the most advanced in the country. It is but one recent improvement in a highly automated tchnique called longwall mining, in which coal is removed not by tunneling like a worm through an apple, leaving more of the target than is removed, but by methodically shuttling back and forth across the width of the deposit and devouring nearly everything.

Longwall mining has been around for decades but mine operators have recently made the technique far more efficient. The method can now extract about 75 percent of the available coal, compared with 50 percent for conventional mining, which is done largely with machines that dig tunnels. Moreover, the coal can be recovered far more inexpensively.

Extensive Deposits
While coal has been hailed as the nation's energy savior since the 1973 Arab oil embargo, the cost of oil has not risen enough to make coal a good substitute beyond the power plant, where it is burned to produce electricity. Cutting the cost of coal production is a small step toward wider use. When costs justify it, coal can even substitute for gasoline.

Already, coal is the nation's biggest indigenous energy source, and its role has been growing. It supplied more than 23.4 percent of all energy consumed in this country, up from 17.5 percent in 1973, the year of the first oil shock, and 19.1 percent in 1979. And it accounted for nearly one-third of all energy produced in this country last year, up from 22.5 percent in 1973. It is the main fuel used to make electricity, providing about 56 percent, and is also the nation's largest energy export by far.

But increased production of

coal also raises intense environmental questions. The issues range from the speculative—like the extent of global warming caused by the burning of carbon-rich fuels like coal—to the spooky, like the collapse of land as robot miners pass beneath. The Government is spending more than $5 billion to find cleaner ways to use coal, and the coal companies have tried harder to ameliorate the effects of the collapse, called "subsidence." . . .

Further Refinements

Engineers are now working on additional refinements to longwall mining. For example, operators of the Blacksville 2 mine hope that even pushing the buttons to make the 153 shields step forward—now done by a human—will soon be taken over by the robot's computer brain.

Workers at this mine do not believe that this refinement will cut payrolls further because someone will be needed to watch the robots. At other mines, however, the prospect of installing a longwall ma-chine brings dread because of the layoffs that will come with it.

High-tech changes are taking place at the surface, too. In a small factory at the mouth of the mine, the coal is washed in water and other liquids, removing some of the sulfur; it is then dried, crushed and sorted by size. Sometimes it is blended with coal from other mines.

—*Matthew L. Wald*

SOURCE: Matthew L. Wald, "Coal Mine Robots Lift an Industry," *New York Times,* February 8, 1990, p. C1. Copyright © 1990 by The New York Times Company. Reprinted by permission.

USE YOUR ECONOMIC REASONING

1. The cost of digging coal appears to be falling, due to technical advances such as the robot described in this article. What will this do to the supply of coal? How would you represent this graphically?

2. When the cost of digging coal is reduced, does this lead to a change in supply or to a change in the quantity supplied?

3. As the price of oil increases relative to the price of coal, does this increase the demand for coal or the quantity of coal demanded? How would you represent this graphically?

buyers would tend to push the price to a higher level, and the higher price of jogging shoes would tend to reduce the quantity demanded while encouraging producers to expand the quantity supplied. In this way, price increases would tend to reduce the shortage of jogging shoes.

Suppose that the price of jogging shoes rose to $20 a pair. At that price, 8,000 pairs of jogging shoes would be demanded and 4,000 pairs supplied. Once again there would be a shortage, but this time it would amount to only 4,000 pairs of jogging shoes (8,000 pairs demanded minus 4,000 pairs supplied). Competition among potential buyers again would bid up the price of jogging shoes. The higher price would lead to a reduction in the quantity demanded and an increase in the quantity supplied, which would reduce the shortage still further.

You can probably see what happens as we move from lower to higher prices. Now let's reverse the process, beginning with the highest price in Exh. 3.9. A price of $50 would tend to encourage production and discourage consumption. Producers would be willing to supply 10,000 pairs of jogging shoes a year, but consumers would demand only 2,000 pairs. The result would be a *surplus*—an excess of quantity supplied over quantity demanded—of 8,000 pairs of jogging shoes a year. How do producers react to a surplus? They begin to cut the price of the product in order to compete for existing customers and lure additional customers into the market. The lower price of jogging shoes tends to increase the quantity demanded and decrease the quantity supplied, thus reducing the surplus. If the price fell to $40, there would still be a surplus of 4,000 pairs of jogging shoes (8,000 pairs supplied minus the 4,000 pairs demanded). Price cutting would then continue, and the surplus would continue to shrink.

EXHIBIT 3.9

The Demand and Supply of Jogging Shoes in Hometown, U.S.A.

PRICE (per pair)	QUANTITY DEMANDED (pairs per year)	QUANTITY SUPPLIED (pairs per year)
$50	2,000	10,000
40	4,000	8,000
30	6,000	6,000
20	8,000	4,000
10	10,000	2,000

Equilibrium Price and Quantity

In our example, $30 is the market-clearing or equilibrium price, and 6,000 units is the equilibrium quantity. The *equilibrium price* is the price that brings about an equality between the quantity demanded and the quantity supplied. The *equilibrium quantity* is the quantity demanded and supplied at the equilibrium price. Equilibrium essentially means stability; once established, the equilibrium price will be maintained so long as the basic supply and demand conditions remain unchanged.

EXHIBIT 3.10

Demand and Supply Curves for Jogging Shoes in Hometown, U.S.A.

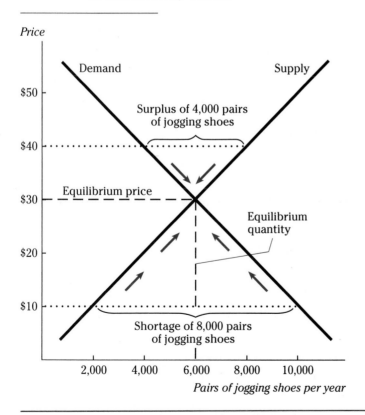

The equilibrium price is the price that equates the quantity supplied and the quantity demanded. In our example, the equilibrium price is $30. Whenever the existing price is above or below equilibrium, pressure exists to push it toward the equilibrium level. For example, at a price of $40 there would be a surplus, and price cutting would take place. At a price of $10, there would be a shortage, and the price would tend to rise in order to eliminate the shortage. The arrows indicate the direction of the adjustments in price and quantity.

In a competitive market the actual or prevailing price will tend toward equilibrium. As you saw in Exh. 3.9, when the price of jogging shoes is above or below equilibrium, market pressures tend to push it down or up toward the equilibrium level. Only when the existing price is at the equilibrium level will there be neither a shortage nor a surplus and no pressure for price to change.

We use supply and demand curves to represent the process of price determination. By graphing the demand and supply schedules in Exh. 3.9, we can construct the demand and supply curves found in Exh. 3.10. These curves intersect at the equilibrium price ($30) and the equilibrium quantity (6,000 pairs of jogging shoes). At any price *above* equilibrium (say, $40) we can measure the amount of the surplus as the horizontal distance between the demand curve and the supply curve. For any price *below* equilibrium ($10, for example) the horizontal distance between the curves tells us the amount of the shortage. As we noted earlier, the shortage or surplus tends to shrink as price approaches the equilibrium level. The graph visually represents these shrinking amounts in the diminishing distance between the demand curve and the supply curve. When price finally achieves equilibrium, the curves intersect. At that point quantity demanded equals quantity supplied, and there is neither shortage nor surplus.

The Rationing, Signaling, and Motivating Functions of Prices

In the preceding example, the equilibrium price succeeds in matching up the quantity supplied and the quantity demanded because it performs three important functions. First, the equilibrium price rations jogging shoes perfectly among the various possible users; at a price of $30, 6,000 pairs are demanded: exactly the quantity made available by producers. Second, it signals or guides producers to supply the correct quantity, the quantity consumers are willing to purchase at $30. Finally, it motivates producers to supply that quantity because it makes it profitable for them to do so.

You may recall from Chapter 1 that because every society faces the basic economic problem of unlimited wants and limited resources, some system must exist for *rationing*—that is, dividing up or allocating the scarce items among those who want them. In the United States and other economies that rely heavily on markets, price is the dominant rationing device. Rationing in a market economy works hand in hand with *signaling*—providing information to producers about how much to supply, and *motivating*—providing incentives to produce the desired output. Let's use Exh. 3.10 to examine this process further, first from the perspective of the consumers demanding jogging shoes and then from the perspective of the producers supplying them.

How does the price of a product ration the supply of it among users? Prices ration because they influence our ability and willingness to purchase the product. The higher the price of jogging shoes, the more of our income it takes to buy them (which means a greater sacrifice in terms of other goods and services we must do without) and the less attractive jogging shoes become in relation to substitute products (tennis shoes, for instance).

To illustrate how price rations, let's begin with a relatively low price for jogging shoes—$10. If jogging shoes were selling for $10 (a price well below equilibrium), consumers would be willing and able to purchase a relatively high quantity—10,000 pairs. But, as we learned earlier, producers are willing to supply only 2,000 pairs at that price, so there will be a shortage and price will tend to rise. As the price of jogging shoes rises toward its equilibrium level, the quantity demanded is reduced—fewer consumers are willing and able to pay the higher price. By discouraging consumers from purchasing the product, the higher price of jogging shoes helps to bring the quantity demanded into line with the number of jogging shoes available; it *rations* jogging shoes. By the same token, at a price initially above equilibrium—for example, $40—the quantity demanded would be too low. But price will tend to decline, and the falling price will encourage consumers to purchase more of the product. Thus higher prices ration by reducing the quantity demanded, and lower prices ration by increasing it.

But changing prices do more than reduce or increase the quantity demanded: They also signal producers to expand or shrink production and motivate them to supply the new quantity. We know from the law of supply that more will be supplied at higher prices than at lower prices. Thus when the price of jogging shoes increases from $10 to $30, the quantity of jogging shoes supplied will increase from 2,000 pairs to 6,000 pairs. At the same time, the quantity of jogging shoes is being rationed among consumers; the quantity demanded is declining from 10,000 pairs to 6,000 pairs. This is how the rationing, signaling, and motivating functions of price work together to balance the desires of consumers and producers and prevent a shortage or surplus. Every consumer who values jogging shoes enough to pay $30 will have them, and every producer who is willing to supply jogging shoes at that price will be able to sell its entire output.

Equilibrium prices balance demand and supply, but they don't make everyone happy. Read "Let's Change: Have Worst Job Pay the Best" on page 88, and see if you can explain why some people who work very hard earn very little.

Let's Change: Have Worst Job Pay the Best

National Public Radio columnist William Hamilton said the other day that we Americans have our priorities all wrong when it comes to salaries.

There's got to be something wrong with a system that pays the lowest salaries to those who do the dirtiest, most abhorrent work, he said. It should be the other way around, he thinks. "Why should I pay $100 an hour to my lawyer, who makes me absolutely miserable, when I pay $4 an hour to my housecleaner, who absolutely makes my heart sing?" he asked. . . .

His reasoning makes perfect sense to me. Everyone wants the good jobs and no one wants the bad ones; so if we pay the highest salaries for the unpopular jobs, we'll have plenty of people to do them, right?

Voila! No more housecleaner shortage! . . .

I heartily endorse Hamilton's request that those who do the ugliest jobs get pretty paychecks. . . . If we want someone to change our dirty sheets and make our beds without any wrinkles, we should raise a competent housecleaner's wage . . . to what we'd pay a plumber, mechanic, bus driver or newspaper reporter. If we want our food brought to us with a smile and our water refilled when we need it, we have to pay a good waitress a decent wage instead of asking her to work for a buck an hour and tips—tips she probably won't get if she has to wait on twice as many customers as is humanly possible.

It's hard to arbitrarily assign a set wage to any given profession and I wouldn't even attempt it. But wages reflect the attitudes we have about jobs, and I think it's about time we afforded proper compensation for a job well done, whether it's mending a broken arm or shoveling out a cow barn.

And it's not only the blue collar professions that get no respect. Many of us have the attitude that teachers should teach our children for altruistic purposes, coming early to the school . . . and staying late to grade papers and take tickets for the basketball game—while we clock in and clock out right at the eight-hour mark. If we strike, it's only because we need a living wage to support our families. If teachers strike, it's because they're selfish and money-grubbing. . . .

You get what you pay for. Next time your coffee cup isn't filled, or your end tables don't shine so that you can see yourself in them, or your lawn isn't mowed in nice, neat rows, or the teacher has a far-off look in her eyes during parent-teacher conference—ask yourself how much you're willing to pay to have it done right. *—Sarah Overstreet*

SOURCE: *The Springfield Leader & Press*, Springfield, Mo., May 31, 1982, p. 4B. Reprinted with permission.

USE YOUR ECONOMIC REASONING

1. **What do you think of Mr. Hamilton's observation? Do the people who perform the "dirtiest, most abhorrent work" receive the lowest pay? Is that always true? Never true?**

2. **Given that the wage rate is the "price" of labor, how would you explain the fact that a housecleaner earns less than a lawyer?**

3. **Some people believe that doctors and lawyers are well paid because they spent so much time preparing for their profession. The average performer in a ballet company or symphony orchestra spends just as much time in training but earns far less. How do you explain the difference?**

4. **Do you agree with Ms. Overstreet that wages reflect society's attitudes about particular jobs? Explain why you agree or disagree.**

Changes in the Equilibrium Price

You have seen that in the absence of artificial restrictions, prices in competitive markets tend toward equilibrium. Once established, the equilibrium price will hold as long as the underlying demand and supply conditions remain unchanged. Of course, such conditions don't remain unchanged forever, often not even for a short time. Anything that causes a change in either demand or supply will bring about a new equilibrium price.

The Impact of a Change in Demand

Recall from earlier in this chapter that the determinants of demand are all the factors that underlie the demand schedule and determine the precise position of the demand curve. These include consumer tastes and preferences, consumer income, the prices of substitutes and complements, expectations regarding future prices, and the number of buyers in the market. Changes in any of these factors will cause a change in demand—a shift of the entire demand curve.

The housing market provides a good example. Increased demand for new houses in your city or town could result from any of several factors: heightened desire for single-family dwellings instead of apartments; an increase in residents' incomes; rent hikes in the area; expectations of higher housing prices in the near future; or a local population expansion. Any of these changes will cause the demand curve for new homes to shift to the right, as depicted in Exh. 3.11.

You can see that 8,000 new houses are demanded and supplied at the initial equilibrium price of $120,000. However, as demand increases from D_1 to D_2, perhaps because of an increased number of buyers in the market, there is a shortage of 4,000 houses (12,000 minus 8,000) at the $120,000 price. This shortage will lead to competition among prospective home buyers, which in turn will push the average price upward toward the new equilibrium level of $130,000. The higher price will perform three functions: it will ration new houses by reducing the quantity demanded, and it will signal and motivate builders to increase the quantity supplied from 8,000 to 10,000. Note here that the increase in demand (the shift of the entire demand curve) causes an increase in the *quantity* supplied (movement along the stationary supply curve). In other words, a *shift* in one curve causes movement *along* the other

EXHIBIT 3.11

The Effect of an Increase in Demand on the Equilibrium Price

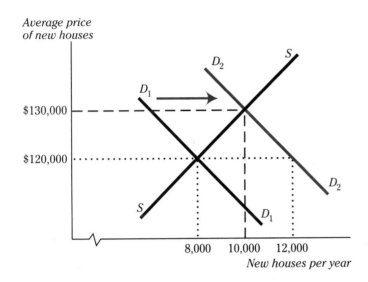

An increase in the demand for new houses will cause the equilibrium price of new homes to rise.

curve. Thus an increase in demand leads to both a higher equilibrium price ($130,000) and a higher equilibrium quantity (10,000 new homes per year).

Now suppose that any of the conditions that might have increased the demand for new houses is reversed, causing demand to decline. As shown in Exh. 3.12, the demand curve will shift to the left, from D_1 to D_2. As demand declines, a surplus of houses develops at the old price of $120,000 (only 4,000 homes will be demanded, but 8,000 will be supplied). This surplus will lead to price cutting as builders compete for buyers and as customers shop around for the best buys. Once again, the price change performs three functions. The falling price convinces home buyers to purchase more than 4,000 homes per year, while it signals and motivates builders to supply fewer than 8,000 homes. Price will continue to decline until the quantity of new houses demanded is exactly equal to the quantity supplied at that price. In our example, the new equilibrium price is $110,000, and the new equilibrium quantity is 6,000 new homes per year.

EXHIBIT 3.12

The Effect of a Decrease in Demand on the Equilibrium Price

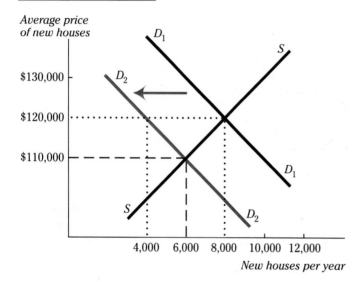

A decrease in the demand for new houses will cause the equilibrium price of new homes to fall.

The Impact of a Change in Supply

Price changes also can be initiated on the supply side. Recall the three determinants of supply: technology, prices of economic resources, and the number of suppliers in the market. Changes in any of these factors that underlie the supply schedule will cause a change in supply. In our example, the supply of housing might be increased by any of the following: (a) the development of new construction methods that enable builders to produce more houses from a given amount of resources; (b) decreases in the cost of land, labor, or materials used in home construction; (c) an increase in the number of builders, enabling the market to produce more houses than before at each possible price.

An increase in the supply of new houses is represented by shifting the supply curve to the right, as shown in Exh. 3.13. When the supply of housing increases from S_1 to S_2, 12,000 new homes will be supplied at a price of $120,000, but only 8,000 will be demanded. As before, the surplus will lead to price cutting downward toward the new equilibrium level of $110,000. Note that here the increase in supply (the shift of the entire supply curve)

EXHIBIT 3.13

Effect of an Increase in Supply on Equilibrium Price

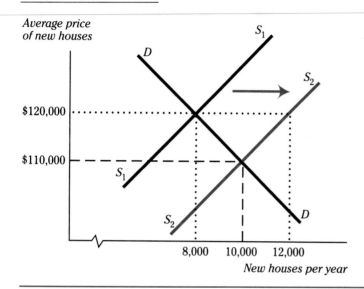

An increase in the supply of new houses will cause the equilibrium price of new homes to fall.

causes an increase in the *quantity* demanded (movement along the stationary demand curve). As we saw earlier, a shift in one curve causes movement *along* the other. This is the process that results in the lower price and the higher equilibrium quantity. A *decrease* in the supply of housing would have the opposite effect; it would raise the equilibrium price and lower the equilibrium quantity.

The Impact of Simultaneous Changes in Demand and Supply

All the price changes we have explored so far have resulted from a single cause, either a change in demand while supply remained constant, or a change in supply while demand remained constant. But in many real-world situations, simultaneous changes occur in demand and supply. Let's consider two examples in the housing market. In the first case, we find an area undergoing a population expansion (a source of increased demand for new houses) at the same time that building-material costs are rising (causing a decrease in supply). In the second case, a period of high unemployment is causing the incomes of area residents to decline (less demand for new houses), while new production methods are reducing the cost of new-home construction (increased supply).

In these two examples, the forces of demand and supply are pulling in opposite directions—the demand curve is shifting one way, while the supply curve is shifting the other. Under these conditions it is relatively easy to determine what will happen to the equilibrium price. In the first example, demand increases while supply decreases; so the equilibrium price tends to rise. In the second example, demand decreases while supply increases; so the equilibrium price tends to fall. Take a minute to draw the diagrams and convince yourself of these results.

Predicting the impact of simultaneous changes in demand and supply becomes a little trickier when both the demand curve and the supply curve are shifting in the same direction. As you can see from Exh. 3.14, when demand and supply are both increasing, the effect on price depends on how much demand increases relative to supply. If demand and supply increase by the same amounts, equilibrium price will not change. If demand increases more than supply, equilibrium price will rise. If supply increases more than demand, equilibrium price will fall. (See if you can predict what would happen to price if demand and supply both *decreased* by the same amount; if demand decreased more than supply; if supply decreased more than demand.)

EXHIBIT 3.14

Effect of Simultaneous Increases in Demand and Supply on Equilibrium Price

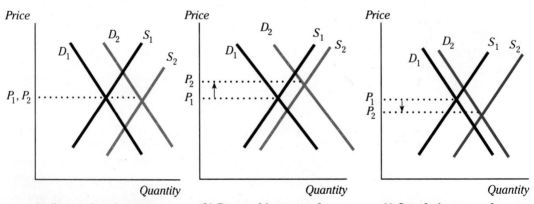

(a) Demand and supply increase by equal amounts; price does not change.

(b) Demand increases by more than supply; price rises.

(c) Supply increases by more than demand; price falls.

In summary, the price of a product can change because of a change in demand, because of a change in supply, or because of simultaneous changes in demand and supply. In all cases the basic principle is the same: Whenever demand increases in relation to supply, the equilibrium price will rise; whenever supply increases in relation to demand, the equilibrium price will fall. By keeping that principle in mind, we can predict what is going to happen to the price of cattle or wheat or any other product whose price is determined in a competitive market. Even illicit drugs are subject to the laws of supply and demand. Read "Costly and Scarce, Marijuana Is a High More Are Rejecting" on page 96, and try to explain why marijuana prices have risen in spite of declining popularity.

Intervention in Price Determination: Supports and Ceilings

Sometimes the prices that result from the interaction of demand and supply may cause hardship for producers or consumers and therefore be perceived as "unfair" by the injured group. Producers may feel that prevailing market prices are too low to provide them with adequate incomes. Consumers may believe that market prices are too high and thus place an unreasonable burden on households—particularly low-income households. To protect their various interests, both consumers and producers form pressure groups and lobby the government to intervene in the process of price determination. Agricultural price supports, minimum-wage laws, interest-rate ceilings, and rent controls are just a few examples that illustrate the success of these campaigns.

Price Supports

Government usually intervenes in pricing by establishing maximum or minimum prices. A *price support* is a legally established minimum price level above the equilibrium price. In the 1930s, for example, the federal government initiated a program of agricultural price supports designed to raise the income of farmers. Under this program the government "supports" the price of the product by agreeing to purchase, at the legally established price, whatever output the farmer is unable to sell at that price.

Exhibit 3.15 shows a hypothetical situation in which the government has established a price support (or support price) for peanuts at $.40, ten cents above the equilibrium price of $.30 per pound. At $.40 a pound customers are willing to purchase only 200 million pounds a year, but

Costly and Scarce, Marijuana Is a High More Are Rejecting

Not long ago, hosts at some Upper East Side dinner parties would set out little silver bowls of home-rolled marijuana cigarettes along with the after-dinner drinks. Rock concerts unfolded under canopies of marijuana smoke, and the drug's syrupy aroma drifted across schoolyards and campuses, construction sites and corporate offices, public parks and private patios.

But as quietly and gradually as the widening of a waistline, America's infatuation with the herb of many names—grass, pot, dope, weed, ganja, sess, sens, smoke, skunk and, quaintly, in the long ago, Mary Jane—has been fading.

In New York and throughout the country, lighting up is no longer hip, not in high school, not at college, not at most social events and, with the advent of widespread random drug testing, certainly not on the job.

"It's Not Cool Anymore"

The great marijuana cloud has grown wispy as rebellion and the quest for nirvana have yielded to conformity and the struggle for survival, as health concerns and a vague fear of getting into trouble have risen above the desire to get giddy.

Part of the shift, undoubtedly, has also been because of relentless police pressure that has transformed an abundant drug once available for $20 or $30 an ounce into a scarce commodity selling in some quarters of New York for $800 an ounce, more than twice the price of gold.

"It's not cool anymore," said a high school senior in Manhattan, capturing the mood of the 90's with the language of the 60's. . . .

Advocates insist that marijuana—the mildest and by far the most widely tried illegal drug in America—is no more harmful than alcohol, not even the latest strains, which are 10 times more potent than the grass of the flower children. Still, it has been as much a target of the national antidrug campaign as cocaine, heroin, LSD and barbiturates, and many people have clearly taken the warnings and prohibitions to heart. . . .

Ultimately, it seems, marijuana just does not fit the personal visions of growing numbers of New Yorkers and other Americans. Nor do most other drugs, including cocaine, alcohol and nicotine, all of which are being increasingly rejected. . . .

And the Manhattan high school senior said that although marijuana was widely accepted as recently as her freshman and sophomore years, she now finds that "everyone is really scared about getting into college and getting good jobs and doing drugs doesn't help." . . .

"Using pot," the high school senior said, "is like dropping out of the race"; which, of course, was precisely the attraction for many in her father's generation.

Former pot smokers—or almost-former pot smokers—are everywhere. Nathan J., a 20-year-old college sophomore, rarely smokes now because he found he was losing his edge in volleyball and Frisbee games. A 28-year-old dancer who said she smoked heavily in high school takes a drag every couple of years and finds to her disappointment that she becomes paranoid and self-conscious and ends up wondering why she tried it again. Her friend, a graphic artist, said she decided she could not tolerate the loss of hand-eye coordination. A lawyer in her 40's said that while she didn't believe smoking was bad, it began to seem "foolhardy" to risk an arrest that "could wreck your career."

Marijuana smoking reached its peak in 1979, when the National Institute on Drug Abuse estimated, based on its survey, that more than 31.5 million Americans had used the drug at least once during that year. By 1990, when the most recent statistics were compiled, the marijuana-smoking crowd had diminished by more than a third, to 20.5 million. . . .

Back in 1979, almost all the marijuana smoked in the United States was grown in other countries. . . .

The United States Customs Service seized more than 3.5 million pounds of marijuana in 1979. Last year, Federal agents intercepted 222,274 pounds, or 15 times less.

The great wall of boats, planes and radar thrown up by the Federal Government may not have dented the cocaine trade, but it nearly killed marijuana smuggling. Marijuana is much bulkier and harder to conceal than cocaine and, until recently, it sold for much less. . . .

Unable to get through the barriers or unwilling to risk jail for the lower profits from marijuana, some smugglers dropped out; others shifted to cocaine. . . .

The war against domestically grown marijuana accelerated in early 1990, after President Bush was embarrassed at a conference on drugs in Colombia at which Alan García, then president of Peru, suggested that Washington could hardly expect Latin America to stop growing the raw material for cocaine when marijuana farmers flourished in the United States.

Government spray planes wiped out 85 to 90 percent of Hawaii's marijuana, administration officials say. . . .

After the air raids in Hawaii, the retail price of marijuana there leaped from $2,000 a pound to $6,000, which is $375 an ounce, or $16 more than an ounce of gold.

Prices fluctuate around the country, but in the Northeast these days it is not unusual to pay $280 an ounce. . . .
—*Joseph B. Treaster*

SOURCE: Joseph B. Treaster, "Costly and Scarce, Marijuana Is a High More Are Rejecting," *New York Times*, October 29, 1991, p. 1. Copyright © 1991 by The New York Times Company. Reprinted by permission.

USE YOUR ECONOMIC REASONING

1. **If the popularity of marijuana is declining, what impact would that trend, by itself, have on the price of marijuana?**

2. **The government has apparently been quite successful in slowing the inflow of foreign marijuana and destroying much of the domestic crop. What impact would these actions alone have on price?**

3. **According to the article, the price of marijuana has risen substantially. What does that tell us about the relative importance of the forces described in questions 1 and 2? Use a graph to help you answer this question.**

4. **Some former marijuana smugglers have turned to smuggling cocaine, even though the demand for cocaine appears to be declining. What impact would you expect these events to have on the price of cocaine? Can you predict the impact on the equilibrium quantity?**

EXHIBIT 3.15

Price Supports and Surpluses

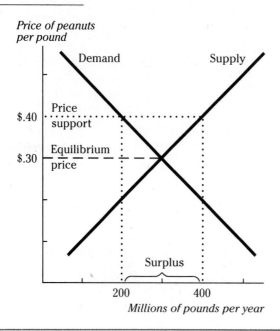

Price of peanuts
per pound

producers are eager to supply 400 million pounds. We know that in a free or unregulated market, sellers of peanuts would deal with the surplus of 200 million pounds by cutting prices down to the equilibrium level of $.30, at which the equilibrium quantity of 300 million pounds would be supplied. However, once the government establishes a price support of $.40, the market remains in disequilibrium with surpluses continuing to accumulate. The government is then required to buy these surplus peanuts, store them, and dispose of them, all at the expense of taxpayers. It usually distributes part of the surplus through such enterprises as supplying peanut butter, cheese, and other commodities to school lunch programs and food pantries that aid low-income families.

Similar problems occur with other price-support programs—the minimum wage, for example. By law, most employers are required to pay their employees at least the government-established minimum wage ($4.25 an hour in 1991). Because this wage is generally above the equilibrium wage for unskilled labor, there are more people willing to work at that wage than employers are willing to hire at that wage. Of course, those who can find jobs are better off because of the minimum wage. But some unskilled workers who would have been able to find jobs at the equilibrium wage will be unemployed at the minimum wage; this occurs because employers simply do not believe that these workers will be able to contribute enough to the production process to justify that high a wage. Just as the support price for peanuts created a surplus of that product, the minimum wage creates a surplus of workers. To the extent that the minimum wage increases unemployment, it conflicts with our objective of raising the incomes of low-income Americans.

Price Ceilings

Government may also intervene in the pricing process when it is convinced that prevailing prices are either too high or increasing too rapidly. In such cases, the government will set *price ceilings,* maximum prices that are established below the equilibrium price. During World War II, for example, price ceilings were placed on most nonfarm prices in order to prevent them from being pushed to exorbitant levels by the demands of the war effort. Price ceilings (or ceiling prices) also have been used during peacetime as a technique both for combating inflation (a general rise in the level of prices) and for controlling specific prices. For instance, in 1971 President Nixon "froze" virtually all wages and prices for a period of 90 days in an attempt to slow the rate of inflation. In the same decade the federal government used price ceilings selectively to limit the price of beef, pork, gasoline, and natural gas, among other products.

Because price ceilings are designed to hold prices below equilibrium, they tend to produce shortages. Consider, for example, the problems that result when interest rates are restricted to artificially low levels. Until 1982, the state of Arkansas did not permit lenders to charge more than 10 percent interest on loans to consumers. Although interest-rate ceilings may seem to be in the best interest of consumers, they frequently create problems for borrowers. Because the interest rate is fixed at an artificially low level, more people will want to borrow money than would desire to do so at the equilibrium rate. In addition, the low rate will make consumer loans less attractive to lenders, who consequently will make available less money than they would provide at the equilibrium rate. The result will be a number of unsatisfied customers, some of whom may borrow from loan sharks—individuals who violate the law by lending money at interest rates above the ceiling.

Exhibit 3.16 illustrates the plight of the Arkansas consumer prior to 1982. As you can see from the diagram, 18 percent is the interest rate at which the amount of money consumers are willing to borrow is exactly equal to the quantity lenders are willing to make available. When the interest rate

EXHIBIT 3.16

Price Ceilings and Shortages

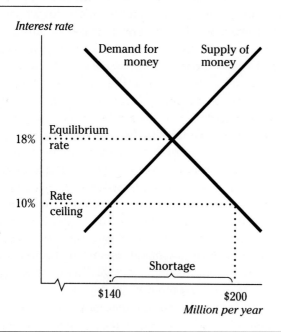

A price ceiling will tend to produce a shortage, since price is legally fixed below the equilibrium level. In this example, an interest rate ceiling of 10 percent leads to a shortage of $60 million in loans.

is held below this equilibrium level, problems occur. At the 10 percent ceiling rate, consumers want to borrow $200 million a year, but lenders are willing to loan only $140 million. There is a shortage of $60 million in loans.[1]

We know that in the market a shortage of any item, including loan money, will lead to a price increase, which signals businesses to supply more of it and consumers to demand less. A ceiling prevents the interest rate from rising to its equilibrium level, so lenders are faced with more potential borrowers than they can satisfy. Consequently they must use some secondary rationing device to decide which consumers will receive loans.

A *secondary rationing device* is a nonprice condition that supplements the primary rationing device, price. The consumer in our example not

---

[1] The 10 percent interest-rate ceiling was repealed in November 1982, yet was replaced by a floating interest-rate ceiling that permits lenders to charge no more than 5 percent above the discount rate determined by the Federal Reserve, the agency which regulates the nation's money supply. While the new ceiling is more flexible, it continues to discourage lenders from making certain loans—particularly loans to less credit-worthy customers. Thus, the floating interest-rate ceiling probably reduces the magnitude of the loan shortage, but does not eliminate it.

only has to be willing to pay 10 percent interest to get the loan, but also has to satisfy some supplementary requirement imposed by lenders. Perhaps lenders will grant loans only on the basis of first come, first served. They may choose instead to lend money only to customers with the very best credit ratings. Or lenders may decide to make loans only to "preferred" customers. In this final situation the definition of "preferred" is seldom precise. It may mean certain customers whom the lender wants to keep; it may mean influential people whom the lender doesn't want to offend; it may include all friends of the bank president or the owner of the business. Whether or not the use of a secondary, nonprice rationing device is preferable to higher interest rates is a matter for you to decide. It is clear, however, that price ceilings do not eliminate the need to ration; they simply force sellers to use secondary rationing devices.

Price ceilings result in shortages in a number of markets. In New York City, for example, where ceilings on rents (rent controls) are enforced to keep rents within the reach of low-income citizens, finding an apartment is a major problem. Because rents are kept below their equilibrium level, New Yorkers face a perpetual shortage of rental housing. For the most part, existing housing is rationed on a first-come, first-served basis, and countless hours are spent in vain attempts to find a vacant apartment. Some frustrated searchers resort to checking obituaries in hope of zeroing in on a newly available rental before anyone else hears of it. Others make secret payments to landlords for the privilege of a new lease. Low rents not only produce a shortage, but also prevent the supply of housing from expanding. In fact, landlords may allow some rental units to deteriorate. If rental income cannot rise, owners cannot profit from money spent on improvements or even break even on money invested in maintenance. In summary, although rent controls succeed in maintaining low rents for those lucky enough to find apartments, they create shortages and prevent expansion, problems that would be eliminated if rents were allowed to rise to their equilibrium level. See "Santa Monica—Only the Elite Need Apply," page 102, for a look at rent control in action.

Economic Efficiency and the Role of Prices

The automatic response of price changes to changes in demand and supply conditions is an important feature of a market economy. As increasing consumer demand pushes the price of a product upward, the higher price rations some consumers out of the market and simultaneously signals and motivates

Santa Monica—Only the Elite Need Apply

When the renters' "underground" alerted Melissa Clare to an apartment vacancy in Santa Monica, the free-lance writer assumed that her chances of getting into the embattled rent-control city were virtually nil.

Living within earshot of the ocean for $280 a month was an alluring proposition. In just three days, the owner of the vacant one-bedroom apartment had talked to more than 200 prospective tenants.

The fact that Clare eventually triumphed over the other applicants is credited to a strong recommendation from the outgoing tenant, a member of Clare's close-knit network of renter friends. Most people are not so lucky.

Five years after Santa Monica voters approved the nation's toughest and most controversial rent-control law—after the so called "renter's revolt" put a lid on spiraling rents and demolitions—the city has experienced an unrelenting demand for apartments. . . .

"Santa Monica has the most comprehensive rent-control law in the country," said John Gilderbloom, an urban studies professor at the University of Wisconsin, Green Bay, and author of

"Rent Control, A Source Book."

"Landlords are realizing that this is where the first battle has got to be pitched, that they have got to knock off this rent-control law because many communities are now trying to emulate it," Gilderbloom said.

Dramatic Effect on City

In its simplest form, rent control acts as a stabilizer on rapidly rising rents. Roughly half of the apartments in California and 10% of the apartments nationwide are covered by some form of rental regulation, according to urban planners. While Santa Monica's law has won the respect of people like Gilderbloom by tightly regulating rents and preventing demolitions, the effect on the city has been dramatic.

• Finding an apartment in Santa Monica has become nearly impossible. It is not uncommon for upward of 400 people to apply for one vacancy, and some people have been on waiting lists for more than two years. Most apartment vacancies are not advertised. Of the ones that are, roughly two-thirds are rented through agencies that charge fees of as much as $1,000 for their services. Because the competition for apartments is so fierce, apartment owners said they most often choose as

tenants young professionals who are more likely to pay for repairs and improvements to their units. While rent control was originally promoted as a way of keeping the city affordable, city planners have estimated that "Santa Monica today has fewer low- and moderate-income people than at any time in its recent history. . . ."

• Maintenance of apartment buildings has declined. Many apartment owners, angry about low profits on their buildings, have decreased general maintenance. Maintenance-related complaints filed by tenants have more than doubled since the passage of rent control, according to the city's building and safety division.

• Apartment building sales and construction remain in decline. Even though new buildings are exempt from rent control (except for units built under special government contracts), a minimal amount of apartment construction has taken place since rent control. . . .

What makes Santa Monica's law unique as well as galling to apartment owners is the Rent Control Board's considerable independence and power. The elected five-member body has the authority not only to regulate rents but to control the demolition or conversion of rental units, and regulate evictions.

Responding to charges that rent control was driving down values of apartment buildings and discouraging construction, the Rent Control Board issued a report last year saying that "rent controls appear to have no demonstrable adverse effect on newly constructed rental units . . . or on the resale value of residential rental properties."

But local realtors maintain that the regulation has had an extremely debilitating effect. Real estate values on Santa Monica apartments have remained about the same since rent control was implemented, while prices of buildings in West Los Angeles generally have doubled. . . .

"We're seeing almost no sales activity," said real estate executive Fred Sands. "No one really wants to buy in Santa Monica unless they can get a steal."

Apartment owners charge that the board has set unnecessarily harsh standards. After five years, board allowed rent hikes are about 24% behind inflation. . . .

Apartment owner Baker said most landlords do not advertise vacancies because the demand is too great, a statement substantiated by several other apartment owners. Landlords said that the majority of the apartments are rented to people who canvass neighborhoods on foot, leaving a citywide trail of applications and resumes. Many owners trade these applica-tions among themselves, Baker said, assuring that they get the best tenants.

As a result of the high demand, apartments are rented mostly to young professionals who earn the most money and campaign the hardest to get them. Baker, who owns three apartment buildings, estimates that the average age of his tenants has declined by about 10 years while their income has more than doubled. . . .

Using pre-rent-control experiences as an example, rent-control supporters answer that Santa Monica's transformation to a population of elite would have occurred faster without rent control. . . .

Deterioration of the housing stock, a fairly common phenomenon in rent-control cities, is another concern in Santa Monica. . . .

For David and Dorothy Merken, both 79, who pay $516 a month for a two-bedroom, two-bathroom apartment with a wet bar and an electric fireplace, that means that shredded curtains, peeling wallpaper and a broken shower head don't get fixed. For others it means having to replace their own water heaters, or even walls and windows.

But with some ocean-front apartments still renting for less than a tenth of what they would fetch on an open market and with homes priced beyond the average person's reach, most tenants aren't complaining. "It's a wonderful law," Dorothy Merken said. "It has stood the test of time. And with these landlords, that's quite a test." . . .

—Alan Citron

SOURCE: *Los Angeles Times*, April 8, 1984, Section II, p. 1. Reprinted with permission.

USE YOUR ECONOMIC REASONING

1. How are apartments being rationed in Santa Monica; what is the secondary rationing device?

2. Why do you suppose the general maintenance of the apartment buildings has declined? Is it solely because apartment owners are angry about their artificially low rents?

3. Why do as many as 400 people apply for a vacant apartment? Try to represent this phenomenon graphically. Would this occur if rents were uncontrolled?

4. Why has rent control not helped to provide housing in Santa Monica for low and moderate income people. How are they being rationed out of the market?

5. Considering the pluses and minuses of rent control, would you support such measures or oppose them? Why?

producers to expand their production of the product. Because these producers are receiving a higher price for their product, they will be able to outbid producers of less-valued items for the resources needed to expand production. In this way price changes help to ensure that businesses produce the goods and services that consumers value the most, in the quantities they desire.

Price changes also help ensure that each product is produced with as few of society's scarce resources as possible. As a particular resource becomes scarcer (due to increased demand or reduced supply), its price tends to rise. This higher cost encourages producers to economize on its use by substituting cheaper resources whenever possible. The end result is the efficient use of society's scarce resources: Producers supply the most-wanted products in the least-costly way in terms of scarce resources.[2] The way that competitive markets promote the efficient use of resources will be explored in greater detail in Chapter 5. Later chapters will examine how factors such as inadequate competition and the ability of firms to ignore the "cost" of the pollution they create can interfere with the ability of markets to achieve this optimal result.

Summary

In a competitive market, prices are determined by the interaction of demand and supply. *Demand* is a schedule showing the quantities of a good or service that consumers are willing and able to purchase at various prices during some given time period, when all factors other than the product's price remain unchanged. Demand may be represented graphically in a *demand curve*, which slopes downward and to the right because the *law of demand* holds that consumers will purchase more of a product at a lower price than at a higher price. *Supply* is a schedule showing the quantities of a good or service that producers are willing and able to offer for sale at various prices during a given time period when all factors other than the product's price remain unchanged. Supply may be represented graphically as a *supply curve*. The supply curve slopes upward and to the right because the *law of supply* states that price and quantity supplied are positively related; that is, a greater quantity will be supplied at higher prices than at lower prices.

---

[2] Note that the fewer the resources an economy needs to produce each product, the more goods and services it can produce with its limited resource stock. Thus an economy that is operating efficiently is producing the goods and services that consumers value the most *and* producing as many of those goods and services as possible from the society's scarce resources.

The demand curve will shift to a new position if there is a change in any of the *determinants of demand:* consumer income, tastes and preferences, expectations regarding future prices, the prices of substitute and complementary goods, and the number of consumers in the market. By the same token, the supply curve will shift if there is a change in one or more of the *determinants of supply:* technology, the prices of resources, or the number of producers in the market.

Economists are careful to distinguish between a change in the quantity demanded and a change in demand. A change in the amount purchased due to a change in the price of the product, while other factors are held constant, is a *change in the quantity demanded* and is represented by movement up or down a stationary demand curve. A change in any of the determinants of demand, while price is held constant, will cause consumers to purchase more or less of a product at each possible price. This is described as a *change in demand* and is represented by a shift of the entire demand curve to the right (in the case of increased demand) or to the left (in the case of decreased demand).

A similar distinction is necessary on the supply side of the market. A *change in the quantity supplied* results from a change in the price of the product and is represented graphically by a movement along a stationary supply curve. A *change in supply* results from a change in one of the determinants of supply and is represented by a shift of the entire supply curve to a new position.

The *equilibrium price* is the price that brings about an equality between the quantity demanded and the quantity supplied, which we call the *equilibrium quantity.* The equilibrium price can be identified by the intersection of the demand and supply curves. If the prevailing price is above equilibrium, a *surplus*—an excess of quantity supplied over quantity demanded—will occur, and sellers will be forced to reduce price to eliminate the surplus. If the prevailing price is below equilibrium, a *shortage*—an excess of quantity demanded over quantity supplied—occurs, and buyers will bid up the price as they compete for the product. Only when the existing price is at the equilibrium level will there be neither a shortage nor a surplus, and no pressure for price to change.

Prices perform three important functions: (1) they *ration* or divide the limited amount of available output among possible buyers; (2) they *signal* producers about how much to supply; and (3) they *motivate* producers to supply the desired quantity. Higher prices ration by discouraging consumers from purchasing a product; they also signal and motivate producers to increase the quantity supplied. Lower prices have the opposite effect. They encourage consumers to purchase more of the product and simultaneously signal and motivate producers to reduce the quantity supplied. The equilibrium price succeeds in matching the quantity demanded with the quantity supplied because it balances the desires of consumers and producers. Every consumer who values the product enough to pay the equilibrium price will have it, and every producer that is willing to supply the product at that price will be able to sell its entire output.

In the absence of artificial restrictions, prices will rise and fall in response to changes in demand and supply. Whenever demand increases in relation to supply, the equilibrium price will tend to rise; whenever supply increases in relation to demand, the equilibrium price will fall. These price changes help to ensure that producers supply the goods and services consumers value the most and that in their production they use as few scarce resources as possible.

Price supports (minimum prices above the equilibrium price) and *price ceilings* (maximum prices below the equilibrium price) prevent price from reaching its equilibrium level in the market. Because these restrictions interfere with the rationing and signaling functions of price, they give rise to surpluses (supports) and shortages (ceilings). Price ceilings also create the need for *secondary rationing devices*—nonprice conditions that supplement the primary rationing device, price.

Glossary

Page 74   ***Change in demand.*** An increase or decrease in the quantity demanded at each possible price and caused by a change in the determinants of demand; represented graphically by a shift of the entire demand curve to a new position.

Page 74   ***Change in quantity demanded.*** An increase or decrease in the amount of a product demanded as a result of a change in its price, with factors other than price held constant; represented graphically by movement along a stationary demand curve.

Page 80   ***Change in quantity supplied.*** An increase or decrease in the amount of a product supplied as a result of a change in its price, with factors other than price held constant; represented graphically by movement along a stationary supply curve.

Page 81   ***Change in supply.*** An increase or decrease in the amount of a product supplied at each and every price; caused by a change in the determinants of supply and represented graphically by a shift of the entire supply curve.

Page 73   *Complement.* A product that is normally purchased along with another good or in conjunction with another good.

Page 69   *Demand.* A schedule showing the quantities of a good or service that consumers are willing and able to purchase at various prices during a given time period, when all factors other than the product's price remain unchanged.

Page 69   *Demand curve.* A graphic representation of demand, showing the quantities of a good or service that consumers are willing and able to purchase at various prices during a given time period, ceteris paribus.

Page 72   *Determinants of demand.* The factors that underlie the demand schedule and determine the precise position of the demand curve: income, tastes and preferences, expectations regarding prices, and the prices of related goods.

Page 78   *Determinants of supply.* The factors that underlie the supply schedule and determine the precise position of the supply curve: technology, resource prices, and number of producers in the market.

Page 85   *Equilibrium price.* The price that brings about an equality between the quantity demanded and the quantity supplied.

Page 85   *Equilibrium quantity.* The quantity demanded and supplied at the equilibrium price.

Page 71   *Income effect.* Consumer ability to purchase greater quantities of a product that has declined in price.

Page 72   *Inferior good.* A product for which demand decreases as income increases and increases as income decreases.

Page 71   *Law of demand.* The quantity demanded of a product is negatively or inversely related to its price. Consumers will purchase more of a product at lower prices than at higher prices.

Page 77   *Law of supply.* The quantity supplied of a product is positively or directly related to its price. Producers will supply a larger quantity at higher prices than at lower prices.

Page 86   *Motivating.* The function of providing incentives to supply the proper quantities of demanded products.

Page 72   *Normal good.* A product for which demand increases as income increases, and demand decreases as income decreases.

Page 99   *Price ceiling.* A legally established maximum price below the equilibrium price.

Page 95   *Price support.* A legally established minimum price above the equilibrium price.

Page 86   *Rationing.* The function of dividing up or allocating a society's scarce items among those who want them.

Page 100   **Secondary rationing device.** A nonprice condition that supplements the primary rationing device, price.

Page 81   **Shortage.** An excess of quantity demanded over quantity supplied.

Page 86   **Signaling.** The function of providing information to producers about how much to supply.

Page 73   **Substitute.** A product that can be used in place of some other product because to a greater or lesser extent it satisfies the same consumer wants.

Page 71   **Substitution effect.** Consumers' willingness to substitute for other products the product that has declined in price.

Page 76   **Supply.** A schedule showing the quantities of a good or service that producers are willing and able to offer for sale at various prices during a given time period, when all factors other than the product's price remain unchanged.

Page 76   **Supply curve.** A graphic representation of supply.

Page 84   **Surplus.** An excess of quantity supplied over quantity demanded.

Page 78   **Technology.** The state of knowledge about how to produce products.

Page 78   **Technological advance.** The discovery of a better way to produce a product, a method that uses fewer resources to produce each unit of output or that produces more output from a given amount of resources.

Study Questions

Fill in the Blanks

1. If the entire demand curve shifts to a new position, we describe this as a change in _____.

2. If a product is a normal good, an increase in income will cause the demand curve for a product to shift to the _____.

3. Movement along a stationary supply curve due to a change in price is called a change in _____.

4. The function of dividing up or allocating scarce items among those who desire to receive them is called _____.

5. The price that exactly clears the market is called the _____ price.

6. Whenever the prevailing price is above equilibrium, a _____ will exist.

7. Prices perform three important functions: They ration scarce items among the consumers who desire to receive them; they _____ producers about the proper quantity to produce; and they _____ producers to supply that quantity.

8. If supply rises and demand declines, we would expect the equilibrium price to _____.

9. If supply increases more than demand, the equilibrium price will _____.

10. We would expect a price ceiling to lead to a _____.

Multiple Choice

1. If the price of automobiles increases and all other factors remain unchanged, it will be reasonable to expect
   a) an increase in the demand for automobiles.
   b) a decrease in the demand for automobiles.
   c) an increase in the quantity of automobiles demanded.
   d) a decrease in the quantity of automobiles demanded.

2. If the demand curve for Heavy Beer shifts to the left, this could be due to
   a) an increase in the price of Heavy Beer.
   b) an increase in consumer income.
   c) an increase in the price of other beers.
   d) a shift in tastes and preferences to light beers.

3. An increase in the price of apples is likely to cause
   a) a decrease in the demand for apples.
   b) an increase in the quantity demanded of apples.
   c) an increase in the demand for other types of fruit.
   d) an increase in the quantity demanded of other types of fruit.

4. If the price of black walnuts increases and other factors remain unchanged, it is reasonable to expect
   a) an increase in the quantity supplied.
   b) a decrease in the quantity supplied.
   c) an increase in supply.
   d) a decrease in supply.

5. If a new labor settlement increases a firm's costs, this will probably
   a) cause a decrease in supply.
   b) cause an increase in supply.
   c) cause a reduction in the quantity supplied.
   d) cause the supply curve to shift to the right.

6. If grasshoppers destroy half of the wheat crop, the result will be
   a) a decrease in the quantity supplied.
   b) a rightward shift of the wheat supply curve.
   c) a leftward shift of the wheat supply curve.
   d) none of the above.

7. If demand increases and supply declines,
   a) the equilibrium price and quantity will both increase.
   b) the equilibrium price will rise, but the quantity will fall.
   c) the equilibrium price will fall, but the quantity will rise.
   d) the equilibrium price and quantity will both fall.
   e) the equilibrium price will rise; quantity will be indeterminate.

8. If the U.S. government were to artificially restrict the price of beef below the equilibrium level, the result would be
   a) a shortage.
   b) a surplus.
   c) an excess of quantity supplied over quantity demanded.
   d) None of the above

9. If the demand for used cars declines, the likely result will be
   a) a reduction in equilibrium price.
   b) an increase in equilibrium price.
   c) an increase in the supply of used cars.
   d) no change in equilibrium price.

10. If the price of cattle feed increases, the result will probably be
    a) an increase in the supply of cattle and lower cattle prices.
    b) a decrease in the supply of cattle and higher cattle prices.
    c) an increase in the demand for cattle and higher cattle prices.
    d) a decrease in the demand for cattle and lower cattle prices.

11. If a shortage exists, it indicates that the existing price is
    a) the equilibrium price.
    b) below the equilibrium price.
    c) above the equilibrium price.

12. If the price of coffee increases, the probable result will be
    a) a decrease in the demand for coffee.
    b) a decrease in the price of substitutes for coffee.
    c) an increase in the price of substitutes for coffee.
    d) a decrease in the supply of coffee.

13. Which of the following statements is *incorrect*?
    a) If demand increases and supply remains constant, the equilibrium price will rise.
    b) If supply rises and demand remains constant, the equilibrium price will fall.
    c) If demand rises and supply falls, the equilibrium price will rise.
    d) If supply increases and demand decreases, the equilibrium price will rise.

14. If additional farmers enter the hog-producing industry, the result will be
    a) lower prices but a higher equilibrium quantity.
    b) higher prices but a lower equilibrium quantity.
    c) lower prices but the same equilibrium quantity.
    d) lower prices and a lower equilibrium quantity.

15. If the supply of cattle is increasing more rapidly than the demand,
    a) cattle prices will rise.
    b) cattle prices will fall.
    c) cattle prices will not change.
    d) any of the above is possible.

Problems and Questions for Discussion

1. My eldest daughter says she really "needs" a new sweatshirt, but she won't use her allowance to buy it. ("I don't need it *that* badly.") How can a "need" evaporate like that? What is the difference between "need" and "demand"?

2. Podunk College experienced a substantial drop in enrollment last year. As an economist, what possible explanations can you offer for what happened? Try to list all possibilities.

3. Why does the supply curve slope upward and to the right? In other words, why will producers supply a higher quantity at higher prices?

4. Which of the following events would cause movement along a stationary supply curve, and which would cause the supply curve to shift? Explain each situation from the producer's point of view.
   a) The price of wheat declines.
   b) The cost of fertilizer rises.
   c) Wheat blight destroys half the wheat crop.
   d) New combines make it possible for one person to do the work of three.

5. Explain the economic reasoning behind the following newspaper headlines:
   a) "Weather Slows Fishing: Seafood Prices Double"
   b) "Sugar: Crisis of Plenty"
   c) "Minimum Wage Costs Jobs"
   d) "Bountiful Wheat Crop Is Hurting Growers"

6. In a competitive market, if the supply of oranges decreases due to severe weather, will there be a shortage of oranges? Why or why not? (*Hint:* Use graphs to help answer this question.)

7. Suppose that your local tennis courts are very crowded and your city is considering charging a fee to ration their use. Who would like to have a fee charged? Would only wealthy individuals feel this way? Why might someone be in favor of a fee?

8. People, including news reporters, often use the terms "supply" and "demand" incorrectly. For example, you will often read that "supply exceeds demand" or "demand exceeds supply." What is wrong with these statements? What does the writer probably mean to say?

9. In a market economy, why is it important that prices be allowed to change in response to changing demand and supply conditions? What functions do these changing prices perform?

10. Assume that consumers are buying equal numbers of hamburgers and hot dogs when these products are selling at the same price. If the supply of hamburger declines, what will happen to the price of hamburgers? What about the price of hot dogs? Graph your conclusions.

Answer Key

Fill in the Blanks

1. demand
2. right
3. quantity supplied
4. rationing
5. equilibrium
6. surplus
7. signal (or inform); motivate
8. fall
9. fall
10. shortage

Multiple Choice

1. d
2. d
3. c
4. a
5. a
6. c
7. e
8. a
9. a
10. b
11. b
12. c
13. d
14. a
15. b

4

THE ELASTICITY OF DEMAND AND SUPPLY

In Chapter 3, we considered how demand and supply interact to determine prices, and we discovered how changes in demand or supply cause prices to change. In this chapter, we investigate the degree of consumer and producer responsiveness to increases or decreases in prices. Economists refer to this degree of responsiveness as the price "elasticity." As you will see, the concept of price elasticity is extremely important; it has many applications in the world around you.

Elasticity of Demand

The law of demand tells producers that if they raise their prices, consumers will buy less, and if they lower their prices, consumers will buy more. But it doesn't tell them anything about the size of the response to a given change in price. If a professional football team decides to raise the price of season tickets by 10 percent, how many fewer tickets will fans buy? If local cable television doubles its rates, how many customers will it lose? To answer these questions, we need some knowledge of how responsive consumers are to changes in the price of a particular product—we need to know something about the price elasticity of demand.

The *price elasticity of demand* is a measure of the responsiveness of the quantity demanded of a product to a change in its price. If a small change in price causes a large change in the quantity demanded, demand is said to be very responsive, or *elastic;* the quantity demanded is either stretching or shrinking a great deal in response to the price change. If a large change in price elicits only a small change in the quantity demanded, demand is not very responsive and is said to be *inelastic;* the quantity demanded is not expanding or contracting very much.

The Coefficient of Demand Elasticity

We can measure the degree of elasticity or inelasticity by calculating a value called the *coefficient of demand elasticity.* We compute the coefficient of elasticity by dividing the percentage change in quantity demanded by the percentage change in price:

$$\text{Coefficient of elasticity} = \frac{\dfrac{\Delta Q}{Q}}{\dfrac{\Delta P}{P}} = \frac{\text{percentage change in quantity demanded}}{\text{percentage change in price}}$$

In this formula for the coefficient, Q stands for quantity, P stands for price, and the Greek letter delta (Δ) stands for "change in." $\Delta Q/Q$ is the percentage change in quantity demanded, and $\Delta P/P$ is the percentage change in price.

Let's apply this formula to the elasticity of demand for Fantastic Cola after a price hike. We'll say that after the price per six-pack rises from $2.50 to $3.00, weekly sales decline from 1,000 six-packs to 900. What is the price elasticity of demand for Fantastic Cola? If the change in quantity demanded (ΔQ) is 100 fewer six-packs per week, and the original quantity demanded (Q) is 1,000 six-packs, the percentage change in quantity demanded (100/1,000) is -10 percent. And if the change in price (ΔP) is 50 cents, and the original price (P) is $2.50, the percentage change in price ($.50/$2.50) is 20 percent. If we divide the 10 percent reduction in quantity by the 20 percent increase in price, we arrive at an elasticity coefficient of -0.5.[1]

$$\text{Coefficient of elasticity } = \frac{\dfrac{-100}{1000}}{\dfrac{\$0.50}{\$2.50}} = \frac{-10\%}{20\%} = -0.5.$$

An elasticity coefficient of 0.5 means that for every 1-percent change in price, the quantity demanded will change by 0.5 percent. Thus if the price of Fantastic Cola goes up by 10 percent, we would expect a 5-percent reduction in the quantity demanded. If it increases by 20 percent, we would expect a 10-percent reduction in quantity demanded. However, if the elasticity coefficient were 2.0 instead of 0.5, each 1-percent change in price would cause a 2-percent change in quantity demanded. For example, a 10-percent increase in price would cause a 20-percent decrease in quantity demanded.

You will note that in our formula the elasticity coefficient (-0.5) carries a negative sign. We know from the law of demand that changes in price normally cause the quantity demanded to change in the opposite direction. Thus price increases cause reductions in the quantity demanded, whereas price reductions cause increases in the quantity demanded. In either case the sign is negative and usually ignored in referring to price elasticity values.

Degrees of Elasticity

Economists use the coefficient of elasticity to define precisely the terms elastic and inelastic. *Elastic* demand exists when the coefficient of elasticity is greater than one, when a given percentage change in price brings about a larger percentage change in the quantity demanded. When the elasticity coefficient is less than one, demand is *inelastic*; a given percentage change in price brings

---

[1] The simple formula we are using to compute the elasticity coefficient produces somewhat ambiguous results. If the sellers of Fantastic Cola raise the price from \$2.50 to \$3.00, the value of the elasticity coefficient is 0.5, the value calculated above. But if the sellers lower their price from \$3.00 to \$2.50, the coefficient will be 0.67, because the initial price and quantity are different.

Economic theory does not suggest any reason why these two coefficients should be different, so we might argue that they should be the same. This can be accomplished by using the average of the two prices and the average of the two quantities as the base values for computing percentages. When this approach is used, the value of the coefficient will be the same regardless of whether the initial price is the higher price or the lower price. In the Fantastic Cola example, the value of the elasticity coefficient would be 0.58. In the modified formula below, we add the two quantities, Q_1 and Q_2, and divide by 2 to arrive at the average quantity. Average price is determined the same way.

$$\frac{\Delta Q/[(Q_1 + Q_2)/2]}{\Delta P/[(P_1 + P_2)/2]} = \frac{100/(1,900/2)}{\$0.50/(\$5.50/2)} = \frac{100/950}{\$0.50/\$2.75} = \frac{10.5\%}{18.2\%} = 0.58.$$

about a smaller percentage change in the quantity demanded. If the coefficient is exactly one, *unitary elasticity* prevails; a given percentage change in price results in an identical percentage change in quantity demanded. The elasticity coefficient can vary from zero to infinity, where zero represents the least elastic demand imaginable, and infinity represents the most elastic demand imaginable.

If the coefficient of elasticity were zero, a change in price would bring no change at all in the quantity demanded. Demand would be described as *perfectly inelastic,* and the demand curve would be a vertical straight line. Over some range of prices, the demand for lifesaving drugs such as insulin may be perfectly inelastic. Another example would be the demand for dialysis treatment by those suffering from kidney failure.

If the coefficient of elasticity approached infinity, a very small change in price would lead to an enormous change in the quantity demanded. Demand would be described as *perfectly elastic* and would be graphed as a horizontal straight line. Perfectly inelastic and perfectly elastic demand curves are depicted in Exh. 4.1. The individual apple farmer faces a situation that illustrates perfectly elastic demand. If the market price of apples

EXHIBIT 4.1

Perfectly Inelastic and Perfectly Elastic Demand Curves

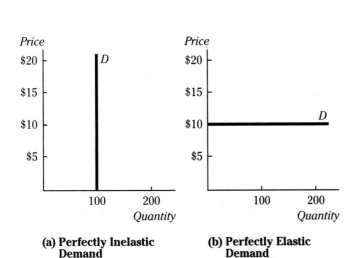

(a) Perfectly Inelastic Demand

(b) Perfectly Elastic Demand

(a) Despite an increase or decrease in price, consumers buy exactly the same quantity. The demand curve for insulin may look like this over some price range. (b) A very small increase in price would cause consumers to reduce their purchases to zero. The individual apple farmer may face a demand curve like this one.

is $10 a bushel, the farmer can sell as much of her production as she desires at that price. But if she attempts to charge more than $10, she will sell nothing; consumers will simply buy their apples from someone else. This is the type of situation we represent with a perfectly elastic demand curve. We will have much more to say about perfectly elastic demand curves in Chapter 5.

Elasticity Along a Straight-Line Demand Curve

In most instances demand curves do not show just one degree of elasticity, they show several. All linear, downward-sloping demand curves show unitary elasticity midway on the curve, with elastic demand above the midpoint and inelastic demand below it. Exhibit 4.2 depicts such a demand curve.

Consider the demand curve in Exh. 4.2 for just a moment. First, note that because it is a straight line, it has a constant inclination or "slope." Therefore a price change of a given size will always bring the same quantity change. In this hypothetical example, each $.60 drop in price brings a 60-million-gallon increase in the quantity demanded, regardless of whether we are at the upper or the lower end of the curve. (Look, for example, at what happens to the quantity demanded when price declines from $2.40 to $1.80, or from $1.80 to $1.20; in both instances quantity increases by 60 million gal-

EXHIBIT 4.2

How Elasticity Changes Along a Hypothetical Demand Curve for Gasoline

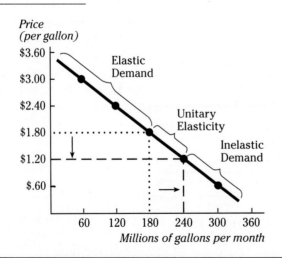

Every straight-line demand curve that is downward sloping displays unitary elasticity at its midpoint, elastic demand above it, and inelastic demand below it.

lons.) That would seem to suggest that consumers are equally responsive to price changes at either end of the curve. But that's not true! We have to remember that the responsiveness or elasticity of demand deals with percentage changes, not with absolute quantities.

If you remember that fact, you will recognize that the responsiveness of consumers changes quite dramatically as we move along this demand curve! For instance, when price drops from $3.00 to $2.40 (a 20-percent decline), quantity demanded increases from 60 million to 120 million gallons (a 100-percent increase). Since the percentage change in quantity is greater than the percentage change in price, demand is elastic at this upper end of the curve. At the other end, the same *absolute* changes in price and quantity represent different percentage changes and consequently produce different elasticities. For instance, when price declines from $1.20 to $.60 (a 50-percent change), the quantity demanded increases from 240 million to 300 million gallons (a 25-percent change). The coefficient of elasticity is 0.5; demand is inelastic. We want to remember, then, that the slope of a demand curve is not the same as its elasticity. A linear demand curve has a constant slope, but it displays many different degrees of elasticity.

Elasticity and Total Revenue

Knowing how responsive consumers will be to price changes is of vital interest to businesses. The elasticity of demand determines what happens to a business's *total revenue*—the total receipts from the sale of its product—when it alters the price of the product it is selling. (Total revenue is equal to the price of the product multiplied by the quantity sold; $TR = P \times Q$).

You can understand total revenue and the importance of the degree of elasticity better if you put yourself in the place of the seller making a pricing decision. Suppose that you're a college president contemplating an increase in tuition from, say, $1,500 to $1,600 a semester. The basic question you face is whether or not the gain in revenue due to the higher tuition per student will be offset by the loss in revenue due to the smaller number of students who are willing and able to pay that higher tuition. To answer that question, you must know how responsive students will be to changes in tuition. In other words, you must have some estimate of the elasticity of demand for an education at your college.[2]

---

[2] In reality, the question faced by a college president or a businessperson would be somewhat more complicated, because any pricing decision may also have an indirect impact on the firm's costs. For example, because a higher price will cause a firm to sell less of its product, the firm may also incur lower costs—since it will not need to produce as much output. Before making any pricing decision, a wise entrepreneur considers its impact on costs as well as on revenues. (The nature and behavior of a firm's costs will be discussed in Chapter 5.)

Case 1: Elastic Demand. Suppose that demand is highly elastic, or very responsive to price changes. If tuition is increased, the college will receive more money from each student, but it will enroll considerably fewer students; the percentage change downward in quantity demanded will be greater than the percentage change in price. As a result, the college will take in less total revenue than it did before the tuition hike. In the face of elastic demand, the logical action for the college to take—assuming there are vacant dormitory rooms and unfilled classes—would be to lower, not raise, tuition. The college will receive less from each student who enrolls, but it will enroll many more students and total revenue will increase.

Case 2: Inelastic Demand. Suppose the demand for an education at your college is inelastic, or not very responsive to price changes. If the college increases tuition, it will lose some students but not very many, and the percentage change in quantity demanded will be less than the percentage change in price. Because each student will pay more than before, the result will be an increase in total revenue. If you decided to reduce tuition under these inelastic conditions, you would probably be fired. The tuition reduction wouldn't attract many new students, and all the students would pay a lower rate than before. As a result, total revenue would be lower than it was before the tuition reduction. (Is the demand for air transportation elastic or inelastic? See if you can answer that question after reading "Car-Rental Firms and Hotels Hit Hard by High Air Fares" on p. 121.)

Case 3: Unitary Elasticity. If the demand for an education at your college is of unitary elasticity, any change in price will be offset exactly by a proportional change in the quantity demanded (enrollment). If you institute a 10-percent tuition increase, 10-percent fewer students will enroll, and total revenue will be unchanged. If you put into effect a 5-percent tuition reduction, 5-percent more students will enroll, and total revenue will be unchanged. As long as demand is of unitary elasticity, total revenue is unaffected by the seller's pricing decision.

The relationship between price changes, elasticity, and total revenue (*TR*) for each of the three cases is summarized in Exh. 4.3. Before continuing, take the time to work through the exhibit. You will see that if demand is inelastic, a price reduction will lead to a decline in total revenue, and a price increase will cause total revenue to increase. If demand is elastic, a price reduction will lead to an increase in total revenue, and a price increase will cause total revenue to decline. With unitary elasticity, a price change up or down is offset by a proportional change in quantity demanded, and total revenue remains unchanged.

Car-Rental Firms and Hotels Hit Hard by High Air Fares

Rising air fares are putting the squeeze on two industries that rely heavily on air travelers—car-rental companies and hotels.

After predicting a strong 1989, car-rental companies and many resorts say business is flat or slightly down this year. Hotels say the timing couldn't be worse: Many properties were just recovering from a long dry spell, caused by a huge surplus of hotel rooms. Things look even worse for the car-rental industry, which after steady growth may be facing its first serious slump this decade. . . .

The dual slump is giving travelers some relief from higher air fares, because many hotels and car-rental companies have been forced to retreat from planned price increases. Budget Rent a Car Corp., for example, had planned to charge $179 weekly on most full-size cars this spring. Now, it is charging only $149. . . .

Such price breaks, however, pale in comparison with air-fare increases. Air fares make up the bulk of total travel costs—and they rose 20% overall in March from a year earlier, a record increase.

That increase has led to a 4% drop in domestic air travel

this year. For airlines, the mix of higher fares and lower traffic has been just right—profits are booming. But the $8 billion-a-year car-rental industry has been hit hard. Seven out of 10 car-rental customers come from airports. "We're the first people to feel it when air traffic goes down," says Joseph Vittoria, chairman of Avis Inc. . . .

The impact of higher air fares on hotels, a $50 billion-a-year industry, has been uneven. Hotel chains with many roadside properties have been doing well, since many people are now taking trips by car. "If anything, the higher fares

have helped us," says Ray Lewis, a senior vice president for Holiday Inns, a unit of Holiday Corp.

But most chains with many airport and resort properties are off to a slow year. "Everything is a bit flat," says Robert Collier, senior vice president, director of marketing for Sheraton Corp., where about 60% of all guests arrive by airline.

—Jonathan Dahl

SOURCE: *The Wall Street Journal,* May 16, 1989, p. B1. Reprinted by permission of *The Wall Street Journal,* © 1989 Dow Jones & Company, Inc. All Rights Reserved Worldwide.

USE YOUR ECONOMIC REASONING

1. How would you graph the impact of higher air fares on the demand for rental cars and hotel rooms? Would the higher fares lead to a change in demand or a change in the quantity demanded of these two products? (Review page 74 in Chapter 3 if you need help with this question.)

2. The article provides percentages that can be used to compute the coefficient of demand elasticity for air travel. What is the value of the coefficient? Does this value suggest that the demand for air travel is elastic or inelastic?

3. Given the elasticity coefficient you computed in question 2, what would you expect to happen to airline revenues when they raise fares? Why would revenues behave in this manner?

EXHIBIT 4.3

Elasticity and Total Revenue

DEGREE OF ELASTICITY	PRICE INCREASE			PRICE DECREASE		
Case 1: Elastic Demand. (The coefficient of elasticity is greater than 1.)	↑ P ×	↓ Q =	↓ TR	↓ P ×	↑ Q =	↑ TR
Case 2: Inelastic Demand. (The coefficient of elasticity is less than 1.)	↑ P ×	↓ Q =	↑ TR	↓ P ×	↑ Q =	↓ TR
Case 3: Unitary Elasticity (The coefficient of elasticity is equal to 1.)	↑ P ×	↓ Q =	No change TR	↓ P ×	↑ Q =	No change TR

Symbols: ↑ increase, ↓ decrease

The elasticity of demand for a firm's product dictates what will happen to total revenue (price × quantity) when the firm alters price. When demand is elastic, a price increase results in a significantly lower *quantity demanded and therefore in lower total revenue, whereas a price decrease leads to a* significantly higher *quantity demanded and therefore results in higher total revenue. When demand is inelastic, a price increase results in a lower quantity demanded,* but not much lower, *so that total revenue increases; a price decrease results in a higher quantity demanded,* but not much higher, *so that total revenue decreases. If demand is of unitary elasticity, any change in price will be exactly offset by the change in quantity demanded, so total revenue will not change.*

The Determinants of Elasticity

As you saw in the preceding discussion, producers need to know whether the demand for their services and products is elastic or inelastic before they can make intelligent pricing decisions. But how can sellers know? Often they can gain insight into the elasticity of demand by considering two major factors that dictate the degree of elasticity: the number of good substitutes available and the importance of the product in consumers' budgets. As you examine these factors, recall our earlier discussion of the *income* and *substitution effects* that underlie the law of demand.

The Number of Available Substitutes for the Product. The primary factor in determining the price elasticity of demand is the number of good substitutes available. Recall that a substitute is a product that can be used in place of another product because to a greater or lesser extent it satisfies the same consumer wants. Some people consider chicken a good substitute for fish, for example, and many would acknowledge that a Ford automobile is an acceptable substitute for a Chevrolet with the same features.

When a large number of good substitutes exist, demand for a product tends to be elastic because consumers have alternatives—they can buy something else if the price of the product becomes too high. On the other hand, if a product has few good substitutes, demand tends to be inelastic because consumers have few options; they must buy the product even at the higher price. Movie tickets, pond-raised catfish, and women's hats have elastic demand because there are a large number of substitutes for each of these items. Cigarettes, electricity, local telephone service, and gasoline tend to have relatively inelastic demand because of the limited options available to consumers.[3]

The Importance of the Product in Consumers' Budgets. The second factor influencing the elasticity of demand for a product is the importance of the product in consumers' budgets. If consumers are spending a significant portion of their income on a particular item (rent or long-distance phone service, for example), a price hike for that item will force a vigorous search for less-expensive substitutes. Demand will tend to be elastic. On the other hand, if expenditures on the product are relatively small (the average family's annual outlay for lemon juice or soy sauce, for instance), consumers are more likely to ignore the price increase. Demand will tend to be inelastic.

Some major budget items persist in having relatively inelastic demand. For example, even though many smokers spend a significant fraction of their incomes on cigarettes, statistical research shows that the demand for cigarettes by adults is quite inelastic. In this case, demand is inelastic because the more important determinant of elasticity is the number of good substitutes. If, like cigarettes, a product has few good substitutes, the fact that it is a major expense item is generally less important to consumers. The article on p. 125, "The High-Price Solution," reveals some interesting and useful facts about the elasticity of demand for cigarettes and beer.

---

[3] The elasticity of demand for a product tends to increase over time. When the price of a product increases, consumers may not be aware of substitutes for that product, so demand initially may be inelastic. But the more time that elapses after the price change, the more opportunities consumers have to discover substitutes and to develop new tastes and new habits. As consumers discover more substitutes, demand tends to become more elastic.

Elasticity of Supply

Thus far we have considered only how the quantity demanded responds to price changes. Now we will explore the supply side of the market. The price elasticity of supply describes the responsiveness of producers to price changes. More precisely, the *price elasticity of supply* is a measure of the responsiveness of the quantity supplied of a product to a change in its price.

The Coefficient of Supply Elasticity

Individual producers of goods and services display varying degrees of response when the price of a product changes. Some are able to expand or contract their supply of the product significantly in a short period of time; others are able to make only minimal adjustments. The more responsive producers are to a change in price, the more elastic their supply.

We measure the elasticity of supply by calculating the *coefficient of supply elasticity,* a value that indicates the degree to which the quantity supplied will change in response to a price change. The coefficient of supply elasticity is computed by dividing the percentage change in quantity supplied by the percentage change in price:

$$\text{Coefficient of elasticity} = \frac{\dfrac{\Delta Q}{Q}}{\dfrac{\Delta P}{P}} = \frac{\text{percentage change in quantity supplied}}{\text{percentage change in price.}}$$

Suppose that the price of coal rises from $40 to $50 a ton, and as a result, coal production in the United States increases from 600 to 900 million tons a year. To compute the coefficient of supply elasticity, we first determine the percentage change in quantity supplied: If the change in quantity supplied (ΔQ) is 300 million tons, and the original quantity supplied (Q) is 600 million tons, the percentage change in quantity supplied (300/600) is 50 percent. Next we take the percentage change in price: If the change in price (ΔP) is $10, and the original price is $40, the percentage change in price ($10/$40) is 25 percent. When we divide the 50 percent increase in quantity supplied by the 25 percent increase in price, we arrive at an elasticity coefficient of 2.[4]

---

[4] As with the elasticity of demand, the more precise formula for calculating the elasticity of supply involves using the average of the two prices and the average of the two quantities as the base values for computing percentages.

The High-Price Solution

We remember being favorably impressed by a study, published five years ago by the National Bureau of Economic Research (NBER), demonstrating that you could substantially reduce smoking by using the price mechanism—specifically, by raising the price of smoking. Although already heavily taxed, cigarettes might be hit harder still. Just as you suspected, higher prices would not substantially deter smoking among the middle-aged addicts; however, the "price elasticity of demand" was quite high for young people not yet addicted, especially young men. (For reasons not explained by the NBER folks, the elasticities were lower for young women.) In effect, higher prices could keep young people from becoming addicts in the first place.

This finding has had zero influence on government policy. Politicians seem to be made uneasy by approaches that rely on market forces, which are diffuse and impersonal, and much prefer programs in which some kind of enforcement mechanism is onstage and dramatically reordering what people do. As in, for example, the federal regulation that is now trying to combat drunk driving by getting the states to raise their drinking ages.

That brings us to some more recent findings of NBER-sponsored research, which are about beer. Prepared by a team of researchers under Professor Michael Grossman of the City University of New York, the paper reflects an analysis of demand elasticities for beer among young persons and concludes that in recent years about 1,000 lives annually would have been saved by a tax of around $2 per case of beer.

The professor's simulations also show that a nationwide age limit of 21 would have been saving only about 555 lives annually. The data are soon to be published in the *Journal of Legal Studies* at the University of Chicago, long a bastion of sound thinking about economics but not yet in control at the political level. —*Daniel Seligman*

SOURCE: *Fortune*, Oct. 27, 1986, p. 127. Reprinted by permission from *Fortune* Magazine. Copyright © 1986 Time Inc. All rights reserved.

USE YOUR ECONOMIC REASONING

1. Keeping the determinants of demand elasticity in mind, how would you explain the fact that the elasticity of demand for cigarettes is higher among young smokers than among middle-aged smokers?

2. If taxing cigarettes more heavily would reduce the number of smokers in the United States (by raising the price of cigarettes), why don't we do it? Can you think of any arguments against this policy? What would be the impact on middle-aged smokers?

3. The Grossman study of beer drinkers seems to suggest that higher prices (as a result of taxes) could also help to reduce drinking by young people. Do you believe the price elasticity of demand for beer would follow the same pattern as cigarettes—higher for younger consumers than for middle-aged consumers? Why or why not?

$$\text{Coefficient of elasticity} = \frac{\dfrac{300}{600}}{\dfrac{\$10}{\$40}} = \frac{50\%}{25\%} = 2.$$

Note that whereas the coefficient of demand elasticity is negative, the coefficient of supply elasticity usually is positive because of the law of supply: an increase in price leads to an increase in the quantity supplied.

Interpreting the Elasticity Coefficient

We interpret coefficients of supply elasticity in essentially the same way we interpret coefficients of demand elasticity. A supply elasticity of 2 means that for every 1-percent change in price, the quantity supplied will change by 2 percent. For example, a 10-percent increase in price would lead to a 20-percent increase in the quantity supplied, and a 20-percent increase in price would lead to a 40-percent increase in the quantity supplied. Of course, reductions in price will have the opposite effect. A 10-percent decrease in price would lead to a 20-percent reduction in the quantity supplied.

An elasticity coefficient greater than one means that supply is elastic, or very responsive to price changes; a given percentage change in price results in a larger percentage change in quantity supplied. When the elasticity coefficient is less than one, supply is inelastic; a given percentage change in price results in a smaller percentage change in quantity supplied. If the coefficient is exactly one, supply is of unitary elasticity; a given percentage change in price results in an identical percentage change in the quantity supplied.

Using Supply Elasticity in Policy Decisions

An understanding of the elasticity of supply can be useful to government policymakers and others seeking solutions to economic problems. Consider, for example, the energy-policy debate that occurred in the late 1970s, a time when the United States was heavily dependent on foreign oil to meet its energy needs. During this period, the price of domestically produced oil was regulated; it could not rise above the government-dictated price. Imported oil was beyond government control, however, and in the mid-1970s it skyrocketed in price. To reduce dependence on foreign oil, some politicians and policymakers began to argue for the deregulation of domestic oil prices, so that U.S. producers would have incentive for increased exploration and production. Deregulation began in 1978–1979 and, in conjunction with consumer conservation (brought about by higher prices), helped to reduce substantially our dependence on foreign oil.

Suppose that the United States would like to increase domestic oil production by 50 percent to reduce its dependence on foreign oil. How much would the price of domestic oil have to rise to make that possible? Since the supply elasticity of oil is about one (actually it's slightly less than one), the price of oil would have to rise by 50 percent. (Remember, when the coefficient is 1, each 1-percent change in price brings a 1-percent change in quantity supplied.) Of course, if supply were more elastic—if producers were more sensitive to price changes—a smaller price hike would accomplish the same result. For example, if the coefficient were 2, the price of oil would have to rise by only 25 percent in order to increase the quantity supplied by 50 percent.

As you can see, the elasticity of supply allows us to determine how much price has to rise to convince suppliers to increase their output by a given amount. That kind of information is very important in making sound decisions about energy policy and addressing a host of other questions.

Time and the Elasticity of Supply

How responsive suppliers are to a change in the price of their product depends on the amount of time they are given to adjust their output to the new price. As a general rule, the longer producers are given to adapt to a price change, the greater the elasticity of supply. We can see the importance of time as a determinant of elasticity by comparing the kinds of adjustments suppliers facing a price change can make in the short run with the changes they can make in the long run.

The Short Run. In economics, the *short run* is defined as the period of time during which at least one of a business's inputs (usually plant and equipment) is fixed—that is, incapable of being changed. Therefore short-run adjustments to a change in price are limited. Producers must use their existing plants and the equipment more or less intensively, adding or eliminating a work shift or using a larger or smaller work force on existing shifts.

The short-run supply curve in Exh. 4.4 shows an increase in the price of oil from $20 to $25 a barrel ($5 equals a 25-percent increase) bringing an increase in the quantity of oil supplied from 800 to 900 million barrels (100 million barrels equals an increase of 12.5 percent). That means the coefficient of supply elasticity is 0.50 (12.5%/25%); supply is quite inelastic in the short run.

The Long Run. The *long run* is defined as the period of time during which all of a business's inputs, including plant and equipment, can be changed. The long run provides sufficient time for firms to build new production

Trying to Cure Shortage of Organ Donors

A rapidly growing gap between the number of people waiting for organ transplants and the supply of organs has educators and researchers searching for ways to increase organ donations.

Some studies suggest that the timing of a physician's or nurse's request to surviving family members can raise consent rates substantially. Other proposals call for some type of federal tax benefit to a donor's estate or assistance with funeral expenses. A physician writing in today's Journal of the American Medical Association broaches the once-heretical notion of paying families outright—say, $1,000—for an organ donation.

Though physicians, medical ethicists and patients differ, sometimes sharply, over the effectiveness of these strategies, there is little dispute about the need for added measures to procure organs.

More people are being recommended for transplants, reflecting soaring success rates for these operations, but organ donations "haven't kept up with demand," says Wanda Bond, a spokeswoman for the United Network for Organ Sharing, a national clearinghouse that maintains the waiting list for organs and matches organs with recipients.

The number of people in the U.S. waiting for a kidney, heart, liver, pancreas, lung, or heart and lung has jumped about 40% in the past two years. Moreover, 2,206 people died in 1990 while awaiting a transplant, 26% more than in 1988.

Altruism—the motivating force on which patients and physicians have long depended for donations—"just doesn't look like it's doing too much" to meet the growing demand, says Ms. Bond. . . .

A partial remedy for that problem may come from a study completed last year by the Kentucky Organ Donor Affiliates, the state's organ-procurement agency, based in Louisville. Researchers found that if a request for organ donation isn't made at the same moment that a family learns of a relative's death, the family is much more likely to agree to donate.

R. Neal Garrison, medical director of the state agency and professor of surgery at the University of Louisville, says the pause "allows the family to accept the fact of death. Then they can start dealing with other options, including the possibility that some good could come from this."

The study found that when an organ request was made separately from a notification of death, 65% of families agreed to donate. When the two were made at the same

Waiting for Transplants

The number of people in the U.S., as of March 4, awaiting a:

	18,163
Kidney	1,884
Heart	1,344
Liver	516
Pancreas	394
Lung	182
Heart/lung	

Source: United Network for Organ Sharing

time, only 18% agreed to the request.

Perhaps the most radical proposals for increasing donations involve some type of reimbursement. (The purchase or sale of human organs is currently a felony, under the National Organ Transplant Act of 1984). In today's AMA Journal, Thomas Peters, a physician at the Jacksonville, Fla., Transplant Center, calls for a pilot program to determine whether payments of $1,000 to families from procurement groups might increase the organ supply—without sparking a process of "organ brokerage or commercialization."

If a family is staunchly opposed to donation, writes Dr. Peters, $1,000 "would not be so great a financial temptation to deter strongly held beliefs." Conversely, if a family is opposed to donation because of "superstition, reaction to the 'Establishment' or belief that the disadvantaged in society are again being exploited," $1,000 might be enough to prompt a donation.

But while many people are starting to view reimbursement as "an option we have to pursue," says Ms. Bond at the United Network for Organ Sharing, resistance to the idea remains substantial.

Trust in the transplant system—not reimbursement—is what's needed, says Mr. Caplan in Minneapolis: "People won't be altruistic if they think their gifts are going to the rich."

A less-divisive possibility might be some form of federal assistance. Felix T. Rapaport, chairman of surgery and director of transplantation services at the State University of New York at Stony Brook, says Congress should subsidize burial costs of organ donors or offer an estate-tax abatement or grant. The key, he says, "is to make it a federally sponsored program that would be standard for all donors." —*Glenn Ruffenach*

USE YOUR ECONOMIC REASONING

1. According to the law of supply, when the price of something goes up, a higher quantity is supplied. Does this law apply to body parts? Would more organs be supplied if families were paid for the organs?

2. Do you believe the supply of organs is highly price elastic? Would a $1,000 payment significantly increase the number of organs supplied? Defend your conclusion.

3. Federal law prohibits the buying and selling of organs. Why do you believe such transactions are prohibited? What are the "normative issues" associated with these transactions? (See Chapter 1 to review the concept of normative issues.)

EXHIBIT 4.4

The Effect of Time on the Elasticity of Supply

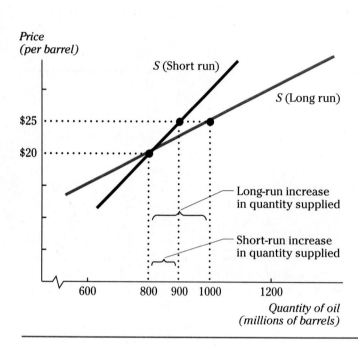

*Price
(per barrel)*

The more time a firm or industry is given to respond to a change in price, the larger the increase or decrease in the quantity supplied and the greater the elasticity of supply. Suppose, for example, that the price of oil rises from $20 to $25 a barrel. In the short run, the quantity supplied can be increased from 800 million barrels per year to 900 million barrels, while in the long run it is possible to increase the quantity supplied from 800 million barrels to 1,000 million barrels per year.

facilities and expand or contract existing facilities. New firms can enter the industry and existing firms can leave. These kinds of adjustments make it possible to alter output significantly in response to a price change.

Note that the long-run response to an increase in the price of oil from $20 to $25 a barrel (a 25-percent increase) is an increase in the quantity of oil supplied from 800 million to 1,000 million barrels (200 million barrels equals a 25-percent increase). The coefficient of supply elasticity in this case is 1.0 (25%/25%), so supply is of unitary elasticity in the long run.

As you can see from our example, the elasticity of supply may vary substantially from the short run to the long run for a given product. Both the short-run and the long-run elasticities of supply also vary from industry to industry and even from firm to firm. What is certain for any particular firm or industry, however, is that the elasticity of supply will increase directly in relationship to the length of time that firm or industry is given to adjust to the price change.

The response of petroleum producers to higher oil prices illustrates the important role that price changes can play in informing and motivating producers. Could financial incentives be used to substantially increase the number of human organs available for transplantation? Read "Trying to Cure Shortage of Organ Donors" on page 128 and form your own opinion.

Summary

To know how much more consumers will purchase at lower prices or how much less they will purchase at higher prices, we need to know how responsive consumers are to price changes. The *price elasticity of demand* is a measure of the change in quantity demanded as a result of a change in price. If a given percentage change in price brings about a larger percentage change in quantity demanded (a coefficient of elasticity greater than one), demand is described as *elastic*. If a given percentage change in price brings about a smaller percentage change in quantity demanded (a coefficient less than one), demand is said to be *inelastic*. If a given percentage change in price brings an equal percentage change in quantity demanded (a coefficient equal to one), *unitary elasticity* prevails.

If demand is perfectly inelastic (the coefficient of elasticity is zero), a very large change in price will bring no change in the quantity demanded; the demand curve will be a vertical straight line. If demand is perfectly elastic (the coefficient approaches infinity), a very small change in price will bring an extremely large change in the quantity demanded; the demand curve will be a horizontal straight line. Most demand curves, however, do not show just one degree of elasticity, they show several. All linear, downward-sloping demand curves will show unitary elasticity in the middle, elastic demand at the upper end, and inelastic demand at the lower end.

The degree of elasticity is important to businesses because it determines what happens to *total revenue,* or total receipts from sales when a business alters the price of its product. If demand is elastic, a price reduction will lead to an increase in total revenue, and a price increase will cause total revenue to decline. If demand is inelastic, a price reduction will lead to a decline in total revenue, and a price hike will cause total revenue to increase.

With unitary elastic demand, any change in price will be offset exactly by a proportional change in the quantity demanded, and total revenue will be unchanged.

The major determinants of the elasticity of demand are the number of good substitutes that exist and the importance of the product in consumers' budgets. The greater the number of substitutes for a product and the more important the item in the budgets of consumers, the greater the elasticity of demand for the product.

Suppliers as well as consumers respond to price changes. The measure of suppliers' responsiveness to a change in the price of their product is called the *price elasticity of supply.* Economists use the *coefficient of supply elasticity* to determine the degree of responsiveness. The formula for the coefficient is the percentage change in quantity supplied divided by the percentage change in price. Supply is elastic if the coefficient is greater than one, inelastic if it is less than one, and unitary if it is equal to one.

As a general rule, the more time a firm or industry is given to adapt to a specified price change, the larger the change in quantity supplied and the greater the elasticity of supply. The *short run* is a time during which at least one input is fixed. In the short run, output can be expanded by employing additional units of labor and raw materials, but time does not permit plant and equipment expansion. Producers have additional options in the *long run,* a period of time sufficient to change all inputs. In the long run new production facilities can be built and existing facilities can be expanded. As a consequence, output can be increased much more in the long run than in the short run.

Glossary

Page 115   ***Coefficient of demand elasticity.*** A value that indicates the degree to which quantity demanded will change in response to a price change.

Page 124   ***Coefficient of supply elasticity.*** A value that indicates the degree to which the quantity supplied will change in response to a price change.

Page 127   ***Long run.*** The period of time during which all of a business's inputs, including plant and equipment, can be changed.

Page 115   ***Price elasticity of demand.*** A measure of the responsiveness of the quantity demanded of a product to a change in its price.

Page 124   ***Price elasticity of supply.*** A measure of the responsiveness of the quantity supplied of a product to a change in its price.

Page 127   ***Short run.*** The period of time during which at least one of a business's inputs (usually plant and equipment) is fixed—that is, incapable of being changed.

Page 119   ***Total revenue.*** The total receipts of a business from the sale of its product. Total revenue is determined by multiplying the selling price of the product by the number of units sold.

Study Questions

Fill in the Blanks

1. If a decrease in the price of the product leads to a decrease in total revenue, demand must be (elastic/inelastic/unitary) _____.

2. If a 10-percent reduction in price leads to a 20-percent increase in quantity demanded, the coefficient of elasticity would be equal to _____.

3. If the coefficient of elasticity is greater than one, demand is _____; if it is less than one, demand is _____ ; if it is equal to one, demand is _____.

4. The major determinant of the elasticity of demand for a product is the number of good _____ that exist for the product.

5. The greater the fraction of the family budget spent for a particular product, the (greater/smaller) _____ the elasticity of demand for that product.

6. A perfectly inelastic demand curve would be a (vertical/horizontal) _____ _____ straight line.

7. Along a downward-sloping linear demand curve, the elasticity of demand is the greatest at the (upper/lower) _____ end of the curve.

8. The degree of responsiveness of suppliers to a price change depends in part on the amount of _____ they are given to adapt to the change.

9. The time period during which all resources or inputs are variable is called the _____.

10. In general, the greater the period of time producers are given to adjust to a change in price, the (greater/smaller) _____ the elasticity of supply.

Multiple Choice

1. If a seller reduces the price of a product and this leads to an increase in the quantity sold, what can be concluded?
   a) Demand is elastic.
   b) Demand is inelastic.
   c) Demand is of unitary elasticity.
   d) Nothing can be concluded about the degree of elasticity.

2. If the demand curve for a product is a vertical straight line, the coefficient of elasticity would be
   a) zero.
   b) one.
   c) infinity.
   d) different between any two points on the curve.

3. If an increase in price causes total revenue to fall, what can be concluded?
   a) Demand is elastic.
   b) Demand is inelastic.
   c) Unitary elasticity prevails.

4. On a downward-sloping demand curve, demand is more elastic
   a) at the upper end.
   b) at the lower end.
   c) in the middle.

5. In general, demand for a product is more elastic
   a) the fewer the substitutes and the larger the fraction of the family budget spent on that product.
   b) the greater the number of substitutes and the larger the fraction of the family budget spent on that product.
   c) the fewer the substitutes and the smaller the fraction of the family budget spent on that product.
   d) the greater the number of substitutes and the smaller the fraction of the family budget spent on that product.

6. The local transit company is contemplating an increase in bus fares in order to expand revenues. A local senior-citizens group, Seniors for Fair Fares, argues that a rate increase would lead to lower revenues. This disagreement suggests that

a) the transit company does not believe the rate increase would reduce the number of riders, but the SFF believes it would.

b) the transit company believes that the demand for bus service is elastic, but the SFF believes it is inelastic.

c) the transit company believes that the demand for bus service is inelastic, but the SFF believes it is elastic.

7. If the supply curve for a product were a vertical straight line,

a) the quantity supplied would not depend on price.

b) supply would be a fixed quantity.

c) supply would be perfectly inelastic; that is, the elasticity coefficient would be equal to zero.

d) All of the above.

8. Which of the following is *not* a short-run adjustment?

a) The purchase of additional raw materials

b) The construction of a new factory building

c) The hiring of additional workers

d) The addition of a second production shift

9. If the coefficient of supply elasticity for widgets is equal to 4, then a 20 percent increase in the price of widgets would cause the quantity supplied to expand by

a) 80 percent.

b) 5 percent.

c) 40 percent.

d) 4 percent.

10. In general, we can say that

a) supply is more elastic in the short run than in the long run.

b) supply is more elastic in the long run than in the short run.

Problems and Questions for Discussion

1. If a college increases tuition as a method of increasing total revenue, what assumption is it making about the elasticity of demand for its service? Do you think that assumption is valid for your college? Why or why not?

2. If the price of Wrinkled jeans is reduced from $10 to $8 a pair, and the quantity demanded increases from 5,000 to 10,000 pairs a month, what is the coefficient of demand elasticity?

3. According to Mark Moore of Harvard's Kennedy School of Government, the ideal demand-side drug policy would make illegal drugs cheap for addicts and expensive for neophytes. What logic can you see for such a policy, and how would it be related to the elasticity of demand for illegal drugs?

STUDY QUESTIONS

4. Which would tend to be more elastic, the demand for automobiles or the demand for Ford automobiles? Why?

5. Suppose that the price elasticity of demand for water is 2.0 and that the government wants to reduce the quantity of water demanded by 40 percent. By how much must they raise the price of water to accomplish this objective?

6. Sales taxes are a major source of revenue for many state governments. But higher taxes mean higher prices, which mean lower quantities sold by merchants. If the government wants to expand its tax revenue yet inflict minimum damage on the sales of merchants, should it tax products with elastic demand or inelastic demand? Why? Can you see any drawbacks to focusing taxes on these products?

7. Suppose that the coefficient of supply elasticity is equal to 2.5 for a particular product. If the price of that product increases by 10 percent, how much will the quantity supplied increase?

8. If price declines by 5 percent, and quantity supplied declines by 20 percent, what is the coefficient of supply elasticity?

9. Why do we expect supply to be more elastic in the long run than in the short run?

10. Suppose that the coefficient of supply elasticity for housing were equal to 1.5. How much would the price of housing need to rise in order to expand the quantity of housing supplied by 30 percent?

Answer Key

Fill in the Blanks

1.	inelastic	4.	substitutes	8.	time
2.	2.0	5.	greater	9.	long run
3.	elastic, inelastic, unitary	6.	vertical	10.	greater
		7.	upper		

Multiple Choice Questions

1.	d	3.	a	5.	b	7.	d	9.	a
2.	a	4.	a	6.	c	8.	b	10.	b

STUDY QUESTIONS

CHAPTER 5

THE PURELY COMPETITIVE FIRM

In Chapter 3, we discussed how demand and supply interact to determine prices in competitive markets. To fully understand the operation of competitive markets, it is necessary to step behind the scenes and examine the decision-making processes of the individual supplier, commonly known as the *firm*.

The *firm* is the basic producing unit in a market economy. It buys economic resources—land, labor, capital, and entrepreneurship—and combines those resources to produce goods and services. A group of firms that produce identical or similar products is called an ***industry.*** Exxon, Gulf Oil, and Mobil are firms in the petroleum industry; McDonald's, Kentucky Fried Chicken, and your local pizzeria are firms in the fast-food industry.

Economists argue that the performance of firms—how effectively they serve consumers—depends on the degree of competition within the industry; the greater the competition, the better the performance. As we have seen in earlier chapters, performing well in a market economy means producing the goods and services that consumers desire the most and selling them at the lowest possible prices. We will begin this chapter by examining the assumptions that underlie the model of pure competition. Then we will investigate the types of production costs the firm incurs and discover how it decides on the level of output that will maximize its profits. Finally, we will examine the factors that cause firms to enter or leave an industry, explaining why this behavior is thought to be in the best interest of consumers.

The Nature of Pure Competition

Since the time of Adam Smith, economists have recognized that a market economy will serve consumers well only if competition exists to protect their interests. The competition economists have in mind, however, is more than mere rivalry among a few sellers. By definition, pure competition must satisfy three basic assumptions:

1. *There must be a large number of sellers, each producing a relatively small fraction of the total industry supply.* This rules out the possibility that a single firm could affect price by altering its level of output.
2. *The firms in the industry must sell identical products.* This condition excludes the possibility of there being any product differences, including those created through advertising, and assures that consumers will view the products of different firms as perfect substitutes.
3. *There can be no substantial barriers (obstacles) to entering or leaving the industry.* Examples of barriers to entry would include patent restrictions, large investment requirements, and restrictive licensing regulations.

If you find these conditions somewhat unrealistic, don't be alarmed. No industries in the United States or any other economy meet all of them perfectly. Pure competition is not an attempt to describe any existing industry. Rather, it is an economic *model* that will allow us to see how an industry would function if it conformed to certain assumptions. In later chapters, we will relax these assumptions and see how the performance of industries will change when they are no longer satisfied.

By using the benefits of pure competition as our standard, or yardstick, we can understand better the problems that may emerge when industries are less competitive. The competitive model also will offer insights into the behavior of industries that come reasonably close to meeting the assumptions of pure competition. These highly competitive industries include building construction, lumber manufacturing, limestone and gravel mining, and the agricultural industries such as hog and dairy-product production.[1]

The Firm under Pure Competition

In a purely competitive industry the individual firm is best described as a *price taker;* it must accept price as a given that is beyond its control. This description follows from two of the basic assumptions of our model. First, because each firm produces such a small fraction of the total industry's supply, no single firm can influence the market price by altering its level of production. Even if a firm withheld its entire output from the market, the industry supply curve would not shift significantly to the left, and the equilibrium price would be essentially unchanged. Second, because all firms sell identical products, no one firm can charge a higher price for its product without losing all its customers; consumers would simply buy cheaper identical products from other firms. As a consequence of both these conditions, the firm must accept, or *take,* the price that is determined by the impersonal forces of supply and demand.

To illustrate how a firm operates under pure competition, we'll consider a producer of pine lumber, an important component in the construction of new homes. There are several thousand sawmills in the United States that produce pine lumber, and they produce virtually identical products. We will assume that the individual lumber producer is such a small part of the total industry that it cannot influence the market price. Whether that price means a gain or a loss in income, the firm can do nothing to alter it. The firm can't charge more than the prevailing price because its product is identical to that of all other producers. Withholding the firm's output from the market in an attempt to drive up prices would be fruitless because its output is just a "drop in the bucket" and would never be missed.

The price the firm receives for its product can change, of course, but price changes under pure competition are due to changes in *industry* demand and supply conditions, not to any actions the firm may take. Price is a given, and the demand curve facing the individual firm is therefore a hori-

---

[1] Although most agricultural industries conform fairly well to the competitive model, price supports and other forms of government intervention in agriculture reduce the usefulness of the model in describing the performance of agricultural producers.

EXHIBIT 5.1

The Firm as a Price Taker

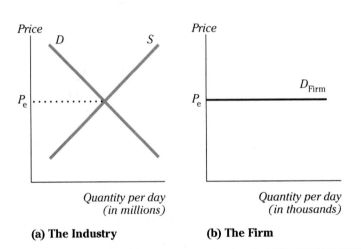

In a purely competitive industry, market forces determine the equilibrium price, and the individual firm is unable to influence that price. The demand curve facing the firm is a horizontal line at the height of the market price because the firm can sell as much output as it desires at the prevailing price, but nothing at a higher price. Note that the industry's quantity is measured in millions, while the firm's is measured in thousands.

(a) The Industry   **(b) The Firm**

zontal line at the equilibrium price. A horizontal demand curve in Exh. 5.1 indicates that the firm can sell as much output as it wishes at the market price, but no output at a higher price. Under conditions of pure competition a firm's demand curve is perfectly, or infinitely, elastic. Recall from Chapter 4 that a high degree of elasticity means that a small change in price will lead to a large change in the quantity demanded. Here a very small change in price leads to an infinitely large change in the quantity demanded, because our lumber mill would lose *all* its customers if it were to raise its price even slightly.

Although an individual competitive firm cannot significantly influence the market price, joint action by a substantial number of firms could affect price. But it is difficult for a large number of producers to agree on a course of action. For example, there have been several attempts by farmers to push up farm prices, but they have always failed. The article on page 142 looks at how farmers attempted to drive up corn prices in 1975 and why those efforts seemed doomed from the start.

Farmer Crusade to Limit '75 Corn Output, Like Efforts in Past, Seems Likely to Fail

Atlantic, Iowa—In what should be his last few days of rest before the start of the planting season, Jim Comes is working harder than ever these days. The 28-year-old farmer is busy driving his muddy Ford pickup truck up and down the hilly roads here in southwest Iowa, trying to enlist his neighbors in a crusade.

Mr. Comes is handing out pale-blue pledge cards asking his fellow farmers to agree to plant 10% fewer acres of corn than they had planned. His neighbors all read the card over carefully and apparently give the matter serious thought. But very few of them are reaching for the pen to sign. So far, only 100 or so of the 1,300 farmers in Mr. Comes's county have pledged to participate in the cutback.

"Most of the rest say they would be glad to go along—if everyone else does," Mr. Comes says wearily. "We've got to bring in the fence-sitters to make this thing work."

Mr. Comes's experience is illustrative of a problem encountered all over the Farm Belt by a hard-working cadre of farmers spearheading the cutback movement. They've been trying to convince their colleagues that the best way to assure decent prices for their corn, soybeans and spring wheat is to reduce production. Some Kansas farmers with similar motives have plowed up part of the winter wheat they planted last fall, but the few thousand acres involved are insignificant in relation to the state's 12.5 million-acre total plantings.

Planting Time Is Near

With planting time almost here, it's becoming increasingly clear that the movement born in the farmers' winter of discontent is failing. As Jim Comes has discovered, there simply are too many fence-sitters and too many farmers who feel that springtime is planting time. . . .

But cutback proponents argue that all-out production is the last thing farmers should be planning if they are to avoid financial disaster this year. . . .

Bumper Crop Outlook

As of March 1, the Agriculture Department says, farmers were planning to plant 76 million acres of corn, the nation's leading feed grain and a bellwether for the farm economy generally. With an estimated normal-weather yield of an average 92 bushels an acre (compared to last year's actual output of 71.3 bushels an acre), farmers would thus produce a bumper crop of more than 6 billion bushels.

That's too much corn, the cutback leaders say. They contend that a harvest of that size would result in farmers getting about $1.75 a bushel for corn that it cost them an average of $2 a bushel to produce. . . .

. . . many nonfarmers, including some philosophically opposed to the cutback, agree with its leaders that enough farmer participation indeed would raise prices. John Roch, a West Des Moines, Iowa, market adviser, who says he is neutral on the cutback issue, estimates that a 10% cutback would result in corn prices of about $2.75 a bushel, compared to the $1.75 that some expect if farmers produce at maximum levels. Iowa State University researchers, who used production and consumption data in a computer study, concluded that a 9% cutback could raise corn prices to a level as much as 40% above the projected bumper-crop price.

If economics is on the side of the cutback proponents, history isn't. Since colonial times, numerous attempts have been made to get farmers to restrict production voluntarily. But these have failed, L. H. Simerl, University of Illinois agricultural economist, says, either because most farmers didn't go along or because those who did idled only their poorest land. Moreover, the movements have occasionally created hard feelings between big and small farmers and sometimes have led to barn-burnings and other acts of violence . . .

—Gene Meyer

USE YOUR ECONOMIC REASONING

1. If the farmers could agree to limit corn output, would that result in higher corn prices? Use graphs to support your answer.

2. Suppose that farmers were successful in driving up the market price of corn. How would that affect the demand curve facing the individual *firm*?

3. Why are farmers reluctant to go along with a restriction on production? Is it just that farmers are independent thinkers, or are there other reasons for their reluctance?

Profit Maximization and Price Takers

The model of pure competition assumes that firms are *profit maximizers;* that is, they are always attempting to earn the most profit possible. *Profit* is the excess of a firm's total revenue over its total cost. When a firm's total costs exceed its total revenue, the firm is incurring a *loss.* (Profit and loss are simple accounting terms; the next section will explain why economists need special terms for different kinds of profits.)

A firm's **total revenue (TR)** is the amount of money it takes in from the sale of its product. *TR* is calculated by multiplying the selling price of the product by the number of units sold. **Total cost (TC)** refers to the sum of all the costs incurred by a business in producing its product and making it available for sale. The behavior of total cost—how rapidly it increases when output is expanded—helps to determine which level of output will maximize a firm's profit. If producing an additional unit of output adds more to a firm's revenue than it adds to cost, the additional unit should be produced. If the unit adds more to cost than it adds to revenue, it should not be produced. In other words, if an extra unit of output is profitable, it should be produced. We'll explore this profit-maximizing rule in greater detail after we discuss the types of costs a firm incurs and how they vary with output.

Short-Run Costs of Production

All firms must incur costs in order to produce the goods or services that they offer in the marketplace. Although this chapter concentrates on the purely competitive firm, the discussion of production costs that is presented here applies to all firms, regardless of the competitive setting in which they operate.

Our discussion of production costs will focus on the short run. The short run, as you learned in Chapter 4, is a time period during which at least one of a business's inputs (usually its plant and equipment) is incapable of being changed. In the short run a business must expand output by using its fixed production plant more intensively, since it does not have sufficient time to build a new plant or expand its existing facilities. In the long run, you will recall, all inputs can be varied, including plant and equipment. There is sufficient time for firms to build new production facilities, and to expand or contract existing ones. We'll have more to say about the firm's long-run adjustments later in the chapter.

Total Costs: Fixed and Variable

Short-run production costs can be classified as either fixed or variable. Total cost *(TC)* is simply the sum of the fixed and variable costs incurred by the firm.

Fixed Costs. *Fixed costs* are costs that do not vary with the level of output. They neither increase when the firm produces more nor decrease when the firm produces less. Fixed costs are often referred to as *overhead* and include such expenditures as insurance payments, rent on the production plant, fees for business licenses, salaries of managers, and property taxes.

The distinguishing feature of fixed costs is that they have to be paid whether or not the firm is producing anything. If our hypothetical sawmill were forced to shut down because of a strike, the firm would still have to pay the salaries of its managers in order to avoid losing them to other companies. It would still have to make interest payments on loans it had taken to purchase the production plant and equipment. It would continue making payments for damage and accident insurance, and it would still require the services of security guards (an expense that might even increase).

Economists also include a normal profit as a fixed cost. *Normal profit* is the amount that the owners of a business could have earned if the money, time, and other resources they have invested in the business were invested elsewhere, in the next best alternative. In other words, normal profit is the opportunity cost of owner-supplied resources. As an example, suppose that the owner of our sawmill had been earning $30,000 a year working for another lumber producer before she decided to buy her own mill. When she quit her job, she withdrew $20,000 from her savings account, which had been earning 10-percent interest per year, and used the money as a down payment to buy the sawmill. Since the earnings she is giving up to launch this venture are her $30,000 supervisor's salary plus $2,000 interest (10 percent of $20,000) on her savings, she will have to make $32,000 in her business (after subtracting all other costs) in order to earn a normal profit.

A normal profit is a fixed cost of keeping a business going. In fact, a firm that is earning a normal profit is said to be *breaking even*. Although some individuals may be willing to work for less than normal profit—perhaps because of the sense of independence they gain by being their own bosses—most owners will keep their resources employed only where they can expect at least a normal return.

Any profit above a normal profit is called an *economic profit.* If, for example, our lumber mill has total revenues of $75,000 and total costs of $57,000 (including $32,000 normal profit), the remaining $18,000 is economic profit. Economic profit is not considered a cost because the owners would remain in the business even at zero economic profit, where the firm would be breaking even.

Variable Costs. *Variable costs* are costs that change with the level of output. They tend to increase when the level of output increases and decline when output declines. Many of a business's costs are variable costs: payments for raw materials such as timber, iron ore, and crude oil, and the manufactured inputs transformed from such materials (lumber, sheet steel, paint); wages and salaries of production workers; payments for electricity and water; and shipping expenses.

In many instances a specific element of cost may be partly a fixed cost and partly a variable cost. For example, although a firm's electricity bill increases as it expands production, some fraction of that bill should be considered a fixed cost because it relates to security lights, running the air-conditioners in administrative offices, and other functions that are independent of the rate of output. Payments for raw materials and other inputs can also have a fixed cost element if the firm has agreed to purchase some minimum amount of these inputs or to make some minimum payment to suppliers each year. Perhaps our sawmill operator has contracted to purchase a minimum of 100,000 pine logs per year in return for a guaranteed price or an assured source of supply. In that case the cost of the 100,000 logs will be a fixed cost, even though it is a payment for raw materials. Because each business is unique, we cannot determine to what extent a particular cost is fixed or variable without knowing quite a bit about the nature of the business and the firm's specific contractual obligations.

Total Cost. Each firm's total cost *(TC)* of production is the sum of its total fixed cost *(TFC)* and its total variable cost *(TVC)*. The first four columns of Exh. 5.2 illustrate how these costs respond to changes in the level of output. The figures in column two show that the firm's total fixed cost (the sum of its expenditures for insurance payments, management salaries, and other fixed expenses) is constant, whereas column three shows the firm's total variable cost (total expenditures for gasoline, oil, labor, and other variable expenses) increasing as the level of output increases. Because total cost (column four) includes this variable cost component, it also increases with the level of production.

EXHIBIT 5.2

Daily Costs of Manufacturing Pine Lumber

OUTPUT (thousands of feet of lumber)*	TOTAL FIXED COST (TFC)	TOTAL VARIABLE COST (TVC)	TOTAL COST (TC)	AVERAGE FIXED COST (AFC)	AVERAGE VARIABLE COST (AVC)	AVERAGE TOTAL COST (ATC)
0	$180	$ 0	$ 180			
1	180	270	450	$180.00	$270.00	$450.00
2	180	510	690	90.00	255.00	345.00
3	180	720	900	60.00	240.00	300.00
4	180	900	1080	45.00	225.00	270.00
5	180	1110	1290	36.00	222.00	258.00
6	180	1350	1530	30.00	225.00	255.00
7	180	1620	1800	25.71	231.43	257.14
8	180	1950	2130	22.50	243.75	266.25
9	180	2340	2520	20.00	260.00	280.00
10	180	2790	2970	18.00	279.00	297.00

*Large quantities of lumber are generally sold in increments of 1000 *board feet;* a board foot measures $12 \times 12 \times 1$ inches.

Average Costs: Fixed, Variable, and Total

Producers are often more interested in the average cost of producing a unit of output than they are in any of the total-cost concepts we've examined. By comparing average, or per-unit, costs with those of other firms in the industry, a producer can judge how efficient (or inefficient) its own operation is.

Actually there are three average cost functions: average fixed cost, average variable cost, and average total cost. *Average fixed cost (AFC)* is computed by dividing total fixed cost by the firm's output. For example, if the firm were producing seven units of output, the *AFC* would be $180/7 = $25.71. As you can see in column five of Exh. 5.2, average fixed cost declines as output expands. This must be true because we are dividing a constant—total fixed cost—by larger and larger amounts of output. The decline in *AFC* is what a business means when it talks about "spreading its overhead" over more units of output.

The figures in column six describe the behavior of the firm's average variable cost. *Average variable cost (AVC)* is calculated by dividing the total variable cost at a given output level by the amount of output produced. For instance, if our lumber mill were producing six units of output (6,000 feet of lumber), its *AVC* would be $1,350/6 = $225. As you can see from the table, average variable cost declines initially and then rises as output continues to expand. The reason for this behavior will be provided a little later.

Average total cost (ATC) is always equal to average fixed cost plus average variable cost. For instance, the average total cost of producing four units of output is equal to the average fixed cost of $45 *plus* the average vari-

EXHIBIT 5.3

The Marginal Cost of Manufacturing Pine Lumber

OUTPUT PER DAY (thousands of feet of lumber)	TOTAL COST *(TC)*	MARGINAL COST *(MC)*
0	$ 180	—
1	450	$270
2	690	240
3	900	210
4	1,080	180
5	1,290	210
6	1,530	240
7	1,800	270
8	2,130	330
9	2,520	390
10	2,970	450

Marginal cost is the additional cost of producing one more unit of output. For example, if it costs the firm $1,290 to produce five units of lumber, and $1,530 to produce six units of lumber, the marginal cost of the sixth unit of lumber is $240.

able cost of $225; that means *ATC* is equal to $270. Average total cost can also be computed by dividing the total cost at a particular level of output by the number of units of output. Using that technique, we find the average total cost of producing four units of output is $1,080/4 = $270, the same answer as before. As you can see from column seven, average total cost declines initially and then rises.

Marginal Cost

Average total cost is useful in gauging a firm's efficiency in production, but the concept of marginal cost plays the more important role in guiding production decisions. The term *marginal* means extra or additional. Thus ***marginal cost (MC)*** is the additional cost of producing one more unit of output. It is equal to the change in total cost from one unit of output to the next. Consider, for example, the marginal cost of the first unit of output—the first thousand feet of lumber—in Exh. 5.3. If it costs the firm $180 to produce zero output (remember fixed costs) and $450 to produce one unit of output, the marginal cost of the first unit of lumber is $270. The *MC* of the second unit of output is $240, the difference between *TC* $450 and *TC* $690. Take a few moments to compute the marginal costs for the remaining units of output, using the total-cost column in Exh. 5.3. Then check your answers against the marginal-cost column in that exhibit.

The Cost Curves

The information scheduled in Exh. 5.2 and Exh. 5.3 is depicted as cost curves in Exh. 5.4. We read cost curves in much the same way we read the demand and supply curves presented in Chapter 3. If we are interested in knowing the average total cost of producing three units of output, for example, we find three units on the horizontal axis, move directly up from that quantity to the *ATC* curve (point *A*), move across to the vertical axis, and read $300. The *ATC* of producing three units of output is $300 per unit. To determine the *AVC* when six units are being produced, we find that quantity on the horizontal axis, move directly up to the *AVC* curve (point *B*), move across to the vertical axis, and read $225. The *AVC* of producing six units of output is $225. The other cost curves are read in the same way.

EXHIBIT 5.4

A Graphic Look at Costs

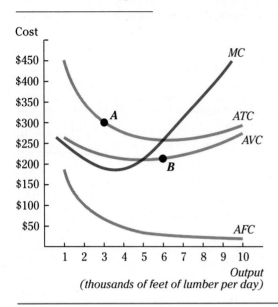

Cost curves show the way that a particular type of cost is related to the level of output. Average fixed cost (AFC) declines as output increases. Marginal cost (MC), average variable cost (AVC), and average total cost (ATC) graph as U-shaped curves; that is, these types of costs decline initially and then rise.

Cost curves help us see how a particular cost behaves as the level of output changes. Note that *AFC* declines as output increases, reflecting the spreading of fixed costs over more units of output. The marginal cost curve and the average cost curve (*AVC* and *ATC*) decline initially and then begin to increase as output expands, giving them a U-shape. As you read the following sections, you will see why the curves behave this way.

The Marginal Cost Curve

Why does marginal cost first decline and then increase? As you've already learned, marginal cost is the additional cost of producing one more unit of output. It is a variable cost because it changes as output changes. The shape of the marginal cost curve, therefore, must be related to some specific variable cost—often the cost of labor.

Let's see how changing labor costs can account for the U-shaped curve in Exh. 5.4. The labor cost of producing an additional unit of output depends on the amount of labor time it takes to produce that unit. If our firm is paying its workers $10 per hour, and it takes eight hours of labor to produce the additional unit, the labor cost of that unit is $80. Keep in mind that the amount of labor time it takes to produce each additional unit of output is not constant. It depends on the degree of *specialization* of labor: the extent to which workers perform a single task rather than several. Workers who specialize do their jobs better, which means lower *MC*.

When a firm is producing relatively little output, the labor cost of producing an additional unit tends to be high, because the low volume permits little specialization. To illustrate, let's think about the variety of tasks you would need to perform if you wanted to run our hypothetical sawmill alone. You would be required to roll the logs onto the saws and cut them into lumber. Then you would have to smooth the rough surface of the boards with a tool known as a plane. Next you would need to stack the lumber for drying. And of course you'd be the one who cleaned and serviced the equipment so that it would continue to operate properly. Many additional tasks would be required, but probably by now you get the point. If you were trying to run the mill by yourself, you would spend a great deal of time moving from one task to the next, and it's likely that you wouldn't become very proficient at any of them. As a consequence, more hours would be required to accomplish each task than would be needed if you were allowed to specialize in one job (or a few jobs) and become more skilled. This is why the marginal cost of producing the first unit of lumber is relatively high ($270).

As output expands, opportunities for specialization increase. For example, if the lumber mill needs to hire two workers to keep up with demand, one of them might do all the sawing while the other planes the boards and stacks them for drying. This greater specialization permits workers to become better at their jobs and reduces the time wasted in moving from one task to another. The result is a lower marginal cost for the second unit of output ($240) and an even lower cost for the third ($210) and fourth ($180), because the amount of labor time required to produce these additional units of output is reduced. Remember, this is a hypothetical example; the numbers are not precise, they are meant only to illustrate a principle. In some businesses, specialization can result in significant reductions in marginal cost; in others, the savings may be minimal.

Marginal cost will not decline infinitely. If the firm continues to expand output, eventually it will start to overutilize its plant and equipment, causing marginal cost to rise. Remember that in the short run the firm must operate with a fixed amount of plant and equipment. If the firm continues to hire additional workers in order to increase output, at some point it will experience congestion, workers waiting for machines, and high breakdown rates as overused machines begin to fail. Then the marginal cost of producing an additional unit of output will rise, as it does in our example when the output is expanded from four to five units of lumber.[2]

In summary, if a firm continues to expand output in the short run, eventually it will overutilize its fixed plant and equipment, causing marginal cost to rise. This principle is simply an extension of the law of increasing costs introduced in Chapter 1.

The Relationship between Marginal and Average Costs

Marginal cost is related to average variable cost and average total cost in a very precise way. In Exh. 5.4, you'll notice that the MC curve intersects the AVC curve at the lowest point, or minimum, of the AVC curve. This point is not a chance intersection but is due to the relationship between marginal and average cost values. A simple example will help clarify this relationship. Let's assume that you want to know the average weight of the students in your class. To determine the class average, you coax each student onto the scales, add up the individual weights, and then divide by the number of students in the class. If an additional (marginal) student who weighs more than the average joins the class, the average will be pulled up. If the additional student weighs less than the previous class average, the average will be pulled down. As you can see, the marginal value determines what happens to the average.

Essentially the same logic applies to the cost curves. Notice that so long as the MC curve is below the AVC curve, the AVC is falling; the marginal value is pulling down the average, just as the thin student pulled down the class average. However, when MC is above AVC, AVC is rising; the marginal value is pulling the average up. When $MC = AVC$—that is, when MC and AVC intersect—the average will remain unchanged. As you can see, the shape of the AVC curve depends largely on the behavior of marginal cost. Thus if MC declines initially and then increases as output continues to expand, AVC must display the same general behavior.

The shape of the ATC curve is also influenced by marginal cost, but in a somewhat more complex manner. Recall that average total cost is the

---

[2] The fixed factor need not be plant and equipment; in agriculture, it might be land. As a farmer adds units of fertilizer (or some other variable input such as labor, irrigation water, or insecticide) to a fixed plot of land, the second unit of fertilizer may increase the output of corn by more than the first unit, and the third unit of fertilizer may increase output by more than the second. Thus the cost of producing each additional bushel of corn declines initially because it takes less fertilizer (and therefore less expenditure on fertilizer) to produce it.

Again, this process can't continue indefinitely. Eventually it will reach the point where the fixed land is being overutilized, the point where the next unit of fertilizer applied to the land will yield less additional output than the unit before it. When that happens, the marginal cost of producing the next bushel of corn will rise. In other words, the marginal cost curve will turn upward.

sum of average fixed cost and average variable cost. Initially, both *AVC* and *AFC* decline, so *ATC* declines as well. But note that *ATC* continues to decline after *AVC* has turned upward. This occurs because *AFC* is continuing to decline, and for a while the downward pull of *AFC* outweighs the upward pull of *AVC*. Eventually the increase in *AVC* will more than offset the decrease in *AFC*, and *ATC* will begin to rise. Thus *ATC* will have the same basic shape as *AVC*, but the minimum point on the curve will occur at a somewhat higher output.

In summary, the marginal cost curve plays a major role in determining the shape of both the average variable and the average total cost curves. As you will see in a moment, marginal cost also plays a major role in guiding the production decisions of the competitive firm.

Profit Maximization in the Short Run

Because the purely competitive firm is a price taker, in effect bound to the price determined by the market, the only variable it can control to maximize its profit (when market conditions permit a profit) or minimize its loss (when a loss is unavoidable) is the level of output.

In the short run, the purely competitive firm can produce any level of output within the capacity of its existing plant and equipment. It adjusts its output by altering the amount of variable resources (labor and raw materials, for example) that it employs in conjunction with its fixed plant and equipment. In the long run, of course, the firm has additional options for expanding or contracting production.

Determining the Profit-Maximizing Output

The profit-maximizing (loss-minimizing) level of output in the short run can be determined by comparing marginal cost with marginal revenue. We have seen that marginal cost is the additional cost of producing one more unit of output. *Marginal revenue (MR)* is the additional revenue to be gained by selling one more unit of output. When the firm is a price taker, *MR* equals price, because the additional revenue to be gained by selling one more unit is exactly the market price.

A firm seeking to achieve the profit-maximizing output will continue to increase production so long as marginal revenue exceeds marginal cost. When *MR* > *MC*, each additional unit "pays its own way" because it adds more to revenue than to cost. In Exh. 5.5, the market price of the

EXHIBIT 5.5

The Profit Maximizing Output

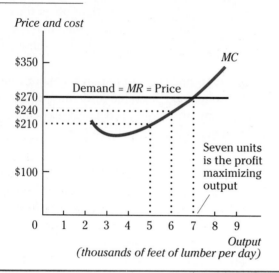

Price and cost

$350

Demand = *MR* = Price

$270
$240
$210

MC

Seven units
is the profit
maximizing
output

$100

0   1   2   3   4   5   6   7   8   9

*Output
(thousands of feet of lumber per day)*

The profit-maximizing firm should continue to expand output until MR = MC. In this case, profit maximization (or loss minimization) occurs at an output of seven units (7,000 feet) of lumber per day.

product is $270, so each additional unit produced will add $270 to revenue. You can see that the marginal cost of producing the fifth unit is $210 and that the firm will be $60 "better off" for producing that unit. In the case of the sixth unit, the company will be only $30 better off, because the marginal cost of that unit is $240. It is important to recognize that although the sixth unit adds less to profit than the fifth unit, it continues to enlarge the firm's *total* profit, so it should be produced.[3]

The seventh unit of output is a little trickier to evaluate. It brings in no more revenue ($270) than it costs to produce ($270), so the firm should be neutral, or indifferent, toward its production. Economists generally assume, however, that the firm will go ahead and produce that unit.

This assumption provides us with a rule for selecting the profit-maximizing output: Produce the level of output where *MC* = *MR*, the output that corresponds to the point where the *MC* and *MR* curves intersect. In instances where there is no whole-number unit of output for which *MC* is exactly equal to *MR*, the firm should produce all the units for which *MR* > *MC*, but no unit for which *MC* > *MR*.

---

[3] With the information provided thus far, we cannot actually determine whether this firm is earning a profit or incurring a loss. But we can say that by producing the sixth unit the firm will either enlarge its total profit *or* reduce its total loss. You'll see how to determine the profit or loss in just a moment.

Evaluating Profit or Loss

By producing where marginal revenue is equal to marginal cost, the purely competitive firm is doing the best it can; it is either maximizing its profit or minimizing its loss. Marginal values alone, however, will not tell us exactly how well the firm is doing; they will not tell us whether the firm is earning a profit or incurring a loss, and they will not tell us the amount of the profit or loss.

To answer those questions, we need to calculate and compare the firm's total revenue and total cost. You already know that total revenue is computed by multiplying the selling price of the product by the number of units sold. To compute total cost, we need the information provided by the average total cost curve. Multiplying the *ATC* by the number of units of output produced gives us the total cost of producing that output level. (Recall that we get our per-unit or *ATC* cost by performing the reverse operation: dividing *TC* at a particular level of output by the number of units.) By comparing total revenue with total cost, we can determine the profit or loss of the firm. Some examples should help clarify this procedure.

Profits, Losses, and Breaking Even. Exhibit 5.6 shows a purely competitive firm in three different short-run situations. As you study the three cases, keep in mind that market price equals *MR* under conditions of pure competition. And the *MR* = *P* curve is the demand curve for the purely competitive firm. In each case the firm is producing where the *MC* curve intersects the demand curve, where *MC* = *MR*; but it is experiencing different degrees of success in these three situations. In part (a), the firm is enjoying an above normal or economic profit. The amount of this profit can be determined by comparing total revenue with total cost. Total revenue is equal to $1,890 (the $270 selling price × 7 units), whereas total cost is only $1,799 (*ATC* of $257 × 7 units). Therefore the firm is earning an economic profit of $91.[4] In part (b), the firm isn't doing as well. Its total revenue of $1,530 ($255 × 6 units) exactly matches its total cost, so the firm is just breaking even; it is earning zero economic profit. Remember that zero economic profit is the same as normal profit, the amount the owners of the business could expect to earn if they invested their resources elsewhere. In part (c), the firm has fallen on hard times. Price is now so low that it will no longer cover average total cost.

[4] An alternative method of determining the profit or loss is to compute the average or per-unit profit (or loss) and then multiply by the quantity of output. For instance, if the firm is producing seven units of output at an average total cost of $257 and a selling price of $270, it would be earning a profit of $13 per unit ($270 − $257 = $13), a total profit of $91 on the seven units sold.

EXHIBIT 5.6

Finding the Profit or Loss

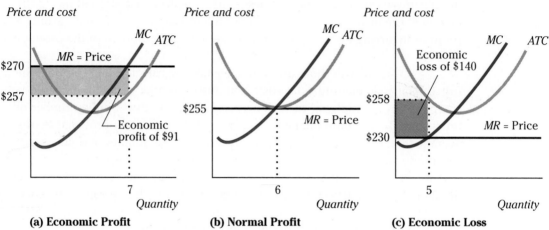

(a) Economic Profit   **(b) Normal Profit**   **(c) Economic Loss**

All firms maximize their profits or minimize their losses by producing the level of output at which marginal revenue is equal to marginal cost. In some instances a firm will be able to earn an above-normal or economic profit. In other instances only a normal profit—zero economic profit—will be possible. Finally, in some cases an economic loss—less than a normal profit—will be the best that the firm can do.

Indeed, the firm will be earning less than a normal profit and therefore facing an *economic loss:* total cost, including all opportunity costs, will exceed total revenue. In our example, the firm's total cost is $1,290 ($258 × 5 units), whereas its total revenue is only $1,150 (*ATC* of $230 × 5 units), a loss of $140.

Operating with a Loss. Why would the company continue to produce in part (c)? Why not simply close down the business and not reopen until conditions improve? The answer has to do with fixed costs, or overhead, which must be paid whether or not any output is produced. If a firm shuts down temporarily—if it stays in the industry but stops producing output—its loss will equal its total fixed costs. But if the price the firm can get for its product is high enough to allow the firm to cover its variable costs (costs that would not exist if the firm shut down) and pay *some* of its fixed costs, the firm will be better off if it continues to operate. This is why U.S. wheat farmers continued to produce in the mid-1980s, despite substantial losses. Doing so resulted

EXHIBIT 5.7

Minimizing a Loss

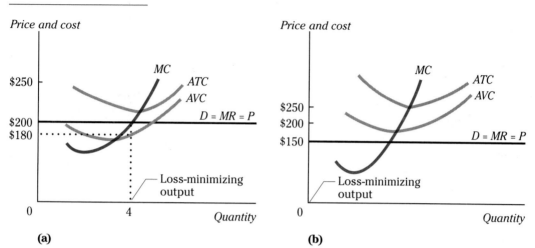

(a)   **(b)**

Whenever price exceeds average variable cost (P > AVC), *the firm will minimize its loss by continuing to operate. This is the situation represented in part (a), where the firm will continue to produce despite an economic loss. When price is less than average variable cost* (P < AVC), *the firm will minimize its loss by shutting down. This situation is represented in part (b).*

in smaller losses than the farmers would have incurred by shutting down. When price reaches so low a level that the firm can no longer recover the variable costs of producing, it will shut down and wait for better times.

Exhibit 5.7 illustrates these two situations. In part (a), the selling price of $200 is greater than the average variable cost of $180, so each unit that the firm produces (up to the point where $MR = MC$) provides it with $20 ($200 − $180 = $20) to help pay its fixed costs. Although the firm will still incur a loss, continued operation will make the loss smaller than it would be if the firm shut down and paid its fixed costs. In part (b), the $150 price is less than the AVC of $170, so each unit the firm produces increases its total loss by $20. This firm would be better off to shut down, accept its fixed-cost loss, and wait for business conditions to improve. Of course, if losses continue period after period, eventually the firm will be forced out of business. In summary, when $P > AVC$, the firm will minimize its loss by continuing to operate; when $P < AVC$, the firm should shut down.

Profit Maximization in the Long Run

Whereas in the short run the purely competitive firm must do the best it can with fixed plant and equipment, in the long run the firm has many more options; all costs are variable in the long run. If the industry has been profitable, the firm may decide to expand the size of its production plant or otherwise increase its productive capacity. If losses have been common, it can sell out and invest in another industry, where the prospects for profits appear brighter. In the short-run the number of firms in an industry remains constant—time is inadequate for firms to enter or leave. But in the long-run there is time for these adjustments to occur, and the industry can expand or contract. In this section, we examine how firms in a purely competitive industry adjust to the presence or absence of short-run profits and how this adjustment process eventually leads to long-run equilibrium for the industry. *Long-run equilibrium* is a situation in which the size of an industry is stable: There is no incentive for additional firms to enter the industry and no pressure for existing firms to leave.

Setting the Stage: The Short-Run Picture

In Exh. 5.8, we follow the path by which a purely competitive firm and industry arrive at long-run equilibrium. Each panel shows the demand and supply curves for the industry on the left and the diagram for a representative firm on the right. In part (a), the industry demand and supply curves establish a price of $300. The representative firm takes that price as a given and maximizes its profits (or minimizes its losses) by producing where $MC = MR$. Here the representative firm is earning an economic profit in the short run, and as a consequence, additional firms will be attracted to this industry in the long run.

The Entrance of Firms: Attraction of Profits

The entrance of additional firms is made possible by one of the assumptions of the purely competitive model—the absence of significant barriers to entry. As additional firms enter the industry, they will increase the industry supply and depress the market price. This adjustment is represented in the left-hand graph of part (b), where supply has increased to S_1 and intersects with the demand curve to establish a new price of $270. Note that at the new price the firms in the industry still are able to earn economic profits; *ATC* is still below

EXHIBIT 5.8

The Long-Run Adjustment Process

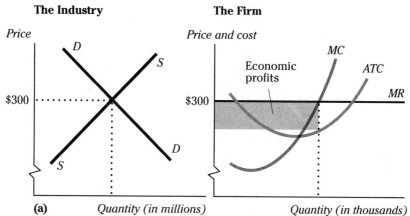

(a) At a price of $300, the firms in the industry will be able to earn an economic profit. Since above-normal profits are being earned, additional firms will be attracted to the industry. This development is reflected in (b).

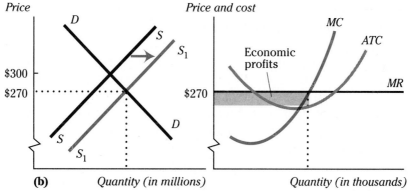

(b) As additional firms enter the industry, the industry supply curve will shift from S to S₁ and price will be forced down to $270. However, since that price still permits an economic profit to be earned, additional firms will enter the industry as revealed in (c) on the next page.

EXHIBIT 5.8 (Cont.)

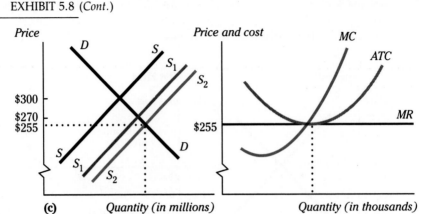

(c) The entrance of additional firms will shift the supply curve to S_2 and depress market price to $255. At that price, the firms in the industry will only be able to earn a normal profit. There will be no incentive for additional firms to enter the industry and the industry will be in long-run equilibrium.

$MR = P$. As a consequence, firms will continue to enter the industry until the price falls to $255, where the demand curve and S_2 intersect in part (c) and price is consistent with normal profits.

Once the price of $255 is established, both the firm and industry are in long-run equilibrium: They have achieved a state of balance, a situation in which there is no tendency for further change. The industry is in long-run equilibrium because at zero economic profit there is no incentive for additional firms to enter it and no incentive for established firms to leave it. The individual firms are in equilibrium because they have no incentive to alter their level of output so long as the market price remains at $255. (In 1991, cattle ranchers were earning nice profits but were concerned about the future. Read "Beef Prices Stay Lofty As Ranchers Avoid Usual Overexpansion" on page 162 to learn something about the competitive nature of the cattle industry.)

The Exit of Firms: Looking for Greener Pastures

If a purely competitive industry undergoes short-run economic losses, a similar adjustment process is likely to result. In the long run, some firms will respond to the short-run losses (less than normal profits) by leaving the industry to search for a better opportunity elsewhere. As these firms exit, industry supply decreases and the market price rises. Firms will continue to leave the industry until the market price has risen sufficiently to afford the remaining firms exactly a normal profit. When that happens, the exodus will cease; the firms and the industry will be in long-run equilibrium.

The Benefits of Pure Competition

As we noted at the beginning of this chapter, economists often use the model of pure competition as an ideal by which to judge other, less-competitive industry structures. Economists hold pure competition in such high esteem primarily because it would lead to an efficient use of our scarce resources.

Production Efficiency

One of the most important features of pure competition is its tendency to promote *production efficiency:* production at the lowest possible average total cost, or minimum *ATC*. As you look at Exh. 5.9, you'll see that the purely competitive firm is in long-run equilibrium when it is producing at the level where its *ATC* curve is tangent to, or barely touching, its demand curve. This tangency occurs at the lowest point on the firm's *ATC* curve, showing that the firm is producing at the lowest possible average cost. In essence this means that the product is being produced with as few scarce resources as possible. Production efficiency is a benefit of pure competition; it allows us to spread our scarce resources across more products, and in so doing it enables us to satisfy more of society's unlimited wants.

Note also that in long-run equilibrium, consumers are able to purchase the product at a price equal to this minimum *ATC*. This must be true because at the tangency point in Exh. 5.9, Price *(MR)* = *ATC*. Thus we can see that the benefits of production efficiency are passed on to consumers. They receive the lowest possible price, given the cost conditions that exist in the industry.

Allocative Efficiency

If pure competition resulted in the efficient production of millions of buggy whips or other products that were not in much demand, consumers obviously would not be pleased. However, pure competition also leads to *allocative efficiency:* producers use society's scarce resources to provide consumers with the proper quantities of the goods and services they desire the most. Economists argue that if pure competition prevailed throughout the

Beef Prices Stay Lofty As Ranchers Avoid Usual Overexpansion

LISCO, Neb.—Michael McGinley's cowboy hat blows off as he barrels across the rolling prairie in a blue pickup truck, kicking up plumes of dust. The 55-year-old rancher is in a frenzied chase after a hot commodity: a three-day-old calf that has run from the herd.

Suddenly, the frantic critter drops from view. Mr. McGinley yelps as he sees the animal has jumped down a steep bluff—and his truck is headed for a terrifying plunge. As the front wheels leap into space, the rear wheels catch on the slope's crest. The vehicle slams to a stop hanging precariously on the ridge. And the calf saunters away.

"Maybe it's the cattle that are getting smarter," Mr. McGinley says. His son returns on horseback to rope the stray.

Ranching has always been hard work, but now ranchers are minding their herds with extra vigilance. The reason: There's a bull market for beef, returning boom times to cattle country. . . .

Lucrative Livestock

Higher beef prices have made ranching extremely profitable. Calves sold at 500 pounds fetched as much as $525 last fall, or about 20% more than they cost to raise. That price—$1.05 a pound—was a record, although not the highest price cattlemen have ever received if inflation is taken into account. So all across the Great Plains, ranchers are rounding up profits—and plowing them into new pickups, tractors or more frequent trips to Las Vegas. . . .

The cattle industry has gone through many boom-and-bust cycles before, but the latest upsurge is something of a surprise because health-conscious consumers have been showing less appetite for beef. Since peaking in 1976, per capita beef consumption in the U.S. has fallen by 28.6%.

Meanwhile, however, the size of the U.S. cattle herd has shrunk to a 30-year low. So the supply of cattle has fallen by even more than demand. Rising beef exports to Japan are also helping to push up prices.

Fixing the Market

Ordinarily, strong cattle prices soon lead to overexpansion, eventually bringing an end to the high prices and the ranchers' prosperity. But the last industry shakeout was particularly rough and wiped out a lot of ranchers, including many of the most aggressive ones. Those still in the business have been more conservative, and haven't stampeded to expand the size of their herds even as prices have risen. . . .

The ranchers vow it won't happen. "Nobody wants to be a cattle baron anymore," says Tom Hansen, a cattleman in North Platte. "We want to be baron-ettes."

This season, Mr. Hansen marched 1,400 cows, each with a calf, to summer range, the same number as last year and the year before that. Rather than get bigger, Mr. Hansen, who is 44, says he is content to spend his money in town to replace an old tractor and corral. He banks the rest.

Likewise, Mr. McGinley says the memory of past boom-and-bust cycles has made him more cautious this time. During the 1980s, he nearly lost his fourth-generation ranch. His father was an old-fashioned rancher who had a grace with cattle but little patience with the ledger. When cattle prices rose, he did what ranchers had always done: got bigger and lived better. When he died in 1976, the 18,400-acre ranch was overextended. That left Mr. McGinley to cope with a wary bank just as consumers' appetite for beef began to slip. . . .

Some economists believe that the advancing age of ranchers is another reason for their reluctance to expand. The farm crisis claimed many of the youngest ranchers. Mr. McGinley, who at 55 is about the age of the average rancher today, says his goal is to reduce the debt on his ranch before the next generation takes over.

In the meantime, he and other ranchers are doing all they can to keep profit margins up. When cattle prices have been this high in the past, farmers from elsewhere got into the business. They could get heifers by buying them from feedlots that fatten the animals for slaughter.

But this time, that isn't so easy. Now many Nebraska ranchers, instead of selling their cattle to feedlots, are paying feedlots to fatten the animals. By retaining ownership, these ranchers guarantee that the cattle end up at the meatpacker. And when they do sell the calves, some ranchers are even going so far as to spay the females so that buyers can't turn them into breeding stock. (Males are routinely neutered.) City slickers, too, have pulled in their horns since tax reform put an end to owning cattle as a tax dodge.

Still, prices of cattle futures contracts at the Chicago Mercantile Exchange have slipped for several weeks on speculation that ranchers can't fight their herd instinct much longer. If even a small number of ranchers expand, the beef supply could rapidly grow. In addition, cattle numbers can be increased more quickly than in the past; because of genetic improvements, a steer can reach slaughter weight of about 1,150 pounds in as little as 14 months—which is several months less than it usually took in the 1970s.

Moreover, some ranchers must be buying land because the price of grazing land has been rising. Mr. McGinley worries that low milk prices could prompt Congress to repeat a program it once enacted of paying dairy farmers to slaughter milkcows, thus creating a meat glut.

"I can't say yet that things have permanently changed," he says as he lifts a bag of salt from the back of his truck and carries it to a wooden feedbox beside a windmill. "If times stay this good I'm not convinced that a bust won't happen again."

For now, that fear is keeping him and other ranchers from expanding.

—*Scott Kilman*

SOURCE: *The Wall Street Journal*, July 23, 1991, p. 1. Reprinted by permission of *The Wall Street Journal*, © 1991 Dow Jones & Company, Inc. All Rights Reserved Worldwide.

USE YOUR ECONOMIC REASONING

1. **Does cattle ranching qualify as a purely competitive industry? Why or why not?**

2. **Even though cattle ranching is presently quite profitable, ranchers seem very concerned about the future. Use the competitive model to explain their concern.**

3. **The cattle industry has historically been characterized by alternating periods of boom and bust. Provide an explanation for this recurring cycle.**

4. **How are ranchers attempting to avoid the "bust" stage of the cycle? Why do continuing high cattle prices make it difficult to avoid an eventual downturn? (Note: Falling prices for cattle futures contracts—contracts to deliver cattle at a specified date in the future—imply that speculators expect cattle prices to fall.)**

EXHIBIT 5.9

The Competitive Firm in Long-Run Equilibrium

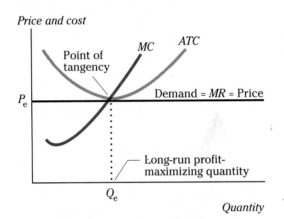

In long-run equilibrium, the competitive firm will earn only a normal profit. This is indicated in the graph by the tangency between the demand curve, or price line, and the ATC *curve at the profit-maximizing output (where* MR(P) = MC*). The equality of price and minimum* ATC *indicates the firm is achieving* production efficiency. *The equality of price and marginal cost signals that the firm is also achieving* allocative efficiency.

economy, all of our scarce resources would be allocated or distributed so as to produce the precise mix of products that consumers desire the most.

How do we know when the correct amount of a product is being produced? Allocative efficiency requires that price equals marginal cost ($P = MC$). To understand why this is true, it is necessary to reexamine the concepts of price and marginal cost. The price of a product reflects the value that consumers place on an additional unit of the item. Marginal cost, on the other hand, represents the opportunity cost of the resources that are used up in producing that additional unit. For instance, if the marginal cost of an additional unit of lumber were $200, society would have to do without $200 worth of alternative goods—whatever products the same amount of raw materials, labor, and capital could have produced—in order to obtain this unit of lumber. When $P = MC$, the value that consumers place on an additional unit of the product is exactly equal to the value of the other things they must give up in order to produce that product.

To illustrate why allocative efficiency is important, consider a situation where resources are being allocated *in*efficiently. Suppose that lumber is selling for $300 a unit, while the marginal cost of producing another unit is $270. The production of an additional unit of lumber would allow consumers to receive something valued at $300, while sacrificing alternative products valued at only $270. Clearly, society would be better off if these resources were allocated to the production of lumber rather than to alternative goods.

Next, consider a situation in which lumber is selling for $300 a unit, but the marginal cost of producing another unit is $330. Here the production of another unit of lumber would require consumers to sacrifice alternative products valued at $330 in order to obtain lumber worth only $300. Society would be better off if these resources were allocated to the production of things other than additional lumber.

Our point is that an efficient allocation of resources requires that each product be produced up to the point at which price is equal to marginal cost. When that occurs, the value of the last unit of output produced is exactly equal to the value of the alternative goods that must be sacrificed for its production. Pure competition ensures this outcome. In order to maximize profits, the purely competitive firm must produce where $MR\ (P) = MC$ (see Exh. 5.9). Therefore pure competition would ensure the efficient allocation of resources.

Let's synthesize what we have just discussed: Under conditions of pure competition, producers seeking their own self-interest are guided by the presence or absence of profits to produce the right amounts of the products that consumers desire the most. The forces of competition also lead to long-run equilibrium, where all firms in the industry operate at the lowest possible average cost (minimum *ATC*) and receive a price just equal to that cost. Thus, in the long run, consumers are able to purchase their most-desired products at the lowest possible prices.

Summary

A *firm* is the basic producing unit in a market economy, and an *industry* is a group of firms that produce similar or identical products. A purely competitive industry is one in which (1) a large number of sellers (firms) each produce a small fraction of the total industry supply; (2) the products offered by the different sellers are identical in the minds of consumers; and (3) no substantial barriers exist to prevent firms from entering or leaving the industry. Although no industries fully meet these conditions, the model of pure competition provides a standard by which to judge the performance of less-competitive industries and helps us to predict price and output behavior in industries that come reasonably close to meeting the assumptions of the model.

The model of pure competition assumes that firms are profit maximizers; that is, they are always attempting to earn the most profit possible. *Profit* is the excess of a firm's total revenue over its total cost. When a firm's total costs exceed its total revenue, the firm is incurring a *loss.*

All costs can be classified as either fixed or variable. *Fixed costs* are costs that do not vary with the level of output. *Variable costs* are costs that do change with the level of output. *Total cost* is simply the sum of the fixed and variable costs incurred by the firm.

The purely competitive firm may be described as a *price taker;* it accepts the price determined by market forces. The only variable that a purely competitive firm can control in order to influence its profit position is the level of output. In order to reach its profit-maximizing level of output, a firm should produce at the point where marginal revenue equals marginal cost. For the purely competitive firm, the price taker, *marginal revenue (MR)* is equal to price or average revenue per unit sold. *MR* is the revenue earned from selling one more unit of output. *Marginal cost (MC)* is the additional cost of producing one more unit. *MC* is a more important concept than *average total cost (ATC)* because *MC* determines the level of output that earns maximum profit.

In the long run, firms in a purely competitive industry tend to earn a *normal profit,* the amount that the owners' resources could earn elsewhere; earning normal profit means breaking even. Above-normal profits are called *economic profits,* and below-normal profits are called *economic losses.* If economic profits exist in the short run, the entrance of additional firms will cause an increase in supply and drive down the market price to the level of zero economic profits, where all firms are breaking even at normal profit. If losses exist, firms will exit the industry until price has risen to a level consistent with normal profits.

When *long-run equilibrium* is finally established, the purely competitive firm will be producing at minimum *ATC,* the point where its *ATC* curve is tangent to its demand curve. When firms operate at minimum *ATC,* *production efficiency* exists. This is a desirable outcome because it indicates that the fewest possible scarce resources are being used to produce the product, and therefore more of society's unlimited wants are being met. In addition to production efficiency, pure competition leads to *allocative efficiency:* the production of the goods and services consumers want the most in the quantities they desire. An efficient allocation of resources requires that each product be produced up to the point at which price is equal to marginal cost. Pure competition ensures this outcome. Thus we can say that the purely competitive firm achieves both production efficiency and allocative efficiency in long-run equilibrium.

Glossary

Allocative efficiency. Using society's scarce resources to produce in the proper quantities the products that consumers value the most.

Average fixed cost (AFC). Total fixed cost divided by the number of units being produced.

Average total cost (ATC). Total cost divided by the number of units being produced.

Average variable cost (AVC). Total variable cost divided by the number of units being produced.

Economic profit. The amount by which total revenue exceeds total cost, including the opportunity cost of owner-supplied resources. (Also called an above-normal profit.)

Economic loss. The amount by which total cost, including all opportunity costs, exceeds total revenue.

Firm. The basic producing unit in a market economy. It buys economic resources and combines those resources to produce goods and services.

Fixed costs. Costs that do not vary with the level of output.

Industry. A group of firms that produce identical or similar products.

Long-run equilibrium. A situation in which the size of an industry is stable: There is no incentive for additional firms to enter the industry and no pressure for established firms to leave it.

Marginal cost (MC). The additional cost of producing one more unit of output.

Marginal revenue (MR). The additional revenue to be gained by selling one more unit of output.

Normal profit. An amount equal to what the owners of a business could have earned had their resources been employed elsewhere; the opportunity cost of owner-supplied resources.

Price taker. A firm that must accept price at a given that is beyond its control.

Production efficiency. Producing a product at the lowest possible average total cost. The essence of production efficiency is that each product be produced with as few scarce resources as possible.

Total cost (TC). Total fixed cost plus total variable cost.

Total revenue (TR). The total receipts of a business from the sale of its product. Total revenue is calculated by multiplying the selling price of the product times the number of units sold.

Variable costs. Costs that change with the level of output, tending to increase when output increases and decrease when output declines.

Study Questions

Fill in the Blanks

1. A purely competitive firm is sometimes described as a _____ _____ because it must accept the price dictated by the market.

2. The demand curve of the purely competitive firm is a _____ _____ line at the price determined in the market.

3. Costs that don't vary with output are called _____ costs; costs that vary with output are called _____ costs.

4. A business that has no output must still pay its _____ costs.

5. _____ cost is the additional cost of producing one more unit of output.

6. Average total cost, _____ cost, and _____ cost all graph as U-shaped curves.

7. If a competitive firm wants to maximize its profits, it should continue to produce additional units so long as _____ is greater than or equal to _____ .

8. If economic profits exist in the short run, they will tend to be _____ _____ in the long run as firms _____ the industry and depress market price.

9. If losses exist in the short run, firms will tend to _____ the industry in the long run. This will reduce market _____ and help to push price back up.

10. When $P = MC$, _____ efficiency exists; when a firm produces its product at minimum ATC, _____ efficiency exists.

Multiple Choice

1. Which of the following is not characteristic of a purely competitive industry?
   a) A large number of sellers
   b) Identical products
   c) Substantial barriers to entry
   d) Relatively small firms

2. Which of the following is the best example of a price taker?
   a) General Motors
   b) Big Bob's Burger Barn
   c) IBM
   d) An average wheat farmer

Answer questions 3, 4, and 5 on the basis of the following information:

QUANTITY	TOTAL COST
0	$10
1	18
2	23
3	30
4	42

3. The firm's fixed cost is
   a) $5.
   b) $42.
   c) $23.
   d) $10.

4. The marginal cost of the third unit would be
   a) $30.
   b) $7.
   c) $10.
   d) $5.

5. If the firm produced three units, average total cost would be
   a) $10.
   b) $30.
   c) $7.
   d) None of the above

6. Which of the following is least likely to be a variable cost?
   a) The cost of raw materials
   b) Insurance payments
   c) The wages of production workers
   d) Shipping expenses

7. *Price and cost*

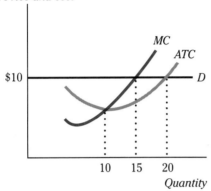

The firm depicted above should
a) produce 10 units and maximize its profits.
b) produce 15 units and maximize its profits.
c) produce 10 units and minimize its losses.
d) produce 15 units and minimize its losses.
e) shut down.

8. *Price and cost*

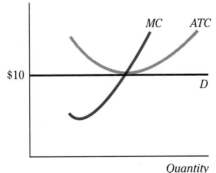

The firm depicted above is
a) facing a loss.
b) making an economic profit.
c) making a normal profit.
d) about to go out of business.

9. *Price and cost*

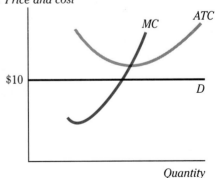

The firm represented above is
a) earning a profit.
b) facing a loss.
c) not a competitive firm.
d) breaking even.

10. If the firms in an industry are earning economic profits,

   a) additional firms will enter the industry and the supply curve will shift to the left.

   b) some firms will decide to leave the industry and the supply curve will shift to the left.

   c) additional firms will enter the industry and the supply curve will shift to the right.

   d) some firms will leave the industry and the supply curve will shift to the right.

Problems and Questions for Discussion

1. Even when an industry does not meet the first two requirements of pure competition, if barriers to entry are low, consumers will still benefit. Why?

2. Complete the following:

QUANTITY	TC	TVC	TFC	MC	ATC
0	$ 50				
1	100				
2	130				
3	180				
4	260				
5	380				

3. One reason for the declining prices of hand-held calculators may be the fat profits earned by early producers. Explain

4. Can you think of any undesirable aspects of pure competition? From the consumer's standpoint? From the producer's standpoint?

5. Why would a firm continue to operate even though it is incurring a loss? When should it decide to shut down?

6.
QUANTITY	TOTAL COST
0	$ 50
1	100
2	130
3	180
4	260
5	380

If the prevailing price of this firm's product is $50, how many units of output should it produce? Would it earn a profit or incur a loss? How much profit or loss?

7.

QUANTITY	MARGINAL COST
1	$20
2	10
3	30
4	40
5	50

If the prevailing price of our product is $35 and our total fixed costs are $15, how many units of output should we produce? What will be the amount of our profit or loss?

8. Draw the diagrams necessary to show the purely competitive firm and industry in long-run equilibrium.

9. In long-run equilibrium, the purely competitive firm is forced to produce where price equals minimum *ATC*. Why is that good news for consumers?

10. What is meant by allocative efficiency? Why must a firm produce where $P = MC$ in order for allocative efficiency to exist?

Answer Key

Fill in the Blank Questions

1. price taker
2. horizontal
3. fixed, variable
4. fixed
5. Marginal
6. average variable, marginal
7. marginal revenue, marginal cost
8. eliminated, enter
9. exit, supply
10. allocative, production

Multiple Choice

1. c	3. d	5. a	7. b	9. b
2. d	4. b	6. b	8. c	10. c

THE FIRM WITH MARKET POWER

In the world of pure competition, the individual firm is a price taker—it has no pricing discretion of its own because price is determined by the impersonal forces of supply and demand. The individual seller manipulates only production output, deciding how much or how little to offer for sale at the given price.

We saw in Chapter 5 that lumber manufacturers, wheat farmers, cattle ranchers, and some other agricultural producers are price takers. However, most sellers in the United States economy possess a degree of pricing discretion or *market power:* some ability to influence the market price of their products. Chapter 6 examines the process through which firms with pricing discretion select their prices and considers how the existence of market power can distort the allocation of scarce resources. It goes on to explore some actual pricing techniques employed by businesses and evaluate the extent to which these techniques make use of economic theory.

The Acquisition
of Market Power

There are two basic ways in which a firm may acquire market power: (1) through *product differentiation,* distinguishing its product from similar products offered by other sellers, and (2) by gaining control of a significant fraction of total industry output. Sellers with either or both of these abilities can exert some influence on the market price of their product; sellers that possess neither ability are powerless to influence price.

Product Differentiation as a Source of Market Power

Product differentiation promotes market power by convincing buyers that a particular firm's product is unique or superior and therefore worth a higher price than the products offered by competitors. By claiming superiority, manufacturers of brand-name aspirin tablets manage to obtain prices that are substantially higher than those charged by sellers of generic and store-brand analgesics. By associating uniqueness with status, the makers of designer-label jeans are able to sell their product at prices much higher than nameless jeans can command.

Sellers can differentiate their products in a wide variety of ways. Some product differentiation is based on real, albeit slight, product differences; in other cases the essential differentiation is created by advertising and promotional efforts. Both types of product differentiation allow the seller to distinguish its product from the competition and thereby acquire pricing discretion that is not available to the purely competitive firm.

Control Over Supply as a Source of Market Power

Firms that cannot differentiate their products successfully must turn elsewhere to acquire market power. Sellers of standardized commodities such as steel and oil can gain pricing discretion by controlling a significant share of the industry output of that product. In the 1970s, for example, when Arab oil producers controlled a substantial fraction of the world's oil production, they drove up prices simply by cutting back on production. The reduced supply created a shortage at the existing price, and users bid up the price as they

The neighborhood pizzeria possesses a modest amount of pricing discretion.

competed for the available supplies. United States steel-producing firms have also cooperated to restrict supply and maintain high prices, though the market power of these firms has declined substantially in recent years due to foreign competition. De Beers Consolidated Mines Ltd., a South African firm, hasn't found competition to be much of a problem. The article on page 178 examines the substantial market power enjoyed by this firm and looks at the methods that it has employed to maintain that power.

Degrees of Market Power

It stands to reason that all firms would like to possess as much market power as possible. But some firms succeed to a greater extent than others. The local telephone company and the local producer of electric power are obvious examples of firms with substantial market power. Here a single firm is the entire industry and has complete control over the industry's output, giving it substantial pricing discretion. Because of the potentially exploitive market power these firms possess, their rates are commonly regulated by state or local government agencies in an attempt to protect the public from unreasonable prices.

Few firms possess the potential market power enjoyed by the local phone company. The neighborhood dry-cleaning establishment and the nearby pizzeria also have market power, but not very much. These establishments can charge somewhat higher prices than their competitors because they offer convenient locations and/or slightly different products. But their prices cannot be much higher than those of other firms because their products are very similar. In Chapter 7, we'll take a closer look at the degrees of market power that exist in different types of industries. For now, the important thing to remember is that most firms possess at least some pricing discretion; they are not price takers.

Price Searching

Firms with pricing discretion are sometimes described as *price searchers,* which means that although they have some freedom in setting prices, they still must search for the profit-maximizing price. A price searcher may possess substantial market power (as the local telephone company) or very little (as the local pizzeria), but all price searchers have one thing in common: Unlike price takers, who will lose all their customers if they raise their prices, price searchers can charge more and still retain some customers. Conversely, while price takers can sell any quantity they desire at the market price, price searchers must reduce price to sell more.

Consider as a hypothetical example Woodstuff Inc., a small manufacturer of executive desks. Although there are a number of firms that produce such office furniture, we can be sure that if Woodstuff raises the price of its desks, it won't lose all its customers so long as it keeps its price within reason. Some customers will prefer the quality or design of the Woodstuff desks to those offered by other sellers. Others may be swayed by the firm's product warranty or by its record for prompt delivery. Still others may be influenced by the firm's policy of accepting old desks in trade or by the variety of payment plans it offers. For all these reasons and others, Woodstuff will still sell some desks despite a price increase. But it won't be able to sell the same quantity; it will have to choose between selling more desks at a lower price or fewer desks at a higher price. That's the fundamental dilemma faced by all price searchers.

The Price Searcher's Demand Curve

Since price searchers have to reduce their prices in order to sell a higher quantity, they must face downward-sloping demand curves, not the horizontal demand curves confronting price takers. Exhibit 6.1 depicts the demand curve facing our hypothetical desk manufacturer. It shows that at $900 a desk, Woodstuff will sell only three desks each week. At $600, it will sell nine desks

How De Beers Revived World Diamond Cartel after Zaire's Pullout

From the mines of Africa to the counters of Tiffany, De Beers Consolidated Mines Ltd. has dominated the diamond business for more than half a century by maintaining an iron grip on supplies. In any given year, at least 80% of the world's uncut diamonds pass through its hands.

Two years ago, however, it appeared that the South African concern's mighty empire was unraveling. A sharp drop in demand sent retail diamond prices plummeting and the market into disarray. Zaire, the world's largest producer of diamonds, dropped De Beers as its marketing agent and began selling diamonds independently. Huge new diamond discoveries in Australia threatened to swamp the market.

De Beers fought back in a globe-spanning campaign. . . . A closer look at just how De Beers acted to protect its interests offers insight into the workings of one of history's great cartels. . . .

The world diamond cartel's success derives in part from its structure and De Beers's role as sole middleman between diamond-producing nations and dealers. By almost single-handedly dictating how the cartel runs, De Beers has been able to moderate the internal discord that has undermined other cartels. Only De Beers buys from producers and sells to dealers, usually setting the price on each end.

De Beers obtains uncut diamonds either from its own mines or other mines that sell through the cartel. It offers the diamonds to the dealers it invites to periodic gatherings known as "sights." Each dealer is offered a box containing various uncut diamonds. De Beers determines which diamonds go into which box, and assigns a single price to each box.

A dealer generally must accept or reject the box he is shown; De Beers rarely negotiates. Those who don't buy risk not being invited back. This arrangement allows De Beers to parcel out diamonds in such a way as to maintain price stability.

By early 1981, however, De Beers's principal concern was to keep prices from collapsing in the face of high interest rates and a world recession in diamonds. Harry Oppenheimer lamented in De Beers's annual report that year: "We haven't gone through such hard times since I entered the business 50 years ago during the Depression of the '30s."

Restricting Supplies

To protect the cartel, De Beers began to restrict supplies, holding as much as 60% of production off the market. By the end of 1982, the inventory of diamonds in De Beers's vaults had risen to $1.7 billion from $570 million in 1979. "De Beers had the guts to commit hundreds of millions of dollars to sop up diamonds," says Allen Ginsberg, the president of the international diamond division of Zale Corp., a major U.S. jewelry retailer.

De Beers also cut production at its own mines and reduced its purchases from diamond mines outside South Africa. According to one source, the company gave financial help to at least one diamond-producing nation hurt by those cutbacks. . . .

Amid this retrenchment came a second blow: one of the most serious internal rebellions in the cartel's history. Zaire, long considered the linchpin of the cartel, had been voicing its dissatisfaction with the arrangement ever since the late 1970s. De Beers had maintained control there through an exclusive concession to market output from the Miba mine, Zaire's largest. But Zaire's complaints intensified, particularly about the 25% sales commission that De Beers charged. Apparently in response, De Beers in 1978 lowered its commission to 20%.

It wasn't enough. . . . Zaire pulled out of the cartel. In May 1981, it signed a five-year agreement with three independent diamond dealers to market Miba's output.

The loss of Zaire had more symbolic than financial effect on De Beers. Most of Zaire's vast output is low-priced, industrial-grade diamonds known as *boart*. In 1980, Zaire's diamonds accounted for less than 5% of the cartel's sales. The real danger was that Zaire's departure might encourage other black African nations to follow suit. "It was a chink in the armor that, if left unrepaired, could grow dangerously," says Zale's Mr. Ginsberg.

De Beers lost no time in making repairs. Though it was then stockpiling most grades of diamonds, the company began selling large quantities of boart from its inventory. This, combined with a generally weakening market, caused boart prices to fall by two-thirds over a two-year period. . . .

Zaire . . . dumped the three dealers in mid-contract and rejoined the cartel.

The other major threat to the cartel began half a world away in the vast state of Western Australia where, in 1979, an epic diamond deposit was discovered.

De Beers could ill afford to let the Argyle mine, as it is known, remain outside the cartel. By 1985, estimated production there could be 25 million carats annually, or about a quarter of current world production. . . .

But De Beers soon hit roadblocks. Rees Towie, then the chairman of Northern Mining Co., a 5% owner of Argyle, publicly charged that De Beers had undervalued diamond samples from the mine. He pressed his partners to consider alternative marketing agents.

De Beers's Victory

Political opposition heated up, culminating in October 1981, when then-Prime Minister Malcolm Fraser told the Australian Parliament he saw "no advantage" in a deal that would "only serve to strengthen a South African monopoly." At the time, his remark was widely thought to have killed De Beers's chances.

Yet the company went on to win the rights to Argyle, with help from its Australian friends. The majority partners pushed ahead on negotiations with De Beers, and the two sides announced a tentative agreement in early 1982. Sir Charles Court, the premier of the state of Western Australia, favored the agreement. The state government—which has a major say in mining matters—eventually ratified the agreement with De Beers.

Sir Charles, now retired, says he favored De Beers because "it is better to deal with people who have strength, especially during times of economic uncertainty." Eventually, the national government backed down. . . .

—John R. Emshwiller and Neil Behrmann

SOURCE: *The Wall Street Journal*, July 7, 1983, p. A1. Reprinted by permission of *The Wall Street Journal.* © 1983 Dow Jones & Company, Inc. All Rights Reserved Worldwide.

BEST FRIENDS

USE YOUR ECONOMIC REASONING

1. **What evidence is there in the article to suggest that De Beers enjoys substantial market power? What is the source of that market power?**

2. **How has De Beers managed to maintain high diamond prices in periods of weak demand?**

3. **Why did Zaire change its mind and decide to once again market its diamonds through De Beers?**

4. **Why was it important to De Beers to control the marketing of the diamonds produced by Zaire and Australia?**

EXHIBIT 6.1

The Price Searcher's Demand Curve

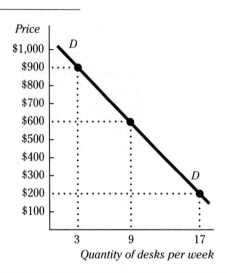

A price searcher can select any price it wants, but it must accept the quantity that results from that price. For example, Woodstuff can charge $900 per desk and sell three desks each week; or it can charge $600 per desk and sell nine desks a week; or it can charge $200 and sell seventeen desks per week.

a week. Of course, at $200 a desk, sales will be even higher—seventeen desks a week. While the price searcher can select any price it wants, it cannot choose a high price ($900 a desk) and expect to sell a high quantity (seventeen desks a week), because that's not a point on the demand curve. Thus even a price searcher finds that its actions are constrained by its demand curve; it cannot choose a price without being locked into a quantity. The firm's task, then, is to decide which of the price-quantity combinations it prefers in order to maximize its profit.

The Profit-Maximization Rule

For a price searcher the profit-maximization rule is essentially the same as it is for a price taker: Produce where marginal revenue equals marginal cost. The difference between a price searcher and a price taker is not in the logic used to maximize profits but in the environment confronting the seller. The price taker has no control over price, so it uses the profit-maximization rule solely to determine the optimal level of output. The price searcher, on the other hand, uses this rule to determine both output and price.

Calculating Marginal Revenue

The first step in determining the profit-maximizing price and quantity is finding the price searcher's marginal revenue curve. Because a price searcher faces a downward-sloping demand curve, it must reduce price to sell more. Consequently the marginal revenue that the price searcher gains by selling an additional unit of output will always be *less* than the selling price of the product (not equal to the price, as under pure competition), and the firm's marginal revenue curve will lie inside its demand curve. Since this idea is conveyed best with an example, let's consider Exh. 6.2.

The first two columns of Exh. 6.2 represent the demand schedule for desks that was graphed in Exh. 6.1. You can see that at a price of $1,000, only one desk will be sold each week. At a price of $950, two desks will be sold each week and total revenue would increase to $1,900. What will be the marginal revenue from selling a second desk? (Remember, marginal revenue is the additional revenue gained by selling one more unit.) The correct answer is $900 ($1,900 − $1,000 = $900), $50 less than the $950 selling price. This relationship—marginal revenue being less than price—holds at all price

---

EXHIBIT 6.2

Marginal Revenue for a Price Searcher

PRICE PER UNIT	QUANTITY DEMANDED	TOTAL REVENUE	MARGINAL REVENUE
$1,050	0	$ 0	
1,000	1	1,000	$1,000
950	2	1,900	900
900	3	2,700	800
850	4	3,400	700
800	5	4,000	600
750	6	4,500	500
700	7	4,900	400
650	8	5,200	300
600	9	5,400	200
550	10	5,500	100
500	11	5,500	0
450	12	5,400	− 100

levels.[1] To understand why, we need to consider the price reduction in more detail.

When Woodstuff reduces the price of executive desks from $1,000 to $950, it allows the first customer—the one who would have paid $1,000—to acquire the product for $950. In return, the seller manages to attract an additional customer who is willing to pay $950, but wouldn't pay $1,000. The marginal revenue from the second desk is $900—the $950 the firm gains by selling one more unit *minus* the $50 lost by having to reduce the price on the first unit. Because marginal revenue is less than price, a price searcher's marginal revenue curve will always lie inside its demand curve (Exh. 6.3).

The Profit-Maximizing Price and Quantity

To maximize its profit (or minimize its loss), Woodstuff must produce at the output where marginal revenue is equal to marginal cost. This rule permits the firm to continue producing additional units only so long as those units add more to revenue than to costs. Exhibit 6.3 graphs Woodstuff's demand and marginal revenue curves along with its marginal cost curve. Note that the marginal cost curve has the U-shape introduced in Chapter 5, marginal cost declines initially and then rises as output is increased.

How many desks should Woodstuff produce and sell in order to maximize its profits? You can tell by studying the graph (or the table accompanying it) that the profit-maximizing (loss-minimizing) output is seven units per week. When output is less than seven units a week, marginal revenue exceeds marginal cost. For instance, the marginal revenue from the fifth unit of output is $600, while the marginal cost of that unit is only $300. That means Woodstuff will be $300 better off if it produces and sells that unit. The sixth unit doesn't make as great a contribution to the firm, but the marginal revenue of $500 still exceeds the marginal cost of $340, so the unit should be produced. The seventh unit adds $400 to revenue and $400 to cost, so seven units represents the profit-maximizing (loss-minimizing) output: the output where $MR = MC$. All subsequent units would add more to cost than to revenue, so their sale would either reduce the firm's profit or increase its loss.[2]

Once the profit-maximizing output has been determined, the profit-maximizing price can be discovered by drawing a line directly up to the firm's demand curve and over to the vertical axis. Remember, the demand curve shows the amount that consumers are willing to purchase at various

---

[1] Note that marginal revenue will always be equal to price for the first unit of output. For all subsequent units, marginal revenue will be less than price.

[2] Actually, in this example, the firm will earn the same profit (or incur the same loss) whether it sells six or seven units of output. The firm wants to operate where $MR = MC$ not because it benefits from the last unit sold, but because it benefits from each unit up to that point.

EXHIBIT 6.3

Determining the Profit-Maximizing Price

PRICE PER UNIT	QUANTITY OF DESKS	MARGINAL REVENUE	MARGINAL COST
:	:	:	:
$800	5	$600	$300
750	6	500	340
700	7	400	400
650	8	300	480
600	9	200	580
:	:	:	:

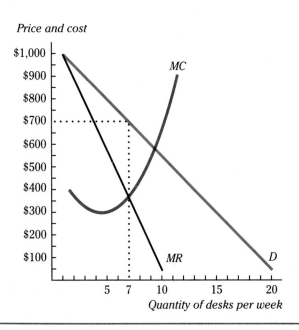

All firms maximize their profits (or minimize their losses) by producing at the output where marginal revenue is equal to marginal cost. In this example, the profit-maximizing output is seven units. Once the profit-maximizing output has been determined, the profit-maximizing price can be discovered by drawing a line directly up to the firm's demand curve and over to the vertical axis. In our example, the profit-maximizing price is $700 per desk.

prices. If we know the price, we can tell how much will be purchased. Conversely, if we know the quantity (output), we can use the demand curve to determine the maximum price that the firm can charge and still sell that amount of output. In our example, Woodstuff should charge a price of $700 per desk. That's the firm's profit-maximizing price.

USE YOUR ECONOMIC REASONING

Pricing Videos: A Rental-or-Sales Gamble

After weeks of speculation, Paramount Home Video is expected to announce on Thursday that "Ghost," one of the largest box-office hits of last year, will be released as a videocassette on March 21. Paramount sets no retail price on its videos, but using an industry formula based on the wholesale price that Paramount will probably charge distributors, "Ghost" should cost about $100.

The high price raises a question heard frequently in video stores. Why are some new hit movies priced low when they are first released and others priced four or five times as high? Why does "Pretty Woman," nearly as big a hit as "Ghost," cost $19.99 and "Total Recall," $24.99, when "Dick Tracy" is priced at $92.99 and "The Hunt for Red October" at $99.50?

"Customers are confused about prices," said Jack Messer, president of the Video Software Dealers Association. "They're particularly confused when two or three movies come out at the same time. How can one be $19 and the others $90?"

The answer, of course, has to do with profit, or rather potential profit. By offering a videocassette at a lower price, a studio is gambling that income from sales direct to consumers will exceed income from sales to rental outlets. Studios normally sell several hundred thousand cassettes to rental dealers at wholesale. . . .

By offering the film at the lower retail price, the studios are hoping that sales to the public will reach into the millions. . . .

Based on its performance in theaters, "Ghost," which many compare to "Pretty Woman" in its audience appeal, would seem a likely candidate for a lower sale price. Officials at Paramount won't comment on the coming release. . . .

. . . while rentals still dominate video, industry figures show that sales of hit movies—along with sales of older films and nontheatrical titles of all kinds—are the fastest-growing area of the industry.

Children's films, animated or otherwise, generally make the strongest candidates for sales. "The things that do best have great kid appeal because kids are the audience that will repeat them over and over," said Ron Castell, a senior vice president at Blockbuster, the nation's largest chain of video stores. Disney, for instance, has had many sales successes with its animated films— "Bambi," "Peter Pan," "The Little Mermaid"—as well as such theatrical titles as

"Honey, I Shrunk the Kids," which was released early last year. Each of those films carried a lower price tag.

"Pretty Woman" a Best Seller

But other types of films also sell well. One notable example is "Pretty Woman," which has been at or near the top of many best-seller lists since its release last October by Touchstone, a Disney company. The sales success of "Pretty Woman" is linked to its popularity among women and its musical score, among other reasons.

Action-adventure also sells strongly—"Indiana Jones and the Last Crusade," "Lethal Weapon 2" and "Total Recall," all released last year, are examples—provided that their helpings of sex and violence aren't objectionable to either consumers or outlets, particularly mass merchandisers anxious to preserve a family image. These films all sold for about $25.

Other sales titles perform well for reasons ranging from their stars to their collectibility as a genre or as part of a series ("Indiana Jones," for example), or suitability as gifts.

But many of those in the video business say it's a rare movie—a "Batman," "E.T.," "Top Gun," "Honey, I Shrunk the Kids," "Peter Pan," to name a few examples—that has sufficient mass appeal to make it more profitable for a studio to sell it than to make it a rental title. . . .

—*Peter M. Nichols*

SOURCE: Peter M. Nichols, "Pricing Videos: A Rental-or-Sales Gamble," *New York Times*, January 29, 1991, p. C11. Copyright © 1991 by The New York Times Company. Reprinted by permission.

USE YOUR ECONOMIC REASONING

1. What comments in the article suggest that Paramount and other producers of videos are price searchers rather than price takers?

2. How do studios decide which films to target for the rental market (with higher prices) and which to aim at the retail market? Can this be related to the price elasticity of demand?

3. Suppose that Paramount determines that it will maximize its profit on a new video by charging a price of $25 and selling one million units. Will the marginal revenue gained from the sale of the millionth unit be greater than, equal to, or less than $25? What can we say about the marginal *cost* of the millionth unit? (*Hint*: Try to picture this situation graphically.)

The article on page 184, "Pricing Videos: A Rental-or-Sales Gamble," illustrates that the search for the profit-maximizing price involves some uncertainty. We'll have more to say about that issue later in the chapter.

Evaluating the Short-Run Profit or Loss

As we discovered in Chapter 5, producing where *MR* = *MC* does not ensure a profit. It ensures only that the firm will do as well as possible in any short-run situation. Recall that we find profits by subtracting total costs from total revenue. In our present example, we can't tell whether Woodstuff Inc. is earning a profit or incurring a loss because we've focused entirely on marginal values.

To compute Woodstuff's short-run profit or loss, we need to know the firm's total revenue and its total costs. Exhibit 6.4 shows our hy-

EXHIBIT 6.4

Calculating the Short-Run Profit or Loss

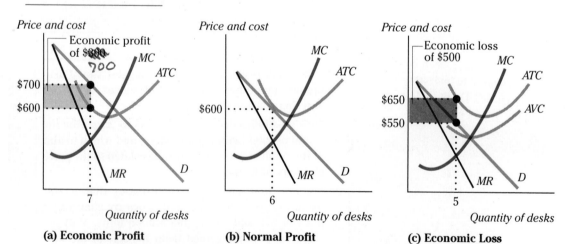

(a) Economic Profit   **(b) Normal Profit**   **(c) Economic Loss**

Case (a): When the profit-maximizing price is above ATC, the price searcher will earn an economic profit. Case (b): When the price is exactly equal to ATC the price searcher will earn a zero economic profit, or a normal profit. Case (c): When the price is less than ATC, the firm will incur an economic loss—it will earn less than a normal profit.

pothetical price searcher in three different situations. In case (a) the firm is earning a profit. As in the previous chapter, the amount of the profit can be determined by comparing total revenue with total cost. Total revenue is equal to $4,900 (the $700 selling price × 7 units—the profit maximizing output). Total cost is equal to $4,200 (the *ATC* of $600 × 7 units). This leaves the firm with an economic profit of $700 ($4,900 − $4,200 = $700).

Case (b) finds our price searcher earning only a normal profit. You can see in the diagram that the *MC* curve intersects the *MR* curve at an output of six desks. At that output, the profit-maximizing price would be $600, so total revenue would be $3,600 ($600 × 6 units). Since the *ATC* curve is tangent to the demand curve at $600, *ATC* must also be $600 when the firm is producing six desks. Therefore the firm's total cost is $3,600 (the *ATC* of $600 × 6 units). This means the firm is earning zero economic profit ($3,600 − $3,600 = $0), or a normal profit. Recall that a normal profit is acceptable; the owners of the business are earning as much as they could expect to earn if they invested their time and money elsewhere.

Case (c) depicts the price searcher facing a short-run economic loss (earning less than a normal profit). At the profit-maximizing (loss-minimizing) output of five desks, the firm's total cost of $3,250 (*ATC* of $650 × 5 units) exceeds its total revenue of $2,750 (the $550 selling price × 5 units). This results in a loss of $500 ($3,250 − $2,750 = $500). Note, however, that the selling price of $550 exceeds the firm's average variable cost of approximately $500, so the firm should continue to operate rather than shut down. Since *P* exceeds *AVC* by $50, each of the five units produced will contribute $50 toward paying the firm's fixed costs. Through continued operation, the firm reduces its loss by $250. Of course, if *AVC* exceeded price (for example, if the average variable cost curve were positioned where the *ATC* curve is presently located) the firm would minimize its loss by shutting down.

Barriers to Entry and Long-Run Profits

We've seen that in the short run a price searcher may gain economic profits, may earn a normal profit, may even sustain a loss. But how do they do in the long run? Is it possible for price searchers to earn economic profits in the long run, or is a normal profit the best that can be expected? (All firms, whether price searchers or price takers, must earn at least a normal profit in the long run, or the owners will sell out and reinvest their money where a normal return is possible.)

If a price searcher is earning an economic profit in the short run, its ability to continue earning that profit in the long run depends on the extent of the barriers to entering that industry. Some price searchers exist in industries with substantial entry barriers—automobile and aircraft manufacturing, for example. Others exist in industries with very modest barriers—shoe retailing, fast photo processing, and dry-cleaning establishments, to cite a few. Because entry barriers differ from industry to industry, we can't generalize about the long-run fate of price searchers as we could about the fate of price takers. (Recall that a normal profit is the *best* that a price taker can expect in the long run. Because there are no significant barriers to entering purely competitive industries, any short-run profits will be eliminated in the long run, as additional firms enter and drive down prices.)

If price searchers are protected by substantial barriers to entry, short-run profits can turn into long-run profits. For instance, it is estimated that Hoffman-La Roche of Switzerland earned multi*billion* dollar profits from the worldwide sale of its Valium and Librium tranquilizers, drugs that were protected by patents and therefore could not be duplicated by competitors.[3] While profits of this magnitude are clearly exceptional, they indicate the impact of entry barriers. In the absence of substantial barriers we expect economic profits to attract additional sellers into the market. This leads to price cutting and other forms of competition that have the potential to eliminate economic profits in the long run.

Thus the fact that a price searcher earns above-normal profits in the short run is no assurance that it will be able to do so in the long run. Unless entry barriers exist, the entrance of additional firms will result in added competition for consumers' dollars and subsequent elimination of all economic profits.

Price Searchers and Resource Allocation

Although the price searcher maximizes its profit by producing the output at which marginal revenue is equal to marginal cost, such a firm actually produces too little output from a societal standpoint.

Recall from Chapter 5 that an efficient allocation of resources requires that firms continue to produce each product up to the precise point

---

[3] F. M. Scherer, *Industrial Market Structure and Economic Performance*, 2d ed. (Chicago: Rand McNally, 1980), p. 449.

where its selling price *(P)* is equal to its marginal cost *(MC)*. This is desirable because *P* is a reflection of the value consumers place on an additional unit of the product in question, while *MC* represents the value of the alternative goods that must be sacrificed to produce the additional unit. If firms produce at the output where *P* = *MC*, the value of the last unit produced is exactly equal to the value of the alternative products sacrificed to obtain that unit. Alternatively, the benefit that consumers expect to derive from an additional unit of this product is exactly equal to the cost of producing that additional unit.

Price searchers distort the allocation of resources because they will not allow output to expand up to the point where *P* = *MC*. To do so would cause them to earn a smaller profit (or suffer a larger loss) than they earn by operating where *MR* = *MC*.

Consider Exh. 6.5. The profit-maximizing price searcher will produce where *MR* = *MC*, at seven units in this example. At that output, marginal revenue and marginal cost are equal. But if you move upward in the exhibit from seven units of output to the demand curve, you find that when

---

EXHIBIT 6.5

Price Searchers and Resource Misallocation

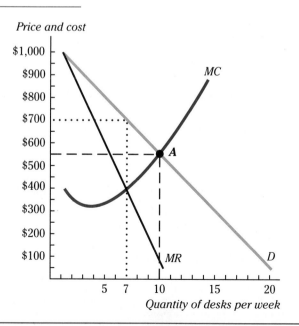

Price and cost

Quantity of desks per week

Allocative efficiency requires that production take place at the output where P = MC, *an output of 10 units in this example. But the profit-maximizing price searcher will produce where* MR = MC, *an output of seven units. By restricting output, price searchers fail to provide consumers with the optimal quantity of this product, and misdirect resources to the production of less-valued goods and services.*

MR and *MC* are equal to $400, price is equal to $700. Therefore price exceeds marginal cost at the profit-maximizing output. This tells us that society values an additional unit of this product more highly than the alternative products that could be produced with the same resources. In short, the price searcher is producing too little output; fewer resources are being allocated to the production of this product than is socially desirable.

An efficient allocation of resources would require the price searcher to produce at the output where the marginal cost curve intersects the demand curve (see point *A* in Exh. 6.5). If our hypothetical price searcher produced ten units of output and charged a price of $550 (so that *P* = *MC*), resources would be allocated efficiently. But that won't happen, because expanding output in this manner would cause the firm to earn a smaller profit. Note that for each unit beyond seven (the profit-maximizing output), marginal cost *exceeds* marginal revenue. Production of these additional units would lower the firm's total profit.

Thus price searchers distort the allocation of scarce resources by producing too little output and thereby forcing resources to be used in the production of less-valued products. In response to this resource misallocation, the federal government has employed a variety of means to encourage competition or correct for the negative impact of market power. (Chapter 7 will include a discussion of these efforts.)

Pricing in Practice

A firm's day-to-day pricing techniques may differ somewhat from the theoretically correct pricing practices that we have discussed thus far. This difference stems in part from the fact that firms are frequently guided by motives other than profit maximization. Ethical considerations, for example, may result in the pursuit of a "satisfactory" profit rather than a maximum profit. The quest for prestige is another motive that may cause the firm or its managers to maximize sales or market share, subject to some minimum profit constraint.[4] Firms pursuing objectives such as these will not select the price where *MR* = *MC*. For instance, if a firm wants to maximize sales, it will

---

[4] While firms may choose to pursue objectives other than profit maximization, they must strive to achieve at least a normal profit in the long run. Otherwise, they won't be able to attract the economic resources they need in order to remain in business. Thus, while some firms may not choose to pursue profit *maximization*, no firm can ignore profitability entirely.

choose a lower price (than the one that maximizes profit) to encourage additional customers to buy the product.

Even those firms motivated by the pursuit of maximum profit may find it difficult to employ the $MR = MC$ rule in precisely the manner we've described. In most real-world situations, pricing takes place in an environment beset with uncertainty. Firms seldom possess precise information about their demand and cost curves. These deficiencies force sellers to rely on other methods for determining price.

Cost-Plus Pricing

The most common technique for determining selling price is probably **cost-plus pricing** (or full-cost pricing, as it is sometimes called). In its simplest form the cost-plus method involves adding some percentage, or markup, to the cost of the goods acquired for sale. For example, a furniture store may pay $100 for a chair, mark it up 150 percent, and attempt to sell it for $250.

Firms using this method do not consider all their costs in arriving at the selling price. They assume that the markup on the **cost of goods sold** (the cost of the items they buy for resale) will be sufficient to cover all other costs—rent, utilities, wages, and salaries—and leave something for profit.

A more sophisticated version of the cost-plus technique attempts to ensure that *all* costs are recovered by building them into the price. Here the seller arrives at a price by determining first the average total cost *(ATC)* of producing the product or offering the service and then adding some margin for profit.

A Cost-Plus Example: Building a Boat. Let's assume that we have just purchased a boat manufacturing facility for $200,000. It has an expected useful life of twenty years and was designed with a production capacity of 1,000 boats per year. The estimated cost of materials is $150 per boat and estimated direct labor cost (the cost of the labor directly involved in the manufacture of the boat) is $200 per boat. Besides these variable costs, we have a variety of fixed costs—everything from utility payments to the salaries of security guards—that amount to $125,000 per year. Since our factory cost $200,000 and has a useful life of twenty years, we must also add $10,000 per year ($200,000/ 20 years) for *depreciation*—the reduction in the value of the production plant due to wear and tear and obsolescence.

Assuming that we expect to sell 1,000 boats this year, which would mean that we would be able to operate the plant at its designed capacity, we arrive at the following costs per boat:

Direct labor	$200.00
Materials	150.00

Depreciation on plant and equipment ($10,000 per year, or $10 per boat—i.e., $10,000 divided by 1,000 boats)	10.00
Fixed costs ($125,000 per year, or $125 per boat—i.e., $125,000 divided by 1,000 boats)	125.00
Total cost per boat (average total cost)	**$485.00**

Now that we have the average total cost of producing a boat, the final step in determining the selling price is adding on the markup that provides our profit margin. A number of factors seem to influence the size of the markup that firms strive to achieve. For instance, executives commonly mention the firm's assessment of what is a "fair" or "reasonable" profit margin.

Custom is another factor that seems to play a major role in some industries. Retailers, for example, often use a particular percentage markup simply because they have always used it or because it is the accepted, therefore "normal," markup in the industry. Obviously, a markup that endures long enough to become customary must be somewhat successful in allowing firms to meet their profit objectives. In fact it may indicate that these firms have discovered through informal means the price and output levels that would have emerged had they applied the theoretical $MR = MC$ rule.

A final factor influencing the size of the markup is the impact of competition. While a firm may desire high profit margins, ultimately the degree of actual and potential competition determines what margins the firm will be able to achieve. The more competitive the industry, the lower the profit margin.

Let's assume that we've considered all these factors and have decided to use a 10-percent markup on cost in determining our selling price. Our final step, then, is to add the 10-percent markup to the average total cost calculated earlier. The resulting value is the firm's selling price as determined by the cost-plus technique:

Total cost per boat (average total cost)	$485.00
Markup on cost (10 percent × $485)	48.50
Selling price	**$533.50**

Cost-Plus Pricing in Action. Cost-plus pricing has been criticized by economists as a naive pricing technique that ignores demand and competition and bases price solely on cost considerations. When the cost-plus technique is used in a mechanical or unthinking way, these criticisms are certainly valid. But that's seldom the case. Most businesses consider carefully the strength of demand and the degree of competition before selecting their markup or profit

Competition—like the competition between the fast-food retailers on this New York street corner—limits the profit margins that firms can achieve.

margin. In addition, the cost-plus price generally is viewed as a preliminary estimate, or starting point, rather than as the final price. Since demand and competition seldom can be measured with precision, the firm must be willing to adjust its price if it has misjudged market conditions. It is through these subjective adjustments that the firm gropes its way closer to the profit-maximizing price. A few examples may help to illustrate this point.

Example 1: The Department Store. A local department store receives its shipment of Nifty Popcorn Poppers just in time for the Christmas gift-buying season. It prices the item at $19.50 in order to earn a 30-percent markup on the popper's cost.

Two weeks later the store has sold 50 percent of the shipment, and Christmas is still six weeks away. The manager realizes that he has a "hot" selling item and that he won't be able to get any more from the manufacturer in time for Christmas. He decides to increase his markup (and consequently the product's selling price) in order to take advantage of the product's strong demand.

Example 2: The Car Dealer. A car dealer in a large metropolitan area has found that in the past several years she has been able to average a 15-percent profit margin on the cost of the automobiles she sells. Her experience has taught her that it is much easier to sell a car at a high markup early in the season, when people will pay to be among the first to own the new model, than later, when the next year's model is about to be announced. So the dealer instructs her sales personnel to strive for a 20–25-percent markup early in the year and settle for a 5–10-percent margin toward the end of the season.

Example 3: The Appliance Manufacturer. Acme Appliance manufactures refrigerators for sale to a regional market. In response to consumers' different budgets and "needs" in terms of optional features, the company offers two models: a basic model that is available only in white, and a deluxe model that offers additional features and comes in a variety of colors.

In pricing its product, Acme feels that a 10-percent markup on average cost will produce the desired rate of return on its investment. Rather than use a single markup percentage, however, Acme has decided to apply a 5-percent markup to the basic model and a 15-percent markup to the deluxe model, for an average markup of 10 percent. This decision was made because previous sales experience indicated that low-income customers are substantially more sensitive to price than intermediate- and high-income customers.

While the cost-plus technique is essentially straightforward, its application requires management personnel to make subjective judgments about the strength of demand and the degree of competition, as these examples illustrate. Both factors are difficult to evaluate and impossible to quantify. As a consequence, pricing remains more an art than a science.

Marginal Analysis and Managerial Decisions

As the foregoing examples indicate, firms that desire to maximize profits must adjust their cost-plus price to reflect market conditions; they cannot use the technique mechanically. Learning to "think marginally" can also lead to better decisions and greater profits.

The major limitation of the cost-plus technique is the fact that it doesn't rely on *marginal analysis:* a comparison of the additional revenue and the additional cost associated with a contemplated action. It concentrates instead on average values, stressing the need to recover all costs plus some markup. That can lead to smaller profits (or larger losses) than necessary, since (as we will see in a moment) marginal costs are the only relevant costs for many business decisions.

Although firms commonly lack the information required to use the *MR = MC* approach to price determination, they generally have some knowledge of marginal values. For instance, even though a firm probably does not know the marginal cost of producing the two hundred thousandth unit of output, usually it can determine the additional cost of producing some block of units—another 10,000 cars, for example. And probably it can discover the additional cost of some contemplated course of action, such as adding or discontinuing a product line. This information will allow a firm to improve the quality of many of its decisions.

To illustrate, suppose that you own a chain of fast-food restaurants that has traditionally opened for business at 11:00 A.M. What costs would you consider in deciding whether it would be profitable to open earlier in order to serve breakfast?

The cost-plus approach implies that the decision should be based on the full cost (or *fully allocated cost,* as it is sometimes called) of the new project—on the project's share of the firm's total costs. In other words, the breakfast meal would be expected to generate enough revenue to pay for the labor, utilities, and food used in the morning meal, plus a share of the firm's overhead costs (rent, insurance, equipment depreciation) and some profit margin. If you anticipate enough business to achieve that objective, you should open for business. Otherwise, you would remain closed.

Marginal analysis yields a different conclusion. According to marginal analysis, the only costs that are relevant to a decision are those that are actually influenced by the decision. In deciding whether or not to open for breakfast, you should *ignore* costs such as rent and insurance because these fixed costs will have to be paid whether or not the restaurants are open for breakfast. The only true cost of serving breakfast is the marginal cost: the increase in the restaurant's total cost that results from the breakfast meal. If the marginal revenue derived from serving breakfast is expected to exceed the marginal cost, you should open earlier. If not, you should continue to serve only the noon and evening meals.

Marginal analysis can often improve the quality of managerial decisions. Many projects that don't appear to be profitable when evaluated on the basis of their fully allocated costs look quite appealing when analyzed in terms of their marginal costs and revenues. By using marginal analysis and applying judgment to cost-plus prices, firms may be able to approximate the profit levels that would be achieved by using the *MR = MC* rule. The article on page 196, "Convenience Stores and Gas Stations Grow More Alike," illustrates how marginal analysis has improved the decisions of some small business owners.

Convenience Stores and Gas Stations Grow More Alike

When Bill Fonda started his chain of convenience stores in 1978, he didn't intend to sell gasoline. Today, all of his stores have gas pumps out front. When Sandy and Troy Smith opened their gas station in 1982, they planned to just "pump gas." Today, their station is a miniature convenience store, selling a variety of snacks as well as milk and other basic food items.

The Smiths attribute their change of heart to the experience they acquired in the first year of running the station. "After we'd owned the station for a while, we saw that we spent a lot of time sitting around doing nothing. We figured we might as well use our time stocking the store and waiting on customers," said Mrs. Smith. Mr. Fonda's experience was very similar. "I could see that our employees could easily handle gas customers without detracting from their other responsibilities," he said. "I couldn't see

any reason to let the gas stations get that business."

Jim Bosley, owner of a small chain of convenience stores in Kansas and Missouri, apparently uses the same logic. "I look at gasoline as an incremental item for my stores. The building is already there. The clerk is already being paid. The additional cost of pumping gas is almost nothing. I'm planning to have gas pumps in place at all of my stores by the end of this year."

Apparently Mr. Bosley's incremental approach has caught on. Most convenience stores are selling gasoline, and gas stations are busily building shelves to display snacks and other convenience items. In the future, the only way to distinguish a gas station from a convenience store may be the sign out front.

Fictitious news article based on events in the late 1980s.

USE YOUR ECONOMIC REASONING

1. Mr. Bosley says that he uses an "incremental approach." What other term might we use to describe his way of thinking?

2. Explain in terms of cost and revenue the logic embodied in the decisions made by Fonda, the Smiths, and Bosley.

3. Mr. Bosley says that the cost of pumping gas is almost nothing. What about the cost of the gas pumps and storage tanks? Should these costs be considered before deciding to sell gas? If so, explain how you would bring them into your decision. If not, explain why not?

Summary

In most U.S. industries individual firms have some pricing discretion, or *market power*. A firm may acquire market power either through *product differentiation*—distinguishing its product from similar products offered by other sellers—or by gaining control of a significant fraction of total industry output. Firms with either or both of these abilities can exert some influence on the market price of their product.

Sellers with pricing discretion are described as *price searchers* because they must search for the profit-maximizing price. All price searchers face demand curves that slope downward and to the right. Unlike the price taker that can sell as much as it desires at the market price, the price searcher has to reduce price to sell more. Therefore the price searcher is forced to choose between selling a low quantity at a high price or selling a high quantity at a low price.

Because price must be reduced in order to sell more, the marginal revenue the price searcher obtains from selling an additional unit of output is always less than the unit's selling price, and the price searcher's marginal revenue curve lies inside its demand curve. The price searcher can determine the profit-maximizing (loss-minimizing) level of output by equating marginal revenue and marginal cost. The profit-maximizing price can then be discovered by drawing a line directly up from the quantity to the firm's demand curve and over to the vertical (price) axis.

Like price takers, price searchers must determine the amount of their profit or loss by comparing total revenue and total cost. If total revenue exceeds total cost, the price searcher is earning an economic profit; if total cost exceeds total revenue, the firm is incurring an economic loss. When total revenue is exactly equal to total cost, a normal profit is being earned.

Although a normal profit is the most that a price taker can hope to earn in the long run, a price searcher may be able to do better. When price searchers are protected by substantial barriers to entry, they may continue to earn long-run economic profits.

The possibility of long-run profits is not the only outcome that distinguishes price searchers from price takers. In addition, price searchers fail to achieve allocative efficiency. Allocative efficiency requires that producers expand output up to the point where $P = MC$. While price takers do produce at this level, price searchers stop short of it. In other words, price searchers produce less output than is socially desirable.

The actual pricing techniques employed by businesses often differ from the theoretically correct procedures described by economists. While the $MR = MC$ approach would enable the firm to maximize its profits, the seller seldom has sufficient information to use this approach in the manner described. As a consequence, most price searchers resort to some other method for determining price. The most common technique is *cost-plus pricing*.

With cost-plus pricing, the seller arrives at the price by determining the average total cost *(ATC)* of producing a product and adding to this figure some margin for profit. While this technique seems quite straightforward, its application requires managers to make subjective judgments regarding strength of demand and degree of competition.

The major limitation of the cost-plus approach is the fact that it doesn't rely on *marginal analysis*. While firms seldom know precisely what their marginal cost and revenue curves look like, they generally have some knowledge of their marginal values. By undertaking activities that are expected to more than cover their marginal costs, firms can enlarge their profits or reduce their losses.

Glossary

Cost of goods sold. The cost of items purchased by a firm for resale.

Cost-plus pricing. The technique of determining price by adding some percentage or markup to the average total cost *(ATC)* of producing an item or acquiring it for sale.

Depreciation. The reduction in the value of a fixed asset (plant or equipment) because of physical deterioration and/or obsolescence.

Fully allocated cost. The full cost of a project or activity; the project's share of the firm's total cost.

Marginal analysis. A comparison of the additional revenue and the additional cost associated with a contemplated action.

Market power. Pricing discretion; the ability of a firm to influence the market price of its product.

Price searcher. A firm that possesses pricing discretion.

Product differentiation. Distinguishing a product from similar products offered by other sellers in the industry; accomplished through advertising, packaging, or physical product differences.

Study Questions

Fill in the Blanks

1. Firms that possess pricing discretion are sometimes described as _____ _____.

2. _____ creates market power by convincing buyers that a particular product is unique and superior.

3. A price searcher maximizes profit by equating _____ and _____.

4. For a price searcher, marginal revenue is (greater/less) _____ _____ than price.

5. In the short run, a price searcher that is incurring a loss will continue to operate rather than shut down, provided that price is greater than _____ _____ cost.

6. A price searcher will not be able to earn economic profits in the long run unless _____ exist.

7. It is difficult to apply the $MR = MC$ technique because firms seldom possess precise information about _____ and _____ _____.

8. One common method by which firms actually determine price is the _____ _____ technique.

9. In the final analysis, the markup used in the cost-plus technique is probably determined primarily by the degree of _____ in a market.

10. A major limitation of the cost-plus technique is the fact that it does not utilize _____ analysis.

Multiple Choice

1. Which of the following would probably *not* be a price searcher?
   a) The local utility company
   b) A Kansas wheat farmer
   c) General Motors
   d) A local movie theater

2. All price searchers
   a) face downward-sloping demand curves.
   b) must reduce price to sell more.
   c) can raise their prices without losing all their customers.
   d) possess some pricing discretion.
   e) All of the above

3. Both price searchers and price takers
   a) must produce homogeneous products.
   b) produce where *MR* = *MC* to maximize profits.
   c) face horizontal demand curves.
   d) must earn normal profits in the long run.

4. If a price searcher is operating where *MR* exceeds *MC*,
   a) it is producing the profit-maximizing output.
   b) it is producing too much to maximize profits.
   c) it is producing too little to maximize profits.
   d) none of the above is true.

Use the following exhibit to answer questions 5–7.

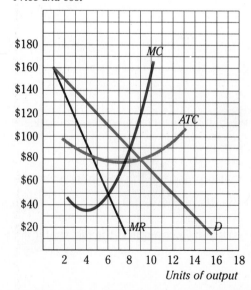

5. To maximize its profit or minimize its loss, this price searcher should
   a) produce six units and charge a price of $50.
   b) produce six units and charge a price of $110.
   c) produce eight units and charge a price of $90.
   d) produce nine units and charge a price of $80.

6. This price searcher is
   a) incurring a loss of $180.
   b) earning a normal profit.
   c) earning a profit of $360.
   d) earning a profit of $180.

7. Allocative efficiency would require this firm to
   a) produce seven and one-half units of output and charge a price of $78.
   b) produce eight units and charge a price of $90.
   c) produce six units and charge a price of $50.
   d) None of the above.

8. If a price searcher's fixed costs have increased,
   a) the firm's profit-maximizing quantity will increase.
   b) the firm's profit-maximizing quantity will not change.
   c) the firm's profit-maximizing quantity will decline.
   d) the firm will operate at a loss.

9. Sonic Waterbeds faces a traditional downward-sloping demand curve (included below), but its marginal cost curve is a horizontal straight line at a height of $600. In other words, marginal costs are constant at $600. How many units should Sonic sell, and what price should it charge to maximize profit?

PRICE (per bed)	QUANTITY (per day)
$1,000	1
900	2
800	3
700	4
600	5
500	6

   a) One unit at $1,000
   b) Two units at $900
   c) Three units at $800
   d) Four units at $700
   e) Five units at $600

10. Last week you purchased a bowling ball for $40. This week you've decided to give up bowling. Marginal analysis would suggest that you sell the bowling ball for
   a) whatever you can get.
   b) anything over $40.
   c) $40.
   d) $40 plus a normal profit.

Problems and Questions for Discussion

1. The price searcher's price and output decisions are one and the same. Explain.

2. Why is marginal revenue less than price for a price searcher? Illustrate with an example.

3. Why should consumers be concerned about the existence of barriers to entry?

4. Explain the cost-plus pricing technique.

5. Why is it often necessary to modify a result determined by the cost-plus method?

6. If a firm includes all its costs in its price by using the cost-plus method, will it ever show a loss? Explain.

7. The Springfield Bouncers, a new professional basketball team, want to rent the high school gymnasium on Sunday afternoons. How would you determine an appropriate rent? If they rejected your first offer, how would you determine the *minimum* acceptable rent?

8. Bland Manufacturing Company manufactures men's suits for sale throughout the Midwest. For the past five years, Bland has operated with about 20-percent unused capacity. Last month, a retailer on the West Coast offered to buy as many suits as Bland could supply as long as the price did not exceed $45 per suit. This price is substantially below the price Bland charges its regular customers. Given the information presented below, should Bland accept the offer? Why or why not?
   ATC at present output level (80,000 units) = $55
   ATC at capacity output (100,000 units) = $50
   Normal markup = 40% on ATC

9. Both price searchers and price takers produce at the output where $MR = MC$. Yet price takers achieve allocative efficiency, whereas price searchers do not. Please explain.

10. Suppose that a price searcher finds itself incurring a short-run loss. How should it decide whether to shut down or continue to operate? What would the price searcher's graph look like if it were in a shut-down situation?

Answer Key

Fill in the Blanks

1. price searchers
2. Product differentiation
3. marginal cost, marginal revenue
4. less
5. average variable
6. barriers to entry
7. demand conditions, cost conditions (or *MR* and *MC*)
8. cost-plus
9. competition
10. marginal (or incremental)

Multiple Choice

1. b
2. e
3. b
4. c
5. b
6. d
7. b
8. b
9. c
10. a

INDUSTRY
STRUCTURE AND
PUBLIC POLICY

Nearly all the firms in our economy enjoy some pricing discretion, or market power. In Chapter 6, we saw how these firms determine their prices, and we considered the impact of market power on the allocation of scarce resources. Chapter 7 takes a closer look at the degrees of market power that exist in different industries and considers how the makeup or structure of an industry influences the amount of pricing discretion enjoyed by its individual firms. This chapter also explores the impact of market power on consumer welfare and examines the role of antitrust enforcement and government regulation in limiting that power.

Industry Structure
and Market Power

You have learned that a firm may acquire market power either through product differentiation—distinguishing its product from similar products offered by other sellers—or by gaining control of a significant fraction of total industry output. The degree of product differentiation and the extent to which a firm is able to control industry output are related to the structure of the industry in which the firm operates. **Industry structure** is the makeup of an industry as determined by certain factors: (1) the number of sellers and their size distribution (all sellers approximately the same size as opposed to some much larger than others); (2) the nature of the product; (3) the extent of barriers to entering or leaving the industry. Note that these factors correspond to the three assumptions of the competitive model discussed early in Chapter 5.

EXHIBIT 7.1

Industry Structure: A Preview

PURE COMPETITION	MONOPOLISTIC COMPETITION	OLIGOPOLY	PURE MONOPOLY
1. Many sellers, each small in relation to the industry. 2. Identical products 3. No substantial barriers to entry. *Examples:* Many agricultural industries and a few manufacturing industries (cotton weaving) come close. **No pricing discretion**	1. Many sellers, each small in relation to the industry. 2. Somewhat differentiated products. 3. No substantial barriers to entry. *Examples:* Retail trade (hair salons, restaurants, gas stations) and a few manufacturing industries (men's suits and women's dresses). **Modest pricing discretion**	1. Few sellers, large in relation to the industry. 2. Identical or differentiated products. 3. Substantial barriers to entry. *Examples:* Steel and aluminum manufacturing (identical products); automobile and cigarette manufacturing (differentiated products). **Modest to substantial pricing discretion**	1. A single firm is the sole supplier. 2. Unique product; no close substitutes exist. 3. Substantial barriers to entry. *Examples:* Local telephone and utility companies. **Substantial pricing discretion**

There are four basic industry structures: pure competition, monopolistic competition, oligopoly, and pure monopoly. Their characteristics are summarized in Exh. 7.1. You are already familiar with pure competition, so we will use that model to open our discussion of the relationship between industry structure and market power.

Pure Competition

As you learned in Chapter 5, firms that operate in a purely competitive industry are price takers and lack market power for two reasons. First, because they produce and sell identical products, no one firm can expect consumers to pay a higher price than they would pay elsewhere. Such firms must be content with the price dictated by the market.

Second, because the purely competitive firm is quite small in relation to the industry, it cannot affect the total industry supply enough to alter the market price. It cannot, for instance, push up prices the way the Arab oil producers did in the 1970s. That cannot happen in wheat or corn production or any other industry that approximates pure competition. In these industries the individual seller supplies such a small fraction of total industry output that the firm is not in a position to alter the market price by reducing production. Once again, the purely competitive firm has no choice but to accept the price that is dictated by the market.

Monopolistic Competition

Few industries in the U.S. economy approximate pure competition. Monopolistic competition is a much more common industry structure. Most of the retailers with whom you do business each week are firms in monopolistically competitive industries: restaurants, gas stations, grocery stores, hair salons, and photo processors, to name just a few examples. In addition, some manufacturers, such as those making wooden furniture, women's dresses, and men's suits, operate in monopolistically competitive industries.

Like pure competition, *monopolistic competition* is characterized by a large number of relatively small sellers and by modest barriers to entering the industry. The feature that distinguishes monopolistic competition from pure competition is product differentiation. Each monopolistically competitive firm sells a product that is slightly different from those of other firms in the industry. Firms compete on price *and* through product differentiation. Products are differentiated by style, quality, packaging, the location of the seller, advertising, the services offered by the firm (free delivery, for example), and other real or imagined characteristics.

As the term suggests, a monopolistically competitive firm is part monopolist and part competitor. It is a monopolist because it is the only firm selling its unique product; it is competitive because there are a large number of firms selling products that are close substitutes. We all have a favorite pizza parlor. It is a monopolist in the limited sense that no other restaurant offers exactly the same food, service, atmosphere, and location. On the other hand, our pizza parlor is in competition with dozens, perhaps hundreds, of other restaurants that sell pizza and substitutes for pizza as well. Your neighborhood hardware store and clothing retailer are in a similar situation. They may have convenient locations and offer some brand names that are not available elsewhere, but they face substantial competition from other sellers of similar products.

Monopolistic Competition and Market Power

Insofar as it sells a unique product, each monopolistically competitive firm has some pricing discretion. In other words, it is a price searcher rather than a price taker. If a monopolistic competitor raises the price of its product, it will lose some customers but not all of them. Some will still prefer the product because they believe it to be superior to that of competitors. We can infer, then, that the firm faces a downward-sloping demand curve, not the horizontal or perfectly elastic demand curve facing competitive firms. However, with many substitute products available, the demand for the monopolistically competitive firm's product will be quite elastic, so consumers will be very responsive to price changes. As a consequence, the market power of the firm is limited; no monopolistically competitive firm can raise its price very much without losing an injuriously large number of customers.

The lack of barriers also functions as a check on market power. Additional firms can easily enter a monopolistically competitive industry to take advantage of short-run economic profits. Consider the monopolistically competitive firm represented in Exh. 7.2. In (a), the firm is earning a short-run profit (price exceeds *ATC* at the output where *MR = MC*). However, in

EXHIBIT 7.2

The Long-Run Adjustment Process in Monopolistic Competition

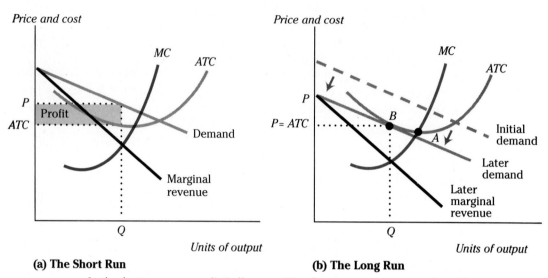

(a) The Short Run

(b) The Long Run

In the short run a monopolistically competitive firm may earn an economic profit, as represented in (a). In the long run, however, the presence of the above-normal profit will cause additional firms to enter the industry, reducing each firm's share of the industry demand and eventually eliminating all economic profit, as in (b). In long-run equilibrium the typical monopolistically competitive firm will earn just a normal profit.

the long run this profit will be eliminated by the entrance of additional firms selling similar but slightly differentiated products. As the new firms enter the industry, the demand curve facing our hypothetical firm will begin to shift to the left because each firm's share of total industry demand will become smaller. If there are now twenty pizza restaurants instead of ten, the typical restaurant will have fewer customers than before. Additional firms will continue to enter the industry (and the individual firm's demand curve will continue to shift leftward) until the typical firm is earning just a normal profit. This situation is depicted in (b). In long-run equilibrium, then, the monopolistically competitive firm will do no better than a purely competitive firm; it will just break even. (The article on page 210, "After Frantic Growth, Blockbuster Faces Host of Video-Rental Rivals," illustrates the long-run adjustment process in a monopolistically competitive industry.)

Evaluating Monopolistic Competition

We discovered in Chapter 6 that price searchers misallocate resources because they fail to produce up to the point where $P = MC$. An examination of Exh. 7.2 confirms that monopolistically competitive firms behave this way. Note that in long-run equilibrium (part b) price exceeds marginal cost, which indicates that society values an additional unit of this product more highly than the alternative products that could be produced with the same resources. In other words, monopolistically competitive firms produce less output than is socially desirable.

In addition to distorting the allocation of resources, monopolistically competitive firms are somewhat less efficient at producing their products and charge slightly higher prices than purely competitive firms with the same costs. These outcomes are at least in part the result of the overcrowding that characterizes most monopolistically competitive industries.

The crowded nature of monopolistically competitive industries is illustrated by the large number of clothing stores, video rental establishments, convenience groceries, and fast-food restaurants that exist in your city or town. By differentiating its product, each of these firms is able to capture a small share of the market. But often there are so many firms sharing that market that it is difficult for any one of them to attract enough customers to use its facilities efficiently—to permit it to operate at minimum ATC.

Because the monopolistically competitive firm underutilizes its production facilities, its average cost of production will be higher than the ATC of a purely competitive firm with identical cost curves.[1] For example, consider the ATC curve in part (b) of Exh. 7.2. In long-run equilibrium a purely competitive firm would earn zero economic profit and produce its product at minimum ATC (point A), whereas we've seen that monopolistically competitive firms will operate at a somewhat higher ATC (point B). As a consequence, the monopolistically competitive firm must charge a higher price than the purely competitive firm in order to earn a normal profit in the long run.

Fortunately for consumers, the difference in price is probably not substantial. Furthermore, consumers gain something for the additional dollars they pay. Remember, purely competitive firms sell products that are iden-

---

[1] This analysis assumes the monopolistic competitor has cost curves that are identical to those of the pure competitor. In fact, the monopolistic competitor probably has higher costs due to advertising expense and other product differentiation efforts. Thus there are two reasons to expect its selling price to be higher: It does not operate at the minimum on its ATC curve (while a pure competitor does), *and* its ATC curve is higher than that of a pure competitor.

After Frantic Growth, Blockbuster Faces Host Of Video-Rental Rivals

FORT LAUDERDALE, Fla.—During a recent roast here for H. Wayne Huizenga, the chairman of Blockbuster Video, Jane Fonda appeared (on tape, of course) to applaud his success and to suggest a joint dieting venture called "Bellybuster."

It's true, Mr. Huizenga has done very well indeed for a guy who got his start driving a garbage truck, who still uses the R-rated language of the refuse trade, and who just four years ago was running a modest little video chain that has since burgeoned into Blockbuster Entertainment Corp., a company that owns and franchises video rental stores with annual sales of $633 million.

Blockbuster is to the video trade what McDonald's is to fast food: a company that created an industry. Blockbuster took a business typified by seedy little mom-and-pop neighborhood rental shops and went national. Its stores are more like supermarkets, they don't have a porno section and they have gobbled up competitors right and left. Blockbuster claims to open a new store, somewhere, every 17 hours. . . .

But is Blockbuster living on borrowed time?

Since the beginning of last year, Blockbuster's year-over-year store revenue growth has slowed each quarter—from a 79% rise in the first three months to a 55% gain in the final quarter, even as the company aggressively opened and acquired stores. (At the end of last year, Blockbuster owned 787 stores itself, and franchised another 795). Then, last week, Blockbuster officials said they expect first-quarter earnings growth to be in the range of 10% to 20%—much less than heretofore and roughly half what analysts had been predicting.

Blockbuster executives claim to be unfazed. "Growth to us is limitless at this point," says Steven R. Berrard, vice chairman and chief financial officer. Blockbuster, big as it is, still has just 11% of the video market, so there's room to bloom. . . .

Attracting Giants

But . . . Blockbuster's growth has made the industry attractive to competitors. Everyone has always expected a shakeout in the industry, but now it's likely to be a clash of titans. . . .

Evidence of that abounds. Qualities that once set Blockbuster apart have been successfully copied by others. With 8,000 titles, Blockbuster used to offer the ultimate in choice. But in some markets, competitors offer even more. Tower Video, based in West Sacramento, Calif., sells the latest in home-movie technology, including 8-mm videos and laser disks, which Blockbuster largely ignores. It sticks pretty much to VHS cassettes.

Blockbuster touted service—longer hours, speedy, computerized checkout. Now it has rivals like the Video Factory in Buffalo, N.Y., where clerks in tuxedos escort shoppers to their cars under umbrellas when it rains. But when Blockbuster was unique, it could charge $3 per tape, against an industry average of more like $2 for an overnight rental. The extra buck contributed to earnings growth.

Lately, Blockbuster has been drawn into price wars. When some Blockbuster stores dropped their rental price to $2 in San Antonio in February, competing HEB Video Central stores dropped their charge for new movies to $1.50 and offers 99-cent specials.

The nation is littered with video stores—28,000, by one count. The biggest and best markets are saturated. In the Pacific and mid-Atlantic states, according to Video Store magazine, a given video store is likely to have six rivals within a three-mile radius. "There is very little key real estate left in the business," says Steve Apple, executive editor of Video Insider magazine. . . .

The crowded field might not matter so much if it weren't for signs that the fast-forward days are over for the video business. Since the mid-'80s, the growth of movie rentals has paralleled sales of videocassette recorders. As hardware prices fell, consumers snapped up 65 million VCRs in six years and surged into

video stores. But with the machines now in about 70% of U.S. households, growth in the rental market last year slipped into single digits for the first time—just 7%. Some expect 1991 to be worse still.

. . . The continuing evolution of pay-per-view television is the ultimate cloud over Blockbuster. Making a trip to the store to rent a film is inherently inconvenient. Ordering it up in your living room is the essence of convenience. Though technology and pricing are problems, pay-per-view appears to be marching inexorably forward, particularly if 150-channel cable systems become a reality for most households.

"I think Blockbuster will do just fine for the next several years," says Robert Wussler, president of Comsat Video Enterprises, a pay-per-view company. "Whether they will still be around 10 to 12 years from now, that's another question."

—*Michael J. McCarthy*

SOURCE: *The Wall Street Journal*, March 22, 1991, p. 1. Reprinted by permission of *The Wall Street Journal*, © 1991 Dow Jones & Company, Inc. All Rights Reserved Worldwide.

USE YOUR ECONOMIC REASONING

1. **New monopolistically competitive industries may remain profitable for quite some time. Why? Has the video rental business followed this pattern?**

2. **As a monopolistically competitive industry matures, it becomes increasingly necessary for firms to differentiate themselves from their rivals. Why? How has Blockbuster attempted to differentiate its outlets from other video rental stores?**

3. **What evidence is there that the video rental business is less profitable than it once was? Use the model of monopolistic competition to explain this outcome.**

tical in the minds of consumers, whereas monopolistic competitors aim for product differentiation. Many of us are willing to pay a little more to obtain the product variety that monopolistic competition provides.

Oligopoly

Millions of firms in hundreds of American retail industries match the model of monopolistic competition reasonably well. However, most manufacturing industries—steel, aluminum, automobiles, and prescription drugs, for example—are more accurately described as oligopolistic. An *oligopoly* is an industry dominated by a few relatively large sellers that are protected by substantial barriers to entry. The distinguishing feature of all oligopolistic industries is the high degree of interdependence among the sellers and the very personal nature of the rivalry that results from that interdependence.

Oligopolists and Market Power

Because oligopolistic firms enjoy a large share of their market, their production decisions have a significant impact on market price. A substantial increase in production by any one of them would cause downward pressure on price; a significant decrease would tend to push price upward. Suppose, for instance, that the Aluminum Company of America (Alcoa) decided to increase production by 50 percent. Since Alcoa is a major producer, this increase in output would expand industry supply significantly and thereby depress the industry price. A substantial reduction in Alcoa's output would tend to have the opposite effect; it would push price upward.

We have seen that soybean farmers, hog producers, and others in purely competitive industries cannot influence price by manipulating industry output: they're not big enough; they don't control a large enough share of the market. In addition, the large number of firms in these competitive industries makes it virtually impossible for them to coordinate their actions—to agree to limit production, for example. As a consequence, changes in the output of a competitive industry are always the unplanned results of independent actions by thousands of producers. Output in an oligopolistic industry, on the other hand, is often carefully controlled by the few large firms that dominate production. This control is one of the keys to the pricing discretion of the oligopolists.

Some oligopolists also acquire market power through product differentiation. Although producers of commodities such as aluminum ingots, steel sheet, and heating oil sell virtually identical products, many oligopolists sell differentiated products. Producers of automobiles, pet food, greeting cards, cigarettes, breakfast cereals, and washers and dryers belong in this category. Oligopolistic sellers of differentiated products possess market power both because they are large in relation to the total industry *and* because their product is somewhat unique.

Mutual Interdependence and the Kinked Demand Curve

Since oligopolistic firms have pricing discretion, they are price searchers rather than price takers. But the high degree of interdependence among oligopolists tends to restrict the pricing discretion of the individual firm and complicate its search for the profit-maximizing price.

Because there are only a few large sellers, each firm must consider the reactions of its rivals before taking any action. For instance, before altering the price of its product, Ford Motor Company must consider the reactions of General Motors and the other firms in the industry. Raising its prices may be ill-advised unless the other firms can be counted on to match the price hike. Price reductions can be an equally poor strategy if other firms respond with matching price cuts or with deeper cuts that lead to continuing price warfare.

Concern over the reactions of rivals may cause the demand curve faced by an oligopolist to be kinked, as in Exh. 7.3. Note that the two segments of this demand curve have quite different slopes. The portion of the curve above the kink is very flat, so a small change in price will bring a large change in the quantity demanded—demand is quite elastic. Below the kink, the curve is steep, so the quantity demanded is not very sensitive to a price change—demand is very inelastic. The significance of these different slopes will become apparent in a moment.

For the firm in Exh. 7.3, the current price is $12,000 and quantity is 3 million units. If the firm raises its price above $12,000, the kinked demand-curve model argues that other firms will *not follow* the firm's lead (will not increase their prices), so it will lose a large number of customers to its rivals. For example, if the firm increases its price from $12,000 to $14,000, the quantity sold will drop from 3 million units to only 2 million. On the other hand, if the firm reduces its price from $12,000 to $10,000, the model contends that other firms *will follow* (they will also reduce their prices), so the firm will not be able to attract customers away from other sellers. (However, the lower price will attract a few additional customers who would not have purchased

EXHIBIT 7.3

The Kinked Demand Curve

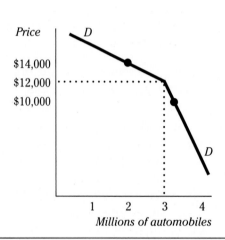

An oligopolist's demand curve may be kinked rather than smooth. Above the kink, the demand curve is flat, or elastic. A price hike will cause a substantial reduction in the quantity demanded. Below the kink, the demand curve is steep, or inelastic. A price reduction will attract few additional customers. Under these circumstances, the oligopolist may be reluctant to alter price.

cars—from anyone—at the higher price. In our example, the quantity sold expands from 3 million to 3.25 million cars.)

The kinked demand curve illustrates how interdependence can constrain the pricing discretion of oligopolists. Oligopolists are inhibited from raising prices by the fear of being undercut and from lowering prices by the fear that their price cuts will be matched. Under these circumstances, oligopolists might be afraid to alter price in either direction and could be forced to maintain a price that did not maximize profit.

Tactics for Limiting Competition

Oligopolists may respond to their interdependence by employing tactics that allow them to cooperate and avoid price competition. One such tactic is *collusion,* a secret agreement among sellers to fix prices, divide up the market, or in some other way limit competition. In the United States such agreements are illegal and punishable by fine and imprisonment. But despite these penalties, firms continue to engage in collusion. Dozens of violators are prosecuted each year, and many others probably go undetected. (Examine "Do

Colleges Collude on Financial Aid?" on page 216 for an example of possible collusion that hits close to home.)

Collusive agreements may be unnecessary when an industry is dominated by a few interdependent sellers. These firms often coordinate their pricing decisions through a more subtle method that requires no direct communication: price leadership. *Price leadership* is much like a game of follow-the-leader. One firm—perhaps the biggest, the most efficient, or simply the most trusted—initiates all increases or decreases in prices. The remaining firms in the industry follow the example set by the leader. This tactic allows the firms in the industry to accomplish price changes legally, without colluding.

As oligopolists attempt to avoid price competition, they channel their competitive instincts into *nonprice competition*—advertising, packaging, and new product development. This form of rivalry has two significant advantages over price competition. First, a new product or a successful advertising campaign is more difficult for a competitor to match than a price cut, so an oligopolist may gain a more permanent advantage over its rivals. Second, rivalry through product differentiation or new product development is less likely than price competition to get out of control and severely damage the profits of all firms in the industry. Thus nonprice competition is seen as a more promising and safer strategy than price-competition.

Factors Limiting Cooperation

Although oligopolists strive to avoid price warfare and confine their rivalry to nonprice competition, these efforts are not always successful. Collusion and price leadership often break down because of the strong temptation to cheat (cut price) in order to steal customers. The likelihood of cheating is greatest in markets where prices tend to be secret (so that price cutting may go undiscovered) and in agreements involving more than a handful of firms. History shows that price cutting is particularly common in periods of weak demand, when firms have substantial excess capacity that they would like to put to work. During such periods, firms will be tempted to undercut their rivals in order to expand sales.

In truth, the success of oligopolists in avoiding price competition varies significantly from industry to industry. Some industries—the breakfast cereal industry, for example—have demonstrated a marked ability to avoid price competition; others—steel, for instance—experience recurring bouts of price warfare. Because the behavior of oligopolists is so varied, it is difficult to generalize about the impact of oligopoly on social welfare. We will attempt some cautious observations after discussing the final industry structure, pure monopoly.

Do Colleges Collude on Financial Aid?

When Angela Walton, a Detroit high-school senior, received acceptance letters and financial-aid offers from a group of colleges last month, her mother, Gloria, was surprised that Harvard University and Princeton University expected her to contribute the same amount to her daughter's education.

After all, in higher education's quest for student diversity, smarts and leadership, Angela is close to the Holy Grail: female, black, from the Midwest and possessed of a superior academic and extracurricular record. The University of Michigan offered a full four-year scholarship, and Stanford's terms would mean that Mrs. Walton would pay "several thousand" dollars less than at the two Ivy League schools.

Angela opted for Stanford. If the Ivy League schools "wanted to compete" for students, Mrs. Walton says, price competition "would make more sense."

No Coincidence
The identical nature of the Ivy offers, however, was no coincidence—as more than 10,000 high-school seniors and their families discovered this year. For the Ivy schools are part of a price-fixing system that OPEC might envy.

Although not widely known outside the tightknit world of college admissions, the price-fixing has existed for some time. The colleges—23 elite Eastern schools—argue that it is the only way to prevent an unseemly bidding war for the best talent and to let students choose a college on the basis of academics.

But with the total costs of a year at some desirable colleges now around $20,000, some academics and education experts question the fairness of an exercise that often denies students the potential of more aid.

"It disturbs some of us a great deal," says Edward Custard, director of admissions at New College, part of the University of South Florida in Sarasota. "The whole thing is designed to save [the schools] grief and save them money. This way they don't have to fight a battle in a pitched way."

To many Americans, especially poorer ones, a college education is a ticket to a good job and a better life. For thousands of families, the price of that ticket was set this year on April 4 and 5 at the alumni club of Wellesley College in Wellesley, Mass. There, the financial-aid officers of the 23 colleges met, as a similar group has done regularly for 35 years, to compare notes on their common applicants seeking financial aid.

Before the Wellesley meeting, the schools sent records of all their financial-aid applicants to Harvard, in nearby Cambridge, Mass. There a closely held, for-profit company owned by some of the schools' admissions officers, Student Aid Services Inc., compiled lists of the applicants who were seeking financial aid at more than one school. . . .

The schools generally refer to their annual spring meeting at Wellesley as "financial-aid overlap." Here's how it works.

Frank Eager, a hypothetical student, has been accepted

both at Harvard, where tuition, room and board for next fall total $19,395, and at Penn, whose costs total $19,100. Both schools agree that the Eagers qualify for financial aid, but they differ on how much. Penn figures the Eager family can afford to pay $6,000 a year for Frank's education, but Harvard arrives at a $7,000 figure. At the meeting, Penn becomes convinced that the Harvard number makes sense and increases its family-contribution amount.

As a result, Frank receives acceptance letters and financial-aid offers that would mean identical $7,000 out-of-pocket, expenses for the Eagers at either school. Had the schools awarded aid independently, the Eagers might have saved $1,000 by choosing Penn. With the same family contribution, Harvard will offer a bigger aid package because its costs are higher. But the burden to the Eagers—their true price of a year's schooling—would be the same.

A further twist toward that end: The Ivy group also tries to match the mix of aid, broadly divided into grants that don't have to be paid back and "self-help" aid such as loans and campus work-study jobs. . . .

Lewis Kaplow, an antitrust-law specialist and Harvard Law School professor, says such activity would be illegal if the parties involved agree to concur on the same family contribution in each case, even if their judgments on the award differ. If, however, they are only agreeing to exchange information to arrive at more informed independent judgments, the activity wouldn't be illegal. . . .

The schools say they are not fixing prices, but just giving one another the option to agree on a family-contribution number. "There's no collusion," says Alfred Quirk, Dartmouth's dean of admissions. Adds Harvard's Mr. Miller: "The purpose of this is the exchange of information—there's no agreement that we agree."

—*Gary Putka*

SOURCE: *The Wall Street Journal*, May 2, 1989, p. B1. Reprinted by permission of *The Wall Street Journal*, © 1989 Dow Jones & Company, Inc. All Rights Reserved Worldwide.

USE YOUR ECONOMIC REASONING

1. How could the 23 elite Eastern schools mentioned in the article benefit from colluding on financial aid awards?

2. How might companies such as Student Aid Services Inc. make it easier for academic institutions to collude?

3. If the alleged collusive agreement omits state universities and lesser-known academic institutions, how can it be effective? Won't the elite institutions find their financial aid packages uncompetitive with institutions outside the collusive agreement?

Author's note: In May 1991, the eight colleges and universities in the Ivy League signed a consent agreement with the U.S. Justice Department agreeing to end their policy of jointly agreeing on financial awards. Other institutions are apparently still under investigation for violating antitrust laws. (Antitrust is discussed later in this chapter.)

Monopoly

Although monopolistic competitors and oligopolists both have some pricing discretion, the classic example of a firm with market power is the monopolist.

Monopoly is an industry structure in which a single firm sells a product for which there are no close substitutes. (Monopoly is sometimes called *pure monopoly* to emphasize that it is the industry structure farthest removed from pure competition.) A firm can become a monopolist in a variety of ways but can remain a monopolist only if barriers prevent other firms from entering the industry. For example, a firm may achieve a monopoly by being the first to produce and sell a specific product, but it must then patent the product to protect it from duplication. A second road to monopoly is the exclusive control of some critical input—a basic raw material needed in the production process, for instance. A third way that a firm may enjoy a monopoly is through sheer size, when larger size brings with it greater efficiency and lower production costs. Entry into the industry is then effectively blocked by the large capital investment a rival would require to begin operating at competitive size. A possible fourth source of monopoly is the government franchise—an exclusive license granted by the government to provide some product or service. Government franchises account for the presence of only one restaurant chain on the interstate highway and a single boat-rental establishment in a state park.

Monopoly and Market Power

Monopolists enjoy substantial pricing discretion because they are the sole suppliers of their products. This enables the monopolist to manipulate industry output and thereby alter the market price. The monopolist's control over output does not provide it with complete or unlimited pricing discretion, however. Complete pricing discretion would result in a vertical, perfectly inelastic demand curve, signifying the ability to increase price without losing *any* customers. This condition would represent the true opposite to the purely competitive firm, which possesses no market power and faces a horizontal, perfectly elastic demand curve.

But a monopolist does stand to lose some customers when it raises its price, because monopolists face a certain amount of competition from rivals in *other* industries. Think about your local telephone and utility companies, for example. These sellers fit the description of a monopolist fairly well, yet neither is without competition. If the telephone company were to charge exorbitant rates for its service, we could communicate by letter or by CB radio or by personal visit. If the utility company were to effect a drastic rate increase for electricity, we could begin by reducing our use of electricity. We could insulate our homes and install energy-saving appliances; ultimately we could even purchase our own electricity generator.

In the face of increasing fuel and electricity costs, many American consumers have already insulated their homes and demanded energy-saving devices. And although none of us wants to resort to a CB radio as a substitute for local telephone service, if rates become high enough, some customers might choose to do just that. The availability of substitutes, however imperfect, constrains the monopolist's pricing discretion. (In the short run, a monopolist's only rivals are firms in other industries. But in the long run, technological change can destroy a firm's monopoly status. Read "The Wireless Wonder" on page 220 to see how the cable television industry is changing.)

Monopoly and Profit Maximization

Because a monopolist stands to lose some customers when it raises its price, the demand curve it faces must be downward sloping like that of other price searchers. This tells us that the monopolist must restrict output to charge a high price; conversely, it must reduce price to sell more. The monopolist will select the profit-maximizing output and price in exactly the same way as other price searchers do; it will produce at the output where $MR = MC$ and find its price by going up to the demand curve. The difference between a monopolist and other price searchers is found not in the rules used to determine their price but in the competitive situation. Monopolistically competitive firms and oligopolists face some degree of competition from other firms in the industry. The monopolist *is* the industry, so its only competition comes from firms in other industries.

Because monopolists enjoy substantial pricing discretion, it is commonly believed that they must earn economic profits. But that need not be the case. In the short run monopolists, like other producers, may experience economic profits, normal profits, or even losses. How well a monopolist will fare depends on the demand and cost conditions that it faces. Imagine, for instance, a firm that has patented a medicine for a very rare disease—an average diagnosis of ten cases a year. This monopolist has substantial pricing discretion with these unfortunate victims, but the demand is so limited that the product probably will be unprofitable to produce. Or consider the boat-rental concession at an isolated state park. The owner enjoys a government-granted monopoly, but if few vacationers frequent the lake, it won't be a very profitable monopoly. The point is that even a monopolist can't earn a profit if the demand for its product is very limited. High production costs can signal

The Wireless Wonder

Pending in Congress are 14 bills that would re-regulate—i.e., cut into the profitability of—the cable television industry. The prospect of re-regulation has been scary enough to wipe billions of dollars off the cable TV companies' market value in recent months. But scarier still is what's happening to cable in Sioux Falls, S.D.

Sioux Falls, South Dakota's largest city (pop. 92,000), was wired for cable in the early 1970s. But if you live a few miles south of town, where only one or two farmhouses per square mile dot the rolling, windswept landscape, no cable passes your home.

Still, Sioux Falls' farmers can receive many of the same programs the townsfolk get. Such popular cable channels as CNN, Nickelodeon and Showtime reach them thanks to "wireless" cable. Since March of last year, Charles Mauszycki's tiny Family Entertainment Network (1989 revenues, $564,000) has signed up 1,200 of Sioux Falls' 8,000 outlying homes for its wireless cable system. Cost: $17.95 a month for basic cable, plus $9.95 a month for Showtime. Mauszycki says that the system, less than one year old, already has positive cash flow.

What is wireless cable? Instead of stringing miles of coaxial cable on telephone poles to reach his far-flung rural subscribers, Mauszycki's wireless cable systems broadcast eight cable channels by microwave to small antennas (about the size of an open newspaper) on the roofs of subscriber homes. A microwave signal broadcasts over a 30-mile radius, meaning a signal from a single tower can cover about 3,000 square miles.

This is not a new technology. The Federal Communications Commission began allocating spectrum for wireless cable channels in 1963. To date, a total of 33 channels per market have been allocated, albeit in a highly convoluted fashion. Licenses for 20 channels are restricted to educational institutions; the rest are awarded in a series of lotteries, with no one person being allowed to apply for more than 4 channels per market. Channel ownership can, however, be consolidated after the lotteries by buying, selling or leasing channels.

Compared with wired cable systems—where about 90% of the capital costs must be laid out before the first paying customer gets switched on, and where systems trade at an average $2,300 per subscriber—the cost to get a wireless system up and running is nominal. Family Entertainment's Mauszycki, for example, has spent about $800,000 to turn on his Sioux Falls system; that's less than $700 per subscriber. And if his company's penetration into the Sioux Falls market reached 40%, the incremental cost of adding those subscribers would bring the cost of the system down to just under $500 a subscriber.

What does wireless cable have to do with all those cable re-regulation bills in Congress? A great deal. Says Federal Communications Commission Chairman Alfred Sikes: "Rather than taking the approach that the market is a monopoly and therefore should be regulated, I take the approach that we should look at ways to point toward a competitive market." And the most viable potential competitor, Sikes adds, is wireless cable. . . .

The wired cable companies are dealing with the wireless threat with closed fists. Their ultimate weapon: control over programming, without which the wireless systems will surely wither.

Tele-Communications, Inc. and Time Warner's American Television & Communications Corp., the two largest U.S. cable companies, control a large chunk of cable's most desirable programming. Time Warner, for example, owns HBO and Cinemax. And TCI owns stakes in a dozen programming companies and has struck a deal to acquire 50% of Showtime from Viacom, another large cable operator. Together, TCI and Time Warner own 38% of Ted Turner's Turner Broadcasting, which owns CNN and TNT, a popular movie channel. . . . And Cablevision, the ninth-largest cable operator, owns Sportschannel, a network of regional sports stations.

So guess which cable stations wireless operators say they are having trouble adding to their rosters? Answer: HBO, Cinemax, Showtime, Sportschannel and TNT.

The wireless operators are hitting back. For example,

four-year-old MetroTen Cablevision in Cleveland, which claims nearly 25,000 subscribers, successfully sued Viacom to have Showtime added to its wireless cable system. Through a public referendum, MetroTen was granted a cable franchise for Cleveland. With franchise in hand, MetroTen President James Theroux was finally able to negotiate a contract with HBO for his wireless system. . . .

Potentially most important, the FCC's Sikes is considering steps to force cable programmers to sell their services to wireless operators. In another effort to encourage competition from wireless, Sikes wants to make it easier for operators to consolidate licenses for wireless systems.

All of which inevitably means that smart money is beginning to follow the local entrepreneurs into the wireless cable business. . . .

In other words, congressmen don't need to control cable's prices. The market will do the job for them.

—*Fleming Meeks*

SOURCE: Fleming Meeks, "The Wireless Wonder." Excerpted by permission of *Forbes* magazine, February 19, 1990, p. 57. © Forbes Inc., 1990.

USE YOUR ECONOMIC REASONING

1. What is "wireless cable," and how does it threaten the monopoly presently enjoyed by many local cable television operators?

2. How are the wired cable companies attempting to defend themselves against wireless cable operators?

3. In June 1991, the Federal Communications Commission voted to permit local governments to regulate cable rates except where cable systems compete with six or more over-the-air TV stations or where communities are served by other multichannel services such as wireless cable. Explain the logic behind these exceptions.

EXHIBIT 7.4

A Monopolist Incurring a Loss

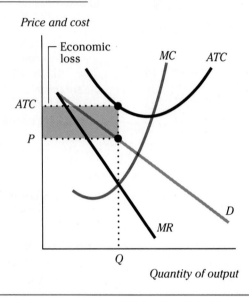

Even a monopolist can incur a loss if there is little demand for its product or if its costs are high.

a similar problem. Exhibit 7.4 depicts a monopolist incurring a short-run economic loss.

When monopolists are able to earn short-run profits, substantial entry barriers help them continue to earn those profits in the long run. Ultimately, changes in tastes and preferences or the introduction of new products may undermine the monopolist's position. But these changes are impossible to forecast. In the meantime, the monopolist can continue to earn the above-normal profit.

The Consequences of Monopoly or Oligopoly

The presence of monopoly can have a significant effect on consumer well-being. Monopolists tend to produce too little output and sometimes charge prices that are inflated by economic profits. These negative effects may be partially offset by lower production costs or greater innovation. Oligopoly can have a similar impact on consumer welfare, though it is much more difficult to generalize about the consequences of this industry structure.

The Problems of Misallocation of Resources and Redistribution of Income

Economists generally agree that monopolists distort the allocation of scarce resources. Like monopolistically competitive firms, monopolists fail to produce up to the point where price is equal to marginal cost—the point where resources would be allocated efficiently. As a consequence, too few resources are devoted to the production of the goods and services produced by monopolists, and too many resources are left over to be used in the more competitive sectors of the economy. For example, if there were only two industries in the economy, a monopolized computer industry and a purely competitive farming industry, society probably would receive too few computers and too many agricultural products.

The redistribution of income is another problem caused by monopolies. Because entrance into these industries is blocked, consumers may be required to pay higher prices than necessary, prices that include economic profits on top of the normal profits that are necessary to convince firms to continue operation. These higher prices redistribute income from consumers (who will be made worse off) to monopolists (who will be made better off).

While economists are fairly confident in generalizing about the consequences of monopoly, they find it more difficult to make blanket statements regarding the impact of oligopoly. This is primarily because the behavior of oligopolists is so varied. To the extent that oligopolists cooperate and avoid price competition, the welfare effects of oligopoly probably are very similar to the effects of pure monopoly. When cooperation breaks down, consumer welfare is enhanced and the negative effects of oligopoly are reduced. Since it is clear that oligopolists do not always succeed in avoiding price competition, the impact of oligopoly on consumer well-being probably lies somewhere between the impacts of monopoly and pure competition.

The Possible Benefits of Size

While monopoly and oligopoly often have undesirable effects on consumer welfare, this is not always the case. Under certain conditions, these market structures may benefit society. For example, if a monopolist's/oligopolist's greater size means that it produces at a lower *ATC* because it can afford more specialized equipment and greater specialization of labor, it may use fewer resources per unit of output and charge a lower price than a competitive firm even as it earns an economic profit. And because monopolists and oligopolists are often able to earn economic profits in the long run, they can afford the investment necessary to develop new products and cost-reducing production techniques. Thus, in the long run, society may receive better products and lower prices from monopolists and oligopolists than from competitive firms.

Studies of the American economy provide limited support for these arguments. For example, in the refrigerator-manufacturing industry a firm needs 15 to 20 percent of the market in order to achieve production efficiency, or minimum *ATC*. This means that for optimal efficiency, room exists for only five or six firms in that industry. The efficient manufacture and distribution of beer requires a somewhat smaller but nevertheless substantial market share: 10 to 14 percent. Fortunately, in more than half the manufacturing industries surveyed, firms with 3 percent or less of the market were large enough to operate at minimum *ATC*. Thus generally it is not necessary for industries to be dominated by one or a few firms in order to achieve production efficiency.[2]

Evidence on business research and development efforts leads to a similar conclusion. Firms in highly competitive industries are not particularly innovative, perhaps because they are unable to earn the profits necessary to finance research and development efforts. But neither do firms in "tightly" oligopolistic industries (wherein a very few firms closely coordinate their actions) tend to be innovative. These firms often have the money but seem to lack the incentive from competitive pressure to invest in research and development. The most innovative tend to be medium-sized firms in "loosely" oligopolistic industries—industries composed of several firms (perhaps ten or twenty) with no single dominant firm. Because some competitive pressure exists, it may be harder for the firms in these industries to coordinate their actions; but because they have some pricing discretion, such firms often earn the economic profits necessary to support research and development efforts.[3]

In summary, lower production costs and greater innovation may compensate for the resource misallocation and income redistribution caused by oligopolists and monopolists. In some cases we may even be able to justify

---

[2] F. M. Scherer, *Industrial Market Structure and Economic Performance* (Chicago: Rand McNally, 1980), p. 119.
[3] Douglas F. Greer, *Industrial Organization and Public Policy* (New York: Macmillan, 1980), p. 598.

a monopoly on the basis of greater production efficiency or other technical considerations, a possibility that will be discussed shortly. However, even when we take these benefits into consideration, we find that manufacturing industries have fewer and larger firms than necessary to achieve the advantages of greater production efficiency and increased innovation. In general, American consumers would be better off if the existing industry structure were more competitive, not less.

Antitrust and Regulation

Because the exercise of market power by monopolists and oligopolists often shortchanges the consumer, the federal government pursues policies designed to promote competition and restrict the actions of firms with market power. The primary weapons used in the battle against market power are antitrust laws and industry regulation. As you will see, these two approaches to the problem differ significantly in both their philosophies and the remedies they propose.

Antitrust Enforcement

Antitrust laws have as their objective the maintenance and promotion of competition. These laws (1) outlaw collusion; (2) make it illegal for a firm to attempt to achieve a monopoly; and (3) ban *mergers,* the union of two or more companies into a single firm, when such mergers are likely to result in substantially less competition.

Virtually all antitrust enforcement in the United States is based on three fundamental statutes enacted around the turn of the century: the Sherman Antitrust Act of 1890, the Clayton Antitrust Act of 1914, and the Federal Trade Commission Act, also passed in 1914. Exhibit 7.5 offers a brief comparison of these laws.

The Sherman Antitrust Act. The Sherman Act, the first of the big three, was a response to the monopolistic exploitation that occurred in the latter half of the nineteenth century. During this period, trusts had become commonplace. *Trusts* are combinations of firms organized for the purpose of restraining price competition and thereby gaining economic profit. So many

---

EXHIBIT 7.5

The Antitrust Laws and What They Do

The Sherman Antitrust Act (1890)	Outlawed agreements to fix prices, limit output, or share the market. Also declared that monopolies and attempts to monopolize are illegal.
The Clayton Antitrust Act (1914)	Forbade mergers between competitors where the impact of merger would be to substantially lessen competition. Also outlawed certain practices such as tying contracts.
The Federal Trade Commission Act (1914)	Created the Federal Trade Commission and empowered it to initiate and decide cases involving "unfair competition." Also declared that deceptive practices and unfair methods of competition are illegal.

---

companies were merging at this time that competitors were disappearing at an alarming rate! Du Pont, for example, achieved a near monopoly in the manufacture of explosives by either merging with or acquiring some 100 rival firms between 1872 and 1912.[4] Monopolies and monopolistic practices translated into higher prices for consumers and inspired a strong political movement that led to the passage of the Sherman Antitrust Act in 1890.

The Sherman Act declared illegal all agreements between competing firms to fix prices, limit output, or otherwise restrict the forces of competition. It also declared illegal all monopolies or "attempts to monopolize any part of trade or commerce among the several states, or with foreign nations." The law was not applied with much force until 1904, when it was used to dissolve the Northern Securities Company, a firm that had been formed to

---

[4] F. M. Scherer, *Industrial Market Structure and Economic Performance* (Chicago: Rand McNally, 1980), p. 121.

Under the leadership of John D. Rockefeller (shown here with an escort of state troopers), the Standard Oil trust acquired a virtual monopoly in petroleum refining.

monopolize railroad transportation in certain northern states. Later, in 1911, the law became the basis for the antitrust suit that resulted in the breakup of Standard Oil, a trust that controlled some 90 percent of the petroleum industry.

As a result of the limits laid down by the courts in the Standard Oil case, businesses became somewhat less aggressive in their monopolistic practices. Rather than strive for monopoly, they were content to become the dominant firms in their respective oligopolistic industries. However, many firms gained dominion not by abandoning practices but by pursuing them in disguised and subtle ways. This led Congress in 1914 to pass two more bills aimed at curbing anticompetitive practices: the Clayton Antitrust Act and the Federal Trade Commission Act.

The Clayton Antitrust Act. The Clayton Act was designed primarily to stem the tide of mergers that had already reduced competition significantly in a number of important industries, such as steel production, petroleum refining, and electrical equipment manufacture. The act prohibited mergers between competing firms if the impact of their union would be to "substantially lessen competition or to tend to create a monopoly." The act also outlawed other practices, if these lessened competition; "other practices" included *tying contracts*—agreements specifying that the purchaser would, as a condition of sale for a given product, also buy some other product offered by the seller. Once again, enforcement was a problem because the courts interpreted this law in ways that permitted mergers between competing firms to continue. Finally, in 1950, the Cellar-Kefauver Act amended the Clayton Act by closing a major loophole, thus effectively eliminating the possibility of mergers involving major competitors.

During the Reagan administration, the government relaxed its restriction against mergers involving major competitors. This more permissive attitude was at least partially responsible for a wave of merger activity in the 1980s. The Bush administration has taken a somewhat tougher stance on antitrust enforcement, including stricter merger guidelines.

The Federal Trade Commission Act. The last of the three major antitrust statutes, the Federal Trade Commission Act, was also passed in 1914. Its primary purpose was to establish a special agency, the Federal Trade Commission, empowered to investigate allegations of "unfair methods of competition" and command businesses in violation of FTC regulations to cease those practices. Although the FTC Act did not specify the precise meaning of "unfair methods of competition," the phrase has been interpreted by the commission to include practices prohibited under the Sherman and Clayton Acts—price fixing and tying contracts, for example—and any other practices that can be shown to limit competition or damage the consuming public. For instance, the FTC has deemed it unfair for a funeral home to fail to provide, in advance, an itemized price list for funeral services and merchandise or to furnish embalming without first informing customers about alternatives.

The Federal Trade Commission is one of the two federal agencies charged with the enforcement of the antitrust statutes. The other agency is the Antitrust Division of the Justice Department. The Antitrust Division is responsible for enforcing the Sherman and Clayton Acts and lesser pieces of antitrust legislation. The FTC is also charged with antitrust enforcement, including civil actions against violators of either the Sherman or Clayton Acts, but its responsibilities are somewhat broader. About half its resources are devoted to combating deception and misrepresentation: improper labeling and misleading advertisements, for example. The overlapping responsibilities of the FTC and the Antitrust Division have posed some problems of coordination, but these are at least partially offset by the fact that one agency's oversights may be picked up by the other.

Industry Regulation

Government regulation of industry approaches the problem of market power from a different perspective and therefore provides a different solution.[5] The basic assumption is that certain industries cannot or should not be made competitive. Hence the role of government is to provide a framework whereby the actions of these less-than-competitive firms can be constrained in a manner consistent with the public interest. This is accomplished by establishing regulatory agencies empowered to control the prices such firms can charge, the quality of service they must provide, and the conditions under which additional firms will be allowed to enter the industry. Exhibit 7.6 summarizes the responsibilities of the major federal regulatory commissions: the Interstate Commerce Commission, the Federal Power Commission, and the Federal Communications Commission. Supplementing these major commissions are smaller specialized federal agencies and numerous state regulatory commissions that govern the businesses that operate entirely within a particular state.

Efficiency and consumer welfare are the rationale for recognizing and regulating industries called natural monopolies. A ***natural monopoly*** exists when technical or cost conditions make it unfeasible or inadvisable to

---

EXHIBIT 7.6

The Major Federal Regulatory Commissions

COMMISSION	JURISDICTION
Interstate Commerce Commission	Railroads, water carriers, trucking, oil pipelines, express companies
Federal Power Commission	Electric power, gas and gas pipelines, waterpower sites
Federal Communications Commission	Telephone, television, cable TV, radio, telegraph

---

[5] Regulation designed to deal with the problems posed by market power is sometimes described as "price and entry regulation" to distinguish it from "health and safety regulation."

have more than one firm in a particular industry. A fairly good example is the telephone industry, wherein the presence of competing local phone companies would mean not only a duplication of investment—telephone poles, cables, and switching stations—but also considerable inconvenience to consumers, who would have to subscribe to the services of each company if they wanted to be able to reach all parties living in the community. Rather than permit duplication, the government allows a single company to become a monopoly but imposes certain restrictions on its actions. As you know, competition is now permitted in long-distance service; however, the phone company still has a monopoly when it comes to the provision of local phone service.[6]

Federal regulation, however, is not confined to natural monopolies. Over the years numerous industries—including airlines, trucking, radio and television, and water carriers (ships and barges)—have been thought to be sufficiently "clothed with the public interest" to justify regulation, even though one would be hard pressed to show that any of these industries qualifies as a natural monopoly.

Criticisms of Government Regulation and Antitrust Policies

Neither antitrust policies nor government regulation has been totally successful in dealing with the problem of market power. In fact it can be argued that consumers would be better off if fewer industries were subject to regulation and fewer antitrust laws were on the books. We'll explore the basis for that argument as we consider criticism against regulation.

What's Wrong with Regulation?

You have seen why there is a fairly strong case for industry regulation of clear-cut natural monopolies—local telephone and utility companies, for example. However, critics argue that regulation outside this arena too often becomes a device for restricting entry and raising prices in industries that might other-

---

[6] At one time, long-distance service was also regarded as a natural monopoly because it was necessary to string expensive copper wire from city to city. Today, microwave communications make it possible to avoid that expense, thus opening the way for competition and eliminating the justification for natural monopoly status.

wise be reasonably competitive. The railroad and trucking industries stand out as examples.

Both railroads and interstate trucking are regulated by the Interstate Commerce Commission (ICC). The ICC was created in 1887 to oversee the railroads, which were believed to have substantial market power. Research suggests, however, that although the railroads clearly enjoyed some pricing discretion, they faced much more price competition than they desired. In fact, the railroads themselves were in favor of regulation as a way of stabilizing price-fixing agreements in the industry.[7] The railroads hoped that the ICC would be able to do for them what they had been unable to do for themselves: restrain price competition.

In 1935, at least partly in response to pressure from the railroads, the interstate trucking industry was brought under the ICC's control. Although the trucking industry at that time was in its infancy, the railroads recognized that competition from trucking might harm them, and they believed that regulation would limit that competition. Available evidence suggests that they were correct; regulated industries are often protected from competition.

Under the ICC regulation, competition within the trucking industry and between trucking and railroads has been significantly restricted. Until recently the commission strictly limited the number of trucking firms that could operate between any two cities. In addition it regulated the routes each firm's trucks were permitted to travel and the number of products each firm could carry. Most important, the commission permitted the trucklines to agree on minimum rates.

Defenders of industry regulation argue that these restrictions were needed to prevent "destructive and wasteful" competition—too many firms serving a particular market, for example. Critics contend that these regulations have resulted in much higher shipping charges than would have been possible in a more competitive environment.

These and similar criticisms of other regulatory agencies resulted in a great deal of pressure for the deregulation of the transportation and shipping industries. In 1978 these pressures led to the passage of legislation to deregulate the airline industry. This process was completed in 1985, when the Civil Aeronautics Board (CAB), the agency that regulated the airline industry, was dissolved. Airlines are now free to compete in whichever markets they choose and free to set their own ticket prices. The Motor Carriers Act of 1980 accomplished essentially the same thing in the trucking industry. Truck-

---

[7] Almarin Phillips, *Promoting Competition In Regulated Markets* (Washington, D.C.: The Brookings Institution, 1975), p. 77.

ing firms are now permitted to decide what markets to serve, what prices to charge, and what products to haul.

The impact of airline deregulation has been the subject of much debate. In the early days of deregulation many new airlines entered the industry, and fares dropped markedly. But today almost all the new airlines are gone, and air fares have risen significantly in some markets. Concern over the shrinking number of major airlines led the U.S. Transportation Department to conduct a study, the results of which were released in February 1990.

According to the study, eight airlines now carry 90 percent of the nation's air traffic. However, because these airlines generally compete vigorously, the study concludes that, on average, Americans now enjoy more flights and pay lower fares than they did when there were a larger number of competitors. This conclusion does not apply to all markets, however. For instance, "The study found that in eight cities where a single airline . . . provides most of the daily flights, fares are on average 18.7 percent higher than at other cities."[8] The eight cities named were Minneapolis, Cincinnati, Dayton, St. Louis, Pittsburgh, Memphis, Salt Lake City, and Charlotte.

Even though most studies show that average air fares have declined as a result of deregulation, not everyone believes it was a good idea. Customers in many small cities have experienced a reduction in the number of available flights and some have lost all jet service. Evidence indicates that the quality of passenger service has declined: there are more flight delays, fewer direct flights, increased overbookings and lost luggage, and so on. Critics of deregulation argue that competitive pressures and an emphasis on price competition are responsible for these problems. When air fares were regulated, the airlines turned to nonprice competition—more frequent flights and in-flight meals, for example. When price competition became legal, price was emphasized because consumer attention tends to focus on prices.

As you might expect, concerns about the quality of service and the high fares in particular markets have caused some critics to call for a return to regulation. The Transportation Department is expected to argue vigorously against such a move.

What's Wrong with Antitrust Policies?

Critics of antitrust policies show less consensus than exists among critics of regulation. At one extreme, economists believe that the antitrust laws are weak and ineffective. At the other, they view these laws as unnecessarily restrictive and counterproductive.

[8] John H. Cushman, Jr., "Support for Airline Deregulation," *New York Times*, February 14, 1990, p. C1.

The first group of economists argues that our existing antitrust laws are virtually useless in a world of oligopolies. These statutes, passed at the turn of the century, were designed to prosecute "attempts to monopolize" and various forms of collusion. But the modern-day antitrust problem is one of oligopoly, not monopoly. As we have seen, oligopolists don't need to resort to collusion to achieve their objectives; they rely instead on price leadership and other forms of *parallel behavior* to achieve the same results without violating the antitrust laws.

Some economists believe that the solution to this problem is to pass legislation that will make "bigness" itself a violation of the antitrust laws. For example, the law might define any firm producing more than 50 percent of an industry's output as being too big and thus subject to being divided into several smaller firms.

The second group of economists, which includes Lester Thurow of MIT, argues that the advantages of bigness—lower production costs and more rapid development of new products—far outweigh the disadvantages. In Thurow's opinion, our antitrust laws force American firms to spend millions of dollars a year defending themselves against government lawsuits, dollars that could be better spent on research and development.

More important, Thurow believes that increased foreign competition has made these antitrust efforts unnecessary and probably even counterproductive. Firms that seem large relative to the U.S. economy are not so large when viewed in the context of the world economy; therefore they possess less market power than is commonly assumed. According to Thurow, even some of America's largest firms are now in danger of being driven out of business by foreign rivals.

> Think, for example, about General Motors. For many years it was the largest industrial firm in the world. Today, even if it were the only American auto manufacturer, it would still be in a competitive fight for its life.[9]

Thurow argues that in this environment American firms need to devote all their efforts to becoming more efficient and developing new and better products. They can't afford to waste money and talent defending themselves against antitrust suits that are based on an out-of-date perception of the dangers posed by big business.

In our discussion of antitrust and regulation, we have tried to remain objective. Some economists believe that our antitrust laws are far too weak; others argue that they are counterproductive. Both sides probably overstate their case. Even though the antitrust laws may deal ineffectively with price leadership, they succeed in discouraging price fixing and other forms of

---

[9] Lester C. Thurow, "An Era of New Competition," *Newsweek*, January 18, 1982, p. 63.

collusive behavior. This effect may be more important than critics believe. Firms in oligopolistic industries may have a difficult time avoiding price competition, particularly when profits are threatened by a recession or by overcapacity in the industry. In such situations, oligopolists are tempted to collude in order to ensure cooperation and avoid price warfare. Vigorous antitrust enforcement can deter such collusion and thereby enhance consumer well-being.

To say that the antitrust laws are counterproductive is also an exaggeration. Although competition from foreign firms has changed the economic environment for some American businesses, many industries do not face competitive pressure from abroad. Some industries that do have already convinced Congress to erect trade barriers to reduce the inflow of foreign products and protect them from foreign competition. Furthermore, statistical studies suggest that most American firms can compete effectively with their foreign rivals. In fact there is little evidence to support the contention that antitrust enforcement places American firms at a competitive disadvantage. For all these reasons, many economists prefer to focus on improving our antitrust laws in ways that will help promote competition without sacrificing efficiency.

Summary

In the American economy, most firms have some market power or pricing discretion. Market power is exercised through product differentiation or by altering total industry output. The extent of the firm's market power depends on the structure, or makeup, of the industry in which it operates. The definitive characteristics of *industry structure* are the number of sellers in the industry and their size distribution, the nature of the product, and the extent of barriers to entry. The four basic industry structures are pure competition, monopolistic competition, oligopoly, and pure monopoly.

At one end of the spectrum lie purely competitive firms, which are totally without market power. Because the competitive industry is characterized by a large number of relatively small firms selling undifferentiated products, each firm is powerless to influence price. The absence of significant barriers to entry prevents purely competitive firms from earning economic profits in the long run.

Monopolistic competition is the market structure most closely resembling pure competition; the difference is that monopolistically competitive firms sell differentiated products. The ability to differentiate its product allows the monopolistically competitive firm some pricing discretion, although that discretion is limited by the availability of close substitutes offered by competing firms. Monopolistically competitive firms misallocate resources because they fail to produce up to the point where $P = MC$. They also are somewhat less efficient at producing their products than are purely competitive firms with identical cost curves. These disadvantages are at least partially offset by the product variety offered by these sellers.

The third market structure, *oligopoly*, is characterized by a small number of relatively large firms that are protected by significant barriers to entry. Although these firms may enjoy substantial pricing discretion, their market power is constrained by the high degree of interdependence that exists among oligopolistic firms. Oligopolists use *collusion*, secret agreements to fix prices, and *price leadership*, informal agreements to follow the price changes of one firm, as tactics to reduce competition.

The market structure farthest removed from pure competition is monopoly, or *pure monopoly*. The monopolist enjoys substantial pricing discretion and dictates the level of output. The monopoly *is* the industry because it is the sole seller of a product for which there are no close substitutes. Unlike that of the purely competitive firm, the monopolist's position is protected by substantial barriers to entry, which may enable monopolistic firms to earn economic profits in the long run.

Like monopolistically competitive firms, monopolists tend to distort the allocation of resources by halting production short of the point where $P = MC$. Monopolists may charge higher prices than necessary—prices that include economic profits. These higher prices redistribute income from consumers to the monopolists. Oligopoly can have a similar impact on consumer welfare, but it is more difficult to generalize about the consequences of that market structure. In some industries the negative consequences of monopoly or oligopoly may be offset by the lower production costs that result from their greater size or by greater innovation due to their ability to invest economic profits in research and development.

Because the market power of monopolists and oligopolists may harm consumers, the U.S. Congress has passed antitrust laws and created regulatory agencies.

Enacted in response to the formation of *trusts* (combinations of firms organized to restrain competition), *antitrust laws* prohibit certain kinds of behavior: price fixing, tying contracts, and *mergers* entered into for the purpose of limiting competition. The major antitrust statutes are the Sherman Antitrust Act of 1890, the Clayton Antitrust Act of 1914, and the Federal Trade Commission Act, also passed in 1914. Industry regulation, the other approach to dealing with potentially exploitive market power, is designed to establish and police rules of behavior for *natural monopolies*, industries where competition cannot or should not develop because of technical or cost considerations. Unfortunately, regulation has been extended to some industries where there is little evidence of natural monopoly status—transportation, for example. Many economists argue that these industries should be deregulated and subjected to the natural forces of competition. The major federal regulatory agencies are the Interstate Commerce Commission, the Federal Power Commission, and the Federal Communications Commission.

Both regulation and antitrust laws have been subject to criticism. Critics argue that regulation too often becomes a device for restricting entry and raising prices in industries that might otherwise be reasonably competitive. Antitrust laws are criticized from two perspectives. Some hold that they are too weak to constrain the behavior of oligopolists. Others contend that such laws are unnecessary because foreign competition provides adequate protection against abuses of firms with market power. Most economists see some truth in each of these criticisms but argue that antitrust is neither as weak nor as counterproductive as critics suggest.

Glossary

Page 225   ***Antitrust laws.*** Laws that have as their objective the maintenance and promotion of competition.

Page 214   ***Collusion.*** A secret agreement among sellers to fix prices or in some other way restrict competition.

Page 205   ***Industry structure.*** The makeup of an industry: its number of sellers and their size distribution; the nature of the product; the extent of barriers to entry.

Page 225   ***Merger.*** The union of two or more companies into a single firm.

Page 206   ***Monopolistic competition.*** An industry structure characterized by a large number of small sellers of slightly differentiated products and by modest barriers to entry.

Page 218   ***Monopoly.*** An industry structure characterized by a single firm selling a product for which there are no close substitutes and by substantial barriers to entry.

Page 229   ***Natural monopoly.*** An industry in which it is not feasible or advisable to have more than one firm due to technical or cost considerations.

Page 212   ***Oligopoly.*** An industry structure characterized by a few relatively large sellers and substantial barriers to entry.

Page 215   *Price leadership.* An informal arrangement whereby a single firm takes the lead in all price changes in the industry.

Page 225   *Trusts.* Combinations of firms organized for the purpose of restraining competition and thereby gaining economic profit.

Page 228   *Tying contract.* An agreement specifying that the purchaser will, as a condition of sale for some product, also buy some other product offered by the seller.

Study Questions

Fill in the Blanks

1. Firms that can influence the price of their product are said to possess _____ _____.

2. An industry dominated by a few relatively large sellers is an _____ _____.

3. The closest market structure to pure competition is _____ _____.

4. In long-run equilibrium, purely competitive firms and _____ firms can earn only a normal profit.

5. The distinguishing feature of oligopoly is the high degree of _____ that exists among sellers.

6. A _____ is the sole seller of a product for which there are no good substitutes.

7. _____ is a secret agreement between sellers to fix prices or limit competition.

8. Monopolists distort the allocation of scarce resources because they produce (more/less) _____ of their product than is socially desirable.

9. The first major antitrust law, the _____ Act, was passed in 1890.

10. Both oligopolists and monopolists may earn economic profits in the long run because they are protected by substantial _____.

Multiple Choice

1. Which of the following is *not* an element of industry structure?
   a) The number of sellers in the industry
   b) The extent of barriers to entry
   c) The existence of economic profits
   d) The size distribution of sellers

2. Which of the following statements about unregulated monopolists is *false*?
   a) They may incur an economic loss in the short run.
   b) They maximize their profit (or minimize their loss) by producing at the output where $MR = MC$.
   c) They sell their product at a price equal to marginal cost.
   d) They face competition from rivals in other industries.

3. Which of the following is *not* a characteristic of monopolistic competition?
   a) Substantial barriers to entry
   b) Differentiated products
   c) A large number of sellers
   d) Small firms

4. Which of the following is probably *not* a monopolistically competitive firm?
   a) A barber shop
   b) A wheat farm
   c) A hardware store
   d) A furniture store

5. American Airlines will not raise prices without first considering how United will behave. This is probably evidence of their
   a) cutthroat competition.
   b) collusion.
   c) interdependence.
   d) price fixing.

6. Which of the following is *not* a characteristic of oligopolistic industries?
   a) Mutual interdependence
   b) Substantial barriers to entry
   c) Relatively large sellers
   d) Fierce price competition

7. Which of the following do monopolistically competitive firms, oligopolists, and monopolists have in common?
   a) All are relatively large.
   b) All have some market power.
   c) All are protected by substantial barriers to entry.
   d) All are concerned about the reactions of rivals to any actions they take.

STUDY QUESTIONS

8. Which of the following statutes outlawed mergers that would substantially lessen competition?
   a) The Sherman Act
   b) The Clayton Act
   c) The Merger Act
   d) The Federal Trade Commission Act

9. What is the primary difference between antitrust enforcement and industry regulation?
   a) Antitrust enforcement attempts to promote competition; regulation does not.
   b) Antitrust enforcement has some critics; industry regulation does not.
   c) Antitrust enforcement is concerned about the public interest; industry regulation attempts to protect the regulated firms.
   d) Industry regulation deals only with natural monopolies; antitrust does not.

10. According to the kinked demand curve,
   a) rival oligopolists will match a price increase but not a price decrease.
   b) rival oligopolists will match a price decrease but not a price increase.
   c) rival oligopolists will match both price increases and price decreases.
   d) rival oligopolists will match neither price increases nor price decreases.

Problems and Questions for Discussion

1. What constrains a monopolist's pricing discretion?

2. What problems might be associated with monopolistic or oligopolistic market structures? That is, how might they harm consumer well-being?

3. How do firms acquire market power? What impact do barriers to entry have on a firm's market power?

4. Why would we expect prices to be somewhat higher under monopolistic competition than under pure competition?

5. Suppose there is only one grocery store in your neighborhood. What limits its market power? If your neighborhood were more isolated, would that increase or decrease the grocery store's market power?

6. In some communities, grocery stores may act as oligopolists, whereas in other communities they may act as monopolistically competitive firms. How is this possible? How would you distinguish the first situation from the second?

7. Under what circumstances might consumers actually be better off with monopoly or oligopoly than with a competitive structure?

8. What is meant by a *natural monopoly*, and how can its existence justify regulation?

9. As a group, economists have been critical of regulation. Why?

10. Why might our existing antitrust laws be ineffective against oligopolistic firms?

Answer Key

Fill in the Blanks

1. market power
2. oligopoly
3. monopolistic competition
4. monopolistically competitive
5. interdependence
6. monopoly
7. Collusion
8. less
9. Sherman
10. barriers to entry

Multiple Choice

1. c	3. a	5. c	7. b	9. a
2. c	4. b	6. d	8. b	10. b

CHAPTER 8

MARKET FAILURE

At times a market economy may produce too much or too little of certain products and thus fail to make the most efficient use of society's limited resources. This, as you might expect, is referred to as *market failure.* In *The Affluent Society,* John Kenneth Galbraith describes numerous instances of market failure:

> . . . The family which takes its mauve and cerise, air-conditioned, power-steered, and power-braked automobile out for a tour passes through cities that are badly paved, made hideous by litter, blighted buildings, billboards, and posts for wires that should long since have been put underground. They pass on into a countryside that has been rendered largely invisible by commercial art. . . . They picnic on exquisitely packaged food from a portable icebox by a polluted stream and go on to spend the night at a park which is a menace to public health and morals. Just before dozing off on an air mattress, beneath a nylon tent, amid the stench of decaying refuse, they may reflect vaguely on the curious unevenness of their blessings. Is this, indeed, the American genius?[1]

---

[1] John Kenneth Galbraith, *The Affluent Society* (New York: New American Library, 1958), pp. 199–200.

In Galbraith's view, the American economy has produced an abundance of consumer goods—automobiles, appliances, sporting goods, and numerous other items—but far too little of other goods that Americans desire: clean air and water, parks, and well-paved roads, for example. Why do such market failures occur? As you will learn in this chapter, there are three major sources of market failure: market power, externalities, and public goods. The passage from Professor Galbraith's book points at two of these, externalities and public goods. In this chapter, we will explore those two sources of market failure in some detail. Because the impact of market power has been examined at length in Chapters 6 and 7, we will review it only briefly here.

Market Power Revisited

As we all know, the American economy does not function in the idealized manner envisioned by the model of pure capitalism; that is, businesses do not always serve the best interests of society as a whole. In part this is because our industries are less competitive than the model requires them to be. Very few U.S. industries are purely competitive; most are monopolistically competitive or oligopolistic. And the less competitive an industry, the greater the market power (pricing discretion) of its firms.

Because firms with market power tend to restrict output in order to force up prices, too few of society's resources are allocated to the goods and services they produce. In simplified terms, this means that because firms like IBM and General Electric have market power, fewer of society's resources are devoted to producing computers and appliances, and too few Americans will be able to own these products. Markets are "failing" in the sense that they are not allocating resources in the most efficient way—the allocation that would occur under pure competition.

While virtually all economists agree that this form of market failure exists, clearly it is not what Galbraith was describing when he wrote the words we quoted. Galbraith seems to believe that Americans have done quite well in the area of consumer goods. How, then, do we explain his criticism of our economy's performance? The answer lies beyond the problems caused by market power, in some shortcomings of the market mechanism itself.

Externalities as a Source of Market Failure

Considerable resource misallocation results from the failure of private, or un-regulated, markets to take into account all the costs and benefits associated with the production and consumption of a good or service.

When producers are deciding what production techniques to use and what resources to purchase, they tend to consider only internal costs, or *private costs*—the costs actually borne by the firm itself. They do not take into account any external costs that are borne by (or spill over on) other parties. Consumers behave in a similar manner; they tend to consider only *private benefits*—the benefits that accrue to the person or persons purchasing the product—and ignore any external benefits that might be received by others.

If businesses and consumers are permitted to ignore these external costs and benefits, or *externalities,* the result will be an inefficient use of our scarce resources: We will produce too much of some items because we do not consider the full costs; we will produce too little of others because we do not consider the full benefits.

Externalities: The Case of External Costs

It's not difficult to think of personal situations where external costs have come into play. Perhaps you've planned to savor a quiet dinner at your favorite restaurant, only to have a shrieking baby seated with its harried parents at the next table. Think about the movie you might have enjoyed if that rambunctious five-year-old hadn't been using the back of your seat as a bongo drum. Why do parents bring young children to these places, knowing that they will probably disturb the people around them? According to the teachings of Adam Smith, they are pursuing their own self-interest—in this case by minimizing the monetary cost of an evening's entertainment. But their actions are imposing different kinds of costs on everyone around them. The frazzled nerves, poorly digested meals, and generally spoiled evenings experienced by you and your fellow diners or movie goers are examples of *external costs:* the costs created by one party or group and imposed, or *spilled over,* onto some other (nonconsenting) party or group.

Pollution as an External Cost. The classic example of external costs is pollution: the contamination of our land, air, and water caused by the litter that lines our streets and highways, the noxious fumes emitted into our atmosphere, and the wastes dumped into our rivers, lakes, and streams. Why does pollution exist? The answer is really quite obvious. It's less expensive for a manufacturer to dispose of its wastes in a nearby river, for example, than to haul that material to a so-called safe area. But it is a low-cost method of disposal only in terms of the private costs borne by the manufacturing firm. If we consider the social cost, there may well be a cheaper method of disposal.

Social cost refers to the total cost to a society of the production and/or consumption of a product. The term includes not only private or internal costs, but also external costs. To illustrate, let's consider the misuse of our water resources. Polluted water means less fishing and fewer people enjoying water sports. It also means less income for the people who rent boats and cottages and sell fishing bait, for example. It further affects the people living downstream, who need water for drinking and bathing; they will have to pay—through taxes—to purify the water. Finally, it may have a deadly effect on the birds and animal life that live off the fish and other creatures in the water. Thus water pollution may create numerous external costs that are ignored by polluters.

External Costs and Resource Misallocation. When the act of producing or consuming a product creates external costs, an exclusive reliance on private markets and the pursuit of self-interest will result in a misallocation of society's resources. We can illustrate why this is so by investigating a single, hypothetical, purely competitive industry.

For the purpose of our investigation, let's assume the paint industry is purely competitive. In Exh. 8.1, demand curve D shows the quantity of paint that would be demanded at each possible price. Supply curve S_1 shows the quantity of paint the industry would supply at each price if all firms considered only their private costs and disposed of their wastes by dumping them into local rivers. As you can see, these demand and supply curves reveal an equilibrium price of $8 per can and an equilibrium quantity of 120,000 cans per year.

Now suppose that the firms are forced to eliminate the external costs they are creating—that is, they must develop production techniques that eliminate the pollution. This will increase their internal (private) costs of production, which in turn will cause them to reduce their supply to S_2. With this supply reduction will come a higher equilibrium price and a lower equilibrium quantity.

So long as paint suppliers were allowed to shift some of their production costs to society as a whole (or to some portion of society), the price of paint was artificially low; that is, it did not reflect the true social cost of producing the product. Consumers responded to this low price by purchasing an artificially high quantity of the product—more than they would

EXHIBIT 8.1

The Impact of External Costs

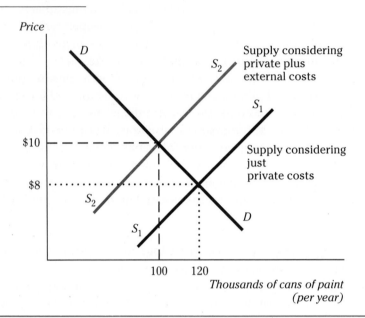

Thousands of cans of paint
(per year)

have purchased if the price reflected the true social cost of production. As a consequence, more of society's scarce resources were allocated to the production of paint than was socially optimal.

When paint suppliers are forced to internalize all costs—that is, when they are forced to consider external as well as internal costs—they must charge a higher price in order to recover these additional costs. To the extent that this higher price reflects accurately the true social cost of production, it will lead to the socially optimal level of output. As you can see from Exh. 8.1, the higher price of paint results in a reduction in the quantity demanded from 120,000 to 100,000 cans per year. Resources must have been misallocated initially, for when consumers are required to pay the true cost of production, their preferences are to use fewer resources in producing paint and allocate more resources to the production of other things.

Correcting for External Costs. Our paint example points out that when manufacturers create external costs, the private market does not record the true costs of production and thereby fails to provide the proper signals to ensure that society's resources are used optimally. In general, problems like this can be corrected only through government intervention. One possibility is for Congress to pass laws that forbid (or limit) activities that impose external costs (like dumping wastes into lakes and streams); another is for government agencies to harness market incentives in an effort to compensate for external costs.

Emissions Standards. The U.S. government has attempted to limit pollution by establishing *emissions standards*—laws that specify the maximum amounts of various wastes that each firm will be allowed to emit into the air or water. To meet these emissions standards, firms have to install pollution-control devices, hire additional personnel to monitor these devices, and take other steps that tend to increase the cost of production and lead to higher product prices. When consumers are required to pay a price that more fully reflects the true cost of production, they purchase fewer units of the formerly underpriced items. Therefore resources can be reallocated to the production of other items whose prices more accurately reflect the full social costs of production.

While government emissions standards have helped reduce pollution, fulfilling their requirements and limiting the discharge of industrial waste to less than some permitted maximum amount can be very costly. Since the polluting firms come from a wide range of industries and employ vastly different production methods, some firms find it much more expensive than others to reduce their discharges. As a consequence, some firms are able to meet their standards at relatively low cost, whereas others face severe financial burdens. The total cost to society of achieving any given level of environmental quality is the sum of the costs incurred by the various firms.

Pollution Taxes. Many economists contend that it would be less expensive to create a *pollution tax,* whereby firms would be required to pay a fee for each unit of waste they discharge into the air or water. Under a system of pollution taxes, firms could discharge as much waste into the environment as they chose, but they would have to pay a specified levy—say, $50—for each unit emitted. Ideally this tax would bring about the desired reduction in pollution. If not, it would be raised to whatever dollar amount would convince firms to reduce pollution to acceptable levels.

A major advantage of a pollution tax is that it would allow the firms themselves to decide who could cut back on emissions (the discharges of wastes) at the lowest cost. For example, given a fee of $50 for each ton of wastes emitted into the environment, those firms that could reduce their emissions for less than $50 per ton would do so; other firms would continue to pollute and pay the tax. As a result, pollution would be reduced by the firms that could do so most easily and at the lowest cost. Society would then

Dumping wastes into a river may minimize private costs, but it can create substantial external costs.

have achieved a given level of environmental quality at the lowest cost in terms of its scarce resources.

A simple example may help to illustrate why the pollution tax is a less expensive approach. Assume that the economy is made up of firms *A* and *B,* and that each firm is discharging four tons of waste a year. Assume also that it costs firm *A* $30 per ton to reduce emissions, while it costs firm *B* $160 per ton.

Suppose society wants to reduce the discharge of wastes by four tons a year. An emissions standard that required each firm to limit its emissions to two tons a year would cost society $380 ($60 for firm *A* and $320 for firm *B*). A pollution tax of $50 a ton would accomplish the same objective at a cost of $120, since it would cause firm *A* to reduce its emissions from four tons to zero. (Firm *A* would opt to reduce its emissions because this approach is less costly than paying the pollution tax. If the firm paid the pollution tax, it would be billed $50 × 4 tons = $200. But it can reduce emissions at a cost of $30 × 4 tons = $120. Thus it would prefer to reduce its emissions rather than pay the pollution tax.) Note that firm *B* will prefer to pay the tax, thus government will receive $200 in pollution tax revenue. This $200 should not be considered a cost of reducing pollution, since it can be used to build roads or schools or be spent in any other way society chooses.

As we noted earlier, the United States has relied on emissions standards to reduce pollution; pollution taxes have been used very sparingly and primarily in an experimental way. But the Clean Air Act of 1990 contains provisions that, like pollution taxes, encourage businesses to reduce pollution in the least costly way. Learn about this new approach by reading "A Marketplace for Pollution Rights" on page 250.

The Optimal Level of Pollution. While emissions standards and pollution taxes are both designed to reduce pollution, neither system is designed to eliminate pollution entirely. The total elimination of pollution would not be in society's best interest, since it requires the use of scarce resources that have alternative uses. Economists support reducing pollution only so long as the benefits of added pollution controls exceed their costs. For example, it makes no sense to force firms to pay an additional $300,000 to reduce pollution if the added benefits to society amount to only $100,000. For that reason, any rational system of pollution control—whether based on emissions standards or pollution taxes—will permit some level of pollution. Unfortunately, because it is difficult to measure the costs and benefits of pollution control in an exact manner, it is also difficult to determine whether efforts to control pollution have been carried too far or not far enough.

Externalities: The Case of External Benefits

Not all externalities are harmful. Sometimes the actions of individuals or businesses create *external benefits*—benefits that are paid for by one party but spill over to other parties. One example is the flowers your neighbors plant in their yard each year. You can enjoy their beauty without contributing to the cost of their planting and upkeep. Another example is flu shots. You pay for them, and they help protect you from the flu. But they also help protect everyone else; if you don't come down with the flu, you can't pass it on to others.

Businesses also can create external benefits. For example, most firms put their workers—particularly their young and/or inexperienced workers—through some sort of training program. Of course, the sponsoring firm gains a more productive, more valuable employee. But most people do not stay with the same employer for their entire working career; when trained employees decide to move on, other employers will benefit from the training they have received.

A Marketplace for Pollution Rights
The Clean Air Act tests a bold new strategy

The new Clean Air Act that President Bush will sign into law this week is long overdue, but for many in the environmental movement it was worth the wait. Major provisions will tighten restrictions on toxic air pollutants, control urban smog and slash emissions of compounds that cause acid rain. But perhaps even more important than any of the specifics for helping Americans breathe easier is a regulatory innovation at the core of the act. Now, companies that clean up quickly will be allowed to benefit financially by selling to their dirtier neighbors tradable permits to pollute. "For the first time, we are unleashing market forces on environmental problems," says Dan Dudek, a senior economist at the New York City-based Environmental Defense Fund.

Bad-air vouchers

This free-market strategy has forged an uncommon alliance of conservatives who are eager to limit the power of government and environmentalists in search of fresh approaches to old problems. The bill's acid-rain provisions place a nationwide cap on sulfur-dioxide emissions from electric utilities, the main cause of acid rain. But instead of relying on the traditional "command and control" strategy of ordering utilities to use a particular pollution-control technology, affected electricity producers will be granted a tradable "right" to emit a certain number of tons of sulfur dioxide each year. Businesses that are cleaner than they're legally required to be are free either to sell their untapped credits or to bank them for future use.

Advocates argue that a system of tradable permits beats command-and-control strategies for a number of reasons.

Under the traditional approach to regulation, they point out, companies had no incentive to go beyond the minimum federal standards. What's more, the government froze innovation in pollution-control technology by in effect specifying how a business was to clean up. But with tradable permits, companies will have an incentive to assign their best engineers to the problem of pollution control. The market approach will also make it advantageous for companies that can clean up most cheaply to do so. This could reduce the overall cost of the nation's effort to clean up acid rain by as much as $2 billion to $3 billion a year, according to Robert Hahn of the American Enterprise Institute in Washington, D.C.

Recent experiments with tradable permits, although limited in scope, have had promising results. For instance, when the Environmental Protection Agency dramatically reduced the lead in gasoline during the mid-1980s, it granted gasoline refiners tradable rights to add a certain amount of lead to each gallon of gasoline they produced. "All evidence suggests that the market was used vigorously and saved hundreds of millions of dollars," says Hahn. . . .

The concept of creating a marketplace for pollution has its critics. Skeptics warn, for instance, that it will be difficult to police the system because the amount of pollutants companies emit may well vary from month to month. "Unless there is stiff vigilance on the part of the government, the loser may be the public," says Richard Ayres, an attorney at the

Natural Resources Defense Council. Others question the wisdom of creating a system of entitlements to pollute, since historically it has been very difficult to take back any legal entitlement once it exists. But even skeptics believe tradable permits deserve a chance. By all accounts, free-market environmentalism can expand the range of regulatory tools, which is bound to be good for the environment.

—*Betsy Carpenter*

SOURCE: "A Marketplace for Pollution Rights," Copyright November 12, 1990, *U.S. News & World Report*, p. 79.

USE YOUR ECONOMIC REASONING

1. What is meant by the "command and control" strategy for reducing pollution? What are the problems associated with this approach?

2. What companies would want to buy permits to pollute rather than simply reduce their own pollution to levels in compliance with the amount permitted? What companies might be willing to sell such permits?

3. In July 1991, the Chicago Board of Trade voted to create a private market in which "permits to emit sulfur dioxide" can be bought and sold. How will the selling price of these permits be determined?

4. How can society benefit from a system that allows companies to buy and sell permits to pollute?

Your neighbor's well-groomed lawn provides external benefits. You can enjoy its appearance without contributing to its upkeep.

External Benefits and Resource Allocation. In a pure market economy, individuals would tend to demand too small a quantity of those products that generate external benefits. To understand why this is so, consider your own consumption decisions for a moment. When you are deciding whether to purchase a product (or how much of a product to purchase), you compare the product's benefits with its price. If you value a unit of the product more than the other items you could purchase with the same money, you buy it. If not, you spend your money on the product you value more highly. In effect, you are deciding which product delivers the most benefits for the money. But whose benefits are you considering? Your own, of course! In other words, you respond to private benefits rather than external benefits. Most consumption decisions are made this way. As a result, consumers purchase too small a quantity of the products that create external benefits, and our scarce resources are misallocated. That is to say, fewer resources are devoted to producing these products than is justified by their *social benefits*—the sum of the private benefits received by those that purchase the product and the external benefits received by others.

Adjusting for External Benefits. To illustrate the underproduction of products that carry external benefits, let's examine what would happen if elementary education were left to the discretion of the private market. Reading, writing, and arithmetic are basic skills that have obvious benefits for the individual, but they also benefit society as a whole. In his prize-winning book, *Capitalism and Freedom*, economist Milton Friedman makes the case as follows:

A stable and democratic society is impossible without a minimum amount of literacy and knowledge on the part of most citizens and without widespread acceptance of some common set of values. Education can contribute to both. In consequence, the gain from the education of a child accrues not only to the child or to his parents but also to other members of the society. . . .[2]

For the sake of our example, let's suppose that all elementary education in the United States is provided through private schools on a voluntary basis. In such a situation the number of children enrolled in these schools would be determined by the forces of demand and supply. As shown in Exh. 8.2, the market would establish a price of $500 per student, and at that price three million students would attend elementary school each year. The market demand curve (D_1) provides an incomplete picture, however. It considers private benefits—the benefits received by the students and their parents—but ignores external benefits. If we include the external benefits of education, society would want even more children to be educated. Demand curve D_2

EXHIBIT 8.2

The Impact of External Benefits

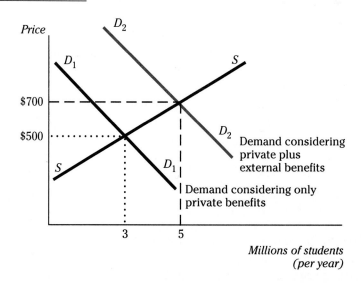

[2] Milton Friedman, *Capitalism and Freedom* (Chicago: The University of Chicago Press, 1962), p. 86.

Return of a Childhood Killer

Two trips to the doctor, two relatively painless shots: Measles prevention is that simple. Yet the virus that in 1983 seemed all but extinct has doctors and public-health officials seriously worried. In Dallas, Los Angeles and Chicago, measles has turned into an epidemic. Some 17,850 people got measles last year, and officials at the federal Centers of Disease Control (CDC) in Atlanta expect to see 25,000 cases by the end of 1990, up from 1,500 in 1983. At least 80 people have died of the disease this year; seven years ago, not one person did. "It's shameful that a country as wealthy as ours has fallen so far behind in fighting a virus we know how to stop," says Dr. Leonard Plotkin, chairman of the American Academy of Pediatrics (AAP) committee on infectious diseases.

The reasons for the flagging fight are hardly mysterious.

Before 1963, when the measles vaccine was introduced, 400,000 people a year became ill. Recent outbreaks have seemed so insignificant by comparison that many parents, especially those who rely on public-health clinics, dismiss the risk and don't have children inoculated when they should; instead, they wait until they have to, when the kids enter school. Sometimes those who do get a shot are not protected, since the vaccine fails to "take" in 5 of every 100 people, according to Dr. William Atkinson, an epidemiologist in charge of measles surveillance at the CDC. Some scientists put the number at 8 in 100. . . .

Because all states now require entering kindergartners to have been vaccinated, school-age children, once hardest hit, are relatively safe this time. Instead, the profoundly contagious virus has grown virulent in two new groups: Children under 5, especially inner-city preschoolers, and adults age 19 to 33 who never had the disease. Seventy percent of the current cases occur in unvaccinated infants and preschoolers, who then spread the virus in day care, in shopping malls, on elevators, in hospital waiting rooms. Because of their immature immune systems, very young children are at a higher risk than other age groups of developing potentially fatal complications such as pneumonia. . . .

In the wake of the 1989 outbreaks, the medical community last year tightened its recommendations on administration of the measles vaccine. The longstanding practice of giving children their first vaccination at the age of 15 months stands. That's the earliest a shot will be effective; in younger infants, antibodies received from the mother through the placenta may prevent the vaccine from causing the mild infection that induces the immune system to produce its own antibodies.

Once an outbreak hits a community, children 12 months old or even younger should get a shot; vaccination within three days of exposure greatly reduces chances of getting sick. . . .

A double shield

Virtually everyone who receives a second shot is assured immunity, which prompted the medical community's announcement last year that every child should be vaccinated twice. . . .

Many adults would be wise to head for the doctor's office, too. The American College of Physicians now recommends one dose of the vaccine for any adult age 33 or under who has neither had measles nor been vaccinated. . . .

Unless you belong to a health maintenance organization, which normally absorbs all or most of the cost of vaccination, the $35-to-$50 office visit and measles shot will come from your pocket.

In theory, at least, public-health clinics will vaccinate any child, usually for free. But many urban clinics are overburdened because doctors are referring more patients to

public facilities. The clinics have often had to turn people away. Once inconvenienced, many people fail to return. In Texas, where officials report a 700 percent rise in referrals from private doctors to public clinics since 1980, there has been nowhere near a corresponding rise in funds to extend clinic hours and add nurses. Last year, Southern California public clinics saw demand for vaccine services jump 24 percent, more than triple the normal 7 percent annual rise. The AAP thinks the federal budget for next year should include $236 million for childhood-immunization programs, compared with $156 million this year; the President is asking for $153 million.

"We're chasing the epidemic rather than trying to stop it," complains Jackie Noyes, a lobbyist for the AAP.

Measles is here to stay, at least for a few more years. But preventing it in your own family demands no more than checking a few records and, if necessary, a trip to get a shot. That's hardly a high price to pay. —*Scott Minerbrook and Francesca Lunzer Kritz*

SOURCE: "Return of a Childhood Killer," Copyright August 20, 1990, *U.S. News & World Report*, p. 64.

USE YOUR ECONOMIC REASONING

1. The article seems to suggest that there are external benefits associated with measles vaccinations. What are those external benefits?

2. If individuals are purchasing too few measles vaccinations (or are waiting to long to have their children vaccinated), how can government attack the problem?

3. Suppose that the only action taken by government was to require that parents have their children inoculated at 15 months. Would this solve the problem? Why or why not?

shows that society would choose to educate five million students a year at an equilibrium price of $700 per student.

As you can see from the Exh. 8.2 diagram, individuals pursuing their own self-interest would choose to purchase less education than could be justified on the basis of the full social benefits. An obvious solution to this problem would be to require that each child attend school for some minimum number of years, allowing the family to select the school and find the money to pay for it. The U.S. government has taken a different approach, however. That is, most elementary and secondary schools are operated by local governments and financed through taxes rather than through fees charged to parents. This spreads the financial burden for education among all taxpayers rather than just the parents of school-aged children. In effect, taxpayers without children "subsidize" taxpayers with children. The rationale for this approach is fairly clear-cut. Since all taxpayers share in the benefits of education (the external benefits, at least), they should share in the costs as well.

In a variety of circumstances subsidies can be used to encourage the consumption of products that carry external benefits. Consider the flu shots again. They protect not only the people inoculated, but also those in contact with them. Still, many people will not pay to receive a flu shot. So if we want more people to get flu shots (but we don't want to pass laws requiring such shots), we could have the government subsidize all or part of the cost. The lower the price of flu shots, the more people who will agree to get them. (Should government subsidize measles vaccinations? Read "Return of a Childhood Killer," on page 254 before you decide.)

There is no reason why subsidized flu shots would have to be provided by government doctors; the government could simply agree to pay private doctors for each flu shot administered. It is precisely this approach that Milton Friedman would like to see implemented in education. Rather than continuing to subsidize public schools, Friedman would prefer a system that permitted students to select their own privately run schools.

> Government could require a minimum level of schooling financed by giving parents vouchers redeemable for a specified maximum sum per child per year if spent on "approved" educational services. Parents would then be free to spend this sum and any additional sum they themselves provided on purchasing educational services from an "approved" institution of their own choice. . . . The role of government would be limited to insuring that the schools met certain minimum standards. . . .[3]

---

[3] Milton Friedman, *Capitalism and Freedom* (Chicago: The University of Chicago Press, 1962), p. 86.

Whether or not you agree with Friedman's particular approach, it should be clear to you by now that subsidies can be useful in correcting for market failure. By encouraging the production and consumption of products yielding external benefits, subsidies help ensure that society's resources are used to produce the optimal assortment of goods and services.

Market Failure and the Provision of Public Goods

Market power and the existence of externalities are not the only sources of market failure. Markets may also fail to produce optimal results because some products are simply not well-suited to sale by private firms. These products must be provided by government or they will not be provided at all.

Private Goods versus Public Goods

In order to understand this problem, we must think first about the types of goods and services our economy produces. Those goods and services fall into three categories: pure private goods, private goods that yield external benefits, and public goods.

Pure private goods are products that convey their benefits only to the purchaser.[4] The hamburger you had for lunch falls in that category, and so does the jacket you wore to class. Most of the products we purchase in the marketplace are pure private goods.

Some products convey most of their benefits to the person making the purchase but also create substantial external benefits for others. These are *private goods that yield significant external benefits.* We have talked about education and flu shots, but there are numerous other examples—fire protection, police protection, and driver's training, to name just a few.

The third category, *public goods,* consists of products that convey their benefits equally to paying and nonpaying members of society. National defense is probably the best example of a public good. If a business attempted to sell "units" of national defense through the marketplace, what problems

---

[4] Note that although pure private goods convey their benefits only to the purchaser, the purchaser may *choose* to share those benefits with others. For instance, you may decide to share your hamburger with another person or allow someone else to wear your jacket. But if others share in the benefits of a pure private good, it is because the purchaser allows them to share those benefits, not because the benefits automatically spilled over to them.

Poverty: A Different Type of Market Failure

The existence of poverty may be regarded as a different type of market failure—a type that is not related to the quest for economic efficiency. Even if a market system were able to achieve an optimal allocation of resources, if it distributed income in a way that a majority of the population saw as inequitable or unfair, we might judge that to be a failure of the market system.

In a market system, a person's income depends on what he or she has to sell. Those with greater skills and more assets (land and capital) earn higher incomes; those with fewer skills and fewer assets earn lower incomes. As a consequence, a total reliance on the market mechanism can produce substantial inequality in the income distribution. Some people are bound to have less while others have much more.

How unequal is the income distribution in the United States? As you can see from the accompanying exhibit,

Percent of Aggregate Income Received by Each Fifth of Families in the United States*			
	1970	1980	1990
Lowest fifth	4.1%	4.2%	3.9%
Second fifth	10.8	10.2	9.6
Third fifth	17.4	16.8	15.9
Fourth fifth	24.5	24.8	24.0
Highest fifth	43.3	44.1	46.6

* Based on money income before taxes. Source: *Current Population Reports: Consumer Income*, Series P-60, No. 174, published by the Bureau of the Census in August 1991.

there is a significant amount of inequality. In 1990, the families in the lowest quintile (the lowest fifth) of the income distribution received less than 4 percent of total money income in the United States, while the families in the upper fifth received more than 45 percent of total income. In fact, the families in the upper fifth of the income distribution actually received more total income than all the families in the bottom three-fifths of the distribution. Moreover, the income distribution in the United States seems to be growing somewhat less equal. As you can see in the exhibit, the fraction of aggregate income going to the richest fifth of U.S. families has increased over the last twenty years, while the shares going to the remaining four-fifths of families have declined.

The existence of inequality may not concern us very much if everyone—including the families in the bottom fifth of the income distribution—is earning enough income to live comfortably. What most of us are really concerned about is families that are living in poverty—those with incomes that are insufficient to provide for their basic needs (according to some standard established by the society).

In the United States we have adopted income standards by which to judge the extent of poverty. For example, in 1990, a family of four was classified as "poor" if it had an income of less than $13,359. By that definition, there were 33.6 million poor people in the United States in

1990—a little less than 14 percent of the population.

Most of us would probably agree that if 14 percent of our population—one person out of every seven—is living in poverty we have some cause for concern. The United States has attempted to address the problem of poverty in a variety of ways. First of all, there are a number of programs designed to get at the source of poverty: the inability of the family to earn an adequate income. For example, there are government subsidized training programs for unemployed workers and policies designed to reduce discrimination in hiring.

Other government programs are designed to reduce the misery of the poor, even if they do not eliminate the cause of poverty. Social Security provides financial assistance to the old, the disabled, the unemployed, and families that are in financial difficulty because of the death of a breadwinner. Aid to Families with Dependent Children (a federal-state program) provides aid to poor families, often with the stipulation that there is not an able-bodied man in the house. In addition to these cash assistance programs there are a variety of in-kind assistance programs that provide the poor with some type of good or service. Food stamps and subsidized public housing are two examples. All these programs are designed to improve the status of the poor and in this way moderate the income distribution dictated by the market.

USE YOUR ECONOMIC REASONING

1. **What accounts for the degree of income inequality in the United States? Why do the families in the highest quintile earn so much more than the families in the lowest quintile?**

2. **How has the income distribution in the United States changed since 1970? Has the income distribution become more equal or more unequal?**

3. **What criteria would you use to decide whether or not the income distribution in the United States is fair? Do the statistics contained in this article provide you with sufficient information to make that determination?**

would arise? The major problem would be that nonpayers would receive virtually the same protection from foreign invasion as those who paid for the protection. There's no way to protect your house from foreign invasion without simultaneously protecting your neighbor's. The inability to exclude nonpayers from receiving the same benefits as those who have paid for the product is what economists call the *free-rider problem*.

The Free-Rider Problem

Why does the inability to exclude certain individuals from receiving benefits constitute a problem? Think about national defense for just a moment. How would you feel if you were paying for national defense and your neighbor received exactly the same protection for nothing? Very likely, you would decide to become a free rider yourself, as would many other people. Products like national defense, flood-control dams, and tornado warning systems cannot be offered in such a way as to restrict their benefits to payers alone. Therefore no private business can expect to earn a profit by offering such goods and services, and private markets cannot be relied on to produce these products, no matter how important they are for the well-being of the society. Unless the government intervenes, they simply will not be provided at all.

Of course we're not willing to let that happen. That's why a substantial amount of our tax money pays for national defense and other public goods. (Not all publicly *provided* goods are public goods. Our tax dollars are used to pay for education and public swimming pools and a host of other goods and services that do not meet the characteristics of public goods.) As we have emphasized, the ultimate objective of government intervention is to improve the allocation of society's scarce resources so that the economy will do a better job of satisfying our unlimited wants. To the extent that government intervention contributes to that result, it succeeds in correcting for market failure and improving our social welfare. (Some economists view the existence of poverty as a form of market failure that's quite different from those described in this chapter. The article on p. 258 provides a brief look at that problem.)

Summary

Market failure occurs when a market economy produces too much or too little of certain products and thus fails to make the most efficient use of society's limited resources.

There are three major sources of market failure: market power, externalities, and public goods. The exercise of market power can lead to a misuse of society's resources because firms with market power tend to restrict output in order to force up prices. As a consequence, too few of society's resources will be allocated to the production of the goods and services provided by firms with market power.

Another source of market failure is the market's inability to reflect all costs and benefits. In some instances, the act of producing or consuming a product creates *externalities*—costs or benefits not borne by either buyers or sellers but that spill over onto third parties. When this happens, the market has no way of taking those costs and benefits into account and adjusting production and consumption decisions accordingly. As a consequence, the market fails to give us optimal results; our resources are not used as well as they could be. We produce too much of some things because we do not consider all costs; we produce too little of other things because we do not consider all benefits. To correct these problems, government must pursue policies that force firms to pay the full social cost of the products they create and encourage the production and consumption of products with external benefits.

Markets may also fail to produce optimal results simply because some products are not well-suited for sale by private firms. Public goods fall into that category. *Public goods* are products that convey their benefits equally to all members of society, whether or not all members have paid for those products. National defense is probably the best example. It is virtually impossible to sell national defense through markets because there is no way to exclude nonpayers from receiving the same benefits as payers. Since there is no way for a private businessperson to earn a profit by selling such products, private markets cannot be relied on to produce these goods or services, no matter how important they are to the well-being of the society.

Glossary

Page 249   ***External benefits.*** Benefits paid for by one party or group that spill over to other parties or groups; also referred to as spillover benefits.

Page 244   ***External costs.*** Costs created by one party or group and imposed on other (unconsenting) parties or groups; also referred to as spillover costs.

Page 244   ***Externalities.*** Costs or benefits that are not borne by either buyers or sellers but that spill over onto third parties.

Study Questions

Fill in the Blanks

1. _____ are instances in which a market economy fails to make the most efficient use of society's limited resources.

2. The term _____ is used to describe costs borne or benefits received by parties other than those involved in the transaction.

3. Social costs are the sum of _____ and _____ _____.

4. One way to encourage the consumption of products with external benefits would be to _____ their purchase.

5. _____ are products that convey their benefits only to the buyer.

6. National defense is an example of a _____.

7. Another word for "private" costs and benefits is _____ costs and benefits.

8. _____ are benefits that are paid for by one party but spill over to other parties.

9. The major reason our rivers and streams have been used as disposal sites is because this approach minimized the firm's _____ costs of production.

10. If an action creates no external costs or benefits, then private costs will equal _____ costs.

Multiple Choice

1. A market economy will tend to underproduce products that create
   a) social benefits.
   b) social costs.
   c) external benefits.
   d) external costs.

2. Which of the following is an example of a pure private good?
   a) A desk
   b) Education
   c) A fence between neighbors
   d) A park

3. Which of the following is most likely to produce external costs?
   a) Liquor
   b) A steak
   c) A flower garden
   d) A storm warning system

4. If the firms in an industry have been creating pollution and they are forced to find a method of waste disposal that does not damage the environment, the result will probably be
   a) a lower price for the product offered by the firms.
   b) a higher product price and a higher equilibrium quantity.
   c) a lower product price and a higher equilibrium quantity.
   d) a higher product price and a lower equilibrium quantity.

5. Which of the following is the best example of a pure public good?
   a) A cigarette
   b) A bus
   c) A lighthouse
   d) An automobile

6. If a product creates external benefits, the demand curve that reflects all social benefits
   a) will be to the left of the demand curve that reflects only private benefits
   b) will be to the right of the demand curve that reflects only private benefits.
   c) will not be downward sloping.
   d) will be the same as the demand curve that reflects private benefits.

7. Public goods can lead to market failure because
   a) they create external costs.
   b) they create social costs.
   c) they cannot be sold easily in markets.
   d) they cannot be paid for through taxes.

STUDY QUESTIONS

8. Banning all pollution may not be the optimal strategy because
   a) the costs may exceed the benefits.
   b) the benefits of this approach are probably limited.
   c) the harm caused by pollution is generally overestimated.
   d) the benefits of a clean environment are generally overestimated.

9. Which of the following is *not* true?
   a) If social costs exceed private costs, external costs are present.
   b) If a product creates external costs, society should devote fewer resources to its production.
   c) If a society fails to consider externalities, it will not use its resources optimally.
   d) Consumers tend to purchase too much of products that create external benefits.

10. Which of the following best describes the free-rider problem?
    a) Your brother always rides home with you but never pays for the gas.
    b) Some private goods create external benefits for those who have not paid.
    c) Some people think that the environment is a free resource and therefore abuse it.
    d) Some goods cannot be sold in markets because the benefits they confer are available to all—whether they have paid or not.

Problems and Questions for Discussion

1. Why should you and I be concerned about whether or not our society's resources are used optimally?

2. What is market failure, and what are the sources of this problem?

3. How can fines and subsidies be used to correct market failure?

4. Most businesses are concerned about our environment, but they may be reluctant to stop polluting unless all other firms in their industry are also forced to stop. Why?

5. If we force firms to stop polluting, the result will probably be higher product prices. Is that good or bad? Why?

6. Why is it important (from society's viewpoint) to encourage the production and consumption of products that yield external benefits?

7. If we're really concerned about external costs, there would be some logic in fining any spectator who insisted on standing up to cheer at football games. What would be the logic? What practical considerations make this an impractical solution?

8. Why is a tornado warning system a public good? What about a flood-control dam? Why does it fall into that category?

STUDY QUESTIONS

9. Milton Friedman suggests that while it makes sense to subsidize a general education in the liberal arts, it makes much less sense to subsidize purely vocational training. What do you suppose is the logic behind that distinction?

10. Explain how the free-rider problem leads to market failure.

Answer Key

Fill in the Blanks

1. Market failures
2. externalities or spillovers
3. private costs, external costs
4. subsidize
5. Private goods
6. public good
7. internal
8. External benefits
9. private or internal
10. social

Multiple Choice

1. c	3. a	5. c	7. c	9. d
2. a	4. d	6. b	8. a	10. d

267

For the past several chapters we have been studying the individual elements that make up an economy. Now we switch from the study of these individual parts of the economy to the study of the overall economy and its operation. In other words, we switch from microeconomics to macroeconomics.

Macroeconomics is the study of the economy as a whole and the factors that influence the economy's overall performance. (If you have a hard time remembering the difference between microeconomics and macroeconomics, just remember that *micro* means small—microcomputer, microfilm, microsurgery—whereas *macro* means large. That should help you keep them straight.) Macroeconomics addresses a number of important questions: What determines the level of total output and total employment in the economy? What causes unemployment? What causes inflation? What can be done to eliminate these problems, or at least to reduce their severity? These and many other considerations relating to the economy's overall performance are the domain of macroeconomics.

In Chapter 9, we begin our study of macroeconomics by examining some indicators, or measures, that economists watch in order to determine how well the economy is performing. Chapter 10 introduces aggregate demand and aggregate supply, and considers how these twin forces interact to determine the levels of prices, output, and employment in the economy. The chapter then uses the aggregate demand and supply framework to examine the views of the classical economists—the earliest macroeconomists—and why their views were challenged in the Keynesian revolution. Chapter 11 takes a closer look at the Keynesian model of income and output determination. It investigates the determinants of consumption and investment spending and the way in which consumption, investment, and saving interact to determine the equilibrium level of output. The possibility of unemployment or inflation is also explored. Chapter 12 takes a detailed look at *fiscal policy*—government spending and taxation policy designed to combat unemployment or inflation. This chapter also considers some of the problems that may be encountered in applying these policies.

Chapter 13 examines how depository institutions—commercial banks, savings and loan associations, mutual savings banks—"create" money, and how the Federal Reserve attempts to control the money supply. Chapter 14 takes a detailed look at the concepts of aggregate demand and supply that were briefly introduced in Chapter 10, and uses the aggregate demand and supply framework to examine the possibility that the economy is self-correcting—that it tends to automatically eliminate unemployment. Chapter 15 concludes the macroeconomics section of the textbook by exploring the debate between "activists," who believe that government should attempt to manage the economy's overall performance, and "nonactivists," who believe that such attempts are ill-advised.

MEASURING
AGGREGATE
PERFORMANCE

Of the economic problems we've talked about so far, which one do you think Americans are most concerned about: The market power of large corporations and labor unions? The distortions caused by agricultural price supports or minimum-wage laws? Environmental pollution?

According to national surveys, none of these problems are foremost in the minds of Americans. Throughout most of the last decade, the major concerns voiced by Americans have been two macroeconomic problems: unemployment and inflation. In the next few chapters we'll be examining the factors that influence the economy's *aggregate*, or overall, performance and how problems such as unemployment and inflation arise. We will also consider policies to combat unemployment and inflation and the difficulties that may be encountered in applying these policies.

This chapter sets the stage for that discussion by examining some *economic indicators*—signals or measures that tell us how well the economy is performing. After all, policymakers can't take actions that lead to better performance unless they know when problems exist. Economic indicators provide that information. The economic indicators we will discuss in this chapter include the unemployment rate, the Consumer Price Index, and the gross national product (GNP)—the indicator that many economists believe is the most important single measure of the economy's performance.

Measuring Unemployment

One dimension of our economy's performance is its ability to provide jobs for those who desire to work. For most of us, that's an extremely important aspect of the economy's performance because we value work not only as a source of income but also to maintain our sense of personal worth. The most highly publicized indicator of performance in this area is the unemployment rate. The *unemployment rate* traditionally reported is the percentage of the civilian labor force that is unemployed. The *civilian labor force* is made up of all persons over the age of sixteen who are not in the armed forces and who are either employed or actively seeking employment. The Bureau of Labor Statistics (BLS), the agency responsible for gathering and analyzing labor force and employment data, surveys some 60,000 households throughout the United States monthly to determine the employment status of the residents. It uses the statistics gathered from this sample (a sample scientifically designed to be representative of the entire U.S. population) to estimate the total size of the labor force and the actual rate of unemployment.

Counting the Unemployed

How does the Bureau of Labor Statistics decide whether a particular person should be classified as unemployed? The first thing it does is determine whether or not they have a job. As far as the BLS is concerned, you are employed if you did *any* work for pay in the week of the survey. It doesn't matter how long you worked, provided that you worked for pay. You are also counted as employed if you worked fifteen hours or more (during the survey week) as an unpaid worker in a family-operated business.

Even if you didn't have a job during the survey week, you are not recognized as unemployed unless you were actively seeking employment. To be "actively seeking employment" you must have done something to try to find a job—filled out applications, responded to want ads, or at least registered at an employment agency. If you did any of those things and failed to find a job, you are officially unemployed. If you didn't look for work, you're considered as "not participating" in the civilian labor force and consequently you won't be counted as unemployed.

The purpose of the BLS monthly survey is to estimate the size of the civilian labor force (the number employed plus those actively seeking employment) and the number of unemployed. Then the bureau computes the unemployment rate by dividing the total number of unemployed persons by the total number of people in the civilian labor force. In 1991, for example, there were 125.3 million people in the civilian labor force, and 8.4 million of them were unemployed. These figures represent averages—the average number of people in the civilian labor force and the average number of people unemployed—for 1991. This means that the average *civilian unemployment rate* for 1991 was 6.7 percent:[1]

$$\text{Unemployment rate} = \frac{\text{total number of unemployed persons}}{\substack{\text{total number of persons} \\ \text{in the civilian labor force}}}$$

$$\text{Unemployment rate (1991)} = \frac{\text{8.4 million unemployed persons}}{\substack{\text{125.3 million persons in} \\ \text{the civilian labor force}}}$$

$$\text{Unemployment rate (1991)} = 6.7 \text{ percent}$$

Types of Unemployment

In general, a high unemployment rate is interpreted as a sign of a weak economy, whereas a low rate is seen as a sign of strength. But in order to recognize a low rate of unemployment when we see it, we have to know what we are aiming for, what is possible or realistic. That in turn requires knowledge of the three basic types of unemployment—frictional, cyclical, and structural—and the extent to which these types of unemployment are unavoidable.

Frictional Unemployment. Even when there are plenty of jobs available, there are always some people out of work because they are changing jobs or searching for their first job. Economists call this *frictional unemployment,* to describe the fact that labor-market adjustments involve time lags or "fric-

---

[1] In 1983 the Bureau of Labor Statistics began to publish a second unemployment rate, one calculated in a somewhat different way. This new method incudes as part of the labor force members of the military who are stationed in the United States (resident armed forces). The result is a slightly lower unemployment rate (6.6 percent in 1991) than the one computed in the traditional way.

  Although government press releases tend to focus on the new, lower rate, it is not strictly comparable to past unemployment rates. Therefore the media, professional economists, and others who track the economy's performance continue to regard the civilian unemployment rate as more relevant.

tion." A certain amount of frictional unemployment is unavoidable and probably even desirable. It is a sign that employers are looking for the most qualified workers and that workers are searching for the best jobs. Neither party is willing to settle for the first thing that comes along. That's good for the economy because it means that the right people are more likely to be matched with the right jobs. But it takes time for workers and employers to find each other, and meanwhile the job seekers are adding to the nation's unemployment rate.

Cyclical Unemployment. *Cyclical unemployment* is joblessness caused by a reduction in the economy's total demand for goods and services. When such a reduction occurs, perhaps because consumers have decided to save more and spend less, businesses that are not able to sell as much output as before usually must cut back on production. This means that some of their workers will become unemployed. We call this unemployment cyclical because we recognize that the economy goes through cycles of economic activity. For a while the economy expands and unemployment declines; then economic activity slows and unemployment rises. You can see this pattern clearly in Exh. 9.1.

When people are cyclically unemployed, the economy is losing the output these workers could have produced, and of course the workers are losing the income they could have earned. Many economists argue that it is possible to reduce the amount of cyclical unemployment by using government policies to stimulate the total demand for goods and services.

Structural Unemployment. *Structural unemployment* is caused by changes in the makeup or structure of the economy that render certain skills obsolete or in less demand. The economy is always changing. New products are introduced and old ones are dropped; businesses continually develop new production methods. These kinds of changes can have a profound effect on the demand for labor. Skills that were very much in demand ten or twenty years ago may be virtually obsolete today. Computerized photocomposition machines have virtually eliminated the need for newspaper typesetters, for example, and robots have begun to replace semiskilled workers in automobile manufacturing plants. Further automation will signal a similar fate for workers in many other manufacturing industries.

The Bureau of Labor Statistics predicts that by the year 2000 the number of jobs in manufacturing will decrease to 18.2 million, from about 19 million in 1990. Moreover, within manufacturing, the nature of the work will change so that many of today's manufacturing workers will find themselves

EXHIBIT 9.1

The Unemployment Rate: 1929–1991

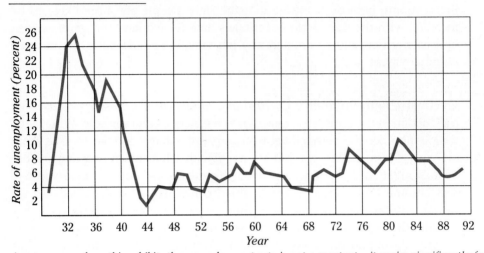

As you can see from this exhibit, the unemployment rate is not a constant—it varies significantly from year to year. But even though the unemployment rate varies, there is a pattern to that variation, an up-and-down cycle that keeps repeating itself. For example, we can see that the unemployment rate dropped from a high of about 25 percent in 1933 to approximately 14 percent in 1937. Then the unemployment rate jumped back up to 19 percent in 1938 and started a steady decline that continued until 1944. The same sort of pattern is evident over other time periods, although the magnitude of the changes certainly is not as great.

The rate reported is the civilian unemployment rate. Sources for these statistics were *Historical Statistics of the United States* (Bureau of the Census) and *Economic Report of the President,* 1992.

unqualified for the jobs of the future—jobs that will require more education and the ability to work with programmable machines.[2]

The changing skill requirements of the workplace are not the only source of structural unemployment. Some people cannot hold a job in the modern economy because they never received much education or training in the first place. We know this is the case with many members of inner-city minorities, who often are educated in second-rate school systems that have a high dropout rate. It is also possible for people to be structurally unemployed even though they have marketable skills. For example, unemployed construction workers in the Midwest (where economic growth has slowed) may have

[2] Doron P. Levin, "Smart Machines, Smart Workers," *New York Times,* October 17, 1988, p. D1.

Structurally unemployed workers may need to be retrained before they can find jobs.

skills that are very much in demand. But if the available construction jobs are in New England or the South Atlantic region of the United States, the Midwestern workers remain structurally unemployed.

All structurally unemployed workers have one thing in common: If they are to find jobs, they must make drastic changes. They will have to acquire new skills or move to a different part of the country. They may even find it necessary to do both. Since such changes cannot be made overnight, economists see structural unemployment as a longer-term problem than frictional or cyclical unemployment. This is also the reason why many social scientists view structural unemployment as one of the most serious problems of our time.

Full Employment Versus Zero Unemployment

Since a certain amount of frictional and structural unemployment is unavoidable, economists consider zero unemployment an unattainable goal. Although no one knows precisely how much unemployment is of the frictional and structural varieties, a common estimate is something in the neighborhood of $5\frac{1}{2}$ percent. For that reason, many economists believe that $5\frac{1}{2}$ percent unemployment ought to be considered *full employment*—the minimum level of unemployment that our economy can achieve in normal times.

A Closer Look at Unemployment Rates

Recognizing that full employment doesn't mean zero unemployment is an important step in learning how to interpret unemployment statistics. The next step is learning to look beyond the overall unemployment rate to see how various groups in our society are being affected. Although we all talk about "the" unemployment rate, in reality the rate of unemployment varies substantially among different subcategories of the American labor force. Historically, blacks have been about twice as likely to be unemployed as whites; women have tended toward slightly higher unemployment rates than men; and teenagers usually have had unemployment rates in the vicinity of $2\frac{1}{2}$ to 3 times the overall rate for their racial group.

Exhibit 9.2 shows the unemployment rates for 1991. Let's consider the figures. First, note that in 1991 the overall unemployment rate for all civilian workers—that is, "the" unemployment rate—was 6.7 percent. Next, let's look at the unemployment rates for the various subcategories of the labor force. The overall rate for black workers (12.4 percent) was more than twice the rate for white workers (6.0 percent), and this relationship held for each of the subcategories: men, women, and teenagers. Note that the rates for teenagers were also within the expected ranges: the rate for white teen-

EXHIBIT 9.2

Unemployment Rates for 1991

WORKER CATEGORY	RATE	WORKER CATEGORY	RATE	WORKER CATEGORY	RATE
All civilian workers	6.7%	*White*	6.0%	*Black*	12.4%
Men (20 and over)	6.3	Men (20 and over)	5.7	Men (20 and over)	11.5
Women (20 and over)	5.7	Women (20 and over)	4.9	Women (20 and over)	10.5
Teenagers (16–19)	18.6	Teenagers (16–19)	16.3	Teenagers (16–19)	36.3

Source: Economic Report of the President, 1992.

agers was approximately $2\frac{1}{2}$ times the overall rate for whites, while the rate for black teenagers was nearly 3 times the overall rate for blacks. The overall unemployment rate for women, however, was slightly *less* than the rate for men, not higher as anticipated. (The differential between the overall rate for women and the overall rate for men has been narrowing for several decades, and may now be a thing of the past. In fact, since a higher proportion of women are employed in service occupations—the fastest growing segment of the economy—lower overall rates for women may become the norm.)

As you can see, the overall unemployment rate conceals a great deal of variation across particular groups. Even when the overall rate is low, the unemployment rate among certain subcategories of our population may be unacceptably high. For that reason, those who rely on unemployment statistics for devising policies to combat unemployment or for helping the unemployed in other ways must be willing to look beyond the overall rate to gain a clearer picture of the nature and severity of the unemployment problem.

Unemployment Rates: A Word of Caution

Before we leave this section on unemployment statistics, a few words of caution are appropriate. Watching the unemployment rate can help you understand whether the economy is growing weaker or stronger. But changes in the unemployment rate from one month to the next may not be very meaningful. In fact, they can sometimes send misleading signals about the state of the economy.

To illustrate that point, suppose that the economy is in the midst of a deep *recession*—a period of reduced economic activity and relatively high unemployment—when the Bureau of Labor Statistics reports a small drop in the unemployment rate. Should that drop be taken as a sign that the economy is growing stronger? Not necessarily. When the economy has been in a recession for quite a while, some unemployed workers become discouraged in their search for jobs and stop looking. Since these "discouraged workers" are no longer actively seeking employment, they are no longer counted as unemployed. That makes the unemployment rate look better, but it's really not a sign that the economy has improved. In fact, it may be a sign that labor-market conditions have become even worse. The article on page 278, "Urban Teen-Agers, Who Often Live Isolated From the World of Work, Shun the Job Market," looks at the discouraged worker phenomenon as it affects teens in our country's major cities.

Of course, we can be misled in the other direction just as easily. Suppose the economy has begun to recover from a recession, and the un-

USE YOUR ECONOMIC REASONING

Urban Teen-Agers, Who Often Live Isolated from the World of Work, Shun the Job Market

NEW YORK—Alex Perez, a Puerto Rico-born 19-year-old on this city's Lower East Side, looks for a job—sometimes.

Much of the time lately, though, the high school dropout has been so discouraged at the prospects that he hasn't even bothered to try. And that makes Alex Perez, unskilled and unsure what to do with himself, one more part of a growing problem in big cities.

There are hundreds of thousands of teen-agers like Mr. Perez, "hanging out," as he says, on city streets and only desultorily looking for work. Nationally, about half of those age 16 to 19 are working or say they are looking for work. But in many of the country's major cities, the labor force includes far fewer teen-agers, reflecting the fact that growing numbers of teens, particularly minorities, not only don't have jobs but aren't looking.

Big City Problem

In Philadelphia, Chicago and Detroit, fewer than 40% of teen-agers are in the labor force. The situation in New York is even worse. In the first half of the year, only one in five teen-agers had work or

were looking for it. Officials say the rate is even a few points lower for Hispanic youths like Alex and for black youths.

"It means many thousands of youngsters don't get the kind of understanding that comes from work experience," says Samuel Ehrenhalt, New York regional commissioner of the Bureau of Labor Statistics. "It affects their understanding of how education relates to your work life and makes it better."

"We haven't even begun to feel the real impact of this on the city," says Josephine Nieves, New York City's commissioner of employment. "We are in for dire things if we have ever more kids on the street who have no knowledge of the working world."

Sociologists and economists aren't completely sure what is causing the problem. Part of it appears to be a decline in demand for teen-age labor as laid-off white collar workers enter the job market and skill requirements grow. In New York at least, part of it is caused by the fact that the types of industries predominant here tend to create fewer part-time jobs. Discrimination is another important factor. So are overly high salary expectations. Then there's the

lure of working in the illegal but lucrative drug industry.

But perhaps the most significant factor that emerges from a number of days spent talking with teen-agers and social workers in New York is the sense of isolation many minority kids feel from the world of work.

Unfamiliar Territory

For instance, the Henry Street Settlement, a Lower East Side social services agency, is only a few minutes away by subway from bustling Wall Street or midtown Manhattan, yet many teen-agers in the area seem frightened by and unfamiliar with those nearby-but-foreign territories. It's an important factor, notes Mr. Ehrenhalt, because of "the simple fact that the places where most black and Hispanic youngsters live don't have that many jobs."

Most kids seem to make at least a perfunctory search for a job. But it is a huge, difficult leap to the working world for teen-agers from the disadvantaged and often troubled families that live in the housing projects.

"A lot of kids from around here don't know where Madison and 42nd Street is," says Carlos Gonzalez, a job counselor at Henry Street. "They've never been there. If I send someone on a job interview in midtown they'll often arrange for a friend to drive them rather than take the subway, which they don't realize is a lot faster."

Mr. Perez, the 19-year-old, is isolated from the working world in more ways than one. A sincere, soft-spoken young man, he lives with his disabled mother in public housing on nearby Delancey Street. His mother can't afford a phone, so he has to list his girlfriend's parents' number when he fills out job applications.

Finding Their Way

Basic job-finding tactics are in short supply. One day, Henry Street social worker Rafael Jaquez suggests Mr. Perez try to get a day construction job at a site in Brooklyn the next morning at 6:30. Mr. Perez is eager to try, but he doesn't know which subway stop would be closest. He says he will guess where it is, go an hour early and hope for the best. Mr. Jaquez has to suggest that Mr. Perez check a street map that shows cross streets, rather than a subway map, to find out.

With so few good role models in the neighborhood, city agencies and social work-

ers find themselves not just scaring up jobs and placing teens but also teaching elemental rules of the working world. "I have a thing about hats," says Nilsa Pietri, head of youth services at Henry Street. "I always have to tell the kids to take their hats off. Employers will write them off if they wear them."

Bill Tomlinson, another Henry Street couselor, leads a session for 20 teen-agers in New York's summer youth employment program. Many are from poor families and seem dumbfounded by his questions about how to act in a job interview. One kid wears a T-shirt that says, "2 Cool 4 School." The gregarious Mr. Tomlinson tells the kids to shake hands firmly, make eye contact, then keep their hands

in their laps. "Ever watch somebody's eyes while your hands are flying?" he asks. "They watch your hands, not you."

Peter Kleinbard, who runs a training and educational program for high school dropouts in Spanish Harlem, says one of his biggest problems is getting kids to show up for job interviews. He attributes the problem less to irresponsibility than to fear. "Minority youth live in such isolation from the culture of work," he says. "Many of the kids I see have never been in an office or a factory.". . .

—*Paul Duke Jr.*

SOURCE: *The Wall Street Journal*, August 14, 1991, p. A10. Reprinted by permission of *The Wall Street Journal*, © 1991 Dow Jones & Company. All Rights Reserved Worldwide.

USE YOUR ECONOMIC REASONING

1. **Based on the second paragraph of the article, would you classify Alex Perez as "unemployed." Why or why not?**

2. **Nationally, about 50 percent of all teenagers were in the labor force in 1991. But in Philadelphia, Chicago, and Detroit the figure was less than 40 percent; and in New York it was only about 20 percent. Explain this discrepancy. Why are fewer teenagers working or seeking work in our major cities?**

3. **According to New York City's commissioner of employment, "We are in for dire things if we have even more kids on the street who have no knowledge of the working world." What problems do you foresee if this trend continues?**

employment rate is falling. Suddenly the monthly survey shows an increase. Does that mean that the economy is headed back toward recession? It may, but a more likely interpretation is that the economy's improved condition has attracted a lot of additional job seekers who have swelled the labor force and pushed up the unemployment rate. Here the unemployment rate has risen not because the economy is worse but because it is better: people are more confident about their prospects for finding jobs.

Because changes in the unemployment rate can send misleading signals about the strength of the economy, they should be interpreted with caution. But even when the unemployment rate seems to be sending clear signals (for instance, when it has risen for several consecutive months), we must be careful not to base our evaluation of the economy's health solely on this statistic. After all, the unemployment rate looks at only one dimension of the economy's performance, its ability to provide jobs for the growing labor force. Other dimensions are equally important. To obtain an accurate picture of our economy's performance, we must consider each of these dimensions by examining several different economic indicators.

Measuring Inflation

Another important dimension of our economy's performance is its success or failure in avoiding inflation. *Inflation* is defined as a rise in the general level of prices. (The existence of inflation does not necessarily mean that all prices are rising, but rather that more prices are going up than are coming down.) We're all concerned about inflation because it means that our dollars won't buy as much as they would before. In general this means that it will take more money to pay the grocery bill, buy clothes, go out for an evening, or do almost anything else.

Unanticipated Inflation and Income Redistribution

Each of us tends to believe that we are being hurt by inflation, but that is not necessarily the case. We forget that at the same time prices are rising, our money incomes are also likely to be rising, sometimes at a faster rate than the increase in prices. Instead of focusing solely on prices, then, we ought to be concerned about what economists call real income. *Real income* is the purchasing power of your income, the amount of goods and services it will buy. Economists argue that unanticipated inflation is essentially an income redistribution problem: It takes real income away from some people and gives it to others. (As you will see later, when people anticipate inflation, they tend to prepare for it and thereby reduce its redistributive effects.)

Keeping Pace with Inflation. The people hurt by unanticipated inflation are ones whose money incomes (the number of *dollars* they earn) don't keep pace with rising prices. If prices rise by 10 percent, but your money income increases by only 5 percent, your real income will have fallen. The actual amount of goods and services that you can buy with your income will be 5-percent less than before.

Whether or not your money keeps pace with inflation depends on a variety of factors. The most important is how flexible your income is, that is, how easily it can be adjusted. Professional people—doctors, lawyers, dentists, and so on—often can adjust the prices they charge their customers and thereby stay abreast (or ahead) of inflation. People who own their own businesses—their own hardware store or motel or janitorial service—may be able to adjust their prices similarly. Of course, whether or not professional people and businesses can successfully increase prices and stay abreast of inflation depends on the degree of the market power they possess. If a seller faces very little competition and therefore has significant market power, it may be able to increase its prices to offset inflation. If it operates in a highly competitive environment, it may not be able to do so.

Workers who are represented by strong unions also may do reasonably well during periods of inflation. Often these unions are able to negotiate cost-of-living adjustment (COLA) clauses, which provide for automatic wage and salary adjustments to compensate for inflation. Other workers may have the forces of demand and supply operating to their advantage. When the demand for workers with a particular skill is strong relative to their supply, those workers often are able to obtain wage or salary increases that more than offset the impact of inflation. Unskilled workers and others in oversupplied fields—those where there are several prospective employees for each job opening—usually find it more difficult to gain wage increases that match the rate of inflation.

Savers and People on Fixed Incomes. The people hardest hit by inflation are those on fixed incomes, since, by definition, their incomes are inflexible. The classic example is a retired person living on a fixed pension or perhaps on his or her accumulated savings. (At the risk of sounding unsympathetic, we have to point out that the plight of retired people can be exaggerated. Many retired persons are not dependent on fixed pensions. For example, Social Security payments are automatically adjusted for increases in the cost of living.)

Savers can also be hurt by inflation. Whether you are relying on your savings to provide retirement income, to make a down payment on a home some day, or to buy a car next summer, inflation can eat away at the value of your savings account and make your saving objective harder to achieve. For example, if your savings account is paying 6 percent interest and the inflation rate is 10 percent, the purchasing power of your savings is declining by 4 percent a year. After you pay taxes on the interest, you're even further behind.

Creditors versus Debtors. Unanticipated inflation can also hurt banks and other creditors, since borrowers will be able to repay their loans with dollars that are worth less than those that were borrowed. Because the federal government is the largest debtor of all, it is probably the biggest gainer from such inflation. Other gainers include families with home mortgages and businesses that borrowed money to purchase factories or equipment.

When Inflation Is Anticipated

The redistributive effects of inflation occur because inflation is unforeseen or unanticipated. To the extent that inflation is anticipated, the redistributive effects will tend to be reduced because individuals and businesses will take actions to protect themselves from inflation.

COLA clauses are one way that we attempt to insulate ourselves from inflation, but there are others. For example, banks try to protect themselves from anticipated inflation by working the inflation rate into the interest rates they set for loans. If a bank wants to earn 5 percent interest on a loan and it expects the inflation rate to be 4 percent, the bank will charge 9 percent interest to get the desired return. If the actual inflation rate turns out to be 4 percent, neither the bank nor the customer will be harmed by inflation. Of course, the bank's inflation forecast won't always be correct. Forecasting inflation has proven very difficult, so bankers and others will make mistakes. As a consequence, inflation is likely to benefit some and hurt others.

Consequences of inflation extend beyond its effect on the income distribution. When inflation is anticipated, individuals and businesses waste resources in their attempt to protect themselves from its impact. Labor time and energy are expended shopping around and shifting money from one financial institution to another in pursuit of the highest interest rate. Restaurant menus and business price lists must be continually revised, and sales personnel must be kept informed of the most recent price information. In short, efforts to stay ahead of inflation use up resources that could be used to produce other things.

In addition to wasting resources, inflation (whether anticipated or unanticipated) can lead to inefficiency because it tends to distort the information provided by the price system. To illustrate, suppose that the price of portable computers increases. Does the higher price indicate greater demand for the product, or does it merely reflect an increase in the overall price level? Because computer manufacturers are uncertain, they may be reluctant to invest in new production capacity. Thus inflation may slow investment spending and retard the economy's rate of economic growth.

In summary, both anticipated and unanticipated inflation impose costs on society. The article on page 284, "Daily Inflation Struggle Obsesses Brazil," examines how individuals behave in an environment of skyrocketing inflation.

Calculating a Price Index

Bankers, union leaders, business executives, and most other people in our society are keenly interested in changes in the general level of prices because they want to try to compensate for those changes; they'd like to build them into the prices they charge their customers and the wages they negotiate from their employers. Government policymakers also want to know what is happening to the price level in order to know when inflation-fighting policies may be necessary.

Economists attempt to measure inflation by using a *price index.* A price index is really nothing more than a ratio of two prices: the price of an item in a base period that serves as a reference point, divided into the price of that item in a period we wish to compare to the base period. For example, if the price of steak was $2.50 a pound in 1985 and $4 a pound in 1992, the price index for steak in 1992 would be 160 if 1985 were used as the base year:

$$\text{Price index} = \frac{\text{Price in any given period}}{\text{Price in the base period}}$$

$$= \frac{\$4.00}{\$2.50}$$

$$= 1.60 \text{ or } 160 \text{ percent}$$

Daily Inflation Struggle Obsesses Brazil
Nation Looks to President-Elect for Relief From Price Shock

RIO DE JANEIRO—It was a balmy evening in Rio, the sort of weather that invites one to relax at an outdoor cafe in Copacabana or Ipanema and take in the beachfront action.

But on this particular recent evening the hottest spot in town wasn't one of the cafes, bars or restaurants that line the city's coast. The place to be was the gas station.

"The price of gas is going up 60% at midnight, so I want to fill up my tank before that happens," explained a taxi driver as he pulled into the line at the Petrobras gas station on Copacabana's Avenida Atlantica. It was close to 11:30 p.m. and there were a good 30 cars ahead of him. "I hope I reach the pump before midnight," he said. "Otherwise, my money will buy only 20 liters instead of 34."

So it goes these days in Brazil as prices continuously test the limits of Brazilians' resiliency—and patience. The question of how to break out of the inflationary spiral will be the biggest challenge facing president-elect Fernando Collor de Mello when he takes office on March 15. His advisers are busy drawing up shock measures to implement in his first days in office.

Inflation of 19,000%

In 1987, inflation was 365%. In 1988, it was 934% and pundits started to say that the country was on the verge of collapse. But in 1989, inflation reached 1,765% and the country has held together. Some wonder how long this can go on. For the month of January, inflation is expected to reach about 55%—an annual rate of about 19,000%. . . .

Investing in Groceries

Every day, the newspapers are full of articles announcing new price rises. Newspapers also offer advice on such matters as whether it's better to stock up on food and consumer products to anticipate price increases or invest one's money. (The answer: go shopping. Since mid-November, supermarket prices have risen an average of 218%, while the stock market and gold rose by 175%, the dollar by 163% and the overnight—a one-day savings account that most Brazilians place their money in as a hedge against inflation—by 137%.) . . .

Inflation has spawned an inflation of work, ideas and even jobs designed to deal with inflation. Isak Marcel Aizim Diamante, the 29-year-old general manager of a Sao Paulo company that makes blinds, says he spends about two hours a day reading business newspapers to decide what to do with his money.

Some don't have the time to do this themselves, so they leave it to their secretaries.

Running to the Bank

"That's all I do in the morning," says 25-year-old Maria Claudia Gebaili, a secretary at a Sao Paulo newspaper. "When I come in, the first thing I do is call the bank. Usually it's busy because everybody else is trying to do the same thing. So I have to go over to the bank and wait on line to talk to the manager and ask him to take money out of my boss's short-term funds and put some in the checking account to cover the checks he wrote overnight. On Fridays, I always have to make sure that my boss's checking account is emptied because the money left there would get devalued over the weekend. But on Monday morning, some of the checks he wrote over the weekend have already appeared at the bank. So I have to race over to make sure he doesn't get an overdraft. It wears you down."

Brazilians are also constantly trying to devise the best way of paying for goods. Daniel Cherman, a 24-year-old employee in a real estate promotion company, has four different credit cards that fall due at different dates. He always tries to use the one payable at the latest date so that by the time his account is debited, the cost of the purchase has been cut in half.

Businesses are wising up however. Most restaurants no longer accept credit cards. And most stores now have price tags with two different prices: one if you pay cash, and one, much higher, if you pay with a credit card. At the Mesbla department store in Sao Paulo, for instance, a pair

of Levi's jeans sells for 859 cruzados novos in cash and 1,561 cruzados novos with a credit card.

For a long time, despite the difficulties involved, Brazilians took all this in stride. They were helped, in large part, by what economist Edmar Bacha calls Brazil's "diabolical indexation system" that protects regular wage-earners from the worst ravages of inflation. . . .

Now, however, there are growing signs that Brazilians are getting fed up. More and more unions are asking that salaries be paid bimonthly, or even weekly, rather than monthly and that salaries be indexed on a projection of the current month's inflation rather than the previous month's inflation.

Businesses are also frustrated by the near-impossibility of making any long-term plans and keeping accounts current. The Pao de Acucar supermarket group keeps its accounts in its own invented currency unit, the real.

Says Mr. Bacha, the economist: "The only reason people don't revolt is that there is a tremendous expectation that the next government will do something quickly." . . .

—*Thomas Kamm*

SOURCE: *The Wall Street Journal*, January 29, 1990, p. A14. Reprinted by permission of *The Wall Street Journal*, © 1990 by Dow Jones & Company. All Rights Reserved Worldwide.

USE YOUR ECONOMIC REASONING

1. **Unanticipated inflation tends to redistribute income. Why? Is Brazil's inflation anticipated or unanticipated? Could inflation be "partially anticipated"?**

2. **Even anticipated inflation imposes costs on society because individuals and businesses must spend time and resources to protect themselves from its impact. What examples are provided in the article?**

3. **According to the article, indexation (the use of COLA clauses) has helped protect workers from "the worst ravages of inflation." How has indexation protected workers? Why are they becoming dissatisfied with this protection?**

EXHIBIT 9.3

Calculating a Price Index: A Hypothetical Example

The average price of indoor-outdoor carpeting was $4 a yard in 1980 and $10 a yard in 1990. What is the price index for indoor-outdoor carpeting if 1980 is used as the base year?

$$\text{Price index} = \frac{\text{Price in any given period}}{\text{Price in the base period}}$$

$$= \frac{\$10.00}{\$4.00}$$

$$= 2.50 \text{ or } 250 \text{ percent.}$$

The price index of 250 tells us that the price of carpeting in 1990 is 250 percent of what it was in 1980. In other words, in 1990 we needed to spend $250 to buy carpeting that cost only $100 in 1980.

(Note that although the price index is actually a percentage, by convention it is written without the percent sign.)

The price index tells us how much the price of the item in question has increased or decreased since the base period. Since the price index in the base period is always 100, an index of 160 means that a price has increased by 60 percent since the base period.[3] By the same logic, an index of 75 would indicate that a price had decreased by 25 percent since the base period. Another example of a price-index calculation is presented in Exh. 9.3.

Three basic price indexes are used in the United States: the Consumer Price Index, the Producer Price Index, and the Implicit Price Deflator. Each index surveys a particular range of goods and services in order to determine the rate of inflation among those items. Each computes an overall index showing the average rate of price change for its assortment (or "basket") of commodities and presents individual price indexes for each major class of items in the survey. This makes it possible to determine which products are most responsible for any change in the overall index.

---

[3] The price index in the base period is always 100 because the numbers in the numerator and denominator of the price-index formula must be the same. For example, if we want to calculate the price index for steak in 1985 using 1985 as the base period, we would have $2.50/$2.50 = 1.00 or 100 percent.

The Consumer Price Index

The best-known index is the Consumer Price Index (CPI). The CPI looks at the prices of some 400 different goods and services that have been chosen to represent the kinds of products typically purchased by urban consumers. In essence, it measures the purchasing power of consumers' dollars by comparing the current cost of this so-called basket of goods and services with the cost of the same basket at an earlier date.

Exhibit 9.4 shows the kinds of items that are included in the Consumer Price Index survey. You can see how the rate of inflation differs from one class of items to another. The top line—i.e., the all-items index—is the CPI usually referred to by economists and the media. It tells us the average rate of price increase for all the items in the market basket. According to the exhibit, the all-items index stood at 137.9 in December 1991. Because the most recent CPI uses the average level of prices between 1982 and 1984 as the base, this means that prices increased by almost 40 percent from the 1982–84 period to the end of 1991. More precisely, it cost $137.90 in 1991 to purchase a market basket of goods and services that sold for $100 in 1982–84. As you can see from the table, some items increased even more than that. For example, medical care rose to an index of 182.6; that means medical care cost almost 83 percent more in 1991 than it did in the 1982–84 period.

Because consumers spend greater percentages of their incomes on certain index items—more, say, on food and beverages than on entertainment—merely averaging all the indexes at face value to arrive at the all-items index would be misleading. Therefore the all-items index is computed as a

EXHIBIT 9.4

Consumer Price Indexes, December 1991 (1982 − 84 = 100)

All items	137.9		
Food and beverages	137.3	Apparel and upkeep	129.6
Housing	135.0	Transportation	125.3
Shelter	148.2	Medical care	182.6
Fuel & other utilities	116.0	Entertainment	139.9
Furnishings & operating	116.3	Other goods and services	177.6

Source: Economic Report of the President, 1992.

weighted average of the individual indexes. That is, the things for which consumers spend more of their incomes are counted more heavily in determining the all-items index. For example, if consumers spend twice as much on food and beverages as they do on entertainment, food and beverage prices will be twice as important in computing the all-items index.

The Producer Price Index and the Implicit Price Deflator

The Producer Price Index (PPI) and the Implicit Price Deflator (IPD) don't receive as much publicity as the Consumer Price Index, which is closely watched because it is used for cost-of-living adjustments in labor contracts and Social Security payments. Nevertheless, they have their particular uses and advantages. The PPI and the IPD are interpreted precisely the same as the CPI. That is, an index of 170 means prices have risen by 70 percent since the base period.

The Producer Price Index is sometimes called the Wholesale Price Index.[4] It reflects the rate of inflation in the wholesale prices of finished products, both consumer goods and capital goods. Economists pay particular attention to the PPI because they think it provides an indication of what will happen to consumer prices in the months to come. The logic here is fairly simple. Eventually, any increases in wholesale prices are going to be passed on to consumers.

The broadest measure of inflation is the Implicit Price Deflator. This index examines the rate of increase in prices for all of the items included in the gross national product (GNP). It is also used to adjust GNP figures for inflation so that we can compare GNP from one year to the next without having that comparison distorted by changes in the price level. But before we say any more about the Implicit Price Deflator, we need to understand what gross national product is and how it functions as an economic indicator.

Measuring Total Output

The fundamental purpose of every economic system is to produce output in order to satisfy human wants. For that reason, many economists argue that gross national product (GNP) is the most important single indicator of our

---

[4] Actually, there are three separate Producer Price Indexes: one for finished goods, one for

The cloth and thread used in manufacturing clothing are intermediate goods, while the finished product is a final good.

economy's performance. ***Gross national product*** is the total monetary value of all final goods and services produced in one year. In other words, it is a measure of the economy's annual production or output.[5]

Calculating GNP: A Sneak Preview

As its definition indicates, GNP is measured in monetary units rather than units of output. That makes it possible to add apples and oranges, so to speak—to sum the economy's output of eggs, stereos, houses, tractors, and

---

semifinished goods, and one for raw materials. The index for finished goods is the one referred to as the Wholesale Price Index. It's also the one commonly referred to in the news.

[5] Another measure of annual output is **gross domestic product** (GDP). GDP is the total monetary value of all final goods and services produced *within a country* during a single year. U.S. GDP includes the value of output produced in the United States by foreign-owned factories and foreign workers, but excludes the value of output produced in other countries by American workers and factories owned by U.S. companies. (U.S. GNP includes the value of final output produced by the resources owned by U.S. citizens, wherever those resources are located.) For the United States, GNP and GDP are virtually identical; GNP exceeds GDP by about two-tenths of one percent. For other countries the difference can be much greater.

so on, to produce a meaningful statistic. The procedure is quite simple: The output of each product is valued at its selling price, and these values are added to arrive at a figure for GNP.

Although GNP is a measure of output, you should note that only the output of final goods and services is permitted to enter the GNP calculation. *Final goods* are those that are purchased for final use rather than for further processing or resale. For example, a new pair of jeans is a final good, but the thread, cloth, zippers, and snaps that are used in manufacturing the jeans are *intermediate goods*. Since the value of the jeans already includes the value of the thread and other intermediate goods, only the value of the jeans should count in GNP. If the value of intermediate goods were to be included in the calculation, the result would be double counting, which would overstate the value of the economy's annual production.

GNP and the Circular Flow

There are two ways to measure gross national product: the expenditures approach and the income approach. The *expenditures approach* measures how much money is spent in purchasing final goods and services; the *income approach* measures the income that is created in producing these goods and services. Since one person's expenditure becomes another person's income, the two approaches must arrive at the same amount. In dollar terms, total output *must* equal total income.

The equality between total output and total income is reflected in the circular-flow diagram in Exh. 9.5, which, like the circular-flow diagram in Chapter 2, is simplified to show the interaction of only the household and business sectors. The expenditures approach measures GNP by summing the various expenditures that make up the flow depicted at the bottom of the diagram. The income approach computes GNP by adding together the various categories of income contained in the flow at the top of the diagram. The circular nature of the diagram indicates that all income spent on final goods and services must be received by someone as income; thus total output must equal total income.

The Expenditures Approach

As you know, the American economy is much more complex than the system depicted in Exh. 9.5. In our economy it's not only households that make expenditures for goods and services, but also businesses, various levels of gov-

EXHIBIT 9.5

Total Output = GNP = Total Income

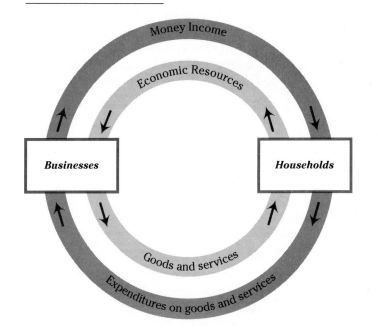

This simplified model of the economy (which ignores government and foreign trade) illustrates that there are two ways to calculate gross national product. The total expenditures made by households on final goods and services (the bottom flow) must equal the sum of the income received by the various economic resources (rent + wages + interest + profits)—the uppermost flow in the diagram. Both the total income received by the economic resources and the total household expenditures must equal GNP.

ernment, and foreign consumers. The categories of expenditures made by these groups are as follows:

1. *Personal consumption expenditures.* This is the total amount spent by consumers for goods and services. It includes both the purchase of consumer *durables*, such as automobiles, refrigerators, and stereos, and the purchase of *nondurables*, such as food, clothing, and entertainment.

2. *Gross private domestic investment.*[6] This category includes all types of expenditures on income-producing assets, including business expenditures for new factories and equipment and household expenditures for new homes and major home improvements. (For accounting purposes, new homes are classified

---

[6] The term *domestic* means "limited to our own country"; for example, domestic investment is investment that takes place within the boundaries of the United States.

as an investment.) It also includes changes in business inventories, since they represent assets that will yield income sometime in the future.[7]

3. *Government purchases.* This category covers federal, state, and local governments' purchases of all kinds of goods and services. For example, it would include purchases of government vehicles, office supplies, weapons, concrete for roads, and even the consulting services of private firms hired to advise various government departments. This category excludes transfer payments such as welfare and Social Security, since these do not represent the purchase of newly produced goods and services.

4. *Net exports.* Some of the output of American businesses is sold in foreign countries, so it doesn't show up in our domestic sales. At the same time,

---

EXHIBIT 9.6

Gross National Product in 1991 (in billions)

EXPENDITURES APPROACH		INCOME APPROACH	
Personal consumption expenditures	$3,889.1	Employee compensation	$3,388.2
		Rental income*	− 12.7
Gross private domestic investment	726.7	Net interest**	493.4
		Corporate profits	307.1
Government purchases of goods and services	1,087.5	Proprietors' income	379.7
		Indirect business taxes	507.1
Net exports of goods and services	− 17.5	Capital consumption allowances	623.0
Gross National Product	$5,685.8	Gross National Product	$5,685.8

* Rental income was negative in 1991 due to depreciation.
** Net interest has been adjusted to reflect net receipts of factor income from the rest of the world.
Developed from information contained in the March 1992 edition of the *Survey of Current Business,* published by the United States Department of Commerce.

---

[7] Counting changes in inventories as part of investment also ensures that total expenditures will equal the value of total output. If a business produces something this year but doesn't sell it this year, that production goes into inventory and is not recorded in total expenditures. So if we just add up the various types of expenditures, we'll miss the portion of GNP that was not sold. To adjust for this problem, we add any additions to inventory that occur from one year to the next in order to make sure that all production is counted. (Decreases in inventories represent the sale of items produced in previous years. Since those items were included in GNP figures for previous years, they must be subtracted from this year's total expenditures if GNP is to reflect current production accurately.)

some of the final goods and services sold in the United States were produced in foreign countries. To adjust for this situation, we subtract the value of imported goods from the value of our exports. The resulting figure, called *net exports*, is then added to our domestic sales. The formula for net exports is

Net exports = total exports − total imports.

The net-exports total will be positive when exports exceed imports and negative when imports exceed exports.

To calculate gross national product by the expenditure approach, we add these four categories of expenditures. This procedure is illustrated in Exh. 9.6, which shows the United States GNP for 1991 as measured by both the expenditures approach and the income approach.

The Income Approach

Calculating GNP by the income approach is somewhat more complicated than the circular-flow diagram would make it appear. In addition to the various forms of income that are created in the process of producing final goods and services (wages and salaries, rent, interest, and profits) there are two *nonincome payments* (indirect business taxes and capital consumption allowances) that account for a portion of the money received by businesses. The categories of income received by the economic resources and the types of nonincome payments are as follows:

1. *Compensation of employees.* In addition to wages and salaries, this income category includes such things as payroll taxes and employer contributions to health plans.
2. *Rental income.* This is the income earned by households from the rental of property such as buildings and land.
3. *Net interest.* This category includes the interest earned by households on the money they lend to businesses to finance inventories, build plant additions, and purchase new machinery.
4. *Corporate profits.* This is the before-tax profit of corporations. It has three components, representing the three things that corporations can do with their profits: (a) *corporate profits tax liability*—profits used to pay federal and state taxes; (b) *dividends*—profits paid out to stockholders; and (c) *retained earnings*—profits kept by businesses for reinvestment (also called *undistributed corporate profits*).

5. *Proprietors' income.* This category includes the income earned by unincorporated businesses such as proprietorships, partnerships, and cooperatives.

6. *Indirect business taxes.* Indirect business taxes include sales taxes and excise taxes. The important thing about such taxes is that they are collected *by* businesses *for* government. Therefore a portion of the money received by businesses must be passed on directly to government; it is not available as a payment to the owners of economic resources. Such taxes are described as *nonincome payments.*

7. *Capital consumption allowances.* Capital consumption allowances are also called *allowances for depreciation.* In essence these are funds set aside for the eventual replacement of worn-out factories and equipment. Like indirect business taxes, they represent a nonincome payment.

To measure gross national product by the income approach, we add together the five types of income and the two nonincome payments. As you can see in Exh. 9.6, the answer we get is the same as the one generated earlier by the expenditures approach.[8] Again, that result is necessary because every dollar spent on output must be received by someone as income or as a nonincome payment.

Interpreting GNP Statistics

Now that we know what gross national product means and how it is measured, we need to note two facts before interpreting GNP statistics. An increase in GNP does not always mean that we're better off. Similarly, a decrease in GNP is not always a cause for concern and corrective action.

Real GNP versus Money GNP. From 1970 to 1980, gross national product in the United States increased from $993 billion to $2,632 billion (or $2.6 trillion). That's an increase of 165 percent in 10 years. On the surface, that seems like a pretty good performance, particularly when you realize that our population increased less than 10 percent in that period. It looks as though the average American had a lot more goods and services at his or her disposal in 1980 than in 1970.

But numbers can be misleading. Because GNP is the physical output of a given year valued at the prices that prevailed in that year, it can

---

[8] Actually, the GNP calculated by the income approach never turns out to be exactly the same as the GNP calculated by the expenditures approach. The difference is what the Department of Commerce calls the *statistical discrepancy.* In Exh. 9.6, the entry for indirect business taxes has been adjusted to incorporate the statistical discrepancy.

increase from one year to another because of increased output, increased prices, or a combination of the two. (To underscore the fact that GNP can change simply due to a change in prices, economists often refer to GNP as *money GNP* or *nominal GNP*.) Therefore, if we want to know how much *physical* output has actually increased, we have to calculate the **real gross national product**—that is, the GNP that has been adjusted to eliminate the impact of changes in the price level.

In order to compare real GNPs in our present example, we would want to value the output produced in 1980 at 1970 prices (or the output of 1970 at 1980 prices). Of course, our economy is much too large to permit us to multiply all the products produced in 1980 by 1970 prices. But we can do something that accomplishes essentially the same thing: We can use the Implicit Price Deflator introduced earlier in this chapter. Suppose that we want to compare the 1970 and 1980 GNPs using 1970 as the base year. That means the price index for 1970 would be 100 because that's the starting point for the comparison. What happened to prices between 1970 and 1980? According to the Implicit Price Deflator, they went up about 90 percent, which means that the price index for 1980 should read 190. (Remember, we start with a base of 100, so an index of 190 means that prices have increased by 90 percent, not 190 percent.) Once we have that price index, we can convert the 1980 money GNP to real GNP. All we have to do is divide by the 1980 price index (expressed as a decimal). The result is real GNP for 1980:

$$\text{Real GNP for year } Y = \frac{\text{GNP in year } Y}{\text{Price index for year } Y}$$

$$\text{Real GNP for 1980} = \frac{\$2{,}632 \text{ billion}}{190}$$

$$\text{Real GNP for 1980} = \$1{,}385 \text{ billion}$$

As you can see, the increase in the real GNP was much smaller than the increase in money GNP. While money GNP increased from $993 billion to $2,632 billion (an increase of 165 percent), real GNP increased from $993 billion to $1,385 billion (an increase of only 39 percent). In other words, much of the increase in GNP was due to inflation. Therefore, when we compare GNPs, we always want to compare real GNPs. This gives us a much better picture of what's actually happening to the economy's output and the nation's standard of living.

What GNP Does Not Measure. Even real GNP figures should be interpreted with caution. They don't measure all of our society's production, and they certainly don't provide a perfect measure of welfare or happiness. Here are some of the things that GNP does not consider.

1. *Excluded production.* GNP does not measure all production or output; it measures only production that is intended to be sold. This means that it excludes the production of homemakers and do-it-yourselfers. It also excludes all barter transactions—transactions in which one person directly exchanges goods or services with another.

2. *Population.* GNP statistics tell us nothing about the size of the population that must share a given output. A GNP of $500 billion means one thing in an economy of 100 million people and something completely different in an economy of 500 million people. (It's like the difference between an income of $20,000 for a single person and an income of $20,000 for a family of five.) Economists generally attempt to adjust for this problem by talking about GNP per capita or per person. That is, GNP divided by the population of the country.

3. *Leisure.* GNP does not measure increases in leisure, but such increases clearly have an impact on our well-being. Even if real gross national product didn't increase, if we could produce a constant real GNP with shorter and shorter workweeks, most of us would agree that our welfare had improved.

4. *Externalities.* We have a very sophisticated accounting system to keep track of all the goods and services we produce, but we have no established method of subtracting from GNP when the production process yields negative externalities—air and water pollution, for example. (See Chapter 8 for a review of this concept.)

These limitations have caused some economists to search for a better measure of output and welfare. Two Yale economists, James Tobin and William Nordhaus, have developed a *measure of economic welfare* (MEW) that attempts to convert the conventional GNP figure into one that measures economic well-being. Among other things, MEW attempts to estimate the value of leisure and adds a correction for negative externalities such as pollution.

While MEW estimates are much larger than conventional GNP (implying that conventional GNP seriously understates economic welfare) MEW has been growing much more slowly than real GNP. In other words, our well-being is not increasing as rapidly as real GNP figures suggest. This should come as no surprise, given continuing concerns about the deterioration of the environment and the increase in the number of women in the labor force (reducing the amount of leisure).

While the MEW concept is a promising idea, it is still in the experimental stage and awaits further refinement. For now, we'll have to be satisfied with GNP statistics and an understanding of their limitations.

Summary

To keep track of the economy's performance, people watch *economic indicators*—signals or measures that tell us how well the economy is performing. Three major economic indicators are the unemployment rate, price indexes (the Consumer Price Index, the Producer Price Index, and the Implicit Price Deflator), and the gross national product. Each of these indicators looks at a different dimension of the economy's performance.

The *civilian unemployment rate* is the percentage of the civilian labor force that is unemployed. (The civilian labor force is made up of all persons over the age of sixteen who are not in the armed forces and who are either employed or actively seeking employment.) Each month the Bureau of Labor Statistics surveys some 60,000 households to determine the employment status of the residents. It then uses the results from this sample to estimate the size of the labor force and the rate of unemployment.

We attempt to measure inflation with something called a *price index*. A price index is a ratio of two prices: a price in some base period that serves as a reference point, divided into the price in whatever period we wish to compare to the base period. For example, if tennis shoes sold for $50 in 1985 and $80 in 1992, the price index for tennis shoes would be 160 if 1985 were used as the base year:

$$\text{Price index} = \frac{\text{price in a given period}}{\text{price in the base period}}$$

$$\text{Price index} = \frac{\$80.00}{\$50.00}$$

Price index = 1.60 or 160 percent

Since the price index in the base period is always 100, an index of 160 means that price has increased by 60 percent since the base period. By the same logic, an index of 75 would indicate that price has decreased by 25 percent since the base period.

The other major indicator, the *gross national product* (or GNP), is the total monetary value of all final goods and services produced in one year. In other words, it is a measure of the economy's annual production or output. GNP can be estimated by the expenditures approach or by the income approach. The expenditures approach sums the categories of expenditures made for final goods and services. The income approach looks at the forms of income that are created when final goods are produced and adds to those income figures certain nonincome payments.

Since GNP is measured in monetary units (dollars), it is possible to add apples and oranges (that is, to sum the economy's output of eggs, stereos, houses, tractors, and so on) and arrive at a meaningful measure of the economy's total output. GNP figures must be interpreted with caution, however. When we compare the GNPs for two different years, we must be sure to correct for the impact of changing prices—to compare real GNPs, not money GNPs. We must also recognize that GNP is not a complete measure of our economy's production because it excludes the work of homemakers and do-it-yourselfers as well as other nonmarket transactions. Nor is it a complete measure of welfare or happiness; it doesn't take into account the value of leisure, for example, or the negative externalities associated with the production of some goods and services.

Glossary

Page 271   *Civilian labor force.* All persons over the age of sixteen who are not in the armed forces and who are either employed or actively seeking employment.

Page 272   *Civilian unemployment rate.* The percentage of the civilian labor force that is unemployed.

Page 273   *Cyclical unemployment.* Joblessness caused by a reduction in the economy's total demand for goods and services.

Page 270   *Economic indicators.* Signals or measures that tell us how well the economy is performing.

Page 272   *Frictional unemployment.* People who are out of work because they are in the process of changing jobs or searching for their first job.

Page 275   *Full employment.* The minimum level of unemployment our economy can achieve in normal times.

Page 289   *Gross national product.* The total monetary value of all final goods and services produced in one year.

Page 280   *Inflation.* A rise in the general level of prices.

Page 268   *Macroeconomics.* The study of the economy as a whole and the factors that influence the economy's overall performance.

Page 283   *Price index.* A measure of changes in the general level of prices. Three basic price indexes are used in the United States: the Consumer Price Index, the Producer Price Index, and the Implicit Price Deflator.

Page 295   *Real gross national product.* Gross national product that has been adjusted to eliminate the impact of changes in the price level.

Page 281   ***Real income.*** The purchasing power of your income; the amount of goods and services it will buy.

Page 273   ***Structural unemployment.*** Unemployment caused by changes in the makeup or structure of the economy that make some skills obsolete or in less demand.

Page 271   ***Unemployment rate.*** See *Civilian unemployment rate.*

Study Questions

Fill in the Blanks

1. The study of the economy's overall performance and the factors that influence that performance is called _Macroeconomics_.

2. Clauses that provide for automatic wage and salary adjustments to compensate for inflation are called _COLA_ clauses.

3. _Economic indicators_ are signals or measures that tell us how well the economy is performing.

4. The price index that is used to adjust union wage contracts and Social Security payments for inflation is the _CPI_.

5. Unemployment caused by a reduction in the economy's total demand for goods and services is called _cyclical_ unemployment.

6. A common estimate for full employment is approximately _5 ½_ percent unemployment.

7. People who stop looking for jobs because they are convinced that none are available are called _discouraged workers_.

8. The two approaches to measuring GNP are the _expenditures_ approach and the _income_ approach.

9. GNP that has been adjusted to eliminate the impact of changes in the price level is called _real_ GNP.

10. The largest component of spending in GNP is _consumption_ spending.

Multiple Choice

1. The civilian labor force is made up of
   a) all persons over the age of sixteen.
   b) all persons over the age of eighteen who are not in the armed forces.
   c) all persons over the age of sixteen who are not in the armed forces and who are either employed or actively seeking employment.
   d) all persons over the age of eighteen who are not in the armed forces and who are either employed or actively seeking employment.

2. If you are out of work because you are in the process of looking for a better job, economists would say that you are
   a) frictionally unemployed.
   b) cyclically unemployed.
   c) structurally unemployed.
   d) None of the above

3. People who are unemployed because they have no marketable skills are said to be
   a) frictionally unemployed.
   b) cyclically unemployed.
   c) structurally unemployed.
   d) None of the above

4. The unemployment rate for blacks is about
   a) three times the rate for whites.
   b) twice the rate for whites.
   c) 2 percent higher than the rate for whites.
   d) the same as the rate for whites.

5. Which of the following is *not* a true statement?
   a) Inflation tends to redistribute income.
   b) Inflation is particularly hard on people with fixed incomes.
   c) No one benefits from inflation.
   d) COLA clauses help protect workers from inflation.

6. If the Consumer Price Index is 250, that means
   a) the average price of a product is $2.50.
   b) prices are $2\frac{1}{2}$ times as high as they were in the base year.
   c) prices have risen 150 percent since the base year.
   d) b and c are correct.

7. The price index that is used to adjust GNP to eliminate inflation is called the
   a) Consumer Price Index.
   b) Wholesale Price Index.
   c) Implicit Price Deflator.
   d) Producer Price Index.

8. Which of the following items would be counted in GNP?
   a) The work of a homemaker
   b) The sale of a used car
   c) A soda you buy at your local drive-in
   d) The firewood you cut for your home last winter

9. If the GNP in 1980 was $2,000 billion and the price index was 150, real GNP (1980 GNP in base-year prices) would be
   a) $1,333 billion.
   b) $3,000 billion.
   c) $1,500 billion.
   d) $2,150 billion.

10. If both output and prices are higher in year 2 than they were in year 1, which of the following is true?
    a) Real GNP declined from year 1 to year 2.
    b) GNP declined from year 1 to year 2.
    c) GNP increased from year 1 to year 2, but real GNP declined.
    d) Both GNP and real GNP increased from year 1 to year 2.

Problems and Questions for Discussion

1. What is the purpose of economic indicators? Can they be of any value to you? Explain.

2. A student could be counted as employed, unemployed, or "not participating" in the labor market. Explain.

3. An increase in the unemployment rate is not always a sign of growing weakness in the economy. Explain.

4. Some frictional and structural unemployment are probably signs of a healthy economy. Why is that true?

5. How does inflation redistribute income?

6. How can savers be hurt by inflation?

7. Why is it true that "the people who are most hurt by inflation are those who have the least bargaining power in the marketplace?"

8. Use the following information to compute the change in real GNP from 1950 to 1960.

YEAR	MONEY GNP	PRICE INDEX
1950	$500	100
1960	700	120

9. Use the following information to compute GNP by the expenditures approach. (Some figures are not required in solving the problem.)

Personal consumption	$500	Exports	$ 10
Gross investment	200	Imports	12
Proprietor's income	450	Government purchases	250
Corporate profits	50		

10. Why must total income always equal total output?

Answer Key

Fill in the Blanks

1. macroeconomics
2. cost of living adjustment (COLA)
3. Economic indicators
4. Consumer Price Index
5. cyclical
6. $5\frac{1}{2}$
7. discouraged workers
8. expenditures, income
9. real
10. consumption

Multiple Choice

1. c
2. a
3. c
4. b
5. c
6. d
7. c
8. c
9. a
10. d

AN INTRODUCTION TO AGGREGATE DEMAND, AGGREGATE SUPPLY, AND THE DEBATE ON POLICY ACTIVISM

Chapter 9 identified some important dimensions of the economy's overall performance and examined techniques used to measure performance in those areas. Now, in Chapter 10, we will begin to explore why the aggregate economy behaves as it does and how its performance changes. We will also examine the origin of an ongoing debate in macroeconomics—the debate about the appropriateness of government attempts to influence or manage the performance of our overall economy.

First we will introduce the concepts of aggregate demand and aggregate supply. Just as demand and supply are important tools in microeconomics, aggregate demand and aggregate supply are important in macroeconomics. We will see how aggregate demand and aggregate supply interact to determine the levels of output, employment, and prices, and how unemployment and inflation arise.

As you discovered in Chapter 9, unemployment and inflation impose costs on our society. Today many Americans assume that it is the federal government's responsibility to reduce those costs by combating unemployment and inflation when they occur. But the issue of government intervention to combat macroeconomic problems provokes sharp disagreement among economists. Economists known as "activists" support a significant role for government. "Nonactivists" are economists who believe that government intervention should be avoided.

After introducing the aggregate-demand–aggregate-supply framework, we will use that framework to explore the origin of the activist-nonactivist controversy. This controversy originated more than 50 years ago with a debate between John Maynard Keynes and the then-dominant classical economists. Our examination of this debate will set the stage for the more detailed discussion of the Keynesian model contained in the next chapter. Examining the classical model offers an additional benefit: some of the views of the classical economists have resurfaced in modern debates about economic theory and policy. The historical debate will provide an important backdrop for understanding the modern controversy about policy activism.

An Introduction to Aggregate Demand and Aggregate Supply

Chapter 3 showed how demand and supply interact to determine the prices and quantities of products in particular markets. In macroeconomics, aggregate demand and aggregate supply determine the general price level and the level of national output, or real GNP. This section presents an overview of the aggregate-demand–aggregate-supply framework. Chapter 14 will consider these concepts in more detail.

Aggregate Demand

One of the forces that determines the economy's level of output, employment, and prices is aggregate demand. *Aggregate demand* is the total quantity of output demanded by all sectors in the economy together at various price levels in a given time period. As we saw in the last chapter, four sectors purchase our economy's output: households, businesses, governments, and foreigners. Thus aggregate demand is the sum of consumption spending by households, investment spending by businesses, government spending for goods and services, and net purchases by foreigners (exports minus imports).

Because the quantity of output demanded by these sectors depends in part on the price level, the *AD* curve slopes downward and to the

EXHIBIT 10.1

Aggregate Demand and Supply Curves

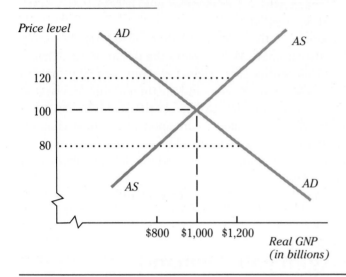

The aggregate demand curve shows the quantity of real output demanded at each price level. The aggregate supply curve shows the amount of real output supplied at each price level.

The intersection of the aggregate demand and supply curves determines the equilibrium level of real GNP and the equilibrium price level in the economy.

right, like the demand curve for a single product (see Exh. 10.1). But the demand curve and the aggregate demand curve are very different concepts. The demand curve shows the relationship between the price of a particular product and the quantity of that product demanded. The aggregate demand curve relates the overall price level in the economy (as measured by a price index, such as the CPI) to the total quantity of real output that consumers, businesses, governments and foreigners want to buy.

The demand curve and the aggregate demand curve slope downward for different reasons. When we are considering the demand curve for a single product, we assume that the prices of all other products remain constant as we reduce the price of the product in question. Consumers, of course, respond by buying (substituting) more of this relatively cheaper product. This *substitution effect* cannot, however, explain the downward slope of the aggregate demand curve. The aggregate demand curve is constructed with the price level for the *entire economy* measured on the vertical axis. A reduction in the overall price level means that the average price of *all* goods and services has fallen. Since all prices are falling, the substitution effect cannot explain the increase in the quantity of real GNP demanded.

The downward slope of the aggregate demand curve is due in part to the ***real balance effect*** (an additional reason will be introduced in

Chapter 14). According to the real balance effect, a reduction in the overall price level will increase the quantity of real output demanded because the lower overall price level will enable people to buy more with their cash and other financial assets. If the prices of goods and services fall, the real value or purchasing power of your financial assets—the cash in your wallet, the balance in your savings account, the wealth you have accumulated in government bonds—will increase. In other words, the same amount of money will stretch farther than before—will buy more than before. As a result, a reduction in the price level will cause people to purchase more goods and services. Of course, an increase in the price level will have the opposite effect; it will reduce spending on goods and services.

Aggregate Supply

The second force determining the economy's overall output and the general price level is aggregate supply. *Aggregate supply* is the total quantity of output supplied by all producers in the economy together at various price levels in a given time period.

Economists have suggested several possible shapes for the aggregate supply curve. For now, we'll assume that it is upward sloping, like the supply curve for a single product. An upward-sloping aggregate supply curve implies that producers will supply more real output at higher price levels than at lower price levels. Why might producers respond to higher prices by expanding output? One reason is that certain input costs—wage rates, for instance—tend to be fixed by contracts in the short run. As a consequence, when prices rise producers can profit by expanding output and pocketing the difference between the higher product prices they receive and the fixed input prices they must pay. We'll have more to say about the shape of the *AS* curve later in the text. For now, the important point is that higher prices induce producers to supply more output. The aggregate supply curve labeled *AS* in Exh. 10.1 depicts this relationship.

The Equilibrium Price Level and Real GNP

The interaction of aggregate demand and aggregate supply simultaneously determines the equilibrium price level and the equilibrium level of real GNP. This process is illustrated in Exh. 10.1, which shows the intersection of *AS* and *AD* resulting in an equilibrium price level of 100 and an equilibrium real GNP of $1,000 billion. The level of employment in the economy is directly related to the level of output; the greater the economy's real GNP, the more workers that are needed (ceteris paribus) and the higher the level of employment. Thus we can say that the interaction of aggregate demand and aggregate supply determines the level of prices, output, and employment in the economy.

Whenever the economy is not in equilibrium, it will tend to move toward it. For instance, if the price level is too high for equilibrium (say, 120 in our example) there will be a surplus of goods and services, causing prices and output to fall. If the price level is too low to provide equilibrium (80, for example), there will be a shortage, and prices and output will tend to rise. The equilibrium combination of the price level and real GNP is the only combination that can be maintained; other combinations will be unsustainable.

Full Employment and Potential GNP

An important question in macroeconomics is whether or not the economy will achieve full employment. In other words, will the aggregate demand and supply curves intersect at a level of GNP sufficient to provide full employment? You will recall that full employment does not mean zero unemployment. As we saw in Chapter 9, some frictional and structural unemployment are unavoidable, perhaps even desirable. Today economists believe that an unemployment rate in the vicinity of $5\frac{1}{2}$ percent should be regarded as full employment because that is the best we can hope to attain in normal times.

The level of output the economy produces when it operates at full employment is called potential GNP. **_Potential GNP_** represents the economy's maximum sustainable level of production; output can expand beyond potential, but it cannot be sustained.

A variety of factors influence the size of the economy's potential GNP. One of the most important is the size of the labor force; the more people who are willing and able to work, the more output the economy can produce. Another important factor is the size of the economy's capital stock—its supply of factories, machinery, tools, and other aids to production. The more capital equipment the labor force has to work with, the more output it is capable of producing.

Of course, labor and machinery won't produce very much output unless businesses also have raw materials. That's the third determinant of the economy's potential GNP—the economy's stock of raw materials. The more timber, iron, coal, and other natural resources the economy possesses, the greater its ability to produce output.

The final determinant of the economy's production capability is technology—the state of knowledge about how to produce products. At any given time, the machinery that businesses use and the production techniques they employ reflect the current technology. The more advanced the technology, the more output businesses can obtain from a given amount of inputs.

In summary, the economy's potential GNP is determined by the size of the labor force, the capital stock, the stock of raw materials, and technology. Whenever the economy is operating at its potential GNP, it is also enjoying full employment.

The Possibility of Unemployment

Exhibit 10.2 is constructed to represent a hypothetical economy that is initially in equilibrium at full employment. As you can see, AD_1 and AS_1 intersect at a real GNP of $1,000 billion (the economy's potential GNP) and a price level of 100. Given this starting point, how would the economy react to a reduction in aggregate demand? Suppose, for example, that business executives become pessimistic about the future and reduce their spending for buildings and equipment. Ceteris paribus, this will cause the aggregate demand curve to shift to the left, since there will now be less output than before demanded at any given price level. This is represented in Exh. 10.2 by the movement from AD_1 to AD_2. The reduction in aggregate demand causes the equilibrium price level to fall from 100 to 80 and reduces real GNP from $1,000 billion to $800 billion. Note that the economy's equilibrium real GNP is now below potential, so the society is no longer enjoying full employment; the reduction in aggregate demand has led to unemployment.

EXHIBIT 10.2

The Impact of a Reduction in Aggregate Demand

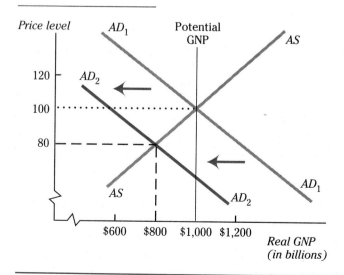

When aggregate demand declines from AD₁ to AD₂, the equilibrium real GNP and the overall price level also decline. This causes real GNP to fall below potential and results in unemployment.

EXHIBIT 10.3

The Impact of a Reduction in Aggregate Supply

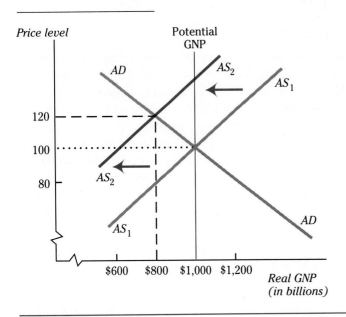

When aggregate supply declines from AS_1 to AS_2, the equilibrium real GNP falls from $1,000 billion to $800 billion, while the overall price level is increased from 100 to 120. The economy experiences unemployment with inflation.

Unemployment can also result from a reduction in aggregate supply. Suppose, for instance, that the economy experienced a supply shock such as the runup in oil prices caused by OPEC in the 1970s or the conflict with Iraq in 1990. The increase in oil prices would mean higher production costs for a wide range of products. As a consequence, producers would require higher prices to supply a given level of output. This is represented graphically by the movement from AS_1 to AS_2 in Exh. 10.3. Again the economy's real GNP is reduced below potential. However, in this instance the overall price level is increased, not reduced as it was in Exh. 10.2. Because supply shocks tend to raise prices while lowering the overall level of output and employment, they are particularly troublesome. We'll have much more to say about supply shocks in later chapters.

The Possibility of Inflation

The preceding examples were intended to show that the interaction of the forces of aggregate demand and aggregate supply can result in an equilibrium level of output that is less than the economy's potential, or full-employment,

EXHIBIT 10.4

The Impact of an Increase in Aggregate Demand

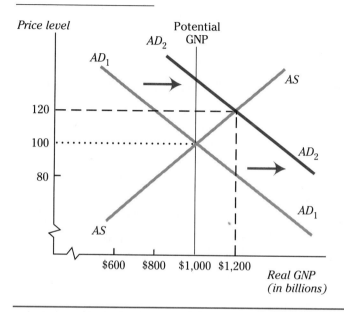

When aggregate demand increases from AD₁ to AD₂, the equilibrium real GNP rises from $1,000 billion to $1,200 billion while the overall price level is increased from 100 to 120.

GNP. It is also possible for the equilibrium level of GNP to *exceed* potential GNP. To see how, suppose the federal government decides to spend several billion additional dollars rebuilding the nation's roads and bridges. This added government spending will shift the aggregate demand curve to the right, from *AD₁* to *AD₂* in Exh. 10.4.

As you can see from the exhibit, this increase in aggregate demand causes the equilibrium level of real GNP to rise from $1000 billion to $1,200 billion—more than the economy's potential. Unfortunately, the price level in the economy has also risen, from 100 to 120 in this example. In short, the increase in aggregate demand has propelled the economy to a higher level of real GNP, but it has also resulted in inflation.

How will the economy respond to these situations—to equilibrium outputs that are greater or less than potential GNP? How can the economy operate beyond its potential, and how long can it maintain such production? If the economy is experiencing unemployment, will it ever return to the full-employment (potential) GNP? If the economy is experiencing unemployment or inflation, should government attempt to improve the economy's performance by influencing aggregate demand or supply? These important questions of theory and policy are the subject matter of subsequent macroeconomics chapters. Many of these questions first emerged in the debate between the classical economists and John Maynard Keynes. The remainder of this chapter is devoted to that debate.

The Classical Model: The Case for Laissez-Faire

We will begin our exploration of the activist-nonactivist debate by considering the views of the classical economists. The term *classical economist* is used to describe the mainstream economists who wrote from about 1776 through the early 1930s. For our purposes, the most important element of classical economic thought was the belief that a market economy would automatically tend toward full employment. Virtually all of the major classical economists held that belief, and apparently people were satisfied with this description of the real world until the Great Depression caused them to question its validity.

Say's Law

The classical economists based their predictions about full employment on a principle known as *Say's Law*, the creation of French economist J. B. Say (1776–1832). Like the laws of demand and supply, Say's Law is nothing more than a theory—one that attempts to explain why a market economy will always tend toward full employment. According to Say's Law, "Supply creates its own demand." In other words, in the process of producing output, businesses also create enough income to ensure that all the output will be sold. Because this theory occupies such an important place in classical economics, we will examine it in more detail beginning with a simple circular flow diagram, Exh. 10.5.

Exhibit 10.5 shows that when businesses produce output, they create *income*, payments that must be made to the providers of the various economic resources. Assume, for example, that businesses want to produce $100 worth of output to sell to households. To do that, businesses must first acquire the economic resources necessary to produce those goods and services. The owners of the economic resources are households, and they expect to be paid—in wages, rent, interest, and profits (remember, profits are the *payment* for entrepreneurship). Therefore $100 in income payments flows to the household sector. If households spend all the income they receive, everything that was produced will be sold. Supply will have created its own demand.

EXHIBIT 10.5

Say's Law: Supply Creates Its Own Demand

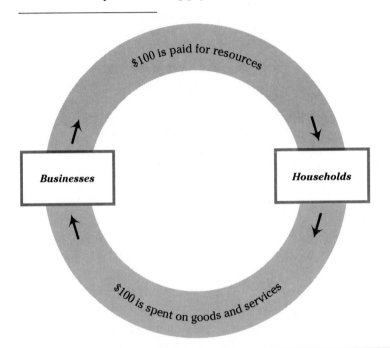

$100 is paid for resources

Businesses

Households

$100 is spent on goods and services

If all the income created in the act of producing output is spent by households, supply will have created its own demand and all the output will be sold.

Because the classical economists accepted Say's Law, they believed that there was nothing to prevent the economy from expanding to full employment. As long as job seekers were willing to work for a wage that was no more than their productivity (their contribution to the output of the firm), profit-seeking businesses would desire to hire everyone who wanted a job. There would always be adequate demand for the output of these additional workers because "supply creates its own demand."

Many students will immediately recognize that saving could disrupt that simple process. If households decided to save a portion of their earnings, not all of the income created by businesses would return in the form of spending. Thus the demand for goods and services would be too small for the supply, and some output would remain unsold. Businesses would then react by cutting back on production and laying off workers, thus causing unemployment.

But the classical economists did not see saving as a problem. Saving would *not* cause a reduction in spending, because businesses would borrow all the saved money for investment—the purchase of capital goods such as factories and machinery. Why were the classical economists so sure that the amount households wished to save would equal the amount businesses wanted to invest? Because of interest rates. In the classical model, the interest rate is determined by the demand and supply of *loanable funds,* money available to be borrowed. If households desired to save more than investors wanted to borrow, the surplus of funds would drive down the interest rate. Because the interest rate is both the reward households receive for saving *and* the price businesses pay to finance investment, a declining interest rate would both discourage saving and encourage investment. The interest rate would continue to fall until the amount that households wanted to save once again equaled the amount businesses desired to invest. At this equilibrium interest rate there would be no uninvested savings. Businesses would be able to sell all their output either to consumers or to investors, and full employment would prevail.

The Role of Flexible Wages and Prices

The classical economists believed that Say's Law and the flexibility of interest rates would ensure that spending would be adequate to maintain full employment. But some critics were unconvinced. Suppose households chose to "hoard" some of their income. Hoarding money is the act of hiding it or storing it. When people are concerned about the future, they may choose to hide money in a mattress or in a cookie jar so that they will have something to tide them over during hard times. (Households may prefer this form of saving if they lack confidence in the banking system—a situation that existed in the 1920s when there were numerous bank failures.) This method of saving creates problems for Say's Law because it removes money from circulation. If households choose to hoard money in cookie jars, that money can't be borrowed by businesses and invested. As a consequence, spending may decline and unemployment may appear.

While the classical economists admitted that hoarding could cause spending to decline, they did not believe it would lead to unemployment. Full employment would be maintained, because wage and price adjustments would compensate for any deficiency in total spending.

The existence of flexible wages and prices implies an *AS* curve that is vertical, not upward sloping as in the initial section of this chapter. Recall that the upward slope of the earlier *AS* curve resulted from the assumption that wage rates and some other input prices remain fixed in the short run. Given these rigidities, an increase in the price level would allow businesses to profit by expanding output, thus producing the upward-

EXHIBIT 10.6

The Classical Aggregate Supply Curve

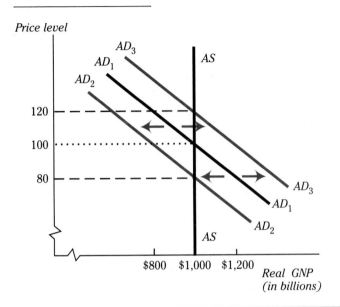

Price level

In the classical model, a
reduction in aggregate
demand would immediately
lead to falling prices and
wages, so that real GNP
would be maintained and
employment would not fall.
Higher aggregate demand
would lead to inflation with
no change in output.

sloping *AS* curve. But the classical economists believed that *all* prices—including wage rates (the price of labor) and other input prices—were highly flexible. An increase in product prices would therefore be quickly matched by higher costs, which would eliminate any incentive to expand output.

Thus the existence of highly flexible wages and prices implies an *AS* curve that is vertical at the full-employment level of output (potential GNP), as represented in Exh. 10.6.

To illustrate how flexible wages and prices guarantee full employment, let us assume that the economy is operating at a price level of 100 and a real GNP of $1,000 billion, the intersection of *AS* and *AD*$_1$. Now suppose that consumers become pessimistic about the future and hide some of their income in cookie jars rather than spend it. What will happen? Aggregate demand will fall—the *AD* curve will shift from *AD*$_1$ to *AD*$_2$—because households are spending less and thus demanding less real output at any given price level. Reasoning from the assumptions of the classical economists, a reduction in aggregate demand leads quickly to falling prices. In our example, the price level will not be maintained at 100; it will fall to 80. If that occurs, businesses will be able to sell the same amount of real output as before, but at lower prices. Wages will also decline because reductions in the demand for goods and services will be accompanied by falling demand for labor, which will lead to labor surpluses and wage reductions. Thus employers will still be able to make a profit at the lower price level.

If *AD* were to increase (due to dishoarding—spending the money that had been hoarded—for example), this entire process would work in reverse. An increase in aggregate demand from AD_1 to AD_3 would quickly push up product prices. On the surface, this would seem to make it attractive for businesses to increase output; if product prices rise while input prices remain stable, producers can make a profit by expanding output to satisfy the higher level of demand. But in the classical model, wage rates and other input prices are also highly flexible, and they would tend to rise because increases in the demand for goods and services would be accompanied by rising demand for labor and other inputs. Thus businesses would have no incentive to expand output. The higher level of aggregate demand would lead to inflation, leaving ouput and employment unchanged.

In summary, the classical economists did not believe that changes in aggregate demand would have any impact on real GNP or employment; they maintained that only the price level would be affected.

Full Employment and Laissez-Faire

As a consequence of their faith in Say's Law and the flexibility of wages and prices, the classical economists viewed full employment as the normal situation. They held this belief in spite of recurring periods of observed unemployment. By the mid-1800s, economists recognized that capitalist economies tend to expand over time, but not at a steady rate. Instead, output and employment fluctuate up and down, growing rapidly in some periods and more slowly, or even declining, in others. Today we call these recurring ups and downs in the level of economic activity the **business cycle.** A period of rising output and employment is called an *expansion*; a period of declining output and employment is called a *recession.*

The occasional bouts of unemployment that accompanied the recession stage of the business cycle were not, however, viewed with alarm or seen as contradicting the classical model. Instead, such unemployment was attributed to external shocks (wars and natural disasters, for example) or to changes in consumer preferences.[1] Because the economy required time to

---

[1] Because the classical economists believed that supply created its own demand, they did not believe that it was possible to have a *general* surplus of goods and services throughout the economy. They recognized, however, that there could be an oversupply of individual prod-

adjust to these events, there might be some unemployment in the interim. But such unemployment would be very short term; it could not persist. Prolonged unemployment would result only if workers' unreasonable wage demands made it unprofitable for firms to hire them. Such unemployment was considered "voluntary"; that is, at the prevailing wage, the people preferred leisure to work. Because prolonged unemployment was regarded as an impossibility and short-term unemployment not deemed a significant social problem, the classical economists focused their energies elsewhere, on studying microeconomic issues and attempting to understand the forces underlying an economy's long-term rate of economic growth (the growth rate of potential GNP).

The classical theorists' belief in the economy's ability to maintain full employment through its own internal mechanisms caused them to favor a policy of laissez-faire, or government by nonintervention. Society was advised to rely on the market mechanism to take care of the economy, and to limit the role of government to the areas where it could make a positive contribution—maintaining law and order and providing for the national defense, for example.

The Keynesian Revolution: The Case for Policy Activism

The classical doctrine and its laissez-faire policy prescriptions were almost universally accepted by economists and policymakers until the time of the Great Depression. Then the massive and prolonged unemployment that characterized the industrialized world challenged the predictions of the classical model.

The term "depression" was coined to describe a severe recession. The Great Depression lived up to its name. In 1929, when it began, unemployment stood at 3.2 percent. By 1933, when the economy hit bottom, the unemployment rate had risen to almost 25 percent. During the same period, the economy's output of goods and services (real GNP) fell by more than 25

---

ucts. For example, automobile manufacturers might miscalculate and produce too many automobiles for the prevailing market. In the short run, this would result in unsold inventories and unemployment: the current number of workers could no longer be profitably employed by the automobile industry. In the long run, however, both problems would be eliminated. The surplus of automobiles would cause their prices to fall, which would shift labor and other economic resources out of the automobile industry and into some other industry, one characterized by shortages and rising prices.

John Maynard Keynes (shown here with his wife, Lydia) contended that the classical economists were wrong in their belief that a market economy automatically tends toward full employment.

percent. Moreover, in 1939, ten years after the depression began, unemployment still exceeded 17 percent and GNP had barely edged back to the levels achieved a decade earlier. Clearly, the classical belief that any unemployment would be moderate and short-lived seemed in direct conflict with reality.

The most forceful critic of the classical model was John Maynard Keynes, a British economist. His major work, entitled *The General Theory of Employment, Interest, and Money,* was first published in 1936. In a sense Keynes stood classical economics on its head. Whereas the classical economists believed that supply created its own demand, Keynes argued that causation ran the other way—from demand to supply. In Keynes's view, businesses base their production decisions on the level of expected demand, or expected total spending. The more that consumers, investors, and others plan to spend, the more output businesses will expect to sell and the more they will produce. In other words, supply (or output) responds to demand—not the converse, as the classical economists suggested. Most important, Keynes argued that the level of total spending in the economy could be inadequate to provide full employment, that the classical economists were wrong in believing interest rate adjustments and wage/price flexibility would prevent unemployment. According to Keynes, full employment is possible only when the level of total spending is adequate. If spending is inadequate, unemployment will result.

In summary, Keynes rejected the classical contention that market economies automatically tend toward full employment, and focused attention on the level of demand or total spending as the critical determinant of an economy's health. We now turn to a more detailed look at his model and the errors he detected in the classical theory.

The Meaning of Equilibrium Output

To understand the Keynesian model, you need to become more familiar with the concept of *equilibrium output* that was introduced earlier in this chapter. As you know, equilibrium means stability: a state of balance or rest. In microeconomics an equilibrium price is a stable price, a price that won't change unless there are changes in the underlying supply and demand conditions. In macroeconomics, an equilibrium output is a stable output, one that is neither expanding nor contracting.

We can illustrate the concept of equilibrium output with the circular flow diagram in Exh. 10.7. Note that this diagram depicts a very simplified economy; there is no government sector (hence there will be no government spending and no taxation) and no foreign sector (so there will be no imports and exports). These simplifications will make it easier for us to grasp the concept of equilibrium. A more complex economy will be introduced in later chapters.

We assume here that businesses expect to sell $1,000 billion worth of output, so they produce that amount. Of course, that sends to households $1,000 billion in income, which they can either spend or save. In this example we imagine that they choose to save $100 billion. Economists refer to saving as a *leakage,* a subtraction from the flow of spending. Leakages mean less money returns to businesses, unless the economy can somehow compensate for the loss. In our example the $100 billion leakage means that only $900 billion will be spent on consumption goods. That $900 billion is what we called *personal consumption expenditures* when we showed you how to calculate gross national product in Chapter 9.

Consumption spending is not the only form of spending for goods and services, even in the simple private economy we are analyzing. Business investors also purchase a substantial amount of our economy's output (GNP). To keep it simple, let's assume that businesses coincidentally desire to purchase $100 billion worth of output. That investment spending is

EXHIBIT 10.7

Equilibrium Output with Saving and Investment

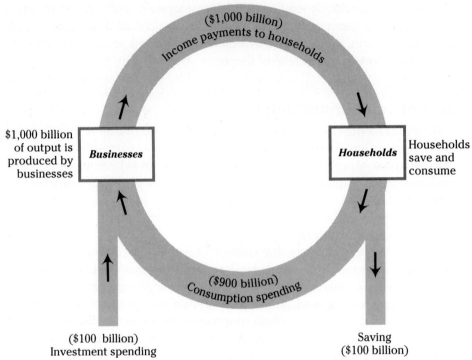

In a simple private economy we can identify the equilibrium output in either of two ways: (1) total spending equals total output, or (2) investment equals saving. In our example, when $1,000 billion worth of output is produced, it creates $1,000 billion worth of spending (consumption of $900 billion plus investment of $100 billion). At the same time, the amount that households desire to save is equal to the amount that businesses want to invest. Hence $1,000 billion is equilibrium output.

described as an *injection,* since it adds to the basic flow of consumption spending. Total spending for goods and services (consumption spending plus investment spending) amounts to $1,000 billion. As you can see from Exh. 10.7, that is just enough to purchase everything that was produced—the entire $1,000 billion. That means the producers' expectations have been fulfilled; they expected to sell $1,000 billion of output, and they have sold precisely that amount. Because producers are usually guided by their successes and failures, this would be an important finding. It would be a signal to produce the same amount next year, a response that would mean the economy was in equilibrium.

As you can see from this example, the economy will be in equilibrium whenever the amount of total spending is exactly sufficient to purchase the economy's entire output (when total spending = total output). When that happens, producers can sell exactly what they've produced, and they have no incentive to alter the level of production.

Note that when the economy is in equilibrium, the amount that households want to save is equal to the amount that businesses desire to invest. The reason for that may be apparent to you. When the amount that is being injected into the spending flow in the form of investment is equal to the amount that is leaking out in the form of saving, the size of the flow is unchanged. The amount returning to businesses will be equal to the amount they paid out; so they will be able to sell exactly what they produced, and the economy will be in equilibrium.

The Problem of an Unemployment Equilibrium

Keynes and the classical economists agreed that the economy would always tend toward equilibrium. We'll save the discussion of the forces that will tend to move the economy toward equilibrium until the next chapter. For now, the important point is that Keynes and the classical economists disagreed about whether the level of output at which the economy stabilized would permit full employment. In the classical model, the economy tends to stabilize at a full-employment equilibrium (at potential GNP). In the Keynesian model, the economy tends toward equilibrium, but not necessarily at full employment. When the economy is in equilibrium at less than full employment, an *unemployment equilibrium* exists.

We can illustrate why Keynes and the classical economists reached different conclusions about the likelihood of full employment by returning to the circular flow diagram found in Exh. 10.7. Recall that in this example households are saving $100 billion, businesses are investing $100 billion, and $1,000 billion is the economy's equilibrium output. To facilitate our comparison between the classical and Keynesian models, let's assume that $1,000 billion is the economy's potential GNP, so the economy is operating at full employment.

Now suppose that households decide to increase their saving from $100 billion to $200 billion. What will happen? Obviously, more money is leaking out of the circular flow in the form of saving. But as we noted earlier, the classical economists did not believe saving would invalidate Say's Law. According to the classical model, this increased saving would simply increase the supply of loanable funds, which would drive down the interest rate and stimulate investment spending. Investment spending would rise from $100 billion to $200 billion, thus maintaining the equilibrium output at $1,000 billion—full employment.

Keynes found fault with this optimistic scenario. According to Keynes, interest rate adjustments cannot be relied on to make saving equal to investment because the interest rate is not the major motivating force in either the saving or the investment decision. In his view, the level of *income* is the primary factor influencing the amount that households plan to save; the higher the income, the greater the level of saving. Changes in interest rates have a relatively minor impact on saving decisions. Investment decisions, said Keynes, are governed by profit expectations. The interest rate is only one factor influencing the profitability of an investment, and not the most important factor. If sales are poor and the future looks bleak, businesses are unlikely to undertake new investment, even if the prevailing interest rate is low. Since the interest rate is not the major force guiding saving and investment decisions, it cannot "match up" the plans of savers and investors. As a consequence, when households want to save more than businesses desire to invest, the level of output and employment in the economy will tend to fall. In short, increased saving (reduced spending) can lead to unemployment.

Rejecting the Wage Flexibility Argument

By itself, Keynes's discrediting of the link between saving and investment was not sufficient to refute the classical claim of a full-employment equilibrium. Remember, the classical economists described *two* forces that ensure full employment in a market economy: interest rate adjustments and wage/price flexibility. If interest rate adjustments fail to synchronize the plans of savers and investors, and if this results in too little spending, wage and price flexibility can still assure full employment. In competitive labor and product markets, inadequate demand would lead to falling wages and prices, which in turn would guarantee that all output was sold and thus prevent involuntary unemployment.

Again, Keynes disagreed. He argued that the classical assumption of highly flexible wages and prices was not consistent with the real world. According to Keynes there are a variety of forces that prevent prices and wages from adjusting quickly, particularly in a downward direction.

EXHIBIT 10.8

The Keynesian Aggregate Supply Curve

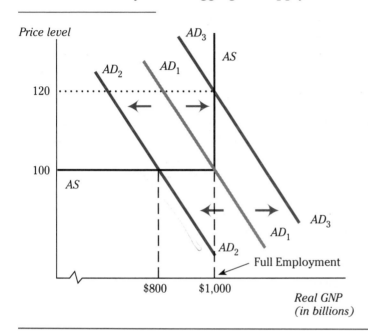

According to Keynes, prices and wages tend to be rigid in the face of falling demand. Thus a reduction in aggregate demand is quickly translated into lower real GNP and reduced employment (greater unemployment). Attempts to purchase more than the full employment output will lead to inflation without increasing real GNP.

First, markets are less competitive than the classical theory assumed. Keynes saw that many product markets were monopolistic or oligopolistic. When sellers in these markets noted that demand was declining, they often chose to reduce output rather than lower prices. And in labor markets, particularly those dominated by strong labor unions, workers tended to resist wage cuts. As a consequence, wages and prices did not adjust quickly; they tended to be rigid or "sticky."

The consequences of rigid prices can be seen in Exh. 10.8, which uses the aggregate-demand/aggregate-supply framework. Let's consider the same scenario outlined in our discussion of the classical model. Assume that consumers become pessimistic about the future and decide to hoard some of their income. Aggregate demand will fall—the AD curve will shift from AD_1 to AD_2—because households demand fewer goods and services at any given price level. This time we will make the assumption that the price level remains stuck at 100 because labor and other contracts prohibit reductions in input costs, which means that firms cannot afford to reduce prices. The assumption of rigid prices and wages implies a flat or horizontal *AS* curve, since any reduction in aggregate demand leads to a reduced level of real GNP but no change in the price level. In this example the level of equilibrium GNP would decline from $1,000 billion to $800 billion. Businesses still want to produce $1,000 billion of output, but since they can only sell $800 billion, they must cut production back to that level. Of course, employment would also decline; if employers produce less real output, they require fewer workers. This is essentially the manner in which Keynes explained the Great Depression—as a prolem caused by too little aggregate demand combined with wage and price rigidity.

Although Keynes was primarily concerned with the problem of unemployment, he agreed with the classical economists that inflation would result if consumers, investors, and others attempted to purchase more than the economy was capable of producing.[2] As you can see, the Keynesian *AS* curve becomes vertical at full employment. If aggregate demand were increased from AD_1 to AD_3, the price level would be pushed up without any increase in real output or employment.

The Case for Government Intervention

Because Keynes did not believe a market economy could be relied on to automatically preserve full employment and avoid inflation, he argued that the central government must manage the level of aggregate demand to achieve those objectives. How could this be accomplished? One approach was through *fiscal policy*—the manipulation of government spending and taxation in order to guide the economy's performance. When unemployment exists, the federal government should increase its spending on goods and services (without increasing taxes). This will shift the aggregate demand curve to the right and increase the equilibrium level of real GNP and employment. A reduction in income taxes (without a reduction in government spending) will accomplish the same thing because it will cause households to spend more at any given price level. When inflation exists, government spending should be reduced or taxes increased. These policies will reduce aggregate demand and thus reduce inflationary pressures.

Another approach would be to use ***monetary policy***: policy intended to alter the supply of money in order to influence the level of eco-

---

[2] Keynes viewed the economy's full employment, or potential GNP, as the maximum output the economy was capable of producing, rather than as the maximum *sustainable* level of production.

nomic activity. When unemployment exists, the Federal Reserve—the governmental agency that regulates the money supply—should increase the amount of money in circulation so that households and businesses will find it easier to borrow funds. This will tend to increase spending for goods and services, which will shift the *AD* curve to the right and raise the level of equilibrium output and employment. Inflation calls for a reduction in the money supply. By making it more difficult to borrow funds, the Federal Reserve can reduce spending and thereby combat inflation. We'll have more to say about fiscal and monetary policy later in the text.

The 1990s: The Debate Continues

Keynesian theory held sway through the 1960s, and many economists remain Keynesians today. But Keynesian thinking began to lose influence in the 1970s, when the Keynesian model seemed unable to explain the stagflation— simultaneous unemployment and inflation—that characterized that period. Since then, Keynesians have been rethinking and modifying their views, and new schools of thought have emerged to challenge their position.

Interestingly, some of these challengers—monetarists and rational expectations theorists—bear a striking resemblance to the classical economists of old. In particular, they generally argue that the economy tends toward full employment and that government intervention is unnecessary and even counterproductive. Thus the debate about economic policy has come full circle; economists are once again arguing about the proper role of government in economic policy: Should government actively attempt to stabilize the economy to prevent unemployment or inflation—or should it keep "hands off"? We will return to the aggregate-demand–aggregate-supply framework and our discussion of the activist-nonactivist debate after taking a closer look at the Keynesian model in chapter 11 and examining Keynesian fiscal and monetary policies in more detail in chapters 12 and 13 respectively.

Summary

In market economies, the interaction of aggregate demand and aggregate supply determines the equilibrium level of real GNP and the overall price level. *Aggregate demand* is the total quantity of output demanded by all sectors in the economy at various price levels in a given period of time. The aggregate demand curve slopes downward to reflect the fact that more aggregate output is demanded at lower price levels than at higher price levels. *Aggregate supply* is the total quantity of output supplied by all producers in the economy together at various price levels in a given period of time. The aggregate supply curve may be horizontal, vertical, or upward sloping; its shape depends on the behavior of wages and prices.

The level of output the economy produces when it operates at full employment is called *potential GNP*. An economy's potential GNP is determined by the size of the labor force, the capital stock, the stock of raw materials, and technology.

The interaction of aggregate demand and supply may give rise to an equilibrium output that is less than potential GNP. When this occurs, unemployment will exist. Economists are in disagreement about the desirability of government efforts to combat macroeconomic problems such as unemployment. Some economists are "activists," who support a significant role for government; others are "nonactivists," who believe that government intervention should be avoided.

The activist-nonactivist controversy originated more than 50 years ago with a debate between John Maynard Keynes and the classical economists who dominated that period. The classical economists felt that a market economy allowed to function without artificial restrictions would provide members of a society with the goods and services they desired while simultaneously maintaining full employment.

The foundation of the classical theory of employment was Say's Law: supply creates its own demand. More precisely, the act of producing output creates the income that will take that output off the market. Because everything that businesses produce will be sold, there should be nothing to prevent the economy from expanding to full employment.

Even an increase in saving was not considered a problem. The increased availability of loanable funds would cause the interest rate to fall, thereby encouraging businesses to borrow those funds and invest them. If the interest rate somehow failed to equate the plans of savers and investors, wage and price adjustments would compensate for any deficiency in spending. Prolonged unemployment would result only if workers made unreasonable wage demands.

The massive and prolonged unemployment that accompanied the Great Depression cast doubt on the predictions of the classical economists and subjected their model to criticism. The most devastating attack came from John Maynard Keynes. Keynes argued that a market economy does not contain any internal mechanism to ensure full employment. In his view, the primary determinant of an economy's health is the level of total spending or total demand for goods and services. If spending is inadequate, unemployment will result; if it is excessive, inflation will occur.

Keynes believed that it was the responsibility of the federal government to combat unemployment or inflation. This could be accomplished through *fiscal policy*—the manipulation of government spending and taxation in order to guide the economy's performance or through *monetary policy*—policy intended to alter the money supply as a method of influencing total spending and the economy's performance.

Glossary

Page 305   ***Aggregate demand.*** The total quantity of output demanded by all sectors in the economy together at various price levels in a given time period.

Page 307   ***Aggregate supply.*** The total quantity of output supplied by all producers in the economy together at various price levels in a given time period.

Page 316   ***Business cycle.*** The recurring ups and downs in the level of economic activity.

Page 312   ***Classical economists.*** The mainstream economists who wrote from 1776 through the early 1930s. They believed that a market economy would automatically tend to maintain full employment.

Page 319   ***Equilibrium output.*** A stable output, one that is neither expanding nor contracting.

Page 324   ***Fiscal policy.*** The manipulation of government spending and taxation in order to guide the economy's performance.

Page 320   ***Injection.*** An addition to the circular flow of spending; e.g., investment spending.

Page 319   ***Leakage.*** A subtraction from the circular flow of spending; e.g., saving.

Page 314   ***Loanable funds.*** Money available to be borrowed.

Page 324   ***Monetary policy.*** Policy intended to alter the money supply in order to influence the level of economic activity.

Page 308   ***Potential GNP.*** The level of output produced when the economy is operating at full employment; the maximum sustainable level of production.

Page 306   ***Real balance effect.*** The increase in the amount of aggregate output demanded that results from an increase in the real value of the public's financial assets.

Study Questions

Fill in the Blanks

1. The level of output the economy produces when it operates at full employment is called _potential GDP_.

2. Economists who support a significant role for government in combating macroeconomic problems are called _activists_; those who believe that government intervention should be avoided are called _nonactivists_.

3. The theory that supply creates its own demand is called _Say's law_.

4. According to Keynes, the primary cause of unemployment is _too little spending_.

5. The classical economists did not believe that saving would lead to too little spending because they felt that all saving would be _invested_.

6. In the classical model, any long-term unemployment must be _voluntary_.

7. In terms of the circular flow diagram, saving is often described as a _leakage_, whereas investment is an _injection_.

8. According to Keynes, the level of output and employment is primarily determined by the level of _total spending_.

9. In the classical model, the flexibility of interest rates was not the only factor ensuring full employment; flexible _wages_ and _prices_ provided an additional safeguard.

10. The classical economists argued that the proper role for government in the economy was a very _limited_ one.

11. According to Keynes, one way to combat unemployment is for the federal government to increase its spending or reduce _____taxes_____.

12. If there is no tendency for the level of output to expand or contract, the economy must be producing the _____equilibrium_____ level of output.

13. Manipulating the level of government spending in order to guide the economy's performance is one form of _____fiscal_____ policy.

14. Keynes believed that a reduction in aggregate demand would lead to lower output and employment rather than to lower _____prices_____, as the classical economists suggested.

15. Altering the money supply in an attempt to influence the economy's performance is termed _____monetary_____ policy.

Multiple Choice

1. The aggregate demand curve is downward sloping because
   a) when the price of a product falls, consumers tend to substitute that product for other things.
   b) certain input prices tend to be fixed by contracts in the short run.
   c) as the price level falls, the real value of financial assets increases.
   d) as the price level increases, the purchasing power of consumers' paychecks rises and they tend to buy more.

2. The aggregate supply curve will be upward sloping if
   a) all product and input prices (including wage rates) are highly flexible.
   b) higher prices lead to more spending for goods and services.
   c) certain input prices tend to be fixed in the short run.
   d) all product and input prices are inflexible due to long-term contracts.

3. Given an upward-sloping aggregate supply curve, a reduction in aggregate demand would tend to
   a) increase the level of equilibrium real GNP and the overall price level.
   b) decrease the level of equilibrium real GNP and the overall price level.
   c) increase the level of equilibrium real GNP and decrease the overall price level.
   d) decrease the level of equilibrium real GNP and increase the overall price level.

STUDY QUESTIONS

4. Given an upward-sloping aggregate supply curve, an increase in aggregate demand, coupled with a decrease in aggregate supply would tend to

   a) increase the economy's equilibrium real GNP and the overall price level.

   b) decrease the economy's equilibrium real GNP but raise the overall price level.

   c) increase the economy's overall price level, but the impact on equilibrium real GNP is indeterminate (depends on the relative magnitude of the two shifts).

   d) increase the economy's equilibrium real GNP, but the impact on the overall price level is indeterminate (depends on the relative magnitude of the two shifts).

5. According to the classical economists,

   a) unemployment is caused by too little spending.

   b) the interest rate will ensure that the amount households plan to save will equal the amount businesses desire to invest.

   c) increasing government spending is the most reliable method of restoring full employment.

   d) the amount households plan to save is primarily determined by their income.

6. During a period of unemployment, Keynes would suggest that government

   a) do nothing.

   b) reduce its spending to stimulate the economy.

   c) increase its spending to stimulate the economy.

   d) take legal action against unions in order to make wages more flexible.

7. The aggregate supply curve implied by the classical model is _____ so a reduction in aggregate demand will mean a lower overall level of _____ _____.

   a) vertical, prices

   b) vertical, output

   c) horizontal, prices

   d) horizontal, output

8. In the Keynesian model, if leakages exceed injections,

   a) the economy is producing the equilibrium output.

   b) the level of output will tend to fall.

   c) the level of output will tend to rise.

   d) the economy must be at full employment.

9. According to the classical model, even when all saving is not invested, full employment will be maintained because

   a) the government will step in and stimulate spending.

   b) the equilibrium wage rate will rise to stimulate spending.

   c) wages and prices will fall to permit businesses to continue hiring everyone who wants to work.

   d) the government will establish special work programs.

10. According to Keynes, the amount that households desire to save is determined primarily by
    a) the rate of interest.
    b) the investment plans of businesses.
    c) the incomes of the households.
    d) None of the above

11. In the Keynesian model, the economy is producing the equilibrium output when
    a) total spending equals total output.
    b) total income equals total output.
    c) total saving exceeds total investment.
    d) surplus inventories are maximized.

12. Perhaps the most important implication of Keynesian economics is that
    a) the economy automatically tends toward full employment.
    b) government should not interfere in the operation of the economy.
    c) the economy always tends toward the equilibrium output.
    d) the economy can come to rest at an unemployment equilibrium.

13. According to the classical economists, prolonged unemployment could only be caused by
    a) too little spending.
    b) workers making unreasonable wage demands.
    c) external shocks.
    d) changes in consumer preferences.

14. In the Keynesian model of a private economy, the equilibrium output exists when
    a) total spending equals total demand.
    b) consumption plus investment equals total spending.
    c) the amount that households want to save equals the amount that businesses want to invest.
    d) All of the above

15. Which of the following is an example of the fiscal policy Keynes would find appropriate for a period of unemployment?
    a) Decrease government spending
    b) Increase the money supply
    c) Reduce personal income taxes
    d) Reduce the money supply

Problems and Questions for Discussion

1. What are the determinants of the economy's potential GNP?

2. Why did the classical economists believe that any long-term unemployment had to be voluntary?

3. What flaws did Keynes find in the classical theory's wage-flexibility argument?

4. In what sense did Keynes "stand classical economics on its head"?

5. Explain the concept of equilibrium output, and describe how to identify equilibrium in the Keynesian model.

6. In the Keynesian model, why is a private economy in equilibrium when the amount that households plan to save is equal to the amount that businesses plan to invest?

7. Why did Keynes believe that the proper response to a period of unemployment was for government to increase its spending? How could this policy help to combat unemployment?

8. How did the classical economists explain the existence of short-term unemployment?

9. Explain the role of interest rates in the classical model.

10. Many economists argue that the Great Depression was actually brought to an end by World War II. In Keynesian terms, how could a war contribute to combating unemployment?

Answer Key

Fill in the Blanks

1. potential GNP
2. activists, nonactivists
3. Say's Law
4. too little spending
5. invested
6. voluntary
7. leakage, injection
8. total spending
9. wages, prices
10. limited
11. taxes
12. equilibrium
13. fiscal
14. prices
15. monetary

Multiple Choice

1. c
2. c
3. b
4. c
5. b
6. c
7. a
8. b
9. c
10. c
11. a
12. d
13. b
14. c
15. c

STUDY QUESTIONS

CHAPTER 11

THE BASIC KEYNESIAN MODEL: DETERMINING THE LEVELS OF INCOME, OUTPUT AND EMPLOYMENT

What determines how much output our economy will produce and how many people will be employed? For Keynesians, the answer is *total spending—total demand for goods and services*. When total spending increases, businesses produce more output and hire more people. As you learned in Chapter 10, that's the central idea in Keynesian macroeconomic theory: *Total spending is the critical determinant of the overall level of economic activity.*

Now we will explore the factors that influence the level of total spending. Why does total spending fluctuate? How can it be too low at some times and too high at others? We take up these questions in the next two chapters as we examine a hypothetical economy. Here in Chapter 11 we confine our analysis to a two-sector economy—households and businesses. We assume that there is no government and no foreign trade. We also assume that all saving is done by households and all investment by businesses. Further, we assume that the price level remains constant until full employment is reached. (Remember, Keynes believed that prices and wages tend to be rigid, not flexible as the classical economists assumed.) These assumptions will make it easier for us to grasp the basics. Later we will allow our hypothetical economy to become more complex.

Our first step will be to explore the determinants of consumption and investment spending. Next we will consider the way in which consumption, investment, and saving interact to determine the level of equilibrium income and output. After we've accomplished those objectives, we will investigate the possibility of an unemployment or an inflationary equilibrium.

Consumption Spending

The largest component of total spending is consumption spending—spending by households for food, clothing, automobiles, education, and all the other goods and services that consumers buy. The most important factor influencing the amount of consumer spending is the level of disposable income. *Disposable income* is your take-home pay, the amount you have left after taxes have been deducted. Because there is no government sector in this chapter's hypothetical economy, no taxes are collected, which means that disposable income will equal total income, or GNP. For both individual households and the society as a whole, a positive relationship exists between the amount of disposable income and the amount of consumption spending: The more people earn, the more they spend.

The Consumption Function

The relationship between disposable income and consumption spending is called the *consumption function.* A consumption function shows the amounts that households plan to spend at different levels of disposable income. Exhibit 11.1 contains a hypothetical consumption function that is consistent with Keynesian theory. Note that the amount households plan to spend increases with income, but by a smaller amount than the increase in income. In other words, households will spend part of any increase in income and save the rest. Whatever disposable income is not spent by households is saved. *Saving* is the act of not spending; putting money in a savings account, buying stocks and bonds, and stashing cash in a cookie jar are all acts of saving.

According to Exh. 11.1, when income is $300 billion, households desire to spend $325 billion. At that income, they are *dissaving* $25 billion; that is, they are dipping into their savings accounts or borrowing to help

---

EXHIBIT 11.1

A Hypothetical Consumption Function (in billions)

TOTAL INCOME* AND OUTPUT (GNP)	PLANNED CONSUMPTION EXPENDITURES	PLANNED SAVING
$300	$325	$ – 25
400	400	0
500	475	25
600	550	50
700	625	75
800	700	100

* In our simplified economy, total income = total disposable income = GNP.

---

finance some minimum standard of living. Higher levels of income involve more consumption spending and more saving, or less dissaving. In our example, $400 billion represents the income level at which every dollar earned is spent; there is neither saving nor dissaving. At higher incomes, households wish to save a portion of their income. For instance, at an income of $500 billion, households plan to save $25 billion; at an income of $600 billion, they desire to save $50 billion.

Exhibit 11.2 plots the consumption function depicted in Exh. 11.1. The consumption function slopes upward and to the right because consumption spending increases with income. We determine the income level where every dollar is spent by using the 45-degree line drawn in the diagram. Because the vertical and horizontal axes meet at a 90-degree angle, the 45-degree line represents a series of points that are equidistant from the horizontal axis (income) and the vertical axis (consumption). Therefore *at every point along the 45-degree line, consumption expenditures equal income.* Where the consumption function crosses the 45-degree line, consumers plan to spend everything they earn and save nothing. In our example, that happens at an income of $400 billion.

At incomes less than $400 billion, there is dissaving, or negative saving. You can see that when income is $300, consumers plan to dissave $25. The vertical distance between the 45-degree line and the consumption func-

EXHIBIT 11.2

Graphing a Consumption Function

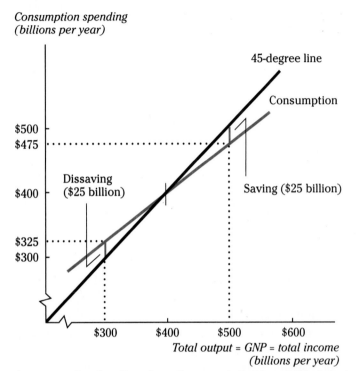

Consumption spending
(billions per year)

45-degree line

Consumption

$500
$475

Dissaving
($25 billion)

$400

Saving ($25 billion)

$325
$300

$300 $400 $500 $600

Total output = GNP = total income
(billions per year)

A consumption function *shows the amounts that households desire to spend at different income levels. According to this hypothetical function, households would spend $325 billion per year if the total income in the economy were $300 billion. That means they would be dissaving—dipping into their savings accounts or borrowing—$25 billion at that income level.*

Note that the amount of consumption spending rises with the level of income. At an income of $400 billion, households desire to spend exactly what they earn. There would be no saving and no dissaving. At an income of $500 billion, households would spend $475 billion each year and save $25 billion.

tion represents the amount of dissaving at that income. At incomes in excess of $400 billion, there is positive saving. When income is $500 billion, saving is equal to $25 billion. The distance between the 45-degree line and the consumption function gets wider as income increases, because the amount of saving increases with income.

The Marginal Propensity to Consume

The way that households react to changes in income depends on their *marginal propensity to consume (MPC)*. The *MPC* is the fraction of each additional earned dollar that households spend on consumption: that is, the change in consumption spending divided by the change in income:

$$\text{Marginal propensity to consume } (MPC) = \frac{\text{change in consumption spending}}{\text{change in income}}$$

If you receive a $1,000 raise and you plan to spend $900 of that increase, your *MPC* is 9/10, or 0.90. In other words, you'll spend 90 percent of any additional income you receive. In our hypothetical economy, the marginal propensity to consume is 3/4 or 0.75. Note that in Exh. 11.1 and 11.2, for every $100 billion increase in GNP (income), consumption spending increases by $75 billion.

$$MPC = \frac{\$\ 75 \text{ billion}}{\$100 \text{ billion}} = \frac{3}{4} = 0.75$$

You can relate the marginal propensity to consume to the consumption function easily if you know that the slope of any line is, by definition, the vertical change divided by the horizontal change. The slope of the consumption function is the change in consumption spending divided by the change in income, which is precisely how we define the marginal propensity to consume. In other words, the slope of the consumption function is equal to the economy's *MPC*. If the *MPC* in our example were higher (0.90 instead of 0.75, for example), the slope of the consumption function would be steeper; if the *MPC* were lower (perhaps 0.50), the consumption function would be flatter.

According to our consumption function, only part of an increase in income is spent; the rest is saved. The *marginal propensity to save (MPS)* is the fraction of each additional earned dollar that is saved, or the change in saving divided by the change in income:

$$\text{Marginal propensity to save } (MPS) = \frac{\text{change in saving}}{\text{change in income}}$$

Calculating *MPS* is no problem once you know *MPC*. The marginal propensity to consume and the marginal propensity to save have to add up to 1.00, or 100 percent: if *MPC* is 0.75, you know that *MPS* must be 0.25. That is, 75 cents from each additional dollar is spent, and 25 cents is saved.

As you study Exh. 11.1 and 11.2, keep in mind that the consumption function indicates the desired—or planned—levels of consumption, not necessarily the actual levels. Just as the demand curves we encountered in

Chapter 3 showed the amount of a product consumers are "willing and able to buy at various prices," the consumption function shows the amounts that households *desire* to consume at various income levels. How much of a product people actually buy depends on the prices that actually prevail. Similarly, the actual level of consumption depends on the actual level of income in the economy.

The Nonincome Determinants of Consumption Spending

Although consumption spending is determined primarily by the level of disposable income, nonincome factors also play a role. These nonincome factors include (1) people's expectations about what will happen to prices and to their incomes, (2) the cost and availability of consumer credit, and (3) the overall wealth of households.

It is easy to see why consumer expectations can have an impact on spending behavior. If people expect prices to be higher next month or next year, they tend to buy now. Why wait to pay $14,000 for a car next year, if you can buy it for $13,000 today? Buying now to avoid higher prices later creates a greater amount of current consumption spending than would normally be expected at each level of income. Similarly, if people expect an increase in income, they will probably spend more from their current income. If you're convinced that you're going to be earning more next year, you'll probably be a little bit freer in your spending habits this year.

The cost and availability of consumer credit also influence the level of consumption spending. Most of us don't limit our spending to our current income. If we really want something, we borrow the money to buy it. But the cost of borrowing money and the ability to get consumer credit can change with the state of the economy. In general, the higher the interest rate and the more difficult it is to get consumer loans, the less consumption spending there will be at any level of total income (GNP).

The third nonincome determinant of consumption spending is the overall wealth of households. A household's wealth includes cash, bank accounts, stocks and bonds, real estate, and other physical assets. Since households can finance consumption spending by depleting bank accounts or selling other forms of wealth, an increase in wealth will permit households to spend more at any given income level. For this reason, an increase in wealth will tend to shift the consumption function upward; a decrease will have the opposite effect.

The consumption function assumes that these nonincome determinants of consumption spending remain unchanged. If that assumption is violated, the entire consumption function shifts. Exhibit 11.3 shows how changing expectations about prices result in different levels of planned con-

EXHIBIT 11.3

Changes in the Nonincome Determinants of Consumption

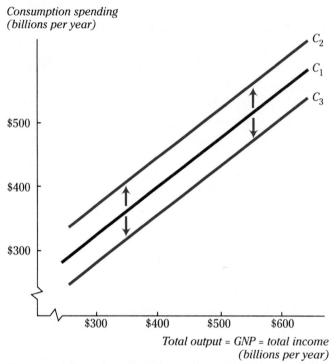

The consumption function assumes that the nonincome determinants of consumption spending remain unchanged. If that assumption is violated, the consumption function will shift to a new position. For example, if consumers expect prices to be higher next year, they will probably choose to purchase more consumer goods this year. The consumption function will shift upward (from C_1 to C_2). If consumers revise downward their expectations regarding future prices, they will probably choose to purchase fewer consumer goods this year. The consumption function will shift downward (from C_1 to C_3).

sumption spending at each level of income. (Suppose that the 1990s turn out to be The Savings Decade. How would the consumption function be affected? Read "Reformed Spenders" on page 342 and see if you can answer that question.)

Except under extreme conditions, such as those that prevailed during the Great Depression or World War II, the consumption function has been relatively stable—it hasn't shifted up or down very much. Knowing that planned consumption has been stable, how do we explain the fluctuations in total spending that occur in our economy? According to Keynes, the major cause of fluctuations in total spending is the ever-changing rate of investment spending.

Investment Spending

The term *investment*, as you saw in Chapter 9, refers to spending by businesses on capital goods—factories, machinery, and other aids to production. Investment spending has a dual influence on the level of economic activity. First, as a major component of total spending, investment spending helps determine the economy's level of total output and total employment. Second, investment is a critical determinant of the economy's rate of growth. We define growth as an increase in real GNP. Investment spending contributes to economic growth because it enlarges the economy's stock of capital goods and thereby helps increase the economy's capacity to produce goods and services.

The Determinants of Investment

As you discovered in Chapter 10, profit expectations are the overriding motivation of all investment-spending plans in a market economy. Those expectations are based on a comparison of costs and revenues.

Suppose you are considering investing in a soft-drink machine for the lobby of the student union. How do you decide whether to make the investment? Like any other businessperson, you compare costs and revenues. On the cost side, you consider the price of the machine and the interest charges on the money you would have to borrow to buy it. If you would be using your own money, you consider the opportunity cost of those funds—the amount of interest you will sacrifice if you withdraw that money from your savings to purchase the machine. On the revenue side, you would include the expected income from selling the soft drinks minus the cost of the drinks. If you expect the machine to generate revenues exceeding all your anticipated costs, you have incentive to make the investment. If not, the investment should not be made. All investment decisions involve a similar comparison.

Interest Rates: The Cost of Money. The rate of interest can be an important factor in determining whether an investment will be profitable. A project that does not appear profitable when the interest rate is 20 percent, for example, may be attractive if the interest rate drops to 15 percent or 12 percent.

Reformed Spenders

Americans Save More and Have Reason to in a Tough Economy

One day six years ago, William McCormick sat at a table with 10 other New Jersey residents and talked about his saving and spending habits. It was all spending, and no saving.

"Pretty impulsive" is the phrase Mr. McCormick used to describe his generation, back in June 1985. The salesman, 31-years-old at the time, said he and his friends were buying bigger houses than they could afford. His family, he said, ran up huge credit-card bills. And they didn't have much money to spare. They counted on income-tax refunds, for instance, to pay their auto insurance premiums. As for savings, he said, "It's almost impossible, really."

Today, Mr. McCormick still sells dairy products to supermarkets and lives in the same house. His wife has an office job now, and their income has about doubled since 1985, to $60,000 a year. But when he talks about money, Bill McCormick sounds like a new man.

'Time to Get Real'

"We're making a concerted effort to put something away—even if it's only a few dollars," the Iselin, N.J., resident says. Why? "I'm 37 years old, not 22. It's time to get real. I was always living on the edge. I'm off it now."

So are many of the other middle-income Americans who got together in a New Jersey conference room six years ago at the request of the Gallup Organization and The Wall Street Journal. A profound change has occurred in most of them, or so it seems. The shop-till-you-drop ethic, so in evidence in 1985, is all but dead. The mood is one of caution, of conserving cash. There is new emphasis on saving, on putting away rainy-day money for an uncertain future.

It may be too early to declare the 1990s The Savings Decade, and some experts doubt that significant change really is afoot. . . . But in an informal, impressionistic survey, this newspaper has found considerable evidence that consumer attitudes *are* changing. And striking change is very much in evidence among the New Jersey residents who gathered around that conference table six years ago to talk about spending and saving.

Things were different then. The U.S. economy was expanding. And around the table, men and women ranging in age from 28 to 68—sales reps and homemakers, a keypunch operator, a systems analyst, a construction worker, an attorney and several others—all expressed optimism about the future, and confidence in their own financial security.

Abe Ash, the systems analyst, told the story of how he and his wife had lost their jobs in 1976 but still qualified for a home mortgage. So they bought a house, and it tripled in value. Others at the table nodded knowingly.

Panelists talked of trading up to bigger houses, of expensive vacations, of proliferating credit cards. The moderator asked the group at one point what everyone would do with a $5,000 windfall. Most of the panelists said they would blow a lot of it on a vacation. . . .

Seven of the 11 original focus-group participants now express a more conservative approach to spending and new determination to save. (The other four members didn't participate in the recent discussion.)

Retirement Planning

Mr. Ash, the systems analyst, admits to having been one of

the "spending pack" before. Today, he says, "I've toned down a bit." He hasn't taken what he considers a real family vacation since 1987, and he and his wife, a teacher, are earnestly trying to put as much of her income as possible away for retirement.

Several others say that, in contrast to the mid-1980s, they are taking fewer vacations, thinking ahead to retirement and waiting until they can afford to pay cash for what they buy rather than go into debt. . . .

Even some young adults in their 20s—typically big spenders on furniture, appliances and cars—are showing a propensity to save these days. Take the unusual case of Kim and George Norris, of Columbus, Ohio, who together earn roughly $50,000 a year. (They were not in the 1985 group.) They seek out $2 movie theaters, avoid expensive restaurant-meals and budget just $40 per week for gasoline and entertainment. They put 40% of their take-home pay into savings. . . .

Texas' Bad Case
The economic shocks of the past few years are probably behind much of the new caution. Texas, particularly, was devastated in the mid-1980s by the collapse of oil prices. An economy built largely on debt came undone as developers went belly up, housing

prices plummeted and deeply indebted homeowners sometimes abandoned houses they couldn't sell or pay for.

Joan Peurifoy, a personal financial planner in Dallas, sees a sharp change in how her clients regard money. Many are two-income couples 35 to 45. Several years ago, when she warned people that they were overspending, many shrugged off her admonitions. No longer.

Ms. Peurifoy says that, nowadays, many of her clients have the same response to a financial problem: "How can we fix it?"

Mindful of the new mood, financial institutions are trying to profit from the new cachet saving seems to have. American Express has begun encouraging card members to remit a little more than they actually owe on their monthly statement.

Under the plan, called Membership Savings, the extra money goes into an FDIC-insured savings account paying half a percentage point more than the average rate paid by commercial banks and thrift institutions. After testing the plan in seven states, American Express is branching out into 20 others. The most enthusiastic response has come from customers in their 20s and 30s.

"Financial responsibility is the thing that is going to play in the 1990s," says Philip Riese, executive vice president and general manager of the consumer card group at American Express. . . .
—*Kathryn Graven*

SOURCE: *The Wall Street Journal*, April 22, 1991, p. 1. Reprinted by permission of *The Wall Street Journal*, © 1991 Dow Jones & Company, Inc. All Right Reserved Worldwide.

USE YOUR ECONOMIC REASONING

1. **Suppose that older adults save more at any income level than younger adults. If the average age of the U.S. population is increasing, how will this affect the consumption function?**

2. **The article suggests that even younger people seem to be saving more of their income. What factors are responsible for this increased interest in saving?**

3. **Think back to Chapter 10. What concerns would Keynes have if he learned that households were saving more?**

To illustrate, suppose that you can purchase a soft-drink vending machine (which has a useful life of one year) for $1,000 and can borrow the money at 20-percent interest. Assume also that you expect to sell 5,000 cans of soft drink a year at $.60 a can and plan to pay $.36$\frac{1}{2}$ for each can you buy. Would your investment be a profitable one? A few calculations show that it wouldn't be.

Anticipated revenue (5,000 cans sold at $.60 per can)		$3,000
Anticipated costs		
Cost of the vending machine	$1,000	
Cost of the soft drinks (5,000 cans at $.36$\frac{1}{2}$)	$1,825	
Cost of borrowed funds ($1,000 at 20 percent)	$ 200	
Total cost		$3,025
Anticipated loss		$ 25

According to these calculations, you could expect to lose $25 on your investment if you had to pay 20-percent interest to borrow the money. So of course you wouldn't make the investment under those conditions. But if the interest rate declined to 15 percent, the cost of borrowing $1,000 for a year would drop to $150, and the investment would earn a profit of $25. If the interest rate declined further, the profit would be even greater. The point we are making is that lower interest rates encourage businesses to undertake investments that would be unattractive at higher rates. Thus we have a negative, or inverse, relationship between the rate of interest and the level of investment spending; the lower the interest rate, the higher the level of investment spending. This relationship is illustrated in Exh. 11.4.

Expectations about Revenues and Costs. While the interest rate influences investment spending plans, it should be clear from our example that it is not the only factor to take into consideration. Businesses will continue to borrow and invest in spite of high interest rates if they are optimistic about future revenues (and costs) and the likelihood of earning a profit. For example, even a 20- or 25-percent interest rate would not discourage you from investing in the vending machine if you were convinced that you could sell 6,000 cans of the soft drink a year. On the other hand, an interest rate as low as 6 percent would be prohibitive if you were forecasting sales of only 4,500 cans. (Take the time to make some calculations and convince yourself of these conclusions.) In short, it is not interest rates themselves, but the interaction of interest rates and expectations about future revenues and costs that determines the attractiveness of investment projects and the level of investment spending in the economy.

EXHIBIT 11.4

Investment and the Rate of Interest

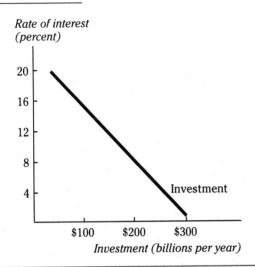

Rate of interest (percent)

Investment (billions per year)

The rate of interest and the level of investment spending are negatively, or inversely, related; the lower the interest rate, the higher the level of investment spending.

The Instability of Investment

From the preceding discussion you may have begun to understand why investment spending is much less stable than consumption spending. There are several reasons. First, the interest rate tends to change over time, and these changes cause businesses to alter their investment plans, as you have seen.

Second, businesses' expectations are quite volatile, or changeable. They are influenced by everything from current economic conditions to headlines in the newspaper. If a wave of optimism hits the country, planned investment may skyrocket. When pessimism strikes, investment plunges.

A third source of instability is the simple fact that plans to invest can be postponed. A business may want to build a more modern production plant to improve its competitive position. But if economic conditions suggest that this may not be the best time to build, the business can decide to make the old plant last a little longer.

Finally, investment opportunities occur irregularly, in spurts. New products and new production processes provide businesses with investment opportunities, but these developments do not occur in predictable patterns. A business may encounter several profitable investment opportunities one year and none the next.

Changing interest rates, the volatility of expectations, the ability to postpone investment spending, and the ups and downs of investment opportunities all lead to fluctuations and instability in the level of investment spending. Because investment spending accounts for more than 15 percent of the GNP, these changes can have a major impact on total output and employment in the economy. We'll have more to say about that impact later in this chapter.

The Equilibrium Level of Output

Now that we have analyzed the individual components of spending in our hypothetical economy, we are ready to combine these components to see how total spending determines the level of output and employment. Remember: According to Keynesian theory, the level of demand—that is, total spending—determines the amount of output that will be produced and the number of jobs that will be made available. To see how the spending plans of consumers and investors determine the level of output and employment, we turn to Exh. 11.5.

The first column in the table shows several possible levels of output (GNP) that our hypothetical economy could produce. Which level will be chosen by businesses depends on how much they expect to sell. Let's assume that businesses believe they can sell $600 billion worth of output. To produce this output, they hire economic resources: land, labor, capital, and entrepreneurship. This transaction provides households with $600 billion of income, an amount exactly equal to the value of total output. Recall that total income *must* equal total output because all the money received by businesses must be paid to someone.

The second column shows the amount households plan to consume for each level of income (GNP) given in column 1. If the tabular data in column 2 were plotted in a graph, you would recognize the consumption function (Exh. 11.1). You can see that when GNP is $600 billion, households desire to consume $550 billion. Moving to column 3, you see that households want to save $50 billion when GNP is $600 billion.

The next category of spending is investment spending (column 4). Our example assumes that investment spending is autonomous, or inde-

EXHIBIT 11.5

Determination of Equilibrium Income and Output (data in billions)

(1) TOTAL OUTPUT AND INCOME* (GNP)	(2) PLANNED CONSUMPTION EXPENDITURES	(3) PLANNED SAVING (1–2)	(4) PLANNED INVESTMENT EXPENDITURES	(5) TOTAL PLANNED EXPENDITURES (2 + 4)	(6) TENDENCY OF OUTPUT
$300	$325	$ – 25	$50	$375	Increase
400	400	0	50	450	Increase
500	475	25	50	525	Increase
600	550	50	50	600	Equilibrium
700	625	75	50	675	Decrease
800	700	100	50	750	Decrease

* In our simplified economy, total income = total disposable income = GNP.

pendent of the level of current output. Unlike consumption spending, investment spending is determined by the factors described earlier: the rate of interest and expectations regarding future revenues and costs. The level of investment spending changes only if those determinants change. Here, we've set the level of investment spending at $50 billion. (Later we'll allow the level of investment to change so that we can trace the impact of that change on the level of output and employment.)

In our simplified economy, total spending (column 5) is the sum of consumption spending and investment spending. Note that the amount of total spending rises with the economy's GNP; higher levels of GNP signal higher levels of total spending because consumption spending increases with income. If the business sector produces $600 billion of output, the result will be the creation of $550 billion of consumption spending and $50 billion of investment spending, or a total of $600 billion. This amount will be precisely enough to clear the market of that period's production. Most important, because businesses can sell exactly what they have produced, they will have no incentive to increase or decrease their rate of output. As you learned in Chapter 10, this means the economy has arrived at its equilibrium output, the output that it will tend to maintain. Businesses can be expected to produce the same amount every year until they have reason to believe that the spending plans of consumers or investors have changed.

Inventory Adjustments and Equilibrium Output

The preceding example demonstrates that the economy will be in equilibrium only when *total spending is exactly equal to total output*.[1] In other words, an economy has arrived at its equilibrium output when the production of that output level gives rise to precisely enough spending, or demand, to purchase everything that was produced. In our example, $600 billion is the only output that satisfies this requirement. At any other output level, there will be either too much or too little demand, and producers will have incentive to alter their level of production.

Consider, for example, an output of $700 billion. As you have seen, producing $700 billion of output means creating $700 billion of income. Note, however, that not all this income will find its way back to businesses in the form of spending. Column 5 in Exh. 11.5 shows that only $675 billion of spending will be created—too little to absorb the period's production. Inventories of unsold merchandise will grow, signaling businesses to reduce the rate of output; this move will take the economy closer to equilibrium.

If spending initially exceeded output, the reaction of businesses would be exactly the opposite. For example, if $500 billion of output were produced, it would generate $525 billion of total spending. Because the amount that consumers and investors desire to spend exceeds the level of output, businesses can meet demand only if they supplement their current production with merchandise from their inventories. This unintended reduction in inventories is a signal to increase the rate of output, which in turn will push the economy closer to the equilibrium GNP.

As you can see, whenever spending is greater or less than output, producers have incentive to alter production levels; there is a natural tendency to move toward equilibrium. The only output that can be maintained is the output where total spending is exactly equal to total output; this is the equilibrium output.

Equilibrium Output: A Graphic Presentation

The data in Exh. 11.5 is graphed in Exh. 11.6. The line labeled "$C+I$" (consumption plus investment) is the total expenditure (or total spending) function. This function is simply a graphic representation of column 5 from Exh.

---

[1] You may remember from Chapter 10 that there is another way to identify the equilibrium output—by finding the output at which planned saving is equal to planned investment. You

EXHIBIT 11.6

Determination of Equilibrium Income and Output

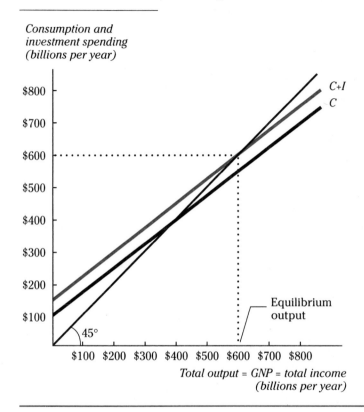

Consumption and investment spending (billions per year)

We can identify the equilibrium output by locating the output where the total expenditures function crosses the 45-degree line.

11.5, showing the total amount of planned spending at each level of GNP. It is easy to understand why the total expenditure function looks so much like the consumption function that we introduced earlier. Because we have assumed investment spending to be an autonomous constant—$50 billion per year—the total spending function can be constructed merely by drawing a line parallel to line C (consumption) and exactly $50 billion above it. The other element of the output-expenditure diagram is the 45-degree line. At every point on this line, total spending equals total output. We locate the equilibrium output where the total spending function intersects the 45-degree line ($600 billion).

can see in Exh. 11.5 that planned saving is equal to planned investment at an output of $600 billion, the output already identified as equilibrium.

Changes in Spending and the Multiplier Effect

Changes in the spending plans of either consumers or investors will alter the equilibrium level of income and output in our hypothetical economy. At any given level of income (GNP) consumers may decide to spend more if they believe that prices are going to rise in the near future or if they expect wage and salary increases. Such a change in consumer expectations would be represented graphically by an upward shift of the consumption function. Similarly, investors may increase their rate of investment spending if they become more optimistic about the future or if interest rates decline. This change in the level of planned investment would be depicted by an upward shift of the investment function.

Because the economy's total expenditure function is nothing more than the sum of the consumption and investment functions, an upward shift of either one would cause an upward shift of the total expenditure function, which in turn would increase the equilibrium level of output. Any change resulting in a downward shift of the consumption or investment functions would reduce the equilibrium output.

To illustrate the impact of a change in the level of planned expenditures, let's assume that the rate of autonomous investment increases by $50 billion per year. This change is represented in Exh. 11.7 by a shift of the total expenditure function from $C + I_1$ to $C + I_2$. The most important thing to notice about this example is the relationship between the initial change in investment spending and the resulting change in total output. When investment spending increases by $50 billion, total output increases by much more than that—by $200 billion to be exact. This phenomenon, the fact that small changes in spending are magnified into larger changes in income and output, is called the *multiplier effect.*

The Multiplier Effect

In order to understand how the multiplier effect operates, let's trace the impact of this increase in investment spending as it works its way through the economy. Exhibit 11.8 illustrates the process. Period one shows the original equilibrium situation from Exh. 11.7 (note that total output equals total spending at $600 billion). In period two, output and consumption spending remain unchanged, but investment spending increases from $50 billion to $100 billion. That pushes total spending up to $650 billion and disturbs the

EXHIBIT 11.7

The Multiplier Effect

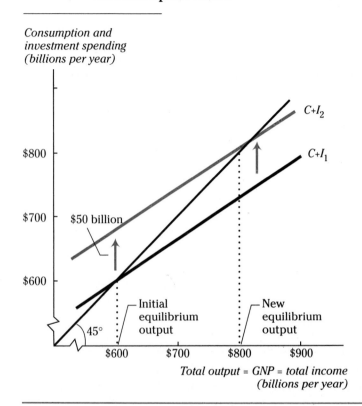

Consumption and investment spending (billions per year)

$C+I_2$

$C+I_1$

$800

$700 $50 billion

$600

Initial equilibrium output

New equilibrium output

45°

$600 $700 $800 $900

Total output = GNP = total income (billions per year)

Because of the multiplier effect, an initial $50-billion increase in spending leads to a $200 billion increase in GNP.

economy's equilibrium. Since the level of total spending in period two exceeds the economy's output, the demand can be met only by drawing inventories below their desired levels.

In period three, producers increase their output to $650 billion in an attempt to catch up with demand. But when producers expand their output by $50 billion, they create an additional $50 billion of new income—the money that is paid to the owners of economic resources. Recall that our hypothetical economy was constructed with a *MPC* of 0.75. Therefore this $50-billion increase in income leads to an additional $37.5 billion of consumption spending (75 percent of $50 billion). As a result, total spending rises by an additional $37.5 billion in period three, and output again fails to keep pace with demand.

EXHIBIT 11.8

Tracing the Impact of a Spending Increase (hypothetical data in billions)

PERIOD	TOTAL OUTPUT AND INCOME (GNP)	PLANNED CONSUMPTION EXPENDITURES	PLANNED INVESTMENT EXPENDITURES	TOTAL PLANNED EXPENDITURES
One	**$600.00**	$550.00	$ 50.00	**$600.00**
Two	600.00	550.00	100.00	650.00
Three	650.00	587.50	100.00	687.50
Four	687.50	615.63	100.00	715.63
Five	715.63	636.73	100.00	736.73
Six	736.73	652.56	100.00	752.56
—	—	—	—	—
—	—	—	—	—
Ultimately	**800.00**	700.00	100.00	**800.00**

In period four, businesses expand their production to $687.5 billion, the level of demand in period three. This $37.5 billion increase in income (output) causes consumption spending to increase by $28.13 billion (75 percent of $37.5 billion). As a consequence, total spending in period four will rise by $28.13 billion and, since total spending continues to exceed total output, inventories again will fall.

As you can see, once equilibrium is disrupted, income and consumption spending continue to feed on one another. Any change in income causes consumption spending to expand, which in turn causes income and output to expand still further. In theory, the new equilibrium would be reached only after an infinite number of time periods. However, the increases in income and consumption become smaller as equilibrium is approached, so most of the expansionary effect is felt after the first half-dozen or so periods. In our example, equilibrium is finally attained when output is equal to total spending at $800 billion. (Note that this is the output level at which the total expenditure function crosses the 45-degree line in Exh. 11.7.) The article on page 354, "The New Look of Capital Spending," examines some of the factors that business executives consider when deciding when and how much to invest. After reading the article, use the study questions to test your understanding of the Keynesian model and how changes in investment spending will influence output and employment.

Calculating the Multiplier

In the preceding example, a $50 billion increase in investment spending led to a $200 billion increase in income and output. That means the *multiplier* is 4. The ***multiplier (M)*** is the number by which any initial change in spending is multiplied to find the ultimate change in income and output.

If we know the marginal propensity to consume in our economy, we can estimate the size of the multiplier before the change in spending has run its course. Either of two simple formulas can be used:

$$M = \frac{1}{1 - MPC}$$

or, since $1 - MPC = MPS$,

$$M = \frac{1}{MPS}$$

Applying the formula to our hypothetical economy (with an MPC of 0.75), we can verify that the multiplier is indeed 4:

$$M = \frac{1}{1 - MPC}$$

$$M = \frac{1}{1 - 0.75}$$

$$M = 4$$

As we've already seen, a multiplier of 4 tells us that any increase in spending will generate an increase in equilibrium output that is four times as large. (The multiplier also works in reverse; so if spending drops, we can expect equilibrium output to decline by 4 times as much.) Of course, the multiplier can take on different values depending on the economy's MPC. If the MPC is 0.5, the multiplier will be 2; if the MPC is 0.8, the multiplier will be 5. As you can see, the size of the multiplier is related directly to the size of the economy's marginal propensity to consume: the larger the MPC, the larger the multiplier. This relationship exists because when the MPC is larger, a greater fraction of any increase in income is spent—meaning that more in-

The New Look of Capital Spending

Mead Corp., like many other U.S. companies, was sitting tight. It had not built a new paperboard plant since 1975. But a little over a year ago top executives met to reconsider. Their mills were operating at capacity, the economy was solid, and the dollar was back down to earth. With two years of research piled on the conference table, the executives finally said yes to a new $556 million project—their first ever to rely heavily on the export market. "It's a big-scale risk," says Thomas Johnson, president of Mead's coated-board division. "But we're investing in a strategy to give us a foothold beyond our borders."

Like Mead, many U.S. companies are opening their wallets after a long spell of caution. Last year business investment rose 9.5% to $487.2 billion after adjusting for inflation. . . .

Though *Fortune* expects that real growth will slow to about 4% this year, capital spending will continue to be one of the strongest sectors in the economy. . . . The re-markable thing about this surge is how different it is from earlier bursts of capital spending. American corporations are rethinking old assumptions about how to invest. The smartest are finding they can do more with less by managing their factories better and adding equipment rather than bricks and mortar. . . .

Today's decisions also reflect lessons hard-learned during the torturous Eighties. In the classic boom-and-bust pattern of capital spending, many companies had overbuilt by the time the 1981 recession hit. . . .

Many companies still have more plant than they need, and for some the problem is global. By most estimates world auto overcapacity stands at better than six million units—enough to supply the entire U.S. market for more than half a year.

Managers have to struggle with extraordinarily difficult questions, such as how long the aging world economic expansion will last, . . . and whether the market can absorb the huge additions to capacity that today's world-scale plants imply. . . .

Recent experience does seem to have taught many of these companies caution about going overboard. . . .

Ford Motor offers a model for companies seeking to resist temptation. The auto star has been running at capacity for three years and could have spent to its heart's content on new factories and robots without exhausting its cash hoard, which now totals some $10 billion. Instead Ford was a tightwad, investing $16.6 billion from 1983 through 1987, less than half as much as General Motors spent, though Ford is three-quarters GM's size. Says treasurer David McCammon: "Sure, we might have missed a few sales, but one of the reasons we've been so successful is that we didn't get carried away in capacity planning and add a lot of extra costs." Instead Ford made its existing plants better. Largely by developing a management system that emphasized teamwork and quality control, the company has lowered its breakeven point in North America by 40% since 1980, and has become the most efficient of the Big Three.

Now Ford is ready to shell out. Capacity is stretched and many of its platforms, the basic foundations upon which cars are built, are aging. Over the next five years Ford plans to spend considerably more than it has in the past five years. Ford won't say how much, but Scott Merlis at Morgan Stanley estimates that spending will total about $29 billion. Ford doesn't want to add another statistic to the column of redundant plants, but it must update vehicles like the Escort, redesign engines, and modernize paint shops. "The name of the game is to stay ahead," says McCammon. "One reason we're being very aggressive is we know the competition is doing a lot." Ford also can expect to get its money's worth because it has already restructured factory operations.

Equipment purchases account for 71% of today's capital spending. Partly that reflects prudence—companies don't want to get caught again with idle plants. But it is also a natural outgrowth of efforts to overhaul factory management. A company that goes to just-in-time inventory, for example, may not need a new building for a long while. The system typically frees up at least a third of the space in existing plants while increasing output, leaving plenty of room for expansion.

The new machinery is often aimed at boosting productivity and making companies able to respond faster to customers' needs. The machine tool industry lagged badly on both counts during the 1980s and lost a lot of business to the Japanese and West Germans as a result. Its leaders are now taking advantage of strong sales to recoup. Cincinnati Milacron, the biggest U.S. producer, increased its capital budget 34% to $21.5 million in 1988 and will increase it again to $37.5 million in 1989. No new factories, of course. Says President Daniel Meyer: "The new manufacturing approach is to improve quality and increase output with less floor space." Milacron plans to cut total manufacturing and design lead time dramatically with its new equipment. Getting a new product to market used to take three years; Milacron's goal is to do it in less than a year. . . .
—*Kate Ballen*

SOURCE: *Fortune*, March 13, 1989, p. 115. © 1989 The Time Inc. Magazine Company. All rights reserved.

USE YOUR ECONOMIC REASONING

1. One reason that Ford Motor Company decided to invest substantially over the next five years is because "its capacity is stretched." Explain. What other reasons do Ford executives offer for their decision to increase investment?

2. This article was written in 1989. In Fall 1990, the economy entered a recession and remained depressed throughout 1991. How would you expect the economy's slowdown to affect investment spending? Explain your conclusion.

3. Why are many firms opting to invest in equipment rather than "bricks and mortar"?

4. If investment spending increases, what impact will that have on output and employment in the economy? Represent this graphically.

come is passed on to the next round of consumers, and the ultimate increase in GNP is larger. Studies of the United States economy show that the actual value of the multiplier in this country is about 2.[2]

Equilibrium with Unemployment or Inflation

Now that we know how the equilibrium output is determined, we want to consider the desirability—from the standpoint of full employment and price stability—of a particular equilibrium GNP. We want to know whether a particular equilibrium is consistent with full employment, unemployment, or inflation.

The Recessionary Gap

Chapter 10 explained that a major conclusion of the Keynesian revolution is that a capitalist economy can be in equilibrium at less than full employment. Consider the economy represented in Exh. 11.9. Let's assume that $(C+I)_1$ represents the economy's total expenditure function and that the existing level of equilibrium GNP is \$600 billion. Let's make the additional assumption that \$700 billion is the full-employment output—the level of output that allows us to achieve our target rate of unemployment. (Recall that our target rate of unemployment is higher than zero because a certain amount of frictional and structural unemployment is unavoidable, even in the best of times.) Given these assumptions, it is obvious that our hypothetical economy is in equilibrium at less than full employment. The problem, in Keynesian terms, is *too little spending.* If full employment is to be achieved, the level of planned spending must be increased so that the total expenditure function intersects the 45-degree line at \$700 billion.

You can see that a function such as $(C+I)_2$ would give such an intersection. The vertical distance between $(C+I)_1$ and $(C+I)_2$ is the ***recessionary gap***—the amount by which total spending falls short of what is needed for full employment. It is called a recessionary gap because a deficiency of spending tends to produce a period of recession, or unemploy-

---

[2] In reality, the calculation of the multiplier is more complicated than this analysis suggests. There are leakages in addition to savings, for example, that reduce the amount of income passed on to the next round of consumers. (Taxes constitute one such leakage.) The estimated value of 2 takes these factors into account.

EXHIBIT 11.9

The Recessionary Gap

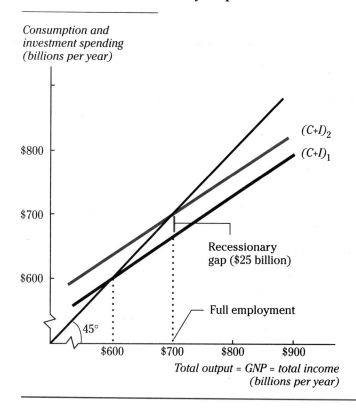

Consumption and investment spending (billions per year)

$(C+I)_2$

$(C+I)_1$

$800

$700

Recessionary gap ($25 billion)

$600

Full employment

45°

$600 $700 $800 $900

Total output = GNP = total income (billions per year)

The recessionary gap is the amount by which spending falls short of what is needed to produce full employment.

ment.[3] In our example, the recessionary gap equals $25 billion. With a multiplier of 4, a $25-billion increase in planned expenditure would increase the equilibrium output by $100 billion and bring about full employment.

The Inflationary Gap

Although Keynes devoted most of his efforts to studying unemployment, the Keynesian framework can also be used to explain inflation. Referring to Exh. 11.10, let's assume that $(C+I)_1$ is the existing planned-expenditure function

---

[3] Technically, a recession is a period of time during which the economy's real output declines. Of course, if less output is being produced, fewer employees are needed, so unemployment tends to rise.

EXHIBIT 11.10

The Inflationary Gap

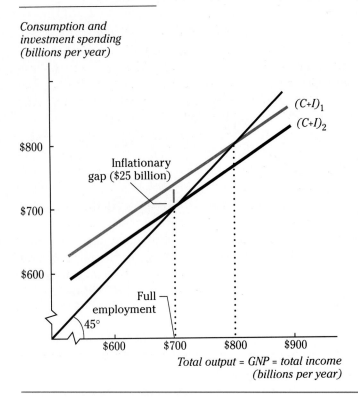

*Consumption and
investment spending
(billions per year)*

$(C+I)_1$

$(C+I)_2$

$800

Inflationary
gap ($25 billion)

$700

$600

Full
employment

45°

$600 $700 $800 $900

*Total output = GNP = total income
(billions per year)*

*The inflationary gap is the
amount by which total
spending exceeds what is
needed to produce full
employment.*

and that the prevailing level of equilibrium GNP is $800 billion. Recalling that
the full-employment output is $700 billion, you will recognize that our hy-
pothetical economy now faces a different problem: inflation.

If $700 billion is the full-employment output, there is no way the
economy can provide more than $700 billion worth of goods and services. In
the Keynesian model, full employment implies that the economy is operating
at full capacity, that it is not capable of producing any more output. If consumers and investors attempt to purchase more output than the economy is
capable of producing, higher prices result as prospective buyers bid against
one another. Real GNP, however, will not increase.

In this simple model, prices are assumed to be constant until full
employment is reached. So long as there are unemployed resources, any increase in spending is translated into an increase in output and employment.
Once full employment is reached, however, further output increases become

impossible. From this point on, increases in spending cannot increase real GNP; they can increase only money GNP. The difference between a GNP of $700 billion and a GNP of $800 billion is not that the larger figure represents more output, but simply that higher prices are being paid for the full-employment output.[4]

If inflation is to be eliminated without sacrificing full employment, the level of planned spending must be reduced so that the total expenditure function intersects the 45-degree line at $700 billion. The expenditure function $(C+I)_2$ would give such an intersection. The vertical distance between $(C+I)_1$ and $(C+I)_2$ is the **inflationary gap**—the amount by which total spending exceeds what is needed to achieve full employment.

In this example, the inflationary gap is $25 billion. With a multiplier of 4 in our hypothetical economy, a $25-billion decrease in planned expenditures would reduce equilibrium GNP by $100 billion while still maintaining full employment.

As you can see, the Keynesian model suggests that a market economy does not always come to rest at a full-employment equilibrium. Instead, the equilibrium output may be consistent with unemployment or inflation. In the next chapter, we will examine how government spending and taxation policy can be used to combat these problems. We will also discuss some of the difficulties associated with attempting to guide the economy's performance.

Summary

According to Keynesian theory, the primary determinant of the level of total output and total employment is the level of total spending. The greater the level of total spending, the more output businesses will want to produce and the more employees they will hire. In a simplified economy with no government sector and no foreign trade, the level of output and employment would be determined by the level of consumption and investment spending.

The most important factor influencing the amount of consumption spending is the level of *disposable income*, or income after taxes. The relationship between disposable income and consumption spending is called the *consumption function*. In Keynesian theory, a positive relationship exists

---

[4] In reality, increases in total expenditures or aggregate demand can lead to increased output *and* higher prices even before full employment is reached. This possibility was previewed in Chapter 10 and will be considered in more detail in Chapter 14.

between disposable income and consumption spending; the more people earn, the more they spend.

The way that households react to changes in income depends on their *marginal propensity to consume (MPC)*. The MPC is the fraction of each additional earned dollar that households spend on consumption. The *marginal propensity to save (MPS)* is the fraction of each additional earned dollar that is saved. The MPC and MPS must add to 1.00 or 100 percent: if MPC is 0.80, MPS is 0.20.

Profit expectations are the overriding motivation in all investment-spending plans. These expectations are based on a comparison of costs (including the cost of the capital equipment and the cost of borrowing the money to buy that equipment) and revenues (the revenues the investment project is expected to generate). If the investment is expected to generate revenues that exceed all anticipated costs, the investment should be made; if not, the investment should not be made.

In deciding how much output to produce, businesses attempt to estimate the spending plans of consumers and investors. If they estimate demand correctly, they will be able to sell exactly what they produced; hence they will tend to produce the same amount in the next period. If not, they will alter their production plans in order to match demand more closely.

The level of output at which the economy stabilizes is the equilibrium output. The equilibrium output is one that is neither expanding nor contracting and that tends to be maintained. It can be identified by finding the level of output at which total spending (consumption plus investment) is equal to total output. The equilibrium output can be determined graphically by finding the output at which the total expenditures function $(C + I)$ intersects the 45-degree line.

Once the equilibrium output has been established, it will be maintained until there is some change in the spending plans of consumers or investors. To determine the ultimate impact on equilibrium of any change in spending, it is necessary to know the value of the *multiplier (M)*, the number by which any initial change in spending is multiplied to get the ultimate change in equilibrium income and output. The multiplier can be calculated by using either of the following formulas:

$$M = \frac{1}{1 - MPC}$$

or, since $1 - MPC = MPS$,

$$M = \frac{1}{MPS}$$

Perhaps the most important contribution made by Keynes was his demonstration that a market economy can be in equilibrium at less than full employment. He attributed this occurrence to too little spending. The amount by which total spending falls short of what is needed to provide full employment is called the *recessionary gap*. When inflation exists, the problem is too much spending. The *inflationary gap* is the amount by which total spending exceeds what is needed to achieve full employment.

Glossary

Page 335   ***Consumption function.*** The relationship between disposable income and consumption spending. A consumption function shows the amount that households plan to spend at different levels of income.

Page 335   ***Disposable income.*** Income after taxes. Disposable income is sometimes described as your take-home pay.

Page 335   ***Dissaving.*** Taking money out of savings accounts or borrowing in order to finance consumption spending.

Page 359   ***Inflationary gap.*** The amount by which total spending exceeds what is needed to achieve full employment.

Page 338   ***Marginal propensity to consume (MPC).*** The fraction of any increase in income that is spent on consumption. The formula for the marginal propensity to consume *(MPC)* is

$$MPC = \frac{\text{change in consumption spending}}{\text{change in income}}.$$

Page 338   ***Marginal propensity to save (MPS).*** The fraction of any increase in income that households plan to save. The formula for the marginal propensity to save *(MPS)* is

$$MPS = \frac{\text{change in saving}}{\text{change in income}}.$$

Page 353   ***Multiplier (M).*** The number by which any initial change in spending is multiplied to get the ultimate change in equilibrium income and output. The formula for the multiplier *(M)* is

$$M = \frac{1}{1 - MPC} \quad \text{or} \quad M = \frac{1}{MPS}.$$

Page 350   ***Multiplier effect.*** The magnified impact on GNP of any initial change in spending.

Page 356   ***Recessionary gap.*** The amount by which total spending falls short of what is needed to produce full employment.

Page 335   ***Saving.*** The act of not spending. Also, the part of income not spent on goods and services.

Study Questions

Fill in the Blanks

1. According to Keynes, the primary determinant of the level of total output and total employment is the level of _total spending_.

2. The _marginal propensity to save_ is the fraction of any increase in income that households plan to save.

3. Keynes believed the primary determinant of the level of consumption spending to be the level of _disposable income_.

4. In the Keynesian model, if the economy is suffering from unemployment, the problem is caused by _little spending_; if the economy is suffering from inflation, the problem is caused by _too much spending_.

5. The _consumption function_ shows the precise relationship between income and consumption spending.

6. The level of output that tends to be maintained is called the _equilibrium_ output.

7. If total spending exceeds the amount necessary to achieve full employment, the economy must be suffering from _inflation_.

8. We can determine the equilibrium output by finding the output where total spending equals _total output_.

9. Graphically, equilibrium exists where the total expenditures function ($C + I$) crosses the _45°_.

10. The amount by which total spending falls short of what is needed to provide full employment is called the _recessionary gap_.

Multiple Choice

1. When Jim's income increased by $1,000, he decided to spend $600 and save the rest. That means his
   a) marginal propensity to save is 0.6.
   b) marginal propensity to consume is $600.
   c) marginal propensity to consume is 0.6.
   d) marginal propensity to consume is 0.4.

2. If the economy's MPS is 0.2, the multiplier would be
   a) 0.8.
   b) 20.
   c) 5.
   d) 4.

   Use the following information to answer questions 3–6.

INCOME	CONSUMPTION
$100 billion	$160 billion
200	240
300	320
400	400
500	480
600	560

3. What is the marginal propensity to consume in this hypothetical economy?
   a) 0.8
   b) 0.5
   c) 0.75
   d) $80

4. At what income level would the consumption function cross the 45-degree line in this hypothetical economy?
   a) $200 billion
   b) $300 billion
   c) $400 billion
   d) $500 billion
   e) None of the above

5. If businesses plan to invest $20 billion, what would be the equilibrium level of output in this economy? (*Hint:* Remember what makes up total expenditures.)
   a) $200 billion
   b) $300 billion
   c) $400 billion
   d) $500 billion
   e) None of the above

6. At an income of $700 billion, how much would households desire to consume? (It's not on the schedule, but you can use your previous answers to figure it out.)
   a) $560 billion
   b) $580 billion
   c) $620 billion
   d) $640 billion
   e) $700 billion

7. Assuming that the economy's *MPC* is 0.8, if autonomous investment spending increases by $15 billion, how much will equilibrium GNP increase?
   a) $15 billion
   b) $30 billion
   c) $45 billion
   d) $60 billion
   e) $75 billion

8. If people expected prices to be higher in the future, this would probably cause
   a) their current consumption function to shift down.
   b) their current saving function to shift up.
   c) their current consumption function to shift up.
   d) the investment function to shift down.

9. Keynes focused particular attention on investment spending because
   a) investment spending is the largest component of total spending.
   b) only investment spending is subject to a multiplier effect.
   c) investment spending is very volatile, or changeable.
   d) investment spending is the most reliable or predictable component of total spending.

10. If the economy produces a level of output that is too small for equilibrium,
    a) there will be an unintended or unplanned increase in inventories.
    b) businesses will not be able to sell everything that they've produced.
    c) there will be an unintended or unplanned decrease in inventories.
    d) there will be a tendency for output to fall (decline) in the next period.

Problems and Questions for Discussion

1. In the hypothetical economy we explored in this chapter, total income equals disposable income. What assumption makes that true?

2. If the consumption function were a 45-degree line, what would that mean?

3. How do businesses decide which investment projects to pursue and which to reject?

4. Discuss the reasons why the rate of investment spending is less stable than the rate of consumption spending.

5. How can a change in the level of investment spending indirectly cause a change in the level of consumption spending?

6. Referring to Exh. 11.5, assume that the level of autonomous investment is $25 billion instead of $50 billion. What would be the equilibrium level of output?

7. What might cause the level of investment spending to decline, as hypothesized in the preceding question?

8. What is the difference between the equilibrium output and a full employment equilibrium?

9. What are the recessionary and inflationary gaps? Represent them graphically.

10. What assumption is made about the behavior of prices in the simple model utilized in this chapter?

Answer Key

Fill in the Blanks

1. total spending
2. marginal propensity to save
3. disposable income
4. too little spending; too much spending
5. consumption function
6. equilibrium
7. inflation
8. total output
9. 45-degree line
10. recessionary gap

Multiple Choice

1. c	3. a	5. d	7. e	9. c
2. c	4. c	6. d	8. c	10. c

CHAPTER 12

FISCAL POLICY

When politicians speak of "stimulating the economy through a tax cut" or "imposing austerity measures to combat inflation" or "creating jobs through government spending," they are talking about *fiscal policy*—the manipulation of government spending and taxation in order to guide the economy's performance.

In the Keynesian model, as you have learned, spending is the key to the economy's aggregate performance. More total spending means more output and more jobs. If there is unemployment, the source of the problem is too little spending—too little demand for goods and services. Keynes pointed out that the federal government can combat unemployment by increasing government spending, reducing taxes, or doing both. These policies will increase the amount of total spending in the economy, which in turn will increase the level of output and employment.

If inflation occurs, a different set of policies is called for. According to the Keynesian model, inflation is caused by too much spending, by people trying to buy more goods and services than the economy can produce. The proper fiscal response to inflation is a reduction in government spending, an increase in taxes, or both.

In this chapter, we take a detailed look at how Keynesians believe fiscal policy can be used to combat unemployment or inflation. In addition, we will consider the limitations of fiscal policy and examine the impact of specific policy measures on the federal budget and the federal debt.

Government Spending and Equilibrium Output

Before we examine fiscal policy we must take a side trip to see how the equilibrium output is determined in a three-sector economy—an economy with households, businesses, and government. This means we will expand the simple two-sector model used in Chapter 11 to include government spending and taxation. In order to keep the presentation as clear as possible, we will introduce government spending first, note the impact on equilibrium output, and then introduce taxation.[1]

For the sake of our analysis, we assume that the level of government spending is determined by political considerations and that it is independent of the level of output in the economy. These assumptions allow us to add government spending to the model as an autonomous constant. Recall from Chapter 11 that investment spending was introduced in the same way, as a component of spending that did not vary with GNP.

Exhibit 12.1 shows how the inclusion of government spending alters the process of determining equilibrium. Let's assume that the government plans to spend $40 billion per year and that it intends to finance its spending by borrowing rather than by imposing taxes. To incorporate this decision into our analysis, we need only add the amount of government spending for goods and services (G) to the total expenditure function (C + I) we constructed in Chapter 11. (You may find it helpful to review Exhs. 11.5

---

[1] We use the term *government spending* to mean purchases of goods and services. Economists always distinguish between expenditures for goods and services and transfer payments. *Government transfer payments* are expenditures made by the government for which it receives no goods or services in return (welfare payments, unemployment compensation, and Social Security benefits, for example). To avoid unnecessary complexity, our model will ignore transfer payments. Later in the chapter, however, we will discuss the role of transfer payments as "built-in stabilizers" of the economy.

EXHIBIT 12.1

Adding Government Expenditures

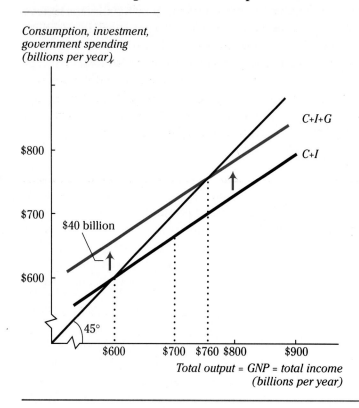

Consumption, investment, government spending (billions per year)

$800

$700

$40 billion

$600

45°

C+I+G

C+I

$600 $700 $760 $800 $900

Total output = GNP = total income (billions per year)

With a multiplier of 4, the addition of $40 billion worth of government spending raises the equilibrium GNP by $160 billion.

and 11.6.) In our two-sector economy, total spending was represented as consumption spending (C) plus investment spending (I). In Exh. 12.1, total spending is labeled $C+I+G$. Adding government spending raises total spending by $40 billion at every level of output.

The equilibrium output is determined by the intersection of the total expenditure function (now $C+I+G$) and the 45-degree line. You can see that the addition of $40 billion of government spending increases the equilibrium output by $160 billion—that is, from $600 billion to $760 billion. Here we see the multiplier effect in operation. Recall from Chapter 11 that in our hypothetical economy the marginal propensity to consume is 0.75. The multiplier $[M = 1/(1 - MPC)]$ therefore is 4. This tells us that any change in spending will produce a change in income and output that is four times larger than the initial spending change.

In practical terms, what happens here is identical to what happened when there was a change in the level of investment spending. The immediate impact of the addition of $40 billion of government spending is to increase the economy's income by $40 billion. With an *MPC* of 0.75, this will cause a $30-billion increase in consumption spending and a $10-billion increase in saving. When the $30 billion is spent, it will provide new income to still another group, which will spend part of what it receives (75 percent of $30 billion) and save the rest. This expansion in spending and output will continue until, eventually, total spending equals total output (where the $C + I + G$ function crosses the 45-degree line) so that the economy is again in equilibrium. In our example, this occurs at a GNP of $760 billion.

Taxation and Equilibrium Output

Now that we've incorporated government spending into our model, we can introduce taxation and note its impact on the equilibrium level of output. To simplify our analysis, we will assume that personal income taxes are the only form of taxation in our hypothetical economy.

Suppose the government decides to collect $40 billion in personal income taxes in order to finance its spending plans. How does this affect the equilibrium level of GNP? The initial impact of this action is to reduce disposable income—income after taxes, or take-home pay—by $40 billion. So long as we ignored taxes, total income (GNP) equaled disposable income (*DI*). But now that we are introducing taxes, this equality no longer holds. The imposition of taxes reduces the amount of disposable income that households have available at any given level of GNP. We have seen that the level of disposable income determines the level of consumption spending. If disposable income declines, consumption spending will decline. Thus the ultimate impact of taxation is a reduction in the amount of consumption spending at any given level of GNP. This can be represented by a downward shift of the consumption function, which in turn will cause a downward shift of $C + I + G$ (the total expenditure function).

Exhibit 12.2 shows that the total expenditure function shifts downward by $30 billion when the government imposes taxes of $40 billion. Why doesn't the total expenditure function shift downward by *$40* billion? The answer is that households react to reductions in disposable income by reducing both their consumption and their saving. If the marginal propensity to consume is 0.75, 75 percent of the reduction in disposable income will

EXHIBIT 12.2

The Effect of Taxation

Consumption, investment,
government spending
(billions per year)

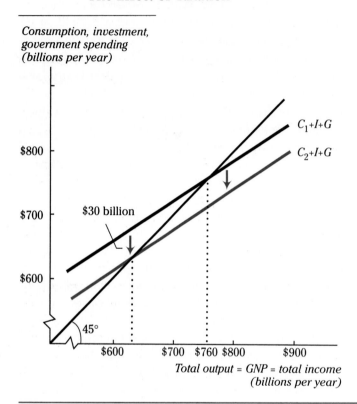

When the government imposes taxes of $40 billion, the total expenditure function shifts down by $30 billion. Because the MPC is 0.75, a reduction in disposable income of $40 billion (the amount of the taxes) will reduce consumption spending by 3/4 of that amount, or $30 billion. This $30 billion is then subject to the multiplier of 4 so that the ultimate impact of the taxation is to reduce the equilibrium GNP by $120 billion.

come from planned consumption spending and 25 percent will come from planned saving. Thus the consumption function—and consequently the total expenditure function—will shift downward by 75 percent of $40 billion, or $30 billion.

Notice that in this case the equilibrium level of GNP falls from $760 billion to $640 billion: a reduction of $120 billion. Once again, this represents the impact of the multiplier. The $30-billion reduction in consumption spending is magnified by the multiplier of 4 and thus produces a $120-billion reduction in GNP.

Given the fact that government spending and taxation affect total spending and equilibrium output, let's see how changes in government spending and taxation can be used as economic policy tools to combat the problems of unemployment or inflation.

Fiscal Policy to Achieve Full Employment

Suppose our economy's full-employment output is $700 billion. With our present equilibrium of $640, some unemployment will result. According to the Keynesian model, the source of the problem is too little spending; in other words, a recessionary gap exists.

One corrective approach is the use of discretionary fiscal policy. *Discretionary fiscal policy* is the deliberate changing of the level of government spending or taxation in order to guide the economy's performance.[2] According to Keynesian theory, if the problem is unemployment, the appropriate policy response is to increase government spending or reduce taxes (or effect some combination of the two). Let's consider these alternatives.

If government spending is increased while taxes remain unchanged, this will increase the amount of total spending in the economy. More spending for goods and services means that businesses will be justified in increasing their production, which will create more jobs.

We must use our knowledge of the multiplier to determine how much more government spending will be necessary. The multiplier in our hypothetical economy is 4; therefore every additional dollar that the government spends will ultimately produce a four-dollar increase in total spending and equilibrium output. If we wish to increase GNP by $60 billion, government spending must be increased by $15 billion ($60 billion ÷ 4 = $15 billion). Exhibit 12.3 shows that a $15-billion increase, when expanded by a multiplier of 4, will produce the needed $60-billion increase in GNP and permit our hypothetical economy to achieve full employment. In an economy with a multiplier of 2, the government would have to increase spending by $30 billion to achieve the same $60-billion increase in GNP. (Recall from Chapter 11 that studies show the value of the multiplier in the U.S. economy to be approximately 2.)

The goal of full employment can also be pursued by cutting taxes and leaving government spending unchanged. If taxes are reduced, consumers are left with more disposable income, which enables them to increase their consumption spending. This increase in the demand for consumer goods stimulates producers to increase their output and creates additional

---

[2] In addition to discretionary fiscal policy, the economy is also influenced by automatic fiscal policy, or built-in stabilizers, that reduce the magnitude of fluctuations in total spending without any discretionary action by decision makers. These built-in stabilizers will be discussed later in the chapter.

EXHIBIT 12.3

Expansionary Fiscal Policy

*Consumption, investment,
government spending
(billions per year)*

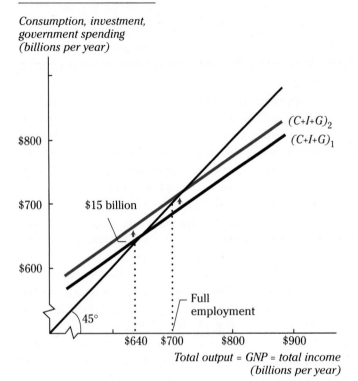

In order to increase the equilibrium output by $60 billion (and achieve full employment), we must either increase government spending by $15 billion or reduce taxes by $20 billion. Either policy will shift the total expenditure function upward by $15 billion. This amount, when expanded by the multiplier of 4, will result in an increase in GNP of $60 billion, the amount needed to reach full employment.

jobs. Determining the precise amount of a tax reduction to combat unemployment is more complicated than determining the right amount to increase government spending. When taxes are reduced, consumers will not spend all of the additional disposable income the reduction provides; they will save some portion of their increased income.

We saw that $15 billion in increased spending is needed to close the recessionary gap. By what amount must we reduce income taxes to prompt consumers to spend an additional $15 billion? If the *MPC* is 0.75, taxes must be reduced by $20 billion (0.75 × $20 billion = $15 billion).[3] Be-

---

[3] To determine the proper amount to increase or decrease taxes, you must divide the needed change in spending by the *MPC* (needed change in spending ÷ *MPC* = amount of tax change). In this example, the needed spending change is $15 billion and the *MPC* is 0.75, so taxes ought to be altered by $15 billion ÷ 0.75 = $20 billion. Remember that to increase spending taxes must be *reduced*, so it is a $20-billion tax reduction.

cause consumers will spend 75 percent of any increase in disposable income, a tax reduction of $20 billion will lead to a $15-billion increase in consumption spending and, via the multiplier, a $60-billion increase in equilibrium GNP. Because not all of it will be spent, a tax reduction used to stimulate spending and promote full employment must be somewhat larger than the increase in government spending that would accomplish the same objective.

Fiscal Policy
to Combat Inflation

When Keynes developed his landmark economic theory in the mid-1930s, his main concern was unemployment. The remedy he prescribed was an expansionary fiscal policy that would increase government spending or reduce taxes to get the economy moving. But Keynes realized that fiscal policy could serve to combat inflation, as well. If society attempts to purchase more goods and services than the economy is capable of producing, a reduction in government spending or an increase in taxes will help reduce inflationary pressures.

If the government spends less, one component of total spending (G) is reduced directly, and consumption spending (C) is reduced indirectly through the multiplier effect. A tax increase has a different impact. Consumers who pay higher taxes find themselves with less disposable income; this forces them to reduce their consumption spending. Either way, total spending is reduced.

As you might expect, the fiscal policy used to fight inflation is considerably less popular than the policy used to combat unemployment. The prescriptions for dealing with unemployment—reducing taxes and increasing government spending—are generally applauded. Inflation-fighting measures usually meet with less widespread approval.

In 1966, when increased defense spending began to push an already strong economy closer to its productive capacity, many economists were calling for a tax increase to slow the growth of spending and prevent inflation.[4] President Johnson decided not to request such an increase at that time, because he believed it would increase opposition to the Vietnam War. When the tax increase was finally requested in 1967, Congress delayed action until 1968. By that time, inflation was well under way and proved very diffi-

---

[4] Concern about a weak economy had prompted a tax *cut* only two years earlier. That 1964 tax cut will be discussed later in the chapter.

Bush's October Surprise
The Economy Has Stalled and a Double-dip Recession Could Be on the Way

George Bush came down with a nasty case of the shakes last week when he—and millions of fearful Americans—were jolted by yet another round of alarming economic news. A disturbing Federal Reserve report shattered any illusions the president may have had about the economy's underlying strength. The survey confirmed what government statistics have clearly indicated over the past few months: Manufacturing has slowed, retail sales are weak and bank lending has plummeted. Unemployment also continued to menace the economy as new claims for jobless benefits jumped to 452,000, the highest weekly level since May. Orders for big-ticket durable goods such as appliances and machinery dropped for the second straight month. And sales of existing homes fell 4.3 percent in September, the third consecutive monthly decline. Even more ominous, the Federal Deposit Insurance Corp. predicted that additional bank failures could triple the amount of money needed to rescue the nation's troubled financial institutions.

These anxiety-producing numbers have raised concerns that the economy may be sliding into another downturn, the second leg of a dreaded double-dip recession. "The fourth quarter will be negative," predicts economist Gary Shilling. "It looks like Christmas [sales] are going to be a real disaster." And if their holidays are spoiled by more bad tidings, Americans are sure to blame President Bush. . . .

The business community has also begun to worry as profits shrivel and staggering corporate losses pile up. Falling demand in an enervated economy triggered General Motors' $1.1 billion deficit during the third quarter, for example, as uneasy customers waited on the sidelines to buy new cars. IBM experienced an 85 percent profit plunge during the same period, because hard-pressed companies put off mainframe computer purchases. . . .

Many corporations would be in far worse financial shape if they hadn't hacked away at payroll expenses and sentenced droves of workers to unemployment. So far, 1.7 million jobs have been lost during this recession, with layoffs permeating a wide range of industries—from banking to baking. Chase Manhattan Corp., which issued pink slips to some 5,000 employees last year, for example, posted a sharp turnaround as its third-quarter earnings climbed to $136 million following a $623 million loss during the same period in 1990. . . .

Slash and burn
A number of struggling firms hope to emulate this success-

ful slash-and-burn strategy. AT&T, a case in point, recently incurred a large restructuring charge from its takeover of NCR that will help fund severance packages for 14,000 employees over the next two years. The telecommunications giant hopes that this write-off, which contributed to its Gargantuan $1.8 billion third-quarter loss, will clear the way for a steady stream of future earnings.

Cutting back on capital expenditures—growing just 1.6 percent in 1991, the smallest increase in five years—is another way that heavily burdened companies are scratching out profits in the slumping economy. Dallas-based AMR Corp., the parent company of American Airlines, for example, managed to register a 7 percent earnings uptick in the third quarter, while many of its competitors remained mired

in bankruptcy. But in order to maintain this scant edge, American has been forced to defer $500 million in new group equipment, while delaying or canceling options on some $3.6 billion worth of new aircraft due for delivery in several years.

Massive layoffs and severe spending cuts enable companies to fatten the bottom line and provide shareholders with better investment returns. But if corporate America, in search of short-term earnings, continues to aggressively scale back its work

force and pare down its outlays, the stalled economy could take a turn for the worse and a double-dip recession could result. . . . —*Robert F. Black, Susan Dentzer and Terri Thompson with Sara Collins*

SOURCE: ''Bush's October Surprise,'' Copyright November 4, 1991, *U.S. News & World Report,* p. 56.

USE YOUR ECONOMIC REASONING

1. **What economic indicators were economists looking at to try to predict the future course of the economy? What do they seem to indicate?**

2. **What are ''slash and burn'' strategies? How do they help corporations? Why could they mean trouble for the economy?**

3. **Suppose the economy continues to weaken. What fiscal policies would a Keynesian support in order to combat the recession and reduce unemployment?**

cult to combat. The reluctance of politicians to employ restrictive policies—to increase taxes or reduce government spending—adds a dimension of uncertainty to the logic of economics where inflation is concerned. (Read "Bush's October Surprise" on page 374 and describe the appropriate Keynesian fiscal policy for the situation outlined in the article.)

Automatic Fiscal Policy: The Built-in Stabilizers

As President Johnson's experience illustrates, significant time can elapse between the appearance of unemployment or inflation and the use of discretionary fiscal policy. Policymakers may respond more promptly to unemployment than to inflation (since the policies for combating unemployment are more palatable politically), but even here some lag exists. It takes time for policymakers to get a clear signal that a problem exists and to gain subsequent legislative approval for a tax or spending bill. Meanwhile the problem may worsen and become more difficult to combat. Fortunately, the fiscal system of the United States economy contains a number of *built-in stabilizers:* automatic changes that reduce the magnitude of fluctuations in total spending and thereby help prevent wide swings in the level of output and employment.[5]

The federal income tax is a powerful built-in stabilizer. As you know, your income taxes increase as your income increases. (Taxes in the real world are not independent of income as they are in our hypothetical economy.) Whenever taxes depend on income, any increase in salaries and wages means higher taxes as well. Thus when incomes rise, consumption spending does not rise as much as it would without taxes. Because this limits the rapid growth of spending during a period of economic expansion, it helps to prevent or slow inflation. As the economy weakens, the tax system operates in reverse. Declines in income mean lower taxes; consumers are left with more income to spend than they would have if taxes remained constant. Thus the income tax helps stabilize spending and retard the weakening of the economy.

Unemployment compensation and welfare benefits also operate as built-in stabilizers. When the level of economic activity declines and the jobless rate begins to rise, the total amount paid out by the government in

---

[5] Built-in stabilizers are sometimes referred to as automatic, or nondiscretionary, fiscal policy.

the form of unemployment compensation and welfare benefits increases automatically. These expenditures for which the government receives no goods or services in exchange are known as *transfer payments.* Government transfer payments compensate somewhat for the declining incomes of the unemployed, and in so doing they prevent a steeper drop in consumption expenditures. This action retards the downward spiral of spending and slows the deterioration of the economy.

When the economy begins to recover and the unemployment rate drops, these transfer payments automatically decrease, which helps prevent inflation by slowing the growth of spending.

While built-in stabilizers do reduce the magnitude of fluctuations in economic activity, they do not ensure full employment and stable prices. They cannot stop severe inflation once it is under way, and they cannot pull the economy out of a deep recession. In fact, the same fiscal features that tend to stabilize the economy can also retard the economy's recovery from a recession. As the recovery begins, personal income starts to rise, but higher taxes reduce the growth of spending and therefore slow the recovery. For these reasons, many economists believe that built-in stabilizers must be supplemented by the kinds of discretionary (deliberate) fiscal policies we have just examined.

Fiscal Policy and the Federal Budget

When we resort to fiscal policy to combat unemployment or inflation, we are deliberately tampering with the federal budget. That's what fiscal policy really is—budget policy.

The *federal budget* is a statement of the federal government's planned expenditures and anticipated receipts for the upcoming year. Using the Keynesian model, our analysis of macroeconomic problems suggests that whenever unemployment exists, the federal government should plan a *deficit budget*—that is, it should plan to spend more than it expects to collect in taxes. By taking this action, the government will inject the economy with additional spending that should help drive it toward full employment. Inflationary times call for the opposite approach, a *surplus budget* wherein the government plans to spend less than it expects to collect in taxes. A surplus budget will help reduce the amount of total spending in the economy and thereby moderate the pressures of inflation. According to our model, a *balanced budget*—a plan to match government expenditures and tax revenues—

is appropriate only when the economy is operating at full employment, when it has achieved a satisfactory equilibrium and needs neither stimulus nor restraint.

While the Keynesian model indicates that budget deficits sometimes make economic sense, that's not the view held by many (perhaps a majority of) Americans. In their opinion, deficit spending is always unwise. A government that cannot balance its budget, they contend, is like a spendthrift who lives continually beyond his or her means; eventually both will suffer financial ruin. But those who voice this blanket condemnation fail to recognize that government deficits arise for a variety of reasons, some of which are legitimate and defensible.

Planned and Unplanned Deficits and Surpluses

In examining government deficits, we find it useful to distinguish between deficits that are deliberate, or planned, and those that are unintentional, or unplanned. No one preparing the federal budget expects the actual level of government expenditures and tax receipts to agree exactly with the estimates. Changes in the level of national income and employment will mean automatic changes in tax revenues and government expenditures, because those income and employment changes trigger the built-in stabilizers we described earlier. The same built-in stabilizers that help reduce the magnitude of economic swings lead to deficits when the economy experiences a downturn and to surpluses during periods of expansion.

Even the most carefully planned budget will be inaccurate if the economy performs in unexpected ways. Consider an experience of the Reagan administration. Early in 1981 President Reagan recommended to Congress a budget with a projected deficit of $45 billion for the 1982 fiscal year. This budget assumed that the economy's real gross national product would grow at a rate of 4.2 percent in 1982 and that the unemployment rate would average 7.2 percent for that year. Both assumptions turned out to be incorrect. Real GNP actually *declined* by 2.1 percent in 1982, and the unemployment rate averaged 9.5 percent. As a result of this unexpectedly weak performance, the federal government's outlay for unemployment compensation and welfare was higher than anticipated, and tax revenues were lower. This produced a budget deficit of approximately $110 billion, a far cry from the administration's $45-billion projection.

Sometimes the economy outperforms the projections of planners. When that happens, the built-in stabilizers have the opposite effect on the government's receipts and expenditures. As the economy expands, tax revenues rise and expenditures for unemployment compensation and welfare decline. Thus the built-in stabilizers tend to increase the size of the surplus or decrease the size of the deficit.

Unemployment and the Federal Budget

Efforts to balance the budget in the face of a recession can have undesired effects on the economy. Suppose the economy is initially operating at full employment, and the federal government projects a balanced budget. What will happen to the budget if the economy suddenly weakens and unemployment begins to rise? As you know, the fiscal system's built-in stabilizers will work automatically to retard the downturn. But what will this do to the balanced federal budget? It will push it into a deficit.

Suppose that Congress insists on restoring a balanced budget. What should be done? The logical response would be to increase taxes and reduce government spending. But wait . . . this response is clearly inconsistent with Keynesian remedies for unemployment. The reduced level of government spending and concomitant higher taxes will mean less total spending for goods and services, which will cause the downturn to deepen and unemployment to worsen. Moreover, because this effort to balance the budget prolongs the recession, it may result in a larger cumulative deficit.

According to our model, whenever the economy is in a recession, the preferred route to a balanced budget entails a deliberate increase in government spending or a reduction in taxes. Obviously, either measure would increase the short-term deficit; but by stimulating output and employment, either action could help pull the economy out of its depressed state. When the economy improves, tax revenues will rise automatically, and government spending for transfer payments will decline automatically. Thus expansionary fiscal policy may create a larger deficit in the short run; but by restoring the health of the economy it can lead to a balanced budget.

We can see how this process works if we look at the tax cut instituted by President Johnson in the mid-1960s. In 1964 the federal budget was already in deficit when Congress finally approved an $11-billion tax reduction (originally requested by President Kennedy in 1963) designed to push the economy closer to full employment. The stimulus provided by this tax cut helped increase GNP by some $36 billion and lower the unemployment rate from about 6 percent to 4.7 percent. According to Arthur Okun, Chairman of the Council of Economic Advisors under President Johnson, the higher tax revenues that resulted from the improved economy brought the federal budget into surplus in the first half of 1965.[6]

---

[6] Arthur M. Okun, *The Political Economy of Prosperity* (New York: W. W. Norton, 1967), pp. 47–48.

Lyndon Johnson's 1964 tax cut helped increase GNP and lower the unemployment rate; the resulting higher tax revenues led to a federal budget surplus in the first half of 1965.

The Public Debt

Whether it be planned or unplanned, whenever the federal government incurs a deficit it must finance that deficit by borrowing. This is accomplished by instructing the United States Treasury to sell government bonds to individuals, businesses, financial institutions, and government agencies. Each of these transactions increases the *public debt*—the accumulated borrowings of the federal government. The public debt is often referred to as the national debt. At the end of 1991, the U.S. national debt stood at $3.6 trillion, a figure so large that it is virtually beyond the comprehension of most of us. That amount represents all the borrowing it took to finance several wars, numerous economic downturns, and a variety of government projects and programs.

Concerns about the Public Debt

The size and growth of the public debt trouble many Americans. Some of their concerns are justified, whereas some are not. In this section, we want to lay to rest some myths and examine the real burden of the debt.

Can we ever pay off the debt? A common misconception about the public debt is that at some time in the future it must be paid off. In reality, there is no requirement that the federal government ever pay off the debt. The government simply refinances the debt year after year with new borrowing. As government bonds become due, the Treasury sells new bonds to take their place. So long as there is a market for government bonds, the government will keep issuing them. And because U.S. Government Bonds are probably the most secure investment in the world, there is really no likelihood that this market will ever disappear.

Does the public debt impose a burden on future generations? Some critics of the public debt suggest that it imposes an unfair burden on future generations. What this logic overlooks is that one person's debt is another's asset. Future generations will inherit not only the public debt, but also the bonds and other securities that make up the debt. When a future generation pays taxes to service the debt, its members will also be the recipients of the interest payments made by the government.

Some of our public debt is owed to foreigners, however, and this portion does threaten to burden future generations. You and your children will pay taxes in order to provide interest payments to foreign investors, whose dollars thus acquired will permit them to claim a share of the goods and services that might otherwise go to Americans. Consequently, our standard of living may be lowered somewhat. Although the fraction of the public debt owed to foreigners has declined modestly since 1980, interest payments to foreign investors have increased slightly as a percent of the federal budget and in relation to our GNP. The next section examines the significance of these changes.

Can Americans afford the interest payments on the growing public debt? Even if the federal government never has to pay off the national debt, it must continue to make interest payments on what it owes. After all, that's why people buy government securities—to earn interest.

We've already discussed the burden of interest payments to foreign investors. Payments to domestic bond owners, too, carry certain negative effects. Because the United States must continue to make interest payments on the debt, either our taxes are higher than they would otherwise be or we must sacrifice some government programs. If we all owned equal shares of the public debt, paying higher taxes would be offset by receiving interest payments on our shares. But while all people pay taxes, only some hold bonds and receive interest on the national debt. To the extent that bond-holders commonly have higher incomes to begin with, this process tends to produce greater inequality. This effect is at least partially modified by our progressive income tax system.[7] Those with higher incomes may receive more in interest payments, but they also pay more in taxes.

The higher tax rates needed to service the debt (that is, to make the interest payments on it) may also have a negative effect on the incentive to work and earn taxable income. If individuals are allowed to keep less of what they earn, some may choose to work less. Others may attempt to avoid taxation by performing work that is not reported to taxing authorities—work for friends and barter transactions, for example.

Until recently, the burden imposed on taxpayers by the interest charges on the public debt was relatively stable. Exhibit 12.4 shows that although annual interest payments were growing, so was GNP—our measure of the economy's income and output. Thus our ability to make those interest payments was growing also. The last column of Exh. 12.4 shows that from World War II until 1975, interest payments on the debt represented a relatively constant percentage of GNP—between 1.6 and 2.1 percent. Then, in the late 1970s and early 1980s, the interest cost of the debt began to grow much more rapidly than GNP (note that interest payments on the debt climbed to 2.8 percent of GNP in 1980 and to 5 percent of GNP in 1991). This was due primarily to the record budget deficits that characterized that period. This rapid growth in the interest cost of the debt relative to GNP is a major concern of economists and politicians.

Will government borrowing crowd out private investment? When the federal government borrows money to finance additional public debt caused by budget deficits, it must compete with private borrowers for funds. Under certain circumstances this increased demand for loanable funds will drive up interest rates, which will discourage private businesses from borrowing for investment purposes. This phenomenon is known as *crowding out:* Government borrowing pushes aside, or crowds out, private borrowing. Since investment spending plays a major role in expanding the economy's productive

---

[7] Existing tax law is somewhat progressive; that is, those with higher incomes pay a higher fraction of those incomes in the form of taxes. Prior to the Tax Reform Act of 1986, taxation was more progressive than it is today.

EXHIBIT 12.4

The Public Debt and Interest Payments in Relation to Gross National Product

YEAR	PUBLIC DEBT (billions)	INTEREST PAYMENT ON DEBT (billions)	GROSS NATIONAL PRODUCT (billions)	INTEREST AS A PERCENTAGE OF GNP
1930	$ 16.2	$ 0.7	$ 90.7	0.8%
1935	28.7	0.8	72.2	1.1
1940	43.0	1.0	100.0	1.0
1945	258.7	3.6	212.4	1.7
1950	256.1	5.7	286.5	2.0
1955	272.8	6.4	400.0	1.6
1960	284.1	9.2	506.5	1.8
1965	313.8	11.3	691.1	1.6
1970	370.1	19.3	992.7	1.9
1975	533.2	32.7	1,549.2	2.1
1980	907.7	74.9	2,631.7	2.8
1985	1,821.0	178.9	4,010.3	4.5
1990	3,206.3	264.9	5,463.0	4.8
1991	3,599.0	286.0	5,685.8	5.0

1995   4,868

Sources: Bureau of the Census, *Historical Statistics of the United States; Statistical Abstract of the United States, 1990; The United States Budget: Fiscal Year 1993.*

capacity, this reduction in the rate of investment spending will tend to reduce economic growth.

According to the Keynesian model, crowding out should be a problem only when the economy is operating at or near full employment. If there are unemployed resources, deficit spending should stimulate the economy, raise incomes, and increase the level of saving. With more savings available to be borrowed, and with more total spending in the economy, business investment may actually increase rather than decrease as a result of the deficit. But when the economy has reached full employment, there can be no further increase in real income or saving; then government borrowing tends to crowd out private borrowing.[8]

The Public Debt: A Look at the Future

According to Bush administration estimates, the federal government will continue to incur substantial deficits through most of the 1990s, but the magnitude of the deficits is expected to moderate after 1992. The Office of Management and Budget predicts a deficit of $367 billion for 1992, but forecasts its decline to $195 billion by 1996. While these deficits imply substantial growth of the public debt—to more than $5.5 trillion by 1996—a downward trend in the size of the deficit would be significant. Smaller deficits imply less government borrowing and consequently less upward pressure on interest rates. In addition, the slower growth of the public debt (caused by smaller deficits) could mean that interest payments on the debt would once again begin to decline as a percent of GNP. Predicting deficits is a difficult task, however, and the administration's projections may be overly optimistic. Forecasts of the deficit are based in part on assumptions regarding the performance of the economy. If the economy grows more slowly than assumed, the budget deficit will be larger than projected. (Can you explain why this is true? How would the government's expenditures and tax revenues be different if the economy experienced slower growth?) In fact, many economists believe that the economy will grow more slowly than assumed in the administration forecasts, causing the deficit to decline at a significantly slower rate than predicted.

The Limits to Fiscal Policy

The federal budget deficit has been a major concern since the early 1980s, when deficits began to soar. (Chapter 15 discusses the initial source of these deficits.) While politicians agreed that the deficit needed to be reduced, they were unable to agree about when and how to accomplish that objective. This impasse ultimately led to the passage of the Gramm-Rudman-Hollings

---

[8] Most studies indicate that borrowing to finance federal deficits did not crowd out much investment in the 1980s. Instead, high interest rates—resulting in part from government borrowing—attracted foreign funds to help us finance our deficit. Unfortunately, the inflow of capital funds increased the value of the dollar in foreign exchange markets, and this harmed American exporters, whose products became more expensive for foreigners. Chapter 17 will consider these issues in some detail.

balanced-budget law in 1985. In its original form, the law mandated that if Congress failed to meet yearly deficit reduction targets, both domestic and military programs (with some exceptions) would be subject to automatic across-the-board cuts designed to bring the budget into balance by 1991.

Even Gramm-Rudman failed to spur Congress to action; the deficits continued at record levels. In 1987, the law was modified to provide Congress with more time to meet the targets. In 1990, the law was modified again. This time the annual deficit targets were replaced with spending ceilings for the military, foreign aid, and most domestic programs. Within each category, new spending is prohibited unless cuts are made elsewhere or taxes are raised. Under the new law, increased deficits are permitted if they are not caused by explicit congressional act—for instance, if they result from recessions.

Keynesian theory calls for budget deficits during periods of high unemployment and surpluses during periods of inflation. But the recent budget history is one of continuing deficits, even during periods of low unemployment. In short, Congress has been unable or unwilling to reduce spending (or increase taxes) even when Keynesian theory suggests that such changes are appropriate. We will conclude our discussion by briefly examining this "expansionary bias" and two other problems that may complicate efforts to use discretionary fiscal policy to guide the economy's performance. (The article on page 386, "As the Economy Sags, Washington Scrambles for Ways to Fix It" illustrates how political and other considerations influence the formulation of fiscal policy.)

The Expansionary Bias

As you know, the Keynesian model calls for an expansionary fiscal policy to combat unemployment and a contractionary policy to combat inflation. But expansionary policies are more attractive politically than contractionary policies. Incumbent officials don't want to sacrifice votes, and voters want neither to pay higher taxes nor to lose the government programs that benefit them. The result is a bias in favor of expansionary fiscal policies. It may be relatively easy for Congress to pass measures to stimulate the economy, but it's quite difficult to muster the votes necessary to trim government spending or increase taxes.

Time Lags

Often a substantial interlude passes between the time when a policy change is needed and the economic impact of any change that is actually made. This lag may reduce the effectiveness of the remedial fiscal policy; in some instances it may even make the change counterproductive.

As the Economy Sags, Washington Scrambles for Ways to Fix It

WASHINGTON — Friday's dismal employment report snuffed out the last hopes for a timely economic recovery, and is likely to create irresistible pressure for government action to boost the lifeless economy.

The employment report came as a shock to White House officials, as well as many private economists, who have argued for months that the economy began a modest upturn last spring. Their arguments rested largely on figures showing that payroll employment began creeping upward in April. But Friday's figures, which registered a drop of 241,000 in payroll workers during November, reversed most of those earlier gains and depicted an economy flat on its back.

Within the Bush administration, officials privately called the numbers "very troubling." . . .

But what can the government do?

Mr. Keynes's Legacy

A quarter century ago, that question seemed an easy one. Economists were in the ascendancy. Time magazine ran a cover photo of British economist John Maynard Keynes in 1965 and declared that his followers "had descended in force from their ivory towers and now sit confidently at the elbow of almost every important leader in government and business." Robert Lekachman wrote that, thanks to Mr. Keynes's ideas, "the sad cycle of boom and bust has been tamed."

Today, that easy confidence has evaporated. The nation has learned that the tools for combating recessions are far less potent than once thought. And their potency is especially limited at the present, with fiscal policy hobbled by a $350 billion federal budget deficit and monetary policy crippled by a banking system under siege. . . .

There's also a timing problem. The recession began 17 months ago, and any effective measures to counter it should have begun shortly thereafter. As it is, the president's plan won't be unveiled until late January, and under even the best of circumstances legislation won't be enacted until late March or April. That means any boost to the economy will be delayed until the second half of next year— more than two years after the recession began and possibly months after it ends.

Feeling the Pinch

Nevertheless, the new numbers raise the risk that this downturn could last far longer than past recessions. And the political pressures for action in an election year have become too strong to ignore.

As a result, an economic rescue package now seems all but certain. The challenge for the government is to fashion proposals that will offer some hope of helping the economy in the near-term, without harming it over the longer run.

That won't be easy. Any measures that make large permanent additions to the nation's huge budget deficit, for instance, could stimulate the economy over the next 12 to 24 months but hobble it well into the next century. Economists across the political spectrum agree the U.S. economy has suffered for decades from insufficient investment. The big budget deficits that soak up the nation's scarce savings—which provide the funds for such investment—are only likely to make that problem worse.

Here's a look at some of the options the government has, and arguments both for and against them.

Middle Class Tax Cuts

This is the clear favorite of the politicians, but wins little praise from the experts. If a tax cut for the middle class is permanent, it could indeed stimulate consumer spending and boost the economy. But because the middle class is so big, the cost to the government of any substantial middle-class tax relief will be immense, swelling an already swollen deficit.

To cut the cost, administration and congressional tax-writers may make any middle-class tax cut they adopt temporary. But economic research suggests that when people know a tax cut is temporary, they will save most of it rather than spend it—thus providing little short-term kick to the economy. "It's well-known by macro economists that temporary tax cuts don't provide much stimulus," says Joel Slemrod, professor of economics at the University of Michigan. . . .

Investment Tax Credit

The investment tax credit, which has been in and out of the tax code three times in the last three decades, is now vying for another run. And it may well get it.

Economic evidence suggests the credit—a tax break for companies that invest in new equipment—has in the past provided a short-term boost to investment spending. And unlike middle-class tax cuts, this tax break is even *more* potent if it's temporary. If companies know the credit is going to expire after two years, they are likely to speed up investment spending they had planned for the future—giving a boost to the economy.

The credit has its draw-backs. It only encourages certain types of traditional equipment investments, and does little, for instance, to boost investment in research or new technologies. Moreover, it is expensive. The one eliminated in 1986 cost the government more than $25 billion a year in lost tax revenue. But the cost can be trimmed substantially if the credit is allowed only for certain types of equipment (the old credit applied to purchases of cars and office partitions, as well as machine tools), and if it is made "incremental"—that is, if a company only gets the credit for investments that exceed a certain threshold. . . .

Increased Spending

The government could choose simply to increase its own spending, thus stimulating the economy. President Bush has already called for a modest speed-up in certain types of federal spending.

Critics say, however, that government bureaucracies tend to be a slow and inefficient means of channeling increased spending to the economy. "You are looking at a lag of a year, maybe two years," says Van Ooms, former chief economist for the House Budget Committee. Moreover, in Washington, "temporary" spending increases—as well as "temporary" tax cuts—have a way of becoming permanent, and thus increasing the budget deficit. . . . Currently, however, both Congress and the White House are focusing most of their attention on tax cuts, rather than spending increases. . . . —*Alan Murray*

SOURCE: *The Wall Street Journal*, December 9, 1991, p. 1. Reprinted by permission of *The Wall Street Journal*, © 1991 Dow Jones & Company, Inc. All Rights Reserved Worldwide.

USE YOUR ECONOMIC REASONING

1. **Why do politicians favor middle-class tax cuts as a method of stimulating the economy? Why do economists generally oppose them?**

2. **Why are policymakers thinking about "temporary" tax reductions and worrying about the speed with which tax cuts or spending increases can be instituted? Why would you be concerned if these measures stimulated the economy after the recession had ended on its own?**

3. **How could measures that help the economy in the "near term" be damaging in the long run? (Hint: Recall the discussion of crowding out.)**

There are several reasons for this time lag. First, the economy does not always provide clear signals as to what the future will bring. This means that some lag may occur before the need for policy change is recognized. Second, even after the need is acknowledged, action is historically slow to transpire. It takes a certain amount of time to draft legislation and get it through Congress, even if lawmakers are in general agreement that action is needed. Third, when the bill is finally passed, more time is required for implementation and still more time is needed for the economy to begin to respond. Some measures take less time than others. Implementing a tax cut is a speedier process than implementing an increase in government spending on highways and parks, for example, but in both situations some lag exists.

These lags mean that by the time the policy effects are felt, they may well be the wrong policies for the state of the economy. For example, it makes no sense to implement a long-awaited tax cut just as the economy has begun to recover on its own from a recession. Extra disposable income at this time could be the stimulus that leads to inflation.

Crowding Out, Again

As you already know, when the federal government borrows money to finance its deficit spending, such borrowing may drive up interest rates. This in turn may reduce private investment. If that happens, the net effect of the increased government spending will not be as beneficial as it would if private investment had not been reduced. In addition, the reduced rate of investment spending will mean a slower rate of economic growth.

By now you can see that discretionary fiscal policy is not without its limitations. The significance of these limitations is open to debate. In general, Keynesians believe that fiscal policy can be useful when employed correctly and selectively. But other economists disagree. A group of economists called *monetarists* believes that the problem of crowding out makes fiscal policy essentially useless. Another group, the *new classical economists,* argues that fiscal policy is ineffective because individuals anticipate its impact and take actions that neutralize the government's efforts. These economists believe that an expansionary fiscal policy does nothing but cause inflation. This isn't the place to take a detailed look at the monetarists and the new classical economists; their views will be examined in Chapter 15. For now, the important point is that economists disagree about the advisability of using discretionary fiscal policy to guide the economy's performance.

Summary

Fiscal policy is the manipulation of government spending and taxation in order to guide the economy's performance. There are two forms of fiscal policy, discretionary and automatic. *Discretionary fiscal policy* requires a conscious decision by policymakers to alter the level of government spending or taxation. Automatic fiscal policy is a system of *built-in stabilizers* that automatically reduce the magnitude of fluctuations in total spending and thereby help prevent wide swings in the level of output and employment.

According to the Keynesian model, the proper discretionary fiscal policy when unemployment exists is to increase government spending, reduce taxes, or do both. These actions increase the amount of total spending, which in turn increases the level of output and employment. If inflation is the problem, the opposite course of action is recommended. Government spending should be reduced, taxes should be raised, or both actions should be taken simultaneously.

When we resort to fiscal policy to combat unemployment or inflation, we are deliberately tampering with the *federal budget*. When unemployment exists, the Keynesian model suggests that the government should plan a *deficit budget* in order to stimulate the economy. When inflation is the problem, a *surplus budget* is called for. Only when the economy is operating at full employment is a *balanced budget* appropriate.

When the federal government incurs a deficit, it finances that deficit by borrowing. This is accomplished by instructing the U.S. Treasury to sell government bonds to individuals, businesses, financial institutions, and government agencies. These transactions result in an increase in the *public debt*—the accumulated borrowings of the federal government.

The public debt is a source of concern to many Americans and does impose some burdens on our society. The fact that the government must make interest payments on the debt means that taxes will be higher than would be necessary otherwise. Since not all taxpayers are bondholders, this results in some income redistribution from taxpayers in general to bondholders in particular. In addition, the dollars that foreign investors acquire as interest payments permit them to claim a share of the goods and services produced in our economy.

The government borrowing necessary to finance additions to the debt (caused by deficit spending) may also drive up interest rates and *crowd out* private borrowing for investment purposes. Because investment spending plays a major role in expanding the economy's productive capacity, this reduction in the rate of investment spending will tend to reduce economic growth.

Discretionary fiscal policy is subject to several limitations and shortcomings: There are often substantial time lags between the appearance of a problem and the economic impact of a remedial policy. Expansionary fiscal policy is more attractive politically than contractionary policy. Elected officials may be unwilling to support the restrictive policies that combat inflation because they fear such support will cost them votes. Finally, when increases in government spending are deficit financed, some investment spending may be crowded out, so the expansionary effect is reduced.

Glossary

Page 377   ***Balanced budget.*** A plan to match government expenditures and tax revenues.

Page 376   ***Built-in stabilizers.*** Automatic changes in taxes and government spending that help reduce the magnitude of fluctuations in the level of economic activity; sometimes called automatic, or nondiscretionary, fiscal policy.

Page 382   ***Crowding out.*** The phenomenon that occurs when increased government borrowing drives up interest rates and thereby reduces the rate of investment spending.

Page 377   ***Deficit budget.*** A plan to spend more than will be collected in tax receipts.

Page 371   ***Discretionary fiscal policy.*** The deliberate changing of the level of government spending or taxation in order to guide the economy's performance.

Page 377   ***Federal budget.*** A statement of the federal government's planned expenditures and anticipated receipts for the upcoming year.

Page 366   ***Fiscal policy.*** The manipulation of government spending and taxation to guide the economy's performance.

Page 380   ***Public debt.*** The accumulated borrowings of the federal government; also known as the *national debt.*

Page 377   ***Surplus budget.*** A plan to collect more in taxes than will be spent.

Page 377   ***Transfer payments.*** Expenditures for which no goods or services are received in exchange.

Study Questions

Fill in the Blanks

1. According to the Keynesian model, if an economy is experiencing unemployment, the federal government should _increase government spending_ _____ or _reduce taxes_ or do both.

2. If the federal government spends more than it takes in from tax revenues, we say that it is incurring a _deficit_ ; if it takes in more in taxes than it spends, it has a _surplus_ .

3. The deliberate changing of government spending or taxation in order to guide the economy's performance is _discretionary fiscal policy_ .

4. The magnitude of fluctuations in total spending is automatically reduced by _built-in stabilizers_ .

5. According to the Keynesian model, the appropriate fiscal policy to combat inflation would be to _reduce spending_ or _increase taxes_ or do both.

6. If the economy is experiencing full employment, deficit spending may lead to _inflation_ .

7. According to our model a _balanced_ budget would be appropriate if the economy were operating at full employment.

8. The accumulated borrowings of the federal government are called the _public debt_ .

9. Our economy's built-in stabilizers include unemployment compensation, welfare benefits, and the _income tax_ .

10. Political considerations may make it particularly difficult to use fiscal policy in combating _inflation_ .

Multiple Choice

1. Let's assume that the economy is in a significant recession, operating $100 billion below the full-employment output. If the marginal propensity to consume is 0.8, in what direction and by what amount should the level of government spending be changed?

    a) Decrease government spending by $100 billion.
    b) Increase government spending by $100 billion.
    c) Decrease government spending by $20 billion.
    d) Increase government spending by $20 billion.
    e) Increase government spending by $80 billion.

2. Select the best evaluation of the following statement: *Increasing government spending by $10 billion will have a greater impact on the level of equilibrium output than decreasing taxes by the same amount ($10 billion).*

    a) False; both changes will have the same impact on GNP.
    b) False; a $10-billion decrease in taxes will have a greater impact than a $10-billion increase in spending.
    c) True; since only part of the tax reduction will be spent, the remainder will be saved and will not stimulate the economy.
    d) True; a tax reduction will always create twice as much stimulus as a spending increase of equal size.

3. If the marginal propensity to consume is 0.75, a $20-billion increase in personal income taxes will initially reduce consumption spending by

    a) $20 billion.
    b) $80 billion.
    c) $15 billion.
    d) $40 billion.

4. The ultimate impact of the tax increase noted in question 3 would be to

    a) reduce the equilibrium GNP by $20 billion.
    b) reduce the equilibrium GNP by $80 billion.
    c) reduce the equilibrium GNP by $60 billion.
    d) increase the equilibrium GNP by $20 billion.

5. Which of the following is *not* an advantage of built-in stabilizers?

    a) They do not involve the political hassle associated with discretionary fiscal policy.
    b) They help speed recovery from a recession.
    c) They go to work automatically, so lags are minimal.
    d) They help prevent a minor downturn from becoming a major recession.

6. Because of built-in stabilizers,
   a) the budget will tend toward surplus during a recession.
   b) the budget will tend toward deficit during an economic expansion.
   c) the budget will tend toward deficit during a recession.
   d) the budget will always remain in balance.

7. According to our model, when the economy is in a recession the shortest route to a balanced budget may entail
   a) higher taxes.
   b) less government spending.
   c) lower taxes and more government spending.
   d) both a and b.

8. Which of the following statements is false?
   a) If the economy is operating at full unemployment, a reduction in taxes may lead to inflation.
   b) If the economy is experiencing unemployment, increased government spending may help combat the problem.
   c) Deficit spending is desirable only when the economy is experiencing inflation.
   d) If we attempt to balance the budget during a period of unemployment, we may aggravate the unemployment problem.

9. A legitimate concern regarding the national debt relates to
   a) the higher taxes that are necessary to make the interest payments on the debt.
   b) our inability to pay off such a large sum.
   c) the fraction of the debt owed to foreign factions.
   d) both a and c.

10. "Crowding out" occurs when
    a) American producers lose sales due to foreign competition.
    b) an increase in taxes results in a lower level of consumption spending.
    c) foreign interests buy government securities.
    d) government borrowing forces up interest rates and reduces the level of private investment spending.

STUDY QUESTIONS

Problems and Questions for Discussion

1. When the government increases spending to combat unemployment, why shouldn't it increase taxes to pay for the increased spending? Why run a deficit instead?

2. Assuming that the economy's *MPC* is 0.666 and that government spending increases by $20 billion, what would be the impact on the equilibrium level of GNP?

3. What is the burden of the national (or public) debt?

4. If Keynes was correct that consumption spending depends primarily on the level of disposable income, then how is it possible for an increase in government spending to lead to an increase in consumption spending?

5. If the prevailing level of output is $800 billion and the full-employment output is $600 billion, we know that the economy is enduring inflation. If the economy's *MPC* is 0.5, how much should government spending be reduced in order to eliminate the inflation without generating unemployment? If taxes were increased instead, how much would the increase have to be?

6. What advantages can you see to using tax reductions rather than government spending increases to combat unemployment? Can your personal values influence which of these approaches you prefer? Explain.

7. George Humphrey, Secretary of the Treasury during the Eisenhower Administration, once declared: "We cannot spend ourselves rich." What do you suppose he meant? Would Keynes agree? Why or why not?

8. List the various types of lags associated with fiscal policy. Why is the existence of lags a serious limitation of such policies?

9. Suppose the federal government decided to pay off the public debt. How would it go about doing it? What do you suppose would be the impact on the economy?

10. Concern over continuing federal deficits has spawned a movement to amend the Constitution of the United States to require the federal government to balance its budget each year. Can you think of any reasons to argue against a balanced-budget amendment? Why would it be difficult to carry out such a rule during a recession?

Answer Key

Fill in the Blanks

1. increase government spending, decrease taxes
2. deficit; surplus
3. discretionary fiscal policy
4. built-in stabilizers
5. reduce government spending, increase taxes
6. inflation
7. balanced
8. public debt (or national debt)
9. income tax
10. inflation

Multiple Choice

1. d
2. c
3. c
4. c
5. b
6. c
7. c
8. c
9. d
10. d

13

MONEY, BANKING, AND MONETARY POLICY

In Chapter 11, we examined the basic Keynesian model. We saw how the level of total spending determines the economy's GNP and its level of employment, and how changes in spending can alter output and employment. Chapter 12 added government to the Keynesian model and explored how fiscal policy can be used to influence the economy's performance.

Chapter 13 completes our expansion of the Keynesian model by considering the role of money in an economy. Most of us take the use of money for granted. We pay our bills in money and expect to be paid in money. We compare prices, incomes, and even our gross national product in terms of money. But exactly what *is* money, and what functions does it perform in our economy? How do banks "create" money, and why can't individuals do the same? These are some of the questions that will be addressed in this chapter. Perhaps most important, you'll learn about the Federal Reserve—the independent government agency responsible for regulating the money supply and performing other duties related to the banking system. And you'll find out how Keynesians believe the money supply can be used as a tool for guiding the performance of the economy. We begin by examining what is meant by "money."

What Is Money?

Economists define money in terms of the functions it performs; anything that performs the functions of money *is* money.

Money performs three basic functions. First, money serves as a *medium of exchange:* the generally accepted means of payment for goods and services. A medium of exchange enables members of a society to transact their business without resorting to barter. In a barter economy, goods are exchanged for goods. A shoemaker who wants to buy a painting must locate an artist in need of shoes. As you can imagine, this requirement makes trading slow and burdensome. Money facilitates trade by permitting the shoemaker to exchange shoes for money and then use the money to purchase a painting or other goods and services.

The second function of money is to provide a *standard of value,* a unit in which the prices of goods and services can be expressed. In a barter economy we would need an almost endless list of prices, one for each possible exchange. For example, we might find that one painting equals (i.e., exchanges for) one pair of shoes, and that one pair of shoes equals four bushels of apples, and that four bushels of apples equals two shirts. Which is more expensive: a shirt or a pair of shoes? It may take you a moment to figure out the answer, because the absence of a standard of value makes the communication and comparison of prices very difficult. The use of money simplifies this process by enabling us to state all prices in terms of a particular standard of value, such as the dollar. Using the dollar as a standard of value, we can easily determine that if a pair of shoes sells for $20 and a shirt sells for $10, the shoes are twice as expensive as the shirt.

Finally, money is a *store of value,* a vehicle for accumulating or storing wealth to be used at some future date. A tomato farmer would find it difficult to accumulate wealth in the form of tomatoes. They don't keep very well! Money is not a perfect store of value, especially in inflationary times, but clearly it is better than a bushel of perishable tomatoes. By exchanging the tomato crop for money, the farmer can begin to build a nest egg for retirement or to save for some major purchase—a tractor or a new barn, for example. In a sense, the availability of a store of value widens the range of spending choices available to individuals and businesses. Their options are no longer limited to what they can afford to buy (trade for) with a single period's income.

Money and Near Money

What qualifies as money in the U.S. economy? We all know that coins and paper currency are money, and a check is usually as good as cash. Checking deposits at commercial banks[1] are known as ***demand deposits,*** since the bank promises to pay at once, or "on demand," the amount specified by the owner of the account. Checks drawn on demand-deposit accounts are an accepted medium of exchange; they are measured in dollars, the standard of value in the United States, and it is certainly possible to accumulate wealth in your checking account. But while it is relatively easy to agree that currency—coins and paper money—and demand deposits are money, some other assets are more difficult to categorize. An ***asset*** is anything of value owned by an entity—that is, by an individual or an organization such as a business. Many assets perform some, but not all, of the functions of money. Others perform all the functions of money but do so incompletely.

One debate among economists concerns the proper classification of ***savings deposits***—interest-bearing deposits at banks and savings institutions. The traditional passbook savings account cannot be used directly to purchase goods and services; hence such deposits do not qualify as a medium of exchange. As a consequence, economists have generally classified savings deposits as ***near money***—assets that are not money but that can be converted quickly into money. Not everyone has supported this position, however. Some economists argue that savings deposits should be considered money because they can be converted easily into cash or demand deposits and therefore have essentially the same impact on spending as do other financial assets.

Recent innovations in banking, moreover, have blurred the distinction between savings deposits and demand deposits. Consider, for example, the NOW account (negotiable order of withdrawal) commonly offered by banks and other financial institutions. The ***NOW account*** is essentially a savings account on which the depositor is permitted to write checks. Here we seem to have the best of both worlds: the convenience of a checking account plus the earning power of a savings account. Banks have also developed automatic transfer service (ATS) accounts, in which funds from savings

---

[1] Commercial banks are so named because in their early days they specialized in loans to businesses. Today they engage in a much wider range of lending, including home-mortgage loans, automobile loans, and other consumer loans.

can be transferred automatically to a checking account. These new types of deposits probably should be considered along with demand deposits as a form of money. But we still face the task of categorizing financial assets that do not function as media of exchange. These include passbook savings accounts, U.S. Government savings bonds, and shares in money-market mutual funds.[2] Are such assets money or not? As you will see in a moment, the answer is not clear, even to the Federal Reserve.

Definitions of the Money Supply

As we noted earlier, the Federal Reserve is responsible for controlling the money supply—the total amount of money in the economy. Naturally, before the Fed (as the Federal Reserve is often called) can attempt to control the money supply, it has to decide what money is.

Rather than settling on a single definition, the Fed has developed several. The narrowest, **M-1,** is composed of currency in the hands of the public *plus* checkable deposits. ***Checkable deposits*** are all types of deposits on which customers can write checks: demand deposits at commercial banks; NOW accounts; credit-union-share draft accounts, which are essentially the same as NOW accounts but are provided by credit unions; and ATS accounts. The primary characteristic of all M-1 money is that it can function easily as a medium of exchange. As you can see from Exh. 13.1, only about 30 percent of this readily spendable money is in the form of currency. Demand deposits account for another 32 percent of the M-1 money supply. The remaining 38 percent—the largest share—is in other checkable deposits.

The Federal Reserve also classifies the money supply according to two broader definitions, M-2 and M-3. **M-2** includes everything in M-1 *plus* money-market mutual fund balances, money-market deposits at savings institutions, and certain other financial assets that do not function as a medium of exchange but can be converted easily into currency or checkable deposits—small savings deposits (less than $100,000) at banks and savings institutions, for example.

M-3 is a still broader measure of the money supply. It includes everything in M-2 *plus* large savings deposits (over $100,000) and other financial assets that are designed essentially to be used as business savings accounts.

---

[2] A mutual fund is an organization that pools people's money and invests it in stocks or bonds or other financial assets. A money-market mutual fund invests in short-term securities, such as U.S. Treasury bills. If you own shares in a money-market mutual fund, you can write checks against your account, but generally they must exceed some minimum amount (commonly $500). This makes money-market funds less useful for everyday transactions involving smaller amounts of money.

EXHIBIT 13.1

M-1, M-2, and M-3 as of January, 1992 (billions of dollars)

M-1

Currency (coins and paper money)	$ 269.4
Demand deposits	293.9
Other checkable deposits	347.3
Total M-1	$ 910.6

M-2

M-1 plus small savings accounts and money-market mutual fund balances	$3,452.1

M-3

M-2 plus large savings deposits and other financial assets that provide an outlet for business saving	$4,180.5

Source: *Federal Reserve Bulletin,* April 1992.

Throughout this chapter and the remainder of the text, we will employ the M-1 definition of money: We assume that money consists of currency plus checkable deposits. These assets function easily as a medium of exchange, the function that many economists regard as the most important characteristic of money.

How Depository Institutions Create Money

Where does M-1 money come from? The currency component is easy to explain. It comes from the Federal Reserve, which supplies depository institutions—commercial banks and savings, or *thrift* institutions[3]—with enough coins and paper money to meet the needs of their customers. But the checkable-deposits element of M-1 is more of a mystery. Checkable deposits are actually created by the various depository institutions that offer such accounts. We will concentrate on explaining how commercial banks create

---

[3]There are three major types of thrift institutions: savings and loan associations, mutual savings banks, and credit unions.

demand-deposit money. But the other forms of checkable deposits—NOW accounts at savings institutions, ATS accounts at commercial banks, and credit-union-share draft accounts—are created in essentially the same way. So once you understand the principles of demand-deposit creation, you really understand how all forms of checkable deposits are created. Keep reminding yourself of that fact as you work your way through this section.

A Bank's Balance Sheet

To demonstrate how commercial banks create demand deposit money, we employ a simple accounting concept known as a balance sheet. A *balance sheet* is a statement of a business's assets and liabilities. The assets of a business are, as we saw earlier, the things of value that it owns. *Liabilities* are the debts of the business, what it owes. The difference between the business's assets and liabilities is the *owner equity.* It represents the interest of the owner or owners of a business in its assets. These accounting statements "balance" because whatever value of the business is not owed to creditors must belong to the owners: assets = liabilities + owner equity.

We turn now to Exh. 13.2 to examine the balance sheet of a hypothetical bank, the Gainsville National Bank. On the left-hand side of the balance sheet we see the bank's assets. The first entry, *reserves,* includes cash in the bank's vault plus funds on deposit with the Federal Reserve. Commer-

EXHIBIT 13.2

A Hypothetical Balance Sheet: Gainsville National Bank

ASSETS		LIABILITIES AND OWNER EQUITY	
Reserves (vault cash plus deposits with the Federal Reserve)	$ 200,000	Demand deposits	$1,000,000
		Savings deposits	360,000
		Owner equity	240,000
Securities	450,000		
Loans	800,000		
Property	150,000	Total liabilities	
Total assets	$1,600,000	+ owner equity	$1,600,000

cial banks are required by law to hold a certain amount of their assets as *required reserves.* The *reserve requirement* is stated as a percentage of the bank's demand deposits and can be met only by cash in the bank's vault and deposits with the Fed. Because reserves earn no interest income, banks understandably try to maintain only the minimum legal requirement. Reserves greater than the minimum requirement are called *excess reserves,* and they play an important role in a commercial bank's ability to create demand-deposit money.

The next two entries on the left-hand side, securities and loans, are the interest-earning assets of the bank. Banks usually have substantial holdings of U.S. Treasury bills and other securities that are both safe and highly liquid—that is, easily converted into cash. Loans offer less liquidity but generally have the advantage of earning a higher rate of interest.

The final entry on the left-hand side of the balance sheet is *property,* which means the physical assets of the bank: the bank building, its office equipment, and any other nonfinancial holdings of the organization.

On the right-hand side of the balance sheet are listed liabilities and owner equity. In our example, the only liabilities entered are *demand deposits* and *savings deposits.* Although both items are assets for customers, they are debts to the bank. If we write a check on our demand-deposit account or ask to withdraw our money from our savings account, the bank has to pay. That makes each of those accounts a liability to the commercial bank.

The only remaining entry on the right-hand side of Exh. 13.2 is *owner equity,* the owners' claims on the assets of the business. As you know, the two sides of the statement have to balance because whatever value of the business is not owed to creditors (the bank's liabilities) must belong to the owners (owner equity).

The Creation of Demand Deposits

Earlier we noted that all commercial banks must meet a reserve requirement established by the Federal Reserve. Let's assume that the reserve requirement for our hypothetical bank is 20 percent. Our bank has $1,000,000 in demand deposits; therefore it is required by law to maintain $200,000 in reserves ($1,000,000 × 0.20 = $200,000). As you can see from the bank's balance sheet, it has precisely $200,000 in reserves.

Even in the absence of bank regulation, commercial banks would need to maintain some reserves against their deposits. If a depositor walks into the Gainsville Bank and writes a check for "cash," the bank must have the currency to pay her. However, the bank does not have to maintain $1 in reserve for every $1 of demand deposits it accepts because it is unlikely that all depositors will request their money simultaneously. In fact, as some depositors are writing checks and drawing down their accounts, others are making deposits and thereby increasing their balances.

The key to a commercial bank's ability to create money is this *fractional reserve principle,* the principle that a bank need maintain only a fraction of a dollar in reserve for each dollar of its demand deposits. Once a bank discovers this principle, it can loan out idle funds and earn interest. That's the name of the game in banking—earning interest by lending money. In the process of making loans, commercial banks create money, specifically demand deposits. We can see how this is true by working through the balance sheet entries of the lending bank. In order to simplify things somewhat, we will show only the changes in assets and liabilities for each entry and not the entire balance sheet.

Step One: Accepting Deposits. Let's assume that one of the bank's depositors, Adam Swift, deposits $1,000 in cash in his demand-deposit account. We would reflect this change by increasing the bank's demand deposits by $1,000 and increasing its reserves by the same amount.

The bank now has an additional $1,000 in cash reserves (clearly an asset) and the liability of paying out that same amount should Mr. Swift write checks totaling $1,000. Because the bank's demand deposits have increased by $1,000, it must now maintain an additional $200 in required reserves (20 percent of $1,000). That means the Gainsville Bank now finds itself with excess reserves of $800.

Gainsville National Bank

Assets			Liabilities	
Reserves		+$1,000	Demand deposits	+$1,000
required	+$200			
excess	+$800			
		+$1,000		+$1,000

What will the Gainsville Bank do with those excess reserves? If the bank simply let them sit in the vault, it would be sacrificing the interest that could be earned on $800. Because the bank wants to show a profit, it will probably use those excess reserves to make loans.

Step Two: Making a Loan. Let's assume that another resident of Gainsville, June Malthus, walks in and asks to borrow $800. How will we record this transaction? On the asset side, we will record a loan for $800. The bank receives this asset in the form of a note, or IOU, agreeing to repay the $800 plus interest. On the liability side of the balance sheet, we increase demand deposits by $800 (from $1,000 to $1,800).

Gainsville National Bank

Assets		Liabilities		
Reserves	$1,000	Demand deposits		$1,800
Loans	+$ 800	Adam Swift	$1,000	
	————	June Malthus	+$ 800	————
	$1,800			$1,800

This last entry may seem puzzling to you if you have not yet borrowed money from a commercial bank. The way you generally receive money borrowed from a bank is in the form of a checking account with your name on it. This is the money-creating transaction of the commercial bank. Ms. Malthus has exchanged a piece of paper (an IOU) that is *not* money for something that *is* money, demand deposits. If you think about this process for a while, you'll see the logic of it: The Gainsville Bank is now using $1,000 in reserves to support $1,800 of demand deposits. And because of the fractional reserve principle, bank officials can be confident that this support is adequate; they know that not all the original depositors will withdraw their money simultaneously.

Not everyone can create money through lending. When you lend money to a friend, your friend ends up with more money, but you have less. The total money supply has not increased. However, when you borrow money from a commercial bank, you end up with more money, but no one has any less. And the money supply actually increases.

How do we explain the difference? Your IOU does not circulate as money, whereas the IOU of a commercial bank does. What happens when you deposit cash in your checking account? You do not reduce your personal money supply as you would if you had made a loan to your friend. Instead, you merely exchange cash (a form of money) for an IOU known as a demand deposit (a different form of money). Your currency then serves as reserves for supporting loans that result in the creation of additional demand deposits. Someone else ends up with more money, but you don't have any less. Once you understand this process, you can see that the commercial bank has really "created" money.

Until the mid-1970s, only commercial banks had the ability to increase the money supply. Thrift institutions, such as savings and loan associations and mutual savings banks, functioned only to funnel money from savers (who agreed not to use it for a while) to borrowers (who wanted to use it immediately). The appearance in the 1970s of NOW accounts and other forms of checkable deposits changed the function of these institutions. Through checkable savings accounts, thrift institutions are now able to create money by lending, just as commercial banks do.

Step Three: Using the Loan. Now that we have seen how commercial banks create money, we can ask what happens to that money when it is used to buy something. Let's assume that Ms. Malthus uses her newly acquired demand-deposit account to buy furniture in the nearby town of Sellmore—at the Sellmore Furniture Store. Let's assume, too, that she spends the entire amount of her loan. She will write a check on the Gainsville Bank and give it to the owner of the Sellmore Furniture Store, who will deposit it in the firm's account at the First National Bank of Sellmore. The Sellmore Bank will then send the check to the district Federal Reserve Bank for collection. (One function of the Federal Reserve is to provide a check collection and clearing service. We'll discuss this and other functions of the Fed later in the chapter.) After the Federal Reserve Bank receives the check, it will reduce the reserve account of the Gainsville Bank by $800 and increase the reserve account of the Sellmore Bank by $800. It will then forward the check to the Gainsville Bank, where changes in assets and liabilities will be recorded. Ms. Malthus has spent the $800 in her demand-deposit account, so demand deposits will be reduced by that amount (from $1,800 to $1,000). The bank's reserves have also fallen by $800 (from $1,000 to $200), the amount of reserves lost to the Sellmore Bank.

Gainsville National Bank

Assets		Liabilities	
Reserves ($1,000 − $800)	$ 200	Demand deposits ($1,800 − $800)	$1,000
required $200		Adam Swift $1,000	
excess 0		June Malthus 0	
Loans	+$ 800		
	$1,000		$1,000

Note that the Gainsville Bank no longer has any excess reserves. It has actual reserves of $200, the exact amount required. If the bank had loaned Ms. Malthus more than $800 (the initial amount of its excess reserves), it would now be in violation of the reserve requirement. But each bank realizes that when it makes a loan it will probably lose reserves to other commercial banks as the borrower spends the loan. For that reason, *individual commercial banks must limit their loans to the amount of their excess reserves.* That's one of the most important principles in this chapter, so be sure you understand it before reading any further.

The Multiple Expansion of Loans and Deposits

Recall that the money lent in the form of demand deposits circulates. Thus the money created when the Gainsville Bank made a loan to Ms. Malthus is not destroyed when she uses the loan. It is simply transferred from one commercial bank to another. The demand deposits and reserves originally represented on the balance sheet of the Gainsville Bank may now be found on the balance sheet of the Sellmore Bank. This means that the Sellmore Bank will now be able to expand its loans.

We know that each commercial bank can expand its loans to create demand deposits equal to the amount of its excess reserves. Assuming that the Sellmore Bank also faces a reserve requirement of 20 percent, and that it had no excess reserves to begin with, it will now have excess reserves of $640. How did we arrive at that amount? The Sellmore Bank increased its demand deposits, and thus its reserves, by $800, the amount deposited by the owner of the Sellmore Furniture Store. With a 20-percent reserve requirement, the increase in required reserves is $160 ($800 × 0.20 = $160). That leaves $640 in excess reserves that can be used to support new loans and create additional demand deposits.

This expansion of loans and deposits continues as the money created by one bank is deposited in another bank, where it is used to support even more loans. In Exh. 13.3, we see that the banking system as a whole can eventually create $4,000 in new loans and new money (demand deposits) from the initial $800 increase in excess reserves received by the Gainsville Bank. We also see the difference between the ability of a single commercial bank and the banking system as a whole to create money. Whereas an individual commercial bank must restrict its loans—and consequently its ability to create money—to the amount of its excess reserves, the banking system as a whole can create loans and deposits equal to some multiple of the excess reserves received by the system. In our example, that multiple is 5; the banking system was able to create loans and deposits five times greater than the initial increase in excess reserves ($800 × 5 = $4,000).

The Deposit Multiplier

Fortunately, we need not work through all the individual transactions to predict the maximum amount of money that the banking system will be able to create. As a general rule, the banking system can alter the money supply by

EXHIBIT 13.3

The Creation of Money by the Banking System

BANK	NEWLY ACQUIRED DEPOSITS AND RESERVES	REQUIRED RESERVES (20 percent of demand deposits)	POTENTIAL FOR NEW LOANS (creating money)
Gainsville	$1,000.00	$200.00	$ 800.00
Sellmore	800.00	160.00	640.00
Third Bank	640.00	128.00	512.00
Fourth Bank	512.00	102.40	409.60
Fifth Bank	409.60	81.92	327.68
Sixth Bank	327.68	65.54	262.14
Seventh Bank	262.14	52.43	209.71
All Others	1,048.58	209.71	838.87
Total amount of money created by the banking system			$4,000.00*

* This figure represents the *maximum* amount of money that the banking system could create from an initial $800 increase in excess reserves. The example assumes that all banks face a 20-percent reserve requirement and that they are all "loaned up" (have no excess reserves) initially.

an amount equal to the initial change in excess reserves times the reciprocal of the reserve requirement:

$$\text{Change in excess reserves} \times \frac{1}{\text{reserve requirement (written as a decimal)}} = \text{maximum possible increase in demand deposits by the banking system as a whole.}$$

The reciprocal of the reserve requirement, one divided by the reserve requirement, yields a number called the deposit multiplier. The ***deposit multiplier*** is the multiple by which demand deposits (in the entire banking system) increase or decrease in response to an initial change in excess reserves. Be careful to distinguish between the deposit multiplier we speak of here and the spending multiplier introduced in Chapter 11. Both multipliers show how an initial change is magnified into a larger amount, but the similarity ends there. The spending multiplier told us the eventual change in income and output (GNP) that would result from any initial change in spending. The deposit multiplier allows us to compute the eventual change in demand deposits resulting from any initial change in excess reserves.

The reserve ratio in our hypothetical example is 0.20, so the deposit multiplier must be 1/.20, or 5. Therefore an $800 increase in excess reserves will permit the banking system to create up to $4,000 of new demand deposits. This $4,000 figure is really the *maximum* possible expansion in demand deposits, given the stated change in excess reserves and the existing reserve requirement. The actual amount may, for a variety of reasons, be less than the maximum predicted.

An illustration will help: Suppose that unlike Ms. Malthus, a borrower chooses to take a portion of the loan in the form of cash rather than demand deposits. Or suppose that the recipient of Ms. Malthus's check decides not to redeposit the entire amount in a checking account. Either of these events will reduce the amount of money being passed on to the remaining banks in the system, and thus reduce the amount the system can create through lending. The expansion in demand deposits will also be less than the maximum if bankers maintain some excess reserves. For instance, perhaps some bankers anticipate deposit withdrawals and prepare for them by holding, rather than lending, excess reserves. Or banks may be forced to hold excess reserves simply because they cannot find enough loan customers. For all of these reasons, the actual expansion in the demand-deposit component of the money supply may be substantially less than the maximum predicted by the deposit multiplier.

The Destruction of Demand Deposits

The deposit multiplier can also work in reverse. Suppose Adam Swift, our original depositor, withdrew $1,000 in cash from his account at the Gainsville Bank and kept it in his wallet. What would this transaction do to the money supply? The initial transaction merely changes its composition: Mr. Swift is giving up his claim to $1,000 in demand deposits (a form of money) and is receiving in return $1,000 in cash (another form of money). The size of the money supply remains the same even though more cash and fewer demand deposits are in circulation.

What happens next? When Mr. Swift withdraws $1,000 from his checking account, the Gainsville Bank loses $1,000 in deposits and reserves.

Gainsville National Bank

Assets		Liabilities	
Reserves	−$1,000	Demand deposits	−$1,000

Assuming that the bank had no excess reserves to begin with, it now finds itself with a reserve deficiency; that is, it doesn't have sufficient reserves to meet the 20-percent reserve requirement. What is the amount of the deficiency? It is $800—the difference between the amount that Mr. Swift has withdrawn from his demand deposit account ($1,000) and the reserve that the bank was required to maintain on that deposit ($200). In order to correct this deficiency, the bank has two choices. Either it will have to sell $800 worth of securities (remember, banks hold securities, particularly government securities, because they earn interest and they can be converted easily into cash), or it will have to allow $800 worth of loans to be repaid without making new loans. In either case, the next bank in the sequence is going to lose $800 worth of deposits and reserves as its depositors buy those securities or repay those loans. That bank will then be faced with a reserve deficiency; it, too, may need to sell securities or reduce the amount of its loans to build up reserves.

As you may suspect, this contractionary process can spread to other banks in the system and result in a multiple contraction of loans and deposits that is similar to the multiple expansion we observed earlier. Once again, the limit to this process is set by the reserve requirement and the deposit multiplier that is derived from that requirement. To predict the maximum contraction in demand deposits, we multiply the initial reserve deficiency times the money multiplier. In our example, that would mean a reduction of $4,000 ($800 × 5 = $4,000).

The Federal Reserve System

Now we are ready to examine the role of the Federal Reserve. As a central bank, the Federal Reserve influences the process of expanding or contracting the entire U.S. money supply. Virtually every industrialized nation in the world has a *central bank*—a government agency responsible for controlling the national money supply. In the United Kingdom, for example, the central bank is the Bank of England; in Germany, it's the Bundesbank; in the United States, it is the Federal Reserve System.

Unlike central banks in other nations, the Federal Reserve is an independent organization that is not required to take orders from any other agency or branch of government. This gives the Fed somewhat greater independence than other central banks.

The Origin of the Federal Reserve

The Federal Reserve System was established in 1913 to provide some stability to the banking system. In 1873, 1884, 1893, and 1907, the United States experienced major financial panics in which people feared for the safety of their deposits. Without a central bank to provide loans to member banks, a shortage of cash reserves meant that banks lacking the funds necessary to satisfy their customers would have to close their doors. Once the banks began to close, the panic would become widespread, resulting in even more bank closings.

Shortly after the financial panic of 1907, a National Monetary Commission was set up to study the problem and make a recommendation. That recommendation led eventually to the passage of the Federal Reserve Act (1913), which created the Federal Reserve System. The original purpose of the Federal Reserve was to act as a "lender of last resort," to make loans to banks only when all other sources had dried up. It was thought that the Federal Reserve, by acting as lender of last resort, would stop any financial panic before it got under way and thus prevent the bank closings and business failures that had attended previous panics. The Federal Reserve was also authorized to provide an efficient mechanism for collecting and clearing checks throughout the United States and to help supervise banks to ensure that their investment and lending practices are prudent.

Today the primary responsibility of the Fed is to help stabilize the economy by controlling the money supply. We expect the Federal Reserve to manipulate the money supply in an effort to prevent (or combat) unemployment or inflation, a responsibility much broader than the one envisioned by Congress in 1913. Because the responsibility for controlling the money supply grew as the federal government assumed a greater role in managing the economy, the modern Federal Reserve organization is far more powerful than Congress intended it to be. Some contemporary economists believe that the Fed's powers to influence the economy should be sharply curtailed, whereas others argue that a strong Federal Reserve is necessary to combat unemployment and inflation. (We'll look further at this debate in Chapter 15.)

The Organization
of the Federal Reserve System

The Federal Reserve System is composed of a Board of Governors, twelve Federal Reserve Banks, and several thousand member banks. The Board of Governors is the policymaking body of the Federal Reserve. It consists of seven members who are appointed by the President of the United States and serve fourteen-year terms. These terms are structured so that only one ex-

The Board of Governors meets at the Federal Reserve Building in Washington, D.C. to make the major policy decisions for the Fed.

pires every two years, which helps to provide continuity and to insulate Board members somewhat from political pressure. The primary function of the Board is to make the major policy decisions that determine how rapidly or slowly the nation's money supply will grow.

To implement these decisions, twelve Federal Reserve Banks (plus twenty-four branches) are located strategically throughout the country. Their primary function is to oversee the actions of the member banks and other depository institutions within their districts. Member banks include all nationally chartered commercial banks, which are required to join the Federal Reserve System, as well as state-chartered banks that have chosen membership.

The Monetary Control Act of 1980

Prior to 1980, the distinction between member and nonmember banks was significant: only member banks were subject to the direct regulation of the Fed. Nonmember banks were subject only to regulations imposed by the states that chartered them. Because the Fed's reserve requirements were generally higher than those imposed by the states, member banks were forced to sacrifice more interest income. (Remember, reserve dollars don't earn interest.)

In the days of relatively low interest rates (4–5 percent), many banks were willing to forgo this interest income in order to obtain the check-collection services and borrowing privileges provided by the Fed. But as interest rates rose, the opportunity cost of those idle reserves increased, and Federal Reserve membership grew less and less attractive. As a consequence, more than 300 banks withdrew from the Federal Reserve between 1973 and 1979; 25 of those were relatively large banks with assets of $100 million or more. Faced with declining membership, the Federal Reserve began to search for some way either to stem the loss of member banks or to establish more effective control over the money-creating activities of nonmember banks.

During this time, the Federal Reserve was concerned also about NOW accounts, which enabled savings and loan associations, mutual savings banks, and credit unions (institutions beyond the Fed's control) to create money. The emergence of NOW accounts further threatened the Fed's ability to monitor and control the money supply. To counter this, the Fed pressed for substantial regulatory changes, and Congress responded with the Depository Institutions Deregulation and Monetary Control Act of 1980.

The Monetary Control Act virtually eliminated the distinction between member and nonmember commercial banks and significantly reduced the distinction between commercial banks and other financial institutions. The act required that all depository institutions—member commercial banks, nonmember commercial banks, savings and loan associations, mutual savings banks, and credit unions—meet the same standards with regard to reserve requirements. It lifted many of the regulations that historically had limited competition among various types of financial institutions, and it opened to all such institutions the option to purchase any of the services offered by the Federal Reserve. As a result of these changes, the Fed is now in a better position to monitor and control the money supply, and there is greater competition among the various types of depository institutions for depositors and loan customers alike.

Deregulation and Bank Failures

Not all of the consequences of the Monetary Control Act and subsequent banking reforms were positive. Many analysts argue that the relaxed regulatory environment contributed to an enormous number of bank and savings and loan failures in the 1980s. With fewer restrictions and more competitive pressure, financial institutions ventured into new lending areas. For instance, many savings institutions began making commercial real estate loans, a type of loan not previously permitted. When real estate markets collapsed, many of these loans became uncollectable, leading to massive losses and the failure of lending institutions. Deregulation was not the only cause of these failures; economic factors such as low oil prices and depressed agricultural markets also played an important role. Poor management and in some instances fraud were also to blame. But reduced regulation and lax supervision clearly were contributing factors. Unfortunately, many financial institutions remain in a weakened condition. Regulators now believe that it may cost $200 to $300 BILLION to close the remaining weak financial institutions or merge them with stronger ones.

The Functions of the Federal Reserve

The foregoing discussion highlights the importance of effectively supervising our financial institutions. That is one of the functions of the Fed, a responsibility it shares with other government agencies including the Federal Deposit Insurance Corporation (FDIC), the primary agency insuring deposits at financial institutions.

In addition to supervising financial institutions, the Fed performs a number of functions. First, the twelve Federal Reserve Banks hold the reserves (other than vault cash) of all the depository institutions in their districts. Second, as the lender of last resort, the Federal Reserve Banks stand ready to make loans to depository institutions in temporary need of funds. Third, the Federal Reserve supplies the economy with coins and paper money. Fourth, as we have seen, the Fed provides a system for collecting and clearing checks throughout the United States, making it possible for checks drawn on out-of-town banks to be returned to the home institution for collection. But all of these functions are secondary to the Fed's primary responsibility: the control of the nation's money supply. That is the topic we will examine next.

Monetary Policy

Monetary policy is policy designed to control the supply of money. More precisely, monetary policy is any action intended to alter the supply of money in order to influence the level of total spending and thereby combat unemployment or inflation.

Although the objective of monetary policy is the same as that of fiscal policy (to prevent or combat unemployment and inflation), its methodology is somewhat different. In Chapter 12, you saw how fiscal policymakers use the government's spending and taxation powers to alter total spending and thereby stimulate employment or reduce inflationary pressures. Likewise, monetary policy works to influence spending, but through a different mechanism: by increasing or decreasing the money supply.

The Fed does not manipulate the amount of money by printing more currency or by removing existing paper money from circulation. Remember, most of our nation's money supply is composed of balances in checking accounts—demand-deposit accounts, NOW accounts, and other forms of checkable deposits. It is this element of the money supply that the Fed's actions are designed to influence. You have seen how depository institutions create checkable deposits when they make loans. Now you will discover how the Federal Reserve can influence the lending ability of depository institutions and thereby alter not only the supply of money, but also the amount of total spending in the economy.

Monetary Policy Tools of the Federal Reserve

The Federal Reserve uses three major policy tools to control the money supply: (1) its ability to alter the reserve requirement in depository institutions, (2) the buying and selling of government securities, a process known as *open-market operations,* and (3) its control over the *discount rate*—the interest rate at which commercial banks and other depository institutions can borrow from the Federal Reserve.

All three policy tools affect the reserve positions of depository institutions. As you have learned, the more excess reserves a bank has, the more loans it can make and the more money (demand deposits) it can create. By altering the volume of excess reserves, the Fed is able to influence the banking system's ability to make loans. Because making loans means creating more money, the Fed's actions influence the money supply.

Changing the Reserve Requirement

The most obvious way to influence the reserve position of depository institutions is to change the reserve requirement. Under existing law, the Federal Reserve has the power to specify reserve requirements between 8 and 14 percent for depository institutions above a specified size. This flexibility provides the Federal Reserve with a tool for influencing the money supply by changing the lending ability of banks and other depository institutions.

Lowering the reserve requirement would convert some required reserves into excess reserves and thereby expand the lending ability of depository institutions. When these institutions increase their loans, they create checkable deposits, and the money supply expands. Increasing the reserve requirement has the opposite effect. As excess reserves are converted into required reserves, lending contracts and the money supply shrinks.

Modifying the reserve requirement is effective but somewhat dangerous. Even changes as small as one half of one percent can alter the banking system's ability to make loans by several billion dollars. Changes of this magnitude, particularly when they are sudden, can jolt the economy severely. Therefore the Federal Reserve uses this tool sparingly, adjusting the reserve requirement only infrequently and relying mainly on other tools to control the money supply.

Open-Market Operations

The Federal Reserve controls the money supply primarily through its open-market operations: buying and selling government securities on the open market. Whenever the United States government runs a deficit, the Treasury finances that deficit by selling government securities. These new securities are sold to individuals, businesses, financial institutions, and government agencies. Most are marketable, or *negotiable,* meaning they can be held until maturity or resold to someone else.[4] Depository institutions find such securities an attractive investment. They not only earn interest, but also convert easily into cash in the event that additional reserves are needed. The Federal Reserve uses the market for negotiable securities as a vehicle for controlling the money supply. Let us see how open-market operations work.

If the Fed wants to increase the money supply by expanding loans, it can offer to buy government securities at attractive prices in the open market. The Fed pays for securities purchased from a commercial bank, for example, by increasing the bank's reserve account at the district Federal Reserve Bank. Because this transaction does not increase the commercial bank's demand-deposit liabilities, the additional reserves are all excess and can be used to expand loans and deposits—up to the maximum predicted by the deposit multiplier. As you know, any change in the excess reserves of one bank will lead eventually to a much larger change in the total system's loans and demand deposits. As commercial banks and other depository institutions make more loans and create more checkable deposits, the money supply will expand.

If the Fed wishes to reduce the money supply, it can shift its open-market operations into reverse and cut the lending ability of depository institutions by selling them government securities. The purchasing banks and thrift institutions will experience a reduction in their reserve accounts at dis-

---

[4] There are different types of marketable government securities. *Treasury bills* are short-term securities with maturities of 91 days to one year. *Government notes* are intermediate-term securities maturing in one to five years. Finally, *government bonds* are long-term securities with maturities of more than five years.

trict Federal Reserve banks. As their reserves decline, these institutions will have to contract loans, or at least limit their expansion. This will cause the money supply to decline or expand at a slower rate.

Changing the Discount Rate

Since the passage of the Monetary Control Act of 1980, any depository institution may ask to borrow reserves from its district Federal Reserve Bank to avoid reducing the number of loans it can grant or to increase its volume of loans and thereby earn additional interest income.[5]

Recall that the rate of interest charged by the Federal Reserve on loans to depository institutions is called the *discount rate*. In theory, increasing the discount rate should discourage borrowing from the Federal Reserve and thus force depository institutions to limit or even contract the number of loans they grant. We know that if banks or thrift institutions contract their loans, the money supply will fall.

Lowering the discount rate should have the opposite effect. By encouraging depository institutions to borrow from the Fed and create additional loans and deposits, the lowered rate should lead to an increase in the money supply.

Please note our use of the terms "in theory" and "should." In practice, changes in the discount rate have proven to be a very weak policy tool. Bankers tend to equate loans from the Federal Reserve with money borrowed from in-laws. It's something you avoid unless you have no other options. This attitude is not surprising when one considers the Fed's corresponding view that borrowing is a privilege and not a right: If Federal Reserve authorities believe that a bank has overextended itself through poor planning or has borrowed too often or for the wrong purposes, they can refuse to lend the needed reserves. This disciplinary action will force the wayward bank to contract loans, sell securities, or look elsewhere for reserves. Because bankers don't like such restrictions, they prefer to borrow through the *federal funds market,* a market that brings together banks that need reserves and banks that temporarily have excess reserves. The rate charged on such loans is called the *federal funds rate* and usually applies to reserves borrowed on a very short-term basis—often overnight to meet temporary reserve deficiencies.

Because banks borrow from the Federal Reserve only infrequently, changes in the discount rate have little impact on the banking system's lending ability and thus register little effect on the money supply. In

---

[5] When depository institutions repay these loans to the Fed, their reserves will decline and they will be forced to contract loans or find other sources of reserves.

fact, many economists tend to view a change in the discount rate more as an indication of the Fed's intentions than as an effective policy move. Increases in the discount rate are thought to indicate the Fed's intention to contract the money supply or slow its rate of growth; decreases signal a desire to expand the money supply or increase its rate of growth.

Money, Interest Rates, and the Level of Economic Activity

Now that we've seen how the Federal Reserve can expand or contract the money supply, let's explore how changes in the money supply affect the economy. According to the Keynesian model, changes in the money supply affect output and employment primarily by altering interest rates and thereby influencing the level of total spending. Because a significant amount of consumption and investment spending is financed by borrowing, changes in the interest rate can affect the amount of spending in the economy. For example, a lower interest rate may encourage more people to buy new cars and new homes and may encourage businesses to invest in new factories and machinery.

Why would changes in the money supply tend to alter the rate of interest? To answer that question we need to think back to Chapter 3, where we discussed price determination in competitive markets. Like the price of wheat or the price of cattle, the interest rate—the price of money—is deter-

Lower interest rates may encourage businesses to invest in new factories and machinery.

mined by the forces of demand and supply. As a consequence, any change in either the demand for money or its supply will affect the rate of interest.[6] If the supply of money increases relative to demand, the interest rate will tend to decline; if the supply of money declines in relation to demand, the rate of interest will tend to increase. (In 1991, many of the nation's top business executives wanted the Fed to bring down interest rates. Test your economic reasoning by reading "Top Executives Urge Fed to Trim Rates" on page 420 and answering the study questions.)

Interest Rate Determination

Individuals and businesses demand money for a variety of reasons. Individuals need money to pay rent, buy groceries, and cover the other expenses that they incur from one payday to the next. Businesses must keep enough money on hand to compensate their suppliers and their employees and pay the other daily expenses associated with running a business.

According to Keynes, the quantity of money demanded by individuals and businesses is inversely related to the interest rate: the higher the rate of interest, the less money demanded. To understand that relationship, remember that the money you hold (cash in your wallet or money in your checking account) generally pays no interest. But other assets you could hold instead of money—bonds, for instance, or bank certificates of deposit—do pay interest. The higher the prevailing interest rate, the more attractive it becomes to hold these assets instead of money. As a consequence, less money will be demanded when interest rates are *high* than when they are *low*. The demand curve in Exh. 13.4 shows that $100 billion dollars would be demanded at an interest rate of 10 percent, whereas $300 billion would be demanded at an interest rate of 6 percent.

The supply of money is depicted as a vertical line in Exh. 13.4 to illustrate that the quantity of money supplied does not respond automatically to changes in the interest rate; instead, it remains constant at the level determined by the Federal Reserve. The intersection of the demand curve and the vertical supply curve determines the equilibrium interest rate: the interest rate at which the amount of money that people want to hold is exactly equal to the amount available. In our hypothetical example, the equilibrium interest rate is 8 percent. At that interest rate, individuals and businesses are willing to hold $200 billion, exactly the amount being supplied by the Federal Reserve.

---

[6] To simplify matters, we will assume a single rate of interest, but in fact there are several. For example, short-term borrowers generally pay a lower interest rate than those who require the money for a longer period. In addition, borrowers with good credit ratings usually pay lower rates than those with poor ratings.

EXHIBIT 13.4

The Equilibrium Interest Rate

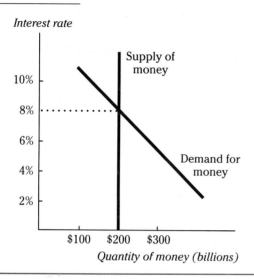

The intersection of the demand curve for money and the supply curve of money determines the equilibrium interest rate—the interest rate at which the amount of money that individuals and businesses want to hold is exactly equal to the amount available. In this example, the equilibrium interest rate is 8 percent.

Monetary Policy and the Level of Economic Activity

In the Keynesian model, monetary policy works primarily through altering the equilibrium interest rate. By adjusting the money supply, the Federal Reserve is able to push the equilibrium interest rate up or down, which influences the level of total spending in the economy and thereby affects unemployment or inflation. This transmission process can be summarized as follows:

$$\text{Money supply} \rightarrow \text{interest rate} \rightarrow \text{spending} \rightarrow \begin{array}{c} \text{output,} \\ \text{employment,} \\ \text{and prices.} \end{array}$$

To illustrate the way monetary policy works, let's assume that the economy is suffering from unemployment. You already know that according to the Keynesian model, unemployment is caused by too little spending. The Federal Reserve can stimulate spending by increasing the money supply. For example, suppose the Fed reduces the reserve requirement, buys government securities, or lowers the discount rate and thereby shifts the money-supply curve in Exh. 13.5 from S_1 to S_2, denoting an increase in the money supply

Top Executives Urge Fed to Trim Rates

Business Council Members Detect Little Evidence of Economic Recovery

HOT SPRINGS, Va.—Unable to find evidence of the much-heralded economic recovery, the nation's top business leaders called on the Federal Reserve to cut interest rates.

"The Fed should ease more and bring interest rates down," said American Express Co. Chairman James Robinson in an interview at the spring meeting of the Business Council. His comments were echoed by chief executives from a variety of industries. "It would be nice if the prime moved down another half point," said General Motors Corp. Chairman Robert Stempel.

Fed Chairman Alan Greenspan was among those who addressed the group of chief executives during their two-day meeting at this mountain resort. But Mr. Greenspan gave them no reason to believe he would answer their pleas for easier credit when the Fed's policy committee meets tomorrow. "He was his usual inscrutable self," Mr. Robinson said.

Many top Fed policy makers believe that the recession has bottomed out and that economic recovery is on the horizon. They are reluctant to ease credit further for fear they would only fuel next year's inflation. As a result, private Fed watchers and government officials believe the Fed won't cut interest rates at its meeting tomorrow.

But the business leaders rejected the Fed's concern about inflation. "I personally don't think the inflation risk is very high now," said Henry Schacht, chairman of Cummins Engine Co.

A group of 20 economists who advise the Business Council also said they expect the economy to turn up in the coming months. But the business leaders generally rejected the optimism of their own consultants. . . .

The chief executives "look at sales, they look at the backlogs, and they look at the pressure they are under—and they are basically pessimistic," said Mr. Robinson. "They are saying that they aren't seeing business picking up."

Automobile industry executives were particularly gloomy. Many economists had predicted the surge of consumer confidence after the Iraqi war would spur car sales. But so far, there's no sign of that. "We are looking at business on a day-to-day basis. We can see it here and now. And it's flat," said Ford Motor Co. Chairman Harold Poling in an interview. Like Mr. Stempel of General Motors, Mr. Poling said he'd "like to see another half-point reduction in the prime"—the base rate banks charge on many loans.

Capital goods makers also were very pessimistic. "Our business is low," said Mr. Schacht. "The industries we serve had production rates in April that are lower than in March. We don't see any sign of an upturn in any of these industries.". . .

At least one of the executives, H. Brewster Atwater, chairman of General Mills Inc., said he did see signs of a turnaround. "Our business is actually quite good," said Mr. Atwater, whose company sells food and operates restaurants. "Consumers certainly feel a whole lot better than they did last October and November."

In his comments to the group, Mr. Greenspan also cited improvements in the housing industry, according to those who attended the closed session.

At their last meeting in March, the Fed's policy com-mittee eliminated the tilt toward easier credit that has characterized their policy directives throughout the early parts of the recession. The group, however, did authorize Mr. Greenspan to cut the key federal funds rate a quarter percentage point if he felt it necessary, and the Fed chairman made that move late last month, in conjunction with a half-point cut in the discount rate. The fed funds rate is what banks charge on loans to each other; the discount rate, largely symbolic, is the rate the Fed charges on loans to financial institutions.

At tomorrow's meeting, the Fed panel is likely to avoid any tilt toward easing but again give Mr. Greenspan the leeway to cut the fed funds rate another quarter point in the coming weeks, if he thinks it is necessary.

—*David Wessel in Washington contributed to this article.* —*Alan Murray*

SOURCE: *The Wall Street Journal*, May 13, 1991, p. A2. Reprinted by permission of *The Wall Street Journal*, © 1991 Dow Jones & Company, Inc. All Rights Reserved Worldwide.

USE YOUR ECONOMIC REASONING

1. **Why do business leaders want the Fed to bring down interest rates? How would that action help their businesses?**

2. **According to the Keynesian model, what impact would lower interest rates have on the overall economy? How would you show this impact graphically?**

3. **If the Fed decided to lower interest rates, what policies would it pursue to accomplish that objective?**

4. **Why is the Fed unwilling to reduce interest rates at this time? What changes in the economy might cause Fed policymakers to desire lower rates?**

421

EXHIBIT 13.5

The Effect of Changes in the Money Supply on the Equilibrium Interest Rate

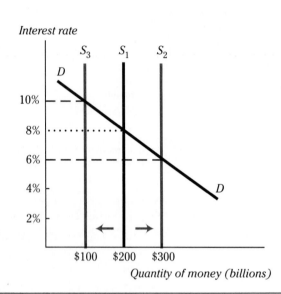

Quantity of money (billions)

By adjusting the money supply, the Federal Reserve may be able to alter the interest rate. For example, if the money supply is increased from S_1 to S_2 (from $200 billion to $300 billion), the equilibrium interest would tend to fall from 8 percent to 6 percent. On the other hand, if the money supply was decreased from S_1 to S_3 (from $200 billion to $100 billion), the interest rate would tend to rise from 8 percent to 10 percent.

from $200 billion to $300 billion. Since the demand for money is unchanged, the equilibrium interest rate will fall from 8 percent to 6 percent. At this lower interest rate, businesses will find it profitable to borrow additional money to invest in plants and equipment; households will be inclined to borrow and spend more on new homes, automobiles, and other consumer goods. An increase in the money supply thus lowers the interest rate and leads to increased total spending, which in turn boosts the level of total output and employment.

To attack inflation, the Federal Reserve must reduce the level of total spending by contracting the money supply. This can be accomplished by increasing the reserve requirement, selling government securities, or increasing the discount rate. You can see in Exh. 13.5 that reducing the money supply from S_1 to S_3, a decrease from $200 billion to $100 billion, pushes the interest rate from 8 percent to 10 percent. What is the effect of the higher rate of interest? Businesses will tend to reduce investment spending, and households will be likely to spend less on new homes, boats, camping trailers, and other items that they buy on credit or through borrowing. Reducing the money supply thus raises the interest rate and leads to a reduction in the level of total spending in the economy, which in turn helps reduce inflationary pressures.

Thus you can see how monetary policy works in the Keynesian model through its impact on the interest rate. By adjusting the cost of money, the Fed is able to influence the level of total spending in the economy and thereby combat unemployment or inflation.

The Limits to Monetary Policy

The Federal Reserve's independent status gives monetary policy some distinct advantages over fiscal policy. When the Fed's Board of Governors decides that action should be taken to combat unemployment or inflation, they need not wait for Congress to agree. The Board members can approve the needed policy changes and have them implemented in a very short time. Their fourteen-year terms also serve to insulate Board members from political pressures, although the insulation is not complete in view of the periodic threats to bring the Fed under the direct control of Congress.

But monetary policy has limitations, as well. (Recall the limitations of fiscal policy that we examined in Chapter 12.) Here we will look at two problems that may be encountered when monetary policy is used in an attempt to guide the economy's performance.

Time Lags

Like fiscal policy, monetary policy is subject to some time lags. Although Federal Reserve authorities don't need the approval of Congress to implement policy changes, they do need time to recognize that a problem exists and agree on the needed action. As we learned earlier, our economic indicators sometimes send mixed or unclear messages, so some time may elapse before members of the Board of Governors identify a problem and prescribe a remedy. Once they take action, additional time passes before their policy change exerts its impact on the economy. If the Board members decide to stimulate the economy, for example, it will take time for an increase in lending to trigger the associated increases in spending, output, and employment. If this time lag is too long, the added stimulus may hit the economy when it is already on the road to spontaneous recovery. In that event, the Fed's actions may contribute to inflation rather than help reduce unemployment.

Uneven Effectiveness

Monetary policy may be less effective in combating unemployment than in combating inflation. When the Fed reduces banks' reserves to combat inflation, banks are forced to restrict (or even contract) lending. However, when it implements an easy-money policy to combat unemployment and makes more reserves available to depository institutions, bankers need not use those reserves to support loans. If bankers doubt the ability of customers to repay loans, they refuse to lend; if households and businesses are pessimistic about the future, they may decide not to borrow. Without greater lending and borrowing, spending will not increase; thus the economy will not receive the stimulus needed to pull it from its depressed state.

How significant are the monetary policy limitations noted here? As with fiscal policy, the issue is open to debate. But the performance of the Federal Reserve in the 1980s seems to provide evidence that discretionary policy can be successful in guiding the economy's performance. After halting inflation early in the decade, the Fed manipulated interest rates to achieve a seven-year expansion without significant inflation. Many economists argue that this experience demonstrates the wisdom of an activist monetary policy.

But all do not agree with this assessment. Monetarists believe that the lags in monetary policy are long and unpredictable. Consequently, they contend that attempts to use monetary policy to guide the economy's performance can result in worse rather than better economic performance. New classical economists also argue against discretionary monetary policy, believing that, as with fiscal policy, the actions of policymakers will be anticipated and neutralized. They argue that an expansionary monetary policy will have no beneficial impact on the economy; it will only lead to inflation. The views of the monetarists and the new classical economists will be considered in detail in Chapter 15.

Summary

Economists define *money* as anything that serves as a *medium of exchange*, a *standard of value*, and a *store of value*. Currency (coins and paper money) and *checkable deposits* (checking accounts at banks and savings institutions) clearly perform all the functions of money. Other *assets*—passbook savings accounts, for example—perform some, but not all, of the functions of money, or perform those functions incompletely. Assets that are not money but that can be quickly converted into money are termed *near money*.

In its role as controller of the U.S. money supply, the Federal Reserve defines that supply according to three classifications. The narrowest is *M-1*, composed of currency in the hands of the public plus all checkable deposits. *M-2*, a somewhat broader definition of the nation's money supply, includes everything in M-1 plus money-market mutual fund balances, money-market deposits at savings or thrift institutions, and small savings deposits. *M-3*, the broadest definition of the money supply, includes everything in M-2 plus savings deposits in excess of $100,000.

Approximately 70 percent of the M-1 money supply is in the form of checkable deposits; the remainder is currency. The Federal Reserve provides depository institutions (i.e., commercial banks and thrift institutions) with the coins and paper currency they need in order to serve their customers. Checkable deposits, on the other hand, are actually created by the depository institutions themselves when they make loans.

According to the *fractional reserve principle*, a bank need maintain only a given fraction of a dollar in *required reserves* for each dollar in demand deposits; the balance of those funds can be loaned out to earn interest. In the process of making these loans, banks create demand-deposit money. For example, when a person borrows money from a commercial bank, he or she exchanges something that is not money (an IOU) for something that is money (a demand-deposit balance). This increases the money supply by the amount of the loan. Other forms of checkable deposits—*NOW accounts* at savings institutions, ATS accounts at commercial banks, and credit-union-share draft accounts—are created in essentially the same way.

Each depository institution must limit its loans to the amount of its *excess reserves*—reserves in excess of the sum it is legally required to maintain in the form of vault cash and deposits with the Federal Reserve. This limitation is necessary because, as loans are spent, reserves are likely to be lost to other depository institutions. Thus each institution can expand the money supply by an amount equal to its excess reserves, but no more than that.

The banking system (including all depository institutions) does not have to worry about losing reserves. Reserves lost by one depository institution must be deposited in some other bank or savings institution in the system. The banking system as a whole, then, can create loans and deposits equal to some multiple of its excess reserves. To be precise, it can expand loans and deposits by an amount equal to the initial change in excess reserves times the reciprocal of the reserve requirement (the *deposit multiplier*).

The Federal Reserve, our nation's *central bank,* influences the ability of depository institutions to expand or contract deposits and thereby regulates the size of the nation's money supply. The Fed's Board of Governors makes all major policy decisions and communicates them to the twelve Federal Reserve banks, which oversee the actions of all depository institutions in their districts.

The Federal Reserve has three major tools with which to control the money supply: (1) the ability to alter the reserve requirement, (2) the buying and selling of government securities, a process known as *open-market operations*, and (3) control over the *discount rate*—the interest rate at which commercial banks and other depository institutions can borrow from the Federal Reserve.

All these policy tools affect the reserve position of commercial banks. By influencing the volume of excess reserves, the Fed is able to affect the banking system's ability to make loans and is thereby able to influence the money supply. This control over the money supply enables the Federal Reserve to alter the interest rate, which in turn influences the level of total spending in the economy.

Monetary policy has some distinct advantages over fiscal policy. The lags in monetary policy tend to be shorter than those in fiscal policy; and because the Fed tends to be somewhat insulated from political pressures, it may have more freedom to pursue long-run goals than does Congress.

Monetary policy is also subject to limitations: (1) While the lags in monetary policy are generally shorter than those in fiscal policy, they do exist and have the potential to make monetary policy counterproductive. (2) Monetary policy may be more effective in combating inflation than in dealing with unemployment.

Glossary

Federal funds market. A market that brings together banks in need of reserves and banks that temporarily have excess reserves.

Federal funds rate. The rate of interest charged by banks for lending reserves to other banks.

Fractional reserve principle. The principle that a bank need maintain only a fraction of a dollar in reserve for each dollar of its demand deposits.

Liabilities. The debts of an entity, what it owes.

M-1. Federal Reserve definition of the money supply that includes currency in the hands of the public plus all checkable deposits; the narrowest definition of the money supply.

M-2. Federal Reserve definition of the money supply that includes all of M-1 plus money-market mutual fund balances, money-market deposits at savings institutions, and small savings deposits.

M-3. Federal Reserve definition of the money supply that includes all of M-2 plus large savings deposits.

Medium of exchange. A generally accepted means of payment for goods and services; one of the three basic functions of money.

Monetary policy. Any action intended to alter the supply of money in order to influence the level of total spending and thereby combat unemployment or inflation.

Near money. Assets that are not money but can be converted quickly to money.

NOW account. A savings account on which the depositor can write checks; NOW stands for negotiable order of withdrawal.

Open-market operations. The buying and selling of government securities by the Federal Reserve as a means of influencing the money supply.

Owner equity. The interest of the owner or owners of a business in its assets.

Required reserves. The amount of reserves a depository institution is required by law to maintain. These reserves must be in the form of vault cash or deposits with the Federal Reserve.

Reserve requirement. The fraction of a bank's demand deposits that must be held as required reserves.

Savings deposits. Interest-bearing deposits at banks and savings institutions.

Standard of value. A unit in which the prices of goods and services can be expressed; one of the three basic functions of money.

Store of value. A vehicle for accumulating or storing wealth to be used at a future date; one of the three basic functions of money.

Study Questions

Fill in the Blanks

1. Money functions as a _____Medium of exchange_____, a ____Standard of value_____ _____, and a ___Store of value_____.

2. Demand deposits, NOW accounts, and ATS accounts are all examples of ___ ____Checkable deposits____.

3. The primary characteristic of all M-1 money is that it can easily function as a ____medium of exchange____.

4. A commercial bank must maintain reserves equal to a specified fraction of its ___demand deposits___.

5. Commercial banks create money when they ___make loans_____; the amount of money that a commercial bank can create is equal to its _____ ____excess reserve____.

6. Today, the primary purpose of the Federal Reserve is to regulate or control the ____money supply____ in order to combat unemployment and inflation.

7. According to the Keynesian model, if the money supply increased, this would tend to (increase/decrease) _____ the interest rate, which would tend to (increase/decrease) _____ investment spending, which in turn would (increase/decrease) _____ _____ GNP.

8. The Federal Reserve controls the money supply primarily through (which policy tool) ___Open market operations___.

9. The rate charged by the Federal Reserve on loans to depository institutions
   is called the _discount rate_.

10. Monetary policy may be less effective in combating _unemployment_
    _____ than _inflation_____.

Multiple Choice

1. Which of the following is the largest component of the M-1 money supply?
   a) Currency
   b) Passbook savings accounts
   c) Checkable deposits
   d) Money-market accounts

2. Which of the following is *not* an example of near money?
   a) A savings account
   b) A government bond
   c) A piece of prime real estate
   d) An account with a money-market fund

3. Which of the following does *not* appear as an asset on the balance sheet of a
   commercial bank?
   a) Demand deposits
   b) Reserves
   c) Securities
   d) Loans

4. Assuming that the reserve requirement is 30 percent, how much additional
   money can the bank represented below create? (All figures are in millions of
   dollars.)

Assets		Liabilities	
Reserves	$23	Demand deposits	$50
Securities	25	Owner equity	40
Loans	17		
Property	25		

   a) $ 8 million
   b) $12 million
   c) $15 million
   d) $25 million

5. Assuming a reserve requirement of 25 percent, how much additional money can the bank represented below create? (All figures are in millions.)

Assets		Liabilities	
Reserves	$35	Demand deposits	$80
Securities	30	Owner equity	20
Loans	25		
Property	10		

a) $20 million
b) $15 million
c) $10 million
d) $ 5 million

6. If the reserve requirement is 25 percent, the money multiplier would be equal to
   a) 4.
   b) 5.
   c) 1/4.
   d) 10.

7. If the balance sheet represented in question (5) were for the banking *system*, rather than for a single commercial bank, the system could expand the money supply by an additional
   a) $15 billion.
   b) $30 billion.
   c) $60 billion.
   d) $80 billion.

8. Which of the following was *not* accomplished by the Monetary Control Act of 1980?
   a) It virtually eliminated the distinction between member and nonmember commercial banks.
   b) It enhanced competition between the various types of financial institutions.
   c) It established uniform reserve requirements for all depository institutions.
   d) It eliminated the "lender of last resort" function of the Federal Reserve.

9. If banks hold demand deposits of $200 million and reserves of $50 million, and the reserve requirement is 20 percent, how much additional money can the banking *system* create?
   a) $20 million
   b) $50 million
   c) $100 million
   d) $200 million

10. Which of the following is *not* a function of the Federal Reserve?
    a) To control the money supply
    b) To make loans to depository institutions
    c) To insure the deposits of customers
    d) To provide a check-collection service

11. If the Federal Reserve wants to reduce the equilibrium interest rate, it should
    a) increase the reserve requirement in order to expand the money supply.
    b) sell securities on the open market in order to expand the money supply.
    c) buy government securities in order to expand the money supply.
    d) increase the discount rate in order to expand the money supply.

12. When the Federal Reserve sells government securities on the open market,
    a) the lending ability of commercial banks tends to decline; the money supply shrinks, and the interest rate tends to decline.
    b) the lending ability of commercial banks tends to decline; the money supply expands, and the interest rate tends to rise.
    c) the lending ability of commercial banks increases; the money supply expands, and the interest rate tends to fall.
    d) the lending ability of commercial banks tends to decline; the money supply shrinks, and the interest rate tends to rise.

13. Let's assume that all banks in the system are loaned up (have no excess reserves) and that they all face a reserve ratio of 20 percent. If the Federal Reserve buys a $100,000 security from Bank A, how much new money can the banking *system* create? (*Hint:* Remember that the Fed will pay for the security by increasing the reserve account of Bank A.)
    a) $100,000
    b) $1,000,000
    c) $400,000
    d) $500,000

14. If the Federal Reserve wanted to reduce inflationary pressures, what would be the proper combination of policies?
    a) Increase the reserve ratio, decrease the discount rate, and sell securities.
    b) Increase the reserve ratio, increase the discount rate, and sell securities.
    c) Increase the reserve ratio, increase the discount rate, and buy securities.
    d) Decrease the reserve ratio, decrease the discount rate, and buy securities.

15. The purpose of an easy money policy designed to expand bank reserves is
    a) to lower interest rates and shift the total expenditures function to a lower level.
    b) to raise interest rates and shift the total expenditures function to a higher level.
    c) to lower interest rates and shift the total expenditures function to a higher level.
    d) to raise interest rates and shift the total expenditures function to a lower level.

Problems and Questions for Discussion

1. Explain each of the functions of money. Which of these functions does a traditional savings account perform? What about a NOW account?

2. Explain what is meant by the fractional reserve principle. How is it related to a bank's ability to create money?

3. Why must individual banks limit their loans to the amount of their excess reserves?

4. If a bank can create money, why can't you?

5. What is the money multiplier, and how is it calculated?

6. If you asked for your loan in cash rather than accepting a checking account, what impact would this action have on the money-creating ability of your commercial bank? What about the banking system as a whole?

7. Suppose that you have a credit card with a $1,000 limit (you cannot charge more than $1,000). Should that $1,000 be considered part of the money supply? Why or why not?

8. Both commercial banks and savings institutions can make loans. But until the appearance of NOW accounts, only commercial banks could create money through the lending process. Why was there a difference in the money-creating abilities of these two types of institutions? How did the emergence of NOW accounts make it possible for savings institutions to create money?

9. Discuss the reasons for the passage of the Monetary Control Act of 1980.

10. According to Keynesians, monetary policy works through the rate of interest. Please explain.

11. Suppose that the Federal Reserve were to increase the reserve requirement. Explain the step-by-step impact of that change on the economy.

12. Why is the discount rate often described as a weak policy tool?

13. What are the advantages of open-market operations over changes in the reserve requirement?

14. Suppose that the housing industry is depressed. What monetary policy actions would you recommend to help the housing industry? Why do you think they would help?

15. If the Fed buys a government security from a private individual, the money supply will immediately be increased. If the Fed buys a government security from a commercial bank, this action will not affect the money supply until a loan is made. Please explain the difference. That is, why does one transaction have an immediate impact while the other does not?

STUDY QUESTIONS

Answer Key

Fill in the Blanks

1. medium of exchange, standard of value, store of value
2. checkable deposits
3. medium of exchange
4. demand deposits
5. make loans; excess reserves
6. money supply
7. decrease, increase, increase
8. open-market operations
9. discount rate
10. unemployment, inflation

Multiple Choice

1. c
2. c
3. a
4. a
5. b
6. a
7. c
8. d
9. b
10. c
11. c
12. d
13. d
14. b
15. c

STUDY QUESTIONS

14

AGGREGATE DEMAND AND SUPPLY: THE MODEL OF THE SELF-CORRECTING ECONOMY

Throughout the last three chapters we have expanded on the Keynesian model that was introduced in Chapter 10. We've examined the forces that determine output and employment in the Keynesian model and considered its policies for combating unemployment and inflation.

The Keynesian model is useful because it calls attention to the level of demand as an important determinant of the economy's performance. But the model is subject to some significant limitations. First, it does not bring the price level explicitly into the analysis. Recall that the Keynesian model assumes that prices remain stable until full employment is reached. As a consequence, the model cannot depict a situation where both real output and prices rise simultaneously, a situation that is commonplace in the real world.

Second, the Keynesian model considers only the demand side of the economy: unemployment results from too little demand for goods and services, inflation results from too much demand. While these observations are valid and important, they don't tell the whole story because they fail to consider the supply side of the overall economy. In short, there are sources of unemployment and inflation that are ignored by the basic Keynesian model.

Finally, the Keynesian model totally dismisses the classical contention that the economy is self-correcting. Because prices and wages refuse to fall, reductions in spending lead to unemployment, which must be attacked by government policy. But modern economists (including modern Keynesians) generally agree that prices and wages will eventually decline in the face of falling demand. This possibility implies that the economy may be self-correcting and calls into question the desirability of discretionary monetary and fiscal policies.

This chapter will address the shortcomings of the basic Keynesian model by expanding the aggregate-demand/aggregate-supply framework that was briefly introduced in Chapter 10. By bringing the supply side of the economy into the analysis, we can obtain a more complete picture of how our economy operates. We will see how the overall price level can change and how changes in aggregate supply can result in simultaneous unemployment and inflation. Finally, the aggregate-demand/aggregate-supply framework will allow us to examine the possibility that the economy is self-correcting.

An Overview of the Model

Understanding the determinants of demand or total spending—the thrust of Keynesian macroeconomics—is only the first step in explaining the economy's overall performance. Modern macroeconomics sees the economy's performance as resulting from the interaction of aggregate demand and aggregate supply. As we discovered in Chapter 10, the intersection of the aggregate demand and aggregate supply curves determines the economy's equilibrium level of real GNP and the overall price level. This is represented in Exh. 14.1, which shows the intersection of *AD* and *AS* determining an overall price level of 100 and an equilibrium real GNP of $1,000 billion.

Chapter 10 provided a brief introduction to aggregate demand and aggregate supply, but neither concept was fully developed. Our first task in this chapter will be to examine these concepts in greater detail. Then we will review the process by which the equilibrium output and price level are determined, and consider the economy's response to changes in aggregate demand and supply. We begin by reviewing and extending our analysis of aggregate demand.

EXHIBIT 14.1

An Overview of Aggregate Demand and Supply

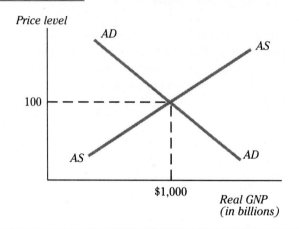

The intersection of the aggregate demand and supply curves determines the equilibrium level of real GNP and the equilibrium price level in the economy.

Aggregate Demand

Aggregate demand is the total quantity of output demanded by all sectors in the economy together (households, businesses, and governments) at various price levels in a given time period. Like the demand curve for a single product, the *aggregate demand curve* slopes downward and to the right, indicating that more real output will be demanded at a lower price level than at a higher price level. But the aggregate demand curve slopes downward for different reasons. When we are considering the demand for a single product—steak, for example—we assume that the prices of all similar products—chicken, fish, and pork, for instance—remain constant as we reduce its price. As steak becomes relatively cheaper than before, consumers tend to substitute it for other products, thus increasing the quantity of steak demanded. When we examine the aggregate demand curve, it is not the price of a single product that falls, but the price level: the average price of all goods and services. Therefore there must be a different reason for the aggregate demand curve's downward slope. In fact, there are two reasons: the real balance effect and the interest rate effect.

The Real Balance Effect

When the price level falls, the real value or purchasing power of the public's financial assets—savings accounts, retirement funds, and other financial assets with fixed money values—tends to increase. This makes people feel wealthier, and they tend to demand more goods and services—more real output. The *real balance effect* is the increase in the amount of aggregate output demanded that results from the increased real value of the public's financial assets.

As an example, suppose that you work each summer to help pay for college. This summer you managed to save $2,000, your share of the year's anticipated expenses. Now, assume the overall price level falls to half of what it was when you established your $2,000 objective. In essence, that means all prices have been cut in half, so your $2,000 will now stretch twice as far as before. How will you react? Chances are you will start buying things you don't normally purchase because you have $1,000 in your savings account that won't be needed for anticipated college expenses. That's the real balance effect in action; the real value or purchasing power of the money balance in your savings account has increased, and this increase in wealth is spurring you to purchase more goods and services. Of course, if the price level increased, everything would work in reverse; your savings would be worth less, so you would feel less wealthy and demand fewer goods and services than before. Either way we describe it, the price level and spending on real output are moving in opposite directions, so the aggregate demand curve must slope downward. Exh. 14.2 depicts the aggregate demand curve for a hypothetical economy.

The Interest Rate Effect

In addition to its impact on real balances, a change in the price level also has an effect on the prevailing interest rate. The interest rate is determined by the demand and supply of money. When the price level falls, consumers and businesses will require less money for their day-to-day transactions because a given amount of money will buy more goods and services than before. In other words, a reduction in the price level will reduce the demand for money. Since each aggregate demand curve assumes a fixed supply of money in the economy, a reduction in the demand for money will tend to reduce the price of money—the interest rate. When the interest rate falls, the lower cost of borrowing money tends to stimulate investment spending and some types of consumer spending. The *interest rate effect* is the increase in the amount

EXHIBIT 14.2

The Aggregate Demand Curve

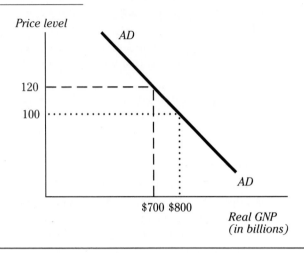

The aggregate demand curve shows an inverse relationship between the overall price level and the quantity of real output demanded. For instance, when the price level decreases from 120 to 110, the quantity of real GNP demanded increases from $700 billion to $800 billion.

of aggregate output demanded that results when a reduction in the overall price level causes interest rates to fall.[1]

To illustrate, let's suppose that the price level—the average price of goods and services—fell to half of what it is today. Homes that had been selling for $200,000 would cost $100,000; automobiles that had been priced at $20,000 would be available for $10,000. As a consequence, consumers would need to borrow only half as much money as before to finance their new homes and automobiles and other credit purchases. This reduced demand for money would tend to lower interest rates and stimulate spending. Thus more real output would be demanded at the lower price level. Of course, if the price level increased (which may seem a more realistic possibility), the demand for money would tend to increase, pushing up interest rates and depressing spending on real GNP.

---

[1] The interest rate effect actually has to do with the impact of a price level change on the "real" interest rate—the interest rate after adjustment for inflation. If the nominal interest rate (the interest rate before adjustment) is 15 percent a year, and the expected rate of inflation is 5 percent, the real interest rate is 10 percent.

Business investment decisions are influenced by real interest rate, not nominal rates. A higher nominal interest rate (resulting from a higher expected rate of inflation) would not necessarily discourage businesses from borrowing, since they would also anticipate receiving higher prices for their products (and thus a higher nominal rate of return). The proof that a higher price level causes a higher real interest rate is beyond the scope of this text.

Changes in Aggregate Demand

As with the demand curve for a single product, we need to distinguish between *movement along* an *AD* curve and a *shift* of the *AD* curve. We've seen that changes in the price level will cause movement up or down along a stationary curve. Any change in the spending plans of households, businesses, or government that results from something *other than a change in the price level* will shift the *AD* curve. Factors that will shift the aggregate demand curve include changes in the expectations of households and businesses, changes in aggregate wealth, and changes in government policy.

Household and Business Expectations

Suppose that households and businesses become less optimistic about the future (perhaps because they anticipate a recession). What impact would that have on aggregate demand? Households might be expected to save more (and thus consume less), while businesses would probably reduce their spending for factories and machinery. Because total spending at any price level would be less than before, the *AD* curve would shift to the left (from AD_1 to AD_3 in Exh. 14.3), a reduction in aggregate demand. More optimistic expectations would have the opposite effect: the *AD* curve would shift to the right.

Aggregate Wealth

An increase in the overall wealth of the society would also tend to shift the aggregate demand curve to the right. Consider, for example, the impact of a stock market boom that increased the value of households' stock holdings. Since consumers can finance spending by selling shares of stock and other forms of wealth, this increase in stock values would tend to spur spending; households might be expected to demand more real output than before at any price level. A reduction in wealth, due perhaps to a decline in the stock market, would shift the *AD* curve to the left.

Government Policy

Government can also influence aggregate demand through its policies. For instance, a reduction in government spending for goods and services would cause the *AD* curve to shift to the left, as would an increase in personal income taxes (since consumers would have less to spend at each price level). A reduction in the money supply would also cause aggregate demand to fall. The size of the economy's money supply is determined by the Federal Re-

EXHIBIT 14.3

Shifts of the Aggregate Demand Curve

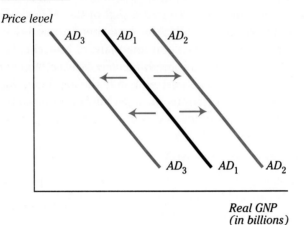

Price level

Real GNP
(in billions)

Any change in the spending plans of households, businesses, or government that results from something other than a change in the price level will shift the AD curve. A shift to the right is an increase in aggregate demand; a shift to the left is a decrease.

serve, or Fed. If the Fed decreases the money supply, the interest rate that businesses and others have to pay to borrow money will tend to increase. This in turn will tend to depress investment spending by businesses and some forms of consumption spending by households, shifting the aggregate demand curve to the left.

Consider an increase in military spending by the federal government. What impact would that have on aggregate demand? It would increase the amount of real GNP demanded at any price level, so it would shift the AD curve to the right (from AD_1 to AD_2 in Exh. 14.3). A tax reduction or an increase in the money supply would also tend to increase aggregate demand.

In summary, the aggregate demand curve will shift due to changes in the expectations of households or businesses, changes in wealth, or changes in government policy. These are the major causes of shifts in aggregate demand, but the list is not exhaustive; other changes could have a similar impact. The important point is that any change in spending plans that stems from something other than a change in the price level will shift the AD curve; changes in the price level will cause movement *along* a stationary curve. The article on page 442, "Rising Mortgage Rates Portend Cutbacks," looks at the impact of Federal Reserve policy on aggregate demand.

Aggregate Supply

Aggregate demand is only half of the model; the other half is aggregate supply. *Aggregate supply* refers to the total quantity of output supplied by all producers in the economy together at various price levels in a given time period.

As we saw in Chapter 10, the shape we assign to the *aggregate supply curve* depends on the assumptions we make about the behavior of wages and prices. If we believe that wages and prices are highly flexible, the *AS* curve will be vertical. If we assume that wages and prices are rigid, the *AS* curve will be horizontal. Most modern economists take a position in the middle; they argue that all wages and prices are flexible in the long run, but that at least some wages and input prices are rigid in the short run. This belief results in an *AS* curve that is upward sloping.

An upward-sloping aggregate supply curve indicates that businesses tend to supply more aggregate output at higher price levels than at lower price levels. Businesses behave in this manner because the wage and input price rigidities we have described cause certain costs to be fixed in the short run. This makes it profitable for businesses to expand output if aggregate demand increases and pushes up the prices they can charge for their products.

EXHIBIT 14.4

The Aggregate Supply Curve

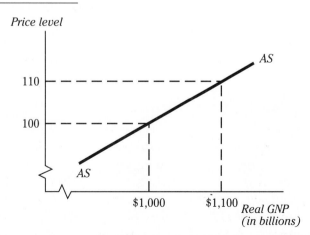

The aggregate supply curve is upward sloping because businesses tend to supply more real output at higher price levels than at lower price levels.

Rising Mortgage Rates Portend Cutbacks
Study Finds Consumers Will Alter Spending Habits

NEW YORK—Economists are starting to get a focus on just how much rising interest rates will squeeze homeowners with adjustable-rate mortgages. And for many, the picture isn't pretty.

"We're right now at the point where people with adjustable mortgages are up against the wall," said A. Gary Shilling, president of the New York-based research firm bearing his name.

To date, much of the evidence has either been narrowly anecdotal or broadly general. Only the most recent consumer spending data has shown any sign of slowing its roaring pace.

But a new study by Mr. Shilling's firm has some ominous implications for the economy, particularly companies that sell durable goods such as cars, appliances and furniture.

The study sought to measure the effect of rising interest rates on the discretionary spending of a variety of household groups, based on income, assets, age and type of debt over several years.

It concludes that for the households most heavily in debt, each percentage-point rise in short-term interest rates could reduce total durable-goods spending as much as 7%. And a five percentage-point move in these rates would slash household durable-goods spending by a sharp 20%, after taking into account offsetting spending by people who would earn more on their investments because of higher rates. . . .

The research found that those who benefit the most from rising rates are people over 65 years old, as they own by far the most assets. Among the worst hit are homeowners with incomes of less than $50,000 and with heavy adjustable-rate mortgage debt and consumer installment debt. . . .

Economists say the adjustable loans, which made up about half of all new mortgages last year, are acting as a sort of grass-roots indicator of current Federal Reserve policy.

The Fed has been raising interest rates in an effort to tame inflation, and one of its goals is to dampen consumer appetites and thereby help cool the economy. With the latest round of tightening, rates on both adjustable and fixed-rate mortgages are approaching their highest levels in 2½ years.

Economists disagree about whether the Fed has tightened

credit enough to get the job done or has pulled the reins too tightly and is steering the country toward recession. But they seem to agree that the increased popularity of adjustable-rate mortgages makes previous experience an unreliable indicator.

Since taking hold in the early 1980s, adjustable-rate mortgages have enjoyed a hefty market share, except for a wave of refinancings in 1986 when interest rates plummeted. In 1983, adjustable-rate loans accounted for less than 5% of all mortgage debt. Today, the Shilling study estimates, they constitute 56% of all existing mortgages for one-to-four-family homes held by thrifts and 33% of all mortgage debt.

Four years ago, Stephen S. Roach, senior economist at Morgan Stanley & Co., stud-

ied the effect of interest rates on spending, and concluded that interest earned on investments would more than cover any drop in consumption caused by rising rates—a traditional view.

But he recently changed his mind. For one thing, the ratio of floating-rate assets to floating-rate debt, 7 to 1 in his first study, has since dropped to 3 to 1, meaning fewer people are earning more when rates rise. For another, "I just recently discovered that a large chunk of this so-called income isn't available to consumers when rates rise," he said. This is because what statisticians consider to be assets is often tied up in un-

touchable pension funds or insurance holdings.

"There is a relatively thin cushion of interest income and it will hurt spending," Mr. Roach said. He believes that "the extent of household resilience to interest rates is overblown.". . .
—*Pamela Sebastian*

SOURCE: *The Wall Street Journal*, March 14, 1989, p. A2. Reprinted by permission of *The Wall Street Journal*, © 1989 Dow Jones & Company, Inc. All Rights Reserved Worldwide.

USE YOUR ECONOMIC REASONING

1. **Rising interest rates apparently harm some households and benefit others. Explain.**
2. **What conclusions did Mr. Shilling's firm reach about the overall impact of rising interest rates on spending? How would you represent this impact graphically?**

The major reason for the rigidity of costs is long-term contracts. Contracts with labor unions, for example, are commonly renegotiated every three years. During the term of the agreement, wage rates are at least partially fixed. The prices paid for raw materials and manufactured inputs may also be governed by long term contracts. Because wage rates and other input prices are commonly fixed in the short run, businesses find it profitable to expand output when the selling prices of their products rise. This positive relationship between the overall price level and the economy's real GNP is reflected in the upsloping *AS* curve depicted in Exh. 14.4.

The Aggregate Supply Curve: A Closer Look

An example from microeconomics may help to illustrate why the *AS* curve is upward sloping. Consider the behavior of the competitive firm. Recall that in the model of pure competition the individual firm is a price taker; it must charge the price dictated by the market. But the firm can sell as much output as it chooses at that price. The firm will continue to expand output so long as the additional (marginal) revenue it will receive from selling an additional unit of output is greater than the additional (marginal) cost of producing that unit. When marginal cost is exactly equal to marginal revenue, the firm will be maximizing its profit (or minimizing its loss). This situation is represented in Exh. 14.5, which shows a firm that is initially maximizing its profit by producing an output of 1,000 units, the output dictated by the intersection of MR_1 and MC_1.

Now suppose the market price of the firm's product increases from \$10 to \$14. This would be represented by shifting the demand curve upward from D_1 to D_2. Note what happens to the firm's profit-maximizing output! It increases from 1,000 units to 1,200 units. The higher price provides incentive for the firm to expand output because the firm can earn a marginal profit on the additional units.

Note that it is not profitable for the firm to expand output indefinitely. Because the marginal cost curve is upward sloping, marginal cost will eventually increase enough to match the new price. Of course, production beyond that point will not be profitable. Why does *MC* increase as the firm expands its output? Why is the *MC* curve upward sloping? Think back to Chapter 5. In the short run, if the firm wants to produce more output it has to squeeze that production from its fixed factory. It does this by hiring more labor and using its factory and equipment more intensively. But this leads to more and more crowding of the fixed facility. Workers have to wait to use equipment; machines are subject to more frequent breakdowns; workers begin to get in one another's way, and so on. As a consequence, successive

EXHIBIT 14.5

Price Level Adjustments and the Individual Firm

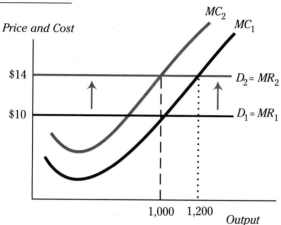

When the price of its product rises and input prices remain unchanged, the competitive firm responds by expanding output. Here, output is increased from 1,000 to 1,200 units when selling price rises from $10 to $14. However, if input prices rise by the same percent as the product price, MC will shift up from MC_1 to MC_2 and the profit-maximizing output will be unchanged.

units of output become more costly to produce; that is, marginal cost rises. Eventually, the cost of producing another unit will have increased enough to match the new product price. At that point, the output expansion will cease; the firm will have achieved its new profit-maximizing level of production.

It is essential to note that the firm would not have expanded output if wage rates and other input prices had increased along with the price of the firm's product. Proportionally higher wages and other input prices would have shifted the marginal cost curve up from MC_1 to MC_2. Note that MC_2 intersects MR_2 (the new, higher product price) at 1,000 units of output, the original profit-maximizing output. The higher input prices have completely offset the higher product price, eliminating any incentive to expand output. In the long run, this is precisely what we expect to happen, since contracts eventually expire and wage rates and other input prices are able to adjust upward. But in the short run, wage contracts and other rigidities provide a gap between product prices and production costs that makes it profitable for firms to expand output.

Changes in Aggregate Supply

The aggregate supply curve is upward sloping because there is a positive relationship between the general price level and the quantity of aggregate output supplied. This relationship assumes that the other factors that influence the amount of real GNP supplied are held constant. Changes in these other factors will cause a change in aggregate supply; the entire *AS* curve will shift to a new position. The factors that will shift the *AS* curve include changes in wage rates, changes in the prices of nonlabor inputs, and changes in labor productivity.

The Wage Rate

Suppose that the average wage rate paid by firms in the economy increases. What will that do to the *AS* curve? If it costs more to produce a given level of output, firms will require higher prices in order to produce that output, thus the *AS* curve must shift upward (leftward). This is represented in Exh. 14.6 by the movement of the aggregate supply curve from AS_1 to AS_2. Lower wages would have the opposite effect; they would tend to shift the *AS* curve

EXHIBIT 14.6

Shifts of the Aggregate Supply Curve

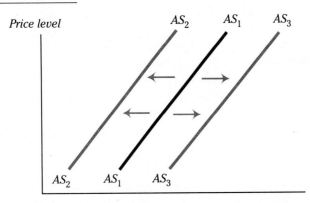

The AS *curve will shift upward (leftward) if there is a hike in wage rates, an increase in the prices of nonlabor inputs, or a reduction in labor productivity. It will shift downward (rightward) if wages or other input prices fall, or if labor productivity rises.*

downward (rightward), from AS_1 to AS_3. Remember that wage rates tend to be fixed by contract in the short term. But when these labor contracts expire, wage rates may be renegotiated up or down, causing the AS curve to shift.

The Prices of Nonlabor Inputs

Labor is only one of the resources required to produce output. Businesses also need capital equipment, raw materials, manufactured inputs, and managerial talent. Changes in the price of any of these inputs will tend to shift the position of the AS curve; increases will shift it upward, decreases will shift it downward.

Consider, for instance, the impact of the increase in the price of petroleum products resulting from Iraq's invasion of Kuwait in 1990. When crude oil prices increased, the cost of producing a given level of output rose, thus the AS curve shifted upward. Bad weather that reduced agricultural output could have a similar impact, since it would tend to increase the price of wheat, corn, and other agricultural products that are inputs in the production of breakfast cereals and other food items.

The Productivity of Labor

The cost of producing output is influenced not only by wage rates and other input prices but also by the productivity of labor—by how efficient labor is at transforming inputs into finished products. If the productivity of labor increases, the cost of producing the finished product tends to fall. Suppose that labor is paid $8 per hour and the average worker is able to produce 10 units of output per hour. The average labor cost of producing each unit of output is $ .80 ($8.00 per hour divided by 10 units per hour). Now suppose that due to improved training or new technology the average worker became able to produce 20 units of output per hour. The labor cost per unit of output would fall to $ .40 ($8.00 per hour divided by 20 units of output per hour). As you can see, an increase in labor productivity reduces the cost of producing a given level of output.

A variety of factors can influence the productivity of labor. If the labor force became more highly educated, we would expect its productivity to rise. An increase in the society's capital stock—its supply of factories and equipment—would also raise labor productivity; as employees work with more capital, they tend to produce more. A technological change that improved the quality of the capital equipment could also raise productivity. For instance, a faster computer will allow more work to be done per hour. In short, a variety of factors can raise productivity, but they all shift the AS curve downward and to the right.

Many Consumers Cut Spending in the Face of Middle East Crisis

George L. Price is a worried man.

"I've completely changed my spending habits. I'm not buying a new car. I've paid off all my bills. I'm starting to stockpile money," the American Airlines flight attendant in Dallas says. Given his seniority, he isn't concerned about job security, but he is pessimistic because "I see a big crash in the economy because of the Middle East. . . . I'm trying to be ready."

Most people interviewed in a nationwide survey by this newspaper aren't quite so worried, but Mr. Price is hardly the odd man out of the spending game. A lot of Americans are cautiously cutting back.

"I won't be purchasing anything except essentials," says Sue Hampton, a 59-year-old retiree in Los Angeles. Mrs. Hampton, who had planned to buy new carpeting and drapes, is holding off because, she says, it doesn't seem right to make "frivolous" purchases while lives are on the line. . . .

Cheerless Numbers

In November, the latest month for which Commerce Department figures are available, consumer spending increased only 0.1%, and it was flat in October. After adjustment for inflation, it fell in both months. December retail sales slipped 0.4% from a year earlier, and early-January sales of domestically built cars and light trucks plunged 31.3% from a year ago.

The slide in spending is largely due to a slide in confidence. The Conference Board's consumer confidence index, which is based on 1985 as 100, fell slightly in December to 61.3 from 61.7 in November but was far below a year-earlier reading of more than 113. The biggest drop came in October, during the budget debate, when it fell to 62.6 from 85.6 in September. Earlier, just after Iraq's Aug. 2 invasion of Kuwait, the index plunged to 83.8 in August from 101.7 in July.

Consumers reacted to the higher oil prices in the wake of the invasion as if the increases matched those in the late 1970s, even though they were only a third as large and oil now is less important in the economy, Roger E. Brinner, executive research director of DRI/McGraw-Hill, commented at a recent conference of the Mortgage Bankers Association of America. "The consumer has panicked," he said, adding that the drop in consumer confidence in one quarter equaled what usually takes two years.

Jobs are clearly a big worry. Of people surveyed in December by the Conference Board, a business-research organization, 34% expected few jobs to be available over the next six months, while only 10% anticipated more jobs. . . .

Not everyone, of course, is holding back. Carol Chua, who sells real estate in Los Angeles, isn't suspending any purchases and plans to go ahead with remodeling her house in the next two months. As for the war, she says, "I don't expect to be affected. I think it will be short term. I think we will be in and out of there. I don't think we will feel the impact." She is also thinking of buying a car. . . .

And the Mideast mess didn't prevent stockbroker Mitchell Eisenberg from skipping out on his lunch break to visit the weekly auction at a Sharper Image store in lower Manhattan. The 34-year-old jumped right in and spent $150 on a Panasonic compact-disc boom box. "It normally sells for $240," he says, showing it

off. He isn't worried about war. He has survived the cutbacks on Wall Street and feels sure that his job won't disappear. "I think without the war the economy would be in trouble. If there is a war, it could be good for the economy," he figures.

Many other Americans also see this as a good time to buy. Robert Snay, who builds automation control panels for Henshaw Electric in Mount Clemens, Mich., even sees a silver lining in the economic clouds. "It might be better for buying a house. People want to sell," says Mr. Snay, who feels secure in his job.

The world looks far different, predictably, to people who lack that assurance. In the past two months, Melanie

Smith, a 23-year-old Atlantan who is working part-time at a magazine store and in the mailroom of a bank, has been cutting back on meals at fast-food restaurants. She is also saving money—about $400 in the past few weeks. "You never know what will happen in a war," she says. "Prices may rise; people may lose jobs.". . . —*News Roundup*

SOURCE: *The Wall Street Journal,* January 19, 1991, p. 1. Reprinted by permission of *The Wall Street Journal,* © 1991 Dow Jones & Company, Inc. All Rights Reserved Worldwide.

USE YOUR ECONOMIC REASONING

1. **War often stimulates the economy. Why? How would you represent this effect graphically using the *AD/AS* model?**

2. **Based on the information contained in the article, what impact did the early stages of the conflict with Iraq appear to have on the U.S. economy? How would you explain this outcome?**

3. **Consumer confidence was clearly hurt by Iraq's invasion of Kuwait. Was there any economic justification for that reaction or was it purely psychological?**

Before continuing, let's review. We've seen that the aggregate demand curve shows the quantity of real GNP that will be demanded at each price level, whereas the aggregate supply curve shows the quantity of real GNP that will be supplied at each price level. The aggregate demand curve will shift to a new position if there is a change in the expectations of households or businesses, the level of aggregate wealth, or government policy. The aggregate supply curve will shift in response to a change in the wage rate, the prices of nonlabor inputs, or labor productivity. What impact did the Persian Gulf crisis of 1990–1991 have on our economy? The article on page 448, "Many Consumers Cut Spending in the Face of Middle East Crisis," looks at that issue.

The Equilibrium Output and Price Level

The interaction of aggregate demand and aggregate supply simultaneously determines the equilibrium price level and real GNP in the economy. This process is illustrated in Exh. 14.7, which shows the intersection of AS and AD resulting in an equilibrium price level of 100 and an equilibrium real GNP of $1,000 billion.

EXHIBIT 14.7

Equilibrium GNP and Price Level

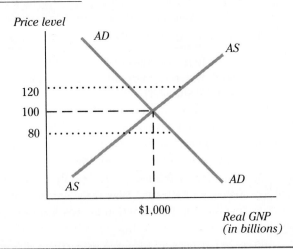

The intersection of the aggregate demand and supply curves determines the price level and the level of output in the economy. Here, the equilibrium real GNP is $1,000 billion and the equilibrium price level is 100.

As you can see in the graph, if the price level was initially above equilibrium (120, for example) the amount of real GNP supplied would exceed the amount of real GNP demanded. This would mean unsold merchandise and pressure to cut prices. The price level would decline until the amount of aggregate output demanded was equal to the amount supplied.

If the price level was initially below equilibrium (80, for instance) the result would be a shortage that would put upward pressure on prices until the equilibrium price level was achieved and the shortage was eliminated.

In summary, only at the equilibrium price level is the amount of real GNP demanded equal to the amount supplied. At any other price level, there will be an overall surplus or shortage that will tend to alter the prevailing price level.

The Impact of Changes in Aggregate Demand or Supply

In a dynamic economy, aggregate demand and supply change frequently. As these changes occur, the equilibrium price and output levels are disturbed and new levels are established. Suppose, for example, that less optimistic expectations caused businesses to cut back on investment spending. Since this would result in less output being demanded at any given price level, the aggregate demand curve would shift to the left. What impact would this have on the economy? As you can see in Exh. 14.8, when aggregate demand declines from AD_1 to AD_2, the level of real GNP in the economy contracts from $1,000 billion to $850 billion, while the overall price level falls from 100 to 90. Since the economy's ability to provide jobs is tied to the level of production, employment in the economy will also tend to fall (which means that, ceteris paribus, unemployment will rise).

If aggregate demand increased due to increased government spending, a tax cut, or some other spur to aggregate demand, the *AD* curve would shift to the right, from AD_1 to AD_3. This would result in higher output and employment, but would also push the price level upward.

Note that the impact of a change in aggregate demand when the *AS* curve is upward sloping is somewhat different from that predicted by the basic Keynesian model we analyzed in preceding chapters. The simple Keynesian model implies an *AS* curve that is flat because prices are assumed to be rigid until full employment is reached. This means that so long as excess capacity exists, any change in aggregate demand will alter output and em-

EXHIBIT 14.8

The Effects of Changes in Aggregate Demand on Real Output and Prices

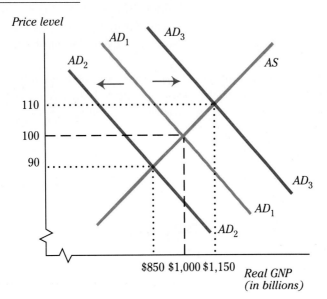

Decreases in aggregate demand will tend to lower the levels of output and employment in the economy while also reducing the overall price level. Increases in aggregate demand will tend to raise output and employment while raising the level of prices.

ployment without changing the price level. The modern aggregate-demand/ aggregate-supply framework provides for price flexibility, so it predicts a different outcome. A reduction in aggregate demand reduces real GNP while putting downward pressure on prices; increased aggregate demand raises output and employment, but also generates demand-side or ***demand-pull inflation.***

The differences between the predictions of the simple Keynesian model and the *AD/AS* model are important. They indicate that policies designed to combat unemployment or inflation do not have entirely beneficial results. Policies to combat unemployment cause inflation; policies to combat inflation cause unemployment.

The economy's equilibrium can also be disturbed by changes in aggregate supply. Suppose that aggregate supply decreased due to a supply shock such as an increase in the price of imported oil or a drought that raised grain prices. Exh. 14.9 shows that when aggregate supply falls from AS_1 to AS_2, the overall price level is driven up, while the equilibrium level of real GNP is reduced.

EXHIBIT 14.9

The Effects of Changes in Aggregate Supply on Real Output and Prices

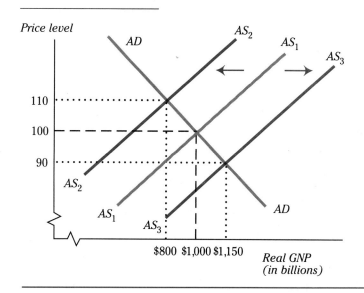

Decreases in aggregate supply will tend to lower the levels of output and employment in the economy while raising the overall price level. Increases in aggregate supply will tend to raise output and employment while lowering the level of prices.

In this instance the economy is experiencing supply-side or ***cost-push inflation***; higher production costs are pushing up prices. Although both demand-pull and cost-push inflation mean higher prices for consumers, cost-push inflation is doubly destructive because it is associated with falling real output. As you can see from Exh. 14.9, when the aggregate supply curve shifts to the left, the level of equilibrium real GNP falls from $1,000 billion to $850 billion. In short, cost-push inflation raises prices while lowering output and employment. This provides us with one possible explanation for the problem of stagflation, high unemployment combined with high inflation.

If reductions in aggregate supply are particularly harmful, increases in aggregate supply appear most beneficial. Suppose that aggregate supply expands due to an increase in labor productivity. As the *AS* curve shifts to the right (from AS_1 to AS_3 in Exh. 14.9), the price level is driven down *and* output and employment are expanded. It is these obviously desirable outcomes that led to a surge of interest in supply-side economics in the 1980s. Supply-siders promoted a variety of policies designed to enhance labor productivity and otherwise lower production costs in an attempt to increase aggregate supply. Chapter 15 will take a closer look at supply-side problems and remedies.

As the preceding discussion indicates, changes in aggregate demand or supply can lead to unemployment, inflation, or even stagflation. The next section examines the economy's response to these problems and considers the possibility that the economy contains a self-correcting mechanism.

The Model of the Self-Correcting Economy

As you will recall from Chapter 10, the classical economists believed in a self-correcting economy that always tended to operate at full employment. According to the classical model, Say's Law and interest rate flexibility would ensure that aggregate demand was always sufficient to maintain full employment. If these defenses somehow failed, reductions in aggregate demand would be quickly met by falling prices and wages, which would keep the economy operating at potential GNP.

When the Great Depression called the classical model into question, Keynes provided an alternative model to explain the widespread unemployment. According to Keynes, interest rate adjustments cannot be relied on to match up saving and investment plans and ensure adequate aggregate demand. Perhaps most important, Keynes did not believe that reductions in aggregate demand would lead to falling prices and wages. Instead, the rigidity of prices and wages would transform these downturns in aggregate demand into lower real GNP and unemployment.

Many economists argue that the crucial distinction between the classical and Keynesian models is their different assumptions about the behavior of prices and wages. Price-wage flexibility is the final line of defense in the classical model; without that assumption, hoarding can result in unemployment. The assumption of rigid prices and wages is equally important to Keynes; if prices and wages are highly flexible, falling demand does not pose a threat to the economy.

Given the importance of these assumptions, it is interesting to note that most modern economists see some validity in *both* the classical and Keynesian positions. In the short run, at least some prices and wages are inflexible as Keynes suggested, so reductions in aggregate demand can cause unemployment. But in the long run, all prices and wages become flexible. Thus reductions in aggregate demand must ultimately result in falling prices and wages, which return the economy to potential GNP and full employment.

The important conclusion of the foregoing discussion is that the economy does contain a self-correcting mechanism. To illustrate that mechanism, let's consider an economy that is presently operating at potential GNP and examine its short-run and long-run reactions to a change in aggregate demand. We will begin with an increase in aggregate demand and then consider a decrease.

Adjustments to an Increase in Aggregate Demand

Suppose that aggregate demand expands because the federal government reduces personal income taxes. Households now have more to spend, so they tend to demand more goods and services at each price level—the aggregate demand curve shifts to the right, from AD_1 to AD_2 in Exh. 14.10.

When aggregate demand increases, the resulting higher price level creates incentive for businesses to expand output. This incentive is provided by the fact that many of a business's costs—particularly wage rates—are fixed by long-term contracts. When product prices rise, these costs do not; thus firms stand to profit by expanding output. In our example, output

EXHIBIT 14.10

Adjusting to Higher Aggregate Demand

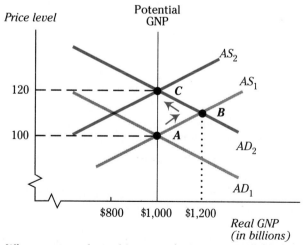

When aggregate demand increases, businesses initially find it profitable to expand output because wage rates and certain other costs are fixed by long-term contracts. Thus equilibrium real GNP expands beyond potential. But when these contracts expire and costs rise, the AS curve shifts upward and eventually reduces equilibrium output to the level of potential GNP.

will be increased up to the point where AS_1 is intersected by AD_2 (point B in Exh. 14.10), well beyond potential GNP.

It may seem contradictory to suggest that the economy can operate beyond its potential. The term "potential" is commonly interpreted to mean "maximum." But the meaning of potential is somewhat different in this context. Potential GNP is not the maximum output the economy is capable of producing, but the maximum *sustainable* level of production. Businesses can run factories beyond their designed or intended capacities for some period of time, and workers may be willing to work overtime. However, neither of these practices is sustainable; ultimately, equipment breaks down and employees become disgruntled and unproductive. But in the short run, these actions permit the economy to operate beyond its potential; that is, they allow actual GNP to exceed potential GNP.

As we've seen, businesses expand output beyond potential GNP because higher prices make it profitable for them to do so. But the higher prices that are attractive to businesses are bad news for employees. Workers find that they must pay more for the goods and services they buy, even though their wage rates are unchanged; thus their *real* wages—the purchasing power of their money wages—has declined.

Eventually firms will have to renegotiate their labor contracts. When that happens, workers will demand higher wages. Other input suppliers, also pressed by higher prices, will demand more for their resources. The result of the higher renegotiated input prices will be an upward shift of the aggregate supply curve. (Remember that a change in input prices will shift the AS curve.) Tight markets for labor and other inputs will put continuing upward pressure on wages and other input prices. The AS curve will continue to shift upward until workers and other input suppliers have regained their original purchasing power. This is represented in Exh. 14.10 by the shift from AS_1 to AS_2. Note that when contracts have been renegotiated, the incentive that originally motivated businesses to expand real output to $1,200 billion will have evaporated. Equilibrium real GNP will return to $1,000 billion (point C in the exhibit), the level of GNP consistent with the economy's potential output. The self-correcting forces have returned the economy to its potential GNP. As you can see, the long-run impact of the increase in aggregate demand is simply a higher price level, since the increase in production cannot be sustained.

Adjustments to a Decrease in Aggregate Demand

The economy's response to a reduction in aggregate demand is similar to its adjustments to an increase, but in the opposite direction. To illustrate, let's again assume the economy is operating at its potential GNP (at point A in

EXHIBIT 14.11

Adjusting to Lower Aggregate Demand

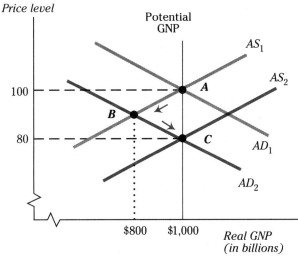

When aggregate demand declines, businesses initially find it necessary to reduce output because wage rates and certain other costs are fixed by long-term contracts. Thus equilibrium real GNP drops below potential. But when these contracts expire and costs fall, the AS curve shifts downward and eventually increases equilibrium output to the level of potential GNP.

Exh. 14.11). If aggregate demand fell from AD_1 to AD_2, firms would initially find their prices falling while some of their costs were fixed by long-term contracts. This would cause them to cut back on output (since output levels that had been profitable at a higher price level are no longer profitable) and reduce equilibrium GNP below potential. This is represented in Exh. 14.11 by the movement along AS_1 from A to B. Of course, when actual GNP falls below potential, the rate of unemployment rises above the full employment level.

Eventually, labor and other contracts will be renegotiated. At that point, the high unemployment rates and unused productive capacity of input suppliers will cause wages and other resource prices to fall. As that occurs, the AS curve will begin shifting to the right, eventually shifting from AS_1 to AS_2 (from B to C) and returning the economy to potential GNP and full employment. The long-run impact of the reduction in aggregate demand is a lower price level; output and employment have returned to their initial levels.

The preceding examples suggest that while the economy can deviate from potential GNP in the short run, these deviations are ultimately corrected, so that in the long run the economy tends to operate at potential GNP and full employment. If the economy always returns to full employment, is there any justification for government intervention to alter the economy's performance? Chapter 15 will address this issue as it considers the modern activist-nonactivist debate.

Summary

Economists use the concepts of aggregate demand and aggregate supply to represent the forces that determine the economy's equilibrium GNP and price level. *Aggregate demand* (*AD*) is the total quantity of output demanded by all sectors in the economy together at various price levels in a given period of time. The *aggregate demand curve* slopes downward and to the right, indicating that more real output will be demanded at a lower price level than at a higher price level. There are two reasons for the downward slope of the *AD* curve: the *real balance effect* and the *interest rate effect*. The factors that will shift the aggregate demand curve include changes in the expectations of households and businesses, changes in aggregate wealth, and changes in government policy.

Aggregate supply (*AS*) refers to the quantity of output supplied by all producers in the economy together at various price levels in a given period of time. The *aggregate supply curve* is upward sloping because higher price levels stimulate businesses to expand output. Since wage rates and some other input prices are commonly fixed by contracts, an increase in the price level provides incentive for firms to increase output. A given aggregate supply curve assumes the existing wage rates, prices of nonlabor inputs, and level of labor productivity. If any of these factors change, the *AS* curve will shift to a new position.

The intersection of the aggregate demand and supply curves simultaneously determines the level of equilibrium real GNP and the equilibrium price level in the economy. Shifts in aggregate demand or supply will tend to alter these equilibrium values. If aggregate demand increases, both real GNP and the price level will tend to increase. The economy enjoys higher levels of output and employment, but it experiences *demand-pull inflation*. If aggregate demand declines, the levels of output, employment, and prices decline.

Changes in equilibrium can also be caused by changes in aggregate supply. A supply shock such as an increase in the price of imported oil will tend to reduce aggregate supply. This will cause *cost-push inflation*, since the higher cost of oil pushes up prices. When aggregate supply is reduced, the levels of output and employment in the economy also decline. Supply shocks provide one possible explanation for *stagflation*, high unemployment combined with high inflation. If aggregate supply increased, the results would be doubly beneficial; the levels of output and employment in the economy would tend to increase, while the overall price level would decline.

Most modern economists agree that to some extent the economy contains a self-correcting mechanism. In the short run, the economy can deviate from potential GNP because certain wages and prices are rigid. In the long run, however, all wages and prices become flexible. As a consequence, reductions in aggregate demand are ultimately met by falling wages and input prices that cause aggregate supply to expand and return the economy to potential GNP. Increases in aggregate demand eventually lead to higher wages and input prices, which cause aggregate supply to contract and output and employment to fall. Thus wage and price adjustments ultimately return the economy to potential GNP and full employment.

Glossary

Page 436   ***Aggregate demand.*** The total quantity of output demanded by all sectors in the economy together at various price levels in a given time period.

Page 441   ***Aggregate supply.*** The total quantity of output supplied by all producers in the economy together at various price levels in a given time period.

Page 453   ***Cost-push inflation.*** Inflation caused by rising costs of production.

Page 452   ***Demand-pull inflation.*** Inflation caused by increases in aggregate demand.

Page 437   ***Interest rate effect.*** The increase in the amount of aggregate output demanded that results from the lower interest rates that accompany a reduction in the overall price level.

Page 437   ***Real balance effect.*** The increase in the amount of aggregate output demanded that results from an increase in the real value of the public's financial assets.

Page 453   ***Stagflation.*** High unemployment combined with high inflation.

Study Questions

Fill in the Blanks

1. The _____ curve shows the amount of real output that will be demanded at various price levels.

2. According to the _____ effect, an increase in the price level will reduce the purchasing power of financial assets and cause society to demand less real output.

3. Any change in the spending plans of consumers, businesses, or government that results from something other than a change in the _____ will shift the aggregate demand curve.

4. A broad-based technological advance will tend to shift the aggregate _____ _____ curve to the _____.

5. According to the interest rate effect, a reduction in the price level will tend to (increase/decrease) _____ the demand for money, which in turn will (increase/decrease) _____ the rate of interest and lead to (an increase/a reduction) _____ in the quantity of real output demanded.

6. Increases in the price level cause businesses to expand output because _____ _____ and other _____ prices are commonly fixed in the short run.

7. An increase in government spending will tend to shift the aggregate _____ _____ curve to the _____.

8. Cost-push inflation is caused by the aggregate _____ curve shifting to the (right/left) _____.

9. The term _____ is used to describe high inflation combined with high unemployment.

10. If the aggregate supply curve remains stationary, policymakers can reduce inflation if they are willing to accept higher _____.

Multiple Choice

1. The type of inflation caused by increased spending for goods and services is
   a) demand-pull inflation.
   b) cost-push inflation.
   c) structural inflation.
   d) expenditure inflation.

2. If a reduction in the price level causes more real output to be demanded, then
   a) the aggregate demand curve will shift to the right.
   b) the aggregate demand curve is downward sloping.
   c) the aggregate supply curve will shift to the right.
   d) the aggregate supply curve is downward sloping.

3. Which of the following will shift the aggregate demand curve to the left?
   a) An increase in government spending
   b) A reduction in labor productivity
   c) An increase in personal income taxes
   d) An increase in society's aggregate wealth

4. Which of the following will increase both the price level and real GNP?
   a) A nationwide drought that drives up the prices of agricultural products
   b) A reduction in government spending for goods and services
   c) A reduction in the money supply
   d) Greater optimism among business executives

5. In 1974, disease killed many anchovies and raised anchovy prices. Anchovies are used in cattle feed as a source of protein. The likely impact of this event would be to
   a) raise both the price level and real GNP.
   b) lower both the price level and real GNP.
   c) raise the price level, but lower real GNP.
   d) lower the price level, but raise real GNP.

6. According to the real balance effect,
   a) a reduction in the price level stimulates spending by lowering interest rates.

b) an increase in the money supply will shift the aggregate demand curve to the right.

c) an increase in the price level reduces spending by lowering the real value of society's financial assets.

d) an increase in society's aggregate wealth will shift the aggregate demand curve to the right.

7. An increase in the productivity of the labor force would be likely to
   a) shift the aggregate supply curve to the right.
   b) shift the aggregate supply curve to the left.
   c) shift the aggregate demand curve to the right.
   d) shift the aggregate demand curve to the left.

8. In the short run, an increase in the money supply will
   a) reduce both real GNP and the price level.
   b) reduce real GNP and increase the price level.
   c) increase both real GNP and the price level.
   d) increase real GNP and reduce the price level.

9. If the prevailing price level was initially below equilibrium,
   a) there would be a surplus of output.
   b) the price level would tend to fall.
   c) the amount of real GNP supplied would exceed the amount demanded.
   d) there would be a shortage of output.

10. Suppose Congress increased government spending at the same time that the price of imported oil (which is used to manufacture gasoline and heating oil) increased. In the short run, this would
    a) clearly increase both the price level and real GNP.
    b) clearly reduce both the price level and real GNP.
    c) clearly increase the price level, but the impact on real GNP is uncertain.
    d) clearly increase real GNP, but the impact on the price level is uncertain.

11. The aggregate supply curve is upward sloping
    a) due to the real balance effect and the interest rate effect.
    b) if all wages and input prices are flexible in the short run.
    c) because increases in the overall price level result in enhanced labor productivity and higher real output.
    d) because input price rigidities make it profitable for firms to expand output when product prices rise.

12. Suppose the economy is operating below potential GNP. According to the self-correcting model, the economy will ultimately return to potential because
    a) the Fed will expand the money supply.
    b) wages and resource prices will fall as contracts expire and are renegotiated.

c) workers will eventually demand higher wages, and resource suppliers will demand higher input prices.

d) aggregate demand will automatically increase enough to push the economy back to potential GNP.

13. When the overall price level rises,

a) businesses tend to reduce output because production becomes less profitable.

b) wage rates and other input prices tend to increase immediately, forcing businesses to cut back on production.

c) businesses have incentive to expand output because many costs are fixed by long-term contracts.

d) businesses may either increase or decrease output, depending on the magnitude of the hike in the price level.

14. According to the self-correcting model, if the economy is producing a level of output in excess of potential GNP,

a) potential GNP will automatically expand to match the actual level of production.

b) workers and input suppliers will eventually negotiate higher wages and prices, which will return the economy to potential GNP.

c) wages and input prices will ultimately fall, which will return the economy to potential GNP.

d) None of the above are correct; the economy cannot operate beyond potential GNP.

15. According to the self-correcting model,

a) unemployment can exist indefinitely.

b) the economy can never operate beyond potential GNP.

c) unemployment is eventually eliminated by falling wages and prices.

d) the economy always operates at potential GNP.

Problems and Questions for Discussion

1. Explain in detail why the aggregate demand curve is downward sloping.

2. Given a stationary aggregate supply curve, policymakers should be able to reduce unemployment if they are willing to accept higher inflation. Explain and supplement your explanation with a graph.

3. What role do contracts play in explaining the upward slope of the aggregate supply curve?

4. Suppose that, on average, wage rates increase less than the increase in labor productivity. What will happen to the overall price level and real GNP? Explain how you arrived at your conclusion.

5. When we use the aggregate-demand/aggregate-supply framework to predict the impact of an increase in government spending, we reach somewhat different conclusions from those obtained when we use the total expenditures model (the basic Keynesian model employed in Chapters 11 and 12). Why are the conclusions different? Would policymakers find these differences important?

6. Explain the difference between demand-pull and cost-push inflation. Use aggregate demand and supply curves to show how each problem would be represented graphically.

7. Suppose the economy is in equilibrium at potential GNP and that policymakers increase aggregate demand (perhaps because they do not recognize that the economy is operating at potential). Discuss the short-run and long-run impact of this change. Supplement your answer with graphs.

8. Consider the short-run impact of the changes listed below. Which changes would cause the economy's price level and real GNP to move in the same direction (both increase, both decrease) and which would cause the price level and real GNP to move in opposite directions (increasing the price level, but reducing real output, for example)? After you have worked through the list, see if you can draw any general conclusions.
   a) An increase in government spending
   b) A severe frost which destroys crops
   c) A large decline in the stock market
   d) An increase in labor productivity
   e) An increase in consumer optimism
   f) Higher prices for imported raw materials

9. Suppose that government spending in support of education were increased. Would this action shift the aggregate demand curve, the aggregate supply curve, or both curves? What would happen to the price level and real GNP?

10. Assume the economy is in short-run equilibrium at less than full employment. Describe the forces that will ultimately return the economy to potential GNP.

Answer Key

Fill in the Blanks

1. aggregate demand
2. real balance
3. price level
4. supply, right

5. decrease,
   decrease,
   an increase
6. wage rates, input

7. demand, right
8. supply, left
9. stagflation
10. unemployment

Multiple Choice

1. a	4. d	7. a	10. c	13. c
2. b	5. c	8. c	11. d	14. b
3. c	6. c	9. d	12. b	15. c

THE ACTIVIST-
NONACTIVIST DEBATE

What are the policy implications of the self-correcting model? If the economy tends to operate at potential GNP and full employment, is there any reason for government intervention to guide the economy's performance? Can demand-management policies be used to speed the adjustment to full employment, or do such policies have a destabilizing effect on the economy? These are the issues that will concern us in this chapter.

As you can see, we have returned to the activist-nonactivist debate that we first encountered in Chapter 10. Just as Keynes and the classical economists disagreed about the advisability of government intervention to guide our economy, today's neo-Keynesians disagree with monetarists and new classical economists (also known as rational expectations theorists). This chapter will introduce you to the views of these competing schools of thought and examine the modern debate about demand-management policies. It will also take a brief look at supply-side economics. We turn first to a short review of the Keynesian, or activist, position.

The Activist Position: Keynes Revisited

As you learned in Chapters 10 and 11, Keynes did not believe that capitalist economies necessarily tend to full employment. Rather, he argued that because of the volatility of spending, particularly investment spending, they could be in equilibrium at a level of output either less or greater than potential GNP. If business executives were pessimistic, they might choose to cut back on investment spending, sending the economy into a tailspin and causing unemployment. If they were optimistic about the future, they might choose to expand investment spending, pushing GNP above potential and causing inflation.

Keynes was an activist economist in the sense that he advocated government action to prevent outbreaks of unemployment or inflation, and to combat these problems should they occur. According to Keynes, the central government should use fiscal and monetary policies to ensure sufficient aggregate demand to achieve full employment without inflation.

Fiscal policy, you will recall, is the manipulation of government spending and/or taxation in order to guide the economy's performance. The appropriate Keynesian fiscal policy for a period of unemployment would be to increase government spending for goods and services, or to reduce taxes. These policies would expand aggregate demand, raise the equilibrium GNP, and lower unemployment. Inflation calls for reductions in government spending or higher taxes. By reducing aggregate demand, these policies will reduce inflationary pressures.

Monetary policy—deliberately changing the money supply to influence the level of economic activity—can also be used to combat unemployment or inflation. If unemployment exists, then the Federal Reserve (recall that the Federal Reserve is the government agency that regulates the money supply) can increase the money supply in order to drive down the market rate of interest. The lower interest rate will tend to stimulate investment spending and certain forms of consumption spending. By stimulating aggregate demand in this manner, monetary policy can raise equilibrium GNP and lower unemployment. Inflation can be attacked by reducing the money supply and thereby raising the prevailing rate of interest. A higher interest rate will cause businesses and consumers to cut back on their borrowing (and spending) and reduce inflationary pressures.

Even if fiscal and monetary policies work in the manner Keynesians suggest, why would anyone consider using them? If the economy is self-correcting in the long run, why not let it take care of itself? In describing the problems posed by an unemployment equilibrium, the neo-Keynesian response echoes that of Keynes himself more than 50 years ago: "In the long run, we are all dead!" The adjustment process described in the last chapter takes time, perhaps a substantial period of time. In the interim, society loses output that will never be regained, individuals suffer the humiliation of being without work, and families deplete their savings or go on welfare. In short, unemployment is costly and the losses incurred as we wait for self-correction may be unacceptable.

Production above potential also imposes costs on society. As we saw in the last chapter, when equilibrium GNP exceeds potential, the price level is pushed up generating inflation. While society benefits from the additional output and employment, unanticipated inflation tends to redistribute income in an arbitrary way. Moreover, the long-run adjustment process will ultimately eliminate the short-term gain in output and leave the economy with a still higher price level.

In summary, Keynesians believe that capitalist economies are inherently unstable so they are always in danger of operating either above or below potential GNP. While the economy will ultimately return to potential GNP, waiting for this long-run adjustment to occur is needlessly costly to society. Instead, fiscal and monetary policies should be used to prevent deviations from potential GNP or to minimize their duration should they occur.

The Nonactivist Position: The Monetarists

Not all economists agree with the activist or neo-Keynesian position. The two major groups, or schools, of nonactivist economists are the monetarists and the new classical economists (rational expectations theorists). We will begin by examining the monetarist position.

Monetarism is the belief that changes in the money supply play the primary role in determining the level of aggregate output and prices in the economy. Economists who hold this belief are called *monetarists*.

According to monetarists, an increase in the money supply will tend to stimulate consumption and investment spending, raising equilibrium output and the price level; a reduction in the money supply will have the opposite effect. Keynesians agree that changes in the money supply can alter output and prices, but they emphasize that other factors—changes in autonomous investment or government spending, for instance—can also influence the economy. Monetarists tend to see these other factors as decidedly secondary; changes in the money supply are what really matter.

Fiscal Policy and Crowding Out

The paramount importance that monetarists attach to the money supply is illustrated by their criticism of Keynesian fiscal policy. According to monetarists, fiscal policy is ineffective unless it is accompanied by monetary policy. To illustrate this view, let's suppose the economy is suffering from unemployment, and Congress decides to increase government spending to combat the problem. What will happen? The monetarists believe that if the money supply is not increased, government borrowing to finance the larger deficit will drive up the interest rate and discourage, or crowd out, investment spending. In an economy with more government spending but less investment spending, the net effect will be no stimulus to the economy. However, if the Federal Reserve were to allow the money supply to expand while the government borrowed, it *would* be possible to provide some net stimulus to the economy. The interest rate would not be bid up, so investment spending would not be discouraged; thus total spending would actually expand. Monetarists are quick to point out that the stimulus in this situation results from the increase in the money supply, not from the added government spending.

Monetary Policy and the Monetary Rule

Because monetarism focuses attention on the money supply, eager students sometimes conclude that monetarists must favor the use of discretionary monetary policy to guide the economy's performance. But that's not the case. Monetarists believe that changes in the money supply are too important to be left to the discretion of policymakers. Instead, they support a *monetary rule* that would require the Federal Reserve to expand the money supply at a constant rate, something like 3 percent a year.[1]

If the Fed were required to increase the money supply at a constant annual rate, it would no longer be free to use changes in the money supply as a policy tool; it could not increase the money supply more rapidly

---

[1] Monetarists believe the money supply should be expanded at 3 percent a year because they think potential GNP expands at about that rate. If sustainable output is growing at 3 percent a year, a 3 percent larger money supply is needed in order to facilitate this greater volume of transactions. But whether we choose to increase the money supply at 3 percent or 4 percent or 6 percent is not too important, so long as we pick *some* rate and stick with it. If the money supply is growing more rapidly than the economy's ability to produce output, inflation will result. But it will be a reasonably constant rate of inflation, so we will know what to expect and will be able to build it into our wage agreements and other contracts. Thus it will not tend to redistribute income the way that unanticipated inflation does.

Milton Friedman, shown here accepting his Nobel prize in economics, would like to see the Federal Reserve adhere to a monetary rule.

to combat unemployment or slow the growth of the money supply to combat inflation. In other words, a monetary rule would eliminate the possibility of the Keynesian monetary policies described in Chapter 14. In a sense, the Fed would be put on autopilot. Monetarists favor this approach because they are convinced that the Fed's attempts to combat unemployment or inflation have often made things worse rather than better.

Policy Lags and the Self-Correcting Economy

According to the monetarists, it is time lags that tend to make Keynesian monetary policies counterproductive. Obviously, Fed policymakers cannot take action until they recognize that a problem exists. Unfortunately, the economy commonly sends mixed signals about its performance. For this reason there is a *recognition lag* before agreement is reached that a problem exists. Even after the problem is recognized and policymakers take action, there will be an *impact lag* before the effect on spending is felt in the economy. Moreover, once the policy does begin to influence spending, the effect will continue for some time. (See "Democracy Comes to the Central Bank, Curbing Central Chief's Power" on page 472 for an illustration of the lags associated with monetary policy.)

The existence of lags would not be a major argument against discretionary monetary policy if the economy tended to remain in an unemployment or inflationary equilibrium indefinitely. But that's not what happens. As our discussion of the self-correcting mechanism indicates, the economy ultimately begins to solve its own problems. When we recognize this self-correcting tendency, lags can mean trouble for policymakers. To illustrate, suppose that the economy gradually weakens and begins to experience a recession. Fed policymakers eventually recognize the problem and take action to expand the money supply. But if the recognition and impact lags are long enough, the economy may begin to recover on its own before these policies start to take effect. That means monetary policy may begin to stimulate spending when such stimulus is no longer welcome. Of course, too much spending can lead to inflation, which is precisely what monetarists believe has happened on several occasions.

In summary, monetarists shun discretionary monetary policy because they believe it often has a destabilizing effect on the economy—creates additional problems—rather than the stabilizing effect that Keynesians predict. In fact, monetarists believe that government tinkering with the money supply may be the major destabilizing force in the economy. For example, Milton Friedman—who is sometimes referred to as the father of monetarist economics—argues that it was inept monetary policy that caused the Great Depression. According to Friedman, the Fed turned what could have been a serious downturn into a major catastrophe by allowing the money supply to fall substantially in the early 1930s. He contends that a policy of stable money growth would have been vastly superior.[2]

Monetarism: Concluding Points

Perhaps the major source of disagreement between neo-Keynesians and monetarists is about the nature of economy. Like Keynes, neo-Keynesians tend to see the economy as inherently unstable and relatively slow to recover from demand and supply shocks. Monetarists, on the other hand, believe that the economy is fundamentally stable and returns fairly rapidly to potential GNP whenever deviations occur. If it persists in deviating from potential GNP, it is due to government tinkering, not to the nature of the economy.

Monetarists emphasize that eliminating the Fed's ability to tinker with the money supply would not completely eliminate unemployment or inflation. Fluctuations in spending would still occur, and some unemployment or inflation would result. But the adoption of a monetary rule would eliminate the major source of fluctuations in spending—fluctuations in the growth of the money supply—and would therefore tend to minimize any unemployment or inflation.

[2] Milton Friedman, "The Case for a Monetary Rule," *Newsweek*, February 7, 1972. Reprinted in M. Friedman, *Bright Promises, Dismal Performance: An Economist's Protest*, published by Thomas Horton and Daughters, 1983.

Democracy Comes to the Central Bank, Curbing Chief's Power

He Can't Shift Course as Fast; Heads of District Banks, Governors Grow Assertive

A Delay in Fighting Recession

WASHINGTON—In the war to liberate the U.S. economy from recession, the key skirmish was fought behind closed doors in the Federal Reserve Board's paneled conference room last Oct. 2.

The Fed's policy committee, meeting as always in secret, was arguing over whether and how much to reduce interest rates. The doves on the panel wanted to cut rates substantially to help the economy. The hawks, determined to fight inflation and still uncertain a recession was at hand, were resisting such a move.

Fed Chairman Alan Greenspan sided with the doves. His proposal was two separate, quarter-point cuts in short-term interest rates. But the hawks would have none of it: They revolted.

After a heated discussion, they forced Mr. Greenspan to retreat. The panel approved only a single quarter-point

drop in short-term interest rates. What's more, the change would be delayed until Congress worked out a new budget-cutting deal—which, as it turned out, was nearly a month later.

It was a startling defeat for Alan Greenspan. With the economy in truble, monetary policy, a potent stimulus, was put on hold for four critical weeks. Credit remained costly. Layoffs mounted. Instead of combating the recession, the Fed's lack of action exacerbated it.

"Greenspan got behind," says Paul Samuelson, the Nobel prize-winning economist. "He's got three or four colleagues who are [anti-inflation] zealots, and he didn't lean on them. You can't be both a good guy and a powerful leader. He was a good guy."

This is life at the new Fed, where the tradition of all-powerful chairmen such as Paul Volcker and Arthur Burns is now a memory. In the last few years, democracy has invaded one of the last bastions of authoritarianism in

the U.S. A sort of *perestroika* has come to the Federal Reserve.

Price of Democracy

There is little doubt these changes move the Fed—long attacked for being arrogant and autocratic—closer to the finest traditions of American governance. Fed officials are unanimous in praising the new spirit of democracy, arguing that it makes for better policy and a more rewarding place to work. "It's now a more collegial group," says Wayne Angell, one of the Fed's governors, "rather than a schoolmarm lecturing third graders."

But there is a price—particularly when the economy is changing rapidly. The new Fed is more cumbersome. The chairman can't rule with Olympian disdain; he must coax rather than command. Forming a consensus isn't always easy and, as the events of last October illustrate, lengthy debates can have serious consequences for the economy.

"Democracy," says Martha Seger, who recently resigned as a Fed governor, "is messier than dictatorship."

For his part, Mr. Greenspan, a former Wall Street economist, shrugs off the October delay. "There is no evidence of which I am aware that suggests accelerating or delaying policy actions by a matter of weeks has any material effect on the outcome," he said. "It is the cumulative thrust of policy that matters.

Moreover, he argues that the best way to manage the central bank is to tolerate different points of view. "The Fed cannot effectively be run by executive fiat. If the Fed chief executive officer cannot persuade his colleagues of the rightness of his policies and recommendations, he cannot prevail." . . .

These days, keeping the Fed on track requires considerable skills of persuasion. Notably, the presidents of the district Fed banks have assumed a powerful new voice in policy. These officials, based in outside-the-Beltway outposts such as Richmond, Minneapolis and Dallas, have become vanguards in the war on inflation. That frequently pits them against the Fed governors who tend to favor easier credit.

His supporters say Mr. Greenspan balances these conflicting interests with skill and that he usually, though not always, gets his way on major issues. Mr. Greenspan himself says that in his 3½ years as chairman, "I cannot recall an important decision which I personally felt was wrong."

The chairman's detractors, on the other hand, worry that he is sometimes blown about by prevailing winds. At the White House, there is even more talk of replacing him when his term expires in August, although top administration officials say he probably will be reappointed.

One thing is clear: The Federal Reserve under Alan Greenspan has changed, and changed dramatically, as was evident at the Oct. 2 meeting. . . . —*Alan Murray*

SOURCE: *The Wall Street Journal*, April 5, 1991, p. 1. Reprinted by permission of *The Wall Street Journal*, © 1991 Dow Jones & Company, Inc. All Rights Reserved Worldwide.

USE YOUR ECONOMIC REASONING

1. **What was the source of the disagreement between Mr. Greenspan and those who opposed his policy moves?**

2. **Recall the two types of lags involved in monetary policy. Which type is illustrated by this article?**

3. **The monetarists believe that lags such as those illustrated here can cause monetary policy to be counterproductive. Why?**

Criticisms of Monetarism

Neo-Keynesian economists disagree with monetarists on several basic points. First, Keynesians believe that monetarists attach too much importance to the money supply. While Keynesians agree that changes in the money supply can alter GNP, they argue that other factors are also important—perhaps even more important. These factors include changes in the level of planned investment or government spending. Keynesians believe that such autonomous changes can lead to inflation or unemployment even if the money supply expands at a constant rate. For instance, Keynesians argue that pessimism about the future might cause businesses to cut back on investment, and this might lead to unemployment even if the money supply continues to expand at a steady rate.

Second, although virtually all Keynesians agree with monetarists that crowding out reduces the effectiveness of fiscal policy, Keynesians believe that only a small amount of investment spending will normally be crowded out, so expansionary fiscal policy can still have a significant impact on equilibrium GNP.

But many modern Keynesians are quite critical of the long lags involved in implementing changes in taxation and government spending. Since the lags in implementing monetary policy are generally shorter than the lags in implementing fiscal policy (though pro-rule monetarists argue that they are still too long), monetary policy is seen as the primary technique for stabilizing the economy.

Third, Keynesians are critical of the monetary rule because they believe it could contribute to greater, rather than less, unemployment and inflation. Because Keynesians believe the economy is *inherently* unstable (due to the volatility of investment spending), they argue that Fed policymakers need discretion to be able to offset fluctuations in spending and maintain full employment without inflation.

The Nonactivist Position: The New Classical Economists

As you probably noted, monetarists have much in common with the classical economists we discussed in Chapter 10. Both groups see the economy as fundamentally stable, and believe in laissez-faire. But another school of modern economists has even more in common with the original classical theorists, so much so that this school has been dubbed the "new" classical school of economics.

The new classical economics is based on two fundamental beliefs- (1) wages and prices are highly flexible, and (2) expectations about the future are formed "rationally." The remainder of this section will investigate the implications of those beliefs.

Wage/Price Flexibility and Full Employment

Like the classical theorists of old, the economists of the new classical school (of which the most prominent members are Robert Lucas of Chicago, Thomas Sargent of Stanford, and Robert Barro of Harvard) believe that wages and prices are highly flexible. This flexibility permits markets to adjust quickly to changes in supply or demand, so shortages or surpluses are prevented. In short, highly flexible prices ensure that the quantity of the good or service demanded will equal the quantity supplied; markets will "clear."

New classical economists believe that the market clearing principle applies not only to individual markets—the markets for shoes or cars or accountants, for instance—but to the aggregate economy as well. Its implications for the overall labor market are particularly important. To illustrate, let's suppose that the economy experiences a decline in aggregate demand. Of course, when the overall demand for products declines, the demand for labor must also fall. But the new classical economists do not believe that this reduction in labor demand will result in unemployment. Because wages are highly flexible, the reduced level of labor demand will cause wages to drop. Lower wage rates will both encourage employers to hire more workers and reduce the amount of labor supplied (at the lower wage, some workers will prefer leisure to work). The reduction in wages will thus restore equilibrium in the labor market; everyone who is willing to work at the new lower wage will find employment, and every employer who is willing to pay that wage will find workers.[3] Any unemployment must be voluntary.

The Importance of Expectations

The belief in highly flexible wages and prices and the voluntary nature of unemployment is not new; this view was held by the original classical economists. But the new classical economists are not clones of the originals; they have made their own distinctive contribution to economic thinking. The dis-

---

[3] The new classical economists do not believe that labor contracts make wages so inflexible as to prevent these adjustments.

tinctive feature of the new classical economics is its focus on expectations and the way that expectations influence people's behavior.

These economists remind us that different expectations about the future can lead to different decisions today. For instance, if consumers expect new car prices to be lower in a few months, they will probably wait to buy; if they expect prices to be higher, they will buy now. These are commonsense observations that few of us would challenge. But the new classical economists go well beyond these observations. They are interested in how expectations are formed; in other words, they want to know how individuals come to expect whatever they expect—higher car prices, lower interest rates, or more rapid inflation, for instance.

Keynesians and monetarists disagree about many things, but both groups have assumed that individuals base their expectations only on experience—by looking backward at past events. The new classical economists argue that this assumption implies individuals are irrational because it presumes they ignore current events that they know will influence the future. As an alternative, the new classical economists have proposed the theory of rational expectations.

The *theory of rational expectations* suggests that people use all available information to develop realistic (rational) expectations about the future. According to this theory, the public is quite perceptive in forming its expectations. Households and businesses do not merely project past trends into the future; they also take current economic developments quickly into account.

For instance, when forecasting inflation, people will consider the inflation of recent years, but they will also consider the potential impact of upcoming labor negotiations, the rate of productivity growth, the anticipated quality of agricultural harvests (and their impact on food prices), developments in the Middle East (and their impact on oil prices), and—perhaps most important of all—the expected government response to inflation.

Rational Expectations and Discretionary Policy

The belief that wages and prices are highly flexible and that expectations are formed "rationally," leads the members of the new classical school to some interesting policy conclusions. According to the new classical economists, *systematic* monetary and fiscal policies cannot alter the level of output or employment in the economy; they can only change the price level. This belief is known as the *policy ineffectiveness theorem.* The implications of the policy ineffectiveness theorem are clear: government attempts to reduce unemployment are doomed to failure; they will result only in inflation.

The problem, according to the new classical theorists, is that systematic policies whereby the government always responds to a particular set of economic conditions in a given way are *predictable*. But if discretionary policies are predictable, individuals will anticipate those policies and alter their behavior in ways that make the policies ineffective. Thus individuals, *acting on rational expectations*, make government stabilization policies ineffective.

To illustrate, let's suppose that historically the Fed has expanded the money supply whenever the measured unemployment rate reached 8 percent.[4] Now let's assume the unemployment rate reaches that magic number and the Fed feels compelled to take action. Of course, when the money supply is expanded, the aggregate demand curve will shift to the right as depicted in Exh. 15.1 by the movement from AD_1 to AD_2. This increase in aggregate demand would, ceteris paribus, tend to raise the level of output in the economy. In our example, output would be expanded from the original equilibrium of $900 billion to $1,000 billion (the intersection of AS_1 and AD_2). Because increased output normally means additional jobs, employment would also tend to expand.

But supporters of the theory of rational expectations believe that the assumption of ceteris paribus is unreasonable in this situation. They argue that workers and businesses have learned to anticipate the Fed's policy response to unemployment. Moreover, they have discovered that when the money supply is increased, inflation inevitably follows. (Note that the increase in aggregate demand pushes up the price level along with the level of output.) So when the public perceives that the Fed is likely to increase the money supply, it takes actions to protect itself from the anticipated inflation. Workers ask for higher wages; suppliers raise their input prices, and businesses push up product prices. Because prices and wages are assumed to be highly flexible, these adjustments occur immediately, the moment the public anticipates higher prices. Of course, if wage rates and other costs rise, the aggregate supply curve will tend to shift upward (from AS_1 to AS_2 in Exh. 15.1), so less real output will be supplied at any given price level. Since the

---

[4] How can the unemployment rate reach 8 percent if wages and prices are highly flexible? According to the new classical economists, this can occur as a result of *unexpected* shocks in aggregate demand or supply—reductions in planned investment, the outbreak of war, or significant crop failures, for instance. Because these events are unexpected, they may be misperceived by workers. For instance, if the economy experiences a reduction in aggregate demand, some workers may mistakenly assume that the downturn has affected only their industry. Equally important, they may fail to recognize that the overall price level has also fallen, so the real wage—the purchasing power of their money wage—is unchanged. Suffering from these misperceptions, they are unhappy with their lower money wage. Thus workers quit their jobs and set out in search of a position that pays as much as they are accustomed to earning. In this way, an unexpected shock may lead to unemployment.

EXHIBIT 15.1

Rational Expectations and Economic Policy

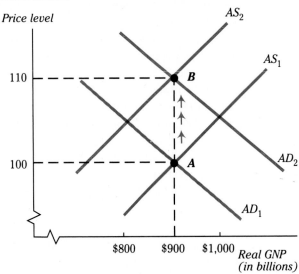

According to the theory of rational expectations, anticipated changes in monetary or fiscal policies cannot alter the level of output or employment; they can only change prices. In this example, the expansionary monetary policy that shifts the aggregate demand curve from AD₁ *to* AD₂ *is anticipated, causing workers to ask for higher wages and suppliers to ask for higher input prices. These changes cause the* AS *curve to shift upward from* AS₁ *to* AS₂ *, neutralizing the output effect of the monetary expansion and raising the overall price level.*

government-mandated increase in aggregate demand has been immediately offset by a *reduction* in aggregate supply, the net effect is to leave output and employment unchanged. The only impact of the expansionary monetary policy has been an increase in the price level from 100 to 110.

The preceding example focused on efforts to combat unemployment, but the theory of rational expectations has equally interesting implications for the the battle against inflation. To illustrate, let's suppose that the inflation rate rises to some level that Fed policymakers have openly designated as unacceptable. According to the theory of rational expectations, if the public is convinced of the Fed's commitment to reducing inflation, it will expect lower inflation; so workers will immediately accept wage cuts and input suppliers will accept lower prices. As a consequence, the *AS* curve will quickly shift downward, lowering the price level but preserving the same level of output and employment. Once again, discretionary policy alters only the price level; it has no impact on real output or the level of employment. (Note that this result is quite different from the effect predicted by neo-Keynesians. Neo-Keynesians would argue that because *some* wages and prices are rigid due to contracts, a reduction in aggregate demand would lower both the *overall* price level and the levels of output and employment. In fact, a major concern of neo-Keynesians has been the unemployment "cost" of combating inflation.) While these examples have dealt with monetary policy, the same conclusions would hold for systematic applications of fiscal policy.

The Need for Policy Rules

What conclusions can we reach from the preceding examples? The primary conclusion is that systematic monetary and fiscal policies affect only the price level; they do not alter either the level of output or employment. Of course, in order for discretionary policies to have the effect intended by neo-Keynesians they must be systematic; it wouldn't make sense to expand the money supply or cut taxes at random time intervals. So, in effect, the new classical economists are arguing that discretionary monetary and fiscal policies cannot be used to reduce unemployment.

Because the new classical economists are convinced that government policies cannot be used to alter employment, they believe that policymakers should concentrate on achieving and maintaining a low rate of inflation. This, they suggest, can be best accomplished by permitting a slow, steady growth of the money supply and avoiding large budget deficits. Thus the new classical economists favor rules much like the monetarists': increase the money supply at a constant rate, and balance the federal budget over some agreed-on period (not necessarily on an annual basis, but over some predictable time frame). These rules will prevent government policymakers from aggravating inflation in their well-intentioned but futile attempts to lower unemployment. (One of President Bush's economists strongly supports rules; is he a new classical economist? See "A Bush Economist is Urging Hands Off" on page 480.)

Criticisms of the New Classical Economics

The new classical economics is quite controversial. Both the assumption of wage/price flexibility and the assumption of rational expectations have been criticized. Few economists seem willing to accept the assertion that wages are sufficiently flexible to ensure that labor markets are constantly in equilibrium. These economists point to the prolonged unemployment of the Great Depression and periods in the 1970s and 1980s as evidence that wages adjust slowly, not rapidly as the new classical model implies.

A Bush Economist Is Urging Hands Off
The Outlook

WASHINGTON—Just when economists are finally being taken seriously in Washington again, those closest to the president are telling him: "Sorry, sir, but the government really can't do much to steer the economy."

If the economy slides into recession, they say, the government shouldn't prop it up with a big public-works program. And, they add, if the Federal Reserve knows what's best, it will worry less about the ups and downs of the economy and more about the long-run goal of reducing inflation.

In language resembling the warning on a cigarette pack, the President's Council of Economic Advisers declares that such attempts to guide the economy "can be detrimental to good economic performance." Instead, the three-member council argues, "policies should be designed to work well with a minimum of discretion."

The man behind this manifesto is John Taylor, the council's macro-economist. He spent years at Stanford University gleaning insights from economists who argue that government economic policy can do zilch (in the short run, at least). Now, Mr. Taylor is trying to practice what he teaches.

His advice to Mr. Bush and Fed Chairman Alan Greenspan: Declare clear and credible goals, devise rules (such as the Gramm-Rudman deficit-reduction law) to reach those goals and deviate from the declared path infrequently.

This is a striking contrast to the days when John F. Kennedy's economists told him that he could, and should, pull the tax and spending strings to control the economy. In those days, John Maynard Keynes rated a *Time* magazine cover.

"Discretionary policy is essential," the council insisted in 1962, proposing to give the president the power to spend as much as $2 billion and to cut taxes temporarily at times of rising employment, as well as the power to reverse course quickly.

Now, that's passe. "Recent economic research and practical experience" show that trying to manage the economy that way is a mistake, Mr. Taylor says, adding that economists don't know enough soon enough to pull the right strings at the right moment.

Not surprisingly, one of the economists who wrote that 1962 report, Nobel laureate James Tobin of Yale University, scoffs at such assertions. "I don't think anything like that has been proved at all," he says.

The economists from whom Mr. Taylor draws inspiration, like Milton Friedman before them, keep urging the Fed not to try to guide the economy around the rough spots. Mr. Taylor differs, admitting that monetary policy still requires much more discretion than simple, fixed rules allow.

In fact, the past decade can be viewed as a triumph of the very sort of fine-tuning of the economy that such economists as Mr. Taylor deplore. After breaking the back of inflation at the beginning of the decade, the Fed has pushed and pulled on interest rates to keep the economy growing for more than seven years without either a recession or a resurgence of inflation.

"For modest fluctuations in the economy, you don't need discretionary fiscal policy as much as we thought you did in the past," concedes Charles Schultze, one of Jimmy Carter's economists and not one of Mr. Taylor's intellectual bedfellows. But the Fed's power to pilot the economy turns out to [be] far greater than he figured.

All this isn't merely an academic argument. Economists were largely ignored at the Reagan White House. But President Bush listens to them. The council is once more a player. Indeed, the influence of economists such as Mr. Taylor is changing the rhetoric and providing intellectual underpinnings for Mr. Bush's economic policy. At the Fed, for instance, the importance of striving for a policy that has credibility is stressed, and the word pops up with a frequency once reserved for "money supply."

In fact, hard-liners at the Fed often borrow from Mr. Taylor and like-minded economists when they say the Fed can reduce inflation to zero without a recession. Once the public believes the Fed is serious, it's argued, the public's behavior will change— inflationary expectations will drop—and the Fed's job will be easier.

With the enthusiastic backing of his boss, Chairman Michael Boskin, Mr. Taylor presses his approach within the administration at every opportunity. He defends Mr. Bush's "no new taxes" pledge as the sort of guiding principle that the government should espouse, and he sees no conflict between this and the administration's proclaimed goal of reducing the budget deficit. "A strong, credible promise to hold the line on taxes is actually better for the deficit," since by limiting revenues it keeps spending under control, he maintains. (Critics, Mr. Tobin included, reply that raising taxes would be far more credible.). . .

The economists' song is far different than the one they sang to President Kennedy, but at least they have their audience back. —*David Wessel*

SOURCE: *The Wall Street Journal*, March 12, 1990, p. 1. Reprinted by permission of *The Wall Street Journal*, © 1990 Dow Jones & Company, Inc. All Rights Reserved Worldwide.

USE YOUR ECONOMIC REASONING

1. Kennedy's economic advisors were obviously Keynesians; how can we recognize that fact from the comments in this article?

2. The article describes the "hardliners at the Fed." To which school of thought do these economists belong? How can you tell?

3. Mr. Taylor's beliefs don't fit any school perfectly. Which school of thought would you place him in and why? Why did you find it difficult to assign him to a school?

The belief that expectations are formed rationally has also been met with skepticism, both by Keynesians and by many monetarists. Critics argue that the public does not gather and analyze information as intelligently as the theory suggests, nor does it always make fully rational decisions based on that information. Studies of the theory of rational expectations have produced mixed results. While some early evidence supported the theory, its performance on more recent tests has not upheld its initial promise.

If either of the basic assumptions discussed above is incorrect, the policy ineffectiveness theorem of the new classical economists is invalidated. In other words, monetary and fiscal policies would be capable of generating short-run changes in the levels of output and employment. This seems to be the view held by most economists. Of course, whether or not such policies should be used to change output and employment still depends on the length of the lags involved in policy implementation—the issue raised by the monetarists.

A New Form of Activism: Managing Aggregate Supply

The debate about the desirability of government efforts to manage aggregate demand has been with us for a long time. And, given that it is very difficult to prove statistically which of the schools of thought has the most accurate model of the economy, the debate is likely to continue. We'll indicate a few areas of consensus among macro economists after we take a brief look at supply-side economics.

Even if monetary and fiscal policies work as Keynesians suggest (which is certainly not the conclusion of the monetarists or the new classical economists), they produce mixed results. As we saw in Chapter 14, efforts to reduce unemployment tend to aggravate inflation, while policies to reduce inflation lead to greater unemployment. In addition, demand-management policies are incapable of offsetting supply shocks—unexpected reductions in aggregate supply. Since supply shocks lead to stagflation, they put pressure on policymakers to combat the two problems instead of one. But once again policymakers are confronted by trade-offs. If they choose to combat inflation, they make the unemployment problem even worse; if they decide to attack unemployment, the inflation rate escalates. In the late 1970s, these limitations led to an intense interest in supply-side remedies.

Supply-Side Economics

Supply-side remedies are policies designed to shift the aggregate supply curve to the right (downward). Remember, a shift of the aggregate supply curve to the right means an increase in aggregate supply: more is being supplied than before at each price level.

Unlike monetary and fiscal policies, supply-side remedies have the very desirable feature of being able to combat unemployment and inflation at the same time. As you consider Exh. 15.2, suppose the economy is operating at point A, the intersection of AD and AS_1. If policymakers can increase aggregate supply from AS_1 to AS_2, they can move the economy to point B; they will have increased equilibrium output (and employment) in the economy while reducing the overall price level. Policymakers will have succeeded in simultaneously reducing unemployment and inflation.

What policies do supply-side economists advocate? The complete list is too long to present here, but the following are illustrative.

1. *Encourage saving and investment through tax policies.* By encouraging saving through a reduction in taxes on interest income, for example, the government can make more funds available for investment purposes. Various techniques can then be used to encourage businesses to borrow this money and invest

EXHIBIT 15.2

The Impact of Supply-Side Remedies

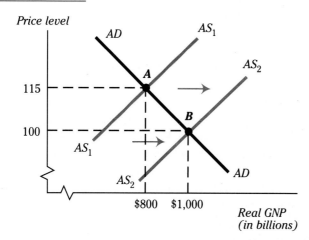

The purpose of supply-side remedies is to shift the aggregate supply curve to the right, thereby reducing the overall price level while increasing output and employment.

it. *Investment tax credits* would allow firms to deduct a certain percentage of their investment outlays from their tax liabilities. To the extent that such policies encourage business to borrow and invest in new factories and equipment, they help to increase the economy's productive capacity so that more output is supplied at any given price level. Of course, if more output is produced at each price level, the aggregate supply curve shifts to the right as depicted in Exh. 15.2.

2. *Reduce government regulations that drive up the cost of doing business.* We all recognize that government regulations are necessary to protect consumers, the environment, and the health and safety of workers. In some instances, however, regulations may add substantially to the cost of producing goods and services, yet provide little real benefit for the society. For example, the Food and Drug Administration has been accused of driving up the cost of developing new drugs by needlessly prolonging the testing that is required to gain FDA approval. Reducing such costs should free resources to produce other goods and services; thus more output can be supplied at each price level.

3. *Encourage individuals to work harder and longer by reducing marginal tax rates.* Marginal tax rates are the tax rates paid on the last increment of income. For example, under a progressive income tax system, an individual earning $15,000 might be required to pay a tax of 15 percent on the first $10,000 and 20 percent on the remaining $5,000. Supply-siders insist that high marginal tax rates discourage work. The way to get people to work more (and thereby increase aggregate supply) is to let them keep more of what they earn by reducing marginal tax rates.

The Reagan Supply-Side Experiment

When President Reagan took office, he presented several supply-side features in his Program for Economic Recovery (announced in February 1981). The cornerstone of Reagan's program was the Economic Recovery Tax Act (ERTA) of 1981. Patterned after legislation proposed by two supply-siders, Representative Jack Kemp of New York and Senator William Roth of Delaware, ERTA called for a 5-percent reduction in tax rates in 1981 and a 10-percent reduction in 1982 and 1983. ERTA also contained provisions to encourage saving and stimulate business investment. According to its supporters, the reduction in tax rates would cause the economy to grow rapidly as the lower tax rates stimulated saving and investment and convinced Americans to work harder. In fact, some supply-siders argued that the economy's growth would be sufficiently rapid that the additional tax revenue generated by the new jobs and expanded hours would more than offset the tax revenue lost through the

President Reagan's Program for Economic Recovery contained several supply-side features.

initial tax cuts. In short, government would take in more revenue at the lower tax rates than it had at the higher rates.[5]

What actually happened? Rather than experiencing the rapid economic growth predicted by supply-siders, the economy began the decade by enduring the worst recession since the Great Depression. The unemployment rate rose from 7 percent in 1980 to 9.5 percent in 1982. The recession ended in 1983, and output and employment expanded rapidly through 1984. However, for the remainder of the 1980s economic growth was unspectacular. Overall, the rate of economic growth experienced in the decade of the 1980s was identical to the experience of the previous decade; in both decades the average annual growth rate of real GNP was 2.7 percent. Clearly, the supply-

---

[5] This possibility was originally suggested by Arthur Laffer, professor of economics at Pepperdine University and one of the early proponents of supply-side measures.

side measures did not lead to the spectacular economic growth that some supporters expected. In addition, there has been little empirical evidence to suggest that the supply-side tax cuts resulted in a significant increase in either saving or investment. Instead, these tax cuts combined with increases in government spending to result in huge government deficits, deficits that tripled the public debt during Reagan's term in office.

Judged by what was initially promised by some supply-siders—an explosion in work effort, investment, and saving—the Economic Recovery Tax Act was clearly a failure. Moreover, Keynesian economists attributed most of the economic expansion of the Reagan years not to the supply-side policies but to the demand-side stimulus provided by the substantial budget deficits.

These economists argue that tax cuts shift both the aggregate demand curve (the traditional Keynesian impact) and the aggregate supply curve (the supply-side impact). However, they believe that in the short run, the supply-side impact tends to be minor in comparison with the demand-side effect. Most statistical studies support this view.

The Long-Run Importance of Supply-Side Measures

Even if Keynesians are correct about the short-run impact of supply-side policies, we should not conclude that measures to enhance aggregate supply should be ignored. On the contrary, virtually all economists agree that policies designed to expand aggregate supply are crucial to the long-run well-being of Americans. The same policies that cause the aggregate supply curve to shift to the right also cause potential GNP to increase. The ability to increase potential GNP is probably the most important impact of supply-side policies. Although studies suggest that supply-side measures contribute little to the short-run battle against inflation and unemployment, the long-run impact of such policies can be quite important.

To understand why supply-side policies may play an important role in the long run, think about the objective of increasing the living standard of Americans. One measure of a society's standard of living is GNP per person (total GNP divided by population). The first step in ensuring a high standard of living is making the most of our potential, ensuring that the economy operates at full employment. That's the objective of monetary and fiscal policies: to push the economy up to its potential. (As we've already seen, monetarists and new classical economists would argue that these efforts to manage aggregate demand are ill-advised.) But another objective is to keep potential GNP expanding so that it grows more rapidly than the society's population. That objective might be thought of as the domain of supply-side economics.

How do we keep potential GNP increasing more rapidly than population? Consensus holds that the key is in improving labor productivity—output per worker. This means providing workers with more and better capital equipment. (Recall that one of the objectives of supply-siders was to stimulate investment spending and spending on research and development.) It also means developing a better educated and more highly motivated work force. Unfortunately, these changes do not occur automatically. The growth of labor productivity in the United States slowed significantly in the early 1970s and has remained sluggish. Economists have been unable to provide a convincing explanation for the slowdown or a palatable plan for remedying the problem. Two things are clear. First, it is more difficult to stimulate labor productivity than the original supply-siders suggested. Second, these efforts generally require society to sacrifice *today* in order to have a higher standard of living in the future. For instance, improving education requires higher taxes, which in turn means less disposable income for households. One reason for the productivity slowdown may be a lessening of our willingness to make these sacrifices.

Summing Up: The Current State of Macro Thinking

Economists obviously disagree about the role of government in attempting to maintain full employment and about the possible benefits of supply-side remedies. This section is the author's interpretation of current thinking.

1. Virtually all economists agree that the economy contains, to one degree or another, a self-correcting mechanism. In the long-run, the economy tends to return to potential GNP and full employment. Economists disagree about how long this adjustment process takes.

2. Economists disagree about the ability of demand-management policies to speed up the adjustment to potential GNP and full employment. Keynesians support such measures; monetarists and new classical economists do not.

    The differences between activists and nonactivists may not, however, be quite as great as they first appear. Even Keynesians recognize that discretionary policies are subject to lags. Thus modern Keynesians believe that it is undesirable to attempt to fine tune the economy—to try to correct every minor increase in unemployment or in the overall price level. Instead, policymakers should confine their efforts to combating major downturns or inflationary threats.

3. The new classical economics has clearly shaken up macroeconomic thinking but hasn't gained very many converts thus far. Most economists do not appear to believe that expectations are formed in a totally "rational" manner. Even fewer economists are willing to accept the classical contention that wages are highly flexible and markets are continuously in equilibrium. If economists reject these arguments, they must reject the policy ineffectiveness theorem that grows from them.

   Although few economists seem willing to embrace the entire new classical model, most tend to agree that the theory of rational expectations is an improvement on the expectations models previously applied by Keynesians and monetarists. Moreover, there appears to be growing support for a weaker version of the policy ineffectiveness theory: fully anticipated policy changes have *smaller* effects than unanticipated changes.

4. Virtually all economists support measures to stimulate aggregate supply. But evidence suggests that supply-side measures do little in the short run to stimulate GNP or lower the price level. The major impact of supply-side policies comes in the long run, where their benefits can be substantial.

Summary

While economists generally agree about the existence of a self-correcting mechanism, they disagree about the speed with which this adjustment process occurs and about the desirability of government efforts to enhance these naturally occurring forces.

Keynesians believe that the economy's self-correcting mechanism works quite slowly. Thus they support an active role for government in speeding the adjustment process through discretionary monetary and fiscal policies.

Monetarists believe that the economy's self-adjustment mechanism works reasonably quickly and that government efforts to aid this process are either ineffective or counterproductive.

According to monetarists, changes in the money supply play the primary role in determining the level of aggregate output and prices in the economy. Government efforts to stimulate the economy through fiscal policy are futile because they lead to the crowding out of investment spending.

The monetarists also argue against the use of discretionary monetary policy. Because of the *recognition lag* and the *impact lag*, the effect of a monetary policy change may be felt when it is no longer appropriate. Thus discretionary monetary policy has a destabilizing effect on the economy: it contributes to greater unemployment and inflation.

Because monetarists believe that discretionary monetary policy tends to intensify the economy's problems rather than lessen them, they support a *monetary rule* that would require the Fed to expand the money supply at a constant annual rate.

Monetarists are not alone in opposing the use of discretionary policies to guide the economy's performance; *new classical economists* also argue against such intervention. The new classical economics is founded on two basic tenets: (1) wages and prices are highly flexible, and (2) expectations about the future are formed rationally.

Because new classical economists believe that wages and prices are highly flexible, they believe that the economy quickly tends toward full employment. Reductions in aggregate demand are met by falling wages and prices which quickly restore equilibrium. Any unemployment is voluntary.

New classical economists emphasize the impact of expectations on behavior; different expectations about the future can lead to different decisions today. The *theory of rational expectations* suggests that people use all available information to develop realistic expectations about the future.

The new classical economists' belief in highly flexible wages and prices and rational expectations led to the *policy ineffectiveness theorem*. According to this theorem, systematic monetary and fiscal policies cannot alter the level of output or employment in the economy; they can change only the price level.

Because the new classical economists are convinced that government policies cannot be used to alter output or employment, they believe that policymakers should concentrate on achieving and maintaining a low rate of inflation. To achieve this objective the new classical economists, like the monetarists, favor rules.

The activist-nonactivist debate has focused on the desirability of demand-management policies. But in the late 1970s, supply-side remedies—policies to increase aggregate supply—attracted a great deal of attention. The desirable feature of such policies is that they can reduce unemployment and inflation at the same time. Available evidence suggests that supply-side measures have a relatively modest impact on aggregate supply in the short run; most of the impact comes in the long run.

Glossary

Page 470   ***Impact lag.*** The time that elapses between the implementation of a policy change and its initial effect on the economy.

Page 468   ***Monetarism.*** The belief that changes in the money supply play the primary role in determining the level of aggregate output and prices in the economy.

Page 469   ***Monetary rule.*** A rule that would require the Federal Reserve to increase the money supply at a constant rate.

Page 476   ***Policy ineffectiveness theorem.*** The theory that systematic monetary and fiscal policies cannot alter the level of output or employment in the economy; they can change only the price level.

Page 470   ***Recognition lag.*** The delay in implementing policy that results from the mixed signals sent by the economy.

Page 476   ***Theory of rational expectations.*** The theory that people use all available information to develop realistic expectations about the future.

Study Questions

Fill in the Blanks

1. Keynesian economists who advocate government intervention to guide the economy's performance are also known as _____.

2. The two modern schools of thought that oppose the use of demand-management techniques are the _____ and the _____ _____.

3. The two types of lags associated with discretionary monetary policy are the _____ lag and the _____ lag.

4. According to the _____ and the _____ , the Fed should be required to expand the money supply at a constant rate.

5. _____ is often called the father of monetarism.

6. According to the _____, expectations are formed rationally.

7. The belief that systematic monetary and fiscal policies cannot alter the level of output or employment is known as the _____ theorem.

8. The requirement that the Fed expand the money supply at a constant rate is known as the _____.

9. The use of monetary and/or fiscal policy in an attempt to eliminate even minor increases in unemployment or inflation is known as _____ the economy and is opposed by virtually all modern economists.

10. Unlike monetary and fiscal policies, _____ remedies can be used to reduce unemployment and inflation at the same time.

Multiple Choice

1. Which of the following schools of economists would be described as "activists"?
   a) Classical economists
   b) Keynesian economists
   c) Monetarist economists
   d) New classical economists

2. Which of the following statements about the activist-nonactivist debate is true?
   a) Monetarists advocate the use of discretionary monetary policy to manage aggregate demand and ensure full employment.
   b) New classical economists support the use of fiscal policy to guide the economy, but believe that monetary policy is ineffective
   c) Keynesians advocate government intervention because they believe the self-correcting mechanism works too slowly.
   d) All of the above

3. According to the monetarists,
   a) fiscal policy is ineffective because of crowding out.
   b) fiscal policy is more effective than monetary policy.
   c) increases in government spending tend to lower interest rates, thus stimulating investment spending.
   d) increases in government spending tend to stimulate investment spending by making business leaders more optimistic.

4. Which of the following is a true statement about the monetarists?
   a) They favor the use of discretionary monetary policy to guide the economy's performance.
   b) They believe that the money supply should be increased at a constant rate.
   c) They favor legislation to provide Fed policymakers with more power to guide the economy's performance.
   d) a and c

5. When monetarists call for a "monetary rule," what they really want is
   a) greater reliance on discretionary monetary policy and less reliance on discretionary fiscal policy.
   b) legislation to provide Fed policymakers with more power to guide the economy's performance.
   c) legislation that would require the Fed to increase the money supply at a constant rate.
   d) bigger paychecks for monetarist economists.

STUDY QUESTIONS

6. The two types of lags in monetary policy are the
   a) policy lag and the implementation lag.
   b) recognition lag and the impact lag.
   c) recognition lag and the policy lag.
   d) identification lag and the implementation lag.

7. The major reason monetarists oppose the use of discretionary monetary policy to guide the economy's performance is
   a) they do not believe that changes in the money supply have any impact on output or employment.
   b) they believe that lags cause monetary policy to have a destabilizing effect on the economy.
   c) they believe that monetary policy is not as effective as fiscal policy.
   d) they believe that rational expectations make monetary policy changes ineffective.

8. Keynesians believe the economy is inherently unstable due to
   a) the instability created by government fiscal policy.
   b) fluctuations in the level of government spending.
   c) the volatility of investment spending.
   d) Federal Reserve monetary policies.

9. Which of the following is not a belief of the new classical economists?
   a) Wages and prices are highly flexible.
   b) Expectations are formed rationally.
   c) Unemployment is voluntary.
   d) Labor markets adjust very slowly to changes in demand.

10. According to the theory of rational expectations,
    a) households and businesses base their expectations only on past experience.
    b) people use all available information in developing their expectations about the future.
    c) it is reasonable for households and businesses to ignore the actions of policymakers.
    d) only policymakers have sufficient knowledge to develop accurate estimates of future price levels.

11. According to the policy ineffectiveness theorem,
    a) anticipated changes in monetary or fiscal policy will alter only the price level.
    b) fiscal policy is ineffective unless it is accompanied by monetary policy.
    c) monetary policy is ineffective unless it is accompanied by fiscal policy.
    d) unanticipated changes in monetary or fiscal policy will alter only the price level.

12. The new classical economists believe that any anticipated increase in the money supply
    a) will expand output and employment
    b) will be immediately offset by a reduction in aggregate supply.
    c) will immediately cause potential GNP to expand.
    d) will lead to an immediate reduction in the price level with no change in output or employment.

13. According to Keynesians, which of the following is true?
    a) When unemployment is caused by inadequate aggregate demand, expanding the money supply will reduce unemployment but intensify inflation.
    b) When inflation is caused by a supply shock, reducing the money supply will lower the rate of inflation but aggravate unemployment.
    c) When unemployment is caused by a reduction in aggregate supply, increasing the money supply will reduce unemployment but aggravate inflation.
    d) All of the above
    e) None of the above

14. Which of the following is *not* a supply-side remedy?
    a) Use tax credits to encourage investment.
    b) Reduce marginal tax rates to encourage people to work longer and harder.
    c) Increase tax rates on interest income in order to discourage saving and stimulate consumption spending.
    d) Eliminate government regulations that do not serve a valid purpose.

15. In the short run, reductions in marginal tax rates probably
    a) increase only aggregate demand.
    b) increase only aggregate supply.
    c) increase both aggregate demand and aggregate supply, but have a greater impact on demand.
    d) increase both aggregate demand and aggregate supply, but have a greater impact on supply.

Problems and Questions for Discussion

1. Given that the economy has a self-correcting mechanism, what is the essence of the Keynesian argument for government intervention to combat unemployment

2. Why do the monetarists believe that fiscal policy cannot be used to stimulate the economy?

3. Discuss the lags involved in the implementation of monetary policy.

STUDY QUESTIONS

4. Keynesians blame the inherent instability of capitalist economies on the volatility of investment spending. Try to recall from Chapter 11 why investment spending tends to volatile.

5. What is the nature of the *monetarist* argument for a monetary rule?

6. The new classical economists sometimes argue that only random monetary policy can alter output and employment. Use their model to explain this conclusion. Does this mean that policymakers should replace Keynesian demand-management policies with random policies?

7. Explain the logic behind the policy ineffectiveness theorem of the new classical economists. Supplement your explanation with a graph.

8. Discuss the similarities and differences between the monetarists and the new classical economists with regard to the issue of demand-management policy.

9. List as many supply-side remedies as you can remember, and discuss the rationale for each.

10. Critics of the Reagan experiment with supply-side economics often argue that it was "oversold." What do they mean? What evidence might they summon to support their position?

Answer Key

Fill in the Blanks

1. activists	5. Milton Friedman	9. fine tuning
2. monetarists, new classical economists	6. new classical economists	10. supply-side
3. recognition, impact	7. policy ineffectiveness	
4. monetarists, new classical economists	8. monetary rule	

Multiple Choice

1. b	4. b	7. b	10. b	13. d
2. c	5. c	8. c	11. a	14. c
3. a	6. b	9. d	12. b	15. c

INTERNATIONAL ECONOMICS: TRADE AND THE BALANCE OF PAYMENTS

In Part 4, we explore economic exchanges between nations and examine the interrelationship between our economy and the other economies of the world. We will consider the benefits of international trade and how trade between nations differs from trade within a nation.

Chapter 16 introduces the economic rationale for international trade and considers the consequences of barriers to free trade. You will learn the meaning of such concepts as "comparative advantage" and "absolute advantage" and see why these concepts are used to summon support for free trade. Arguments for and against free trade will be presented, and we will look closely at the impact of foreign competition. Chapter 17 considers the financial dimension of international trade and the role of exchange rates. You will see how exchange rates are determined and how changes in exchange rates influence international trade. You will learn the difference between a nation's "balance of payments" and its "balance of trade" and discover how these concepts are related to the exchange rate.

INTERNATIONAL TRADE

For fifteen chapters we have explored economics without a word about international trade and our economic relationships with other nations. Although this has simplified our approach to economic reasoning, we can't continue to ignore those topics if we expect to understand fully the modern American economy and the issues that concern citizens, politicians, and policymakers. Today many Americans see foreign competition as a destructive force that threatens their jobs and their way of life. But others view foreign competition as a blessing that provides quality products at prices lower than domestic producers charge. Economic policymakers must weigh these costs and benefits as they develop policies to promote or retard international trade. In this chapter, we will explore the theoretical basis for free or unrestricted international trade, and we'll take a closer look at the costs and benefits associated with it.

Interdependent Economies and American Trade

Statistics show that the economies of the world are becoming more interdependent. American consumers are buying more foreign products, and foreign consumers are buying more American goods. Producers around the world are using more imported parts and raw materials in the products they manufacture. In short, foreign trade is already more important than most Americans realize, and current signs indicate that it will gain even more importance in the future.

Import and Export Patterns

The Sony television sets, Nike tennis shoes, and Raleigh bicycles we see in American stores are all *imports*—goods or services purchased from foreign producers.[1] In the last two decades, trade between the United States and other nations has expanded significantly. More Americans are driving Saabs, Nissans, Peugeots, and Isuzus. They are listening to stereos made in Japan; they are drinking wine from France and Italy; they are wearing clothes from Korea, Romania, Taiwan, and other countries. As you can see from Exh. 16.1, imports almost tripled as a fraction of GNP between 1960 and 1991.

American exports are expanding as well. *Exports* are goods and services produced domestically and sold to customers in other countries. Exports of goods and services accounted for less than 6 percent of our gross national product in 1960; by 1991, that figure had climbed to approximately 13 percent of GNP. That percentage is low when compared with Ireland (63 percent of GNP), Sweden (30 percent of GNP), and Canada (26 percent of GNP), but it is a significant fraction of GNP and one that undoubtedly will increase in the future.[2]

[1] The services component of imports includes such items as transportation charges for moving goods and passengers between nations and expenditures made by tourists while traveling in foreign countries.

[2] The percentage figures for Ireland and Sweden are for 1990 and come from *Foreign Economic Trends and Their Implications for the United States,* published by the U.S. Department of Commerce, June 1991. The figure for Canada is for 1987 and is from The Organization for Economic Cooperation and Development, *Economic Surveys,* 1989.

EXHIBIT 16.1

Trends in U.S. Imports and Exports

	1960	1970	1980	1991
Exports of goods and services	$29.9 billion (5.8% of GNP)	$68.9 billion (6.8% of GNP)	$351.0 billion (12.8% of GNP)	$726.3 billion (12.8% of GNP)
Imports of goods and services	$24.0 billion (4.7% of GNP)	$60.5 billion (6.0% of GNP)	$318.9 billion (11.7% of GNP)	$743.8 billion (13.1% of GNP)

Source: Developed from data contained in *The Economic Report of the President, 1991* and the *Survey of Current Business,* March 1992.

Interdependence and American Attitudes

We are constantly reminded of the many ways that national economies are linked to one another. Consumers the world over felt the impact of the oil cutbacks that resulted from Iraq's invasion of Kuwait in August of 1990. When there is a poor harvest in Brazil, we all pay higher prices for coffee. Consider, too, the many products of American manufacture that require foreign parts or materials. Many of our automobiles, for example, have foreign-made engines and other components. American steel producers rely on imported coke, and our refineries use imported oil to manufacture gasoline and other petroleum products.

Countries often react strongly, almost resentfully, to the actions of foreign nations with whom they trade. When Japanese automobile producers step up production, American producers cry foul. When Federal Reserve policies drive up interest rates in the United States and attract investment funds, complaints ring out from other nations. With increasing frequency, economic events in one part of the world have global repercussions—repercussions that affect each of us.

How should Americans react to this growing interdependence? Does the availability of Japanese automobiles and Taiwanese shoes and other foreign products make Americans better off? Or does the inflow of foreign products simply mean less demand for American products and fewer jobs in domestic manufacturing industries? Should we support American steel and automobile producers and shoe manufacturers when they appeal to our gov-

Domestic workers often protest against imported products.

ernment for protection from "cheap foreign labor"? To respond intelligently to these questions, it is necessary to have some understanding of international economics. We need to understand why countries trade. What are the benefits of trade? Does trade help one country at the expense of another, or is it mutually beneficial? What are the arguments for and against trade barriers? These are the questions we now take up.

The Basis for International Trade

Why do countries trade? The various nations of the world are not all equally blessed in terms of either natural resources or capital and labor endowments. Therefore different nations have different production abilities. Great Britain may be self-sufficient in petroleum products because of oil discoveries in the North Sea. If the British want oranges and grapefruit, however, they will probably have to trade for them, because Britain's climate is ill-suited to growing citrus fruits. American consumers have no trouble buying domestically grown fruits and vegetables, but they must rely on other nations for items like tin, tea, and teakwood furniture. One reason why countries trade, then, is to acquire the products they cannot produce themselves. But that is not the sole—or even the most important—reason for trade.

The Opportunity Cost
of Domestic Production

Virtually every country is capable of producing almost any product its citizens desire—if it is willing to expend the necessary resources. Lacking alternative sources of supply, the British probably could grow hothouse oranges and grapefruit, and Americans probably would find some way to produce tea domestically. The important point is that neither country chooses to expend its resources this way because other countries can produce these products so much less expensively.

Think of the resources the British would need to use to produce hothouse oranges. More important, think of the other products that Britain could produce with those same resources. Whenever economists talk about the true cost of producing something, they mean the *opportunity cost.* As you will recall, the opportunity cost of anything is what you have to give up to obtain it. The opportunity cost of hothouse oranges would be whatever products the British would sacrifice to produce those oranges. By the same token, the cost of tea or coffee produced in the United States would be whatever other domestic products we could have produced with the same resources.

By making comparisons based on opportunity cost, we can determine which country is the low-cost producer of a particular product without becoming confused or misled as we would if we made comparisons in dollars or some other currency. Economic logic dictates that each country should specialize in the products it can produce at a relatively low opportunity cost and trade those products for the items that other countries can produce more cheaply. This logic is called the principle of *comparative advantage,* and it is the key to understanding how countries can benefit from trade.

The Principle of Comparative Advantage

The classic example of comparative advantage doesn't involve foreign countries, it has to do with a lawyer and the lawyer's secretary. The lawyer, Ms. Legal Wizard, is not only the best legal mind in the country, but also types better than anyone else around. We could say she has an *absolute advantage* over her secretary (and everyone else in the community) in both jobs. That means the lawyer is more efficient at those jobs; she can accomplish more work in a given amount of time. If that is the case, why does the lawyer have her secretary, Mr. Average Typist, do the typing? By having the secretary do the typing, the lawyer frees her own time to do legal work.

Consider the high opportunity cost of having the lawyer do her own typing. It would mean the loss of the additional income she could have generated by handling more cases. The secretary, who has almost no talent for legal work, has a comparative advantage in typing because the amount of legal work he gives up to perform the typing duties is insignificant. The secretary does the typing not because he is a better typist than the lawyer (absolute advantage) but because he is better at typing than at legal work (comparative advantage). By allowing individuals to concentrate on the jobs they do the best—the jobs where their absolute advantage is the greatest or their disadvantage the least—the firm is able to handle more clients, earn more money, and thereby raise the standard of living of all its members.

Comparative Advantage as a Basis for Trade

Countries can benefit from specialization and trade in much the same way that the lawyer and the secretary benefit from their relationship. Consider the possibility of trade between the United States and France. Even if the United States were more efficient than France in the production of everything, specialization and trade along the lines of comparative advantage would allow each country to achieve a higher standard of living than it could possibly attain if it remained self-sufficient.

In order to illustrate that conclusion as simply as possible, let's assume that the United States and France are the only two countries in the world, and that they produce only two products: microcomputers and champagne. Exhibit 16.2 summarizes the production abilities of these two nations in terms of a hypothetical unit of resources, with each unit representing some combination of land, labor, capital, and entrepreneurship, some set amount of those resources. For instance, each resource unit might contain 10,000 hours of labor, 1,000 units of raw materials, the use of 10 machines for a year, and 500 hours of entrepreneurial talent. While each unit contains the same quantities of these resources, the quality of these inputs would vary from nation to nation, giving rise to differences in productive abilities.

With each unit of resources, the United States can produce either 50 microcomputers or 100 cases of champagne. With the same unit, France can produce either 20 microcomputers or 80 cases of champagne. Because the

---

EXHIBIT 16.2

Production Possibilities per Unit of Economic Resources

	MICROCOMPUTERS	CASES OF CHAMPAGNE
United States	50	100
France	20	80

United States can produce more microcomputers and more champagne per unit of resources, we know that it has an absolute advantage over France in the production of both products, just as the lawyer had an absolute advantage over her secretary in both typing and legal work. How is it possible for both countries to benefit from trade when one of them is more efficient, or has an absolute advantage, in producing both products? To answer this question, we must explore the concept of comparative advantage.

In our example, the United States has a comparative advantage in the production of microcomputers because the opportunity cost of producing that product is lower in the United States than in France. The United States must sacrifice two cases of champagne in order to free the resources necessary to produce one additional microcomputer. (Each resource unit can produce either 50 microcomputers or 100 cases of champagne, so each additional computer costs us two cases of champagne.) In France, however, the opportunity cost of each additional microcomputer is four cases of champagne because each unit of French resources can produce either 80 cases of champagne or 20 microcomputers. The United States can produce microcomputers at a lower opportunity cost and therefore has a comparative advantage in that product.

If we switch our attention to champagne production, we note that the French have a comparative advantage in this area. In the United States, the production of one additional microcomputer forces the society to sacrifice two cases of champagne. The opportunity cost of producing one more case of champagne is therefore half a computer. In France, the cost is lower. Each additional microcomputer requires the sacrifice of four cases of champagne. Therefore the opportunity cost of each case of champagne is one-fourth of a computer. The French do indeed have a comparative advantage in the production of champagne.

The Benefits
of Trade

Now that you understand how to determine a nation's comparative advantage, let's see how trade based on the principle of comparative advantage can result in a higher standard of living for both trading partners. In the absence of product specialization and trade, both France and the United States would produce some microcomputers and some champagne, the exact amounts of each depending on the strength of demand for the two products. Prior to trade, we can't say with precision what those amounts would be, but we know that one microcomputer would exchange for two cases of champagne in the United States and for four cases of champagne in France.

Suppose the United States decides to specialize in the production of microcomputers and offers to trade one microcomputer to France for three cases of champagne. Would the French agree? Of course they would agree! Through trade they can acquire a microcomputer for three cases of champagne, whereas they would have to sacrifice four cases of champagne to produce one domestically. Under such circumstances they are better off to specialize in producing champagne and to trade for the microcomputers they desire.

As U.S. citizens, would we be better off with this arrangement? We certainly would be. We would be getting three cases of champagne for each microcomputer we traded, whereas we would be able to manufacture only two cases of champagne from the resources we used to produce each microcomputer. Clearly, trade based on the principle of comparative advantage will allow both countries to enjoy a higher standard of living.

The Production Possibilities Curve
and the Gains from Trade

We can see the gains from trade more clearly by using the production possibilities curve introduced in Chapter 1. A production possibilities curve shows the combinations of goods that an economy is capable of producing with its present stock of economic resources and existing techniques of production.

Let's assume that the United States and France each have 100 units of economic resources to use in producing either microcomputers or champagne and that these resources are equally suited to the production of either product. When resources are assumed to be equally productive, the production possibilities curve appears as a straight rather than a bowed-out line (recall Chapter 1). In the United States these 100 resource units can be used to produce either 10,000 cases of champagne or 5,000 microcomputers or any other combination of champagne and microcomputers found on its production possibilities curve [see Exh. 16.3(a)]. In France the 100 resource units can be used to produce either 8,000 cases of champagne or 2,000 micro-computers or any other combination of champagne and microcomputers found on France's production possibilities curve [see Exh. 16.3(b)]. Recall that any combination of products we can plot either on or within the production possibilities curve (*PPC*) is available to the society. Combinations falling outside the *PPC* are beyond the economy's production capability and therefore unattainable unless we can trade for them.

Suppose that prior to trade the United States chooses to produce and consume 2,000 cases of champagne and 4,000 microcomputers, whereas the French choose a combination of 5,000 cases of champagne and 750 computers. Total world production would then be 7,000 cases of champagne (2,000 produced by the United States and 5,000 by France) and 4,750 microcomputers (4,000 produced by the United States and 750 by France).

Suppose next that the two countries decide to specialize along the lines of comparative advantage, agreeing to trade with each other at our hypothetical exchange ratio: one microcomputer = three cases of champagne. The United States has a comparative advantage in microcomputers, so it will use all its 100 resource units to produce microcomputers and will trade for champagne. The French will produce champagne, their product of comparative advantage, and will trade for microcomputers.

We know that the United States is producing 5,000 microcomputers and France is producing 8,000 cases of champagne. What will be the result if the United States trades 1,000 microcomputers for some champagne? With an exchange ratio of one microcomputer to three cases of champagne, the United States will receive 3,000 cases of champagne in return for its 1,000 microcomputers and still have 4,000 microcomputers left over. France will have 5,000 cases of champagne left over plus 1,000 microcomputers. The United States will have 1,000 more cases of champagne than it had prior to trade, and France will have 250 more microcomputers.

Trade and specialization have made it possible for each country to move beyond its *PPC* and enjoy a combination of products that it could not obtain on its own. Moreover, total world production has increased from 7,000 to 8,000 cases of champagne and from 4,750 to 5,000 microcomputers. The principle of comparative advantage has allowed each of the trading partners to obtain more goods from each resource unit and to enjoy a higher standard of living.

EXHIBIT 16.3

Production Possibilities Curves and the Gains from Trade

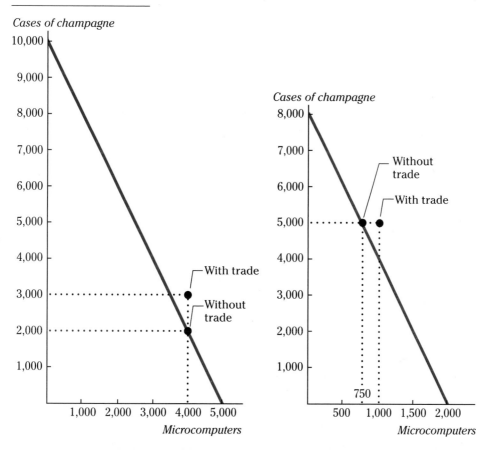

(a) The Production Possibilities
of the United States

(b) The Production Possibilities
of France

The two production possibilities curves show the combinations of champagne and
microcomputers that the United States (a) and France (b) can produce. Without trade, each
nation is forced to select a combination of the two products that lies either on the production
possibilities curve or inside it. For example, the United States might choose to produce and
consume 2,000 cases of champagne and 4,000 microcomputers, while France might select a
combination of 5,000 cases of champagne and 750 microcomputers. Through specialization and
trade, each of these nations can enjoy a higher standard of living. If the United States
specializes in producing microcomputers and France specializes in champagne, each of these
nations can move to a point beyond its production possibilities curve. For example, if the two
countries agree on an exchange ratio of one microcomputer for three cases of champagne, the
United States can exchange 1,000 microcomputers for 3,000 cases of champagne. That will
leave the United States with 4,000 microcomputers and 3,000 cases of champagne, while
France will have 1,000 microcomputers and 5,000 cases of champagne; both countries will be
better off than they were without trade.

The Transition to Greater Specialization:
Winners and Losers

Trade based on comparative advantage clearly makes sense. And in the absence of *trade barriers*—legal restrictions on trade—we can be confident that the pursuit of self-interest will automatically lead producers to specialize in the products for which their country has a comparative advantage. Consider again our hypothetical world economy. Prior to trade, microcomputers were selling for twice as much as a case of champagne in the United States, but four times as much as a case of champagne in France. Enterprising French and American businesses would take advantage of these international price differentials to increase their profits. For instance, suppose that microcomputers were selling for $1,000 in the United States, while a case of champagne was selling for $500. In France, on the other hand, microcomputers were selling for 4,000 francs, while a case of champagne was selling for 1,000 francs. American businesses could make a substantial profit by selling microcomputers in France and using the money to buy champagne for resale in the United States. French businesses could do the reverse; they could sell champagne in the United States and use the proceeds to buy computers for resale in France. Because French producers can sell champagne for less, ultimately they would force American champagne producers out of business. The same fate would befall French computer manufacturers: They would be eliminated by competition from the United States.[3]

What would happen to the workers displaced from the French computer industry and the U.S. champagne industry? Our model assumes that all resources are equally suited for champagne production or computer manufacturing, and that they move freely between those industries within each country but not between countries. Thus the economic resources—workers, factories, and equipment—no longer needed by the American champagne industry would flow to the American computer industry, and the resources released by the French computer industry would flow to the French champagne industry. With greater specialization, workers in both countries

---

[3] Even in the absence of trade barriers, specialization may be less than complete. The United States might continue to produce some champagne, and France might continue to produce some microcomputers.

In order to conclude that foreign trade along the lines of comparative advantage will lead to complete specialization, we have to assume that (1) the products offered by French and American manufacturers are identical—i.e., French champagne is the same as American champagne; (2) all economic resources are equally productive in both uses; (3) economic resources can move freely from one industry to the other but not between countries; (4) transportation costs are not large enough to outweigh the differences in production costs in the two nations; and (5) the computer and champagne industries are purely competitive. To the extent that these assumptions are not met, specialization will be less than complete.

would become more productive, and they would be paid higher wages by their employers. In this way, the benefits of trade would be shared by all members of the society; everyone would benefit from specialization and trade based on comparative advantage.

The transition to greater international specialization, however, is never painless. When a domestic industry is eliminated or reduced in size by foreign competition, difficult adjustments follow. Unemployed workers need time to find other jobs, and factories must be put to other uses. Some of these resources will never be reemployed because firms are reluctant to invest money to retrain a 55-year-old winemaker, for example, or remodel a 30-year-old computer plant. Even though the total output of both countries will be greater than before trade (see Exh. 16.3), not every individual or group will be better off. Thus specialization has costs as well as benefits.

Lower Prices through International Competition

Even when specialization is incomplete and several countries continue to produce the same products, international trade can benefit consumers by providing them with a wider variety of products from which to choose. Furthermore, the availability of foreign products limits the pricing discretion of domestic producers and forces them to be more responsive to consumer demands.

Consider the American automobile market. Foreign competition has not only given American consumers more brands from which to choose, but also spurred domestic manufacturers to develop small, fuel-efficient cars. In addition, competition from foreign producers has helped to keep automobile prices in the United States lower than they would be otherwise. A 1980 study by the Council of Economic Advisors concluded that if automobile imports were limited to 10 percent of the U.S. market, new-car prices would increase between 13 and 17 percent. The Federal Trade Commission and the International Automobile Dealers Association have conducted studies that predicted even greater price hikes—up to $3,000 a car.[4] As you can see, international competition can be a powerful force in restraining the market power of domestic oligopolists and promoting a higher standard of living for consumers.

When we consider the benefits of trade in permitting greater specialization along the lines of comparative advantage and fostering greater

---

[4] Murray L. Weidenbaum, with Michael C. Munger and Ronald J. Penoyer, *Toward a More Open Trade Policy* (Center for the Study of American Business, Formal Publication Number 53, January, 1983), p. 5.

Competition from foreign automobile manufacturers has helped to hold down new car prices in the United States.

competition, we can understand why economists generally agree on the desirability of *free trade*—trade that is not hindered by artificial restrictions or trade barriers of any type.

Types of Barriers to Trade

We have seen that free trade benefits consumers but often imposes substantial costs on particular groups in a society. Moreover, the benefits of free trade are widely diffused across a large number of people, each of whom is made a little better off, whereas the losses tend to be concentrated in a relatively small segment of the society. Workers who are forced out of jobs by foreign competition provide the best example.

Not surprisingly, the segment that is significantly harmed by foreign competition is likely to be more vocal than the group whose welfare is slightly improved. That's why politicians in the United States and elsewhere hear more often about the costs of free trade than about its benefits. As Michael Oldfather, former Chairman of the Kansas Council on Economic Education, has noted,

[R]emoving import barriers on cars . . . might save every car-buying family a few hundred dollars a year. On the other hand, several thousand families would lose a great deal each (the families of U.S. automobile workers). Even though the total gains of car buyers would far exceed the total losses of car makers, it's not hard to guess whose voice will be the loudest.[5]

Virtually all the nations of the world impose trade barriers of one sort or another, partly in response to political pressure. These trade barriers are designed primarily to limit competition from imports, although export restrictions are sometimes established. The most common devices for limiting import competition are protective tariffs and import quotas.

Tariffs

A *tariff* is a tax on imported products. Its purpose is either to generate revenue for the taxing country through a *revenue tariff* or to protect domestic producers from foreign competition by means of a *protective tariff*. Historically, revenue tariffs were the major tool for financing government expenditures. Such tariffs served as the principle source of revenue for the United States government through the nineteenth century and remain the principle source in some less-developed countries.

Today, most developed countries rely on other forms of taxation for revenue—income and sales taxes, for example. When developed countries such as the United States employ tariffs, their main purpose is to protect domestic producers. A tariff on a foreign product increases its price and makes it less competitive in the marketplace, thereby encouraging consumers to buy domestic products instead. In this way, tariffs help to insulate domestic producers from foreign competition.

Quotas

Quotas restrict trade in a different way. An *import quota* specifies the maximum amount of a particular product that can be imported. The volume of imported wine, for example, might be limited to 50 million gallons per year, or the quantity of imported steel could be limited to 100,000 tons each year.

Import quotas can be either global or selective. A *global quota* limits the amount of a product that can be imported from the rest of the world. When the limit is reached, all further imports of that item are prohibited. A *selective quota* specifies the maximum amount of a product that can be

---

[5] Michael Oldfather, "Cost of any import ban outweighs gain," *Springfield* (MO) *News-Leader*, March 9, 1983, p. 7E.

Brazil Set to Lift Electronics Import Ban
Nationalist Laws Backfire on Computer Industry

SAO PAULO, Brazil—He is president of the Brazilian unit of Italian computer maker Ing. C. Olivetti & Co., but Enrico Misasi doesn't have an Olivetti computer. Instead, the system behind his desk is made by two Brazilian firms: the monitor by Elebra Computadores and the computer by ABC-Bull.

"It costs three times more than what an Olivetti would cost and doesn't do as much," says Mr. Misasi. So why does he have it? "It seems very strange to me too," says Mr. Misasi, whose company makes only typewriters and calculators in Brazil. "But I can't have one because of the market reserve."

"Market reserve" is the polite phrase Brazilians use to avoid saying "import ban." But in fact, importing a foreign personal computer—or a microchip, a fax or dozens of other electronic products—has been prohibited informally since 1975, and by law since 1984, when Brazil, then under military rule, passed the so-called Informatics Law. The law was designed to foster a home-grown electronics industry. Instead, even its beneficiaries admit it has engendered an uncompetitive and technologically outdated industry.

Brazilian-made computer equipment on average costs 2½ times what it would cost in the U.S., and a country such as Mexico, which produces one-third as much as Brazil, exports twice as many computers.

But now, Brazil is about to strike the "delete" key on the market reserve. If, as is likely, the Senate and President Fernando Collor de Mello approve a recently passed congressional bill, Brazil will rescind the market reserve and other controversial aspects of its Informatics Law in October of next year, scrapping a cornerstone of Brazil's nationalistic approach and signaling a new desire to liberalize its economy.

"Oct. 29, 1992, is a new liberation day," exults consultant Carlos Langoni. "Finally, I can buy a laptop."

By lifting the market reserve, Brazil is acknowledging that closing its markets to foreign electronic goods has also closed off the country to major technological innovations and new products, delaying its modernization, adding to production costs and reducing its global competitiveness.

"It was the worst thing that could have happened to this country," says Sergio Haberfeld, president of Toga S.A., a packaging company.

Nowhere was Brazil more zealous in applying its import-substitution model than the electronics business.

"It was enough for a Brazilian company to say that it was planning to develop the same thing eventually and imports were banned," says Jose Goldemberg, Brazil's secretary for science and technology. Not only were imports banned, but foreign companies willing to invest in manufacturing plants in Brazil also were banned.

"We repelled the products and the producers," says deputy Roberto Campos. Even joint ventures were deterred as foreign partners were kept from owning more than 30% or transferring technology.

"It was a chauvinistic reaction," admits Mr. Goldemberg. "The interests of consumers played no role whatsoever."

The cost is visible today: Almost no Brazilian cars are equipped with anti-skid brake systems or electronic fuel injection, both commonplace elsewhere. Products such as Apple Computer Inc.'s Macintosh computer still haven't made it to Brazil. Brazil preferred to see Texas Instruments Inc. close down its semiconductor plant here, throwing 250 people out of work, rather than allow TI to invest $133 million to modernize its product line.

By shooting itself in the foot in this way, Brazil ended up a largely computer-unfriendly nation. A recent study by the newsweekly *Veja* showed that only 0.5% of Brazilian classrooms are equipped with computers, while 96% of U.S. classrooms have computers, and a mere 12% of small and medium-sized Brazilian companies are at least partly automated, compared with 90% in the U.S. Many companies delayed modernization because machines available abroad weren't produced here and couldn't be imported. Many others resorted to smuggling in equipment. Some trading firms specialized in putting made-in-Brazil labels on foreign machines. . . .

Even companies that owe their creation to the market reserve say they now suffer from it. "Our models cost twice what they would cost outside because of taxes and because locally made components cost more," says Touma Elias, president of the

Sao Paulo microcomputer company Microtec. "Our quality is less than satisfactory, but how can I offer good quality when I can't use a Toshiba drive if I want to?"

Microtec illustrates how the law went awry. "We made PCs before the Taiwanese and the Koreans," says Mr. Elias. "But instead of being a $1 billion company, like [Taiwan's] Acer or [the U.S.'s] AST or Dell, we're a $35 million one hoping to be a $100 million one. Why? Because our market wasn't open," which made components more expensive, pricing Brazilian exports out of the market. "We were locked into our little market, and that was the error of our policy."

In addition to lifting the market reserve—though continuing to protect domestic industry with high import duties—the new law also allows foreign joint-venture partners to raise their stakes to 49%

from 30% and to transfer technology. . . .

Free-marketeers say the new law still doesn't go far enough. Local companies, defined as 51% Brazilian, will get preference for public procurement and various tax incentives, and a supervisory body has life-and-death power over joint ventures. Foreign companies also have to apply 5% of sales to local research. But even defenders of the market reserve admit the new law will spur competition and give consumers more choice and better quality.

—*Thomas Kamm*

SOURCE: *The Wall Street Journal*, August 8, 1991, p. A7. Reprinted by permission of *The Wall Street Journal*, © 1991 Dow Jones & Company, Inc. All Rights Reserved Worldwide.

USE YOUR ECONOMIC REASONING

1. **Brazil's computers are more expensive and less sophisticated than those available in the United States. How did the "market reserve" policy contribute to that outcome?**

2. **Brazil's protectionist policies backfired on some of the firms they were designed to protect. How?**

3. **How did Brazil's protectionist policies cause it to become a "computer-unfriendly nation"? What are the likely consequences of that status?**

imported from a particular country. For example, the United States might set a global quota of 500,000 imported automobiles per year and further specify selective quotas: 250,000 cars from Japan and 50,000 from France, perhaps, and the remaining 200,000 from other countries.

Domestic producers generally support import quotas over tariffs. Both trade barriers reduce competition from imported goods, but quotas are considered more effective. If consumers prefer foreign products to those offered by domestic producers, they may continue to buy relatively large amounts of these products in spite of the higher prices caused by the tariff. On the other hand, a quota will completely prohibit imports once the limit has been met.

Other Restrictions

While tariffs and quotas are the primary tools for restricting import competition, a wide variety of secondary methods are used: Health and safety laws are invoked to prevent or complicate the importation of certain products; the acquisition of import licenses can be difficult or expensive; and many government agencies are required to purchase domestic products whenever possible. The state of New York requires that state agencies buy American-made steel, for example, and New Jersey requires that all state cars be produced in the United States.[6] These and other techniques are used to restrict the inflow of imported goods and protect domestic producers. The article on page 512, "Brazil Set to Lift Electronics Import Ban," examines the far-reaching consequences of Brazil's protectionist policies.

Trade Barriers and Consumer Welfare

Economists generally condemn all forms of trade barriers. By reducing competitive pressures on domestic producers, such barriers allow firms with market power to charge higher prices yet be less responsive to the demands of consumers. Moreover, trade barriers interfere with the principle of comparative advantage: They prevent countries from concentrating on the things they do best and enjoying the best products produced by other countries.

---

[6] Murray L. Weidenbaum, *Confessions of a One-Armed Economist* (Center for the Study of American Business, Formal Publication Number 56, August 1983), p. 25.

Consider the impact of the tariffs imposed by the United States on television sets imported from Japan and elsewhere. These tariffs not only increase the prices consumers have to pay for imported TV sets, but also permit American producers to charge more for their sets. If Japanese sets were not taxed, they would sell for less, and American producers would be forced to reduce their prices in order to compete. Therefore American producers desire tariffs even though tariffs are harmful to American consumers.

Tariffs are less damaging to consumer welfare than quotas are, however. When increased demand causes the prices of domestic products to rise, comparable tariff-bearing foreign products become more competitive because the price differential between the foreign and domestic products is reduced. Because foreign products are now a more viable alternative for consumers, domestic producers may be restrained from raising prices further, lest they lose sales to foreign rivals. This is not the case with import quotas. When domestic producers are protected by quotas rather than tariffs, rising domestic prices cannot call forth additional units from foreign suppliers once the quotas have been met. As a consequence, domestic producers have more freedom under a quota system to increase prices without fear of losing their market share to foreign firms.

Another point in favor of import tariffs is that they provide governments with additional revenue, whereas import quotas do not. This added revenue can make it possible to reduce personal taxes or provide additional government services. Suppose, for example, that we imposed a $1,000 tariff on all imported Japanese cars. If two million cars were imported annually, that would amount to an additional $2 *billion* in revenue, not an insignificant sum. None of this is meant to suggest that tariffs are desirable, only that they are preferable to quotas.

The impact of trade barriers on the prices that consumers pay is only part of the story. When the United States erects trade barriers to keep out Japanese television sets or South Korean clothing or Canadian lumber, it interferes with the pursuit of comparative advantage. Not only do American consumers get less for their dollars; the United States and the other nations of the world get less from their scarce resources. When we establish import quotas to protect high-cost American producers of television sets, for example, we allow those firms to stay in business and use resources that could be put to better use in producing airplanes or machinery or other products in which the United States has a comparative advantage. We can acquire more television sets by producing aircraft and trading for TV sets than by producing the TV sets American consumers demand. If we insist on protecting our television manufacturers and Japan insists on protecting its aircraft turers, both societies lose. Their people will have to settle for fewer goods and services than free trade could produce. The price tag for this kind of protection is a lower standard of living for the average citizen.

Common Arguments for Protection

In spite of the costs imposed by trade barriers, they continue to exist. They exist because they serve the interests of certain powerful groups, even though they penalize society as a whole. Anyone who reads the newspaper or watches television is aware of the ongoing efforts of American shoe manufacturers to maintain import protection against cheaper products from Taiwan and South Korea and Italy. Automobile producers, clothing manufacturers, and steel firms also lobby for protection. They argue that removing import restrictions would mean eliminating some producers and shrinking the output of others. The workers in these industries would have to look for new jobs, learn new skills, and perhaps even relocate to other parts of the country. These adjustments would be easy for some but difficult for others, particularly older workers. For these reasons, employers and employees in industries that suffer from foreign competition have a strong personal interest in lobbying, or appealing to Congress for protection. Invariably, the arguments that are used to justify protection mix some truth with at least an equal amount of misunderstanding or distortion. Let's consider three of the most popular arguments.

1. *Infant industries need protection from foreign competition.* The infant-industry argument suggests that new industries need protection until they become firmly established and able to compete with foreign producers. This argument makes little sense in a diversified and sophisticated economy like that of the United States, but may have some relevance in less-developed countries. Even in that setting there are dangers. There is no assurance that the new industry will ever be able to compete internationally, and once protection has been granted it is difficult to take away.

2. *Defense-related industries must be protected to ensure our military self-sufficiency.* This argument suggests that we must protect certain critical industries so that the United States will not be dependent on foreign countries for the things it needs to defend itself in time of war. The national-defense argument is commonly used to summon support for the protection of a long list of industries, including steel, munitions, rubber, and petrochemicals. There is no way to

decide which industries are critical to our national defense and which are not. The longer the list, the more expensive protection becomes for American consumers.

3. *American workers need protection from cheap foreign labor.* The cheap-labor argument is heard often today. It claims that American producers and their workers need protection from firms operating in countries with much lower wage rates than the United States, wage rates that constitute an unfair advantage that protection should offset.

   There are two major flaws in this argument. First, low wages do not necessarily mean cheap labor. Labor is cheap only if the value of the output it produces is high relative to the wage rate. In many industries, the United States is very competitive internationally, despite its high wage rates. Workers produce more output per hour than their foreign counterparts because American workers tend to work with more and better machinery and tend to be better trained than workers in many other countries.

   Second, we must remember that no country can have a comparative advantage in everything. The United States has a comparative *disadvantage* in the production of products whose manufacture requires large amounts of unskilled labor. On the other hand, we tend to have a comparative advantage in goods that are produced using highly skilled labor or large quantities of land or capital.

   If we insist on protecting our labor-intensive industries, other nations have every right to protect their capital-intensive industries. Of course, such protectionism will deprive everyone of the benefits of comparative advantage, and we'll all be poorer for having resorted to protectionist measures. (Recently, some industries have been lobbying not for tariffs or quotas but for "managed" trade. Read "What is 'Managed Trade'—and Will It Work?" on page 518.)

Reducing Trade Barriers: The Role of Adjustment Assistance

For the most part, arguments in support of trade barriers amount to little more than pleas that we protect the incomes of certain groups in our society. In the past, pressure from various interest groups has been successful in maintaining tariff and quota protection for vulnerable industries. When the federal government gives in to pressure for protection, it forces society as a

What Is 'Managed Trade'—and Will It Work?

It's the latest buzzword in foreign-policy circles: "managed trade." Once a philosophy reserved for hard-line trade hawks, it is now favored in some form by such establishment heavyweights as Henry Kissinger and Cyrus Vance. In essence, "managed trade" means conceding that the Japanese system is fundamentally different from ours—and relying on negotiated results, rather than market forces, to improve the trade balance.

The phrase covers a range of approaches. Under the most common one, a country that discriminates against foreign goods would be forced to buy a specific amount of imports, with the total rising each year until a target is met.

If the country failed to buy the set amount, the United States would retaliate by limiting the offender's exports to America.

A second variation would focus on specific industries. The United States might demand that Japan buy a set amount of supercomputers, or communications satellites. Still another calls for "strict reciprocity": if a country delays in issuing contracts or patents for U.S. products, America responds in kind. Or, in the words of trade expert Lawrence Krause of the University of California, San Diego: "Anything they do to us, we do to them."

To free-traders, such ideas are anathema. Taken too far, they warn, managed trade could cause overall world trade to shrink and prices in "managed" industries to rise. "Managed trade is a terrible idea," says Michael Boskin,

head of the Council of Economic Advisers "It threatens trade wars. It sets governments up to dictate what people can buy and sell. It will make everybody poorer."

As the debate rages on, some groups are seeking middle ground. The Advisory Committee for Trade Policy and Negotiations, a group consisting of heads of major American corporations, has proposed a "results-oriented trade strategy." Under this plan, the United States would identify sectors in which it is competitive in most places except Japan. Then U.S. negotiators would set targets for the percentage of goods that it expects Japan to import, and work toward those objectives.

Can such tactics really work? Some economists believe that even in its modified form, the managed-trade concept will backfire. Jagdish Bhagwati, an economics professor at Columbia University, fears that managed trade would create a bureaucratic nightmare. "It becomes a matter of horse-trading between countries," he says. "Bureaucrats and politicians will take control."

Perhaps. But managed trade may be an unpalatable idea whose time is coming. Strong evidence exists that the Japanese would respond positively; they yield to European pressures all the time. And last year Tokyo resolved a dispute over South Korean knitware by granting Seoul an agreed-upon share of the Jap-anese market. As Chalmers Johnson, an Asia scholar at the University of California, San Diego, puts it, "[to date] Japan has found a rich uncle who bitches a lot but continues to send the check." If managed trade can ever be successfully implemented, the check may no longer be in the mail. —*Annetta Miller* with *Rich Thomas* and *Lourdes Rosado*

SOURCE: From *Newsweek*, March 5, 1990, p. 25, and © 1990, Newsweek, Inc. All rights reserved. Reprinted by permission.

USE YOUR ECONOMIC REASONING

1. What is meant by "managed trade"? Describe the type of policies that would be pursued under such a system.

2. According to Michael Boskin, managed trade would cause the prices in "managed" industries to rise and could lead to trade wars. Why do these outcomes seem likely?

3. Jagdish Bhagwati argues that managed trade would create a bureaucratic nightmare. Why?

4. Under one form of managed trade the United States might demand that Japan (or some other country) buy a set amount of a particular U.S. product to help correct a trade imbalance. How would politicians select the U.S. product?

whole to sacrifice the additional income and output that free trade could produce. On the other hand, there is no denying that the removal of trade barriers would hurt industries that are vulnerable to foreign competition. For this reason, many economists believe that efforts to reduce trade barriers should be accompanied by programs to help retrain workers and otherwise assist those harmed by foreign competition.

The Trade Adjustment Act of 1962 took an important first step in this direction. Under that act, workers who have lost jobs because of increased competition from imports become eligible for *trade adjustment assistance* in the form of higher unemployment compensation and funds for retraining. Businesses are granted money to modernize and better prepare to compete with foreign producers. About $3 billion worth of assistance was given in 1981, primarily to displaced automobile workers. The program was cut back during the Reagan administration, which supported increased spending for job-training programs rather than assistance targeted specifically toward workers hurt by foreign competition. The Bush administration has also relied on general programs rather than targeted assistance.

Even with the proper incentive, the process of retraining and relocation is much more complicated than it appears. In some cases displaced workers have very poor educational backgrounds, which makes retraining difficult and expensive. Sometimes there are no other industries in the area for which the workers can be retrained. Additional factors such as age, family ties, and limited personal savings often mean that relocation can be accomplished only at the cost of considerable personal hardship.

All of these problems complicate the transfer of labor to other industries and increase the human suffering associated with the removal of trade barriers. In fact, some critics argue that the case for free trade is commonly overstated because economists forget the assumptions of their models—that resources can shift easily from one industry to another, for example—seldom hold true in reality. This important criticism reinforces what we learned earlier in the chapter: Free trade tends to benefit consumers in general, but it usually imposes substantial costs on particular groups in the society. Such criticisms point to the need for adjustment assistance (perhaps available to any worker in need of retraining or relocation) and other programs and policies designed to improve the mobility of the work force—better general education for high school students and more effective retraining and job placement programs, for example—so that there will be a greater likelihood that workers released by one industry can find employment elsewhere without an unbearable delay. By approaching the problem this way, we can move closer to the ideal of free trade while we minimize the distress of workers who are displaced by foreign competition.

Summary

The economies of the world are becoming more interdependent. Americans are buying more *imports*—goods or services purchased from foreigners—and foreign consumers are buying more of our *exports*—products produced domestically and sold in other countries. Furthermore, many American-made products have foreign-made components. To know how to react to this growing interdependence, it is necessary to have some understanding of international economics—of why nations trade and how countries can benefit from trade.

One reason why nations trade is to acquire products that they cannot produce domestically. However, this is not the most important reason. Most countries can produce any product their citizens desire, *if* they are willing to expend the necessary resources. But trade may permit countries to acquire products much more cheaply—at a lower opportunity cost—than they can produce them domestically. This is the major benefit of international trade.

According to the theory of *comparative advantage*, each country should specialize in the products it can produce at a relatively low opportunity cost and trade for the items that other countries can produce more efficiently. This principle will permit each nation to achieve a higher standard of living than it could possibly attain if it remained self-sufficient.

Even when specialization is incomplete, trade can benefit consumers by providing them with a wider variety of products, limiting the pricing discretion of domestic producers, and forcing domestic producers to be more responsive to consumer demands.

Although free or unrestricted trade generally benefits consumers, it often imposes substantial costs on particular groups in any society—workers forced out of jobs by foreign competition, for instance. At least partly in response to pressure from these groups, countries erect *trade barriers*—legal restrictions on trade—to protect their domestic industries.

The most common devices for restricting imports are protective tariffs and import quotas. A *tariff* is a tax on imported products. A tariff on a foreign product increases its price and makes it less competitive in the marketplace, thereby encouraging consumers to buy domestic products instead. An *import quota* specifies the maximum amount of a particular product that can be imported.

Economists tend to condemn all forms of trade barriers. Such barriers allow domestic producers to charge higher prices and be less responsive to consumers. They also prevent countries from concentrating on the things they do best and trading for the best products produced by other countries.

In spite of the costs imposed by trade barriers, they continue to exist. Three common arguments are used to support trade barriers:

1. Infant industries need protection from foreign competition.
2. Defense-related industries must be protected to ensure our military self-sufficiency.
3. American workers need protection from cheap foreign labor.

For the most part, these arguments amount to little more than pleas to protect the incomes of certain groups in our society.

There is no denying that the removal of trade barriers will hurt industries that are vulnerable to foreign competition. For that reason, efforts to reduce trade barriers should be accompanied by programs to retrain workers and otherwise assist those harmed by foreign competition.

Glossary

Page 502   *Absolute advantage.* One nation's ability to produce a product more efficiently—with fewer resources—than another nation.

Page 502   *Comparative advantage.* One nation's ability to produce a product at a lower opportunity cost than that of other nations.

Page 499   *Exports.* Goods and services produced domestically and sold to customers in other countries.

Page 510   *Free trade.* Trade that is not hindered by artificial restrictions or trade barriers of any type.

Page 499   *Imports.* Goods and services that are purchased from foreign producers.

Page 511   *Import quota.* A law that specifies the maximum amount of a particular product that can be imported.

Page 511   *Tariff.* A tax on imported goods.

Page 520   *Trade adjustment assistance.* Aid to workers and firms that have been harmed by import competition.

Page 508   *Trade barriers.* Legal restrictions on trade.

Study Questions

Fill in the Blanks

1. Economists advocate that countries specialize in the products they can produce at a lower _____ than other countries.

2. If country *A* can produce all products more efficiently than country *B*, country *A* is said to have a(n) _____ in the production of everything.

3. If country *A* can produce a given product at a lower opportunity cost than country *B*, country *A* is said to have a(n) _____ in the production of that product.

4. A _____ is a tax on imported products.

5. An _____ specifies the maximum amount of a particular product that can be imported.

6. The _____ argument suggests that new industries need protection until they are firmly established.

7. A _____ quota simply limits the amount of a product that can be imported from the rest of the world, whereas a _____ quota specifies the maximum amount of a product that can be imported from each country.

8. Aid to workers who have been harmed by foreign competition is called _____.

9. In most situations, the (benefits/costs) _____ of free trade are widely diffused, while the (benefits/costs) _____ tend to be concentrated.

10. Most economists would like to see trade barriers eliminated. However, if they are forced to choose between tariffs and quotas, they would probably agree that _____ are less damaging to consumer welfare.

Multiple Choice

Use the following table in answering questions 1 through 4.

Production Possibilities per Unit of Economic Resources

	Food	Clothing
Country A	60	240
Country B	100	300

1. Which of the following statements is true?
   a) Country A has an absolute advantage in the production of both food and clothing.
   b) Country B has an absolute advantage in the production of both food and clothing.
   c) Country A has an absolute advantage in food, and country B has an absolute advantage in clothing.
   d) Country B has an absolute advantage in food, and country A has an absolute advantage in clothing.

2. In country A, the opportunity cost of a unit of food is
   a) 4 units of clothing.
   b) 60 units of clothing.
   c) 240 units of clothing.
   d) 1 unit of clothing.

3. According to the table,
   a) country A has a comparative advantage in food.
   b) country B has a comparative advantage in clothing.
   c) country A has a comparative advantage in clothing.
   d) country B has a comparative advantage in both food and clothing.

4. According to the principle of comparative advantage,
   a) country A should specialize in food, and country B should specialize in clothing.
   b) countries A and B should each continue to produce both food and clothing.

c) country *A* should specialize in clothing, and country *B* should specialize in food.

d) country *B* should specialize in clothing, and country *A* should specialize in food.

5. Which of the following is *not* a correct statement about trade barriers?
   a) Import tariffs are taxes on imports.
   b) Tariffs encourage consumers to buy domestic products.
   c) Quotas specify the maximum amount of a product that can be imported.
   d) Tariffs are probably more harmful to consumer welfare than quotas.

6. Which of the following is a true statement about trade barriers?
   a) They tend to enhance competition and benefit consumers.
   b) They benefit society as a whole but penalize small groups.
   c) They are needed to protect American workers from cheap foreign labor.
   d) They serve the interests of certain powerful groups, even though they penalize society as a whole.

7. The purpose of trade adjustment assistance is to
   a) assist foreign countries when a tariff or quota is used to reduce imports from that country.
   b) assist domestic workers who are harmed when a quota is levied.
   c) assist domestic workers who are harmed when a tariff is reduced or a quota is eliminated.
   d) a and c

8. Which of the following is an accurate description of the impact of tariffs?
   a) They tend to raise the prices of imported products that are subject to the tariff.
   b) They tend to raise the prices of domestically produced products that are comparable to those being taxed.
   c) They permit inefficient industries to continue to exist.
   d) All of the above

9. Suppose that Britain can produce either 20 bicycles or 100 calculators with a unit of resources, and that Taiwan can produce either 10 bicycles or 80 calculators. Which of the following statements is true?
   a) Taiwan has a comparative advantage in calculators.
   b) Taiwan has an absolute advantage in bicycles.
   c) Britain has a comparative advantage in calculators.
   d) Taiwan has an absolute advantage in calculators.

10. Why do economists prefer tariffs to quotas?
    a) Consumers may continue to buy imported products in spite of the tariff.
    b) Tariffs do not really hinder trade; in fact, they may enhance trade.
    c) As domestic products increase in price, foreign products become more competitive.
    d) a and c

Problems and Questions for Discussion

1. Suppose that your roommate can make a bed in three minutes, whereas it takes you six minutes. Suppose also that your roommate can polish a pair of shoes in ten minutes, whereas it takes you fifteen minutes to do the same chore. What can we say about comparative advantage and absolute advantage in this example? How could the principle of comparative advantage be used to make you both better off? Does it make any difference how often each of these tasks must be performed?

2. Explain the difference between comparative advantage and absolute advantage. Why do economists emphasize the concept of comparative advantage (rather than absolute advantage) as the basis for trade?

3. How is the concept of opportunity cost related to the principle of comparative advantage?

4. The chapter mentions that politicians in the United States and elsewhere often hear more about the costs of free trade than the benefits. Why is that the case?

5. How can specialization and trade allow countries to consume beyond their own respective production possibilities curves?

6. How do trade barriers contribute to the inefficient use of a society's scarce resources?

7. Some economists have suggested that interference with free trade may be legitimate if it is used as a "bargaining chip" to convince another country to lower its trade barriers. Economist Robert Lawrence has criticized this approach because "it's something like a nuclear deterrent—it only applies if it isn't used." ("New Theory Backs Some Protectionism," *New York Times*, September 9, 1985, page D1.) Explain Mr. Lawrence's comment.

8. If resources (including labor) could move freely from one industry to the next, there would be less opposition to the removal of trade barriers. Please explain.

9. Wisconsin University economist John Culbertson once suggested that "There is little comparative advantage in today's manufacturing industries, since they produce the same goods in the same ways in all parts of the world." ("'Free Trade' Is Impoverishing the West," *New York Times*, July 28, 1985, page F3.) How could less-developed countries gain access to the same type of capital equipment employed by the United States? Could they operate it if they could obtain it? What are the implications of Mr. Culbertson's statement?

10. State the three most common arguments for trade protection. What are the limitations of each of these arguments?

Answer Key

Fill in the Blanks

1. opportunity cost
2. absolute advantage
3. comparative advantage
4. tariff
5. import quota
6. infant industry
7. global, selective
8. trade adjustment assistance
9. benefits, costs
10. tariffs

Multiple Choice

1. b
2. a
3. c
4. c
5. d
6. d
7. c
8. d
9. a
10. d

INTERNATIONAL FINANCE

What are exchange rates, and how do they influence the prices we pay for imported products and even for travel? What do news commentators mean when they say that the dollar has "depreciated in value" or that the "appreciation of the yen" has made Japanese cars more expensive for Americans?

In Chapter 16, our simplified trade model assumed an arrangement whereby two countries exchanged their products directly. In reality, however, international transactions almost always involve money—the currencies of the two nations participating in the exchange. As we examine the financial dimension of international transactions, we'll learn how the dollars we spend on imported products are converted into the currencies desired by foreign producers, and we'll explore the systems used to determine exchange rates. We'll consider the factors that can cause the exchange value of a nation's currency to change and examine the impact of those changes on the nation's economy. In short, this chapter extends the analysis of Chapter 16, allowing us to gain a more complete understanding of international trade and our economic relationships with other nations.

International Trade and Exchange Rates

If you want to buy a Japanese radio, you can pay for your purchase with cash or check or credit card. Ultimately, however, Japanese producers want to receive payment in yen, their domestic currency, because their workers and domestic suppliers expect to be paid in yen. That's why French perfume manufacturers seek payment in francs, and Scottish producers of cashmere sweaters expect payment in pounds. The need to convert dollars into some foreign currency (or foreign currency into dollars) is the distinguishing feature of our trade with other nations.

The rate at which one currency can be exchanged for another currency is called the *exchange rate;* it is simply the price of one nation's currency stated in terms of another nation's currency. If you have traveled abroad, you know that the exchange rate is of more than passing interest. Suppose you are having dinner at a quaint London restaurant where steak and kidney pie costs ten pounds (£10). How much is that in American money? If the exchange rate is £1 to $3, you'll be spending $30.00; if it's £1 to $1.75 (about the current exchange rate), the same meal will cost you only $17.50.

American importers also want to know the dollar cost of British goods. A wool sweater that sells for £25 will cost the importer $75 if the exchange rate is £1 to $3, but it will cost $100 if the exchange rate is £1 to $4. Whenever the pound is cheaper (whenever it takes fewer dollars to purchase each pound), American tourists and importers will find British goods more attractive. If the pound becomes more expensive, fewer tourists will opt for a British vacation and fewer British products will be imported into the United States.

Foreign Exchange and the Balance of Payments

Before we examine how exchange rates are determined, we should be more familiar with the various sources and uses of foreign currency, or *foreign exchange.* This will give us a better picture of the forces that influence exchange

American businesses must acquire foreign currency to pay for the televisions and other products they import.

rates and will set the stage for our discussion of the existing exchange-rate system and the systems that preceded it.

Earning and Using Foreign Exchange

When American businesses import foreign products, they can pay for their products either by sending dollars, which the seller can exchange for domestic currency, or by sending payment in the seller's own currency. Either way, the importation of products will require ultimately that we obtain foreign currency. Additional reasons why we must acquire foreign currency are to make investments in other countries, to provide gifts to foreign citizens and governments, and to make dividend and interest payments to foreign investors.

One source of this foreign exchange is exports. When people in other countries purchase American-made blue jeans or tractors or computers, American businesses acquire the currencies of those countries. We also obtain foreign exchange when citizens and businesses of other countries invest in the United States (for example, when foreign automobile firms establish assembly plants in our country) and when Americans receive interest and dividend payments on investments they have made in other countries. Finally,

Americans can receive foreign exchange through gifts from individuals or groups in other countries. If your wealthy British aunt dies and leaves you two million pounds, your inheritance brings an inflow of foreign exchange. Similarly, U.S. holdings of foreign exchange would increase if the Japanese government endowed an American university with ten million yen to promote the study of Japanese culture.

The Balance of Payments Statement

Each nation keeps track of its economic transactions with other countries by recording them in a balance of payments statement. A *balance of payments (BOP)* statement is a record of *all* economic transactions between a particular country and the rest of the world during some specified period. It shows the various ways that a nation acquires and uses foreign exchange.

The payments side of Exh. 17.1 shows that our primary use of foreign exchange is in the purchase of imported products. In 1991 the United States spent $490 billion of foreign exchange in order to acquire imports, ap-

EXHIBIT 17.1

The U.S. Balance of Payments, 1991 (in billions)

U.S. PAYMENTS TO OTHER COUNTRIES		U.S. RECEIPTS FROM OTHER COUNTRIES	
Merchandise imports	$490.1	Merchandise exports	$416.5
Military expenditures abroad	15.7	Military sales abroad	10.5
Travel abroad and transportation on foreign carriers	72.2	Foreign travel in the U.S. and transportation on U.S. carriers	82.5
Income earned by foreigners on investments in the U.S.	105.9	Income earned by U.S. citizens on investments in other countries	115.3
Other services purchased by foreigners	20.9	Other services purchased from the U.S.	51.7
Gifts and grants to foreigners	19.7	Foreign investment in the U.S.	58.9
Investments in other countries	77.1	Errors and omissions	-3.1
Total	**$801.6**	**Total**	**$732.5**

Source: Adapted from *Survey of Current Business*, March 1992.

proximately 60 percent of our total payments to other countries. The major source of that foreign currency was our sale of exports. Merchandise exports earned the United States $416 billion in 1991, roughly 57 percent of our total receipts from other countries.

The relationship between a country's merchandise exports and its merchandise imports is called its **balance of trade (BOT).** When exports exceed imports, a country experiences a favorable balance of trade (BOT), or a **trade surplus.** When imports exceed exports, it experiences an unfavorable balance of trade, or a **trade deficit.** In 1991 the United States trade deficit was equal to $73.6 billion, the difference between merchandise imports (left-hand column) and merchandise exports (right-hand column).

Before the 1970s, U.S. trade deficits were virtually unheard of. In fact the United States enjoyed a favorable balance of trade in every year from 1946 through 1970. It was in the early 1970s that substantial OPEC price increases and our increased dependence on foreign oil led to trade deficits. Then, in the mid-1980s, the high value of the dollar—the fact that it took more foreign currency than before to buy each dollar—contributed further to our trade deficits. A strong dollar means more expensive American products for foreigners and cheaper imported products for Americans. (We'll explore the factors that influence the exchange value of the dollar later in the chapter.)

Merchandise exports and imports are only two of the transactions recorded on a nation's balance of payments statement. As we have seen, nations acquire and use foreign exchange in a variety of other ways. For example, on the payments side (left-hand column) of the balance of payments statement, we find among other items foreign travel by Americans, income earned by foreigners on investments in the United States, and foreign investments by U.S. citizens and businesses. For each of these transactions, Americans must obtain appropriate foreign exchange before they can make payment. When you travel abroad, for example, you must convert dollars into foreign currencies so that you can pay for meals, lodging, and souvenirs of your trip. All these transactions show up under the "Travel abroad . . ." category of the BOP statement.

As you learned earlier, the primary source of foreign exchange is the currency received by American firms that sell their products to buyers in foreign countries. When these exporters exchange their yen or francs or pounds for dollars to pay their employees and other domestic expenses, banks acquire foreign exchange that they can make available to others. Other sources of foreign exchange are listed in the right-hand column in Exh. 17.1. Among these are military sales abroad, travel by foreigners in the United States, and income earned by U.S. citizens on investments they have made in other countries. The entry entitled "Errors and omissions" is an adjustment to compensate for our government's inability to monitor every single transaction between our country and the rest of the world.

BOP Deficits and Surpluses

You can see from Exh. 17.1 that the two sides of the balance of payments statement don't necessarily balance. Total receipts from other countries do not always equal total payments to other countries.[1] When a nation earns more in foreign exchange than it needs to finance its transactions with other countries, it enjoys a favorable balance of payments or a *balance of payments surplus.* When it spends more abroad than it receives from other nations (when total payments exceed total receipts), it experiences an unfavorable balance of payments or a *balance of payments deficit.* In 1991 the United States experienced a BOP deficit of approximately $69.1 billion.

Don't confuse the balance of payments (BOP) with the balance of trade (BOT). A nation's BOT compares its merchandise exports with its merchandise imports, only one part of the BOP, whereas the BOP includes *all* financial transactions between the nation and the rest of the world. Exhibit 17.1 shows that the United States experienced both a balance of trade deficit and a balance of payments deficit in 1991, but this represents only one possibility. For example, it is possible for a nation to have an unfavorable BOT and a favorable BOP, or the converse—a favorable BOT and an unfavorable BOP.

Financing a Balance of Payments Deficit

Balance of payments deficits have been the norm for the United States since the 1970s. Over that period, the amount that we paid to other nations was not being offset by foreign payments to the United States. Where did we get the money to make up the difference—to pay off such debts? Think about your own financial situation for just a moment. Whenever you spend more than you earn in a given period, you either have to dip into your savings or borrow the money to make up the difference. When the United States pays

[1] Technically, total payments must always equal total receipts, much as total income must equal total output when we calculate gross national product (Chapter 9). If one country experiences a balance of payments deficit with some other country, the deficit nation must somehow make up the difference—it must finance the deficit. The transaction that finances the deficit is called a *compensatory* transaction because it allows one nation to compensate another nation in order to make up for the deficit in the balance of payments. When this compensatory transaction is taken into consideration, we can say that the two sides of the balance of payments statement do indeed balance.

out more than it takes in, it finances its international deficits in much the same way. One option is to reduce our reserves of foreign currencies, such as the German deutsche mark or the Japanese yen, currencies so widely accepted that they can be used to finance deficits with almost any country. Another option, if our foreign exchange holdings have been depleted, is to ask foreign nations to hold our dollars until some later date when they may be needed or use them to buy U.S. government securities.[2] At one time, deficits were also financed by the payment of gold from one country to another. Today such transfers are relatively rare.

An example may help to clarify the options available for financing a deficit. To simplify the example as much as possible, let's focus on our balance of payments with France and ignore the rest of the world for just a moment. Let's assume further that transactions are restricted to merchandise imports and exports, so that each nation's balance of payments is the same as its balance of trade (BOP = BOT). Now suppose that the United States wants to buy more from France than France wants to buy from the United States. Where will the United States find the additional francs to pay for the deficit? We might use reserves of francs held from an earlier period when we had a BOP surplus, or reserves of other currencies that France is willing to accept. Lacking such reserves, the United States probably will ask France to hold its excess dollars or convert those dollars into U.S. government securities, loan instruments that pay interest.

Why would the French agree to the arrangement described above? If the United States does not have a chronic balance of payments problem, the rationale is fairly obvious. By lending the United States the francs it needs today, France is able to acquire a stock of dollars (dollars in excess of what France now needs to buy our products) that can be used to finance future purchases of U.S. products. In other words, by helping us finance our current BOP deficit, France will be able to create a reserve of U.S. dollars that will help finance any balance of payments problems France might face in the future. Of course, if the United States is continually running BOP deficits and continually asking France to lend its francs, eventually the French may refuse to go along; at some point they may begin to wonder if their growing reserve of dollars will ever be worth anything in terms of goods and services. If that happens, France may demand that we take actions to eliminate our balance of payments deficit and thereby eliminate the need for additional borrowing.

---

[2] Actually, asking the foreign nations to buy our government securities is just a different way of asking them to hold our excess dollars—those in excess of what they need to buy American products. That's true because the value of U.S. government securities is stated in terms of dollars. Of course, the nations will prefer our securities to the dollars themselves because the securities pay interest.

In some respects the United States has greater flexibility in financing BOP deficits than most countries have, because the dollar is a *reserve currency* for many of the nations of the world. The dollar is one of the currencies that nations accumulate in order to settle balance of payments deficits with nations other than the United States. Thus France may be more willing to hold excess dollars than to hold excess pesos (Mexico) or lire (Italy). The status of the dollar as a reserve currency gives the United States more time to correct its balance of payments problems. Lesser economic powers such as Mexico and Italy are under greater pressure to eliminate BOP deficits because other trading nations have little use for their currency.

Exchange Rate Systems and Balance of Payments Problems

How do balance of payments problems arise, and how can a country correct them when they do appear? In order to answer those questions we need to understand the process by which exchange rates are established. We will examine two types of systems for determining exchange rates: flexible and fixed.

Flexible Exchange Rates

In a system of *flexible exchange rates* the exchange rates are determined by market forces—that is, by the interaction of demand and supply for each currency in question. Because rates are free to change in response to new demand or supply conditions, this is described as a system of flexible or floating exchange rates.

Americans demand foreign currencies in order to purchase imports, to make investments in other countries, to provide gifts to foreign citizens or foreign governments, and to make interest and dividend payments to foreign investors. To make any of these payments, Americans must exchange dollars for specific foreign currencies.

On the supply side, we see a similar list. Americans acquire foreign exchange from sales of American products abroad, from investments that foreign citizens make in the United States, from gifts to U.S. citizens, and from interest and dividend payments received by Americans on their investments abroad. The interaction of these demand and supply forces determines the rate at which the U.S. dollar will exchange for various foreign currencies.

Establishing the Equilibrium Exchange Rate. In order to illustrate this process, let's return to our discussion of trade between the United States and France. Exhibit 17.2 shows hypothetical demand and supply curves for francs. According to the exhibit, market forces produce an exchange rate of $.20 to 1 Fr (alternatively, the exchange rate may be stated as 5 Fr to $1.00). That's the *equilibrium exchange rate*—the exchange rate at which the quantity of francs demanded would exactly equal the quantity supplied. At this equilibrium exchange rate, neither the United States nor France would have balance of payments problems because neither currency would be in shortage or in surplus.

Suppose the exchange rate temporarily became $.30 to 1 Fr. At that exchange rate, the franc would be *overvalued*—the dollar price of the franc would be too high for equilibrium. You can see from the exhibit that fifteen

---

EXHIBIT 17.2

The Equilibrium Exchange Rate

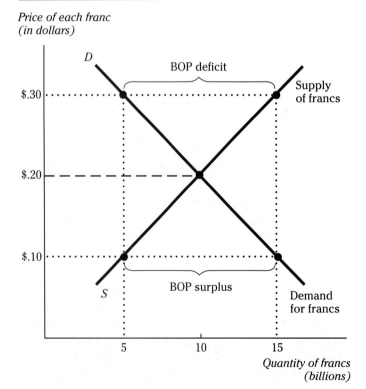

*Price of each franc
(in dollars)*

*Quantity of francs
(billions)*

At the equilibrium exchange rate ($.20 = 1 Fr), the quantity of francs demanded is exactly equal to the quantity supplied, and France has neither a BOP deficit nor a BOP surplus. If the dollar price of the franc is too high for equilibrium, France will face a BOP deficit; if it is too low, France will experience a BOP surplus. When the exchange rate is allowed to seek its own level, it will move to the equilibrium rate.

billion francs would be supplied at that rate, but only five billion francs would be demanded. Because less French currency is being demanded than supplied, France must be paying out more than it is earning from the United States. Thus France would have a balance of payments deficit of ten billion francs (three billion dollars) at that exchange rate. In a free market, this excess supply, or surplus, of ten billion francs would tend to drive down the price of the franc, just as a surplus drives down the price of wheat or cattle or anything else. In this way, market forces would tend to push the exchange rate toward its equilibrium level.

Now consider an exchange rate of $.10 to 1 Fr. At that exchange rate, the franc would be *undervalued*—the dollar price of the franc would be too low for equilibrium. According to the exhibit, fifteen billion francs would be demanded at that rate, but only five billion supplied. Therefore France would have a balance of payments surplus of ten billion francs (one billion dollars). But in a free market the excess demand, or shortage of francs, would tend to push up the price of the franc until it reached the equilibrium level. In summary, if the exchange rate is left to seek its own level, ultimately it will reach equilibrium. At the equilibrium exchange rate, the quantity of francs demanded will exactly equal the quantity supplied, and France will have neither a BOP deficit nor a BOP surplus.

Changes in the Equilibrium Exchange Rate. Now suppose that the demand for French francs increases. Why might that happen? Here are some possible reasons:

1. Perhaps Americans are demanding more French products—more wine and perfume and designer fashions—because the U.S. economy is expanding and the incomes of Americans are growing. (Remember, consumption spending is related to the level of income; higher incomes mean more consumption spending for imported products as well as domestic products.) If that's the case, the demand for francs will increase because more francs will be needed to purchase more French imports.

2. Perhaps the U.S. government has decided to expand its military operations in France and must spend more money to support our military personnel. The U.S. government will then exchange more dollars for francs.

3. Perhaps an increase in American income brings more American tourists to France, where they stay in French hotels, eat in French restaurants, travel on French ships and airlines, and spend money in all the other ways that tourists do. More spending on French goods and services means exchanging more dollars for French francs.

4. Perhaps more Americans are investing money in France because French interest rates have become higher than interest rates in the United States. If the

prevailing interest rate in France is 20 percent and the U.S. rate is 15 percent, you can bet that many Americans are going to exchange dollars for francs in order to invest their money in France.

Any of these changes would increase the demand for francs and therefore shift the demand curve for francs to the right, from D_1 to D_2 in Exh. 17.3. If the demand for francs increases and the exchange rate remains at $.20 to 1 Fr, we have a problem. At that rate twenty billion francs will be demanded, while only ten billion will be supplied. Thus France will have a balance of payments surplus, and the United States will have to finance a balance of payments deficit of ten billion francs (two billion dollars).

Under a system of flexible exchange rates, however, balance of payments deficits and surpluses are eliminated automatically by changes in the exchange rate. In our example, the increase in the demand for francs results in an increase in the dollar price of francs from $.20 to $.30 per franc, the equilibrium rate where the quantity demanded equals the quantity supplied. The dollar has *depreciated* (lost value) against the franc because it now takes a larger fraction of a dollar to buy each franc. Conversely, the franc has

---

EXHIBIT 17.3

An Increase in the Demand for Francs

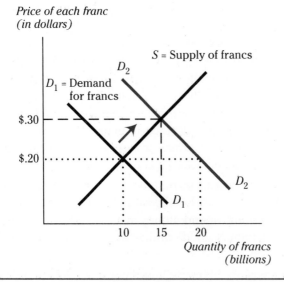

Price of each franc (in dollars)

If the demand for francs increases, the franc will tend to appreciate in value; it will take more American money to buy each franc (or, conversely, it will take fewer francs to buy each dollar).

appreciated (gained value) against the dollar because each franc now buys more dollars (cents).

This adjustment process automatically eliminates the balance of payments deficit. At the new exchange rate of $.30 to 1 Fr, French products are less attractive, and Americans will purchase fewer of them. Fewer Americans will find French vacations, champagne, and designer clothing a good buy. At the same time, French consumers will take advantage of the cheaper dollar—the converse of a more expensive franc—and buy more American goods, thus helping the United States earn the additional francs needed to pay for more French imports. By automatically equating the quantity demanded and the quantity supplied of each currency, flexible exchange rates eliminate balance of payments problems.

Suppose that American blue jeans became more popular with the French, or that investments in the United States became more attractive. How would those changes alter the exchange rate? Either of those changes would require that French citizens obtain additional dollars. To obtain those dollars, they would need to supply francs. Remember that! *An increase in the demand for dollars leads to an increase in the supply of francs.* This will shift the supply curve of francs to the right (see Exh. 17.4 on page 542) and reduce the dollar price of a franc. Does that mean that the *dollar* has appreciated or depreciated? It means that the dollar has appreciated in value, since it now buys more francs than before. Alternatively, the franc has depreciated; it takes more francs to buy each dollar.

As before, the change in the exchange rate automatically matches up the quantity demanded and supplied of this currency, eliminating BOP problems. Our graphs make it appear that this adjustment process occurs instantaneously, but that's not really the case. When there is a change in the exchange rate, it takes a while for trade to adjust to the new rate. If a product has become more expensive due to an exchange rate change, importers must look for a new source of supply. In addition, long-term contracts may bind them to suppliers for some time into the future. The article on page 540, "Caterpillar Sees Gains in Efficiency Imperiled by Strength of Dollar," looks at the impact of exchange rate changes on U.S. manufacturing firms.

As you can see, the system of flexible exchange rates has the desirable feature of eliminating balance of payments problems automatically. However, the system contains a flaw. Many business and government officials believe that the daily variation in exchange rates makes the outcome of international transactions less predictable for trading partners and therefore may restrict the overall volume of international trade. Because exchange rates are free to fluctuate, exporters face some of the risks of speculation. They can't know precisely how much they will receive in their own country's

Caterpillar Sees Gains in Efficiency Imperiled by Strength of Dollar

EAST PEORIA, Ill.—Caterpillar Inc.'s tough battle to remain the international leader in heavy machinery is being waged here at plant KK, where yellow-helmeted workers are ripping out antiquated machine tools and putting in dozens of octopus-shaped robots. The work is part of a $2 billion overhaul of Caterpillar's manufacturing operations.

But across the Illinois River at Caterpillar's world headquarters, executives fret that a force beyond their control is undermining this efficiency drive: the weakening Japanese yen. Over the past 16 months, the dollar has climbed 30% against the yen, making Japanese goods comparably less expensive in the U.S. and third-country markets and giving Caterpillar rivals such as Komatsu Ltd. a substantial competitive edge.

Indeed, the difference in the exchange rates alone has slashed Komatsu's costs by a greater percentage than the reductions Caterpillar antici-

pates from its entire modernization program.

Worsening Problem

"It gets tougher and tougher to compete," complains James W. Wogsland, a Caterpillar executive vice president. "We're concerned about the [dollar's] trend, and we don't see how it's going to stop."

Caterpillar's factories obviously aren't the only ones likely to be hurt. C. Fred Bergsten, the director of the Institute for International Economics in Washington, estimates that if the yen-dollar exchange rate remains at its current level, U.S. exporters could lose $5 billion to $10 billion in business annually. In addition, billions more could be lost as Americans buy more Japanese-made goods.

"It's a matter of great concern when you work so hard to see it wiped out by something you don't control," says G. Mustafa Mohatarem, the director of trade and competitive analysis at General Motors Corp., which also has invested heavily to modernize its U.S. manufacturing. . . .

Corporate Lone Wolf

Caterpillar also has become something of a lone wolf

among major U.S. companies. In the past 10 years, many American corporations have built more overseas factories, increased purchases of Japanese materials and components, and become more sophisticated in using financial hedging instruments—all moves that lessen the impact of a strengthening dollar. . . .

So, even though major multinationals' U.S.-based manufacturing operations suffer when the dollar rises, the companies can still look good in their financial reports. In fact, their overseas operations become more profitable, in dollar terms, when the firms convert them into dollars to bring them home.

The result: There are fewer fired-up corporate advocates for industrial America. The attitude among many companies today is "Who cares where I make my money?" says Ben Fischer, a former Steelworkers union official who directs the Center for Labor Studies at Carnegie-Mellon University. "You do not have sharp, black-and-white motivations in terms of what happens in U.S. operations." Even Timothy L. Elder, Caterpillar's chief lobbyist, concedes that "there aren't a whole lot of folks getting concerned" about the declining yen. . . .

Like many U.S. companies, Caterpillar has taken some steps to protect itself from currency gyrations, but it also has retained a singular commitment to succeeding as a predominantly American manufacturer. More than two-thirds of its 60,400 employees work in the U.S., where it has 17 production sites. . . .

In the mid-1980s, it was Caterpillar that led corporate America's charge against the then-sky-high dollar. (It was much higher then than it is now.) Enlisting the aid of such potent groups as the National Association of Manufacturers and the Business Roundtable, Caterpillar Chairman Lee L. Morgan waged a crusade on Capitol Hill and met more than a dozen times with top administration officials, including President Reagan. The lobbying helped lead to the landmark Plaza Agreement in 1985, when industrial-

ized nations agreed to try to drive down the dollar.

Trying Again

Now, Caterpillar is again revving up its exchange-rate activism. Its executives are warning any bureaucrat who will listen that the dollar's rise against the yen damages American competitiveness. . . .

Caterpillar officials acknowledge, however, that there aren't any clear solutions to their problems. . . .

Caterpillar and other U.S. companies would welcome a reduction in U.S. interest rates, which could make the dollar less attractive and bolster their business. But the Fed fears that if it acts to lower rates, U.S. inflation probably would increase. . . .

But that doesn't stop Caterpillar from pressing its point. And if the yen doesn't stop slumping, more manufacturers may join Cat's chorus. Vows Mr. Elder, the company's lobbyist: "In the next couple of months, we'll turn up the heat."

—*Robert L. Rose*

SOURCE: *The Wall Street Journal*, April 6, 1990, p 1. Reprinted by permission of *The Wall Street Journal*, © 1990 Dow Jones & Company, Inc. All Rights Reserved Worldwide.

USE YOUR ECONOMIC REASONING

1. If the dollar has "climbed 30% against the yen," does that mean that the dollar has appreciated or depreciated?

2. Explain how exchange rate changes can wipe out the efficiency gains achieved by Caterpillar.

3. Why is Caterpillar more concerned than many other U.S. companies about the strength of the dollar?

4. Why does Caterpillar want the Fed to reduce U.S. interest rates? How would that help Caterpillar's competitive position?

EXHIBIT 17.4

An Increase in the Supply of Francs

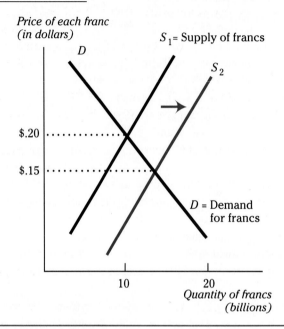

An increase in the supply of francs will tend to depreciate the franc; it will take less American money to buy each franc.

currency for the goods they export. To the degree that this uncertainty discourages foreign trade, nations lose the advantages of specialization based on comparative advantage.[3] Despite this shortcoming—or perhaps because of it—the system that has operated since the early 1970s is best described as a quasi-flexible exchange rate system. Exchange rates have been allowed to change or float within limits agreed on by the central governments concerned.

Fixed Exchange Rates

Prior to the emergence of flexible exchange rates, the international monetary system was characterized by one form or another of *fixed exchange rates,* rates established by central governments rather than by market forces. We will look

---

[3] Many economists have pointed out that exporters and importers can protect themselves against exchange rate changes by buying and selling foreign currency in what is called the *futures market* for foreign exchange. For example, if an importer wanted to protect itself against a change in the exchange rate, it would buy forward foreign exchange of the country whose

first at the gold standard and then at its successor, the Bretton Woods system, instituted after World War II.

The Gold Standard. From the early 1800s to the end of the Great Depression, the international fixed exchange rate system was the ***gold standard;*** each country's currency was linked to gold. A central government agreed to buy and sell gold to anyone and everyone at a specified price stated in terms of that country's currency. For example, if the United States agreed to buy gold for $20 an ounce and France agreed to pay 100 Fr per ounce, the exchange rate of dollar to franc was $20 to 100 Fr, or $1 to 5 Fr. That rate would prevail until either the United States or France changed the price it was willing to pay for gold.

In those days, a central government changed the price only in response to persistent balance of payments problems. For example, if France continually bought more from the United States than the United States bought from France, France might ***devalue*** its currency by agreeing to pay more francs for each ounce of gold.[4] By reducing the value of its currency in terms of gold, France would also establish with the United States a new exchange rate that would encourage Americans to import more French products and discourage French citizens from importing as many American goods and services.

According to supporters of the gold standard, balance of payments problems normally would not require devaluation of currency because a mechanism of the system would restore balance of payments equilibrium automatically whenever it was disrupted. The system of the gold standard was thought to work in the following way: Whenever a country experienced a balance of payments deficit, it would be required to ship gold to the surplus country to finance the deficit. Because all currencies were tied to gold, this action would reduce the money supply in the deficit country, which in turn would reduce the demand for goods and services (including imports) and increase unemployment. Lower domestic demand would tend to reduce prices, which would help to stimulate exports. The surplus country would experience the opposite effects. The inflow of gold would lead to an increase in the country's money supply, which would stimulate spending (including spending for imports), employment, and prices. Higher prices would tend to reduce exports, since the surplus country's products would not be such good

products it was importing. What this means is that the importer buys foreign currency to be received in the future at an exchange rate agreed upon now.

[4] By convention, economists use the term *devalue* in connection with fixed exchange rate systems and *depreciate* when speaking of flexible exchange rate systems. When the value of a currency in terms of gold is increased, it has been *revalued upward* under a fixed exchange rate system, rather than having *appreciated,* as under a system of flexible rates.

buys as they were before. In this way, the transfer of gold was thought to eliminate the underlying source of the balance of payments problem.

The gold standard worked reasonably well as a fixed exchange rate system so long as the economic adjustments required to maintain BOP equilibrium were not sudden or severe. However, following World War I, the system fell apart. Nations with substantial balance of payments problems refused to subject their domestic economies to widespread unemployment in order to restore the value of their currency. Instead, they devalued their currency in an attempt to stimulate exports and discourage imports. These decisions by central governments led to round after round of competitive devaluations, in which one country devalued its currency only to see its competitive edge wiped out as other nations followed suit. As a result of the uncertainty created by sudden devaluations, trade virtually ceased until a new fixed exchange rate system was devised to restore some stability.

The Bretton Woods System. From the end of World War I until after World War II the international economy experimented with a variety of temporary exchange rate systems, none of which gained acceptance. Then an international monetary conference held in 1944 at Bretton Woods, New Hampshire, developed a new fixed exchange rate system in which the U.S. dollar played a prominent role. Under what became known as the *Bretton Woods system,* most governments agreed to maintain a fixed value for their currency in terms of the dollar, while the United States agreed to redeem dollars (from foreign central banks) for gold at $35 an ounce. This linked all major currencies directly to the dollar and indirectly to one another. For example, if France and the United States agreed that $1.00 would exchange for 6 Fr, and the United States and Germany agreed that $1.00 would exchange for 2 DM (deutsche marks), then 3 Fr would exchange for 1 DM.

Once these exchange rates were established, each nation was required to maintain its exchange rate unless it experienced a chronic balance of payments problem, which could be corrected only through a change in the official rate. To maintain its exchange rate, a nation was expected to intervene in foreign exchange markets whenever necessary. The process of intervening in foreign exchange markets is illustrated in Exh. 17.5.

Under the terms of the Bretton Woods system, suppose there is a decrease in the demand for French products, represented by the shift from D_1 to D_2. At the official exchange rate of $.20, only eight billion francs are being demanded while ten billion are being supplied. In other words, there is a surplus, or excess supply, of two billion francs. Under free-market conditions, the value of the franc would decline from $.20 to $.15. But this would violate the Bretton Woods agreement to maintain a stable rate. To offset this

EXHIBIT 17.5

Intervention in Foreign Exchange Markets

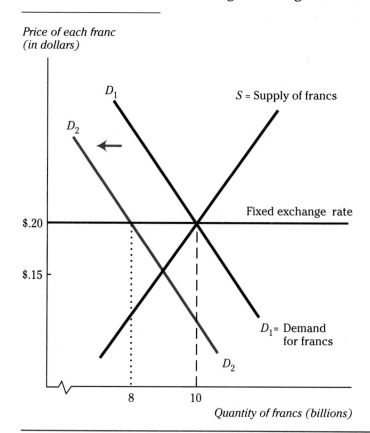

*Price of each franc
(in dollars)*

D_1

D_2

S = Supply of francs

Fixed exchange rate

$.20

$.15

D_1= Demand
for francs

D_2

8   10

Quantity of francs (billions)

*If the demand for francs
declines under a fixed
exchange rate system, the
nation must buy up the
surplus currency in order to
maintain the official
exchange rate. Here, France
must use its reserves of
dollars to purchase two
billion surplus francs.*

change and maintain the official exchange rate of $.20, the French central bank is expected to intervene in the foreign exchange market by using its reserves of dollars and other currencies to buy these excess francs. In effect, it is expected to increase the demand for francs artificially, forcing the franc back to its initial position.

If this change in the demand for French products is short-lived, there will be no problem. Later the French will be able to rebuild their reserves of currency when the demand for their products is strong. But if the French are confronted with a long-term decline in demand, they will eventually run out of currencies with which to buy francs.

In 1944, a conference at Bretton Woods, New Hampshire led to a new fixed exchange rate system.

Under the Bretton Woods system, intervention was intended to correct temporary and modest changes in the demand for a country's currency; it was not viewed as a cure-all for fundamental disequilibrium. When currencies were clearly overvalued or undervalued, the Bretton Woods system provided for a change in the official rate. Thus the system was intended to be more flexible than its predecessor, the gold standard. Whereas the gold standard expected nations to deflate their economies if necessary to maintain the exchange rate, Bretton Woods provided for a realignment of exchange rates when fundamental disequilibrium existed.

In order to assist central governments in making short-term adjustments, the Bretton Woods agreement established the International Monetary Fund (IMF). Member nations were required to contribute funds to the organization, which then made loans to countries that faced short-term balance of payments problems. The IMF also granted formal permission for devaluation in cases of fundamental or long-term disequilibrium.

The Emergence of the Managed Float

As time passed and conditions changed, the fixed exchange rates established at Bretton Woods gradually began to deviate from equilibrium exchange rates, and nations began to experience balance of payments problems. By the 1960s, the currencies of Japan and Germany, for example, had become significantly undervalued, and these nations had BOP surpluses. On the other hand, the dollar was overvalued, and the United States experienced chronic balance of payments deficits.

Despite these chronic problems, the nations were unable to agree on who should take the initiative in reestablishing exchange rates. Should the United States devalue its currency, or should surplus countries appreciate their currencies against the dollar? Instead of devaluing its currency, many nations wanted the United States to deflate, or depress, its economy in order to reduce import demand and strengthen its currency. The United States was unwilling to take this action. At the same time, most surplus nations were unwilling to appreciate their currencies because this action would depress their export industries. The resulting impasse led to no changes in the official exchange rates, and BOP problems continued.

Because the United States was experiencing chronic balance of payments deficits, nations were no longer willing to hold our surplus dollars. Instead, they started asking the United States to redeem those dollars for gold. (Recall that at the Bretton Woods conference the United States had *agreed* to redeem dollars for gold.) By the late sixties, it was apparent that our gold supply would soon be exhausted. Thus, in August 1971, President Nixon announced that the United States would no longer buy or sell gold at any price. In effect, the dollar was left to *float*—to find its own value in foreign exchange markets. By 1973, most of the major trading nations were letting their currencies float. As a consequence, the system that has emerged bears a strong resemblance to the system of flexible exchange rates that we described earlier.

Under the present system, exchange rates are determined to a great extent by market forces—by the supply and demand for the currencies in question. There is, however, a significant amount of government intervention in foreign exchange markets. Central banks attempt to smooth out, or moderate, short-term fluctuations in exchange rates. In some instances they may even attempt to reverse exchange rate changes that they consider inappropriate, or hasten exchange rate changes that they see as desirable. This system of quasi-flexible exchange rates is sometimes described as a ***managed float.*** The article on page 548, "Dollar's Speedy Ascent Slowed by Intervention," looks at efforts to manage exchange rate changes.

Dollar's Speedy Ascent Slowed by Intervention
Foreign Exchange

A second day of dollar selling by central banks slowed the dollar's speedy ascent from its record lows against some currencies only four weeks ago.

Though yesterday's selling barrage was more successful than a similar effort on Monday, when the dollar rose strongly anyway, the U.S. currency remains in strong demand.

In late New York trading, the dollar stood at 1.5695 marks and 135.80 yen, down from 1.5815 marks and 138.24 yen on Monday but still near the levels at which the central banks intervened. The British pound rose to $1.8635 from $1.8515 the day before.

In intraday activity Monday, the dollar climbed to 1.5875 marks and 138.63 yen, its highest levels in six months. At that point, the dollar was up about 10% against the mark from its post-World War II low of 1.4425 set Feb. 11.

Attempts to slow the dollar's advance yesterday began in Asian markets, where traders said the Bank of Japan bought yen and sold dollars when the U.S. currency was trading at about 136 yen. Later, in Europe, the Bundesbank along with at least seven other European central banks intervened at 1.57 marks.

Both the level of the dollar and the speed with which it rises or falls is important.

Some economists contend that wildly fluctuating exchange rates inhibit international trade and investment. And although currency markets usually "overshoot" to some degree, a fast-rising currency can begin to feed on itself and accelerate as it climbs through important levels on traders' charts. . . .

Over a longer period, a strong dollar could threaten to choke American economic growth just as, many analysts are predicting, the U.S. begins to pull out of recession. That's because a rising dollar makes U.S. goods less competitive on world markets by increasing their cost while reducing the costs of products priced in foreign currencies.

Moreover, a rising dollar adds to inflationary pressures in other countries by increasing the cost of imports. "The Bundesbank is always paranoid about inflation, and they need a strong mark to fight it and to keep the 3% to 3.5% inflation rate they want," said Claus Wagner, chief trader at Citibank in Frankfurt. . . .

The same logic would apply to other European economies that are either directly or indirectly linked to the mark. "But if the dollar's rise proved to be unstoppable, it might force the Bundesbank to raise interest rates" to defend the mark, said Gisela Kurtz, a senior vice president at Deutsche Bank AG in Frankfurt. That, in turn, would put upward pressure on rates elsewhere in Europe, which are already high because of German spending to prop up its eastern states. "This is a very delicate situation," she said. . . .

—*Michael R. Sesit*

SOURCE: *The Wall Street Journal*, March 13, 1991, p. C13. Reprinted by permission of *The Wall Street Journal*, © 1991 Dow Jones & Company, Inc. All Rights Reserved Worldwide.

USE YOUR ECONOMIC REASONING

1. **When the Bank of Japan buys yen and sells dollars, how does that alter the exchange rate between the dollar and the yen? What is the purpose of this intervention?**

2. **What policies should the Fed pursue if it wants to slow the ascent (appreciation) of the dollar?**

3. **The article suggests that the German central bank, the Bundesbank, may feel compelled to raise German interest rates in order to "defend the mark." What is meant by "defending the mark"? How would higher interest rates in Germany accomplish this objective?**

4. **What groups in the United States are harmed when the dollar appreciates? What groups are helped?**

Even before the United States forced the shift to flexible rates, many nations supported such a move. They believed flexibility would be preferable to the old fixed rate system, which sometimes put pressure on central governments to slow the growth of their domestic economies in order to maintain equilibrium exchange rates. When the price of a stable exchange rate was domestic unemployment, few nations could see the benefits exceeding the costs.

But the system of flexible exchange rates adopted in the mid-1970s has not been without problems. At times, exchange rate movements have been quite volatile. Moreover, the adjustments to exchange rate changes have not transpired as rapidly as proponents of flexibility predicted, so balance of payments problems have persisted longer than anticipated. In addition, governments have discovered that, even under a regime of flexible exchange rates, balance of payments considerations can limit their ability to manage their domestic economies. In the late 1980s, for example, the Federal Reserve was reluctant to expand the money supply, even though a recession threatened. To do so would have driven down domestic interest rates, which would have reduced capital inflows into the United States and contributed to a weaker dollar. Thus the Fed's ability to stimulate the domestic economy was handicapped by concern for the exchange rate and the U.S. balance of payments.

Because flexible exchange rates have not proven to be the panacea that was hoped for in the mid-1970s, a vocal minority of economists have argued for a return to some form of fixed exchange rate system. But most believe that although the existing system is far from ideal, it represents an improvement over fixed regimes. At this time no major changes appear likely.

Summary

The feature that distinguishes international trade from trade within a nation is the need to convert the currency of one nation to the currency of some other nation. The rate at which one currency is exchanged for some other currency is called the *exchange rate*. The exchange rate plays a critical role in determining each country's level of imports and exports. Whenever the dollar is cheaper—that is, whenever it takes fewer pounds or yen or francs to purchase each dollar—importers will find American goods more attractive and Americans will find British and Japanese and French goods more expensive. On the other hand, if the dollar becomes more expensive, American goods will become less attractive and foreign goods a better buy.

The relationship between a country's merchandise exports and its merchandise imports is called its *balance of trade (BOT)*. When exports exceed imports, a country experiences a favorable balance of trade, or a *trade surplus*. When imports exceed exports, it experiences an unfavorable balance of trade, or a *trade deficit*.

A nation's balance of trade is one part of a broader accounting record called a balance of payments (BOP) statement. A balance of payments statement looks at all financial transactions between a nation and the rest of the world, not just merchandise imports and exports. It shows the various ways that a nation acquires and uses foreign currency, or *foreign exchange*. When a nation earns more in foreign exchange than it needs to finance its transactions with the rest of the world, it enjoys a *balance of payments surplus*. When it spends more abroad than it receives from other nations, it experiences a *balance of payments deficit*.

Whenever a nation has a balance of payments deficit, it must finance that deficit in some way. One option is to reduce its holdings of foreign currencies. Some currencies (e.g., the dollar, the deutsche mark, and the yen) are so widely accepted that they can be used to finance deficits with almost any country. Another option is to ask foreign nations to hold the deficit country's currency until some later date when it may be needed. Finally, the deficit country may ask the surplus country to buy its government's securities; under this approach, the deficit country in effect would be paying interest on a loan from the surplus country.

Under a system of *flexible exchange rates*, wherein exchange rates are determined by market forces, balance of payments deficits and surpluses tend to be eliminated automatically. At the *equilibrium exchange rate*, the quantity demanded of a particular currency is equal to the quantity supplied, and neither a deficit nor a surplus exists in the balance of payments. There is one problem with this system, however. Because exchange rates are free to fluctuate, the outcome of international transactions is less predictable for trading partners. Because of this shortcoming and because central governments want to moderate fluctuations in exchange rates, the system that has been in existence since the early 1970s is best described as a quasi-flexible exchange rate system. Exchange rates have been allowed to change, or float, but within limits.

Prior to the emergence of flexible exchange rates, the international monetary system was governed by one form or another of *fixed exchange rates*, rates established by central governments rather than by market forces. The first system was the *gold standard*. Each central government agreed to buy and sell gold at some specified price stated in terms of that country's currency. Since each currency was linked to gold, all of the currencies of the world were linked indirectly to one another. After World War II, the gold standard was replaced by the *Bretton Woods system*. Under this system, most governments agreed to maintain a fixed value for their currency in terms of the dollar, while the United States agreed to redeem dollars for gold at $35 an ounce. Since all currencies were linked directly to the dollar, they were also linked indirectly to one another.

Under both of these fixed exchange rate systems, each nation was expected to maintain its exchange rate unless it encountered a balance of payments problem that only devaluation would correct. If a nation was facing a BOP deficit, it was expected to accept unemployment and falling prices as the necessary cost of maintaining a stable exchange rate. In the final analysis, most nations were unwilling to accept this cost; their reluctance led to the emergence of the quasi-flexible exchange rate system that exists today.

Glossary

Page 539   *Appreciation of currency.* Under a system of flexible exchange rates, an increase in the value of a currency.

Page 533   *Balance of payments deficit.* Total payments to other countries exceed total receipts from other countries for an unfavorable balance of payments.

Page 533   *Balance of payments surplus.* Total receipts from other countries exceed total payments to other countries for a favorable balance of payments.

Page 531   *Balance of payments (BOP) statement.* A record of all economic transactions between a particular country and the rest of the world during some specified period of time.

Page 532   *Balance of trade (BOT).* The relationship between a country's merchandise imports and its merchandise exports during some specified period of time.

Page 544   *Bretton Woods system.* A fixed exchange rate system in which member nations agreed to fix a value on their currency in terms of the dollar, and the United States agreed to redeem dollars from other central banks for gold.

Page 538   *Depreciation of currency.* Under a system of flexible exchange rates, a decrease in the value of a currency.

Page 543   *Devaluation of currency.* Under a system of fixed exchange rates, an official reduction in the value of a currency.

Page 536   *Equilibrium exchange rate.* The exchange rate at which the quantity of a currency demanded is equal to the quantity supplied.

Page 529   *Exchange rate.* The price of one nation's currency stated in the terms of another nation's currency.

Page 542   *Fixed exchange rate.* An exchange rate that is established by a central government rather than by market forces.

Page 535   *Flexible exchange rate.* An exchange rate that is determined by market forces, by the supply and demand for the currencies in question.

Page 529   *Foreign exchange.* The currency of another country.

Page 543   *Gold standard.* A fixed exchange rate system in which the value of each country's currency is tied directly to gold.

Page 547   *Managed float.* The quasi-flexible exchange rate system that has been in place since 1973. Under this system, exchange rates are determined essentially by supply and demand conditions, but central banks intervene to a significant degree in order to manage exchange rate changes.

Page 535   *Reserve currency.* A widely accepted currency that nations accumulate to use in settling up balance of payments deficits with other nations (e.g., the dollar or the deutsche mark).

Page 532   *Trade deficit.* Imports exceed exports for an unfavorable balance of trade.

Page 532   *Trade surplus.* Exports exceed imports for a favorable balance of trade.

Study Questions

Fill in the Blanks

1. The price of one currency in terms of another currency is called the _____ _____.

2. Another term for foreign currency is _____.

3. When imports exceed exports, a country is experiencing a _____ _____ ; when exports exceed imports, a country is experiencing a _____.

4. The _____ refers to merchandise imports and exports, while the _____ refers to all economic transactions between nations.

5. There are essentially two types of exchange rate systems: those involving _____ exchange rates and those involving _____ exchange rates.

6. Under a system of flexible exchange rates, if it takes more French francs than before to buy an American dollar, we can say that the dollar has _____ _____ and the franc has _____.

7. If per capita incomes increased in the United States due to an economic expansion, U.S. imports of foreign products would probably (increase/decrease) _____.

8. Under the gold standard, a country with a balance of payments deficit would tend to (lose/gain) _____ gold, which would serve to (expand/contract) _____ the domestic money supply and reduce imports into that country.

9. If interest rates are higher in the United States than they are abroad, foreign investors will tend to invest more money in the United States, and the dollar will tend to (appreciate/depreciate) _____ in value.

10. If the dollar appreciates in value, it will be (harder/easier) _____ for American producers to sell their products abroad.

Multiple Choice

1. If total exports by the United States exceed total imports, the United States is experiencing a
   a) balance of payments deficit.
   b) balance of payments surplus.
   c) balance of trade deficit.
   d) balance of trade surplus.

2. Which of the following is not a source of foreign exchange for the United States?
   a) Foreign tourists visiting the United States
   b) U.S. exports to France
   c) U.S. imports from Japan
   d) German investments in the United States

3. For which of the following transactions must the United States acquire foreign exchange?
   a) Buying Japanese automobiles
   b) Investing in French companies
   c) Paying dividends to Arabs on their U.S. investments
   d) All of the above

4. If Americans decide to buy more Japanese automobiles,
   a) the demand curve for Japanese yen will shift to the left.
   b) the demand curve for American dollars will shift to the right.
   c) the demand curve for Japanese yen will shift to the right.
   d) the supply curve of Japanese yen will shift to the right.

5. The Bretton Woods system
   a) preceded the gold standard.
   b) was identical to the gold standard.
   c) was established after World War II.
   d) lasted until 1982.

6. If the British decide to purchase more American products,

a) the demand curve for the British pound will shift to the right.
b) the supply curve of the British pound will shift to the right.
c) the supply curve of the American dollar will shift to the right.
d) the supply curve of the American dollar will shift to the left.

7. If a $40,000 American computer costs a German importer 120,000 DM, the exchange rate must be

a) 1 deutsche mark to 3 dollars.
b) 1 deutsche mark to 1/4 dollar.
c) 1 dollar to 1/3 deutsche mark.
d) 1 dollar to 3 deutsche marks.

8. Under a system of flexible exchange rates, if U.S. citizens started buying more British goods,

a) the dollar would tend to appreciate relative to the pound.
b) the price of the pound (in dollars) would begin to fall.
c) the dollar would tend to depreciate relative to the pound.
d) the price of the dollar (in pounds) would begin to rise.

9. If the yen price of the dollar (the price of a dollar stated in terms of Japanese yen) declined,

a) Japanese cars would cost Americans fewer dollars.
b) Japanese tourists would find American meals less expensive.
c) American cars would cost Japanese consumers more yen.
d) American tourists would be encouraged to tour Japan.

10. The existing exchange rate system is best described as a

a) gold standard.
b) system of fixed exchange rates.
c) system of flexible exchange rates.
d) managed float.

Problems and Questions for Discussion

1. How is it possible for a country to experience a favorable balance of trade and an unfavorable balance of payments at the same time?

2. In 1984 some American business executives were complaining about the strong dollar—about the fact that it took more units of foreign exchange than before to buy each dollar. Why would Americans complain about a strong dollar?

3. If you are visiting London, which exchange rate would you prefer: $4 to £1 or $3 to £1? Why?

4. Suppose that we are operating under a system of flexible exchange rates. If Americans demand more British automobiles, will the dollar tend to appreciate or depreciate? Show this result graphically. What about the pound? Show the result graphically.

5. How was the use of the gold standard supposed to correct balance of payments problems "automatically" without the need for devaluation?

6. How was the Bretton Woods system different from the gold standard? What did the two systems have in common?

7. Why would central banks want to intervene in the foreign exchange market? Explain how they would do so if their country's currency were (1) overvalued or (2) undervalued.

8. The United States had been running a balance of payments deficit almost continuously for more than 30 years. How do we get away with it? Why are countries willing to give us valuable goods and services while they accumulate pieces of paper called dollars?

9. Both the gold standard and the Bretton Woods system eventually failed. Why? What did these failures have in common?

10. How can monetary and fiscal policies be used to eliminate a BOP deficit?

Answer Key

Fill in the Blanks

1. exchange rate
2. foreign exchange
3. trade deficit; trade surplus
4. balance of trade, balance of payments
5. fixed, flexible
6. appreciated, depreciated
7. increase
8. lose, contract
9. appreciate
10. harder

Multiple Choice

1. d   3. d   5. c   7. d   9. b
2. c   4. c   6. b   8. c   10. d

Index